Nagy, Gregory.

Pindar's Homer.

$38.95

PINDAR'S HOMER

The Mary Flexner Lectures, 1982
Bryn Mawr College

□□ GREGORY NAGY

Pindar's Homer

The Lyric Possession of an Epic Past

THE JOHNS HOPKINS UNIVERSITY PRESS
BALTIMORE AND LONDON

This book has been brought to publication with the generous assistance
of Bryn Mawr College.

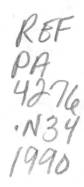

© 1990 The Johns Hopkins University Press
Printed in the United States of America

The Johns Hopkins University Press, 701 West 40th Street, Baltimore, Maryland 21211
The Johns Hopkins Press Ltd., London

The paper used in this publication meets the minimum requirements of
American National Standard for Information Sciences — Permanence of Paper
for Printed Library Materials, ANSI Z39.48 – 1984.

Library of Congress Cataloging-in-Publication Data

Nagy, Gregory.
   Pindar's Homer: the lyric possession of an epic past / Gregory Nagy.
        p.   cm.
   Includes bibliographical references.
   ISBN 0–8018–3932–7
   1. Pindar—Criticism and interpretation. 2. Homer—Influence—Greek—History
and criticism. I. Title.
PA4276.N34   1990
884′.0109—dc20   89–19938 CIP

□□ Contents

▣▣ Acknowledgments

This book stems from the Mary Flexner Lectures in the Humanities at Bryn Mawr College, which I delivered in the autumn of 1982. I am grateful to Bryn Mawr College for the invitation and for the allocation of a generous subsidy that has helped make this book more affordable. I offer my thanks to Mary Patterson McPherson, President of Bryn Mawr, to Judith Shapiro, the Provost, and to Mary M. Dunn, Academic Deputy. Also to Ellen F. Reisner, Assistant to the President, and to Dr. Deborah A. Goldstein. Special thanks go to my esteemed colleagues at Bryn Mawr, most notably to Professors Mabel Lang, Richard Hamilton, and Gregory W. Dickerson. I have fond memories of lively exchanges with them and other colleagues, especially in the Pindar seminar that I was invited to conduct during my stay at Bryn Mawr. Among those who attended the seminar sessions was the late Richmond Lattimore, whose kind interest I recall with nostalgia.

I wish to record my deep gratitude to all those who gave me advice at various stages in the evolution of this book. They include Margaret Alexiou, Nancy Andrews, Danielle Arnold, Mary Moffitt Aycock, Ann Batchelder, Victor Bers, Deborah Boedeker, Martha Cowan, Gregory Crane, Olga Davidson, Marian Demos, Carol Dougherty-Glenn, Robert O. Doyle, Thomas J. Figueira, John M. Foley, Douglas Frame, John Hamilton, Albert Henrichs, Thomas Hubbard, Leslie Kurke, Vassilis Lambropoulos, Nicole Loraux, Albert B. Lord, Richard P. Martin, Kenneth Morrell, Leonard Muellner, Michael Nagler, Blaise Nagy, Joseph Nagy, Sarah Nolan, Hayden Pelliccia, Dan Petegorsky, William Race, Ian Rutherford, James Shirky, Dale

Sinos, Laura Slatkin, Nancy Sultan, Holly Thomas, Emily Vermeule, Brent Vine, Calvert Watkins, Michael Witzel.

A compressed version of many of the ideas formulated in this book appeared in a chapter entitled "Ancient Greek Views on Poets and Poetry," part of volume 1 of the *Cambridge History of Literary Criticism*, edited by George Kennedy.

The final printed version of this book was achieved by Gary Bisbee, master compositor and scholar.

Finally, I dedicate this book to my genial son, László, whose radiant company has been for me a priceless treasure.

▣▣ Abbreviations

The following abbreviations identify works frequently cited in the notes:

CEG	See Hansen 1983
DELG	See Chantraine 1968+
DK	See Diels and Kranz 1951–1952
EG	See Page 1975
FGH	See Jacoby 1923+
GP, GP II	See Gentili and Prato
IG	= Inscriptiones Graecae . . . Berlin, 1873+
KA	See Kassel and Austin 1983+
LSJ	See Liddell, Scott, and Stuart Jones 1940
LSS	See Sokolowski 1962
MW	See Merkelbach and West 1967
N	See Nagy
PMG	See Page 1962
PSI	= Papyri Greci e Latini, Pubblicazioni della Società italiana per la ricerca dei papiri greci e latini in Egitto, 1912+
PW	See Parke and Wormell 1956
SIG	See Dittenberger 1915–1924
SLG	See Page 1974
SM	See Snell and Maehler
V	See Voigt 1971
W	See West 1971/1972

PINDAR'S HOMER

☐☐ Introduction: A Word on Assumptions, Methods, and Aims

This effort is a continuation of two earlier books. One of these, *The Best of the Achaeans*,[1] centered on the role of oral tradition in early Greek achievements of poetic artistry and precision of expression, with Homer in the forefront. The task was difficult, in that I was challenging two influential stances that remain fashionable among experts in Greek literature. One of these can be described as an eagerness to explain whatever we admire in Homer as something that must transcend any oral traditions. This is to ignore, I argued, the communicative power of tradition itself: in seeking to discover the genius of invention in the surviving examples of early Greek epic, we run the risk of underrating the continuum of oral tradition from which these examples had emerged.[2] To say this much is not to go so far as to say *das Volk dichtet*: it is a romantic notion to make generalized claims about folk creativity — claims that in fact blur the observable dynamics of oral tradition within society.[3] It is just as romantic, however, for latter-day critics to attribute the evidence of artistry in Homeric poetry to a genius who is emancipated from oral tradition. Such an attitude is reminiscent of Chateaubriand's notion of "mother-geniuses" (*génies mères*), as dissected by M. M. Bakhtin.[4]

The other influential stance that I challenged in *Best of the Achaeans* is a general reluctance to recognize artistic values that belonged only to the

---

1. N 1979.
2. Two most important studies of oral tradition in epic poetry: Parry [1971] and Lord 1960.
3. On this subject, I recommend the balanced judgment of Bausinger 1980.
4. Bakhtin [1984b] 123–124.

ancient Greeks and no longer to us. This attitude presumes that we are the heirs to everything of theirs that qualifies as artistic and sophisticated, and whatever fails to match our own criteria of these qualities is more "primitive" and therefore less sophisticated. I am reminded of "God's library," as Voltaire pictures it (*Temple du goût*, 1732), where the Muses must busy themselves with revising and abridging the existing great books.

Such an attitude encourages the rejection of any interpretation that recognizes precision and subtlety in early Greek poetics. One critic, after disagreeing in detail with various points that I made about allusions in early Greek literature, decided to call a halt after reading the first three of my twenty chapters; he questioned whether he should even have made the effort of going that far into the book since "I felt sure (and I believe many would agree with me) that so sophisticated a technique of allusions is quite alien to the early epic and would hardly be found even in Hellenistic poetry."[5] I cling to the hope of persuading such critics with my present effort, in which I propose to widen the scope of inquiry.[6] Whereas *The Best of the Achaeans* concerned primarily the epic tradition, this book is an attempt to confront, at least in broad outlines, the full range of poetic and song-making traditions in early Greek civilization. Without such a confrontation, I now fear, my efforts in the previous books may be permanently misunderstood by some. *Pindar's Homer* provides the background for *The Best of the Achaeans*.

In widening the scope, I shift the focus from epic to lyric, as represented primarily by the compositions of Alcman, Stesichorus, Alcaeus, Sappho, Ibycus, Anacreon, Simonides, Bacchylides, and Pindar.[7] The conventional dating of these figures covers a period stretching roughly from 650 to 450 B.C.,[8] and hereafter I refer to this period as the age of Archaic Greek lyric. The task becomes even more difficult, in face of yet another influential line of thought: I am challenging the tenaciously fashionable notion, which takes shape in many variations, that Archaic Greek lyric represents the rise of individual innovation over collective tradition. It can be said straightaway that such a notion lacks the perspectives of social anthropology. Beyond that, it

5. Solmsen 1981.83. Cf. Griffin 1984.134, where he refers to "some scholars" who "are now finding in the epics meanings of great subtlety which have been undetected for three millennia."

6. In the case of Professor Solmsen, it gives me a sense of permanent loss that he died before this book was finished.

7. I take note here of a convention in spelling. Greek authors whose names have survived in our inherited Classical canon will be spelled in Latin: thus *Ibycus* and *Stesichorus*, not *Ibykos* and *Stesikhoros*. Or in anglicized Latin: thus *Pindar* and *Homer*, not *Pindaros* and *Homeros*. The same goes for figures whose names are normally pronounced according to the Latin spelling, such as *Croesus* and *Phoenix*, not *Kroisos* and *Phoinix*. Otherwise, Greek names will be spelled in a modified transliteration of the Greek alphabet: thus *Peisistratos* and *Polykrates*, not *Pisistratus* and *Polycrates*. I regret that this convention frustrates the eternal reciprocity of fame promised by Ibycus to the tyrant Polykrates, as discussed in Ch.6.

8. Cf. Kirkwood 1974.3.

would be premature at this point to enter into the controversy, which would engulf the reader in a bibliographical quagmire. Instead this notion is challenged by a variety of arguments, both explicit and implicit, that extend throughout this book.

Which brings me to mention the other of the two earlier books that the present work continues, *Comparative Studies in Greek and Indic Meter*.[9] The basic thesis was that the meter known as the dactylic hexameter of Greek epic originated from lyric meters and that these lyric meters have an ancient heritage that can at least be partially recovered through the comparative method of Indo-European linguistics.[10] This is not to say that lyric is necessarily older than epic or that epic did not influence lyric as well as the other way around. Rather the point is simply that Greek lyric represents a tradition — or various traditions — in its own right, and that the form of Greek epic can be explained as a differentiation of various forms that we find in Greek lyric. This thesis, however, raises many questions about the very concepts of lyric and epic, and it is to these questions that I now turn.[11]

As the work proceeds, the definition of *lyric* will progressively broaden, to the point that lyric becomes, for all practical purposes, the basis for defining *epic*, rather than the other way around. This point is reflected in the subtitle: *The Lyric Possession of an Epic Past*. I chose the word *possession* because the preoccupation of Greek poetry with the application of the past to the here and now is in itself an exercise of political power.[12] Moreover, there is a side connotation of the poet's "possession," or inspiration, *by* the spirits of the heroic past.[13] In using the word this way, I have in mind the celebrated passage retelling the ecstatic "seizure" of the composer in Diderot's *Le neveu de Rameau* — a seizure that activates a panorama of musical, poetic, and dramatic performance.

Of all the poets of Archaic lyric, I choose Pindar as the centerpiece. Along with his near-contemporary, Bacchylides, Pindar is not only the latest but also the last in the canon of lyric poets as transmitted by the Alexandrian editors. The last securely datable poem of Pindar, *Pythian* 8, was composed

9. N 1974.

10. Cf. p. 37. Unlike most other attempts at tracing the history of the epic hexameter, my approach takes into account the phraseological as well as the metrical heritage: cf. Ritoók 1987.4, 6–7 (with an important reference at p. 6n17 to Monroe 1972.35). A central element of my argument is the noun + adjective combination κλέος 'fame' [**kleos**] + ἄφθιτον 'unfailing' [**aphthiton**], as attested in *Iliad* IX 413, the antiquity of which has recently been questioned by a variety of critics. For an effective answer to some of these questions, see Risch 1987, especially p. 4, where he points out a crucial oversight on the part of most experts who have expressed their views on this subject. See also Edwards 1988. Further discussion at p. 244.

11. For other views on such questions, cf. Gentili and Giannini 1977.30n64, with reference to Peabody 1975.

12. Cf. p. 172 and following.

13. Cf. p. 329.

for performance in 446 B.C. (for Bacchylides, the last datable compositions are *Odes* 6 and 7, performed in 452 B.C.).

There are two reasons for my focus on Pindar. One concerns the specific form — or, better, forms — of his lyric poetry, specifically its metrical forms, and the relationship of these forms to the form of epic. The other reason relates to the content of this poetry, in particular, what it says both explicitly and implicitly about the connections between epic and lyric.

Which brings me to a point of principle. Throughout I shall pay close attention to the relationship between poetic form and content. This relationship reveals the tradition that shapes both the poet and the poetry, and for me it is the poetic tradition itself that serves as the primary empirical evidence at my disposal. For others, however, what the poet says about anything counts as raw data, serving as the basis for a "scientific" reconstruction of the poet and the poet's world, as also for any educated second-guessing about the poet's reasons for saying what is said in the poetry. The second-guessing can then lead to various opinions about what we are or are not permitted to believe about the poet's testimony — all in accordance with our own privileged sense of verisimilitude. It is as if the poet's words existed in a vacuum, just waiting to be discovered as direct information about the past, for the exclusive use of future generations. I prefer instead to treat the poetic tradition itself as the primary evidence, as manifested mainly in the language of the surviving texts.

Treating the actual language of poetic tradition as my primary evidence, I must refer, and refer often, to the perspectives of linguistics. I hope to do so, however, without encumbering the reader with an overabundance of technicalities. The few explicit linguistics concepts that do occur in this book are fundamental, and it makes sense to prepare the reader for two of them immediately.

One of these concepts of linguistics is the distinction between *synchronic* and *diachronic*. By *synchronic* I mean the workings of a system as it exists at a given time and place; by *diachronic,* the transformations of this system through time.[14] To avoid confusion, I choose to use these terms consistently from the standpoint of an outsider who is thinking about a given system, not from the standpoint of an insider who is thinking within that system. The diachronic perspective, as we see throughout this book, is essential for understanding the relationship of form and content in terms of such categories as *theme, formula,* and *meter.*[15] I should warn at the outset, however, that the

14. For a particularly accessible discussion of these concepts, with essential bibliography, see Ducrot and Todorov 1979.137–144. In the realm of metrics, the dichotomy of synchrony and diachrony corresponds to what West 1982.64 distinguishes as *definition* and *etymology.*

15. On the diachronic hierarchy of theme (in the sense of "a traditional unit of composition on the level of meaning") over formula (in the sense of "a traditional unit of composition on the level of wording") over meter (in the sense of "a traditional unit of composition on the level of rhythm"), see N 1976 and the useful commentary of Cantilena 1982.41–45, 55–56. In the

diachronic perspective cannot suffice for the description, the classification, of a *system* as it exists at a given time and place. For that, the synchronic perspective is essential.

The second of the two basic concepts of linguistics that I use throughout this book is the distinction, from a synchronic perspective, between the *marked* and *unmarked* members of any opposition within the system of language. These terms are defined as follows by Roman Jakobson: "The general meaning of a marked category states the presence of a certain (whether positive or negative) property A; the general meaning of the corresponding unmarked category states nothing about the presence of A."[16] The unmarked category is the general category, which can include the marked category, whereas the reverse situation cannot hold. For example, in an opposition of the English words *long* and *short*, the unmarked member of the opposition is *long* because it can be used not only as the opposite of *short* ("I am reading a long book, not a short one") but also as the general category ("how long is this book?"). In an opposition of *interesting* and *boring*, the unmarked member is *interesting*: if we say "A is more interesting than B," we do not necessarily mean that both A and B are interesting or that B is boring, whereas "A is more boring than B" presupposes that both A and B are boring. To ask a question like "how interesting is this?" does not commit the questioner, unlike "how boring is this?" Further, in an opposition of *day* and *night*, the unmarked member is *day*, which serves not only as the opposite of *night* ("it is daytime, not nighttime") but also as the general category ("there are seven days in the week").[17] To ask "how short?" is to presuppose shortness, whereas "how long?" does not presuppose either shortness or length. Thus the marked member, as in the case of *short*, is defined in terms of the unmarked member, in this case, *long* — and not the other way around.

Where the marked member is a semantic subcategory of the unmarked member, we may be witnessing the reflex of an older situation where the form of the marked member had once been assigned the function currently held by the form of the unmarked member. Such a pattern of semantic evolution is known in linguistic theory as Kuryłowicz's fourth law of analogy: when two forms come into competition for one function, the newer form may

---

present work I have tried to answer some interesting points raised by Cantilena, pp. 42–43n30.

16. Jakobson (1957) 1984.47; also Jakobson 1939. I omit the final segment of Jakobson's definition, "the general meaning of the corresponding unmarked category states nothing about the presence of A, *and is used chiefly, but not exclusively, to indicate the absence of A*," in light of the discussion by Comrie 1976.122 and n2 (thanks to H. Pelliccia). For further updating on the semantic applications of the terms *marked* and *unmarked*, with bibliography, I recommend Waugh 1982.

17. For these and similar examples, see Waugh, pp. 307–308; also Ducrot and Todorov 1979.112–114. For a discussion of right-left as unmarked-marked categories, with useful bibliography, see Markey 1982.

take over that function while the older form may become relegated to a sub-category of its earlier function.[18]

The unmarked member is inclusive, in that the marked member can be an aspect of the unmarked. It can be exclusive, however, if it negates the marked member, as when we say "that is not *short*, it is *long*." The negation of the marked by the unmarked has been called the *minus interpretation* of the unmarked (for example, "long, not short"), as distinct from the *zero interpretation* (for example, "long"); the assertion of the marked member is the *plus interpretation* (for example, "short," or "short, not long").[19] The term *plus interpretation* designates not "positive" but "marked, either negatively or positively."

The zero interpretation of the unmarked member includes, as an overarching principle, both the minus interpretation of the unmarked member and the plus interpretation of the marked member. The opposition of *long* and *short* is a matter of length. Further, the opposition of unmarked *order* and marked *disorder* is a matter of overall order. I cite a particularly interesting example from Greek metrics, an Archaic eight-syllable metrical unit known as the *choriambic dimeter*:

$$\underline{\cup}\,\underline{\cup}\,\underline{\cup}\,\underline{\cup}-\cup\cup-\,{}^{20}$$

This unit consists of a "disordered" first half, four syllables that display a wide variety of possible combinations of long ($-$) and short ($\cup$) quantities, such as $----$, $---\cup$, $-\cup--$, $-\cup-\cup$, $\cup---$, $\cup--\cup$, $-\cup-\cup$,[21] followed by an "ordered" second half, four syllables that rigidly follow the pattern $-\cup\cup-$. There is a principle of order even in the disorder of the first half, as

---

18. To quote his own words: "Quand à la suite d'une transformation morphologique une forme subit la différentiation, la forme nouvelle correspond à sa fonction primaire (de fondation), la forme ancienne est réservée pour la fonction secondaire (fondée)" (Kuryłowicz [1966] 169). By older form I mean simply the form that is *already* assigned to a given function, whereas by newer form I mean the form that is *about to be* assigned. As an example, I cite English *quick*, cognate of Latin *uīuos* 'alive': *quick* was ousted from the sphere of meaning 'living, alive', becoming semantically specialized in the sense of 'lively' and, eventually, 'quick' (the older meaning is still evident in such fossils as *the quick and the dead*, or *bite the nails to the quick*). Kuryłowicz's fourth law is pertinent to the following formulation of Bakhtin [1984] 410: "The object that has been destroyed remains in the world but in a new form of being in time and space; it becomes the 'other side' of the new object that has taken its place." There are of course patterns of development that may be described as alternatives to Kuryłowicz's fourth law. For one, there will be situations where the competition between newer and older forms leads to the ousting of the older form by the newer form altogether. Or else the newer and older forms may achieve coexistence in a suppletive relationship (as in Latin *ferō / ferre / tulī / lātus*, where the first two principal parts are "older," while the second two are "newer"; similarly in *tollō, tollere, sustulī, sublātus*) or as morphophonemic variants (on which see Householder and Nagy 1972.758).

19. For a brief history of the varying terminology used for these concepts, see Waugh, p. 303.

20. Further details about this unit at p. 445.

21. Poultney 1979.139. Cf. Itsumi 1982.60–61 (who does not cite Poultney).

we can see from a constraint that escapes notice at first sight. The constraint is this: the first half does not allow just any possible combination of longs and shorts. One pattern in particular, −∪∪−, is avoided in the disordered first half, and this pattern −∪∪− is precisely the ordered pattern of the second half.[22] In other words it is a matter of overarching order that the first half be disorder as opposed to the order of the second half. The first half is the plus-interpretation of disorder, the second half is the minus interpretation of order, while the two halves together comprise the zero interpretation of order.[23] As we shall see later, such an arrangement on the level of form is typical of the

22. Further details in N 1974.37–38. Other patterns that tend to be avoided in the first half are ∪−∪− and −−∪− (also −−∪∪ and ∪∪−−): Poultney, p. 139. These other patterns, as we shall see in the Appendix, are actually related to −∪∪−, which is the primary pattern to be excluded from the disordered first half. Itsumi 1982.60 has found two exceptional cases of choriambic dimeter with the pattern −∪∪− in the first half; both occur in the choral lyrics of Euripides (*Orestes* 839 and *Iphigeneia in Tauris* 435). Given that Itsumi has collected some 400 attestations of the choriambic dimeter in the corpus of Euripides (p. 61), and that he can point to only two examples where the pattern −∪∪− occurs in the first half, I find that his own statistical findings reinforce my observation that the pattern −∪∪− is traditionally avoided in the first half of the choriambic dimeter. Moreover, Itsumi himself stresses that Euripides is in many respects an innovator in his use of the choriambic dimeter (e.g., p. 72). Since he can cite no exceptions to the pattern of avoiding −∪∪− in the first half of choriambic dimeter in Archaic Greek metrics and a strikingly low percentage of exceptions in the more innovative metrics of Euripides, I fail to see the validity of his disagreement (p. 60) with the formulation offered in N 1974.37, where I say that "the opening of the choriambic dimeter must be free, and therefore it is not allowed to be a choriamb itself." Also, it is misleading for Itsumi to say that the first half of choriambic dimeter "should not be regarded as a separate component" since it "does not appear in isolation" (p. 69). A comparative analysis of the available metrical evidence, as in the discussion at N, pp. 37–38, is not predicated on the notion that the first half of choriambic dimeter is a "separate component." It is a component, yes, but not a separate component.

23. This interpretation differs from the approach of Itsumi 1982 to the choriambic dimeter. He assumes that rhythmical freedom in the first half of the choriambic dimeter can be posited only if we find every possible combination of long and short quantitites there. No such assumption is necessary since the freedom of the first half is already assured by the simple fact of variability in its rhythmical patterns, as opposed to the invariability of the patterns in the second half. Even if the third of the first four syllables in attested choriambic dimeters is regularly long (Itsumi, p. 60), the variety of patterns in the first, second, and fourth syllables still constitutes a sector of variability in the entire first half of choriambic dimeter, as opposed to a sector of invariability in the second half. There is a symmetry in the opposition between a variable opening half and an invariable closing half. I recommend a close reading of Allen 1973.106, with its enhanced perspective of comparative evidence on the topic of interaction between rhythmically flexible openings and rigid closings in metrical units, as a counterweight to the limitations imposed by Itsumi's strictly descriptivist interpretations of available metrical data. On the general tendency of maintaining a tension between ideal and actual patterns at the beginning of the line and of solving this tension at the end of the line, see Allen, p. 110. Cf. also p. 446. Moreover, the notion that an initial pattern of ∪∪−∪ in choriambic dimeter precedes the pattern ∪∪−∪ historically (Itsumi, p. 71) seems to me counterintuitive from the standpoint of comparative metrics. I also disagree with the notion that the choriambic dimeter may have been "created" by way of changes in the glyconic (ibid.); cf. p. 445.

thought patterns of myth making on the level of content: in the stories of myth, the opposition of disorder and order, of discord and concord, serves to achieve an overall concept of *order, concord*.[24] More specifically the opposition of social division and integration serves to achieve an overall concept of *integration*.[25] Further, the opposition of alien and native serves to achieve an overall concept of *native*.[26]

The distinction of *marked-unmarked* can be further applied in a variety of contexts, starting in Chapter 1 with an extended discussion of song and poetry as distinct from "everyday" language. I apply it even here with the intent of challenging a common misconception about a term that is central to the whole book, *oral poetry*. The descriptive term *oral* in *oral poetry* has come to have an overly narrow meaning, restricted by our own cultural preconceptions about writing and reading. We feel the need to define *oral* in terms of *written*: if something is *oral*, we tend to assume a conflict with the notion of *written*. From the general standpoint of social anthropology, however, it is *written* that has to be defined in terms of *oral*. *Written* is not something that is not *oral*; rather it is something in addition to being oral, and that additional something varies from society to society.[27] It is dangerous to universalize the phenomenon of literacy.[28] To restate the problem in terms of the distinction between *marked* and *unmarked:* if we juxtapose *oral* and *written*, it is *written* that functions as the marked member of the opposition, while *oral* is unmarked. The definition of *written* is predicated on the given of *oral*.

In this book we have ample opportunity to consider the many variations of interaction between two fundamental aspects of oral traditions: composition and performance. Already at this point, however, I call attention to a general tendency in contemporary thinking to undervalue the aspect of performance by overvaluing the aspect of composition. In seeking to put the act of performance into a balanced perspective, I find it useful to bring into play J. L. Austin's notion of a performative utterance or *speech-act*, where the antithesis of word and action is neutralized, in that the word *is* the action.[29] I invoke also Barbara Johnson's application of Austin's notion of speech-act to *poetry*—an application that Austin resisted—and her insistence on the self-referential quality of the performative: "The performative, then, acts like a 'shifter' in that it takes on meaning only by referring to the instance of its

24. Cf. p. 365.

25. Cf. p. 367.

26. Cf. Ch.10.

27. For a crucial discussion from the standpoint of ancient Greek society, see Svenbro 1987 (1988); cf. also Detienne 1988.

28. A common pitfall is the failure to observe the drastic changes in the very notion of literacy that were occasioned by two historical events: the diffusion of the technology of printing and the Reformation. See Ong 1982.117–138; also Ong 1986.168–169. Cf. also Zwettler 1978.24.

29. Austin 1962. Cf. also Searle 1979.

utterance."[30] Johnson adds her own translation of Emile Benveniste's formulation: "An utterance is performative insofar as it *names* the act performed. . . . The utterance *is* the act; the utterer performs the act by naming it."[31]

If indeed performance "takes on meaning only by referring to the instance of its utterance," then this instance, this occasion, must be the basis for the intent of the utterance, for its rhetoric.[32] If, further, the occasion should ever be lost or removed, then the intent of the utterance is destabilized. We may say that the very notion of genre serves as compensation for the lost occasion.[33]

I take it, then, that questions of meaning in the composition of a song or poem cannot be settled in terms of the composition alone: we must keep in mind what the composition says about its performance or potential performance, and what that says about whoever is the composer, whoever is the performer.[34] Only this way can we begin to do justice to questions of authorship and even of authority.[35]

What makes words authoritative is the value that the given society attaches to their performance. And the authoritativeness of speech is a central issue in this book. The notion of authoritative speech, as we shall see, is conveyed in Greek by such key words as **ainos**.[36]

Bringing to a close this brief review of technical elements in the book, I take this opportunity to stress my awareness that there is no one method, no one theory, that could ever suffice for comprehending the totality of any piece of Greek literature, or of any literature. This is no excuse, however, for being hostile to theory, a stance that is perennially fashionable among Classicists. I agree with Eagleton that "hostility to theory usually means an opposition to other people's theories and an oblivion of one's own."[37]

In the end the critic can do no better than to discover and then apply the criteria of those who create, or better, re-create, the tradition. I take to heart the reaction of Elroy Bundy to the imperative of **phuē** 'nature' in the poetry of Pindar:[38]

30. Johnson 1980.56. On the term *shifter*, referring to forms where the referent can be determined only from the standpoint of the interlocutors, see Jakobson 1957. For an application of speech-act theory to Archaic Greek poetics: Martin 1989.

31. Ibid. Benveniste 1966.274.

32. For a working definition of *occasion* in terms of ritual and myth in small-scale societies, see p. 31.

33. On the Hellenistic concept of genre as a form that re-creates the lost occasion, see p. 362.

34. Cf. Bauman 1977.

35. More at Ch.2, Ch.12.

36. Cf. pp. 31, 147.

37. Eagleton 1983.viii.

38. Bundy 1972.90n113.

Pindar's φυά [**phuē**] has nothing to do with the natural, unschooled, unconscious genius of the eighteenth and nineteenth centuries, but denotes schooling by experience in the truth of words and actions in a living tradition; the [negative concept of] "learning" he speaks of . . . is mere rote imitation of things not understood. You must not, he means, apply systems of method but elicit your method from the thing to be investigated; do not, armed with a detached system, go in search of a subject, but, having chosen a subject, refusing to bury it under an avalanche of terms, allow it to reveal the unity in its manifold as you "draw together the strands of many matters in brief."

The choice of subject in this book is clear. As the title says, the central concern is not Pindar, but Pindar's Homer. What interests me primarily is the relationship of Pindar's tradition to other lyric traditions and to the epic tradition of Homer. A major task that I have set for myself is to seek whatever the epic of Homer really means to Pindar as a master of his own medium of poetry, which is lyric; the search must engage Pindar's own words, which I hold to be the prime evidence for the independent lyric tradition that lives on through his art. In searching for a unified vision of what Homer means to Pindar, I hope to achieve an insight into a broader literary question, that is, what epic means to lyric.[39] Since the unified vision that is sought — what Bundy calls the unity to be revealed — is complex, a variety of strategies in presentation is needed, and that variety makes it necessary to offer here, for the sake of clarity, an outline of the chapters that follow.

39. For exemplary works on Homeric references in Pindar, where the emphasis is not so much on the independence of Pindar's lyric tradition as on the independence of Pindar himself as an individual poet, see, for example, Race 1986.58–62 and Pelliccia 1987. Cf. also Nisetich 1989; at pp. 1–5 he offers a survey of works that address the question of Homer's influence on Pindar, e.g. Fitch 1924, Young 1968, Stoneman 1981. I object, however, to the remark in Nisetich, pp. 4–5: "The transformation of Arctinus' Leuce into Pindar's Island of the Blest necessarily escapes notice if we insist on treating the one as if it were the equivalent of the other." As a case in point he refers to N 1979.167, 207, among other discussions. This is to misconstrue what was being analyzed in those pages. I was not treating one myth as if it were the "equivalent" of another: rather, I was comparing variant myths that are cognate with each other. To argue that given variants are cognates is a far cry from treating one myth as if it were the equivalent of another and failing to notice differences. The very concept of variation, of multiformity in myth making, requires the recognition of differences as well as similarities between traditional patterns. The existence of multiforms in myth, however, leads to serious methodological difficulties. I cite N, pp. 42–43, for example, where I discuss the pitfalls of trying to establish an "Ur-form" on the basis of multiforms in a given tradition. To assume that variation results merely from multiple instances of personal artistic creation, as implied for example by Nisetich's reference to "Arctinus' Leuce," is to risk the slighting of tradition itself as a vital component of the creative process in Archaic Greek poetry. I fail to see why Nisetich thinks that anyone would have a problem with the idea of "transformation" in comparing one version with another. The real problem is: to what extent is tradition involved in such transformation? My book seeks answers.

To begin, Chapter 1 examines the criteria for differentiating oral *poetry* and *song* in early Greek society, as exemplified by the epic of Homer and the lyric of Pindar, respectively. The aim is to set up the concept of *lyric poetry* or *lyric* as a default category for those types of song that are *not* poetry, in a stricter sense of the word. Conversely it is argued that the meters known to us as the hexameter, the elegiac distich, and the iambic trimeter are the formal markers, in the Classical period, of poetry in this stricter sense, that is, of verse that is not sung. In contrast lyric typifies what is sung, what is potentially danced and potentially accompanied by **aulos** 'reed' or **kitharā** 'lyre'. It is also argued that just as song becomes differentiated into a dichotomy of poetry and song, so also poetry becomes further differentiated into a dichotomy of prose and poetry. In the process of arriving at an understanding of all these differentiations, the meanings of the key words **mūthos** 'myth' and **mīmēsis** 'mimesis' are reassessed, while another key word, **ainos**, is assigned a working definition, 'speech-act'.[40]

With reference to the Appendix, Chapter 1 goes on to argue that the three prime meters of poetry in the Classical period, however distinct the medium of poetry may have become from the medium of song, can nevertheless be derived from the attested meters of song. The two major categories of meters that comprise the song-making traditions of Pindar, the so-called Aeolic and dactylo-epitrite, are shown to contain the building blocks of the iambic trimeter, the elegiac distich, and even the hexameter. In this sense it can even be said that Pindar's inherited meters are the parents of Homer's hexameter, though the parent in this case has experienced a longer evolution, culminating with Pindar, than the child, culminating with Homer.

Chapter 2 investigates the general characteristics of oral poetry, as established by the cross cultural perspective of field work in living traditions, and compares these with the specific characteristics of oral poetry in the social context of early Greece. Whereas the two factors of composition and performance are essential in all oral poetry, with varying degrees of recomposition in performance depending on the form of poetry and on the given phase of its evolution, the early Greek evidence calls for a third factor to be taken into account, the factor of diffusion. The diffusion of early Greek poetry, as exemplified primarily by Homer, is analyzed in terms of two emerging social patterns in early Greece, culminating in the institution of the **polis** 'city-state' and in the correlative impulse of Panhellenism. These patterns destabilize the concept of **mūthos** 'myth' and promote an alternative truth value, the privileged concept of **alētheia** 'truth'. Also, the factors of diffusion and recomposition in performance have a profound effect on the very concept of authorship.

40. Cf. pp. 31, 147.

Chapter 3 shifts attention to the characteristics of oral songmaking, as distinct from nonlyric "poetry" in the stricter sense of the word. The striking diversity of melodic patterns in early Greek traditions of songmaking is examined in terms of chronologically successive but overlapping criteria, deduced from both the internal evidence of the songs and the available external evidence. These criteria are reflected in the technical words **nomos, harmoniā, tonos,** and **genos.** The progressive systematization reflected by these words is correlated with the progressive canonization of melodic patterns, a reflex, it is claimed, of Panhellenization in songmaking traditions. The trend of Panhellenization also accounts for the emergence of a Classical canon of nine lyric poets, corresponding to the earlier canons of nonlyric poets. In the forefront of the "lyric nine" is Pindar.

Chapter 4 offers an introduction to the medium of Pindar, with *Olympian* 1 as the centerpiece. This composition of Pindar's affords a premier illustration of the victory ode, or epinician, the only lyric genre to survive from Pindar's vast lyric repertoire as a near-complete corpus. The choice of *Olympian* 1 as illustration is specially suited for the book since the central myth of this ode, the story of Pelops, is connected with the ritual dimension of the Olympic Games, the premier athletic festival of the ancient Greek world. It is argued that Pindar's presentation of the Pelops myth, including his explicit rejection of some details inherited from past versions of the narrative, reflects not his private invention but rather his public acceptance of the narrative in its then-current version, as formalized in the mythological and ritual dimensions of a most complex institution, the Olympics.

Chapter 5 connects the ritual dimension of athletics with the ritual dimension of the epinician itself, as presented in Pindar's own words. The efforts of the poet, in glorifying the occasion of the athletic event, are presented by the song as a ritual speech-act that serves as compensation for the efforts culminating in the athlete's victory, which in turn serve as compensation for the primordial efforts or experiences of heroes in the heroic age, as glorified by Homer. All these efforts, of poets, athletes, and heroes, are treated by the poetry as *ordeals*, a ritual concept conveyed by words like **agōn,** shared by Pindar and Homer.

This topic of a ritual ideology linking athletes, heroes, and poets sets the stage for Chapter 6, an extensive survey of the relationship between Pindaric song and Homeric poetry. While Homer's medium of epic poetry glorifies heroes, Pindar's medium of lyric song glorifies simultaneously the heroes of the past and the athletes of the present. By collapsing the distinction between hero and athlete, the epinician of Pindar becomes a genuine occasion of prestige for the contemporary figure who is being glorified, and this poetic glorification is correlated with the realities of wealth, power, and prestige in the here and now. These three realities of wealth, power, and prestige ultimately preserve the identities of Pindar's patrons. Conversely the identity of

Pindar is a function of his authority, which is simultaneously the authority of the epinician, to confer prestige. The authority of the epinician, as a form of authoritative speech, is conveyed by the word **ainos**.[41] It is this authority that guarantees the authorship of Pindar.

Chapter 7 concentrates on three different occasions when the world of heroes merges with the world of the here and now through the authority of the **ainos**. The three occasions correspond to three Pindaric epinicians: *Pythian* 8, *Isthmian* 8, and *Pythian* 6. Here are three different compositions enhancing in three different ways the prestige of real people whose prestige or **kleos** 'glorification' depends on an ideological merger between the **kleos** of Pindar's **ainos** and the **kleos** of Homer's epic, the world of heroes.

Chapter 8, resuming the discussion in Chapter 1, takes up the subject of prose, to be explained as one further stage of differentiation in types of speech-act. This time, the argument goes, poetry becomes further differentiated into a dichotomy of prose and poetry, just as song had earlier become differentiated into a dichotomy of poetry and song. The prime example of early Greek prose is the discourse of Herodotus, whose language makes it implicit that he is a **logios** 'master of speech', a description that is pertinent to the dichotomy, made explicit in Pindar's language, between **logios** 'master of speech' and **aoidos** 'master of song'. The prose of Herodotus, like the poetry and song of the **ainos**, is a speech-act of authority. Such authority is parallel to that of Solon, a historical figure who becomes part of the canonical Seven Sages tradition. The dramatized words addressed by Solon to Croesus the Tyrant in Book I of Herodotus are tantamount to an **ainos** contextualized by the narrative frame of the *Histories*.

The very word **historiā** 'inquiry, history', used by Herodotean discourse in referring to itself, is traced in Chapter 9 to the traditions of juridical prose, especially in the context of international (that is, inter-polis) arbitration. These traditions of juridical prose are shown to parallel those of sacred juridical poetry, as exemplified by Hesiod. There are parallels between the moral message of such discourse and the moral message of the **ainos**, as exemplified by the poetry of Theognis and the song making of Pindar. Herodotean prose reveals its affinities with the **ainos** of poetry and song in its deployment of the word **sēmainō** 'indicate', derivative of **sēma** 'sign, tomb of a hero'.

In Chapter 10 the parallelism between modes of discourse in Pindar and Herodotus is explored further, with the theme of Croesus the Tyrant as a test case. Special attention is given to what is traditionally left unsaid in such a theme, reflecting as it does the diplomatic stance of the **ainos**, where implicit warning is an aspect of explicit praise. It becomes clear that the theme of Croesus the Tyrant is pertinent to the actual occasion of epinicians, to the

41. Cf. p. 147.

here and now of Pindar's contemporaries who commissioned him to compose songs to enhance their prestige. Since the diplomatic format of the **ainos** allows implicit warning in the context of explicit praise, the very trappings of a tyrant can be acknowledged as powerfully attractive, without any diminution of the moral impact in the overall message. Tyranny has its charms. It also becomes clear that the figure of the tyrant, overtly alien to Hellenic ways, is intended by the **ainos** as a latent reflection of what is native. The explicit other is the implicit self. This theme of "alien is native," which has its origins in the straightforward ethnocentric tendency of appropriating what is foreign as a form of self-reassurance for the community, can thus be turned into a form of warning: if what you want to find from the outside is already available on the inside, then perhaps whatever you do not want to enter from the outside has already emerged from within. This moral message is relentlessly persistent in the prose narrative of Herodotus, as if in an **ainos**.

Chapter 11 shows that the parallelism between the messages in the prose of Herodotus and the lyric poetry of Pindar can best be observed in situations where Herodotus quotes or paraphrases poetry, particularly the nonlyric poetry of oracular utterances. Similar patterns of quoting or paraphrasing poetry can be found in the *Lives of the Seven Sages* tradition, as typified by the *Life of Solon* tradition. In the Herodotean sequences of prose and poetry, the train of thought matches the train of thought in Pindaric sequences of uninterrupted lyric poetry. In other words the framing of poetry by prose in Herodotus matches the continuum of lyric poetry in Pindar. Thus the **logios** 'master of speech' conveys **ainos** indirectly by framing poetry while the **aoidos** 'master of song' conveys it directly. This chapter brings to a close the comparison, ongoing since Chapter 9, of Pindar and Herodotus. The final point of emphasis is the sheer variety of poetic traditions, both nonlyric and lyric, that is quoted or cited by Herodotus. For Herodotus, the general category of poetry can accommodate even the *Fables* of Aesop and the *Seven Sages* tradition. What makes Herodotus a particularly rich resource for understanding the fullest possible range of fifth-century traditions in poetry and song is that he makes the themes of poetry and song a part of his own repertoire of composition and even of organization.

Chapter 12 takes another look at the actual authority of the epinician in the larger context of the social function of the **khoros** 'song-and-dance ensemble, chorus' in the polis. It is argued that the chorus is the ultimate mimesis of authority in early Greek society, and that the very concept of authorship is ultimately defined by choral authority. In this light the argument is repeated that Archaic Greek poetry is the result of a differentiation of monodic song, which in turn had become differentiated from choral song and dance.

Chapter 13 confronts the major historical phenomenon that stands between us and the vast repertoire of poetic traditions available to Herodotus and exemplified by Pindar. That phenomenon is the evolution of Athenian State Theater, pioneered by tyrants and perfected by the democracy. State Theater appropriated the repertoire of older poetic traditions and transformed it, in a vast and ongoing synthesis described by Plato as "theatrocracy." It is argued that the evolution of democratic poetics in Athenian State Theater is analogous, albeit on a much more complex level, to the evolution of aristocratic poetics in the choral medium of Pindar and even in the nonchoral medium of a figure like Archilochus. As the focus shifts to the later phases of the democracy in Athens, it becomes clear that the old-fashioned repertoire represented by the likes of Pindar could still survive in the context of monodic reperformances at symposia. Also the Classics of the old masters were still being taught in private schools. Nevertheless, the domain of public choral performance had become the primary domain of State Theater. The poets of State Theater, such as Aristophanes, could still express nostalgia for the more aristocratic choral medium of Pindar and even borrow from it, either directly or in parody, but the audiences at Athens were ultimately theirs, not Pindar's. Yet the lyric poetry of Pindar survived, because it became a textbook for those inner circles that wanted to perpetuate an old-fashioned and aristocratic choral medium of composition and performance. Pindar's actual *medium* of performance ultimately did not survive, but his words did, thanks to another kind of medium, what I have just described as the textbook. Pindar's aristocratic medium of performance, even down to its last attested phases of extinction, was ever redolent of potential or real tyrants, the sort of social circles that had indeed once upon a time reshaped this medium by dint of their authority in the glory days of Pindar's prime.

This point leads finally to Chapter 14, a retrospective summary of the relationship between the lyric heritage of Pindaric song and the epic heritage of Homeric poetry. For the Pindaric tradition, it is clear that Homer is the representative of all epic, not just the *Iliad* and *Odyssey*. For Pindar, the epic repertoire of Homer can be freely generated from his own inherited lyric repertoire, much as we can derive the Homeric hexameter from the inherited building-blocks of Pindar's meters. Whatever the merits of Homer, he is always held up as a foil for Pindar's own artistry.

In ending my summary of the book on this particular note, which sets the tone for beginning the exposition in detail, I can do no better than quote Pindar himself on the tales of heroes told by Homer:

καὶ ταῦτα μὲν παλαιότεροι | ὁδὸν ἁμαξιτὸν εὗρον· ἕπομαι δὲ καὶ αὐτὸς ἔχων μελέταν· | τὸ δὲ πὰρ ποδὶ ναὸς ἑλισσόμενον αἰεί κυμάτων | λέγεται παντὶ μάλιστα δονεῖν | θυμόν. ἑκόντι δ' ἐγὼ νώτῳ μεθέπων δίδυμον ἄχθος | ἄγγελος ἔβαν

Pindar *Nemean* 6.53–57

All these things are a highway [**amaxitos**] which the men of old time [**palaioteroi**] discovered, and I follow it also, with premeditation [**meletē**]. But on a ship, they say, the wave that ever rolls nearest the keel [**to ... par podi**] most concerns every man's heart. Gladly have I taken on my back a twofold burden [**didumon akhthos**] and come as messenger [**angelos**].[42]

Pindar is following in the path of epic with his own epinician themes. An expert in the art of Pindar writes about this passage:[43]

The word **palaioteroi** refers primarily to the epic poets; the word **amaxitos** 'highway' points to the expansiveness and, in both senses, popularity of epic; the word **meletē** 'premeditation' refers to his own craft or training ground; **to ... par podi** '[the wave] nearest the keel' represents the here and now of the epinician occasion in opposition to the heroic past; the **didumon akhthos** 'twofold burden' is the double duty of praising the victor and praising the community at large;[44] and the word **angelos** refers to his own role as lyric "messenger."

All of which "draws together the strands of many matters in brief."

42. The translation of Pindar here, as also elsewhere, is based primarily on the work of Lattimore 1976, though I have attempted several adjustments. I offer special thanks to W. H. Race for helping me with many of these adjustments.

43. W. H. Race *per litteras* 7/5/1988.

44. Cf. Bundy [1986] 82. Alternatively, as T. K. Hubbard suggests to me, the "twofold burden" may be the praising of both the epic past and the epinician present.

1 ▫▫ Oral Poetry and Ancient Greek Poetry: Broadening and Narrowing the Terms

The theory of oral poetry as set forth by Milman Parry and Albert Lord resists application to Archaic Greek poetry only if oral poetry is defined too narrowly by the opponents of the theory — and if the surviving poetry of Archaic Greece is treated too broadly as a general example of oral poetry. In what follows, I attempt not only to sketch a concept of oral poetry that is broad enough to accommodate the various forms of ancient Greek poetry but also to redefine these forms in terms of specific sub-types of oral poetry.[1]

The most secure basis for inquiry into the varieties of oral poetry is that of social anthropology.[2] From the vantage point of social anthropologists, various forms of song, poetry, and prose have functioned and continue to function in various ways in various societies without the aid of — in most cases without the existence of — writing.[3] From this vantage point we should

---

1. An earlier version, with ad hoc application to the theories of Wolfgang Kullmann, was printed in *Critical Exchange* (16 [1984] 32–54), a periodical committed to the publication of tentative versions of work still in progress.

2. For my methodology, a particularly influential work has been Jacopin 1981, with its balanced treatment of *parole* as well as *langue*. Cf. also Leach 1982, especially p. 5, with incisive comments on the impact of Jacopin's work.

3. For a forceful presentation, with an emphasis on oral song and poetry, see Zumthor 1983. At p. 34 the author stresses that oral poetry is not poetry minus writing. As an introduction to the characteristics of oral poetry, the standard works remain and will surely remain Parry [1971] and Lord 1960. The intellectual and emotional resistance to the findings of Parry and Lord stems for the most part from various cultural preconceptions of our own times concerning "folk poetry"; for an illuminating historical account of such preconceptions, centering on the dichotomy of "Volkspoesie" and "Hochpoesie," see Bausinger 1980.41–55 ("Folklore und gesunkenes Kultur-gut"). Cf. also Nettl 1965.13: songs can travel not only from "high" culture to "low," but also the other way around. In the case of German traditions the two-way travel between "art music"

not even be talking about oral poetry, for example, as distinct from poetry but rather about written poetry as possibly distinct from poetry: in other words, written poetry is the marked member of the opposition, and the poetry that we call oral is the unmarked.[4]

From the vantage point of our own times, however, *poetry* is by definition written poetry, and what we need to do first is to broaden our concept of poetry. Aside from questions of oral poetry and written poetry, the very word *poetry* becomes a source of confusion, in that it excludes dimensions normally included in the word *song*.

The semantic differentiation between *poetry* and *song* affects the nomenclature of constituent elements common to these two differently perceived media: for example, whereas poetry is said to have *meter*, song has *rhythm*. This conventional distinction has a long history. There are traces attested in the scholarship of the fourth century B.C., where proponents of a rhythmical approach to poetry had an ongoing argument with proponents of a metrical approach.[5] The argument continues to this day, with the "metricians" emphasizing the patterns of alternating long and short syllables in the text as it is composed, and the "rhythmicians," the patterns of rhythm in the song as it is performed. In their argumentation the rhythmicians tend to define poetry in terms of song while the metricians tend to define song in terms of poetry.[6] My position is closer to that of the rhythmicians, to the extent that the affinities between song and poetry in ancient Greece can be viewed in terms of an evolution of various kinds of song into something differentiated from song — let us call it *poetry* — so that song and poetry can then coexist as alternative forms of expression. This point is elaborated as the discussion proceeds.

Another point to be elaborated concerns Archaic Greek poetry and song in general, which I define for the moment as all attested poetry and song from Homer to Pindar: throughout this book, I argue against the need to assume that the medium of writing was necessary for the medium of composition or for the medium of performance and reperformance.[7]

---

and "folk music" is particularly intense (Nettl, p. 69). As songs travel "up" and "down," there can be commensurate patterns of tightening or loosening, either way, in the built-in rules of song making.

4. Cf. p. 8.

5. Cf. Pöhlmann 1960.29–48, especially 29–32, 47–48; also Henderson and Wulstan 1973.48–49 on the different systems of notation used by the rhythmicians and metricians.

6. Cf. Allen 1973.96–125, especially pp. 98–100.

7. On the role of the written text as an alternative to performance, see the discussion in Ch.6, especially with reference to the work of Svenbro 1988. My argument that writing is not essential for either the composition or the performance of poetry and song in the Archaic period of Greece requires, already at this point, one major modification: a notable exception is the Archaic epigram, which does indeed require the medium of writing as an alternative to performance, though not for composition. As Alexiou 1974.13 and 106 argues, the epigram is a poetic form that com-

Let us begin the extended discussion by considering the level of poetry, proceeding from there to the level of song. My premise stems from the observation of Albert Lord, based primarily on ethnographic field work in South Slavic traditions, that composition and performance in oral poetry are aspects of the same process, in that each performance is an act of recomposition.[8] Suffice it for now to add that so long as the traditions of oral poetry are alive in a given society, a written record cannot by itself affect a composition or a performance, and that it cannot stop the process of recomposition in performance.[9]

The basic forms of ancient Greek poetry are traditionally classified in terms of metrical types:

1. dactylic hexameter (Homeric epic and hymns,[10] Hesiodic wisdom- and catalogue-poetry)[11]
2. elegiac distich = dactylic hexameter + "pentameter" (as in Archilochus, Callinus, Mimnermus, Tyrtaeus, Theognis, Solon, Xenophanes, and so on)

---

pensates for emerging patterns of restriction against antiphonal types of lamentation performed in two choral subdivisions, where one subdivision took the role of the dead, engaging in a "dialogue" with another subdivision that took the role of the living; the medium of writing was necessitated as a substitute for actual performance, in the wake of social pressures, exerted within the new context of the emergent city-states, against ostentatious degrees of lamentation on the part of families with powerful ties to the older phases of the existing social system. Even in the case of the epigram, it can be argued that writing had no direct role in the actual composition of the poetry: it appears that the built-in mechanics of composition, which can be ascertained from the diction of the various attested epigrams, do not necessarily correspond to the various local patterns of spelling reflected by these epigrams. Two notable examples in Archaic epigrams are (1) the spelling-out of elided vowels (e.g., CEG 13.4) and (2) the spelling of "movable ν" in violation of the meter (e.g., CEG 288; cf. Kock 1910.22). For an internal cross reference to the genre of the epigram within Homeric poetry, cf. *Iliad* VII 89–90 and the commentary (with bibliography) of Gentili and Giannini 1977.22–25. As for the various other forms of song and poetry, which were not dependent on writing as their primary vehicle of expression, I agree with the general arguments of Herington 1985.41–57 (especially pp. 46–47) against presupposing the necessity of writing as an aid for the performance of songs in what he calls the "song culture" of the Archaic and Classical periods. I disagree, however, with his postulating the necessity of writing for the actual compositon of songs (especially p. 41).

8. Cf. Lord 1960.13–29, 99–123; cf. Nettl 1983.247–258 on the concept of fieldwork.

9. Cf. also pp. 53, 57, 60, 84, 382, 404, and following.

10. For the moment, I shall include under the rubric "Homer" not only the *Iliad* and *Odyssey* but also the Homeric *Hymns* and the poems of the Epic Cycle, such as the *Aithiopis* and *Destruction of Ilion* attributed to Arctinus of Miletus (Proclus, p. 105.21–22 and p. 107.16–17 Allen, Suda s.v.), the *Little Iliad* attributed to Lesches of Mytilene (Proclus, p. 106.19–20; Phaenias F 33 Wehrli, in Clement *Stromateis* 1.131.6), and so on. I reserve for p. 72 a discussion of the patterns of differentiation between Homeric and Cyclic Epic. As we see in that discussion, as also later in Ch.14, the patterns of attribution to Homer become progressively more exclusive as we move forward in time, from the Archaic to the Classical period and beyond.

11. I use the term *wisdom poetry* to encompass both the *Theogony* and the *Works and Days*.

3. iambic trimeter (as in Archilochus, Hipponax, Semonides, Solon, and so on; also as in fifth-century Athenian tragedy and comedy).

In each of these metrical types of Greek poetry, I propose that the format of performance was *recitative* as opposed to *melodic*. This is not to say that such forms of poetry had no prescribed patterning in pitch. But patterns of pitch in poetry were formally and functionally distinct from the patterns of pitch that we, on the basis of our own cultural conditioning, recognize as melody in song. On the level of form, the difference is not as drastic as suggested by the contrast of *monotone* with *song*. I find the term *recitative* more suitable than *monotone*, to the extent that it does not necessarily convey the absence of melody. I use the term *recitation* to indicate either the absence or the reduction of melody. The contrast between not-sung (or recitative) and sung (or melodic) is attested most clearly in fifth-century Athenian tragedy, where the iambic trimeter of dialogue was "spoken" by actors while a wide variety of other meters were sung and danced by a **khoros** 'chorus', to the accompaniment of an **aulos** 'reed'.[12] It bears emphasis that **khoros** 'chorus' in Greek is a group that sings *and* dances, to the accompaniment of wind or string instruments, and that, in Greek traditions, the concept of song is fundamentally connected with the concept of the chorus.[13]

In the claim just made for the iambic trimeter of Athenian tragedy, the argumentation is relatively secure. What follows, however, is a matter of controversy. I am proposing that an absence or at least a reduction of melody—and an absence of instrumental accompaniment and dance—eventually developed not only in the iambic trimeter of dialogue in Athenian drama but also in the iambic trimeter of the old iambic poets (Archilochus, Hipponax, Semonides, Solon, and so on), in the elegiac distich of the old elegiac poets (Archilochus, Callinus, Mimnermus, Tyrtaeus, Theognis, Solon, Xenophanes, and so on), and in the dactylic hexameter of Homer and Hesiod. This proposition may at first seem startling, in view of such internal testimony as Homer's bidding his Muse to *sing* the anger of Achilles (*Iliad* I 1) or Archilochus' boasting that he knows how to 'lead a choral performance' (verb **exarkhō**) of a dithyramb (F 120 W).[14] The significance of this evidence, however, is not what it may first appear, and we must examine it more

---

12. As the discussion proceeds, we shall see that some types of meter that are performed by the chorus are transitional between not-sung and sung, such as the so-called **parakatalogē**, with reduced rather than full melody (p. 27) and with reduced dancing (p. 46).

13. Details in Ch.12, where I also reckon with various lines of argumentation that have been invoked to challenge the notion of an inherited correlation of song and dance in the **khoros**.

14. The meter in which this utterance is composed is trochaic tetrameter catalectic, on which see pp. 45, 46; also p. 395. Also in the same meter is Archilochus F 121 W, where the description 'leading the choral performance' (again, verb **exarkhō**) applies to the choral leader of a paean. Further discussion of the concepts of dithyramb, paean, and choral performance (verb **exarkhō**) in Ch.3 and Ch.12. For more on Archilochus F 120 W, see N 1979.252n.

closely. To begin, the internal evidence of Homeric and Hesiodic diction tells us that the word **aeidō** 'sing' (as in *Iliad* I 1) is a functional synonym, in contexts where the medium refers to its own performance, of the word **e(n)nepō** 'narrate, recite' (as in *Odyssey* i 1), which does not explicitly designate singing.[15] For some, the functional synonymity of **aeidō** 'sing' and **e(n)nepō** 'narrate, recite' is proof that the narrative format must be song — that the Homeric (and presumably Hesiodic) poems were sung and accompanied on the lyre.[16] For others, however, the equating of a word that refers to strategies of narrating Homeric and Hesiodic poetry with a word that refers to the format of singing to the accompaniment of a lyre proves only that such poetry had such a format in some phase of its evolution.[17] Self-references in Archaic Greek poetry may be diachronically valid without being synchronically true.[18] This phenomenon may be designated as *diachronic skewing*.

For example, the epic poetry of Homer refers to epic poetry as a medium that was performed in the context of an evening's feast. Yet we know that the two epic poems of Homer, by virtue of their sheer length alone, defy this context.[19] If we look for the earliest historical evidence, we see that the actually attested context for performing the *Iliad* and *Odyssey* was already in the sixth century not simply the informal occasion of an evening's feast but rather the formal occasion of a festival of Panhellenic repute, such as the Panathenaia in Athens.[20] The performers at such festivals were **rhapsōidoi**

15. Thus for example the **aoidē** 'song' of the Muses at Hesiod *Theogony* 104 is in the context of the poet's bidding them to 'narrate' (**espete**: *Th.* 114) and to 'say' (**eipate**: *Th.* 115). On ennepō as 'recite', see N 1974.11n29.

16. See for example West 1981, who makes this additional observation at p. 113: "We cannot make a distinction between two styles of performance, one characterized as **aeidein**, the other as **enepein**."

17. Again, N 1974.11n29.

18. I am using the terms *diachronic* and *synchronic,* on which see p. 4, not as synonyms for *historical* and *current* respectively. It is a mistake to equate *diachronic* with *historical*, as is often done. Diachrony refers to the potential for evolution *in a structure*. History is not restricted to phenomena that are structurally predictable.

19. For further exploration of this subject, see N 1979.18–20. Note Kirk's (1962.281) comparison of the size of the Homeric compositions with the "leap from the largish pot to the perfectly colossal one" in the evolution of monumental amphoras/craters during the Geometric Period. What interests me in this comparison is that the colossal size of a utensil defies its own utility (N, p. 20 §5n5).

20. For a convenient collection of testimonia concerning the performance of Homeric poetry at the Panathenaia, see Allen 1924.226–227: Lycurgus *Against Leokrates* 102 (the law requires the performance of the poetry of Homer at the Panathenaia, to the exclusion of other poets), Isocrates *Panegyricus* 159, "Plato" *Hipparchus* 228b, Diogenes Laertius 1.57 (Life of Solon). Cf. also Hesychius s.v. **Braurōniois**. Herington 1985.139 calculates that the running time of the *Oresteia* trilogy of Aeschylus "could be more than a quarter of that of a full-length Homeric epic." He concludes: "These and similar figures seem often to be overlooked in discussions about the practicability of delivering the Homeric epics complete on any one occasion" (p. 269n58). A dynasty of tyrants in Athens, the Peisistratidai, played a major role both in the shaping of the Panathenaia and in making this festival the context for performance of epic (scho-

'rhapsodes'.[21] In Plato's *Ion* the rhapsode Ion is dramatized as just having arrived at Athens in order to compete in the rhapsodic contest of the Panathenaia (*Ion* 530ab). That the rhapsodes who performed at such festivals were in competition with each other is evident also from the reference in Herodotus (5.67.1) to **agōnes** 'contests' (ἀγωνίζεσθαι) in the public performance of "Homer's words" by **rhapsōidoi** 'rhapsodes' in the city-state of Sikyon, which were banned under the reign of the tyrant Kleisthenes.[22]

In the case of Homeric poetry, the earliest phases of rhapsodic transmission are associated with the **Homēridai**, a corporation of rhapsodes who traced themselves to an ancestor called **Homēros** (Pindar *Nemean* 2.1; Plato *Phaedrus* 252b; Strabo 14.1.33–35 C 645; *Contest of Homer and Hesiod*, p. 226.13–15 Allen).[23] The basic testimony is most clearly set forth in the scholia to Pindar (*Nemean* 2.1c, III 29.9–18 Drachmann), while the equation of the Homeridai with rhapsodes is specified in the actual text of Pindar (*Nemean* 2.1–3).

The scholia to Pindar (again *Nemean* 2.1c, III 29.9–18 Drachmann) also specify that rhapsodes such as Kynaithos of Chios, credited with the final form of the Homeric *Hymn to Apollo*, could no longer trace themselves to Homer. In other words the tradition continued by Kynaithos is here being

lia to Aristides *Panathenaicus* 3.123; "Plato" *Hipparchus* 228b). The involvement of the Peisistratidai in the institutionalization of Homeric performance at Athens has been explained in terms of a "Peisistratean Recension" (for an introduction to this concept, with bibliography, see [S.] West 1988.36–40). The present book develops an alternative explanation that does not require the textual notion of a "recension." For more on the Peisistratidai and their connection with the performance of Homeric poetry at the Panathenaia, see especially pp. 73, 75, 160, 174, 192.

21. For example, "Plato" *Hipparchus* 228b, concerning the **rhapsōidoi** 'rhapsodes' at the Panathenaia. It appears that some cities were later than others in instituting formal occasions for rhapsodic performance: see Maximus of Tyre 17.5a concerning the "latecomers" Sparta, Crete, and Cyrene (ὀψὲ γὰρ καὶ ἡ Σπάρτη ῥαψῳδεῖ, ὀψὲ δὲ καὶ ἡ Κρήτη, ὀψὲ δὲ καὶ τὸ Δωρικὸν ἐν Λιβύῃ γένος).

22. On **agōn** as 'contest' in poetry, see *Homeric Hymn* 6.19–20 (cf. p. 137). When Heraclitus (22 B 42 DK) says that Homer and Archilochus should be banned from **agōnes** 'contests' in poetic performance, what is really being said is that **rhapsōidoi** 'rhapsodes' (as suggested by the playful use of ῥαπίζεσθαι) should not be allowed to perform Homer and Archilochus. The expression Ὁμηρείων ἐπέων 'Homer's words' in Herodotus 5.67.1 probably refers to the *Seven against Thebes* tradition, not to the *Iliad* or *Odyssey*; see Cingano 1985, whose argumentation meshes with a line of thought that pervades this book: that the patterns of attribution to Homer become increasingly less exclusive as we move further back in time.

23. Cf. Brelich 1958.320–321. Elsewhere I have argued that the "signature" in the Homeric *Hymn to Apollo* 172, where the speaker refers to himself as 'the blind man of Chios', is an idealized self-reference to Homer: see N 1979.5 and 8–9 (for a similar conclusion, from a different point of view, see Burkert 1979.57); the verb οἰκεῖ 'he has an abode' (from noun **oikos** 'house, abode') at line 172 suggests that Homer, as ancestor of the Homeridai, had a hero cult at Chios (cf. N 1985.76–77, 81 §79n1). For other references to the Homeridai of Chios, see Acusilaus FGH 2 F 2, Hellanicus FGH 4 F 20 (both by way of Harpocration s.v.); Isocrates *Helen* 65; Plato *Republic* 599d, *Ion* 530c.

discredited by the sources as no longer authorized by the Homeridai. This Kynaithos is said (ibid.) to have been the first rhapsode to recite Homeric poetry at Syracuse, in the 69th Olympiad (504/1 B.C.), according to Hippostratus (FGH 568 F 5). By implication, Kynaithos was the first recorded winner in a seasonally recurring festival at Syracuse that featured a competition of rhapsodes.[24] As other possible examples of Homeric transmission not authorized by the Homeridai, I cite the traditions about the introduction of Homeric poetry to Sparta by Lycurgus the Lawgiver: he is said to have received the tradition not from the **Homēridai** of Chios but from the **Kreōphūleioi** (Kreophyleioi) of Samos, who traced themselves back to an ancestor called Kreophylos of Samos (Plutarch *Life of Lycurgus* 4).[25]

The ancient sources make it explicit that the rhapsodes, in performing Homeric poetry at the Panathenaia, were constrained by law to take turns in narrating the poetry in its proper sequence ("Plato" *Hipparchus* 228b and Diogenes Laertius 1.57).[26] In other words, even if the size of either the *Iliad* or the *Odyssey* ultimately defied performance by any one person at any one sitting, the monumental proportions of these compositions could evolve in a social context where the sequence of performance, and thereby the sequence of narrative, could be regulated, as in the case of the Panathenaia.[27]

From this rapid survey of rhapsodic traditions in the performance of Homeric poetry, I conclude that the model of simultaneous composition and performance by an oral poet at a feast had evolved organically into a quite different model, with the continuity of composed narrative achieved through a continuum of performance by rhapsodes who take turns at occasions like a Panhellenic festival.[28] The point that I am making about the context of

24. For a defense of the reported date, 504/1 B.C., cf. West 1975, Burkert 1979, and Janko 1982.261–262n88; Burkert adduces, for comparison, a tripod with an epigram dedicated by Simonides on the occasion of his victory in a dithyrambic competition at Athens in 476 B.C. (Simonides EG 28). The relative lateness of the date here assigned to Kynaithos is puzzling to those who posit a relatively early date for Stesichorus, supposedly the earliest attested poet in the Hellenic West. But note the juxtaposition of Homer and Stesichorus in, for example, Simonides PMG 564 (Burkert 1979.56n16); also in Isocrates *Helen* 64–65. I interpret such references to imply the appropriateness of conventionally juxtaposing performances of Homeric and Stesichorean compositions at a given festival.

25. Further details at p. 74. Cf. Burkert 1972, who offers an analysis of myths that connect the transmission of Homeric poetry by the Kreophyleioi with the transmission of Homeric poetry by the Homeridai. This testimony about the reception of Homeric poetry at Sparta may be compared with the remark of Maximus of Tyre 17.5a, cited at p. 22.

26. This detail about taking turns is apparently not taken into account in the arguments of Schnapp-Gourbeillon 1982.720 against N 1979.18–20 (et passim).

27. It remains to ask whether, in the case of the Panathenaia, the reported law about consecutive recitation (cf. also p. 21) was a reinforcement or extension of something that might already have been a convention of, say, the Homeridai. Cf. also Lycurgus *Against Leokrates* 106–107 about a customary law at Sparta concerning the performance of the poetry of Tyrtaeus.

28. Cf. p. 21. I infer that the rhapsodes who took turns reciting within the sequence were in competition with each other. I cite again the reference in Herodotus (5.67.1) to **agōnes** 'contests'

Homeric performance applies also to the medium of performance: just as the Homeric testimony about the performance of epic by singers at feasts belies the synchronic reality of the performance of epic by rhapsodes at Panhellenic festivals, so also the Homeric testimony about the singer's singing to the accompaniment of the lyre belies the synchronic reality of the rhapsode's reciting without any accompaniment at all. On the basis of available evidence, it appears that rhapsodes did not sing the compositions that they performed but rather recited them without the accompaniment of the lyre.[29] So also with Hesiodic poetry: the internal testimony of the composition represents a theogony that is simultaneously *sung* and *danced* by the local Muses of Helikon (*Theogony* 3–4, 8),[30] and yet we know that the *Theogony*, as also the other Hesiodic compositions, was in fact recited by rhapsodes.[31] This is not to say that hexameter could not be sung in the Archaic period:[32] only that hexameter evolved into *poetry* as distinct from *song,* and that its fundamental form of rendition, as poetry, was recitation.[33]

Similarly with old iambic and elegiac poetry we see that the internal testimony refers to choral singing and dancing to the accompaniment of the lyre (as in Theognis 791; cf. 776–779),[34] or singing to both the lyre and the **aulos**

(ἀγωνίζεσθαι) in the public performance of "Homer's words" by **rhapsōidoi** 'rhapsodes' (cf. p. 22). As H. Pelliccia suggests to me, the requirement for consecutive performance by rhapsodes has the effect of ensuring that competition does not result in the arbitrary selection, by ambitious rhapsodes, of the most popular sequences. [S.] West 1988.39–40 leaves room for the possibility that the division of the *Iliad* (and, by extension, of the *Odyssey*) into twenty-four "books" reflects traditional units of performance by rhapsodes at the Panathenaia. On the usage of **rhapsōidiā** in the sense of a 'book' of the *Iliad*, see, e.g., Plutarch *Apophthegmata* 186e.

29. The expression ἄλυρα 'without lyre' in Plato *Laws* 810bc furnishes explicit testimony (cf. also Plato *Ion* 533b5–7). For testimonia about reciting rhapsodes holding a staff instead of a lyre, see West 1966.163–164 (though I disagree with his application of these testimonia to Hesiod *Theogony* 30). The iconographic evidence of vase paintings showing rhapsodes either with a lyre or with a staff (West ibid.) can be viewed as another example of the phenomenon that I have called the *diachronic skewing* of perspective on an evolving institution (on which see p. 21).

30. See Ch.12 on the diachronic correctness of the description, in Hesiod *Theogony* 3–4, 8, of *song* and *dance* in the performance of the Muses.

31. For testimonia on the rhapsodic recitation of Hesiodic poetry, see Plato *Ion* 531a, 532a, *Laws* 658d; also p. 29. For an overview of the evolution from singer (**aoidos**) to reciter (**rhapsōidos**), see N 1982.43–49. Conversely, the concept of rhapsode can be retrojected all the way back to Homer and Hesiod, as when Plato refers to both as rhapsodes (*Republic* 600d).

32. For example, the hexameters attributed to Terpander, which counted as a lyric form, were sung: "Plutarch" *On Music* 1132c (Heraclides Ponticus F 157 Wehrli) and the commentary of Barker 1984.208n18. On the lyric hexameters (and quasi-hexameters) attributed to the archaic figure called Terpander as a model for those of the post-Classical poet Timotheus (including his attested *Persians*): see *On Music* 1132de and the commentary of Barker, p. 209n25.

33. See, for example, Aristotle *Poetics* 1447a29–b8, 1448a11, 1449b29; Plato *Laws* 669d–670a. Cf. Else 1957.37–39.

34. Cf. p. 368.

'reed' (531–534, 759–764),[35] or singing to the **aulos** alone (825–830, 943–944, 1055–1058, 1065–1068).[36] But in fact the external evidence points in another direction, namely, that the attested traditional format of performing the iambic trimeter and the elegiac distich in the Classical period and beyond was simply recitative. The crucial passage is Aristotle *Poetics* 1447b9–23,[37] about which it has been said that "it is our earliest explicit testimony about the mode of performance of elegiac."[38] This is not to say that elegiac distich and iambic trimeter had not in earlier stages been compatible with instrumental (and vocal) melody. In the case of elegiac we can cite not only the internal evidence of references to the **aulos** but even the possible external evidence of testimony in Pausanias and elsewhere for such earlier stages.[39]

The fact remains that the professional performers of old iambic and elegiac poetry were not singers but rhapsodes.[40] The crucial passages in this regard are Plato *Ion* 531a, 532a, with references to rhapsodic performance of the poetry of Archilochus, and Athenaeus 620cd, 632d, a difficult set of references to which we shall return presently. The notion of **rhapsōidos** 'rhapsode' can refer to amateur performances as well, as in Plato *Timaeus* 21b1–7, a passage that describes how the young Critias took part in "rhapsodic" contests in performing the poetry of Solon and others.[41]

---

35. Cf. p. 368.

36. Ibid. See also Archilochus F 58.12 W, where we read ᾄδων ὑπ' αὐλητῆρος 'singing to the accompaniment of the **aulos**-player'; cf. Theognis 533, 825. Note Hipponax F 153 W and Mimnermus T 5 GP, by way of "Plutarch" *On Music* 1134a: the author is discussing an unattested passage of Hipponax where the poet cross-refers to Mimnermus as an **aulos**-player (cf. T 2 and T 4 GP); this cross reference leads the author to assert that in earlier times elegiac poetry was sung to the accompaniment of the **aulos**. See also the report in Pausanias 10.7.5–6 that at an early stage elegiac distichs were performed to the accompaniment of the **aulos** at the Pythian Games, and that this practice came to an end in 582 B.C. Also, the testimony of "Plutarch" *On Music* 1134a suggests the possibility that at an early stage elegiac distichs were performed to the accompaniment of the **aulos** at the Panathenaia. In the case of Pausanias, Bowie 1986.23 argues that the specification of **elegeia** 'elegiac distichs' may have resulted from a misunderstanding of the word **elegoi** in the Echembrotus epigram quoted by Pausanias (Echembrotus, p. 42 GP II).

37. See the commentary of Else 1957.56–57, who integrates the evidence of this passage with that of *Poetics* 1459b32–1460a2 and *Rhetoric* 1409a7; cf. also Lucas 1968.61.

38. Rosenmeyer 1968.218 (by "elegiac" he is referring to the metrically determined category of elegiac distich). Rosenmeyer's 1968 article (following Campbell 1964) concentrates on the elegiac distich because his purpose is to challenge the widespread view, encouraged by the internal testimony sketched in the preceding discussion, that elegiac distich was regularly accompanied by the **aulos**. As for iambic trimeter, it is more generally agreed that it was recited, not sung (cf., e.g., Gentili 1985.45–46).

39. Cf. n36.

40. I suggest that the repertoire of rhapsodes would include such lengthy compositions in elegiac couplets as the *Smyrneis* of Mimnermus, on which see Bowie 1986.27–30.

41. Cf. Brisson 1982.61.

All this is not to say that the references made in Archaic iambic or elegiac poetry to choral performance or instrumental accompaniment are diachronically wrong: as I have been arguing, they are in fact diachronically correct,[42] and it is not without reason that even the performance of a rhapsode is from a traditional point of view an act of "singing" (e.g., Plato *Ion* 535b).[43] Still, such references are synchronically inaccurate, becoming a source of confusion.

In one particular case, the testimony of Athenaeus 620cd, 632d,[44] we must make a special effort to sort out the chronologically diverse strata of information. For example, Athenaeus 620c quotes Clearchus (F 92 Wehrli) as saying that one 'Simonides of Zakynthos used to perform, rhapsode-style, the compositions of Archilochus in theaters, while seated on a stool [**diphros**]' (τὰ Ἀρχιλόχου, φησίν, Σιμωνίδης ὁ Ζακύνθιος ἐν τοῖς θεάτροις ἐπὶ δίφρου καθήμενος ἐρραψῴδει).[45] Also, there is a report of a rhapsode called Mnasion who performed the iambic poetry of Semonides (Athenaeus ibid.)[46] and of a rhapsode called Kleomenes who performed the *Katharmoi* of Empedocles at the Olympics (Dicaearchus F 87 Wehrli, by way of Athenaeus ibid. and Diogenes Laertius 8.63).[47] Similarly we read at Athenaeus 632d that the poetry of Xenophanes, Solon, Theognis, and the like was composed without melody (cf. also Aristoxenus F 92 Wehrli, with commentary). But we also read at Athenaeus 620c (= Chamaeleon F 28 Wehrli) that the poems of Homer, Hesiod, and Archilochus could be sung melodically. This statement follows up on the immediately preceding discussion, at Athenaeus 620b, of **Homēristai**. These **Homēristai** seem to be distinct from the **rhapsōidoi**,[48] and they represent the innovative practice of taking passages that were traditionally recited and setting these passages to music (cf. the references to Homer at Athenaeus 632d; there is also a similar reference to Hesiod in Plutarch *Sympotic Questions* 736e). Such activity was charac-

42. See p. 24. This formulation expands on the positions taken by Campbell 1964 and Rosenmeyer 1968. It can also serve as a friendly amendment to Bowie 1986.27, with whose basic point about the compatibility of the **aulos** 'reed' and the elegiac distich I agree.

43. On this point, see the survey by West 1981.114n8 on attestations of **aeidō** 'sing' as designating the performance of a rhapsode. Cf. also *Timaeus* 21b1–7, as cited immediately above. I agree with Campbell 1964.66 that the expression ἐν ᾠδῇ 'in song [**ōidē**]' in Plutarch *Solon* 8.2 (with reference to Solon F 1 W) refers to "formal recitation like that of a rhapsode." A similar point can be made about the use of **āidō** 'sing' in Philochorus FGH 328 F 216 (by way of Athenaeus 630f). These considerations affect the arguments of Bowie 1986.19n29.

44. Cited at p. 25.

45. Cf. West 1981.125.

46. For the reading "Semonides" instead of "Simonides," see West ibid.

47. West 1981.125 dates these testimonia to the fourth century B.C., or the end of the fifth at the earliest. On the setting for the performance of the rhapsode Kleomenes, we may compare the report that Dionysius I of Syracuse engaged rhapsodes to perform his poetry at Olympia (Diodorus Siculus 14.109).

48. See the useful references of West 1970.919.

teristic of the post-Classical era,[49] about which it has been said: "So great is the ascendancy of song over speech that, in the [Hellenistic] revivals of tragic and comic texts of the 5th and 4th centuries B.C., it even takes over the parts composed in iambic trimeters, intended originally for simple recitation."[50]

Once such a phase is reached, where traditionally recited pieces of poetry are being set to music, it becomes easy to confuse and reinterpret the diachrony of various sung and recited meters that are obviously related to each other. For example, apparently on the basis of parallelisms in meter and diction between Homer and Terpander, a representative of Archaic lyric who was credited with the composition of songs sung to the lyre,[51] Heraclides Ponticus is cited as saying that Terpander set his own poems and those of Homer to music (F 157 Wehrli in "Plutarch" *On Music* 1132c). So also Stesichorus is described as having set what are described as his **epē**, loosely to be translated as *hexameters*, to music ("Plutarch" *On Music* 1132c). As we see later, this hexameter of Stesichorus is cognate with, but not identical to, the Homeric hexameter.[52] Further, Archilochus is credited with the invention of the **parakatalogē**, that is, a delivery characterized by reduced rather than full melody, with the accompaniment of a musical instrument ("Plutarch" *On Music* 1141a).[53] In "Aristotle" *Problems* 19.6, the **parakatalogē** is described as a form of delivery that explicitly contrasts with song.[54] Archilochus is generally credited with 'introducing the practice of having some iambics spoken with instrumental accompaniment and others sung with it' (ἔτι δὲ τῶν ἰαμβείων τὸ τὰ μὲν λέγεσθαι παρὰ τὴν κροῦσιν, τὰ δὲ ᾄδεσθαι, Ἀρχίλοχόν φασι καταδεῖξαι "Plutarch" *On Music* 1141b).

The reported distinctions, with reference to the "inventions" of Archilochus, between iambics that are sung as well as instrumentally accompanied and those that are not sung, that is, with reduced melody, though instrumentally accompanied, are valuable in revealing an intermediate stage in what I argue is an evolution from sung to spoken forms in the Archaic period. The claim that Archilochus was the actual inventor of the sung and the intermediate forms can be discounted as readily as the parallel claim that he invented the iambic trimeter (see *On Music* 1140f). What is essential is that these

49. As we see from a survey by Gentili 1979.26–31, with a focus on the performance of drama. Cf. also West 1986 on the hexameters of a newly-discovered inscription from Epidaurus, a fragment of a hymn that he dates "not later than the third century B.C." (p. 45; cf. p. 44n19). The melodic notations preserved in this inscription reflect, in West's opinion, a uniform instrumental cadence, hexameter after hexameter.

50. Gentili, p. 26.

51. See p. 24.

52. Cf. p. 458.

53. Cf. the commentary of Barker 1984.212nn183, 185.

54. Cf. Aristides Quintilianus, pp. 5.25–6.7 (ed. Winnington-Ingram) on the recitation of poetry as an intermediate category, to be placed between the categories of speech and song. See further at p. 39. Cf. also Barker, p. 234n183.

"inventions" are then correlated with historically attested innovations that start with the late fifth century, such as those of Crexus, in setting iambic meters to music (*On Music* 1141b); Crexus was a contemporary of Timotheus and Philoxenus (1135c).[55] In the post-Classical period, when poetry is being set to music — that is, the period starting with the likes of Crexus, Timotheus, and Philoxenus — we see that the archaic forms of song, as also of reduced song, like **parakataloge**, are being treated as if they too were such "innovations".[56]

We can be satisfied with the diachronic correctness of ancient Greek poetry's references to itself as song by noting that such self-references are traditional, not innovative. The traditional phrases in Homeric poetry and elsewhere about the subject of singing and song have an Indo-European ancestry.[57] Even the word **rhapsōidos** 'rhapsode', designating the professional reciter of poetry, is built on a concept of artistic self-reference ('he who stitches together the song') that is likewise of Indo-European provenience.[58] The institutional reality of formal competition among rhapsodes, immortalized for us in Plato's dialogue *Ion* (530a),[59] seems to be a direct heritage of formal competition among singers, as reflected directly in passages like *Homeric Hymn* 6.19–20[60] and indirectly in the numerous myths about such competitions.[61] There is enough evidence, then, to conclude that what the rhapsodes recited was directly descended from what earlier singers had sung.[62]

---

55. Cf. the comments of Barker, p. 52n20.

56. For a similar line of thinking, note the report of Timomachus (FGH 754 F 1 in Athenaeus 638a), who says that one Stesandros was the first to set Homer to the lyre for a performance at Delphi; it is as if the medium of "Homer" had never been *sung* before, only *spoken*.

57. Cf. N 1974.10n29 and 244–261.

58. Durante 1976.177–179. The notion of **rhapsōidos** 'rhapsode' as 'he who stitches together the song' is made explicit in Pindar *Nemean* 2.1–3. On the concept of **oimē** as a sort of textual "fil d' Ariane," see Svenbro 1976.45n135.

59. Cf. also Herodotus 5.67.1, on which see also p. 22. For further testimonia from inscriptions recording various contests of rhapsodes, see West 1981.114n13. Cf. also Brisson 1982.62–63, with a convenient summary of details, gleaned from the *Ion* of Plato, about the competition of rhapsodes at the Panathenaia.

60. Quoted at p. 77. Further details on this passage at p. 137.

61. For a survey of the institution of competition among singers, see Dunkel 1979; cf. N 1979.311 §2n6. For an example of a myth about such a competition, I cite the story of a contest between Arctinus of Miletus and Lesches of Mytilene, two of the poets of the Epic Cycle (Phaenias F 33 Wehrli, in Clement *Stromateis* 1.131.6). A more famous example is the *Contest of Homer and Hesiod* tradition (pp. 225–238 Allen); for bibliography, see Janko 1982.259–260n80; cf. also Dunkel 1979.252–253. On the interrelationship of narrative structure between the Homeric *Iliad* and *Odyssey* on the one hand and the Epic Cycle on the other, see p. 72.

62. For further arguments, see N 1982.43–49.

There is no compelling reason to believe that the medium of writing had anything to do with the traditions of the rhapsodes.[63] In fact there is positive evidence that their mnemonic techniques were independent of writing. The textual tradition of Homeric poetry as we have it stems from Hellenistic Alexandria, where the practice of accentual notation was invented. This textual tradition bears witness to certain archaic patterns of Homeric accentuation that were no longer current in the everyday Greek language— patterns that can now be verified through the application of Indo-European linguistics.[64] This comparative evidence leads to the conclusion that these patterns were preserved through norms of recitation inherited by the rhapsodes; the factor of writing seems to be ruled out, since a textual tradition for the notation of accents was evidently lacking before Alexandrian times.[65] Even in such matters of minute detail, we may infer that the oral tradition of the rhapsodes was inherited—albeit in an ossified or crystalized phase— from the oral tradition of the singers who came before them.[66]

Up to this point, I have used the term *oral tradition* only in a broad sense—to the extent that the medium of writing is not to be taken as a prerequisite for either composition or transmission. As we approach the subject of oral poetry in particular, I am for the moment more interested in the applicability of the term *poetry*, as distinct from *song*, to the oral traditions of ancient Greece. We have seen that a differentiation seems to have taken place, which can be represented in the following diachronic scheme:[67]

63. This is not to say that in historical times they could not have owned texts of what they recited (cf. Xenophon *Memorabilia* 4.2.10); in any case, it is clear that the rhapsodes recited from memory (Xenophon *Symposium* 3.6).

64. N 1982.45 and 69, citing Wackernagel [1953] p. 1103; also West 1981.114n12.

65. Ibid.

66. Note also the bits of information adduced by Allen 1924.48 about the **sunthutai Mousōn Hēsiodeiōn** 'fellow-sacrificers to the Hesiodic Muses' (IG VII 1785; cf. also 4240), a corporation that "owned the land at Thespiae which contained the sacred spots": Allen offers the theory that this corporation was analogous to the **Homēridai** in that it seems to have exercised authority over the corpus of Hesiodic poetry. At p. 72 of Allen's book, we find a parallel, not adduced at p. 48, that can serve as a powerful additional argument in favor of Allen's theory: in Plutarch *Banquet of the Seven Sages* 149f-150a, there is mention of one Ardalos of Trozen, supposedly a contemporary of the Seven Sages and described as both an **aulōidos** 'aulos-singer' (aulos = 'reed') and a ἱερεὺς τῶν Ἀρδαλείων Μουσῶν 'priest of the Ardalean Muses'. The cult of these "Ardalean Muses" had been supposedly established by the ancestor of this Ardalos, also called Ardalos of Trozen (Plutarch 150a), who is elsewhere reported to be the inventor of the **aulos** (Pausanias 2.31.3). This parallelism suggests that the 'fellow-sacrificers to the Hesiodic Muses' are **rhapsōidoi** who transmit the compositions of Hesiod, just as the 'priests of the Ardalean Muses' are **aulōidoi** who transmit the compositions of their ancestor Ardalos—and just as the **Homēridai** 'sons of Homer' transmit the compositions of their ancestor Homer.

67. I print *song types*, not just *song*, to indicate the potential plurality of song types in opposition with any single given type of poetry. I elaborate on this point in what follows.

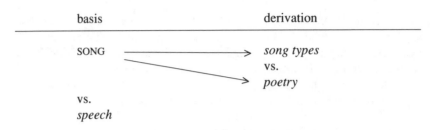

basis	derivation

SONG ⟶ *song types*
vs.
poetry

vs.
speech

By *speech* I mean everyday or unmarked language, and by SONG I mean special or marked language that is set off from *speech* on the formal level of
phonology, morphology, syntax, or any combination of these three.[68] From a
functional point of view, SONG would be any speech-act that is *considered* set
apart from plain or everyday speech from the standpoint of a given society.[69]

The perception of plain or everyday *speech* is a variable abstraction that
depends on the concrete realization of whatever special speech, or SONG, is
set apart for a special context. In small-scale societies, the setting apart
would normally happen in terms of myth and ritual.

I use the word *ritual* here not in terms of our own cultural preconceptions but in terms of the broadest possible anthropological perspective.[70] For
the moment, I invoke the working definition of *ritual* offered by Walter
Burkert: "Ritual, in its outward aspect, is a programme of demonstrative acts
to be performed in set sequence and often at a set place and time — sacred
insofar as every omission or deviation arouses deep anxiety and calls forth
sanctions. As communication and social imprinting, ritual establishes and
secures the solidarity of the closed group."[71] The insistence of ritual on a set
order of things should not be misunderstood to mean that all rituals are static
and that all aspects of rituals are rigid. Even when a given society deems a
given ritual to be static and never changing, it may in fact be dynamic and
ever changing, responding to the ever changing structure of the society that it
articulates. Also, even within the strict framework of a given ritual, the various rigid patterns that conform to an ideology of unchangeability may be
combined with various flexible patterns that conform to the needs of the here
and now. Such is the case with the festivals of Greek city-states.

---

68. On the distinction between unmarked and marked members of an opposition, see p. 5.

69. On the notion of *speech-act*, see p. 8.

70. Cf. Leach 1982, especially pp. 5–6. For further elaboration, see p. 117. Most Classicists
of my generation tend to resist the very concept of *ritual* in the wake of the earlier excesses of the
so-called Cambridge School: see, for example, Herington 1985.123–124. Herington's important
contributions to our understanding of the earlier forms of Athenian tragedy could be further
enhanced through a broader perspective of ritual. In this regard I find it helpful to cite the sketch
offered by Seaford 1984.10–16. I agree with Seaford that his findings help confirm "the
unfashionable view that the performance of tragedy originated in the practice of ritual" (p. 14).

71. Burkert 1985.8.

As for *myth*, it can be defined for the moment as "a traditional narrative that is used as a designation of reality. Myth is applied narrative. Myth describes a meaningful and important reality that applies to the aggregate, going beyond the individual."[72]

In small-scale societies — rather than complex ones — we can observe most clearly the symbiosis of ritual and myth, how neither is to be derived from the other, and how the language of ritual and myth is *marked*, let us call it SONG, while everyday language, *speech*, is *unmarked*. To repeat, the perception of plain or everyday speech is a variable abstraction that depends on the concrete realization of whatever special speech is set apart for a special context, let us call it *occasion*. In small-scale societies, the setting apart is normally a matter of ritual and myth, and the idea of ritual includes not only such basic activities as sacrifice and prayer but also such diverse occasions as meeting, eating and drinking, courtship, hunting, gathering, farming, building, and traveling.[73] The marked speech-acts associated with the special occasions of ritual and myth are what we are calling SONG. Internal criteria for marked speech-acts can be expected to vary from society to society: what may be marked in one may be unmarked or everyday in another. A striking example is the Bahutu convention of singing one kind of song while paddling upstream, another while paddling downstream.[74] There are potential differentiations of marked and unmarked categories within everyday language as well.

Marked speech-acts could be a matter of denial as well as affirmation or reinforcement, as in the case of the Greek word **an-ain-omai** 'deny', opposed to an unattested *ain-omai 'affirm'. The form *ain-omai conveys that the thing affirmed is a social contract, in the broadest sense, as we can see from the derivative of *ain-omai, ainos, in the sense of 'legislative decision or resolution'.[75] In other words **ainos** is authoritative speech: it is an affirmation, a marked speech-act, made by and for a marked social group.[76]

In complex societies — and the situation in Archaic Greece can already be described as such — the pervasiveness of myth and ritual, as well as their connectedness with each other, may be considerably weakened. Still, the marking of speech, that is, the turning of unmarked *speech* into marked SONG, may persist as the basic way to convey meaning in the context of ritual and myth. There is a reflex of this pattern in the usage of the Greek verb **muō**, which means 'I have my mouth closed' or 'I have my eyes closed' in

---

72. My translation, with slight modifications, of Burkert 1979b.29. For an illuminating discussion of myth, especially useful to those who are unfamiliar with the perspectives of social anthropology, I cite Leach 1982.

73. Cf. Leach, pp. 5–6.

74. Nettl 1965.120.

75. For example, SIG 672.15. Commentary and further discussion by Edmunds 1985.105.

76. Further details at p. 147.

everyday situations,[77] but 'I say in a special way' or 'I see in a special way' in marked situations of ritual. The latter meaning is evident in the derivatives **mustēs** 'one who is initiated' and **mustērion** 'that into which one is initiated, mystery [Latin *mysterium*]'.[78] So also the word **mūthos** 'myth', it has been argued, is a derivative of the same root from which **muō** is derived;[79] its special meaning seems to be 'special speech' as opposed to everyday speech.[80] For an illustration of the semantics underlying the usage of these Greek words, I cite Sophocles *Oedipus at Colonus* 1641–1644: the visualization and the verbalization of whatever it was that finally happened to Oedipus in the precinct of the Eumenides at Colonus are restricted, in that the precise location of his corpse is a sacred secret (1545–1546, 1761–1763).[81] Only Theseus, by virtue of being the proto-priest by hindsight for the Athenians of the here and now, is to witness what happened, which is called the **drōmena** (1644).[82] Here the visualization and the verbalization of the myth, what happened to Oedipus, is restricted to the sacred context of ritual, controlled by the heritage of priestly authority from Theseus.[83]

From an anthropological standpoint, *myth* is indeed *special speech* in that it is a given society's way of affirming its own reality through narrative.[84] In Homeric diction, we see that the ancestor of our word *myth*, Greek **mūthos**, actually designates speech-acts, such as formal boasts, threats, laments, invectives, prophecies, prayers, and so on.[85] Let us for the moment

77. Chantraine DELG 728: from onomatopoeic **mū**, with the primary meaning of opening and closing the lips (cf. Aristophanes *Knights* 10: see Chantraine, p. 717).

78. We may compare the semiotics of whispering, which may count as a form of not-speaking in everyday or unmarked situations and as a form of special speaking in marked situations of secrecy, sacredness, and the like.

79. See Chantraine, pp. 718–717, with bibliography in support of the argument that **mūthos** 'myth' is likewise derived from onomatopoeic **mū**. Despite the morphological grounds for accepting this derivation, Chantraine expresses doubts on semantic grounds. I hope that my interpretation here helps dispel that doubt.

80. For more on **mūthos** 'myth', see pp. 65 and following. "Surviving examples" in social institutions tend to reflect a general pattern in earlier stages but only a particular situation in later stages of attestation.

81. For the belief that the corpse of the hero was a talisman of fertility for his native or adoptive community, see p. 178. On the hero cult of Oedipus at Colonus as represented by the tragedy of that name, see Edmunds 1981, especially p. 223n8 (a reference that is accidentally omitted in N 1985.76–77).

82. The participle **drōmena** is from the verb **draō**, which means 'do, perform' within the world of tragedy but also 'sacrifice, perform ritual' within the "real world," the outer world that frames the world of tragedy. See p. 387. The participle **drōmena**, as used outside of tragedy, designates 'ritual' (e.g., Pausanias 9.27.2, 9.30.12; cf. Burkert 1983.33n14). Inside tragedy, as here at Sophocles *Oedipus at Colonus* 1644, it bears the more inclusive and ambiguous sense of 'things that are done', 'things that are happening'.

83. N 1982b. The key lines are in Sophocles *Oedipus at Colonus* 1641–1644.

84. On the truth-value of myth: Leach 1982.2–7.

85. Detailed demonstration in Martin 1989.12–42. On the concept of *speech-act*, see p. 8.

take as a given, then, that the function of marked speech is to convey meaning in the context of ritual and myth.

In most societies, not only the smaller-scale but the more complex as well, the pattern of opposition between marked and unmarked speech takes the form of an opposition between SONG and *speech* respectively, with the "singing" of SONG being marked by a wide variety of patterns resulting from constraints on available features of *speech* in the given language. From the standpoint of our own cultural preconceptions, singing is a patterning of both melody (stylized tone or intonation)[86] and rhythm (stylized duration and/or intensity).[87] From a cross cultural survey of a variety of societies, however, it is evident that singing may also be equated with many other available types of stylized phonological patterning, such as isosyllabism, rhyme, assonance, and alliteration, and that the patterning of SONG extends to the levels of morphology and syntax as well.[88] Moreover, there is a potential reinforcement of SONG with motor activity, as minimal as muscular tension[89] or as maximal as corresponding movement of the body in the form of dance.[90] With reference to dance, from this point onward, I argue that the activity of dancing *to* the

86. When differences in pitch have a lexical function (as in ancient Greek), it is a matter of tone; where they have a syntactical function (as in English), it is a matter of intonation: cf. Devine and Stephens 1985.151.

87. On duration and intensity as aspects of "stress," cf. Devine and Stephens, p. 152. Further discussion at p. 34.

88. See Guillén 1985.93–121, especially pp. 103–104, and Bright 1963.29. One feature of the fusion of experience in ritual, as Tambiah 1985.165 suggests, is "the hyper-regular surface structure of ritual language: the poetic devices such as rhyme, meter, assonance, and alliteration generate an overall quality of union and a blurring of grammatical boundaries." Cf. also Jakobson 1960.358.

89. Note the following remark of Merriam 1964.119: "Some connection is made between pitch and muscle tension; the musician becomes accustomed to the muscle tension which he knows to be correct. One Basongye musician expressed this by saying that he chooses a pitch 'which does not make me sweat', and the same musician very logically noted that he comes to know the voices of the people with whom he sings and thus chooses a starting pitch 'in the middle' which he knows will suit all the voices."

90. Cf. Allen 1973.100. The concept of *dance* should not be defined narrowly on the basis of our own cultural preconceptions. The categories of stylized bodily movement corresponding to our notion of *dance* vary from society to society. Cf. Royce 1977. Further details are at p. 38. On dance as an optional element in ballad performance, see Nettl 1965.56; for more details, with reference to Faroese culture, see Wylie and Margolin 1981.99, 115, 117. I note in particular the following description, p. 99:

> At the village dancehall—or, before villages had dancehalls, in a house rented for the occasion—men and women link arms to form a long, twisting circle. Anyone may join the circle at any point. They dance with a rhythmically shuffling, kicking step to the singing of the ballads. There is no instrumental accompaniment. A *skipari* (leader) sings the verses of a ballad, while the rest of the singers join in on the verses (if they know them) and on the refrain. When one ballad ends, the ring keeps moving round for a few moments until a new *skipari* starts up a new one.

words of SONG is primary, while dancing without the subtext, as it were, of SONG is secondary.[91]

This topic brings us to yet another type of markedness, yet another level of reinforcement for SONG, instrumental music. I also argue that instrumental accompaniment of the words of SONG is primary, while instrumental solo is secondary.[92] In the case of instrumental music, there can even come about a transition from marking speech as special to imitating special speech.[93] In making these arguments, my central point remains that the essential characteristic of SONG is the simple fact of its actual markedness or distinctness from everyday *speech*.

Let us pursue the argument with a tentative formulation on the level of phonology, considering the elements of rhythm and melody, prime constituents of our notion of singing. From the standpoint of the Greek language, what potentially sets SONG apart from *speech* is a differentiation in patterns of duration/intensity (eventually rhythm) and pitch (eventually melody).[94] In a

91. Cf. the ethnographic testimony discussed briefly by Merriam 1964.275.

92. Cf. Herzog 1934, Schneider 1957.32–33, and especially Sultan 1988.396–397. Note too Bake 1957.196–197 on the Indic traditional teaching that vocal music is "pure" sound while instrumental music is a "manifestation" of sound. As Nettl 1965.51 points out, the limitations of the human voice (not to mention the limitations of the human ear), as contrasted with the relatively greater freedom of sound-range in musical instruments, lead to differences in the patterns of evolution for vocal and instrumental music. In this connection it is useful to ponder the discussion of Bright 1963.27. See in general the survey of the relationships between language and music in Nettl 1964.281–292. On the tendency of specialization and even professionalization in the social position of those who perform SONG with instrumental accompaniment and, by extension, of those who perform musical instruments, see Nettl 1965.50. On the development of instrumental solo playing on the **aulos**, so that the **aulōidos** 'he who sings to the accompaniment of the **aulos** [reed]' gives way to the **aulētēs** 'he who plays the **aulos**', see Pausanias 10.7.4, with the terminus of 582 B.C. at the Pythian Games.

93. Hence the notion of "talking instruments," as discussed by Stern 1957; cf. also Ong 1977b. On instrumental music as imitation of the "special speech" of bird song, see Merriam 1964.75. Conversely, at one step further removed, unusual vocal techniques like Alpine yodeling can be traced back to the imitation of instruments: cf. Nettl 1956.58.

94. On "stress" in ancient Greek, which includes the phonological features of duration and intensity but not pitch, see the fundamental work of Allen 1973; for an updated defense of Allen's formulation, see Devine and Stephens 1985. From the standpoint of general phonetics, stress may be a matter of duration, intensity, and pitch. From a survey of typological evidence, Devine and Stephens, p. 152, point to "instances of languages in which intensity is independent of both pitch and duration (Japanese), languages in which intensity is independent of duration and combines with pitch as an exponent of stress (Estonian, Komi), and languages in which intensity combines with both pitch and duration as an exponent of stress (English)." When differences in pitch have a lexical function, as in ancient Greek, it is a matter of tone; where they have a syntactical function, as in English, it is a matter of intonation: see p. 33. In ancient Greek, pitch is thus a matter of morphology as well as phonology. This is being taught today as the sum total of Greek accentuation. Allen's discovery, that ancient Greek also had a system of duration and intensity that was independent of its system of pitch, suggests that the two systems merged in Modern Greek, where the inherited patterns of pitch are correlated with both duration and intensity (Devine and Stephens, p. 146n83).

later stage of development what sets *song* apart from *poetry* is a further differentiation on the level of pitch (melody), so that *song* is plus melody while *poetry* is minus melody or reduced melody. The notion of *plus melody* is in line with such terms as *lyric poetry* or *melic poetry*, applicable to the medium of the main figure of this book, the poet Pindar.

My view of *poetry* as something derived from SONG and differentiated from *song* runs counter to the view of metricians for whom song is poetry set to music. According to this second of two possible lines of thought, music would be extrinsic to language. This other view, however, runs counter to the experience of fieldwork in ethnomusicology, a discipline that has built a strong case against the fallacy of treating music as a "universal language."[95] Our own cultural prejudices in favor of such a concept can be traced to medieval Europe, where the eventual dissociation of language and music was already under way.[96] Toward the end of the fourteenth century, Eustache Deschamps already made a distinction between the "natural music" of language and the "artificial music" of traditional melodies.[97] But it is clear in this case that the association of language and music is primary. For example, a study of attested traditions of Provençal singing has shown that only with the eventual divorce of melody from "text" can melody take on the characteristics that we, from the standpoint of our own cultural preconceptions, can recognize as music.[98] With the advent of polyphony, the motet can triumph over its libretto; but before that, in the twelfth and thirteenth centuries, the melodic traditions were still bound to phraseological traditions of song.[99] From the standpoint of medieval poetics, recognition as one good at melodies merely required a good vocal register;[100] a singer could be good at producing melodies and still be bad at producing words — and therefore a bad singer.[101]

Of the two terms, *lyric* and *melic*, the first is the more elusive in that it tends to be applied in contemporary academic usage to practically all Archaic Greek poetry except Homer and Hesiod. For my purposes, however, *lyric* is still the more useful term since it is more general. As such, *lyric* is suitable for distinguishing the general notion of song from the more specific one of poetry, which is restricted to the recitative medium of epic, elegiac, and iambic trimeter. From here on I use the word *lyric* as a parallel to *song*, exclud-

---

95. Cf. Merriam 1964.10–11.

96. See Zumthor 1972.100.

97. Ibid.

98. Zink 1972.24: "Quand le divorce entre le texte et la musique sera comsommé, la musique, paradoxalement, pourra prendre plus d'importance; elle sera développée pour elle-même et pour l'effet extérieur qu'elle produit, indépendamment des exigences internes du poème."

99. Zink, pp. 17–24; especially p. 23n2.

100. Examples in Zink, p. 23n1.

101. Zink, p. 20n3.

ing the elegiac and the iambic trimeter. In current usage such exclusion is generally not observed. It is instructive to notice, however, one particular constraint even in current usage against the application of the term *lyric*: we cannot say that the iambic trimeter of Athenian tragedy and comedy is *lyric* for the simple reason that it is patently recited as opposed to sung. As for what is sung, we call that *lyric* by way of opposition to what is recited. Thus the opposition of lyric meters and iambic trimeter in Athenian drama is that of song and poetry. We may note the dictum of Aristotle to the effect that iambic trimeter approximates, more closely than any other meter, everyday speech in real life (*Poetics* 1449a22–27; cf. *Rhetoric* 1408b33). Thus the opposition of song and poetry in tragedy not only recapitulates diachronically an earlier opposition of SONG and *speech*: it also imitates synchronically the actual opposition of *song* and *speech* in "real life."

Whereas the iambic trimeter of tragedy regularly imitates *speech*, the dactylic hexameter of epic occasionally imitates SONG, whenever Homeric poetry "quotes" a speech-act like a song of lament.[102] Thus the dactylic hexameter of epic, unlike the iambic trimeter of drama, is not used as a contrast to song; rather it can be used as an imitation of song. This distinction between these two kinds of poetry helps explain Aristotle's perception that the rhythms of dactylic hexameter, unlike those of iambic trimeter, are not close to those of everyday speech (*Poetics* 1449a27–28). In any case, the art of imitating *speech*, as achieved in the medium of the iambic trimeter, can be measured by its realistic effects: the more the realism, the greater the artifice.[103]

Undifferentiated SONG as opposed to *speech* can be imagined as having had features that ranged all the way from what we see in differentiated *song* to what we see in *poetry*. Thus, for example, SONG in any given society may or may not require melody. In other words what counts as *poetry* for us may in another given society count as *song* if there are no melodic prerequisites. In this light, I cite a particularly useful formulation by Dan Ben-Amos, based on a wide cross cultural variety of ethnographic data:

> The existence or absence of metric substructure in a message is the quality first recognized in any communicative event and hence serves

---

102. A prominent example is *Iliad* XXIV 723–776, where the narrative gives a direct quotation of three different laments, performed by three of Hektor's female next of kin on the occasion of the hero's funeral. At this funeral there are also professional **aoidoi** 'singers' (XXIV 720) who sing a more stylized kind of lament, called the **thrēnos** (721), while the nonprofessional singers, next of kin to the deceased, are singing a less differentiated kind of lament, called the **goos** (XXIV 723, 747, 761). Correspondingly, at the funeral of Achilles, his next of kin, the Nereids, sing undifferentiated laments (*Odyssey* xxiv 58–59), while the Muses sing a differentiated **thrēnos** (xxiv 60–61). Cf. N 1979.112.

103. On the concept of *imitation* as a narrowed version of the concept of reenactment, see p. 43.

as the primary and most inclusive attribute for the categorization of oral tradition. Consequently, prose [= what I have been calling *speech*] and poetry [= what I have been calling SONG] constitute a binary set in which the metric substructure is the crucial attribute that differentiates between these two major divisions. It serves as the definitive feature that polarizes any verbal communication and does not provide any possible intermediary positions. A message is either rhythmic or not. However, within the category of poetry [in my sense of SONG], speakers may be able to perceive several patterns of verbal metrical redundancy which they would recognize as qualitatively different genres.[104]

This statement, useful as it is, can be made more precise with reference to the term *metric substructure*. First, I turn to the cross cultural linguistic evidence assembled by W. S. Allen, showing that all phraseology has built-in rhythm.[105] In line with this thinking, I would argue that the inherited words of SONG *contain* the rhythm, from a diachronic point of view. In an earlier work on Greek and Indic metrics, I had put it this way:

> At first, the reasoning goes, traditional phraseology simply contains built-in rhythms. Later, the factor of tradition leads to the preference of phrases with some rhythms over phrases with other rhythms. Still later, the preferred rhythms have their own dynamics and become regulators of any incoming non-traditional phraseology. By becoming a viable structure in its own right, meter may evolve independently of traditional phraseology. Recent metrical developments may even obliterate aspects of the selfsame traditional phraseology that had engendered them, if these aspects no longer match the meter.[106]

Such a formulation, to be sure, presupposes that the traditional phraseology of SONG, generating fixed rhythmical patterns, is itself already regulated by principles of phonological, morphological, and syntactical parallelism and repetition that serve to differentiate SONG from *speech*.[107]

104. Ben-Amos 1976.228. He quotes at this point Andrzejewski and Lewis 1964.46, who note, as an example: "the Somali classify their poems into various distinct types, each of which has its own specific name. It seems that their classification is mainly based on two prosodic factors: the type of tune to which the poem is chanted or sung, and the rhythmic pattern of the words." The formulation of Ben-Amos may be compared with that of Aristotle *Poetics* 1447b9–23, as discussed at p. 25.

105. Allen 1973.99–101, who prefers in the end not to use the word *rhythm* (p. 101). I continue to use it here in the sense of "a system that operates in terms of stress (duration or intensity or both)."

106. N 1974.145. Parts of this statement are already quoted in Allen 1973.14, 258 (cf. also p. 13) with the bibliographical tag "Nagy 1970b," listed as "Monograph (unpub.) on Indo-European metrics" (Allen, p. 378). Without Allen's generous acknowledgment, the existence of an unpublished 1970 version of N 1974 would not be a matter of public record (in N 1979b.629n1 I list those to whom I had sent copies of this unpublished version).

107. On the fundamental role of parallelisms and repetitions in differentiating what I am

Granted, a factor like rhythm may become stylized to the point that it can become transferred from the words of song, in the forms of dance and instrumental music.[108] I am arguing, however, that patterns of convergence and parallelism between the rhythm in the words of SONG and the rhythm in the forms of dance and instrumental music are primary, while patterns of divergence and contrast are secondary. In any case the *perception* of rhythm depends ultimately on the innate human capacity for language.[109] In that sense the very process of dance is related to the inner rhythms of language. The linguistic factor of stress, which seems to be the basis of rhythm in languages like Greek, is psychologically perceived in terms of body movement.[110] We may compare the discussion in Plato *Laws* 653e-654a (also *Laws* 665a), where the combination of rhythmic and melodic idiom is synthetically visualized as **khoreiā** 'choral song and dance'.[111] I am proposing that the phraseology of SONG tends to stylize and regularize its own built-in rhythms, and that these regularizations result diachronically in what we call *meter*.[112]

---

calling here SONG and *speech*, see again Guillén 1985.93–121, especially pp. 103–104 with reference to the work of Žirmunskij 1965 following Steinitz 1934.

108. There is a particularly interesting example cited by Allen 1973.259n1: in the Luganda traditions of accompaniment, short syllables are regularly accompanied by one drumbeat and long syllables, by two drumbeats. See also Ong 1977b.

109. Allen, pp. 99–101.

110. I cite the formulation of Allen, p. 100 (where "stress" is intended to include the components of duration and intensity: cf. p. 34): "Implicitly or explicitly underlying this identification of stress as the basis of rhythm is the conception of rhythm as movement, and of stress, in the production of audible linguistic phenomena, as the motor activity par excellence." Cf. Wylie and Margolin 1981.115, quoting from a 1906 description of Faroese ballad performance and dancing, where the dancers coordinate their voices and movements: "What, moreover, should be well looked after in the ballad singing is to 'get the word under the foot', as the old ones used to say. One gets the word under the foot when one stresses one word or syllable at the same time that one steps along with the foot."

111. In light of this image I would translate **skhēma** as 'dance-figure' in Plato *Laws* 654e and 655a, despite the fact, noted by Barker 1984.142n60, that the usage of Plato does not restrict **skhēma** to the context of the dance. For the notion of **skhēmata** as 'dance-figures', postures and gestures that *represent,* see Barker 119n10 on Xenophon *Symposium* 2.15. With reference to **skhēma** as a pose that *represents*, D. Arnold draws my attention to the use of the verb **ekhō**, from which the noun **skhēma** is derived, in Herodotus 1.31.5: at the moment that the brothers Kleobis and Biton die after their ordeal in the service of the goddess Hera, it is said that ἐν τέλεϊ τούτῳ ἔσχοντο 'they were held fast in this sacred accomplishment' (the context is discussed further at p. 245). The narrative goes on to say that this precise moment, with the pose of the brothers in perfect synchrony, is captured as if in a "freeze frame" by the people of Argos, who witnessed the event: they commission the making of **eikones** 'images' of the brothers, presumably in their completed pose, which they dedicate at Delphi (Herodotus ibid.).

112. This formulation allows for the possibility that some rhythmical types, in the process of becoming purely metrical types, will have developed into a state of incompatibility with dance or instrumental accompaniment or both. On Aristotle *Poetics* 1448b21–22, where meters are described as **moria** 'parts' of rhythms, Hardison 1981.71n4 observes: "The passage simply

Similarly, I also propose that the phraseology of SONG can stylize and regularize its own built-in tones or intonations, resulting diachronically in what we call *melody*.[113] If we combine the two proposals, we get a scheme where both rhythm and melody in SONG could be viewed as regularized outgrowths of *speech* that serve eventually to distinguish SONG from *speech*. In terms of this composite scheme, I am now ready to substitute *rhythm or melody or both* for *metric substructure* in the formulation of Ben-Amos. The result is a formulation that is not alien to ethnomusicology. On the general topic of the connections discovered by ethnomusicologists between music (what I have been calling SONG) and language, I cite a general theory, built on a broad cross cultural sampling of ethnographic data, offered by Bruno Nettl:

> My own theory is based on the assumption that an undifferentiated method of communication existed in remote times, one which was neither speech nor music [= SONG] but which possessed the three features that they hold in common: *pitch*, *stress* [which I reinterpret in the specialized sense of *intensity*], and *duration*. . . . There must have been a long, gradual stage of differentiation and specialization in culture, during which the two [= language and "music"] became distinct. . . . This theory, then, postulates three stages in the development of music: (1) undifferentiated communication, (2) differentiation between language and music, and (3) differentiation between various musical styles. The

---

asserts that meters share ('are parts of') certain forms derived from dance music ('the rhythms')." This observation is conditioned by Aristotle's description of a particular meter used for imitating speech, the trochaic tetrameter catalectic, as a rhythm originally associated with dance that later became displaced by another meter, the iambic trimeter, which was dissociated from dance: *Poetics* 1449a22–24, *Rhetoric* 1404a31–33. See further at p. 45. Lucas 1978.86 emphasizes the fact that the scholia to Aristophanes *Clouds* 1352 mention dancing to tetrameters. Aristotle's linking of the trochaic tetrameter catalectic with dance may well be extrapolated from such self-references as in Archilochus F 120 W, on which see p. 20. See also Menander *Dyskolos* 879, with a reference to the accompaniment of iambic tetrameters catalectic by the **aulos** 'reed'.

113. Cf. p. 102. For a pioneering discussion of the relationship between pitch accentuation in the ancient Greek language and melodic patterns in ancient Greek song, see Allen 1973.231–234, especially p. 233, where he cites such testimony as that of Aristoxenus *Harmonics* 1.10 (and following) concerning the difference beween (1) the **sunekhēs** 'continuous' pattern, with gradual shifts of tone in the accentual patterns of everyday speech and (2) the **diastēmatikē** 'intervallic' pattern, with stylized shifts of tone in song, by way of intervals. According to Aristoxenus (ibid.), the **diastēmatikē** pattern is singing, not speaking. Aristides Quintilianus, pp. 5.25–6.7 (ed. Winnington-Ingram), posits an intermediate pattern, between the **sunekhēs** and the **diastēmatikē**, *for the recitation of poetry*. For similar evidence in Indic melodic traditions and elsewhere concerning the distinctions between tone, that is, pitch accent, and melody, see Allen, pp. 233–234. On zones of overlap and non-overlap in patterns of tone and melody, see Allen, p. 234. On the difference between tone and intonation, see p. 34. I expect that languages with fixed patterns in tone would generate melodic traditions different from languages with patterns in intonation only. Cf. p. 40.

last stage is, of course, the only one for which we have any data at all, and even that . . . is fairly recent.[114]

In this connection, consider the earlier theories of Curt Sachs,[115] postulating three kinds of origins for melodic traditions: "logogenic" (from language), "pathogenic" (from motion), and "melogenic" (from "music"). On the basis of what we have noted about the relationship of language and motor activity, the category "pathogenic" is unnecessary. As for the category "melogenic," it may be useful for describing historically attested situations where a given melodic tradition has lost or at least outgrown its "logogenic" moorings, and where such a tradition is then recombined with or superimposed on originally unrelated phraseology.[116] Still, I would offer a formulation for melody that parallels what I have offered for rhythm: that the primary situation is that of convergence and parallelism between the patterns of tone or intonation or both in the words of SONG on the one hand and the patterns of melody, dance, and instrumental accompaniment on the other hand.[117] I would also argue, conversely, that the secondary pattern is that of divergence and contrast.[118]

It should be stressed, however, that contrastive patterns between dance or instrumental accompaniment on the one hand and song on the other, even

114. Nettl 1956.136. Cf. also Bright 1963, especially p. 27; also Merriam 1964.285. There are important elaborations in Nettl 1964.281–292; note in particular his analysis of the correlation between the pattern of strong word-initial accent in the Czech language and the pattern of stressed notes beginning musical phrases in Czech folk music, both vocal and instrumental (1964.283); also his observation that, in English folk songs, the melodic contour "tends to descend at the end of a section, phrase, sentence, or song," corresponding to intonational patterns in the language.

115. Sachs 1937.181–203, 1943.30–43.

116. Cf. Herskovits and Herskovits 1947 on Trinidad melodies: "But not all melodies are rephrasings of old ones. Sometimes a tune heard, a European tune, can be 'swung' into a desired rhythm, with perhaps a change of a few measures, or no change at all. In this case, the words to a traditional song might be joined to the new melody, or a proverb might be used and to it added lines from older songs."

117. Note the description of "logogenic" melodies: they are "narrow of range, using small intervals," whereas corresponding dances are "tight, controlled, expressed through narrow steps" (Merriam 1964.253). See Bake 1957.200 on the Indic tradition of the bhāṣikasvara 'speech tone', which has the narrowest pitch compass and is employed, according to tradition, in performing the words of the (White) Yajur Veda. Note too the following formulation: "The melodic line follows the text in every detail; the words prescribe the rhythm and the flow; there is one note to each syllable, pitch is independent of duration. One might say that the melody only supports the words" (Bake ibid.; cf. West 1981.115 and 116, who draws particular attention to the old three-pitch and four-pitch patterns).

118. In the case of Balinese music lessons for the young, Merriam 1964.152 notes: "Those instruments which do not play the melody are ignored for the moment, for the melody must be learned first." On patterns of primary convergence and secondary divergence between SONG and speech, cf. the bibliography assembled by Nettl 1964.290–291. Cf. also the discussion of the factor of "tension" in Allen 1973.110–112.

if they are diachronically secondary, are even more effective than parallel patterns in marking off the language of SONG from the language of *speech*. Intensified contrast in form further marks what is already marked in function. We should expect partial contrast, for example, in the patterns of *melody* in the song and of *tone* or *intonation* in the words of the song, or in the patterns of *ictus* in the verse and of *stress* (duration and intensity) in the words of the verse, or in the patterns of the *colon* in the stanza and of the *clause* or *phrase* in the words of the stanza, and so on.[119]

In light of these arguments, supported by the insights of ethnomusicologists, I offer a broadened outline of possible developments, with special reference to the development of Greek music. Whereas SONG may or may not have required melody, *song* must be plus melody as opposed to *poetry*, which is minus melody or reduced melody. Whereas SONG may or may not have required dance and instrumental accompaniment, given forms of *song* may be plus dance or plus instrumental accompaniment or plus both.

Let us pursue further the point, made earlier, to the effect that the parallelisms between patterns of dance or instrumental accompaniment and patterns of rhythm or melody in SONG are diachronically primary and that the contrasts between them are secondary.[120] If indeed SONG is marked *speech*, then such elements as dance and instrumental accompaniment can be viewed as ramifications of SONG that can in turn be further differentiated as either parallel to the SONG or contrasting with it or, even further, parting with it altogether, as in forms of dance or instrumental music that exist independent of SONG. This is not to say something altogether naive and pseudo-historical, such as "in the beginning there was song, which was both danced and instrumentally accompanied." Rather it is to speak of the linguistic foundations of singing, dancing, and instrumental accompaniment. It is to speak of diachronic potential: SONG, as a marked form of language, is *structurally* capable of generating differentiated subforms such as dance and instrumental music. From a diachronic point of view, then, dance and instrumental music are optional realizations of the stylized speech-act. From the standpoint of traditions with song, dance, and instrumental accompaniment surviving together, analogous forms with any of these constituents missing are liable to be viewed as the result of a tearing away of that constituent from a unified whole, as we read in Plato *Laws* 669d-670a. In this connection, we may follow the formulation of A. M. Dale, who makes use of Milton's concept of

---

119. Cf. Allen, p. 111: "One could envisage a form of which the pattern is determined by some prosodic feature *x*, such that there is another feature *y* whose distribution in the language is partially coincident with that of *x*. In such a situation one could speak of tension between *x* and *y* where the two factors failed to coincide in composition, and of 'concord' or 'harmony' where they coincided and so reinforced the metrical pattern; and such a 'counterpoint' between the patterns of the two features could arguably be manipulated by the poet for artistic ends."

120. Cf. pp. 38 and following.

Voice and Verse as uniting to form Song: "For the Greek lyric poet Voice and Verse were not a pair of sirens; Verse was merely the incomplete record of a single creation, Song."[121]

To set up language as the diachronic foundation of dance and instrumental music is in line with A. M. Dale's view that "song, with its dance, was a function of the words themselves when they were alive — that is, in performance."[122] More fundamentally, it is in line with Aristotle's view that the basis of musical rhythm is the syllable (*Metaphysics* 1087b33 and following).[123] Still, the fundamental function of dance and instrumental music, whether their patterns are parallel or contrastive with the patterns of language that they accompany, is to mark special speech as opposed to everyday speech, that is, SONG as opposed to *speech*.[124] An ideal example is Athenian drama, in which the dancing and instrumental accompaniment further distances the words sung in the lyric meters by the **khoros** 'chorus' from the words recited in the iambic trimeter by the actors.

Let us examine more closely the medium of the chorus, as attested in Athenian drama, in which song, dance, and instrumental accompaniment survive together. To repeat, analogous forms that happen to lack any of these constituents are viewed as a tearing away of that constituent from a unified whole (Plato *Laws* 669d–670a). Wherever song has the capacity of being danced, as in the case of Greek choral lyric, dancing to the song is dancing to its rhythms and melodies on the level of form and to its words on the level of content. In Greek, this correspondence is **mīmēsis** or mimesis, which can best be translated as 'reenactment' or 'impersonation'.[125]

In general the noun **mīmēsis**, as well as the corresponding verb **mīmeisthai**, designates the reenactment, through ritual, of the events of myth (e.g., Lysias 6.51).[126] In the case of a highly stylized ritual complex like

121. Dale 1969.166.

122. Dale 1969.168. For reinforcement of this view on the level of testimony about the actual performance of song, see Pratinas *PMG* 708 (in Athenaeus 617b-f) and Plato *Republic* 398d.

123. Cf. also Plato *Republic* 400a and *Cratylus* 424c. See the comments on these and other passages by Pöhlmann 1960.30.

124. On patterns of primary convergence and secondary divergence between SONG and *speech*, I cite again Nettl 1964.281–292.

125. Cf. Koller 1954 on the inherited concept of **mīmēsis**; for a balanced updating of Koller's synthesis, addressing the criticism of Else 1958, see Nehamas 1982. Following Halliwell 1986.110, I concede that the semantic range of mimesis was shifting, even before Plato, away from the notions of reenactment or impersonation, to accommodate such distinct notions as imitation or the reproduction of appearances. As I shall argue presently, however, such distinct notions are more limited in scope. For Plato's views on mimesis, see Halliwell, pp. 116–122 (also p. 53). As for Aristotle, Halliwell, p. 128, begins his account by mentioning as a possibility "that Aristotle's guiding notion of mimesis is implicitly that of enactment: poetry proper (which may include some works in prose) does not describe, narrate or offer argument, but dramatises and embodies human speech and action."

126. In the case of Lysias 6.51, **mīmeisthai** refers to the misuse rather than proper use of a

Athenian drama, the act of reenactment, **mīmeisthai**, is equivalent to acting out the role of a mythical figure (e.g., Aristophanes *Women at the Thesmophoria* 850).[127] The acting out can take place on the level of speech alone or else on the level of speech combined with bodily movement, that is, dance: hence the force of πρός 'corresponding to' in the expression πρὸς τὰ πάθεα αὐτοῦ 'corresponding to his sufferings [= **pathos** plural]' at Herodotus 5.67.5, describing the singing and dancing by **tragikoi khoroi** 'tragic choruses', at Sikyon in the time of the tyrant Kleisthenes, in reenactment of the **pathea** 'sufferings' of the hero Adrastos.[128]

While the fundamental meaning inherent in **mīmēsis** is that of reenacting the events of myth in ritual,[129] by extension **mīmēsis** can also designate the present reenacting of previous reenactments. This narrowed view of reenactment, where the focus is on the the present reenactment of a previous reenactment without considering the whole chain of reenactments extending from the past into the future, corresponds to the more specialized and episodic notion of *imitation*. In that the newest instance of reenacting has as its model, cumulatively, all the older instances of performing the myth as well as the "original" instance of the myth, **mīmēsis** is a current imitation of earlier reenactments. This is the sense of **mīmēsis** in the Homeric *Hymn to Apollo* 163, where a choral group called the Deliades are described as being able to 'imitate',' **mīmeisthai**, the voices and musical sounds of a wide variety of Ionians who are described as assembling for a festival on the island of Delos (162–164).[130]

---

priestly costume by Andocides; still, as Halliwell, p. 113, points out, Andocides is "acting out the part of a priest *in full*."

127. Cf. Halliwell, p. 114, on the nuances of mimesis in Aristophanes *Women at the Thesmophoria*: "Aristophanes' parody involves, and deliberately confuses, both an ordinary usage of mimesis terms (for impersonation) and a newly developing application of the language of mimesis to the fictional status of dramatic poetry."

128. Further discussion of this passage at p. 387. Cf. the discussion of Royce 1977.73, including this interesting quotation from Boas 1944.14–15 concerning the dance traditions of the Kwakiutl: "In the Cannibal Dance, the women's War Dance, and some others, there is a fixed fundamental gesture like a basso ostinato that is broken at intervals by special gestures of pantomimic character which is descriptive of the text of the song."

129. For the perspective of a social anthropologist on the reenactment of myth in ritual: Leach 1982.5–6.

130. I single out the helpful commentary of Barker 1984.40n4, especially with respect to the reading κρεμβαλιαστύν at *Hymn to Apollo* 162, which he interprets as "the locally grown rhythmic form, since rhythm is what **krembala** were used to emphasize." Barker argues that this passage is "advertising the rhythmic and linguistic versatility of the Delian chorus, who might be asked to perform pieces from any of the literary and musical traditions of Ionia and the islands" (ibid.). Cf. Burkert 1987.54: "Contrary to what both others and I myself have written [Burkert 1985.110], I am inclined now to take this [= lines 162–165] as indicating mimetic elements in [the] performance of choral lyrics." Cf. also Bergren 1982.93.

The sense of wonder about the **mīmēsis** performed by the Deliades concerns the accuracy or exactness of their reenactment: everyone will say, when they hear the sound of their own voices reenacted by the Deliades, that they are hearing their own way of speaking (*Hymn to Apollo* 163–164).[131] This line of thought corresponds to the celebrated description of **mīmēsis** in the *Poetics* of Aristotle as the mental process of identifying the representing 'this' with the represented 'that': οὗτος ἐκεῖνος 'this *is* that' (1448b17).[132] In the performance of the Deliades, the represented 'that' is not only whatever the visiting Ionians have sung before. Whatever they have sung before is simply the latest in an ongoing series of previous reenactments, ultimately reenacting a given myth. So also with the formulation of **mīmēsis** by Aristotle (again *Poetics* 1448b17): the represented 'that' identified with the representing 'this' can be perceived not only as the previous experience but also as the sum total of previous experiences. 'This', then, is particular, the experience in the here and now, whereas 'that' is potentially universal, a cumulative synthesis of all previous experience. Aristotle goes on to say that the mental process whereby 'this' is being identified with 'that', by way of **mīmēsis**, is a source of pleasure (*Poetics* 1448b11, 13, 18). This pleasure is not incompatible with an anthropological understanding of ritual: "Fixed rhythm and fixed pitch are conducive to the performance of joint social activity. Indeed, those who resist yielding to this constraining influence are likely to suffer from a marked unpleasant restlessness. In comparison, the experience of constraint of a peculiar kind acting upon the collaborator induces in him, when he yields to it, the pleasure of self-surrender."[133]

Such a formula of equating the particular 'this' with the universal 'that', as implied by the use of the verb **mīmeisthai** in the Homeric *Hymn to Apollo* and as explicitly linked with the concept of **mīmēsis** in the *Poetics* of Aristotle, is a fundamental expression of assent in many languages: besides the many attestations in Greek (e.g., τοῦτ' ἐκεῖν' 'this is that' = 'yes' in Aristophanes *Lysistrata* 240), there is a particularly striking example in the Latin combination *hoc illud* 'this is that', which is the ancestor of the French *oui* 'yes' (and of the Southern French *oc*, as in *Languedoc*). Such a *yes* can serve as the *amen* of a participant in a given ritual, who assents to the realities of myth as reenacted in the context of ritual.[134]

131. Cf. Aeschylus *Libation-Bearers* 564 and the commentary of Nehamas 1982.56–57. Cf. also Theognis 367–370, as discussed at p. 374.

132. On which see Sifakis 1986, especially p. 218.

133. Tambiah 1985.123.

134. I cite the description of an all-female ritual, as attested in an Ismaili community south of Mashhad in Eastern Iran, which entails the narration of a story as the central event of a ritual meal (Mills 1982). At crucial moments in the retelling of this story (described as a combination of Aarne-Thompson tale type 480, "The Kind and the Unkind Girls," and 510A, "Cinderella"), the girl who is the chief participant, to whom the story is primarily addressed, has ritual food spooned into her bowl by the widow who tells the story, to which the girl answers *yes* at each of these crucial moments (as recorded in Mills, pp. 185–186).

From the standpoint of ritual, then, the activity of the chorus in an institution like Athenian drama, where, song, dance, and instrumental accompaniment can function as a unified whole, is a matter primarily of reenactment, insofar as the performers reenact the events of myth, and only secondarily of imitation, insofar as the performers at one given occasion imitate the performances of previous occasions.

This is not to say, however, that reenactment is not imitation. All ritual reenactment is imitation, though of course not all imitation is ritual reenactment. Moreover, imitation is pertinent to the differentiation of SONG into *song* as opposed to *poetry*: we see a synchronic use of such a differentiation in Athenian drama, where the opposition between sung or lyric meters on one hand and the spoken iambic trimeter on the other hand imitates the real-life opposition of SONG on the one hand, with its ritual context, and *speech* on the other, with its nonritual context. The imitation is effective: poetry actually seems closer than song to *speech* in that it does not have the same degree of specialized patterning in melody. Nor is it correlated with dance or in most cases with instrumental accompaniment.[135]

And yet, if indeed poetry is to be derived from SONG, it is really one step further removed from *speech*: to repeat the diachronic construct, song is specialized by retaining and refining melody from SONG, while poetry is specialized by losing or failing to develop the melody that is potential in SONG.[136] In terms of differentiation, some form of SONG had to lose melody, or fail to develop melody, so that poetry could be differentiated from song. In Athenian drama, this form was the iambic trimeter. From a diachronic point of view, however, this meter did not have to be the form that imitated *speech*: we hear from Aristotle (*Poetics* 1449a21) that the trochaic tetrameter catalectic had been the earlier format of spoken poetry as opposed to song.[137] But the conventions of Athenian tragedy seemed to allow only one meter to serve as the canonical format for imitating *speech* at any one given time:[138] in attested tragedy, for example, the trochaic tetrameter catalectic is not isofunctional with the iambic trimeter — it is marked off from it by virtue of being associated with "scenes of heightened tension."[139] Moreover, there is

135. Cf., for example, Dale 1968 on recitative anapaestic meters in drama.

136. There are parallels in medieval traditions: poetic genres where melody is absent are characterized by patterns of prosodic elaboration that seem to serve as compensation for the lost melodic component: see Zumthor 1972.99. On the old French distinction between *dit* and *chant*, see Zumthor, p. 406.

137. On the use of the trochaic tetrameter catalectic as a medium of dialogue, that is, imitated speech, see Pickard-Cambridge 1968.158–160. This is not to say that this meter could not be sung, danced, or instrumentally accompanied: see Pickard-Cambridge, pp. 156–158.

138. We may recall the primary nature of the opposition SONG and *speech*, as discussed by Ben-Amos (quoted at pp. 36–37).

139. West 1982.78, following Pickard-Cambridge, p. 159, who cites, for example, Sophocles *Oedipus at Colonus* 887–890, Euripides *Herakles* 855–874.

evidence that the trochaic tetrameter catalectic was in certain situations delivered in a reduced melodic form known as **parakatalogē**.[140] There is no need to argue, however, that iambic trimeter could never be sung after having become the imitative format of *speech*: there are sporadic traces, even in Athenian drama, of sung iambic trimeter[141] as also of sung dactylic hexameter[142] and sung elegiac distich.[143] Still, the appropriate way to imitate the single format of *speech* with the multiple formats of SONG is to contrast a single spoken meter with the plurality of sung meters. If Aristotle *Poetics* 1449a21 is right in saying that the trochaic tetrameter catalectic used to be the medium for imitating *speech*, then I am ready to posit a stage where even iambic trimeter, like the trochaic tetrameter catalectic, used to be delivered in the format of **parakatalogē**, and where this type of modified melodic delivery used to be the only approximation of *speech*.[144] Then another stage of differentiation could have led to the iambic trimeter of Classical tragedy, with its non-melodic delivery, while trochaic tetrameter catalectic persisted with a modified melodic delivery. At such a stage of differentiation, only iambic trimeter could imitate *speech*, whereas the trochaic tetrameter catalectic would be imitating something that is now more than just *speech*.

At another stage further removed, the appropriate way to imitate the single format of *speech* with the multiple formats of SONG would be to contrast a non-metrical form with the plurality of metrical forms. The nonmetrical form would be prose:

basis	derivation	further derivation

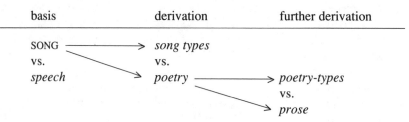

140. See Pickard-Cambridge 1968.158–160 (also Comotti 1979.21). It may be misleading to some that West 1982.77 uses *recitative* to translate **parakatalogē**. To repeat, I view **parakatalogē** as an intermediate stage between sung and spoken: the **parakatalogē** is described as a form of delivery that explicitly contrasts with song in "Aristotle" *Problems* 19.6. See p. 27.

141. Dale 1968.86 and 208.

142. Dale 1968.25–31. Cf. West 1982.98, 128 (especially n125).

143. As in Euripides *Andromache* 103–116.

144. In line with this argument it is crucial to note that **parakatalogē** is incompatible with dance, as Rossi 1978 has argued on the basis of Aristophanes *Wasps* 1528–1537. To put it more accurately: **parakatalogē** is compatible only with a special kind of stylized dance, a mimesis of dance (in this sense, a mimesis of a mimesis), not with dance itself. That is to say, **parakatalogē** is one stage removed from dance, just as it is one stage removed from singing. Dance becomes reduced, just as melody, in a format of reduced song. Moreover, it may well be that the ritual content itself is correspondingly reduced.

I suggest that the opposition between *recited* meters on one hand and *spoken* prose on the other hand once again imitates the real-life opposition of SONG vs. *speech*. Again, the imitation is effective: prose seems closer than poetry to *speech* in that it does not have the same degree of specialized patterning in rhythm. And yet, if indeed prose is predicated on poetry, as Herodotus implies in the first sentence of his *Histories*,[145] then prose is really one step further removed from *speech*: to extend the diachronic construct, while *song* is specialized by retaining and refining melody from SONG, poetry is specialized by detaching melody from SONG, and prose is specialized by at least partially detaching rhythm from poetry.[146] Further, just as one form of poetry can coexist and interact with many forms of song in the medium of Athenian drama, so also the form of prose coexists and interacts with forms of poetry in such forms of expression as represented by the *Lives of the Seven Sages* tradition and even by the *Histories* of Herodotus.[147]

Before proceeding any further in our consideration of the distinctions between song and poetry, we must confront a semantic problem occasioned by our own cultural preconceptions. Whereas the stylized rhythms of poetry are known to us as *meter*, we think of the stylized rhythms of song simply as *rhythm*. This mode of nomenclature is hardly appropriate to the traditions of Greek lyric, where song operates on principles of rhythm that are clearly cognate with the principles of meter in the recitative poetry of, say, Greek epic. In fact it is common practice to speak of the rhythms of Greek lyric in terms of meter.

This much said, I should note that my theory about poetry as a differentiated derivative of SONG can be supported by the ancient Greek metrical evidence. To make this point, I offer in the Appendix a survey of two fundamental types of Greek lyric metrical patterns, the so-called Aeolic and dactylo-epitrite meters. All the attested lyric poetry of Pindar, with only a few exceptions, is composed in one or the other of these two kinds of meters.[148] In the Introduction, I singled out Pindar's compositions as the

---

145. Full discussion in Ch.8.

146. We may also adduce the prose of Gorgias (82 DK). For a parallel phenomenon in medieval traditions, where poetic compositions can be subjected to a conscious process of *dérimage* or "un-rhyming" into prose, see Zumthor 1972.99–100; also Kittay and Godzich 1987. In light of a distinctly juridical function associated with much of early medieval prose, and the fact that the form of an "un-rhymed" composition is perceived as conveying the content of a different level of truth-value from the "rhymed" (Zumthor, p. 98), it is interesting to compare the juridical dimension of early Greek prose authors like Herodotus, as discussed at Ch.9.

147. On which see p. 332. We find a parallel in the medieval genre of the *chantefable*, such as *Aucassin et Nicolette*, with alternating song (the melody of the *laisses* has been preserved) and prose: see Vance 1986.161–163. I note in particular the following summary: "Prose is unmarked speech 'at large', while verse is the marked speech of a social constituency with precise boundaries" (Vance, p. 163). For the Chinese analogue known as *chu-kung-tiao*, see Chen 1976.

148. For a convenient metrical overview, see the analysis of Snell in the SM edition of Pin-

centerpiece for illustrating the traditions of lyric poetry, that is, song. In later chapters we see that the actual content of this poetry reaffirms both explicitly and implicitly the thematic connection between epic and lyric, which reflects on the formal connection between poetry and song. In the Appendix, finally, I present the case for arguing that these connections are verified by the form — or, better, forms — of lyric poetry.

Specifically, I argue that the dactylic hexameter, the meter of epic, took shape from the phraseology of the two basic metrical systems inherited by Pindar, the Aeolic and the dactylo-epitrite (both surveyed at length in the Appendix). More generally, I also argue that the three major types of meter in Greek poetry, that is, dactylic hexameter, elegiac distich, and iambic trimeter, are differentiated equivalents of cognate types of meter found in Greek song, as in the inherited medium of Pindar. Whereas elegiac distich and iambic trimeter can be connected with dactylo-epitrite, dactylic hexameter is more easily explained in terms of both the Aeolic and the dactylo-epitrite heritage of Pindar.[149]

Further, it can be shown that the three basic meters of poetry, dactylic hexameter, elegiac distich, and iambic trimeter, are not only derived from SONG but also differentiated from the corresponding meters of *song*. To begin, we may note that the meters of Greek song are either *strophic*, built on the principle of the *colon*, the constitutive element of both the relatively simpler stanzas of monody and the more complex stanzas of the choral medium, or *stichic*, built on the principle of the *verse*.[150] Other available terms of description are *asynartetic*, where the divisions between cola are overt, and *synartetic*, where they are latent.[151]

The notion of *asynartetic* is compatible with that of **parakatalogē**, a category of song where both melody and dance become reduced or

---

daric fragments, pp. 162–174. In only one case, Pindar *Olympian* 13, is there a coexistence of the two types *within one composition* (Aeolic modulating into dactylo-epitrite; cf. Bacchylides *Epinician* 3). For an exceptional case of a Pindaric song composed in neither Aeolic nor in dactylo-epitrite meters, I cite *Olympian* 2, composed in Ionic meters.

149. Cf. Appendix pp. 439 and following.

150. On the concept of *colon*, see Appendix p. 439. For *stikhos* in the sense of *verse*, cf. Aristophanes *Frogs* 1239. On the concept of a distinction between the monodic and the choral medium, see pp. 84–85.

151. Cf. West 1982.43. It is important, however, not to confuse *synartetic* with *strophic* and *asynartetic* with *stichic*, in that the category of asynartetic accommodates not only verse but also strophes where the colon is clearly delineated; conversely, the category of *synartetic* does not accommodate strophes where the colon is clearly delineated. Granted, there are cases where the direction of development is from asynartetic to synartetic (cf. Wilamowitz 1921.421). Still, it hardly follows that the constituents of the strophe are built from the constituents of the verse. As the discussion proceeds, it in fact becomes evident that the direction of development is the reverse: from colon to verse portion, not from verse portion to colon. In any case *asynartetic* is a category that is roughly half-way between *strophic* and *stichic*. Cf. p. 394.

eliminated altogether.[152] Whereas both melody and dance are bound to a strophic framework, the category of **parakatalogē** is associated with an asynartetic or stichic framework.[153]

The stichic meters of lyric are a transitional point of differentiation from song, whereas total differentiation is achieved in the stichic meters of non-lyric, that is, of poetry proper.[154] The stichic rather than strophic meters of lyric are actually attested as usable for extended narrative of a type parallel to epic, composed in the dactylic hexameter, which is the stichic meter of non-lyric par excellence. A worthy example is Sappho F 44 V, a poem with a heroic setting: it is composed in a stichic meter[155] that is clearly cognate with various strophic meters of Lesbian lyric poetry.[156] Such stichic meters of narrative lyric poetry, conventionally sung to the accompaniment of the lyre, are doubtless more closely related than is the spoken meter of hexameter to the format of the South Slavic *guslar* who sings to the accompaniment of the *gusle*.[157]

Let us reformulate in terms of the concepts just introduced. The fundamental argument in the Appendix is that the sequences of cola in the strophic meters of song are cognate with the verses in the stichic meters of poetry. Perhaps the clearest example is the case of the strophic sequences of Stesichorus, which are built from units such as the following:[158]

a	$\underset{\smile}{} - \smile -$	=	*ia*
b	$\underset{\smile}{} - \smile - \underset{\smile}{}$	=	*ia˜*
c	$- \smile -$	=	*˜ia*
d	$- \smile - \underset{\smile}{}$	=	*˜ia˜*
L	$\underset{\smile}{} - \smile - \underset{\smile}{} - \smile -$	=	*ia&IA*
M	$- \smile - \underset{\smile}{} - \smile -$	=	*˜ia&IA*

152. Reduction of melody: p. 27; reduction of dance: p. 46.

153. Cf. Rossi 1978 on Aristophanes *Wasps* 1528–1537.

154. On the Alexandrian poetic practice of generalizing units taken from the synartetic framework of strophic *song* into the stichic units of verse in *poetry*, see Rossi 1971.86. For later developments in the genres of the **nomos** and the **dithurambos**, where the principle of strophic responsion is abandoned, see Gentili 1985.35. As it is pointed out in "Aristotle" *Problems* 19.15, the abandonment of responsion entails greater freedom for experimentation in both the rhythms and the melodies.

155. The meter in question is *glyc@2da*, on which see Appendix p. 440. All of Book II of the canonical Sapphic corpus was composed in this meter: Hephaestion 7.7, p. 23.14–17 Consbruch.

156. For example, *glyc@da* in Sappho F 94 V, on which see Appendix p. 440.

157. Cf. West 1973.188: "If there was epic or heroic balladry in (say) 1600 [B.C.], its characteristic verse was most likely the glyconic [= *glyc*], whose cognates are used in Sanskrit and Slavic epic." On the Middle High German evidence for melodic traditions of epic sung in strophic form, see Brunner 1970.160.

158. Cf. Appendix pp. 452 and following. For the metrical symbols, see Appendix p. 439.

A	⏕–⏑⏑–⏑⏑–	=	*pros*
B	⏕–⏑⏑–⏑⏑––	=	*pros˜*
B″	⏕⏕–⏑⏑–⏑⏑––	=	*pros˜*
C	–⏑⏑–⏑⏑–	=	*˜pros*
D	–⏑⏑–⏑⏑––	=	*˜pros˜*

These shapes are not only prototypical of those found in, say, the so-called dactylo-epitrite meters of a Pindaric strophe: they are also identical with some of the major components in the meters of poetry, that is, in the dactylic hexameter (CB″), in the elegiac distich (CB″ICC), and in the iambic trimeter (bM).[159]

These meters of poetry are not only derived from SONG but also differentiated from the corresponding meters of *song*. As a finishing touch of differentiation between poetry and song, meters of song can avoid patterns that have been appropriated for poetry: thus, for example, the dactylo-epitrite metrical repertoire of Pindar's compositions contains the ingredients needed to generate equivalents of the dactylic hexameter, elegiac distich, and iambic trimeter, and yet it is precisely these patterns of spoken poetry that the lyric poetry of Pindar, let us call it *song*, consistently avoids.[160] It appears that the parent forms were covering their tracks. The poetic structure of the parent forms shades over, within that structure, those of its aspects that match various aspects that have become distinctive features of the respective daughter forms.

With any differentiation of poetry from song through the loss of melody, there would have to come about a new structural strain in the oral tradition. Melody can be an important feature in the mnemonics of oral tradition in song, as we know from the studies of folklorists who scrutinize the transmission and diffusion of song: melody helps recall the words.[161] We are reminded of the anecdote about the Athenians captured after the debacle at Syracuse who ingratiated themselves with their captors by singing passages from Euripides: these memorable passages were evidently parts from choral lyric, not iambic trimeter (as we see from the wording τῶν μελῶν ἄσαντες 'singing from his lyrics' in Plutarch *Nicias* 29.3).[162] In terms of a differentia-

159. See Appendix pp. 451 and following.

160. Cf. Rosenmeyer 1968.230. One apparent exception is Pindar *Pythian* 9.4, 12. Another is *Pythian* 1.92 (–⏑⏑–⏑⏑–⏑⏑–I⏑⏑–⏑⏑I––I––, on which see Gentili and Giannini 1977.17), where part of the sequence looks like a dactylic hexameter; it is not in fact a hexameter since there is no correspondence with the final word boundaries of hexameter. There is an analogous situation in Pindar *Nemean* 9: at the beginning of each strophe is a unit –⏑⏑–⏑⏑–––⏑⏑–⏑⏑–– matching the hexameter in its initial and final word boundaries but clashing with the primary caesura patterns of hexameter.

161. Cf. Klusen 1969.72–83, cited in an interesting discussion by Rösler 1980.104n176. As a counterweight to the notion of *gesunkenes Kulturgut* in Klusen's work, see Bausinger 1980.41–55.

162. Cf. also Satyrus in *Oxyrhynchus Papyri* 1176 fr. 39 col. xix.

tion of oral SONG into oral poetry as opposed to oral song,[163] I offer this axiom: with the structural strain brought about by the loss of melody in poetry, there would come about, for the sake of mnemonic efficiency, a compensatory tightening up of rules in the poetic tradition.[164] This tightening up would entail an intensification of both phraseological and prosodic regularities, as we see in the formulas and meters of Homer, Hesiod, and the old elegiac and iambic poets. I also suggest that the concept of *formula*, stemming ultimately from Milman Parry's study of Homeric phraseology, applies primarily to such regularities stemming from the differentiation of oral poetry from oral song. In other words the formula is to be seen as characteristic primarily of oral poetry as opposed to song. In order to account for the distinct regularities of oral song as opposed to poetry, the concept of *formula* could be considerably broadened.[165]

For song, it seems most useful to distinguish three dimensions of regularity: *phraseological*, *rhythmical*, and *melodic*. These three dimensions correspond to the tripartition of **melos** 'lyric poetry' into **logos, rhuthmos,** and **harmoniā** in Plato *Republic* 398d (cf. Aristotle *Poetics* 1447a21–23). The rhythmical dimension would be represented by meters and the melodic, by modes.[166] The process of oral composition in song, then, can be conceived as an interaction of phraseology, rhythms, and modes.

163. On which see p. 45.
164. See, for example, Dale 1968.25–31, especially p. 29, on phraseological and prosodic irregularities in the sung varieties of dactylic hexameter—which are irregularities only from the standpoint of the regularities in the nonsung variety. Cf. West 1982.98, 128 (especially n125). See also Zumthor 1972.99 on a comparable situation in medieval European traditions: "Dans les genres non chantées, le perfectionnement des effets sonores semble une sorte de compensation de la perte de la mélodie." As for Zumthor's list (ibid.) of formal features that serve to differentiate poetry from song, I should emphasize that all these formal features are potentially present in song.
165. See N 1979b.614–619.
166. For more on the notion of *mode*, see pp. 82 and following.

2 ◫◫ The Poetics of Panhellenism and the Enigma of Authorship in Early Greece

I have been attempting both to distinguish poetry from song and to broaden the current concept of oral poetry in such a way as to include song. Since the conventional semantic range of our word *poetry* tends to exclude song, however, I prefer not to use the actual term *oral poetry* in this broader sense. Instead, I confine myself for now to the more narrow concept of oral poetry as distinct from oral song. But even this more narrow concept is not accurate enough to account for Homeric and Hesiodic poetry, or old elegiac and old iambic poetry. There is another characteristic of such poetic traditions that makes it a special kind of oral poetry. That characteristic is the phenomenon of Panhellenism.

Panhellenism can be most readily defined in terms of the distinctively Greek institution of the **polis** or 'city-state', the importance of which for defining the concepts of Hellenism and even civilization can be most simply illustrated with Aristotle's dictum, ὁ ἄνθρωπος φύσει πολιτικὸν ζῷον 'man is by nature an organism of the polis' (e.g., *Politics* 1253a2–3). With the **polis** 'city-state' as frame of reference, the phenomenon of Panhellenism can be summed up as follows.[1]

On the basis of archaeological and historical evidence, A. M. Snodgrass applies the concept of Panhellenism to the pattern of intensified intercommunication among the city-states of Hellas, starting in the eighth century B.C., as evidenced in particular by the following institutions: Olympic Games,

---

1. The next paragraph is a reworking of N 1985.35 §17n3. From here on the Greek word **polis** is no longer printed in boldface.

Delphic Oracle, and Homeric poetry.[2] I have extended the concept as a hermeneutic model to help explain the nature of Homeric poetry, in that one can envisage as aspects of a single process the ongoing recomposition and diffusion of the *Iliad* and *Odyssey*.[3] I have further extended the concept to apply to Hesiodic poetry[4] and to Theognidean poetry.[5] Finally, as we see in Chapter 3, the concept can be extended still further to apply to lyric poetry in general, that is, to song.

Essentially, the hermeneutic model of Panhellenism must be viewed as an evolutionary trend extending into the Classical period, not some fait accompli that can be accounted for solely in terms of, say, the eighth century. In other words the concept of Panhellenism as I use it here is a relative one. Thus various types of Archaic Greek poetry, such as the elegiac tradition preserved by Theognis, make their bid for Panhellenic status considerably later than Homeric and Hesiodic poetry. Still I see in such poetry as the Theognidea a parallel pattern of ongoing recomposition concomitant with Panhellenic diffusion. The most obvious reflex of this ongoing recomposition in diffusion is the ultimate crystalization of a body of poetry like the Theognidea, composed not in the native Doric dialect of a polis like Megara but in an accretive Ionic dialect that is for all practical purposes the same as we see in the poetry of Archilochus, Callinus, Mimnermus, Tyrtaeus, Solon, Xenophanes, and so on.[6]

From here on I refer to this process, described here as crystalization, simply as textual fixation. I apply this notion of textual fixation to oral traditions with an emphasis on gradual patterns of fixity in an ongoing process of recomposition in diffusion, and without presupposing that the actual composition of the "text" required the medium of writing.[7] In applying this notion I would stress the interconnected development of traditions alongside each other.[8]

2. Snodgrass 1971.421, 435; cf. Snodgrass 1987, especially pp. 160, 165, and Morris 1988, especially pp. 754–755.

3. N 1979.5–9.

4. N 1982.43–49, 52–57, 59–60.

5. N 1985.34–36.

6. Ibid. Gentili 1985.45 discusses a poem for the Corinthian dead at Salamis: the inscription is Doric (CEG 131; Simonides EG 11), but the transmission is Ionic (Plutarch *On the Malice of Herodotus* 870e).

7. For the related notion of *intertextuality*, in a specialized sense as applied to Homeric poetry, see Pucci 1987.29n30.

8. This interconnected development of traditions is reflected in cross references from one tradition to another. I suggest that the notion of "cross reference" is indeed workable in the study of oral poetics, provided we understand that any references to other traditions in any given composition/performance would have to be *diachronic* in nature. On such cross referencing between the *Iliad* and the *Odyssey* traditions, see N 1979.35–58; also Pucci, pp. 240–242. For analogous cross referencing in Hesiodic poetry, I cite *Theogony* 87, where the assertion that an ideal king can resolve even the greatest possible **neikos** 'quarrel' seems to presuppose a thematic association with the **neikos** between Hesiod and Perses at *Works and Days* 35, which is treated

By Panhellenic poetry, then, I mean those kinds of poetry and song that operated not simply on the basis of local traditions suited for local audiences. Rather, Panhellenic poetry would have been the product of an evolutionary synthesis of traditions, so that the tradition that it represents concentrates on traditions that tend to be common to most locales and peculiar to none.[9]

Such a synthetic tradition would require a narrower definition than suitable for the kind of oral poetry and song described by Albert Lord on the basis of his field work in the South Slavic oral traditions. The difference is that such a tradition is in the process of losing the immediacy of the performer-audience interaction expected in the context of ongoing recomposition in performance. The teleology of this loss is attested: in the historical period Homeric and Hesiodic as well as old elegiac and iambic poetry is being performed verbatim by **rhapsōidoi** 'rhapsodes' at Panhellenic festivals.[10] In the same context of Panhellenic festivals, what we have been calling song or lyric poetry is being performed verbatim by **kitharōidoi** 'lyre singers' and **aulōidoi** 'reed singers'.[11] Each new performance is now aiming at a verbatim repetition — not at an act of recomposition.[12]

Earlier I argued that the rhapsodes were direct heirs to earlier traditions in oral poetry.[13] But we see that over a long period their role has become differentiated from that of the oral poet. Whereas the oral poet recomposes as he performs, the rhapsode simply performs. In contemplating the recitation of Homer by rhapsodes, I am reminded of the following description of the recitation of "historical" poetry in Rwanda society: "Unlike the amateur,

---

by the *Works and Days* as an ultimate criterion, as the quarrel to end all quarrels; cf. N 1982.58–59. In fact cross references can serve to distinguish one tradition from another. To cite an example: the description of the funeral of Achilles in *Odyssey* xxiv makes references to Patroklos and Antilokhos (77–79) in such a way as to signal that the *Odyssey* follows the *Iliad* tradition, not the *Aithiopis* tradition: see Edwards 1985b.223–225 (cf. N 1979.21; also p. 211). A veritable network of cross references establishes the complementarity of the Homeric *Iliad* and *Odyssey* traditions, of the Hesiodic *Theogony* and *Works and Days* traditions (cf. Slatkin 1987). It may be that the distinctness of two separate major compositions within each of the two traditions resulted from evolutionary differentiations within the Homeric and the Hesiodic traditions. Moreover, the *Contest of Homer and Hesiod* tradition (*Certamen*, pp. 225–238 Allen), and the myth behind it (see further at p. 76), implies an even more fundamental pattern of evolutionary differentiation between the Homeric and the Hesiodic traditions.

9. See N 1982.48–49.

10. See p. 21, where I discuss the notion of *Panhellenic* as applied to international (that is, inter-polis) festivals like the Panathenaia. On the performance of old elegiac and iambic poetry by rhapsodes, see p. 25.

11. References and further discussion in Ch.3, where we shall see that the patterns of Panhellenization in song are even more complex than they are in poetry.

12. That the rhapsodes may not be able to accommodate the compositions that they perform to the current political requisites of the audience is suggested in Herodotus 5.67.1, as interpreted by Svenbro 1976.44; for more on this passage, see p. 75.

13. Cf. pp. 28–29.

who gesticulates with his body and his voice, the professional reciter adopts an attitude of remoteness, a delivery that is rapid and monotone. If the audience should react by laughing or by expressing its admiration for a passage that is particularly brilliant, he stops reciting and, with the greatest detachment, waits till silence has been reestablished."[14] Such a description need not rule out the potential for variation from performance to performance. Still, variation is counteracted by the ideology of fixity. To that extent we see at least the impetus toward the notion of textual fixation without writing.[15]

The differentiation of composer and performer is attested in many cultures, as illustrated most succinctly by the incipient semantic split of *trobador* as 'composer' and *joglar* as 'performer' in Old Provençal usage.[16] In this case there is still evidence for some overlap.[17] With Homeric poetry, in contrast, the notion of composer is drastically retrojected, from the standpoint of the performers themselves, to a protopoet whose poetry is reproduced by an unbroken succession of performers; Socrates can thus envisage the rhapsode Ion as the last in a chain of magnetized metal rings connected by the force of the original poet Homer (Plato *Ion* 533d-536d). More accurately we may say that Ion is the next to last in the chain with relation to his audience, who would be the last link from the standpoint of the performance (*Ion* 536a). The implication of Plato's construct is that the magnetic force of the poetic composition weakens with each successive performer. Ion then, by virtue of being the last or at least the latest reproducer of Homer, would also be the weakest.

In contrast, during phases of a given tradition where both composition and performance can be "owned" by the same person at a given occasion,[18] the advantage of the immediate composer-performer, as conferred by the occasion at hand, can be conventionally contrasted with the relative disadvantage of his predecessors, who are at this point deprived of their own occasion. Such an attitude is expressed this way in one particular Eskimo song: "All songs have been exhausted. He picks up some of all and adds his own and makes a new song."[19] We may note the juxtaposition made by Ferdowsi,

14. Coupez and Kamanzi 1962.8, quoted by Finnegan 1970.6.
15. See p. 53.
16. Cf. Boutière and Schutz 1950, p. xii.
17. Cf. Stevens 1986.43. Cf. Zwettler 1978.84–88 on the Arabic concept of the *rāwī*.
18. On categories of ownership of song (and/or dance), see Kunst 1958.2.
19. Boulton 1954.4–5. Note here the oral performance's reference to the newness of its composition. It would be deceptive, here as elsewhere in oral traditions, to equate such "newness" with our own general notions of *innnovation*. We must be on guard against projecting into oral traditions an anxious modernist vision of the creative self, which can lapse all too easily into romantic scenarios of creation out of self-contained genius. We may achieve a more balanced formulation from the vantage point of anthropology: I cite Barnett 1953.39–95 on the concept of innovation, where he offers a cross cultural survey of nine possible social factors that promote innovation. Barnett's book has strongly influenced ethnomusicologists like Merriam (e.g., 1964.312–313), especially with his observation that whereas innovation in oral traditions may be

poet of the *Shāhnāma*, with his predecessor, Daqiqi: 'In transmitting, his [= Daqiqi's] words became weak. Ancient times were not renewed by him' (VI 136.18).[20] A variant reads: 'Now I will tell what he [Daqiqi] has told. For I am alive and he has become united with the dust' (same citation).[21] The poet is presenting himself as owning the composition on the grounds that he, not his predecessors, now has access to the occasion, which is stylized as a series of performances before assemblies: 'These stories, grown old, will be renewed by me in all assemblies' (III 6.9).[22]

In the case of Plato's *Ion*, the myth-making retrojection of Homeric composition back to the strongest protopoet belies the evolutionary progression of a tradition where the aspect of recomposition gradually diminishes in the process of diffusion entailed by performance in an ever-widening circle of listeners.[23] The wider the diffusion, the deeper the tradition must reach within itself: the least common denominator is also the oldest, in that a synthesis of distinct but related traditions would tend to recover the oldest aspects of these traditions.

A key to such Panhellenic synthesis is the ever-increasing social mobility of the poet or **aoidos** 'singer' by virtue of his being a **dēmiourgos** 'artisan in the community [**dēmos**]', as he is described in *Odyssey* xvii 381–385.[24] In Homeric poetry other professions besides the **aoidos** belong to this category of **dēmiourgoi**: the **mantis** 'seer', the **iētēr** 'physician', the **tektōn** 'carpenter' (*Odyssey*, ibid.), and the **kērux** 'herald' (*Odyssey* xix 135).[25] The **dēmiourgoi** are socially mobile, traveling from one **dēmos** to another.[26] For

---

initiated by individuals, the cultural background must allow it (for example, by way of collaboration of effort, expectation of change, and the like). On the relativity, from society to society, of the descriptive term *improvisation*, see the useful discussion of Merriam, p. 179.

20. Davidson 1985.110; also in general pp. 103–142. The textual references here to the *Shāhnāma* follow the volume and page numbers of Bertel´s 1966–1971. Again I draw attention to the "renewal" claimed by the composer.

21. Ibid.

22. Davidson, p. 109. Note again the notion of "renewal."

23. I note the interesting ethnographic typologies discussed in Bausinger 1980.52.

24. Commentary in N 1979.233–234. On the **dēmos** 'administrative district, population' in Archaic Greek poetic diction in the sense of 'local community', with its own traditions, customs, laws, and the like, see N, p. 149 §11n6; also p. 251.

25. Cf. Hesiod *Works and Days* 25–26, where the **aoidos** 'singer' is juxtaposed with the **tektōn** 'carpenter' and the **kerameus** 'potter'; also with the itinerant **ptōkhos** 'beggar', ibid. Such a juxtaposition of **aoidos** and **ptōkhos** is also built into *Odyssey* xvii 381–385.

26. There is clearly a hierarchy of professions within the category of **dēmiourgoi**, supplemented by the notion that the **ptōkhos** 'beggar' is at the bottom. The association of the **ptōkhos** with the category of **dēmiourgoi** relates perhaps to the notion that beggars, like **dēmiourgoi**, could appeal for immunity as they traveled from **dēmos** to **dēmos**, or perhaps to a poetic topos concerning the social scale as ranging all the way from the king at the very top to the beggar at the very bottom. It could be argued that such a mention of beggars on one end of of the social scale is intended as a symmetrical implication of kings on the other end: just as beggars can be listed at the bottom of a hierarchy of **dēmiourgoi**, so also kings can be listed at the top. The slid-

an example of a cognate institution, I cite the Old Irish *áes cerd* 'people of crafts [*cerd*]' the designation for artisans, including poets, who enjoyed a legal status even outside their own *tuath* 'tribe' as they traveled from one *tuath* to another.[27] Old Irish *cerd* 'craft' is cognate with Greek **kerdos** 'craft, craftiness; gain, advantage, profit'; the same Greek word, in the diction of poetry, can refer to the craft and the potential craftiness of poetry.[28]

Given the social mobility of the poet, who is teleologically evolving into the rhapsode, his cumulative exposure to multiform traditions in many places is analogous to the experience of an ethnographer who attempts to reconstruct back to a prototype the distinct but cognate versions of traditions in different but neighboring locales. What I am offering in effect is a hermeneutic model for explaining how the myth-making mind can become critical of variants in myth. I am arguing that such a faculty for criticism arises primarily from the factor of the poet's social mobility, which I offer as a substitute for what has been posited by others, namely, the factor of the poet's ability to write.[29]

A synthetic and critical tradition purports to represent a prototype of variant traditions, and the diachrony of its evolution thus becomes its own synchrony. Homeric synchrony, to take the clearest example, operates on the diachronically oldest recoverable aspects of its own traditions.[30]

The synthetic tradition, in order to survive, must prevail over the countless variant traditions from which it was constituted. And in order to prevail, the tradition must be performed. We turn to an observation of Claude Lévi-Strauss in his book on masks, where he confronts, perhaps more explicitly than elsewhere, the question of the relationships between localized myth-variants and localized ritual-variants, with particular reference to ritual objects such as masks: each performance of a myth, he notes, entails a re-creation of that myth, so that the latest version of the myth, in the context of its performance in the here and now, takes precedence over all previous versions.[31]

The latest performance is by necessity a crisis point for the traditions of myth, in that the latest performance determines what continues to be

---

ing scale in the social status of Odysseus from king to beggar back to king in the *Odyssey* may be connected with a poetic topos concerning the relationship between the king and the **dēmiourgoi**. On the **ainos** 'fable' of the Hawk and the Nightingale in Hesiod *Works and Days* 202–212, where the hawk is to a king as the nightingale is to a poet as **dēmiourgos**, cf. N 1979.238–241.

27. Old Irish *tuath* 'tribe' (as ruled by a king) is cognate with Umbrian *touto* 'civitas' and German *Deutsch*. On the *áes cerd*, see [J. F.] Nagy 1985.33, 35 and 239n48; cf. also Meid 1974.

28. Cf. p. 188.

29. For the theory that literacy is the primary impetus toward a critical faculty, see, for example, Goody and Watt 1968.

30. N 1982.47–49, 52. For a particularly compelling formulation with regard to Arabic traditions, I cite Zwettler 1978.221.

31. Lévi-Strauss 1979.153–163, especially pp. 162–163.

transmitted and what does not. There may be at any given time a multitude of latest performances by a multitude of performers in a multitude of places. Still, each latest performance is a crisis for what has been said in all previous performances, and the cumulative trends of latest performances determine what ultimately survives and what is lost. The crisis can be expected to deepen whenever the number of performances decreases or the occasions for them become progressively restricted. In any case each latest performance helps determine what is highlighted and what is shaded over, with the ever-present possibility that the shading will lapse, with the passage of time, into total darkness.

In this evolutionary vision of change in oral traditions, I have deliberately used the imagery of light in order to bring home a point that is actually made by the poetic traditions of Greek myth making, although there the view is episodic, not evolutionary. As Marcel Detienne has documented in his survey of Archaic Greek poetics, the poetic power of **mnēmosunē** 'remembering' is traditionally associated with light, which is in conflict with the darkness of **lēthē** 'forgetting'.[32] What is illuminated or obscured by poetry is what is respectively preserved or lost in the tradition.

The concept of **lēthē** 'forgetting', however, is not only negative. As Detienne points out, **lēthē** is not only the opposite of **mnēmosunē** 'remembering': it can also be an aspect of **mnēmosunē**.[33] For example, the goddess **Mnēmosunē** is described in the *Theogony* of Hesiod as giving birth to the Muses, divine personifications of the poet's power, so that they, through their poetry, may provide **lēsmosunē** 'forgetting' of sadnesses and of worries for humankind (53–55); whoever hears the Muses no longer **memnētai** 'remembers' his own ills (*Theogony* 98–103). By implication the highlighting of the glory of poetry is achieved by shading over anything that detracts from it. A bright light needs a background of darkness.

Such a concept of **mnēmosunē** can be achieved only through an ever-present awareness of its opposite, **lēthē**. Without the obliteration of what need not be remembered, there cannot be memory — at least, from the standpoint of Archaic Greek poetics.

Let us reformulate these thought patterns in terms of an opposition between unmarked and marked categories.[34] In an opposition of **mnē-** 'remember' vs. **lēth-** 'forget', **mnē-** would be the unmarked member and **lēth-**, the marked, in that **lēth-** can be included by **mnē-** as an aspect of **mnē-**. Besides the passage just considered from the *Theogony*, I cite another striking illustration, from a different source: in the ritual of incubation con-

32. Detienne 1973.22–27. For example, **Lēthē** or 'Forgetting' personified is descended from Night in Hesiod *Theogony* 227/224; **Mnēmosunē** 'Remembering' is contrasted with darkness in Pindar *Nemean* 7.12–16.

33. Detienne, pp. 69–80.

34. For these terms, see the Introduction, p. 5.

nected with the cult of Trophonios, the initiate drinks from the springs of both **Lēthē** and **Mnēmosunē**; this way the undesired mental state can be shaded over while the desired mental state is highlighted (Pausanias 9.39.8).[35]

To pursue the subject of these thought patterns even further, I cite an example of unmarked and marked opposition in the English language. In an opposition of the pronouns *he* and *she, he* is the unmarked member and *she*, the marked, in that *she* is included by *he* as the feminine aspect of being *he*. The masculine aspect of being *he*, by contrast, has to be achieved through an ever-present negation of the feminine. We may say something like: this is not a *she*, this is a *he*. Otherwise *he* does not, of and by itself, convey a masculine aspect. In generalizing statements, for example, *he* can stand for both *he* and *she*, as in "everyone may interpret as he chooses."[36]

Where the unmarked member excludes the marked member through a negation of the marked, the unmarked member receives a minus interpretation; where the unmarked member includes the marked, it receives a zero interpretation.[37] The minus interpretation of the unmarked member is ever-present in the context of a given Archaic Greek poem's references to itself as absolute truth, conveyed by a specialized **mnēmosunē** 'remembering' that excludes **lēthē** instead of including it. These relationships can be visualized as a larger circle of **mnēmosunē** 'remembering' that includes an inner area of **lēthē** 'forgetting' surrounding a smaller circle of specialized **mnēmosunē** 'remembering' that excludes the outer area of **lēthē** 'forgetting'. The area of forgetting is visualized as the ongoing erasure of things not worth remembering, erasure by way of **lēthē** 'forgetting'; the smaller circle of remembering, within the larger circle, is highlighted by the area of darkness surrounding it, the area of forgetting. In fact, a special word in the diction of Archaic Greek poetry formalizes this specialized and exclusive kind of remembering: that word is the negation of **lēthē** 'forgetting', namely **a-lētheia**, normally glossed in English as 'truth'. A comparable case of minus interpretation in English can be seen in the word *unforgettable*. The **alētheia** 'truth' of the poet is the nonerasure of the poetic glory that is his to confer.[38] The same concept is evi-

35. See the discussion by Detienne, p. 74.

36. Waugh 1982 compares the French usage of the masculine gender as the unmarked member of an opposition with the feminine, in that the masculine can stand for the category as a whole: thus an adjective describing both masculine and feminine categories will be put into the masculine: *des hommes et des femmes intelligents*.

37. For these terms, as used by Waugh 1982 following Jakobson 1939, see again the Introduction. Waugh, p. 302, pictures the marked-unmarked relationship as "a subset-set relationship where the marked category is the subset and the unmarked category is the set," or alternatively as "a figure-ground relationship where the marked pole is the figure and the unmarked pole is the ground."

38. Given that the smaller circle within the larger circle symbolizes the specialized sort of **mnē-**, that is, **a-lētheia**, I would say that the larger circle that contains **lēth-** would correspond to the function of the Muses, who help humans forget some things so that they may remember oth-

dent in the periphrastic expression **oude me/se/he lēthei** 'it does not escape my/your/his-her mind', which conventionally reinforces injunctions to be **memnēmenos** 'mindful, remembering'.[39]

Besides contrasting with negative thoughts about human ills,[40] or erroneous thoughts that lead to injustice,[41] the **alētheia** of Greek poetry tends to contrast with the divergence of local poetic versions in the overarching process of achieving a convergent version acceptable to all Hellenes.[42] This argument brings us back to the observation of Lévi-Strauss that the latest performance of myth is in principle an occasion for selecting from and thereby potentially erasing versions available from countless previous performances.[43] In what survives of Archaic Greek poetry — and now I am using the word *poetry* in the broadest sense — what we keep finding is the ultimate extension of this principle, to the point where the latest version becomes the last version, a canonization that brings to a final state of crystalization what had been becoming an ever-less fluid state of variation in performance.[44] I attribute this canonization not so much to the phenomenon of incipient literacy as to the broader social phenomenon of Panhellenization.[45] I reiterate that this phenomenon is relative from the standpoint of an outsider to the tradition, in that some compositions are more Panhellenic in scope than others. From the standpoint of the insider to the tradition, however, in the here

---

ers. The root *mnā- of **mnē-** 'remember' may in fact be related to the root *mon-t- (or *mon-th-) of **Mousa** 'Muse' (Hesiod *Theogony* 53–55, 98–103). The etymological connection is certain if **Mousa** is to be derived from the root *men-, expanded as *mon-t- (or *mon-th-), which is one of several possibilities entertained by Chantraine DELG 716. The relationship of the root *men- with the expanded form *mnā-, as in **mnē-**, is clear: Chantraine, p. 703.

39. The pertinent passages are discussed in N 1983.44. This expression **oude me/se/he lēthei** 'it does not escape my/your/his-her mind' implies a synchronic understanding of the word **alētheia** as a compound consisting of privative **a-** and the root **lēth-**. In the formulation of Cole 1983.12, the reference of **alētheia** is "not simply to non-omission of pieces of information . . . but also to not forgetting from one minute to the next what was said a few minutes before, and not letting anything, said or unsaid, slip by without being mindful of its consequences and implications." (For a critique of Heidegger's celebrated explanation of **alētheia**, see Cole, pp. 7–8.) Cf. also Detienne 1973.48n107.

40. I cite again Hesiod *Theogony* 53–55, 98–103.

41. On this theme, see Detienne 1973.29–50.

42. This is not to say, of course, that the convergent version may not be complex, containing multiformities within its overarching uniformity.

43. Cf. p. 57; cf. also p. 80.

44. Royce 1977.104 points out, with reference to traditions of dance, that various structures of performance, as they become progressively more rigid, can suffer "abrupt confrontation and loss."

45. The threat of "abrupt confrontation and loss," to use the expression quoted immediately above, could help promote an impetus for recording by way of writing. But a critical attitude toward myth is caused not by the technology of writing but rather, more fundamentally, by the crisis of confrontation between variants of myth. See p. 57.

and now of performance, the Panhellenic perspective is the absolutist perspective of **alētheia** 'truth'.[46]

This notion of *canonization*, as I have just outlined it,[47] is analogous to a concept used by scholars associated with the Museum housing the great library of Alexandria.[48] This concept is **krisis**, in the sense of *separating, discriminating, judging* (verb **krīnō**) those works and those authors that are worthy of special recognition and those that are not.[49] The Alexandrian scholars who inherited the legacy of this process of separation, discrimination, judgment were the **kritikoi** 'critics',[50] while the Classical authors who were recognized as the survivors of this process of **krisis** were called the **enkrithentes**,[51] a term that corresponds to the Roman concept of the Classics, the *classici*, who are authors of the 'first class', *primae classis*.[52] The **krisis** of the **enkrithentes**, however, starts not with the Alexandrian scholars, nor even with the likes of Aristotle.[53] The *crisis* of this **krisis** happens to be already under way in the Archaic period. We must remind ourselves that songs and poetry were traditionally performed in a context of competition.[54]

46. We may well ask: how does the local perspective contribute to the Panhellenic, and to what degree does the Panhellenic perspective recognize the local? From the standpoint of the local tradition, the best chance for self-assertion is a process of self-selection that accommodates the Panhellenic tradition. Note the discussion by Royce 1977.164 of the repertory of some 90 *sones* (dances) among the Zapotec of the Isthmus of Tehuantepec: in asserting their identity to outsiders, the Zapotec tend to select just three of these 90 *sones*. Royce notes (ibid.) that "these three are the dances that any non-Zapotec would name if asked about 'typical' dances of the Isthmus," and that it is these three dances that are synthesized by the Ballet Folklórico in its suite "Wedding in Tehuantepec."

47. For a history of the usage of *canon* to designate a selective listing of authors and works, see Pfeiffer 1968.207.

48. For an introduction to the era of Alexandrian scholarship, see Pfeiffer, pp. 87–233.

49. For a survey of this usage, see Pfeiffer, p. 117.

50. See Pfeiffer, pp. 89, 242.

51. Pfeiffer, pp. 206–207. Cf. Horace *Odes* I 1.35, and the comments of Pfeiffer, p. 206.

52. Pfeiffer, p. 207. The canon as conceived by the Alexandrian scholars is not to be confused with the actual collection of works housed in the great library of the Museum at Alexandria. The *Pinakes* or 'Tables' of Callimachus, in 120 books, was intended not as a selection but as a complete catalogue of the holdings of the Museum, generally organized along the lines of formal criteria, including meter. For an informative discussion, see Zetzel 1983.98–100, who stresses that the Alexandrian system of classification was "eminently suitable for describing the literature of pre-Alexandrian Greece" (p. 99).

53. On the principles of selection, from Aristotle to the Alexandrians, see Pfeiffer, pp. 117, 205. This is not to assume that there was an ongoing process of actual selecting of *Classical* (as opposed to current) authors in the period of Alexandrian scholarship; I cite Page 1953.68, who doubts that "any ancient lyrical poet whose works were in circulation up to the Alexandrian era was omitted by the Alexandrian editors from their collection" (for a critique of this formulation, see p. 83). In the case of epic, Quintilian *Institutio oratoria* 10.1.55 notes explicitly that the Alexandrian editors Aristophanes and Aristarchus included no contemporary poets into the *ordo*, or canon, barring even Apollonius of Rhodes.

54. See p. 28.

A striking example is the tradition of dramatic festivals at Athens, with the **krisis** 'judgment' of winners by **kritai** 'judges'.[55] But the *criteria* of the *crisis* are different. The very evolution of what we know as the *Classics* — as both a concept and a reality — was but an extension of the organic Panhellenization of oral traditions. In the Archaic period, I argue, the general principle that determines what is worthy of special recognition and what is not can be formulated as a question: what is Panhellenic, **alētheia**, and what is not?

For illustration, let us turn to the "Days" portion of the *Works and Days* of Hesiod, which begins with the following injunction:

ἤματα δ' ἐκ Διόθεν πεφυλαγμένος εὖ κατὰ μοῖραν
πεφραδέμεν δμώεσσι

> Hesiod *Works and Days* 765–766

Take care to mark the days[56] [of the month], which come from Zeus, giving each day its due, for the household-servants.

The very first day of the month to be mentioned is a crisis point for the Panhellenic perspective, since it is the day when each polis is most idiosyncratic, with local traditions prevailing:

... τριηκάδα μηνὸς ἀρίστην
ἔργα τ' ἐποπτεύειν ἠδ' ἁρμαλίην δατέασθαι,
εὖτ' ἂν <u>ἀληθείην</u> λαοὶ <u>κρίνοντες</u> ἄγωσιν.

> Hesiod *Works and Days* 766–768

The thirtieth day of the month is best
for inspecting different kinds of work that have to be done and for
    apportioning food-supplies.
This is the day that people spend by <u>sorting out</u> [= verb
    krīnō] what is <u>truth</u> [**alētheia**] and what is not.

A commentator on the *Works and Days* remarks: "Civil calendars often fell out of step with the moon . . ., and it was on the thirtieth that errors arose. Each month had to be allowed either 29 or 30 days, but the last day was called **triākas** (or in Athens **henē kai neā** [meaning 'the old and the new']) in either case, the preceding day (?) being omitted in a 'hollow' month. So it

---

55. For the wording, see, for example, the description in Plato *Laws* 659ab. There is a stylization of this institution in the *Frogs* of Aristophanes, in the form of a competition between Aeschylus and Euripides (see p. 401); in this context, we may note the usage of the word **krisis** and the corresponding verb **krīnō** at *Frogs* 779, 785, 805, 873, 1467, 1473. Cf. also Dunkel 1979.252–253.

56. First we had the "works"; now we have the "days."

was always a question of when to have the thirtieth."⁵⁷ In other words each polis had its own traditions about the calendar. At the thirtieth, there is a crisis about arriving at a Panhellenic norm from the standpoint of each polis. This norm is conveyed here by the notion of **alētheia** 'truth', which, I argue, is the criterion of Panhellenism. Then the poet embarks on a catalogue of those days of the month that share the highest degree of consensus in local traditions, with the catalogue proceeding in a descending order of consensus. The thirtieth may be a crisis point, varying from polis to polis, but the crisis leads to a shared Panhellenic perspective. The poet has blotted over the differences, simply noting that **alētheia** 'truth' is being 'sorted out' [= is in a crisis: the verb is **krīnō**] on the thirtieth. After the thirtieth it is possible to arrive at a fixed sequence of given days traditionally spent in given ways by all Hellenes.⁵⁸

The poet now highlights this fixed sequence, which is the Panhellenic perspective. Zeus, the god who is the planner of the universe, is an appropriate symbol for the organizing principle that underlies the Panhellenic perspective. With Zeus the poet begins the catalogue, as he then proceeds to present a synthetic overview of the days of the month:

αἵδε γὰρ ἡμέραι εἰσὶ Διὸς παρὰ μητιόεντος·
πρῶτον ἔνη τετράς τε καὶ ἑβδόμη ἱερὸν ἦμαρ
(τῇ γὰρ Ἀπόλλωνα χρυσάορα γείνατο Λητώ) ὀγδοάτη τ' ἐνάτη τε.
δύω γε μὲν ἤματα μηνὸς
ἔξοχ' ἀεξομένοιο βροτήσια ἔργα πένεσθαι
. . .
ἐν δὲ τετάρτῃ μηνὸς ἄγεσθ' εἰς οἶκον ἄκοιτιν,
οἰωνοὺς κρίνας οἳ ἐπ' ἔργματι τούτῳ ἄριστοι.
. . .
παῦροι δ' αὖτε ἴσασι τρισεινάδα μηνὸς ἀρίστην
ἄρξασθαί τε πίθου καὶ ἐπὶ ζυγὸν αὐχένι θεῖναι
βουσὶ καὶ ἡμιόνοισι καὶ ἵπποις ὠκυπόδεσσιν,
νέα ⟨τε⟩ πολυκλήιδα θοὴν εἰς οἴνοπα πόντον
εἰρύμεναι. παῦροι δέ τ' ἀληθέα κικλήσκουσιν.
τετράδι δ' οἶγε πίθον — περὶ πάντων ἱερὸν ἦμαρ —
μέσσῃ. παῦροι δ' αὖτε μετεικάδα μηνὸς ἀρίστην
ἠοῦς γεινομένης. ἐπὶ δείελα δ' ἐστὶ χερείων.
αἵδε μὲν ἡμέραι εἰσὶν ἐπιχθονίοις μέγ' ὄνειαρ·
αἱ δ' ἄλλαι μεταδούπιοι, ἀκήριοι, οὔ τι φέρουσαι,
ἄλλος δ' ἀλλοίην αἰνεῖ, παῦροι δέ τ' ἴσασιν·
. . .
. . . εὐδαίμων τε καὶ ὄλβιος, ὃς τάδε πάντα

---

57. West 1978.351.
58. For the apparent exception on the island of Keos, see the passages quoted by West, p. 351.

εἰδὼς ἐργάζηται ἀναίτιος ἀθανάτοισιν,
ὄρνιθας κρίνων καὶ ὑπερβασίας ἀλεείνων

Hesiod *Works and Days* 769–774, 800–801, 814–824, 826–828

For what I now tell you are the days of Zeus the Planner.
To begin with, the first,[59] the fourth,[60] and the seventh[61] are each a holy
day
(it was on the seventh that Leto gave birth to Apollo of the golden
sword).
So too the eighth[62] and the ninth.[63] And yet, these two days of the wax-
ing part of the month
are particularly good for various kinds of work by mortals.[64]
. . . On the fourth of the month bring home your wedded wife,
having sorted out [verb **krīnō**] the bird omens,[65] which are best for
doing this.
[. . .]
Further, few people know that the thrice-nine of the month is best
for opening a wine jar and for putting yokes on the necks
of oxen, mules, and swift-footed horses,
or for hauling a swift ship with many oars down to the wine-colored
sea.
Few give it its true [**alēthēs**] name.[66]
Open your jar on the fourth. The fourth of the midmonth is the most
holy of them all.
Again, few do it [= give it its true name].[67] I mean the after-twenty

59. In the *Odyssey*, the new moon is the context for a festival of Apollo (xiv 162 = xix 307; xx
156, 276–278, xxi 258): West 1978.352.

60. For example, Aphrodite was specially worshipped on this day: sources in West, ibid.

61. The most important holy day of Apollo: sources ibid.

62. For example, the eighth at Athens was the day for honoring Poseidon and Theseus: West,
p. 353.

63. For example, the ninth at Athens inaugurated the City Dionysia: ibid.

64. That is, they may be holy days, but they are not necessarily holidays. This hedge suggests
that the eighth and the ninth are less "Panhellenic" than the first, fourth, and seventh. This reading differs from that of West, p. 132, whose punctuation indicates that he takes δύο γε μὲν ἤματα
as referring to what follows (the 11th and 12th at line 774) rather than to what precedes (the 8th
and the 9th at line 772). I take δύο γε μὲν ἤματα at 772 and ἄμφω γε μὲν at 774 to be parallel in
referring to what precedes in the syntax.

65. Note the parallel expression concerning bird-omens at *Works and Days* 828, as discussed
at p. 65.

66. The Hesiodic name 'thrice-nine' would be the Panhellenic designation, as implied by the
word **alēthēs**. Note the observations at ##T89 about **alētheia** at *Works and Days* 768. Local
designations of this day may have been subject to tabu. The number thrice-nine is particularly
sacred: see the references collected by West, p. 361.

67. This interpretation differs from what is found in the standard editions.

[= the twenty-first],[68] which is best
when dawn comes. As evening approaches, it is less good.
These, then, are the days, a great blessing for earth-bound men.
The others fall in between. There is no doom attached to them, and
they bring nothing.
Different people praise different days,[69] but few really know.[70]
. . .

With respect to all of these days, fortunate and blissful is he who
knows all these things as he works the land, without being responsible
to the immortals for any evil deed,
as he sorts out [= verb krīnō] the bird omens,[71] and as he avoids any
acts of transgression.

For further illustration of the concept of **alētheia** as a Panhellenic truth-
value, I offer five additional passages. This truth-value is associated not just
with poetry in the narrower sense but also with song, as in the lyric poetry of
Pindar, and even with prose, as in the *Histories* of Herodotus. The five passages that follow, then, are selected from the widest possible range of Greek
verbal art and range all the way from song to prose:

1

ἢ θαύματα πολλά, καί πού τι καὶ βροτῶν | φάτις ὑπὲρ τὸν ἀλαθῆ
λόγον | δεδαιδαλμένοι ψεύδεσι ποικίλοις ἐξαπατῶντι μῦθοι. Χάρις
δ᾽, ἅπερ ἅπαντα τεύχει τὰ μείλιχα θνατοῖς, | ἐπιφέροισα τιμὰν καὶ
ἄπιστον ἐμήσατο πιστὸν | ἔμμεναι τὸ πολλάκις

Pindar *Olympian* 1.28–32

Indeed there are many wondrous things. And the words that men tell,
myths [**mūthoi**] embellished by varied falsehoods, beyond wording
that is true [**alēthēs**], are deceptive. But **Kharis**,[72] which makes every-

---

68. Note again the periphrasis, as in the case of thrice-nine at line 814.

69. Here we see the localized perspective.

70. Here we see the Panhellenic perspective. 'Know' is in the sense of **histōr** 'the
knowledgeable one', as at *Works and Days* 792.

71. Note the parallelism between verse 828 here and verse 801, p. 64, where again the verb
krīnō 'sort out' is used with reference to divination by birds. The *crisis* of sorting out the right
and the wrong bird-omens is implicitly parallel to the *crisis* (again, verb **krīnō**) of sorting out
what is **alētheia** 'truth' and what is not. In order to appreciate the importance of
ornithomanteíā 'divination by birds' in the whole poem, we may note that *Works and Days* 828
had served as a lead-off for a concluding stretch of verses, now lost, containing instructions on
the interpretation of bird omens (West 1978.364–365). A bird omen is central to the entire ethical message of the *Works and Days*, that is, the **ainos** 'fable' (202) of "The Hawk and the
Nightingale" (202–212), on which see p. 256.

72. That is, **kharis** personified. For the specific purposes of this book, I consistently interpret
kharis as a 'beautiful and pleasurable compensation, through song or poetry, for a deed

thing pleasurable for mortals, brings it about [= verb **mēdomai**],[73] by way of conferring honor [**tīmē**], that even the <u>untrustworthy</u> [**apiston**] oftentimes becomes <u>trustworthy</u> [**piston**].

Here we see the juxtaposition of what purports to be a unique and true Panhellenic version with a plethora of false versions, described as **mūthoi** 'myths'.[74] The **mūthoi** 'myths' are the outer core, containing traditions that are **apista** 'untrustworthy', while **alētheia** 'truth' is the inner core, containing traditions that are **pista** 'trustworthy'. In referring to itself, the **alētheia** of Panhellenic poetics represents **mūthoi** as if they were additions to the kernel of truth as formulated by **alētheia**.[75] I would argue, however, that **mūthoi** 'myths' stand for an undifferentiated outer core consisting of local myths, where various versions from various locales may potentially contradict each other, while **alētheia** 'truth' stands for a differentiated inner core of exclusive Panhellenic myths that tend to avoid the conflicts of the local versions.

If we symbolize the exclusive sort of **mnēmosunē** 'memory' (which excludes **lēthē**: so **a-lēth-eia**) in terms of a smaller circle surrounded by an area of **lēthē** within a larger circle of inclusive **mnēmosunē** (which includes **lēthē**), we may imagine an ongoing erasure of **mūthoi** by **lēthē** within the outer circle, resulting in **a-lētheia**. Thus **a-lētheia** 'truth' is 'un-forgettable'. It cannot be emphasized enough that such a model of Panhellenic tradition is dynamic, not static. Through time, the inner and outer circles, along with the area of **lēthē** between them, keep shifting.

Myths that are epichoric, that is, local, are still bound to the rituals of their native locales, whereas the myths of Panhellenic discourse, in the process of excluding local variations, can become divorced from ritual. The word **mūthos** 'myth' is associated with the epichoric rather than Panhellenic phase of myth making; its remaining links with ritual can be seen even in its etymology, if indeed **mūthos** is to be derived from the verb **muō** in the sense of 'I say in a special way' or 'I see in a special way', where the special way

---

deserving of glory'. This word conveys both the beauty ("grace") and the pleasure ("gratification") of reciprocity.

73. West 1978.49 observes: "The aorist of **mēdomai**, unlike the imperfect, means not 'planned' but 'wrought'." In the range of meaning from 'planned' to 'wrought', I submit, we see the range of meaning within the single word **kerdos** 'craft', on which see p. 57.

74. I shall argue in Ch.4 below that Pindar's "unique and true Panhellenic version" represents the official aetiology of the Olympics in Pindar's time.

75. In visualizing an outer core of 'falsehoods' and an inner core of 'truth', I am following the interpretation of Young 1986, who adduces, besides Pindar *Olympian* 1.28–32, Plato *Republic* 377a, Pausanias 8.2.6 and Strabo 1.2.9 C20. I would add Thucydides 1.21.1: οὔτε ὡς ποιηταὶ ὑμνήκασι περὶ αὐτῶν ἐπὶ τὸ μεῖζον κοσμοῦντες μᾶλλον πιστεύων. These parallels help put Pindar *Nemean* 7.20–23, also adduced by Young, in a new light; note the singularity of the Pindaric πάθα at *Nemean* 7.21 as opposed to the plurality of the Homeric πολλὰ ... πάθεν ἄλγεα in the prooemium of the *Odyssey* (i 4). See p. 203.

is the marked procedure of ritual.[76] Local traditions in ritual, and the myths that go with them, seem to be unfit for Panhellenic discourse. Thus Hecataeus of Miletus, at the beginning of his discourse, dismisses the local tales of the Greeks as πολλοί τε καὶ γελοῖοι 'many and laughable [**geloioi**]', as distinct from the things that he has to say, which are ἀληθέα 'true [**alēthea**]' (FGH 1 F 1). Pollux uses the same notion of 'laughable' (**geloio-**) in referring to such distinctly epichoric concepts as the herm or the evil eye (7.108). All of which helps account for the negative implications of **mūthos** in the discourse of figures like Pindar (again *Olympian* 1.29; also *Nemean* 7.23, 8.33) and Herodotus (2.23.1, 2.45.1).[77] Moreover, earlier versions that claim Panhellenic authority can be dismissed by later versions as **mūthoi**: for example, the authority for the **mūthos** that is discredited by Herodotus at 2.23.1 is his own predecessor, Hecataeus.[78]

All this is not to say that a local or epichoric version, as distinct from a Panhellenic version, can be equated with the version that is supported and promoted by the polis. As an institution, the polis mediates between the epichoric and the Panhellenic: although it *contains* what is epichoric, it also *promotes* what is Panhellenic.[79] In the development from tribe to polis, certain older institutions, no longer compatible with any individual polis, coalesce to form Panhellenic institutions in which a variety of city-states may participate. A prime example is the institution of athletic games, which preserve aspects of tribal initiation patterns no longer suited to the ideologies of any Greek city-state.[80] Another case is the institution of poetry and song. The polis can best promote its prestige by promoting its own traditions in poetry and song on a Panhellenic scale. I have already cited the example of Theognis of Megara.[81] What is particular to Megara alone, grounded in Megara's own rituals and its own myths, tends to be shaded over; what is shared by Megara and by a wide variety of other city-states is highlighted.[82] Thus the polis is in such cases incompatible with **mūthoi**, in the narrow sense of "myths" that reflect the given city's diversity from other cities. For such reasons the implied concept of **poliētai** 'people of the polis, citizens' is explicitly

---

76. Cf. p. 31.

77. The verb **mūtheomai** 'say', derivative of **mūthos**, seems less susceptible to such negative implications: see Pindar *Pythian* 4.298 and Hecataeus FGH 1 F 1. On Aristotle's rehabilitation of the word **mūthos**, see Halliwell 1986.57–58, especially n16. On **mūthos** in Plato: Brisson 1982.

78. How and Wells 1928 I 170.

79. This point is developed further at p. 144. It is no coincidence that the decline of the polis in the fourth century and thereafter coincides with the decline of Panhellenism.

80. At p. 144 and following, I refer to this phenomenon in shorthand as the exoskeleton of the polis.

81. Cf. p. 53.

82. Detailed discussion in N 1985.

opposed by the neologism **mūthiētai** 'people of **mūthos**' (Anacreon PMG 353).[83]

2

ἴδμεν ψεύδεα πολλὰ λέγειν ἐτύμοισιν ὁμοῖα,
ἴδμεν δ᾽, εὖτ᾽ ἐθέλωμεν, <u>ἀληθέα</u> γηρύσασθαι

Hesiod *Theogony* 27–28

We know how to say many false things that look like <u>genuine</u>
[**etuma**] things,
but we also, when we are willing, know how to announce things that
are <u>true</u> [**alēthea**].

These words are spoken to Hesiod by the Muses, who are conferring
upon him his power as a poet. To 'announce things that are true [**alēthea**]' is
a model for the evolution of a unique Panhellenic *Theogony* out of an untold
number of local theogonies, which seem **etuma** 'genuine' but are here set
apart as a plethora of falsehoods.[84]

3

ἀλλὰ παλαιὰ γὰρ   εὕδει χάρις, ἀμνάμονες δὲ βροτοί,   ὅ τι μὴ
σοφίας ἄωτον ἄκρον   κλυταῖς ἐπέων ῥοαῖσιν ἐξίκηται ζυγέν

Pindar *Isthmian* 7.16–19

But the **kharis** [= pleasurable compensation, through song or poetry,
for a deed deserving of glory][85] of the past is asleep, and mortals are

83. Cf. Detienne 1981.92–94. As the scholia to *Odyssey* xxi 71 make clear, the **mūthiētai**
'people of **mūthos**' in the island-polis of Samos are the people who represent **stasis** 'discord'
(στασιασταί). On the theme of **stasis** as a negative way of achieving a definition of the polis,
see pp. 365 and following.

84. See N 1982.47–49. The phrase ἀληθέα γηρύσασθαι 'announce things that are true
[**alēthea**]' at *Theogony* 28 is one of a set of variants, including ἀληθέα μυθήσασθαι 'tell [verb
mūtheomai] things that are true' at *Iliad* vi 382, *Homeric Hymn to Demeter* 121, etc. (also
attested as a textual variant at *Theogony* 28) and ἐτήτυμα μυθήσασθαι 'tell [verb **mūtheomai**]
things that are real [**etētuma**]' at *Homeric Hymn to Demeter* 44. I suggest that these variations
result from a chain of differentiations setting off a marked Panhellenic version from unmarked
versions that are ostensibly local or at least more local. The variant γηρύσασθαι 'announce'
represents a differentiation of marked **gērūsasthai** 'announce' from unmarked **mūthēsasthai**
'tell'; also, the variant ἀληθέα 'things that are true [**alēthea**]' represents a differentiation of
marked **alēthea** 'things that are true' from unmarked **etētuma** 'things that are real'. In each case,
the marked member differentiates a concept that is Panhellenic (**alēthēs**, **gērūsasthai**) from an
earlier concept that is perceived as obsolete (**etētumo-** [or **etumo-**], **mūthēsasthai**) with reference to the new marked member. At each stage of differentiation, we must allow for the proba-
bility that the unmarked member of the opposition had once been the marked member in earlier
sets of opposition.

85. Cf. p. 65.

<u>unaware</u> [= negative of **mnē-**] of whatever does not attain[86] the cresting blossom of the art of songmaking by being wedded to the glory-bringing streams of sung words.

The tradition that informs this song is realized only in the here and now of performance, which is visualized as blossoming from the irrigating waters of the tradition.[87] The '**kharis** of the past' is the cumulative response to all other potential realizations of the tradition, with the adjective **palaio-** 'of the past' implicitly contrasting the present performance.[88] In the diction of Pindar the present performance is conventionally described as **neo-** or **nearo-** 'new', which refers not to the novelty of a theme but to the ad hoc application of a myth to the here and now of those who attend and are the occasion of performance.[89]

4

> τὴν γὰρ ἀοιδὴν μᾶλλον ἐπικλείουσ᾽ ἄνθρωποι
> ἥ τις ἀκουόντεσσι νεωτάτη ἀμφιπέληται

Odyssey i 351–352

Men would most rather give glory [**kleos**] to that song
which is the newest to make the rounds among listeners.

Telemachus says these words to his mother Penelope, who had tried to stop the singer Phemios from singing what is described as the **nostos** 'homecoming' of the Achaeans (i 326).[90] Here too, as in the diction of Pindar, the concept **neo-** 'new' refers to the appropriateness of the myth to the situation in the here and now.[91] In this case Odysseus is both a prime figure in the myth and about to become a prime figure in the here and now narrated by the poem. His **nostos** is literally in the making, which is precisely the subject of the singer. Naturally the Panhellenic **Nostos** of Odysseus in the *Odyssey* is one to end all **nostoi**.[92]

86. Here I am following the interpretation of Race 1986.108.
87. On water as a symbol of poetry or song, see p. 278.
88. The word **palaio-** 'of the past' implies a contrast specifically with **neo-** 'of the present, new': cf. Chantraine DELG 851.
89. Cf. [A. M.] Miller 1982.114. Cf. p. 55.
90. On **nostos** as both 'homecoming' and 'song about homecoming', see N 1979.97 §6n2.
91. Cf. again [A. M.] Miller 1982.114.
92. Cf. N 1979.98. Telemachus is "wrong" in not understanding that the myth applies to the situation in the here and now. For him, the "newness" of the song has the surface-meaning of mere novelty (cf. the interpretation in Plato *Republic* 424bc). But he is "right" in insisting that the singing proceed. This way, the **nostos** sung by the singer may ultimately be fulfilled in the **nostos** of Odysseus, which is the "novelty" of the *Odyssey*—the "news" of what finally happened in the *Odyssey*. Penelope, by contrast, is "right" in understanding that the song applies to the present, but she is "wrong" in interpreting it at this particular moment in the overall narrative

5

τῶν δὲ ἄλλων βασιλέων οὐ γὰρ ἔλεγον οὐδεμίαν ἔργων ἀπόδεξιν,
κατ' οὐδὲν εἶναι λαμπρότητος, πλὴν ἑνὸς τοῦ ἐσχάτου

Herodotus 2.101.1

About the other kings, they [= the Egyptian priests] had no public statement [**apodeixis**] to tell of their deeds [**erga**], since there was nothing
distinguished [= literally 'bright'], except for the last [king].

The word **apodeixis** 'public display' refers to the medium for performing what we see written in Herodotus.[93] Since this medium makes public the
deeds of men, what men do is also **apodeixis**, in that their deeds are being
publicly witnessed.[94] In this case the **apodeixis** of the priests — and of Herodotus in turn — erases the deeds of all kings except one. To put it in terms of
the passage, the making public of a tradition by way of performance — or at
least by way of a written record that simulates performance — highlights the
deeds of an exceptional figure as it darkens over the deeds of other figures.[95]

In light of these illustrations, let us return to the notion of a single
Panhellenic tradition as opposed to a plethora of local traditions. It should be
clear that this notion of *Panhellenic* is absolute only from the standpoint of
insiders to the tradition at a given time and place, and that it is relative from
the standpoint of outsiders, such as ourselves, who are merely looking in on
the tradition. Each new performance can claim to be the definitive Panhellenic tradition. Moreover, the degree of Panhellenic synthesis in the content
of a composition corresponds to the degree of diffusion in the performance of
this composition. Because we are dealing with a relative concept, we may
speak of the poetry of the *Iliad* and *Odyssey*, for example, as more Panhel-

---

of the *Odyssey*. What is absolutely right, not wrong, can emerge only from the overall narrative
in progress.

93. Cf. pp. 218 and following.

94. Ibid.

95. As the narrative of Herodotus proceeds, the spotlight keeps shifting. At the beginning of
this account, the spotlight is on a figure described as the very first king of Egypt (2.99.1–4); after
he is named and his deeds are accounted for, it is said that the priests who were the informants of
Herodotus had records of a sequence of 330 other names that followed the first pharaoh, including one woman (2.100.1). This woman is then highlighted, with a recounting of her name and
some of her deeds (2.100.2–4). Then follows the statement just quoted: 'About the other kings,
they [= the Egyptian priests] had no public statement [**apodeixis**] to tell of their deeds, since
there was nothing distinguished [= literally 'bright'], except for the last [king]' (2.101.1). At this
point, the spotlight falls on the last in this sequence of 330 pharaohs, with a recounting of his
name and some of his deeds (2.101.1–2), capped off by a reaffirmation that this king at least had
these deeds to 'show for himself' (2.101.2; the verb is **apo-deik-numai**, on which see pp. 218
and following), whereas the other kings did not (again 2.101.2). Then the spotlight shifts again,
to the king who came after this last one, and there follows a particularly lengthy and detailed
accounting of this pharaoh's name and some of his notable deeds (2.102.1–2.111.1).

lenic than the poetry of the Epic Cycle. To put it conversely: a Cyclic poem like the *Aithiopis*, attributed to Arctinus of Miletus, is clearly less Panhellenic and more regional, focusing on the local traditions of Miletus.[96] Whereas both the *Iliad* and *Odyssey* refer to the immortalizing **kleos** 'glory' of Panhellenic epic that is to serve as compensation for the death of Achilles,[97] the *Aithiopis* is concerned rather with the personal immortalization of Achilles after death, on the island of Leuke (*Aithiopis*/Proclus, p. 106.12–15 Allen; Pindar *Nemean* 4.49–50). This myth, as espoused by the *Aithiopis*, is anchored in local cult: Leuke is not only a mythical place of immortalization for Achilles but also the ritual place of his hero cult, localized in the territory of Olbia, daughter city of Miletus.[98] I have argued elsewhere that "the Cyclic

96. On the Milesian orientation of the *Aithiopis*, see Pinney 1983, who argues convincingly that the iconographic theme of Scythian archers on Attic late sixth-century vases is akin to local epic traditions specifically associated with Milesian colonization on the northern coast of the Black Sea, and that these local epic traditions are reflected in the *Aithiopis* of Arctinus of Miletus. In the mythological traditions of the mother city, Miletus, the notion of "the Other" apparently became particularized as "the Scythian" in the social context of the daughter cities on the northern coast of the Black Sea (on the subject of Milesian colonization in this area, notably at Olbia, see Bravo 1974). Just as the mother city tends to replicate its social structure, divisions and all, in the daughter city, so also the new social experiences of the daughter city, such as contacts with "new" kinds of barbarians (in this case, Scythians), become incorporated into the ideology of the mother city (see Figueira 1981.192–202, especially p. 199). In light of the fact that Archaic Miletus and Megara were as a rule linked together in rivalry against Corinth and were both predominant as the colonizers of the coastline of the Propontis and the Black Sea (Figueira 1985.276), I note that the poetic traditions of Megara, like those of Miletus, draw attention to the theme of Scythians. These Megarian poetic traditions are preserved in the corpus attributed to Theognis of Megara, where the ideology of Megara incorporates the ideologies of the daughter cities of Megara along with those of the mother city (N 1985.51 §38n1 and Figueira 1985.127–128), and I cite here in particular the Scythian reference at Theognis 825–830 (with the commentary of Figueira 1985.146). Even the Theognidean vision of the **kakoi**, the ethically inferior, as sociopolitically inferior savages who threaten the polis from the outside (Theognis 53–68; cf. N 1985.44 §29n4, 51 §39n2, 54), may convey a colonial point of view adopted from a daughter city on the coast of the Black Sea (cf. Figueira 1985.129). In contemplating the partial "Scythian" characteristics of the Achilles figure in the mythological traditions of Miletus/Olbia (as surveyed by Pinney 1983, especially pp. 133–139; cf. Alcaeus F 354 V), I see a typological parallelism in the figure of Rostam in the *Shāhnāma* of Ferdowsi: this national hero of Iranian epic traditions has partial "foreign" characteristics that give form to his function as both "the Other," an outsider, and "the Self," an insider to the body politic as represented by the ruling *shāh* (see Davidson 1985, especially pp. 61–103). On the equation of the **ephēboi** 'pre-adults' of Elis with Scythians in Photius *Lexicon* s.v. συνέφηβοι, see Hartog 1980.59–79 (especially pp. 71–72) and Vidal-Naquet 1986.133.

97. Discussion in N 1979.29, 35–36, 38–40, 184, especially with reference to *Iliad* IX 413 and *Odyssey* xi 489–491.

98. Details in Pinney 1983.143n56 and 145n94, who accepts as early a dating as the late sixth century B.C. (p. 133); cf. N 1979.167 (I agree with the reservations expressed by Pinney, p. 144n64, about the thesis that Achilles was originally a god of the underworld). On names like **Elusion** 'Elysium' and **Makarōn Nēsoi** 'Islands of the Blessed' as simultaneous designations of a mythical place of immortalization and a ritual place of hero cult, see N, pp. 189–192.

epics are so different from the two Homeric epics not because they are more recent or more primitive but rather because they are more local in orientation and diffusion."[99]

To explain the superior prestige of the Homeric poems on the basis of their greater Panhellenic orientation and diffusion would also help account for the dependency of the whole Cycle on the narrative structure of the *Iliad* and *Odyssey* combined: the Cycle fills in the portions of the tale of Troy that had not already been told in its own way and on its own terms by the poetry of the *Iliad* and *Odyssey*.[100] In other words the text of the Epic Cycle is built around that of the *Iliad* and *Odyssey*.[101]

Clearly the poems of the Cycle, as also the Homeric *Hymns*, become fixed texts at various times that are all later than the textual fixation of the *Iliad* and *Odyssey*.[102] So we must assume either that poems like the *Aithiopis*, *Little Iliad*, and *The Destruction of Ilion* developed parallel to the *Iliad* and *Odyssey* or that they are derived from them. The latter alternative is an impossibility. The basic achievement of the "neoanalytic" approach as advocated by Wolfgang Kullmann and others is their cumulative demonstration that any given Homeric treatment of a given tradition may entail a refinement of that same tradition as attested in the Cycle.[103] In terms of my argument, such refinements are a reflex of further Panhellenization in Homeric poetry as distinct from other related poetry. Such refinements cannot be accounted for merely by invoking the genius of a poet who stands out from among the rest.

Paradoxically the textual fixation of the Homeric poems is older than that of the Cycle, in that the overall narrative of the Cycle is built around the *Iliad* and *Odyssey*, and yet the inherited themes of the Cycle appear consistently older than those of the Homeric poems.[104] I propose to account for this state

---

99. N 1979.8 §14n1: there I make clear that I part company with Griffin 1977, who thinks that the Homeric epics have screened out most of "the fantastic, the miraculous, and the romantic" (p. 40) elements characteristic of the Cycle because Homer was a superior or "unique" poet. (For a useful critique of Griffin's position, see Young 1983.166n32.) Instead I would stress that the fantastic and the miraculous elements in the Cycle characterize the religious ideology of local cults, reflecting the more localized interests of individual city-states or groups of city-states. The same goes for the romantic element of love stories, again for the most part screened out by the Homeric epics: it goes without saying that love affairs lead to conceptions of heroes, a basic theme of genealogical poetic traditions that promote the localized interests of the status quo. On the relationship of Panhellenic poetic traditions with the more localized **ktisis** ('foundation, colonization') poetic traditions of various city-states, see N 1979.8 §14n1 (with cross references) and especially pp. 139–141; also N 1982.63–64 and 1985.51 §38n1 and 63 §51n2.

100. For a helpful survey, see Allen 1924.72–75.

101. I use the concept of *text* in the broadened sense outlined at p. 53.

102. For a comprehensive survey of linguistic and other criteria that can be applied for an overall relative chronology, see Janko 1982.

103. Kullmann 1985, especially pp. 17–18n37.

104. A survey of Archaic Greek iconographical evidence, as assembled by Fittschen 1969 and juxtaposed by Kannicht 1982 with the evidence of Archaic Greek poetry, shows that the earliest

of affairs by arguing that the Panhellenization of the Homeric tradition entailed a differentiation from older layers of Panhellenic epic tradition, and that these older layers were gradually sloughed off in the process of Homeric streamlining. Such an explanation would account for not only the artistic superiority of the *Iliad* and *Odyssey* but also the thematic archaism of the Cycle.[105] The older layers represented by the Cycle kept developing alongside the emerging core of the Homeric tradition and, being the more local versions, had the relative freedom to develop for a longer time, albeit at a slower pace, toward a point of textual fixation that still seems like a case of arrested development in contrast with the ultimate Homeric form.[106]

This sloughing off of older layers could have been expressed in terms of myth as a break in genealogical continuity with the Homeridai, the descendants of Homer.[107] We earlier witnessed the explicit articulation of such a break in the case of Kynaithos the rhapsode: according to the scholia to Pindar (*Nemean* 2.1c, III 29.9–18 Drachmann), Kynaithos of Chios, credited with the final form of the Homeric *Hymn to Apollo*, could no longer trace himself to Homer. In other words the tradition continued by Kynaithos is here being discredited by the sources as no longer authorized by the Homeridai.[108]

Myth can provide for indirect as well as direct heirs to the Homeridai. According to one version Stasinus, reputedly the poet of the *Cypria* (e.g., scholia A to *Iliad* I 5), was not the author of that poem but instead received the *Cypria* as a dowry from his father-in-law, Homer (Tzetzes *Chiliades* 13.636–640; Pindar F 265 SM, in the fuller context of Aelian *Varia Historia*

---

identifiable pictorial responses to epic concern predominantly the themes of the Cycle, not those of the *Iliad* or *Odyssey*.

105. This explanation differs from the one offered by Kannicht, p. 85, who accounts for the relative absence of early pictorial references to the Homeric *Iliad* and *Odyssey* by arguing that the artistic limitations of early Greek iconographical traditions made it too difficult for these traditions to react to the great artistic achievements of the *Iliad* and *Odyssey*.

106. A similar point can be made in the case of the contrast between *Iliad* II 557–570 and Hesiod F 204.44–51, where both passages describe the extent of the dominion of the hero Ajax. As Finkelberg 1988 argues, the Homeric passage from the *Iliad*, part of the *Catalogue of Ships*, is more innovative than the Hesiodic passage in drastically restricting the realm of Ajax, even though the text fixation of the Homeric passage is presumably earlier than that of the Hesiodic. As Finkelberg also argues (pp. 39–40), the Homeric version is politically advantageous to Athens under the Peisistratidai and, secondarily, to Argos in the era of Pheidon, as also to Corinth and even to Sparta, while it is disadvantageous primarily to Megara. Such a version, which suits the politics of the more powerful city-states, is clearly more Panhellenic in scope than the Hesiodic version (which itself is distinct from the overtly pro-Megarian version: Finkelberg, p. 40). I should add that the parallelisms between *Iliad* II 557–570 and Hesiod F 204.44–51 (as illustrated by the underlinings in Finkelberg, pp. 32–33) suggest that the Homeric version reduces the realm of Ajax not so much by deleting elements found in the Hesiodic version but by augmenting the traditional elements and then reassigning the greater portion to figures other than Ajax.

107. On the Homeridai, see p. 22.

108. Cf. p. 22.

9.15). According to another myth Homer had taught the composition called the *Capture of Oikhalia* to Kreophylos of Samos, founder of the corporation of rhapsodes known as the Kreophyleioi, as a gift in return for the hospitality of Kreophylos when Homer had traveled from Chios to Samos (Strabo 14.1.18 C638; cf. Callimachus *Epigram* 6 Pfeiffer).[109] From the standpoint of the Homeridai, the Kreophyleioi were left out of Homer's genealogy, perhaps because they were rivals. The rivalry would concern the basic question: who is the authoritative representative of the epic tradition in a given community? In Archaic Sparta, for example, it appears that the Kreophyleioi of Samos were more authoritative than the Homeridai of Chios: tradition has it that the introduction of Homeric poetry took place in Sparta by way of the Kreophyleioi of Samos (Aristotle F 611.10 Rose).[110]

Wherever a given succession of rhapsodes is left out of the direct genealogy of Homer, we can expect that they may have to relinquish the central repertory of the Homeridai and make do with what is left over. Such is the case, it seems, with the distinct repertories attributed to Arctinus of Miletus, Lesches of Mytilene, Stasinus of Cyprus, and the other poets of the Cycle.[111]

109. The basic testimonia are conveniently available in Allen 1924.228–229 and Burkert 1972.76n10. Cf. N 1979.165–166.

110. Tradition also has it that it was Lycurgus, lawgiver par excellence, who brought to Sparta the Homeric poems, which he acquired from the descendants of Kreophylos at Samos, according to Plutarch *Life of Lycurgus* 4. It is said of the poems that Lycurgus 'had them written down', ἐγράψατο, and that he then 'assembled' them (ibid.). I draw attention to a further detail in the narrative of Plutarch (ibid.): ἦν γάρ τις ἤδη δόξα τῶν ἐπῶν ἀμαυρὰ παρὰ τοῖς Ἕλλησιν, ἐκέκτηντο δὲ οὐ πολλοὶ μέρη τινά, σποράδην τῆς ποιήσεως, ὡς ἔτυχε, διαφερομένης· γνωρίμην δὲ αὐτὴν καὶ μάλιστα πρῶτος ἐποίησε Λυκοῦργος 'for there was already a not-too-bright fame attached to these epics among the Greeks, and some of them were in possession of some portions, since the poetry had been scattered, carried here and there by chance, and it was Lycurgus who was the first to make it [= the poetry] well-known' (ibid.). For an alternative tradition, according to which Lycurgus met Homer directly, see Ephorus FGH 70 F 103 and 149 (by way of Strabo 10.4.19 C482). The notion of a disassembled book, scattered here and there throughout the Greek world, and then reassembled for one particular time and place by a wise man credited with the juridical framework of his society, is parallel to the story about the making of the Book of Kings in the Iranian epic tradition. According to Ferdowsi's *Shāhnāma* I 21.126–136, a noble vizier assembles *mubad*-s, wise men who are experts in the Law of Zoroaster, from all over the Empire, and each of these *mubad*-s brings with him a "fragment" of a long-lost Book of Kings that had been scattered to the winds; each of the experts is called upon to recite, in turn, his respective "fragment," and the vizier composes a book out of these recitations. As Davidson 1985.123 points out, "It would seem from this passage that the authority of the unified Empire and of the unified Book of Kings is one." The vizier reassembles the old book that had been disassembled, which in turn becomes the model for the *Shāhnāma* 'Book of Kings' of Ferdowsi (*Shāhnāma* I 23.156–161). We see here paradoxically a myth about the synthesis of oral traditions that is articulated in terms of written traditions, as Davidson argues in detail (pp. 111–127). For a comparable myth in Irish traditions, concerning the recovery of the "lost" *Cattle Raid of Cúailnge*, see [J. F.] Nagy 1986.292–293.

111. So also, perhaps, in the case of Kynaithos of Chios: it may well be that his "Homeric" repertory was not the *Iliad* and *Odyssey*. This Kynaithos, as we have seen, is said to have been

To judge by the repertory of the Cycle, what was indeed left over was already finite[112] in that the Panhellenism of the Cycle, however less developed than that of the *Iliad* and *Odyssey*, still entails the preservation of a few variants at the expense of the extinction of many others. Just as the *Iliad* and *Odyssey* had prevailed over the Cycle, so also the Cycle had teleologically prevailed over countless other epic traditions. In terms of myth, however, as long as a given tradition can somehow survive after losing to another tradition, the loser can be presented as the winner: it is as if the surviving tradition, deprived of the repertory of the prevalent tradition, had won its own remaining repertory as a concession from the prevalent one.[113] Such is the case in the myth that tells of the contest between Arctinus of Miletus and Lesches of Mytilene, which is won by Lesches (Phaenias F 33 Wehrli, in Clement *Stromateis* 1.131.6).[114]

---

the 'first' rhapsode to recite Homeric poetry at Syracuse, in the 69th Olympiad (504/1 B.C.), according to Hippostratus (FGH 568 F 5). By implication Kynaithos was the first recorded winner in a seasonally recurring festival at Syracuse that featured a competition of rhapsodes. Cf. p. 22. As another possible example of a distinct repertory, see p. 22 on Herodotus 5.67.1, where the reference to the "Homeric" repertory of the rhapsodes who were banned from Sikyon implies not the *Iliad* and *Odyssey* but rather an overall *Seven against Thebes* epic tradition. In the *Contest of Homer and Hesiod* 287–315 Allen, a myth tells how Homer visited the people of Argos, gave a performance there, and was subsequently given great honors by that city-state. In Callinus F 6 W, the *Seven against Thebes* is attributed to Homer. In contrast Herodotus 4.32 may be taking a stance that is detrimental to Argos when he expresses doubt whether the poet of the *Epigonoi,* the sequel of the *Seven against Thebes,* is indeed Homer.

112. Eleven books of the *Cypria* (Proclus summary, p. 102.10 Allen), five of the *Aithiopis* (p. 105.21), four of the *Little Iliad* (p. 106.19), two of the *Destruction of Ilion* (p. 107.16), five of the *Nostoi* (p. 108.15), and two of the *Telegonia* (p. 109.7).

113. A clear example is the Homeric *Hymn to Hermes,* where the functions that Hermes "wins" from Apollo correspond to earlier stages in patterns of differentiation involving the **aoidos** 'singer' and the **mantis** 'seer'. The later stages of these patterns were taken over by the figure of Apollo. Discussion in N 1982.56–57.

114. See p. 28. On the associations of the *Little Iliad* of Lesches with the local traditions of Lesbos, see the discussion and bibliography in Aloni 1986.120–123. In general, Aloni's book offers an interesting case in point illustrating the interdependence between two distinct narrative traditions owned by two distinct communities in conflict. The communities in question are the cities of Mytilene in Lesbos on the one hand and on the other Athens in the era of the Athenian dynasty of tyrants, the Peisistratidai. The focal point is "Trojan" Sigeion (cf. Herodotus 4.38.2), an outpost of Athenian power, founded by the Peisistratidai as an intrusion into a geographical area controlled by Mytilene, whose rival outpost was the Akhilleion (Herodotus 5.94.1–2; Sigeion was at the mouth of the river Skamandros: Herodotus 5.65.3). Aloni argues that the contemporary winners of the conflict, the Athenians, needed to appropriate at least part of the narrative traditions owned by the losers, the Mytilenaeans, in order to legitimize their own expansionistic presence in Sigeion (see especially pp. 65n8, 91). In the context of the conflicting claims of the Athenians and Mytilenaeans, note the use of the word **apo-deik-numi** at Herodotus 5.94.2; cf. p. 162 (also p. 316). Note too the story of the duel to the death between the Athenian Phrynon, an Olympic winner, and the Mytilenaean Pittakos, tyrant and lawgiver, as recorded in Diogenes Laertius 1.74 and Strabo 13.1.38 C599–600 (and omitted in Herodotus 5.95: cf. Plutarch *On the Malice of Herodotus* 858ab). Both sources agree that the Mytilenaeans won in this

A similar point may be made about the *Contest of Homer and Hesiod* tradition (*Certamen*, pp. 225–238 Allen).[115] Here Hesiod is represented as the victor on the basis of the specialization of Hesiodic poetry: telling of peacetime pursuits is deemed superior to telling of wartime ones (*Certamen*, p. 233.205–210 Allen). By implication, the telling of wartime pursuits is not open to Hesiod, whereas it is to Homer. The myth of this victory compensates for the fact that the poetry of Hesiod is relatively less Panhellenic than that of Homer. For example, we hear only of Homeric poetry, not of Hesiodic, in connection with reports about recitations that are privileged by law at the Panathenaia.[116]

This point about relative Panhellenism brings us back to the Epic Cycle. The story about the contest between Arctinus and Lesches, which Lesches wins (Phaenias F 33 Wehrli), may have a symbolic bearing on the interrelationship of narratives in the poetry attributed to Arctinus and Lesches. Both the *Aithiopis* and the *Destruction of Ilion* are attributed to Arctinus, whereas the *Little Iliad* is attributed to Lesches. On the basis of this story of a contest, combined with the fact that the story line of the *Little Iliad* of Lesches intervenes between that of the *Aithiopis* and that of the *Destruction of Ilion*, the two compositions attributed to Arctinus, it has been supposed that Arctinus, who "has the lion's share of the Cycle," had been "forced by Lesches' rising merits to yield him the [*Little Iliad*]."[117] This interpretation assumes that the story of a contest between Lesches and Arctinus is a historical fact, whereas I argue that it is a myth reflecting the historical relationship between the poetry attributed to these two figures. As we look at the narrative coverage of the *Little Iliad* as attributed to Lesches, this poet from the island of Lesbos, it seems at first to be an intrusion into the narrative of Arctinus of Miletus. But it would be more accurate to say that the narrative of Arctinus envelops the narrative of Lesches at both ends, almost engulfing it. Just as the Epic Cycle is built around the Homeric *Iliad* and *Odyssey*, so also, within the Cycle, the repertoire of Arctinus seems to be built around that of Lesches. There seems to be a stratification here, as if an earlier repertoire represented by Lesches of Mytilene were being enveloped by a later repertoire represented by Arctinus of Miletus.[118]

---

conflict, only to lose later in an arbitration undertaken by Periandros, tyrant of Corinth (this aspect of the tradition is not omitted in Herodotus 5.95.2). The accretion of narrations concerning an earlier victory and a later loss by the Mytilenaeans recapitulates, it seems, a hierarchy of accommodations between rival narrative traditions: the ultimately losing side is pictured as having won first.

115. For a possible allusion to *Contest of Homer and Hesiod* tradition in Hesiod *Works and Days* 657, see N 1982.66.

116. Cf. pp. 21 and following.

117. Allen 1924.64.

118. Cf. Kuryłowicz's fourth law of analogy, as discussed at p. 5.

This observation, made on the level of content, has an analogy on the level of form: the Ionic diction of Homer, as also of the Cycle, envelops an earlier stage of Aeolic diction, so that Aeolic forms tend to survive only where they are not replaceable, in the metrical frames that they occupy, by corresponding Ionic forms.[119] From the linguistic point of view an even earlier layer of Homeric diction is closely akin to the surviving local dialect of Cyprus.[120] In this connection, we may take note of the fact that the *Cypria* makes explicit localized references to Cyprus (see, e.g., Lysimachus FGH 382 F 12; cf. "Apollodorus" *Epitome* 3.3–4); also, Stasinus, the reputed poet of the *Cypria*, is conventionally described as 'the Cypriote' (e.g., at *Suda* s.v. Ὅμηρος; cf. Athenaeus 334b).[121] Since the themes of the *Cypria* constitute the narrative basis for the entire epic tradition of the Trojan War, its Cypriote associations may be connected to an early phase in the Panhellenic diffusion of epic traditions on the island of Cyprus.[122]

In sum the Cycle may be viewed as a vestigial recapitulation in content of the chronological layering of the entire Homeric tradition, even though much of this layering has been sloughed off by the actual *Iliad* and *Odyssey*. The traditions of these sloughed-off layers, as represented by the Cycle, could have kept growing alongside the Homeric tradition, becoming even more Ionian in diction than Homeric diction itself.[123] In the few remaining fragments of the Cycle, an Ionic layer is clearly superimposed on the arguably Aeolic traditions represented by Lesches of Mytilene and the Cypriote traditions represented by Stasinus of Cyprus.[124]

The overarching Panhellenism of the Homeric poems, as we have seen, is evident from the differentiation of these poems from those of the Cycle. But the differentiation must be asserted on the basis of whatever distinct tra-

119. Cf., for example, Householder and Nagy 1972.785. For a restatement of the facts that necessitate the positing of an Aeolic phase in the evolution of Homeric diction: West 1988.162–163 (with bibliography).

120. Householder and Nagy, pp. 783–785.

121. As Huxley 1969.134–135 points out, there are also traces of Cypriote localization as the setting for *Homeric Hymn* 10, where the poet, in praying to Aphrodite as the queen of Salamis in Cyprus (10.5), treats her as a local Muse in asking her to give him a song that brings gratification (ibid.); also in *Homeric Hymn* 6, addressed to Aphrodite as queen of all Cyprus (6.2–3), where the poet prays that the goddess grant him victory in the competition: δὸς δ' ἐν ἀγῶνι Ι νίκην τῷδε φέρεσθαι 'grant that I carry away victory in this contest [**agōn**]' (6.19–20).

122. Janko 1982.176 gives reasons for estimating 750 B.C. or thereabouts as the terminus post quem for any possible proliferation of early phases of the *Cypria* tradition on the island of Cyprus, but he doubts that Cyprus was "the area in which this tradition grew to maturity."

123. The case is clear in Hesiodic poetry: despite its ultimate local provenience, Aeolic Boeotia, this poetry is more Ionic in diction than even Homeric poetry. See Janko 1982.85, 197; cf. N 1982.70–72.

124. In *Little Iliad* F 12 Allen, however, as quoted by Clement *Stromateis* 1.21.104.1, the occurrences of α in place of η may suggest an Aeolic layer of transmission: see West 1971.308n3. Alternatively such occurrences may reflect editorial aeolicisms.

ditions are offered by the Cycle. Without such a pattern of assertion, the distinction between the Homeric poems and those of the Cycle poems can lapse into indifference in face of Homeric Panhellenism. Thus whereas the poems of the Epic Cycle could be attributed to individual poets like Arctinus and Lesches, they could also be attributed to the central figure of textual fixation, Homer.[125] According to one particular myth, for example, Homer himself was commissioned to "dictate" the *Little Iliad*, along with another composition called the *Phokais*, when he traveled to Phokaia (Herodotean *Life of Homer* 15, pp. 202–203 Allen). In this version any attribution of the *Little Iliad* to Lesches of Mytilene is wanting. For another example, I cite again Pindar F 265 SM, referring to the myth that told how the composition of the *Cypria* was Homer's dowry for his daughter (who was married to Stasinus: Aelian *Varia Historia* 9.15, Tzetzes *Chiliades* 13.636–640). Further, Herodotus goes out of his way to argue, apparently against certain traditions in his own time, that the poet of the *Cypria* is not Homer (2.116–117).[126] The words of Callinus apparently referred to the *Seven against Thebes* as Homer's poem (F 6 W); or again, Herodotus feels bound to express doubt whether the poet of the *Epigonoi*, the sequel of the *Seven against Thebes,* is indeed Homer (4.32).[127] By the time of Aristotle the safest thing was to say simply 'the author of the Cypria' or 'the author of the *Little Iliad*', as opposed to the prototypical and idealized Homer (*Poetics* 1459b). One latter-day critic puts it this way: "If Homer had a kind of claim to all this epic literature — a rather strong claim to the Hymns, a weaker one to the Cycle — and the alternatives to admitting his claim were either anonymity or naming a definite poet, what explanation can be given of the phenomenon except that the whole literature was the work of a school?"[128] For the phrase *the work of a school*, elsewhere deemed *the Homeric canon* by the same author,[129] I would substitute *a Panhellenic tradition*. Whereas the *Aithiopis* and the *Destruction of Ilion* are claimed by Miletus by way of attribution to Arctinus of Miletus, and the *Little Iliad* is claimed by Mytilene by way of attribution to Lesches of Mytilene in Lesbos, no single polis has an unequivo-

125. This point is stressed by Allen 1924.75.

126. It is the more complex pattern of the Homeric poems, where one level of narrative is being subordinated to another, as contrasted with the more simple pattern of the *Cypria*, that convinces Herodotus that the poet of the *Cypria* cannot be Homer. Further discussion in p. 420.

127. We have already seen that the city-state of Argos apparently attributed to Homer the entire *Seven against Thebes* tradition. See p. 75.

128. Allen 1924.71, who adds that the "work" of such a poet could have been "gradually taken from him" by the "survival and revelation of local tradition" (ibid.). I disagree with this additional point to the extent that I interpret the "revelation of local tradition" not as something that is taken away from Homeric poetry but rather as something that is generally rejected by Homeric poetry.

129. Allen, p. 76, where he speculates that, by the time of Peisistratos, "the Cycle was all but finished and the Homeric canon all but closed."

cal claim on Homer (though his cult as hero at Chios seems definable by way of the Homeridai at Chios).[130]

In offering this sketch of the synthetic tradition that produced the Homeric poems, I should close by stressing that I do not deny the notion of "poets within a tradition."[131] The oral composer in the context of performance can execute considerable refinements in the act of recomposition.[132] The composer can even appropriate the recomposition as his own composition, as if it emanated exclusively from an owned authority: "This is my song."[133] But the gradual replacement of divergences in local oral traditions by convergences in Panhellenic oral tradition leads to an internal idealization of the very concept of the composer. If indeed Panhellenization gradually eliminates opportunities for recomposition in performance, we should then expect a commensurate elimination of opportunities for successive generations of performers to identify themselves as composers. I therefore do not argue generally that tradition creates the poet.[134] Rather I argue specifically that the Panhellenic tradition of oral poetry appropriates the poet, potentially transforming even historical figures into generic ones who represent the traditional functions of their poetry. The wider the diffusion and the longer the chain of recomposition, the more remote the identity of the composer becomes. Extreme cases are Homer and Hesiod.[135] To put it another way: the person of the poet, by virtue of being a transmitter of tradition, can become absorbed by the tradition.[136] Then the poet as an exponent of his poetry can become identified with and even equated with that poetry. Thus, for example, when Heraclitus (22 B 42 DK) says that Homer and Archilochus should be banned from contests in poetic performance, **agōnes**, what is really being said is that rhapsodes should not be allowed to perform Homer and Archilochus.[137]

The appropriation of a historical person by the poetic tradition in which that person is composing can be visualized hypothetically in the following general schema of progressive phases, constructed from specific examples of performance conventions taken from a variety of traditional societies:

130. For references on the Homeridai, cf. N 1979.165 §25n4.
131. As Griffith 1983.58n82 suggests that I do in N 1979.5–6, 296–297.
132. To call such refinements "innovation," however, can be deceptive: see p. 55.
133. Cf. p. 55. For a survey of conventions expressing the simultaneous appropriation of authority and authorship in Iranian poetic traditions, see Davidson 1985.103–142. In the conventions of Greek oral poetic traditions, self-identification is particularly appropriate in the context of the **prooimion** or 'prelude': brief discussion in N 1982.53.
134. As Griffith 1983.58n82, again, suggests that I do in N 1979.5–6, 296–297.
135. Cf. N 1979.295–300.
136. I explore this topic at length in N 1985.
137. See p. 22.

1. At a phase of the tradition where each performance still entails an act of at least partial recomposition, performer L publicly appropriates a given recomposition-in-performance as his own composition.[138]

2. At a later phase of the tradition, performer M stops appropriating the recomposition of the recomposition as his or her own composition and instead attributes it to the predecessor L; this attribution is then continued by successors NOPQ.[139]

3. In the process of successive recompositions by NOPQ, the self-identification of L is recomposed often enough to eliminate the historical aspects of identity and to preserve only the generic aspects (that is, the aspects of the poet as defined by traditional activity as a poet; also by being the ancestor or at least predecessor of those who continue in the tradition).[140] The definitive stages of Homeric text fixation, I would suggest, correspond to this stage 3.[141]

The key to loss of identity as a composer is loss of control over performance. Once the factor of performance slips out of the poet's control — even if the performers of the poet's poetry have traditional comments about the poet as a composer — the poet becomes a myth; more accurately the poet becomes part of a myth, and the myth-making structure appropriates his or her identity. Such is the case with the poetry of a Homer or a Hesiod or an Archilochus, as performed by **rhapsōidoi** 'rhapsodes' like Ion of Chios.[142]

138. On categories of ownership of song (and/or dance), see Kunst 1958.2. See also the examples cited at p. 55. On the ownership, in North American Indian traditions, of personal songs obtained in the vision quest, see Merriam 1964.83. Cf. also Merriam and d'Azevedo 1957.623: "Most songs seem to have been embellished, consciously or unconsciously altered over time, combined, improvised, forgotten and 'caught' again in new form as one's own. The last are thought of as 'new' or 'my' songs, but the singer has no inclination to hide the fact that he was influenced by another song, and that 'I just changed it a little'. Nevertheless, it does become a 'new' song." For bibliography on the relativity of the descriptive term *improvisation*, see p. 56.

139. As in Rwanda praise poetry, with memorization and remembering of the "original" composer by name: Finnegan 1977.79; cf. also p. 75. In Somali poetry: "A poet's composition . . . becomes his own property, under his own name, and another poet reciting them has to acknowledge from whom he has learnt them" (Finnegan, p. 74). For a possible trace of this type of attribution in the South Slavic traditions, see Lord 1960.19–20.

140. Rwanda and Somali examples: Finnegan, p. 83. Cf. Merriam 1964.83 on the ownership of songs by kinship groups. See Boutière and Schutz 1950.xii on the Provençal convention that requires the *joglar* 'performer' to narrate the *vida* 'life story' of the *trobador* 'composer' whose composition he is about to perform. On the related genre of the *razo* (from Latin *ratiō*) as a sort of prelude, see Boutière and Schutz, p. xiii. The purpose is to recover the *context* of composition.

141. Kirk 1962.88–98 offers a different model of Homeric transmission, where his division into various successive stages presupposes a general pattern of decline. For a critique, see Jensen 1980.113–114.

142. There are instances where we have specific evidence that the transmission is regulated in the context of a hero cult in honor of the poet. See N 1979.304 §4n3 on the cult of Archilochus;

In sum, Panhellenism affects not only the form and the content of Archaic Greek poetry. It affects also the very identity of the poet. As the poet's composition is successively reperformed, the poet's identity is successively reenacted and thereby reshaped.[143]

---

cf. also p. 124 §9n1 on what appears to be a cult of a clearly historical figure, Pindar himself. See also the discussion in N 1982.49–51 on the cult of Hesiod, to be supplemented with the comments at p. 29. In this discussion it is argued that the traditions of Archaic Greek poetry already contain, as a built-in program, so to speak, the ideology that makes cult heroes of poets.

143. On the reenactment of the poet through reperformance, see p. 373.

3 ▣▣ The Panhellenization of Song

The concept of Panhellenism helps explain not only how the multiple traditions of Archaic Greek oral poetry became a synthetic tradition but also how this tradition, as visualized in the hypothetical schema that has been offered, tended to counteract the emergence of historically verifiable authorship. Further, the concept of Panhellenism also helps explain why the oldest body of Greek literature to survive — the poetry of Homer and Hesiod — is representative of oral poetry, not song. I argue that the Panhellenization of poetry preceded the Panhellenization of song because the traditions of song were more diverse than the traditions of poetry. In the Archaic and even the Classical period of Greece, it appears that the greatest diversity in local oral traditions was on the level of song, with a wide variety of different melodic patterns native to different locales.[1] In their diversity, the local traditions of song were less adaptable to the evolving synthesis that I call Panhellenization.

The earliest attestations of a critical mass of actual compositions in Greek song — which we may also call *lyric poetry* — are represented by the surviving texts attributed to Alcman, Stesichorus, Alcaeus, Sappho, Ibycus, Anacreon, Simonides, Bacchylides, and Pindar; in the era of Alexandrian scholarship, these nine names constituted the inherited canon of lyric poetry

---

1. There is a useful survey by Comotti 1979.15–25 (see especially p. 18). For an insight into the character of local melodic patterns, consider the expression δημώδη μουσικήν 'songmaking of the locale [**dēmos**]' at Plato *Phaedo* 61a, in the context of the discussion by Brisson 1982.55–56. In the discussion that follows, I use the same notions of *pitch* and *melody* that I have set up in the working definitions at p. 34.

(cf. *Palatine Anthology* 9.184, where all nine are enumerated).[2] The relative dating of these poets covers a period stretching roughly from 650 to 450 B.C.[3] These attestations of song are the reflex of what we may call a second wave of Panhellenization, achieved through an ongoing synthesis as represented by the myths about the "inventions" of figures like Terpander and Olympus, to whom we turn presently. As with the first wave, namely, the Panhellenization of oral poetry, the relatively later Panhellenization of oral song would entail a progressively restricted series of recompositions, in ever-widening circles of diffusion, with the streamlining of convergent local traditions at the expense of divergent ones.[4] In this way, a preexisting multitude of local traditions in oral song could evolve into a finite synthetic tradition of fixed lyric compositions suited for all Hellenes and attributed by them all to a relatively small number of poets.

Wilamowitz was struck by the limited number of poets just listed, nine, whose lyric compositions were being edited in the era of Alexandrian scholarship,[5] and he was ready to conclude that these Archaic poets were for all practical purposes the only ones whose texts of lyric poetry had survived from the Classical into the Hellenistic period.[6] This line of thinking fails to

2. See Pfeiffer 1968.205. On the concept of *canon* as used here, see p. 61.

3. Cf. Kirkwood 1974.3. The dating of Corinna as roughly contemporaneous has been a matter of controversy, discussed impartially by Page 1953.68–84. If indeed this lyric poetry is Archaic (cf. Gerber 1970.394–395), like the canon of the nine lyric poets, the question remains: why was Corinna ignored in the canon? I agree with the reason offered by Page: by the time that we reach the era of Alexandrian scholarship, Corinna would have "long ceased to rank among οἱ πραττόμενοι, the poets whose works survived in universal and unbroken circulation (p. 69)." If then we suppose that Corinna is an Archaic poet, I would further suppose that the transmission of her lyric poetry happened not on a Panhellenic but on a more localized Boeotian level. (On the localized nature of the compositions attributed to Corinna, I cite the useful discussion of Davison 1968.300–302.) The absence of an ultimately Panhellenic transmission could perhaps be connected with the possible absence of an Athenian transmission. We would not expect Corinna, as a local poet of Boeotia, to be a "Classic" in the **paideiā** 'education' of Athenian youths, on which see further at p. 97. On the likelihood that the canon inherited by the Alexandrian scholars reflects primarily the traditions of Athenian **paideiā**, see in general Ch.13. In any case it is important to distinguish between the selective canon inherited by the Alexandrian scholars and the nonselective repertory of works housed in their Museum: see p. 61. For the Alexandrian scholars, exclusion of an author from the canon does not preclude an active interest in that author, even as a model for imitation. As Zetzel 1983.99 points out, "one of the most striking characteristics of Alexandrian poetry was its tendency to avoid the major classical genres and even to elevate to literary status forms probably not recognized previously as literature at all." This way the classifier sets himself apart as one who is beyond classification (Zetzel ibid.; cf. also Rossi 1971.83–86).

4. This is not to say that we should expect the patterns of recomposition in poetry and song to be neatly parallel in every way.

5. Wilamowitz-Moellendorff 1900.63–71, especially p. 65.

6. Ibid. See also Page 1953.68, who doubts that "any ancient lyrical poet whose works were in circulation up to the Alexandrian era was omitted by the Alexandrian editors from their collection." For bibliography on reactions to this view, see Pfeiffer 1968.205n4.

distinguish between the relatively small selective canon inherited by the Alexandrian scholars and the massive nonselective collection of works that was at their disposal in the Museum;[7] it is enough to say that the canon of nine lyric poets was inherited from the Classical period.[8] I argue that this limited number of nine lyric poets is due to the Panhellenization of preexisting traditions in oral song, just as the comparably small number of canonical Archaic poets who are credited with compositions in hexameters (predominantly two, Homer and Hesiod)[9] or in iambics (Archilochus, Hipponax, Semonides, Solon, and so on) and elegiacs (Archilochus, Callinus, Mimnermus, Tyrtaeus, Theognis, Solon, Xenophanes, and so on) is due to the Panhellenization of preexisting traditions in oral poetry.[10]

I have suggested that the very evolution of what we know as the Classics—as both a concept and a reality—was but an extension of the organic Panhellenization of oral traditions.[11] In line with this reasoning, the evolution of an ancient Greek canon in both poetry and song need not be attributed primarily to the factor of writing.[12] Granted, writing would have been essential for the ultimate preservation of any canon once the traditions of performance were becoming obsolete; still I argue that the key to the actual evolution of a canon must be sought in the social context of performance itself.

In Archaic Greece the form of song or lyric poetry was functionally divided into two distinct media of performance. This division is most explicitly formulated in a hypothetical discussion, as framed by Plato *Laws* 764c-

7. See p. 61.

8. What Zetzel 1983.98 writes about the three canonical iambic poets (Archilochus, Hipponax, and Semonides of Amorgos: cf. Quintilian *Institutio oratoria* 10.1.59) can be applied also to the nine canonical lyric poets: "it was a selection and not, as has sometimes been thought, a complete list of all early authors—it was explicitly a list of earlier authors, *stopping with the fourth century B.C.*" (emphasis mine). I would also compare the canonical notion of Seven Sages, datable all the way back to the Archaic period, where the number seven is a constant while the actual membership is variable, in that we witness attestations of different "members" at different times and different places (see p. 243).

9. As we have already observed in the case of Homer, the patterns of attribution to such a given "author" become progressively more exclusive as we move forward in time: see p. 19. Thus the Epic Cycle, for example, becomes reassigned to distinct poets, whose canonical status is considered inferior to that of Homer: see pp. 72 and following. On Orpheus and Musaeus, presented as if they were earlier than Hesiod and Homer, cf. Aristophanes *Frogs* 1032–1035 (further references at pp. 216). By contrast Herodotus 2.53.3 argues against the notion that there might be such poets older than Homer and Hesiod (cf. p. 216). It is clear from the context that Herodotus places Homer and Hesiod as the earliest because he deems their canonical status the very highest.

10. Ch.2 above. By the time of the first century A.D., the entire surviving corpus of Greek lyric in the broader sense, including iambic and elegiac poetry, was ranked as a nonpractical aspect of education in the Classics (cf. Dio of Prusa *Orations* 18.8, p. 478 R).

11. Cf. p. 62.

12. See pp. 57, 60.

765b, of an idealized system of festivals in an idealized polis; the presuppositions of this discussion, however, are based on the institutional realities of the polis. On the one hand is **monōidiā** 'monody' (764de, 765b), that is, performance by a single professional such as a **rhapsōidos** 'rhapsode' or **kitharōidos** 'lyre singer' (764de). On the other hand is **khorōidiā** 'choral song' (764e), that is, performance by a nonprofessional **khoros** 'chorus', a singing and dancing ensemble of selected men, boys, or girls (764e),[13] who represent some aspect of the polis as a whole.[14] The essential context of public performance in both the monodic and the choral media is competition — among rhapsodes, among lyre singers, among choruses. This competition is called **krisis** (765b), and those who are officially chosen to select the winners are **kritai** 'judges' (ibid.).[15] Granted, there is no traditional distinction made between a monodic and a choral mode of *composition*.[16] Still the medium of both monodic and choral composition is public *performance*. Moreover, it is possible to explain the distinctiveness of solo lyric poetry, or monody, in terms of choral lyric poetry, rather than the other way around.[17] For now, however, I confine myself to observing the traditions of melody in singing and instrumental accompaniment and postpone till later my account of the complex patterns of differentiation in choral and monodic performance.[18]

Because of the diversity of localized traditions in melody, oral poetry, not oral song, was better suited for Panhellenic diffusion in that rhythmical (metrical) and phraseological systematization would not violate localized perceptions of what is correct as readily as the synthesis of diverse melodic patterns. Granted, the melody of song would have promoted diffusion from the standpoint of mnemonic utility.[19] Still, melody would also have impeded diffusion from the standpoint of contextual sensitivity. Thus the process of Panhellenization took effect relatively later for oral song than it did for oral poetry.

---

13. The element of dancing is made explicit in this context: ὀρχήσεσι (*Laws* 764e). In Ch.12, we shall consider various patterns of differentiation between singers and dancers in the context of the **khoros**.

14. The valuable testimony in Plato *Laws* 764c-765b on the given of institutional differentiation, in terms of public performance, between the monodic and choral media is too readily dismissed by commentators. I stress also the crucial testimony in Aristophanes *Frogs* 1329–1364, with parodies of the monodic technique (note **monōidiā** at 1330) as distinct from the choral lyric technique, parodied in 1248–1329.

15. Cf. also Plato *Laws* 659ab, as cited at p. 62.

16. This point is stressed by Kirkwood 1974.10, 212n16 (with specific reference to Plato *Laws* 764c-765b); cf. also Harvey 1955.159n3 and Färber 1936.16. Davies 1988.61 observes that "it is dangerously misleading to talk of choral or monodic *poets*."

17. Cf. pp. 339 and following.

18. Ibid.

19. See p. 50.

The Panhellenization of song required an ongoing synthesis of patterns in vocal and instrumental traditions. Within the actual traditions of song, however, what I am calling a *synthesis* is treated as if it resulted from inventions by prototypical figures. The two names most commonly associated with these "inventions" are differentiated in terms of instrumental accompaniment: Terpander in the realm of string instruments, to which I refer with the general term **kithara** 'lyre',[20] and Olympus in the realm of wind instruments, that is, the **aulos** 'reed'.[21] The most comprehensive direct account of the relevant traditions is to be found in "Plutarch" *On Music* 1032cd-1034b. Even before we consider this account, however, I should stress that instrumental accompaniment does not require the point-for-point following of the vocal part by the instrumental part: in "Plutarch" *On Music* 1137b, with a description of an Archaic musical style associated with Terpander and Olympus, it is made clear that the instrumental part calls for complexities that do not match the vocal part.[22]

Let us begin with Terpander, that is, **Terpandros** 'he who gives pleasure to men.'[23] Tradition has it that he was a singer from Lesbos who moved to Sparta, where he was the first of all winners at the Spartan festival known as the **Karneia** (Hellanicus FGH 4 F 85 by way of Athenaeus 635e). The Feast of Karneia was reportedly founded in the twenty-sixth Olympiad, that is, between 676 and 672 B.C. (Athenaeus 635ef).[24] In other words the inception of the Karneia, an institution that was recognized by tradition as the oldest established festival of the Spartans, was reckoned in terms of Terpander's victory in a contest of singing to the accompaniment of the lyre (Athenaeus 635ef). That Terpander was eventually thought to be a solo singer is clear from his being regularly designated as a **kitharoidos** 'lyre [**kithara**] singer' ("Plutarch" *On Music* 1132d, 1133b-d).[25]

---

20. For a useful survey, see Barker 1984.14. References to string instruments in Archaic Greek poetry tend not to differentiate **kithara** from, for example, **phorminx**: see Barker, p. 25n19, who also takes note of the later taxonomy of differentiation, as in Aristotle *Politics* 1341a. Cf. also Maas and Snyder 1989.5, 202.

21. Survey in Barker, p. 15.

22. Also I should caution against any general assumptions of parity between instrumental and vocal intervals: for a cross-cultural survey, see Nettl 1956.50.

23. As the discussion that follows makes clear, I interpret this name as generic, in line with the programmatic use of the verb **terpō** 'give pleasure' *in poetry* to describe the effects *of poetry*, as in the case of Phemios at *Odyssey* i 347. The name **Terpandros** is analogous to the expressive patronymic **Terpiadēs**, derived from verb **terpō** 'give pleasure', as applied to the singer Phemios at *Odyssey* xxii 376. More details in N 1979.17 ¶4n1.

24. Athenaeus also reports a variant tradition according to which Terpander was a contemporary of Lycurgus (635f, on the authority of Hieronymus *On Kitharōidoi*). Lycurgus is credited with being one of the founders of the first numbered instance of the Olympic Games, that is, at 776 B.C. (Athenaeus ibid.).

25. In this connection, "Plutarch" *On Music* 1133d mentions one Periclitus, who was at some undetermined later point likewise a winner at the Spartan Feast of Karneia in the contest of singing to the accompaniment of the **kithara**: like Terpander, he was a **kitharoidos** 'lyre singer'

Tradition also has it that Terpander "invented" what are called the **nomoi** of **kitharōidiā** 'lyre singing': Boeotian, Aeolian, **Orthios, Trokhaios, Oxus, Kēpiōn, Terpandreios, Tetraoidios** ("Plutarch" *On Music* 1132d; cf. 1132c; supplemented by Pollux 4.65).[26] For the moment the word **nomoi** has been left untranslated. It is enough to observe at this point that Terpander's "invention," as discussed in "Plutarch" *On Music* 1132cd and Pollux 4.65, is traditionally seen as the forerunner of a specific genre[27] known in the time of Plato as the **kitharōidikos nomos** 'citharodic nome' (*Laws* 700b). In this context the word **nomos** is specific to the given genre: thus it is reported in "Plutarch" *On Music* 1132c that Terpander was the "inventor" of the **kitharōidikos nomos** 'citharodic nome', which is to be compared with the tradition, as reported in Herodotus 1.23, that ascribes to Arion the "invention," in Corinth, of the **dithurambos** 'dithyramb'.[28] Arion is described in Herodotus (ibid.) as the premier **kitharōidos** 'lyre singer' of his era, who was the first to name, compose, and teach the dithyramb at Corinth in the era of the tyrant Periandros. In this early description, we see that the word **kitharōidos** originally did not exclude involvement in choral performance.

That the strict distinction in genres between citharodic nome and dithyramb may be relatively late is suggested by a detail in the story of Arion: when he is abducted by pirates and performs for them a solo lyric composition that ultimately saves his life, this composition is described as an **orthios nomos** (Herodotus 1.24.5).[29] This naming of Arion's tune corresponds to one of Terpander's **nomoi** in the list of his citharodic nomes (Pollux 4.65). Still,

---

from Lesbos, and after his death the continuous tradition at Lesbos of singing to the **kitharā** supposedly came to an end (ibid.). On the preeminence of **kitharōidoi** from Lesbos, see also Aristotle F 545 Rose and Hesychius s.v. μετὰ Λέσβιον ᾠδόν.

26. See the commentary of Barker 1984.96n16; also p. 251. The list of seven **nomoi** in "Plutarch" *On Music* 1132d omits the **Orthios**, present in the list of eight given by Pollux 4.65. In *Suda* s.v. ὄρθιος νόμος, it is specified that there are seven **nomoi**; the account goes on to mention the **Orthios** along with the **Trokhaios**. In *Suda* s.v. νόμος, the **Tetraoidios** and the **Oxus** are mentioned. Perhaps the number seven may have been a constant within some traditions, whereas the constituents were variable over the course of time. In Timotheus *Persians* (PMG 791) 225, there is a reference to *ten* **ōidai** 'melodies' of Terpander.

27. On the appropriateness of the term *genre* here, see Svenbro 1984.225 and n135. See also Pfeiffer 1968.184 on **eidos**.

28. On the "invention" of the dithyramb in Corinth, see also Pindar *Olympian* 13.17–19.

29. This reference in Herodotus 1.24.5 to the lyric performance of Arion as a **nomos** suggests that the earlier meaning of this word was broad enough in scope to designate simply a lyric composition that followed a set mode or melodic pattern, in this case specified as **orthios** 'shrill'. There is another reference to **orthios nomos** in Aristophanes *Knights* 1279. As for the story about the attempt by greedy sailors to rob Arion of his great wealth (Herodotus 1.24.1–2), we may compare the *Homeric Hymn [7] to Dionysus*, where Dionysus is abducted by pirates. This thematic connection between Arion and Dionysus is parallel to the connection between Arion and the dithyramb (again Herodotus 1.23), which is associated with the cult of Dionysus (e.g., Archilochus F 120 W).

for Plato, the **kitharōidikos nomos** 'citharodic nome' and the **dithurambos** 'dithyramb' are to be treated as parallel genres inherited from the Archaic period (again *Laws* 700b).

Let us move beyond the use of the term **nomos** in the Terpander tradition, in the context of Terpander's having supposedly invented the various categories of **nomoi** just listed. In this context **nomos** is a matter of a specific genre and reflects a specialization of usage. In other contexts, however, the word **nomos** refers more generally to various types of local melodic patterns. In generalized references to song within song, **nomos** has the general sense of 'localized melodic idiom' (as in Aeschylus *Suppliants* 69);[30] such a usage meshes with the basic meaning of **nomos**, which is 'local custom'.[31] Just as **nomos** as 'local custom' refers to the hierarchical distribution or apportioning of value within a given society (root *nem-, as in **nemō** 'distribute'), so also **nomos** as 'localized melodic idiom' refers to the hierarchical distribution or apportioning of intervals within the melodic patterns of song.[32]

In line with the earlier argument concerning melodic traditions as extensions of patterns in pitch or intonation,[33] I suggest that the various Greek systems of **nomoi** evolved in symbiosis with the patterning of pitch accent in the phraseology of song.[34] As a melodic pattern that is characteristic of distinct speech in distinct habitats, **nomos** serves as the ideal metaphor for conveying the distinctiveness of bird song, as when the voice of Alcman declares that he knows the **nomoi** of all the different kinds of birds in the world (PMG 40). This theme can best be understood in the context of Alcman PMG 39, where the poet names himself as the "discoverer" of melody and words that put into human language the voices of partridges. In other words, the song of Alcman is being conceived as a mimesis of bird song, and the varieties of bird song resemble the varieties of **nomoi**. Thus song, as a mimesis of speech, can extend into a mimesis of the "speech" of birds.[35]

In the context of Terpander's "invention" of **nomoi**, however, **nomos** takes on more restricted meanings. From the standpoint of our main source, "Plutarch" *On Music* (1132de), the **nomoi** of Terpander are the result of a

---

30. Cf. Comotti ibid. Cf. also Aristophanes *Birds* 745 and the commentary of Fraenkel 1962.209–212.

31. Chantraine DELG 742–743.

32. On the specific parallelism between the hierarchical distribution of intervals within a melody and the hierarchical distribution of sacrificial meat within a community, see Svenbro 1984 and N 1985b.

33. Cf. p. 39.

34. The phraseology of song, from the synchronic standpoint of Greek metrics, is organized along the lines of a stylized syntactical unit, the colon; cf. p. 439.

35. On the basis of the self-references, I infer that this extension is not just a matter of metaphor: the mimesis of bird song seems to be part of an actual musical tradition. Cf. Nettl 1964.284 on a Shawnee song tradition imitating the call of the turkey, where the sound patterns "still fit into the musical structure."

systematization of preexisting melodic patterns.[36] The figure of Terpander represents the common denominator of these patterns. The fitting of these patterns into a system attributed to Terpander is formalized in the tradition that attributes to this figure the "invention" of a seven-note scale that accommodates his **nomoi** ("Aristotle" *Problems* 19.32; "Plutarch" *On Music* 1140f, 1141c).[37]

Corresponding to Terpander's "invention" of this scale is his "invention" of the seven-string lyre, displacing the older four-string type (Strabo 13.2.4 C618, quoting Terpander PMG, p. 363; "Plutarch" 1141d). The iconographical evidence of the eighth and early seventh centuries B.C. corroborates this tradition: the norm during this period is a four-string instrument, which is replaced after this period by a seven-string instrument.[38] It has been said that the spread of the seven-string lyre in the seventh century "betokens a revolution in music."[39] In terms of the Panhellenic synthesis that I am proposing,

36. In this source, the **nomoi** of Terpander are understood anachronistically as equivalent to the **nomoi** of Timotheus of Miletus, a virtuoso composer of the late fifth century, who is said to have composed his earliest **nomoi** in dactylic hexameters: "Plutarch" *On Music* 1132e. At 1132de (see Barker 1984.209n25) the source infers that Terpander too composed primarily hexameters (though it would be more accurate to say, on the basis of Terpander PMG 697, that Terpander composed in meters related to the hexameter: Gentili and Giannini 1977.35–36). Timotheus was famed for a performance of a composition of his that happens to be a **kitharōidikos nomos** 'citharodic nome', known as the *Persians*, at the Feast of the Panathenaia at Athens, around 408 B.C. The composition is attested as Timotheus PMG 788–791, and we do indeed find a prominent deployment of dactylic hexameters alongside various lyric meters, even at the beginning of the song (PMG 788). In his *Persians* Timotheus overtly refers to Terpander as his predecessor (PMG 791.225–236). For more on the *Persians* of Timotheus, see in general the interesting discussion of Herington, pp. 151–160, who has enough information to calculate even the running time for the performance of the complete composition (thirty-five or forty minutes: p. 275n25).

37. I should stress that the values within any scale at this particular stage of development in Archaic Greek song have to be considered in terms of relative rather than absolute pitch.

38. There is a summary of the evidence in Wegner 1968.16, with helpful observations about the nonsignificance of occasional deviations from the number of four. I find it unnecessary to adopt, however, Wegner's restricted nomenclature of **phorminx** for the four-string and **kitharā** for the seven-string instrument. On the still earlier use of seven- and eight-string lyres in the Minoan and Mycenaean periods, see Wegner, pp. 26–27. Also, I disagree with the theory of West 1981 that Homeric poetry was sung to a four-string instrument: the reasons for my disagreement have to do with the diachronic skewing of Homeric self-references, as discussed in p. 21.

39. West 1981.120. For a particularly early representation of a seven-string lyre, on a seventh-century Greek sherd found at Smyrna, see Boardman 1980.97–98, with illustration. For a comprehensive survey of evidence concerning ancient Greek stringed instruments, see now Maas and Snyder 1989; at pp. 27–28 and 203, they argue that the post-Mycenaean iconographic attestations of four-string instruments may be a matter of iconographic convention rather than reality, and that seven-string instruments may have been the norm even in the post-Mycenaean period. From the standpoint of comparative ethnomusicology, however, it is logical to expect the diachronic sequence of morphological development in stringed instruments to proceed from the four- to the seven-string configuration, though there is no reason to rule out even the coexistence of four- and seven-string instruments in any given era.

the older four-string lyre would be adequate for any single local **nomos**, while the newer seven-string lyre, which represents the "revolution" of the seventh century, would fit a wide variety of **nomoi**, irrespective of local provenience, within a new interrelated system.[40] In the diction of Pindar, Apollo is represented as leading the choral performance of 'all sorts of **nomoi**' (παν-τοίων νόμων *Nemean* 5.25) as he plays on the seven-string lyre, which is described as **heptaglōssos** 'having seven languages' (5.24).

Parallel to the tradition about Terpander's "invention" of the seven-string lyre is the story in *Homeric Hymn to Hermes* 51: when Hermes "invents" the lyre, it has seven strings. In the narrative, Hermes gives the **kitharis** 'lyre' to Apollo (*Hymn to Hermes* 499, in the context of 475 and following), the figure conventionally associated with this instrument (e.g., *Hymn to Apollo* 131, 188). We may note, in connection with the traditional provenience of the Terpander figure from Aeolic Lesbos, the actual form κίθαρις 'lyre' in the *Hymn to Hermes* (e.g., 499) and in Homeric diction in general (e.g., *Odyssey* i 153): the accentuation of this word follows a clearly Aeolic pattern.[41] In yet another version Amphion "invents" the seven-string lyre in Thebes (Pausanias 9.5.7). In this case two of the **nomoi** "invented" by Terpander for **kitharōidiā** 'lyre singing' are precisely the Aeolian and the Boeotian (again "Plutarch" *On Music* 1132d). This tradition squares with the linguistic facts: the dialectal heritage of Thebes is Aeolic in general and Boeotian in particular.

Before we pursue further the topic of an implicit Panhellenization as reflected by the "inventions" of Terpander in the realm of the lyre, let us consider the counterpart of Terpander, Olympus, and his corresponding "inventions" in the realm of the **aulos**. Just as Terpander is a prototype of the **kitharōidos** 'lyre [**kitharā**] singer', so Olympus is presented as a parallel prototype of the, **aulōidos** 'reed [**aulos**] singer' (cf. "Plutarch" *On Music* 1137b, 1133def; Aristotle *Politics* 1340a).[42] Like Terpander, Olympus is credited with the "invention" of specific **nomoi** ("Plutarch" 1133d).[43]

40. Cf. Barker 1984.49: "A four-stringed instrument, perhaps tuned to a pair of fourths separated by a whole tone, does little to fix a clear-cut form of scale. A seven-stringed instrument must do so, though later writers were in doubt as to exactly which notes Terpander's scale incorporated." The interval of a fourth, known as a tetrachord, is the basis of formulating the three categories of *genus*, to be discussed below.

41. Schwyzer I 385. The variant of this Aeolic form κίθαρις is κιθάρη = **kitharā** (e.g., Herodotus 1.24.5, referring to the lyre of Arion), which is not even attested in the *Iliad* and *Odyssey*. Cf. Shelmerdine 1981.41n73.

42. See also the commentary on "Plutarch" *On Music* 1133e in Barker 1984.212n51.

43. "Plutarch" *On Music* 1133d marks a transition from the discussion of **nomoi** as sung to the accompaniment of lyre or **aulos**: now the subject shifts to **nomoi** for solo **aulos**. It is made clear that Olympus is credited with inventions of both kinds of **nomoi**, those for solo **aulos** and those for voice accompanied by the **aulos** (1133e). The distinction between an earlier and a later Olympus (1133de) reflects an attempt to resolve conflicting relative chronologies. On the reference to a **nomos** of Olympus in Aristophanes *Knights* 8–10, see Bowie 1986.24.

Olympus is a decidedly mythical figure, a disciple of the mythical **aulos** player Marsyas of Phrygia ("Plutarch" 1133e). Olympus too is said to be a Phrygian (ibid.);[44] this detail becomes more significant as our discussion proceeds.[45] Besides Olympus, there are later figures who are less remotely mythical in appearance and who tend to be synchronized with Terpander. One such figure is Clonas, described as an inventor of **nomoi** for **aulōidiā** 'reed [**aulos**] singing' ("Plutarch"1132c), who supposedly lived shortly after the time of Terpander (1133a).[46]

The systematizations attributed to figures like Terpander and Olympus are comprised of **nomoi**. Thus the **nomoi**, from the standpoint of these traditions about "inventors" and their "inventions," are no longer separate melodic idioms: they are patterns that are already integrated with each other into a larger system that controls its constituents. In other words we see here an early stage in the ongoing Panhellenization of local traditions in song.

In considering the performance traditions of Archaic Greek song, I concentrate on the internal and external references to the performance of compositions attributed to the canonical nine poets of lyric. In these references we can find clear traces of Panhellenic systematization, as we have seen in the example from Pindar: the seven-string lyre, presented as a symbol of systematization, allows Apollo to lead the choral performance of 'all sorts of **nomoi**' (παντοίων νόμων *Nemean* 5.25).

The word **nomos**, however, is hardly adequate for designating the actual process of systematization since its basic meaning of *local custom* retains a built-in emphasis on the local origins of the constituents of the system. A more adequate word is **harmoniā**, in the specific sense of a tuning or *accordatura* that fits a given melodic idiom, as attested in Aristophanes *Knights* 994. In a more general sense **harmoniā** can be understood as a 'system of intervals in pitch', as in Plato *Republic* 397d, where the point is that the traditional **harmoniā** and rhythm of song is regulated by the words of song. Plato's usage in this passage, it has been observed, "points to the fact that the existence of melody depends on the prior existence of an organised scheme

---

44. On the myth of Marsyas, cf. Plato *Symposium* 215bc.

45. For more on the Phrygian connection of Olympus and Marsyas, see Barker 1984.210n32.

46. The text does not say that Clonas actually originated **aulōidiā**, so that the emendation of αὐλητικῶν for αὐλῳδικῶν at the end of "Plutarch" *On Music* 1132f, entertained as a possibility by Barker 1984.210n35, seems to me unnecessary. If we keep the text as it is, the source is giving the following relative chronology: Olympus/Terpander/Clonas. Our source claims that Clonas composed elegiacs and hexameters ("Plutarch" *On Music* 1132c). We have already seen a parallel claim, that Terpander composed hexameters (p. 89). Also, our source gives two variant traditions about the provenience of Clonas: he is a Tegean according to the Arcadians, a Theban according to the Boeotians ("Plutarch" 1133a). Also named in this same context is one Polymnestus of Colophon (ibid.). We know that Polymnestus was mentioned in the songs of Alcman and Pindar ("Plutarch" 1133a). A Pindaric mention of Polymnestus is quoted by Strabo (14.1.28 C643: Pindar F 188 SM).

of pitches standing to one another in determinate relations, on the basis of whose relations the selection that generates a melody is made."[47] We must distinguish this notion of **harmoniā** from the later notion of **tonos**, especially as developed by Aristoxenus, pupil of Aristotle, who himself was the son of a professional musician from Tarentum (*Suda* s.v. Ἀριστόξενος). The difference has been formulated as follows: "each **tonos** had the same pattern of intervals: they differed one from another, as modern keys do, only in respect of pitch."[48] In contrast the **harmoniai**, as Plato understands them in the passage under consideration, "were distinguished from one another primarily by being constituted out of different sequences of intervals."[49] Correspondingly "rhythm" in this passage means "the element of rhythmic organisation that any composition must possess, an individual rhythm being the formal rhythmic structure underlying an individual piece or type of piece, its overall pattern of movement."[50]

Let us consider the six names of various **harmoniai** as discussed in Plato *Republic* 398e–399a: the *Ionian* [= "Iastian"], the *Dorian*, the *Phrygian*, the *Lydian*, the *Mixolydian*, and the *Syntonolydian*. From other testimonia, to be cited later, we see that such **harmoniai** were the basic melodic patterns of Archaic Greek lyric in its attested phase of development. Moreover, Plato's list of Archaic **harmoniai** corresponds to actual self-references found in Archaic Greek lyric poetry.

On the basis of these self-references, it becomes clear that there were in fact other such **harmoniai**, besides the ones listed en passant by Plato in *Republic* 398e-399a. Most notably missing from Plato's list is the **harmoniā** named as the *Aeolian* in the Archaic diction of lyric poetry. I cite the specific reference to a **harmoniā** described as *Aeolian* in Lasus of Hermione PMG 702.3, where it is described as **barubromos** 'deep-roaring', suggesting that the *tessitura* of the *Aeolian* was marked by its frequency of lower notes.[51] Plato's omission of the *Aeolian*, in view of his inclusion of the *Ionian* and the *Dorian*, is asymmetrical from the standpoint of the Greek language, the major dialectal subdivisions of which are Aeolic, Ionic, and Doric.[52] But this

47. Barker 1984.130n18.

48. Barker, p. 164.

49. Barker ibid., with a survey of references. This working definition corresponds to my understanding of *mode*, as discussed in p. 51. In modern Greek folk music there is an analogy in the notion of δρόμος 'road, mode', which is parallel to Arabic *maqām* 'mode' and Turkish *makam* 'mode': see Beaton 1980b, especially p. 8, emphasizing the independence of the systems of δρόμοι from the Byzantine Oktoechos. On the difference between **harmoniai** and **tonoi**, Solomon 1984.249 notes: "Aristoxenus no doubt had to squeeze some of the intervallic leaps used originally in the native, tribal **harmoniai** and then in the **tonoi** into or out of the great system, but such is the universally compromising force of standardization. The difference between our own tempered and nontempered systems provides somewhat of a parallel."

50. Barker ibid.

51. Cf. West 1981.126.

52. The dialectal subdivisions correspond to political subdivisions as well: cf. the narrative

very asymmetry reflects the transformations over time in the systematization of Greek modes. The *Aeolian* **harmoniā** was already replaced by Plato's time with the so-called *Hypodorian*. The Archaic nature of the *Aeolian* **harmoniā** within the newer systematization of the **harmoniai** is indicated by the older concept of an *Aeolian* **nomos** within the framework of an older systematization of **nomoi** ascribed to Terpander.[53]

Not only the names of the **harmoniai** listed by Plato but even the descriptive modifications associated with them, such as **suntono-** 'tense' in *Syntonolydian*, correspond to actual contrastive self-references found in Archaic Greek lyric poetry. For example, in the words of the Archaic poet Pratinas of Phleious, an older contemporary of Aeschylus, what are described in terms of lyre tuning as **suntono-** 'tense' and **aneimenē-** 'lax' melodic patterns or "Muses" are rejected for the moment as extremes in favor of a "moderate" *Aeolian* **harmoniā** (PMG 712). Plato uses the notion of **khalarā-** 'lax' in describing the *Ionian* **harmoniā** (*Republic* 398e).

In our present survey of Archaic references to **harmoniai**, I draw particular attention to a quotation from Terpander, where the frame of quotation specifies that the song is being composed in the *Dorian* **harmoniā** (PMG 698, in Clement *Stromateis* 6.88). Thus Terpander is associated with not only the *Aeolian* melodic tradition, compatible with an older system of modes known as **nomoi**, but also the *Dorian,* compatible with a newer system of modes known as **harmoniai**, which accommodate both *Dorian* and *Aeolian*. This accretive combination of older *Aeolian* and newer *Dorian* tuning or accordatura dovetails with the myth that tells how Terpander came from *Aeolic* Lesbos to *Doric* Sparta.[54] It dovetails also with a linguistic given: that the dialectal texture of the medium that we know as choral lyric is dominantly *Doric,* with significant recessive elements of *Aeolic*.[55] This dialectal texture is most evident in the choral lyric poetry of Pindar.[56] In fact the medium of Pindar provides the following explicit self-reference:

Αἰολεὺς ἔβαινε Δωρίαν κέλευθον ὕμνων

Pindar F 191 SM

An Aeolic man went along the Dorian path of songs.[57]

---

master plan of subdividing the notion of "Hellenes" into Ionians, Aeolians, and Dorians in Herodotus 1.6.2 et passim.

53. See p. 87. In this connection, R. Hamilton points out to me the fact that we know of no **nomos** that is *Dorian*. Again I invoke Kuryłowicz's "fourth law of analogy," discussed at p. 5.

54. Cf. p. 86.

55. Survey in Palmer 1980.119–130; a basic work in this regard is Forssman 1966. Further discussion at p. 418.

56. Palmer, pp. 123–127.

57. The 'Aeolic man' need not be Pindar (as claimed in the apparatus of Snell in SM, p. 130); it could be Terpander himself, as a reputed founder of the choral lyric medium.

Appropriately these words are framed in the metrical system known as *dactylo-epitrite*, which is the Doric counterpart to the other major metrical system used in Pindar's choral lyric compositions, the *Aeolic*.[58] All the attested lyric poetry of Pindar, with only a few exceptions, is composed in one or the other of these two kinds of meters.[59]

From such evidence I infer that the choral lyric traditions represented by Pindar resulted from an accretive blend of Aeolic and Doric poetic language, where all the various elements of mode, rhythm, and the words themselves can be seen participating in the synthesis. The model that I posit here for the choral lyric tradition of Pindar can be extended to the lyric tradition of Sappho and Alcaeus. In this case the available evidence points to a diachronic blend of Aeolic and Ionic poetic language.[60]

The synthesis of Aeolic and Doric traditions is expressed overtly in Pindar's *Olympian* 1, where a *Dorian* lyre is playing (17) while the **molpē** 'singing and dancing' is described as *Aeolian* (102). In this particular case I infer that the actual mode is *Aeolian* since the meter of this composition is Aeolic. Elsewhere self-references to the *Aeolian* mode correspond to the actual composition of the given ode in Aeolic meter (Pindar *Pythian* 2.69, *Nemean* 3.79).[61] So also with the *Dorian* mode: we have already seen an example of a reference to this mode within a song composed in dactylo-epitrite, that is, Doric meter (Pindar F 191 SM), and there are other examples (e.g., Pindar *Olympian* 3.5).[62] Such a neat pattern of convergence between the given meter and the self-reference to a mode seems to work only where the mode is *Aeolian* or *Dorian*. Other Pindaric compositions in the Aeolic meter contain self-references to the *Lydian* mode (*Olympian* 14.17, *Nemean* 4.45; cf. *Olympian* 5.19). Also, one composition in dactylo-epitrite meter contains a possible reference to the *Lydian* mode (*Nemean* 8.15). The *Lydian* mode may be adaptable to more than one native metrical tradition. After all, in Plato's list of six **harmoniai** in *Republic* 398e–399a, we hear of three different kinds of Lydian mode: *Lydian*, *Mixolydian*, and *Syntonolydian*. Perhaps these differentiations result from different adaptations to different native meters.

What seems at first to interfere with a coherent picture of melodic patterns in the development of traditions in Archaic Greek song is the traditional

---

58. The Doric affinities of the dactylo-epitrite are best illustrated by the metrical heritage of Stesichorus, as discussed at p. 452.

59. Cf. pp. 47–48.

60. On the evidence for Ionic in Lesbian poetic diction, see the summary in Bowie 1981.136. In the corpus of Sappho and Alcaeus there is probably more of an Ionic element than meets the eye; such an element can easily become blurred by the efforts of Alexandrian scholars in re-aeolicizing the transmitted text (on which topic see also Palmer 1980.115–116).

61. Cf. Most 1985.100n26.

62. The latter example is cited by Most ibid.

naming of seemingly "foreign" modes or **harmoniai**, such as the *Lydian*, which are distinct from the three native names of *Aeolian*, *Ionian*, and *Dorian*. For example, there is a reference to the *Phrygian* melodic patterns in Alcman PMG 126, as also in a fragment from the *Oresteia* of Stesichorus, PMG 212. Elsewhere Alcman is said to have named some famous *Phrygian* **aulos**-players in his compositions (Athenaeus 624b). In Pindar's own words (F 125 SM) a string instrument called the **barbiton** was "discovered" by Terpander at the feasts of the *Lydians*, the sound of which would answer to that of the **pēktis**, another *Lydian* string instrument. Alternatively the "invention" of the **barbiton** is attributed to Anacreon (Athenaeus 175e). On the authority of Posidonius, Anacreon is said to have referred to three kinds of melody, which were supposedly the only three he used: the *Dorian*, *Phrygian*, and *Lydian* (Athenaeus 635cd). We may compare the repertoire of Pindar, as gleaned from the self-references surveyed above: *Dorian*, *Aeolian*, and *Lydian*. As for the *Lydian* **pēktis**, noted by the words of Pindar (F 125 SM) in the context of praising Terpander as a forerunner, we may compare the report that credits Sappho with being the first to use this instrument (Athenaeus 635e).[63] On the authority of Aristoxenus (F 81 Wehrli), Sappho is also credited with the "invention" of the **harmoniā** called *Mixolydian*, which the composers of tragedies supposedly learned from her songs ("Plutarch" *On Music* 1136cd).[64]

The contrastive nature of these "foreign" **harmoniai** turn out to be a key to our understanding the systematization of Archaic Greek modes. I draw attention to the contrastive mentions of explicitly local **harmoniai**, in particular Pindar F 140b SM, with its mention of a local **harmoniā** of the Locrians that is described as a rival of the *Ionian* "Muse."[65] In order to explore further the principle of contrastiveness as it operates within a system of **harmoniai**, let us return to Plato's list of **harmoniai** in *Republic* 398e–399a: *Ionian* [= "Iastian"], *Dorian*, *Phrygian*, *Lydian*, *Mixolydian*, and *Syntonolydian*. These six **harmoniai** are described in terms of fixed scales by Aristides Quintilianus, p. 19.3–10 (ed. Winnington-Ingram), whose testimony seems to be a genuine reflex of old traditions in the actual performance of Archaic Greek lyric poetry.[66] Notable for its omission in both Plato *Republic* 398e-

63. Note that Sappho's own words (F 106 V) acknowledge the primacy of Terpander, the 'singer from Lesbos'.

64. For a remarkable anecdote that pictures Euripides singing μιξολυδιστί 'in the *Mixolydian* manner' to the members of his chorus in preparing them for performance of one of his compositions, see Plutarch *On Listening to Lectures* 46b. See also West 1981.125n73 on the reference by the *Phrygian* slave to his song as a **harmateios nomos** in Euripides *Orestes* 1384; according to Glaucus of Rhegium ("Plutarch" *On Music* 1133f), Stesichorus is credited with compositions in the **harmateios nomos**, derived from Olympus of Phrygia, and we have already seen a reference to a *Phrygian* tune in Stesichorus PMG 212.

65. Commentary by Barker 1984.60–61.

66. See especially West 1981.117–118. Cf. also Barker 1984.165–168. From the standpoint of someone like Aristides Quintilianus, the notion of scales is no longer anachronistic. The pro-

399a and Aristides Quintilianus, p. 19.3–10 is the *Aeolian* mode, specifically designated as a **harmoniā** in Pratinas of Phleious PMG 712[67] and Lasus of Hermione PMG 702.[68] Heraclides Ponticus (F 163 Wehrli, by way of Athenaeus 624e) equates the *Aeolian* of Lasus with a new replacement category, the *Hypodorian*. Other sources (e.g., Cleonides, p. 198.13 Jan) equate the *Aeolian* specifically with *Locrian*, as "invented" by Xenocritus of Locri (scholia to Pindar *Olympian* 11.17); clearly such an old category as *Locrian* would be out of step with any newer systematization. According to Athenaeus 625e the *Locrian* became obsolete after Pindar. Which brings us back to our point of departure, the reference in Pindar F 140b SM to a local **harmoniā** of the Locrians that is a rival of the *Ionian* "Muse."

There is much confusion arising from the fact that such terms as *Dorian* and *Phrygian* earlier used to designate the **harmoniai**, were later adapted to the newer theoretical notion of **tonos**, as used by Aristoxenus.[69] In the so-called Greater Complete System of Aristoxenus, some earlier terms reflecting regional differentiation were replaced by newer terms designed to connect even more explicitly the various systems that had at earlier stages been separate from one another: thus the categories of *Aeolian* and *Ionian* were replaced respectively by *Hypodorian* and *Hypophrygian*.[70] In the case of *Hypodorian* we have noted the explicit testimony of Heraclides Ponticus (F 163 Wehrli, by way of Athenaeus 624e), who equates the *Aeolian* of Lasus of Hermione PMG 702 with *Hypodorian*, a component of a newer system of interrelations as recognized by Aristoxenus. Such names of **harmoniai**, as reused in the later classification-systems of Aristoxenus and the like,[71] reflect not the local melodic idioms themselves but the eventual Panhellenic systematization of categories that resulted from the ongoing juxtaposition of the local melodic idioms.[72]

Such categories as *Phrygian* and *Lydian* are particularly indicative: they convey identification of the locale indirectly, not by way of naming what is native but by way of representing what is alien to the native — in this case

---

gressive systematization of relations between distinct **harmoniai** leads to a paradigm-shift from *modes* to *scales*.

67. Cf. p. 93.

68. Cf. p. 92. Cf. also West, p. 126.

69. On which see p. 92.

70. For more on the *Aeolian* **harmoniā**, see pp. 92 and 95. Cf. Anderson 1966.48; also West 1981.128–129. Still, the nomenclature of the **tonoi** retains the notion of regional differentiation. Thus Aristoxenus *Harmonics* 46.20–47.1 compares the confusion of relationships between **tonoi** with the confusion of relationships between various days of the month in various regional calendars: what counts as the tenth day of the month for the Corinthians is the fifth for the Athenians and the eighth for yet others.

71. See p. 92.

72. For possible traces of various stages in this process of systematization, see the interesting discussion of West 1981.127.

not just alien but "barbarian" as well. It has been pointed out that the **harmoniai** with barbarian names have no common feature that distinguishes them from the ones with Greek names, or the other way around.[73] The same sort of mentality is at work in the distinctions among **harmoniai** with Greek names. In the case of *Ionian*, for example, this **harmoniā** would represent a synthesis of what is alien to, say, native Locrian traditions (again I cite Pindar F 140b SM). Still the synthesis implied by a concept such as the *Ionian* **harmoniā** could take place in terms of local traditions. In other words the local traditions are the frame of reference.[74] In this way the alien is appropriated because it can be performed. In other words *alien* becomes native, in a broader and inclusive sense of *native*.[75] Such thought patterns of inclusion reflect the real beginnings of Panhellenism.

It has been calculated that changing from any one **harmoniā** to another meant re-tuning at least five strings on a seven-string instrument.[76] Which leads to the following inference: "To minimize the inconvenience which such re-tunings involved, musicians must have striven to find as much common ground between different modes [= **harmoniai**] as they could, and to identify certain notes in one where possible with notes in another."[77]

Still the various **harmoniai** were distinct enough to require considerable effort in the development of a performer's repertoire. In the comedies of Aristophanes we see the ridiculing of a character on the grounds that he could learn only the *Dorian* **harmoniā** when he had been a boy in school (*Knights* 985–995).[78] The context for such learning of the **harmoniai** can best be observed in the *Clouds* of Aristophanes, with its informative description of old-fashioned Athenian **paideiā** 'education' (τὴν ἀρχαίαν παιδείαν 961), the kind that purportedly produced the men who fought at the Battle of Marathon (985–986).[79] Boys learn selected compositions of old lyric masters in the house of the **kitharistēs** 'master of the **kithara**' (964), who teaches them to learn by heart (**promathein**: 966) the performance of famous lyric compositions (967)[80] and who insists on their adherence to performing these

---

73. West, p. 126.

74. The synthesis may require sub-categories: there were "more or less co-ordinated 'families' of **harmoniai**, grouped together under headings such as 'Lydian', etc." (Barker, p. 167).

75. For more on this type of thought pattern, see Ch.10.

76. West 1981.127.

77. West ibid. I would have preferred the words *pitch* or *tone* over *note* here.

78. Anderson 1966.234n65 argues that it was singing different **harmoniai** that was difficult, not learning to play them. On the appropriateness of the *Dorian* **harmoniā** in teaching the young, see Aristotle *Politics* 1342a-b.

79. The "old" **paideusis** 'education' (*Clouds* 986) is associated with the era that produced the fighters at Marathon (985–986).

80. The composition to which reference is made here in *Clouds* 967 is apparently that of Stesichorus (see Sommerstein 1982.207).

compositions in the proper **harmoniā** 'mode' that had been 'inherited from their forefathers' (968; cf. 969–972).[81]

In the same context, Aristophanes *Clouds* 969–972, there is mention of a composer, called Phrynis, who is ridiculed for modernizing the old conventions of **harmoniā**. This Phrynis belongs by our standards still to the Archaic period: he was a **kitharōidos** 'lyre [**kitharā**] singer' from Mytilene who won first prize in a contest at the Panathenaia of 456 (or possibly 446).[82] He was primarily known for his virtuosity in the genre of the **kitharōidikos nomos** 'citharodic nome' (Athenaeus 638c). According to "Plutarch" *On Music* 1133b, he was the first to introduce the practice of modulating between **harmoniai** within a single composition (apparently a citharodic nome: ibid.; see also Pherecrates F 145.14–18 Kock). Such testimony implies that the contemporaries of Phrynis, such as Pindar, did not yet compose songs that modulated between **harmoniai**. We have already seen a parallel on the level of meter: Pindar generally avoids modulating between the Aeolic and the Doric or dactylo-epitrite meters. Moreover, we have seen that the Doric and Aeolic meters of Pindar seem to be correlated respectively with self-references to the Dorian mode on one hand and to the Aeolian or the various "foreign" modes on the other. It appears that, to this extent, Pindar keeps his meters and his **harmoniai** distinct in any given composition, and that only on the level of dialect are the Aeolic and Doric elements accretively merged. Still the report that the *Locrian* mode, to be equated with the *Aeolian* (Cleonides, p. 198.13 Jan), had become obsolete after Pindar (Athenaeus 625e), combined with the fact that the concept of *Hypodorian* eventually replaced that of *Aeolian* (Athenaeus 624e, citing Heraclides Ponticus F 163 Wehrli), suggests that the distinction between the *Aeolian* and the *Dorian* modes had become obsolete after Pindar. The new nomenclature of *Hypodorian* suggests that the old *Aeolian* melodic tradition had become at best a residual subcategory of *Dorian*.[83]

Such shifts in classification might help explain what seem at first to be contradictions in the later testimony about the melodic pattern of various genres.[84] For example, there is a report in "Plutarch" *On Music* 1136f that the **partheneia** 'maiden-songs' of Alcman, Simonides, Bacchylides, and Pindar were composed in the melodic pattern of *Dorian*.[85] Yet, in the few fragments

81. Each **harmoniā**, as Sommerstein (p. 207) emphasizes, "required a different tuning (the literal sense of **harmoniā**) of the instrument."

82. Pickard-Cambridge 1962.43–44n4; on the date 446 see Davison 1968 [1958] 61–64.

83. Again we may apply Kuryłowicz's fourth law of analogy, as discussed at p. 5.

84. The genres about to be named are discussed in further detail at a later point, p. 108.

85. Cf. also Aristoxenus F 82 Wehrli on the practice of Simonides, who reputedly used the *Dorian* pattern for **partheneia** 'maiden-songs', **prosodia** 'processional songs', and **paiānes** 'paeans'. In *Etymologicum Magnum* 295.53 and following, there is a report that Apollonius the so-called Eidographos classified the compositions of the lyric masters by distinguishing the following categories: *Dorian, Phrygian, Lydian, Mixolydian, Ionian*, and so on (cf. Rossi 1971.92n63).

of attested **partheneia** collected as Pindar F 94a-104b SM, the metrical pattern is Aeolic, which suggests an *Aeolian* melodic pattern. If indeed such a pattern is perceived as *Hypodorian*, the term *Dorian* here may be viewed as inclusive of *Aeolian*.[86] An alternative explanation is that the **partheneia** of Pindar, like his **epinīkia** 'victory odes', may have been composed in either the *Dorian* or the *Aeolian* melodic patterns, and that the formulation offered in "Plutarch" *On Music* 1136f is overly restrictive. Still there seem to be clear signs of correlation between given genres and given melodic patterns, parallel to the well-known correlation between given genres and given metrical patterns. Thus, for example, Aristotle says explicitly that the *Phrygian* **harmoniā** is natural to the **dithurambos** 'dithyramb' (*Politics* 1342b); he notes an anecdote about Philoxenus, who tried to compose a dithyramb in the *Dorian* **harmoniā** and who could not help but fall back into the *Phrygian* (ibid.).[87] Further, we hear that the *Hypodorian* and the *Hypophrygian*, described as having relatively less melody than other patterns, are inappropriate for the choruses of tragedy ("Aristotle" *Problems* 19.48), and that the *Hypodorian* is the most suited of all **harmoniai** for solo **kitharōidiā** by principal actors (ibid.). We may note the remark in Plato *Republic* 398e that **thrēnoi** 'laments' are associated with such **harmoniai** as the *Mixolydian* and the *Syntonolydian*.

Before we end this discussion of relationships between melodic systematization and the content of songs, it is important to consider yet another set of categories for melodic traditions, organized under the heading of **genos** 'genus'. Classification by way of genus was systematized by Aristoxenus. According to this system (Aristoxenus *Harmonics* 21.31–27.14, 46.19–52.34) there is a fundamental unit of composition, the tetrachord, which consists of four notes and which is divided into three genera: (1) enharmonic, (2) chromatic, and (3) diatonic. The two outer notes of the tetrachord are constant for all three of the genera while the two inner ones are variable; the different locations of the inner notes within the tetrachord of four notes constitute the differences in genera. A tetrachord has different interval patterns according to its genus: in the enharmonic it is quarter-tone, quarter-tone,

---

86. The various existing patterns of inclusion led to various doctrines reducing the "original" number of **harmoniai** to three. According to Heraclides Ponticus (F 103 Wehrli, by way of Athenaeus 624c), the "original" three **harmoniai** were the *Dorian*, *Aeolian*, and *Ionian*; Heraclides makes the explicit equation of *Aeolian* with *Hypodorian* (F 163 Wehrli, by way of Athenaeus 624e). By contrast, according to the more prevalent doctrine, apparently espoused by Aristoxenus (cf. Athenaeus 635e, 637d), the "original" three **harmoniai** were rather the *Dorian*, *Phrygian*, and *Lydian*. Further references and commentary in Barker, p. 213n62. According to the doctrine of Aristoxenus, I would infer, *Hypodorian* was treated as not only a subcategory but also a derivative of *Dorian*. According to the doctrine of Heraclides, on the other hand, it seems to have been derived from the *Aeolian*, in defiance of the nomenclature. The latter doctrine comes closer to a true diachronic scheme.

87. Cf. Barker, pp. 95, 181. On the genre of **dithurambos** 'dithyramb', see p. 87.

ditone (that is, 1/4, 1/4, 2); in the chromatic it is predominantly semitone, semitone, tone-and-a-half (1/2, 1/2, 1 1/2); in the diatonic it is semitone, tone, tone (1/2, 1, 1).[88] Although these categories themselves are late,[89] they clearly contain old patterns: it has been plausibly argued that the tetrachord, which is the basis of the three genera, is related to the system of tuning for the older four-string lyre.[90] Within the later system of tuning for the newer seven-string lyre, as reflected by the **harmoniai**, it is possible to find embedded the earlier system of tuning for the older four-string lyre, as reflected by the tetrachord, with its three categories of genus.[91] This diachronic hierarchy seems to be supported by the synchronic fact that "the tetrachord, whether it came high or low in the scale [of the **harmoniā**], had primary status in the melody, it was a nucleus, while the notes outside the tetrachord derived their significance from their relation to it."[92]

We might say that the containers known as the three genera are new, but they contain three redistributed sets of old patterns.[93] Moreover, the actual distribution into containers reflects a relative ranking of features that are at least perceived as ranging from old-fashioned to innovative. The most old-fashioned features, clearly, fall into the category of the enharmonic genus. There are reports about later musicians who imitated Pindar and Simonides by deliberately avoiding the chromatic genus, thereby "sounding" enharmonic ("Plutarch" *On Music* 1137f; cf. 1145a). The enharmonic genus was considered typical of tragedy ("Plutarch" 1137de).[94] In the fourth century B.C., as we know from the testimony of Aristoxenus, the chromatic genus was the prevalent mode (*Harmonics* 23.9–22);[95] moreover, Aristoxenus specifies that it tended to displace the enharmonic genus, which was becoming obsolete (ibid.).[96]

When Aristoxenus discusses the order in which the genera came into being (*Harmonics* 19.17–29), he places the diatonic as the first and oldest on the grounds that it sounds more universal, as if the diatonic genus were the first system that would occur to human nature (πρῶτον γὰρ αὐτοῦ ἡ τοῦ ἀν-θρώπου φύσις προστυγχάνει ibid.); then comes the chromatic, and finally the enharmonic, on the grounds that human perception has the hardest time in

---

88. Cf. Barker, p. 216n77.
89. See Barker, p. 184n8, for a collection of references.
90. West 1981.115–121.
91. Ibid.
92. West, p. 118.
93. Cf. Kuryłowicz's fourth law of analogy, as discussed at p. 5.
94. See also "Aristotle" *Problems* 19.15, *Hibeh Papyrus* 13 (see Barker, p. 184), and other sources listed by West, p. 117n30. According to Plutarch (*Sympotic Questions* 645de) the chromatic genus was first used in tragedy by Agathon. On the interpretation of **khrōma** 'coloration' as a "deviation from the standard," see West, p. 117.
95. Cf. Barker, p. 225n132.
96. Cf. Barker, p. 183.

getting accustomed to the enharmonic (ibid.). In "Plutarch" *On Music* 1134f–1135 there is a convergent formulation, attributed to Aristoxenus, according to which the mythical master of the **aulos**, Olympus the Phrygian, supposedly "invented" the enharmonic genus by experimenting with the diatonic genus and adjusting it; all music before Olympus was supposedly diatonic or chromatic (ibid.). According to Aristoxenus this "experimentation" of Olympus, "transforming" the diatonic genus into the enharmonic, led to a system of composition in the Dorian **tonos** ("Plutarch" 1135a).[97] The account goes on to admit that such a system, as attested in the compositions attributed to Olympus, cannot readily be classified under any one single genus, whether it be diatonic, chromatic, or even enharmonic, because the interval patterns reveal areas of nondifferentiation that do not correspond even to current enharmonic standards (*On Music* 1135ab). Thus the Archaic musical style of Olympus is to be considered a sort of early enharmonic (ibid.). This admission makes it clear that the enharmonic was in fact the basis for differentiation, and that the hierarchy in terms of myth has to be reversed in terms of the actual development of patterns.[98]

The hierarchy of myth, which is based on contemporary musical perceptions of what comes naturally, must be juxtaposed with actual contemporary musical trends. Despite the thought-pattern of myth, which insists on the invention of the chromatic out of the diatonic, it is generally agreed by present-day musicologists, on the basis of other indications in the ancient sources, that the diatonic genus superseded the chromatic as the prevailing musical style in post-Hellenistic times.[99] One such indication is the explicit testimony of Aristides Quintilianus, p. 16.10–15 (ed. Winnington-Ingram). Moreover, we have also seen the testimony of Aristoxenus to the effect that the chromatic genus tends to displace the enharmonic in his own time (*Harmonics* 23.9–22). Thus it would appear that the enharmonic is more Archaic in its interval patterns than the chromatic. Similarly, if indeed composers avoid the chromatic in order to imitate the older masters — and we have seen that Aristoxenus verifies this practice as a contemporary one — then the chromatic genus must surely be less Archaic than the enharmonic. We may infer then that the Archaic masters like Pindar and Simonides "sounded" more enharmonic than chromatic or anything else.

---

97. Clement *Stromateis* 6.88 attributes to Aristoxenus the observation that the enharmonic genus suits the *Dorian* **harmoniā** and the diatonic genus, the *Phrygian* (cf. West 1981.128). He then proceeds to cite a *Dorian* **harmoniā** in a hymn to Zeus attributed to Terpander, the beginning of which he quotes (PMG 698).

98. Note that the reason given by Barker, p. 165, for his choice of the enharmonic genus in his own description of **harmoniai** is that "the members of the 'unsystematic' group are more nearly enharmonic than they are anything else."

99. Henderson and Wulstan 1973.30; cf. West 1986.44.

From the standpoint of the Archaic masters of lyric, it may even be enough to describe their *enharmonic* melodic patterns as simply *harmonic*.[100] In setting up a chronological hierarchy of (en)harmonic as the oldest, followed by chromatic and then by diatonic, we may perhaps draw some inferences from the presence of the so-called **puknon** in the enharmonic and chromatic genera, as opposed to its absence in the diatonic. The word **puknon** refers to a pattern where the two lowest intervals of the tetrachord, when added together, are less than the remaining interval of the tetrachord. Thus in the chromatic genus 1/2 plus 1/2 is less than 1 1/2, and in the enharmonic genus 1/4 plus 1/4 is less than 2. By contrast in the diatonic genus 1/2 plus 1 is not less than 1. In other words the distinctive feature of enharmonic and chromatic genera is the consecutive sequence of two small intervals, the **puknon**, while the rest of the tetrachord is occupied by one single large interval. In addition there is an auxiliary rule according to which the **puknon** cannot be followed in traditional melody by an interval that is shorter than one tone.[101] The smaller intervals in the enharmonic and the chromatic, which are relatively older genera, seem to resemble more closely the "speech melody" of ancient Greek accentuation than the larger intervals of the diatonic, which is relatively younger.[102] The smaller intervals in the enharmonic and chromatic are the very factors that would make ancient Greek music sound foreign from the standpoint of the tempered tones and semitones of the modern Western musical traditions.[103]

If indeed the enharmonic tetrachord were once simply the harmonic, preceding any differentiations leading to the chromatic and thereafter to the diatonic, then we may look for the clearest traces of preserved affinities with the pitch accent system of the Greek language precisely in the enharmonic genus. On the authority of "Plutarch" *On Music* 1135ab and 1137ab (especially 1137b), we know that some of the oldest melodic patterns, attributed to Olympus and Terpander, were trichords, not tetrachords.[104] It can even be argued, on the basis of such testimony, that certain types of tetrachords developed out of trichords.[105] The affinity of the (en)harmonic tradition with trichords, that is, three-note systems, suggests even closer links between the

---

100. Cf. Henderson 1957.389.

101. See Henderson, pp. 364–366.

102. Cf. p. 39; cf. also Allen 1987.123 on the speech melody of ancient Greek accentuation, "which gradually rises towards the high pitch, whether by steps or glide, and then returns to the low." If there is more than one low pitch in a Greek word, that is, in polysyllables, there will be one lowest pitch while the other lows will be intermediate (ibid.). The smaller intervals in the enharmonic and chromatic may be a reflex of the distinction between lowest pitch and intermediate low pitch.

103. Mountford and Winnington-Ingram 1970.707.

104. West 1981.117.

105. West ibid.

interval patterns of the enharmonic genus and the interval patterns of pitch accentuation in the Greek language.[106]

Rounding out this survey of the chronologically overlapping melodic systems of **nomoi, harmoniai, tonoi,** and genera, we may say that they all reflect in various degrees an ongoing process of mutual assimilation and systematization, to which I have applied the overall concept of Panhellenization. The present list is hardly exhaustive. For example, another important factor that contributed to the systematization of melodic traditions was the innovative interaction of conventions in accompaniment by lyre and reed (**aulos**),[107] and the actual conflation of distinct melodic patterns associated with the lyre, the **aulos**, and the voice, as pioneered by such antecedents of Pindar as Lasus of Hermione (Theon of Smyrna, p. 59.4 Hiller, Suda s.v.; "Plutarch" *On Music* 1141c).[108] This particular figure is reputed to have been a teacher of Pindar (scholia to Pindar *Olympian* 1, p. 4.13–15 Drachmann) and a rival of Simonides (cf. Aristophanes *Wasps* 1409–1411). Given that the provenience of Lasus is the *Dorian* city of Hermione, we may note again the specific reference to a **harmoniā** described as *Aeolian* in Lasus PMG 702.3;[109] there is a comparable self-reference to an *Aeolian* song and dance in Pindar *Olympian* 1.102 (Αἰοληΐδι μολπᾷ), the same composition in which the voice of the poet, at the beginning, asks that the *Dorian* lyre be handed over to him (Δωρίαν ... φόρμιγγα 17).[110]

With this survey of melodic traditions in Greek song serving as background, we may pursue further the notion of a *canon* in our ongoing discussion of Panhellenization in poetry and song. What I have proposed is that the formation of a canon in song — which we can also call *lyric poetry* — started relatively later than the formation of a canon in nonlyric poetry proper. Once the Panhellenic breakthrough of song did happen, however, its transmission would have been facilitated to rival that of poetry not only because of the mnemonic utility of melody but also because of the relative brevity of song as opposed to the potentially open-ended length of poetry. In any inherited distinction between SONG and *speech*, we would expect that the pressures of regularization in SONG would tend to delimit the length of production in contrast with the potentially open-ended length of speaking everyday *speech*. So also in any differentiation of SONG into song vs. poetry, we would expect that song would be more clearly delimited in length of production by contrast with the potentially open-ended length of poetry in its imitation of *speech*.[111]

---

106. See p. 102.

107. For a reference to patterns of tuning the lyre that corresponded to tunes played on the **aulos**, see Xenophon *Symposium* 3.1 and the commentary of Barker 1984.120n13.

108. Cf. Comotti 1979.27–28 and Seaford 1984.15.

109. Cf. p. 92.

110. Cf. p. 94.

111. A similar point is made, with illustrations from Arabic traditions, by Monroe 1972.40–41; cf. Zwettler 1978.212–213, 217.

With these considerations, let us examine the social context of performance. If indeed the transmission of Panhellenized song coexists with that of poetry, it stands to reason that the professional performer of such song, the **kitharōidos** 'lyre [**kitharā**] singer' and the **aulōidos** 'reed [**aulos**] singer', would be valued on a scale comparable to that of the professional performer of poetry, the **rhapsōidos** 'rhapsode'. In fact the epigraphical evidence shows that **rhapsōidoi, kitharōidoi**, and **aulōidoi**, as they perform in competition at festivals, are awarded comparable sums for their prizes.[112]

In the following chapters, we have occasion to observe a recurrent pattern where the composer/performer of song or lyric poetry is eventually differentiated into a mythical protocomposer on the one hand and a contemporary professional performer, the **kitharōidos** or **aulōidos** on the other. But this pattern is just one of many other possible patterns of evolution. The category of lyric poetry includes performance not only by a single professional or nonprofessional performer but also by a nonprofessional group of specially selected natives of the polis, the **khoros** 'chorus', who both sang and danced the song.[113] In Pindar's time, as we see later, the nonprofessional chorus would be performing, on commissioned occasions, songs composed by professional poets of Panhellenic prestige, such as Pindar.[114] As we also see later, the institution of the chorus plays its own role in the emerging concept of authorship in Archaic and Classical Greece.[115]

Of all the composers of song, or lyric poets, I single out Pindar as the focus of our attention. Along with his near-contemporary, Bacchylides, Pindar is the latest and the last in the canon of lyric poets inherited by the Alexandrian editors. The last securely datable poem of Pindar, *Pythian* 8, was composed for performance in 446 B.C. (for Bacchylides, the last datable compositions are *Odes* 6 and 7, performed in 452 B.C.). With this date of 446 we have an imprecise but revealing terminus in the history of ancient Greek poetry.

A striking feature of this terminus is the fact that the canon of lyric poetry excludes poets who flourished in the second half of the fifth century or thereafter. This fact will in due course be linked with the argument that the canon of lyric poetry results from patterns of Panhellenization in oral tradi-

112. Cf., for example, IG II² 2311, an inscription concerning prizes at the Panathenaia (first half of the fourth century B.C.); also IG XII ix 189 (Eretria, ca. 340 B.C.). The most marked difference is that the **kitharōidoi** outrank the **aulōidoi** in the value of the prizes. To be compared is the hierarchy of listing in Plato *Laws* 658b: **rhapsōidiā kitharōidiā tragōidiā kōmōidiā**. Note too the use here of the verb **epi-deiknunai** in the sense of *public performance*. Homer is specified as the exponent of **rhapsōidiā**; exponents of the other three media are left unspecified. See also *Laws* 834e–835a. There is a **kitharōidos** featured in the representation of the Panathenaic procession on the Parthenon Frieze (Shelmerdine 1981.80).

113. Cf. p. 85.

114. More on the professionalism of Pindar at pp. 340 and following.

115. Cf. pp. 339 and following.

tions of song. Although there is ample evidence for the existence of poets who composed song in the second half of the fifth century and thereafter — the most prominent of whom are Timotheus of Miletus and Philoxenus of Cythera —[116] there is also evidence that their song was a medium that had evolved beyond the lyric poetry represented by Pindar and the other canonical lyric poets. In particular the differences can be seen in the genres known as the citharodic nome and the dithyramb.[117] I quote from a brief summary of the situation:[118]

> One point about the development of lyric poetry in the latter part of the fifth century . . . is both clear and relevant to the question [of why this poetry was excluded from the canon]: two kinds of lyric poetry, the [citharodic] nome and the dithyramb, began to dominate nondramatic poetic composition. Both were different from all the earlier lyric types, including the earlier nome and dithyramb,[119] in signficiant respects: they were nonstanzaic, the relative importance of music to words suddenly and greatly increased, and their affinity to drama was recognized; Aristotle groups them with tragedy and comedy in his classification of the mimetic arts at the beginning of the *Poetics*. It may be that the Alexandrian critics did not consider this new poetry, which continued dominant in the fourth century, to be of the same genre as lyric poetry (nearly all of which was stanzaic),[120] and for this reason excluded Timotheus, Philoxenus of Cythera, Cinesias, and the other writers of dithyrambs and nomes.

I propose a different reason for the exclusion of these poets in the canon

116. See Kirkwood 1974.3–4.

117. Cf. p. 87.

118. Kirkwood ibid. Cf. Herington 1985.228n39: "By the time that Aristotle was composing his *Poetics*, about 330 B.C., the dithyramb seems to have been the only kind of choral lyric that was still alive enough to deserve his notice in that work." On the performance of a citharodic nome, the *Persians* of Timotheus (PMG 788–791), at Athens around 408 B.C., see the informative discussion of Herington, pp. 151–160.

119. I take note of the explicit contrast in "Plutarch" *On Music* 1142bc between the dithyrambs of Philoxenus and those of Pindar as representatives of the new and old styles, respectively. Kirkwood 1974.4 argues that the dithyrambs of Bacchylides represent a transitional phase, being more innovative than his victory odes in revealing a greater proximity to the new styles associated with drama. On the appropriateness of dithyramb for expressing the author as speaking in his own person, cf. Plato *Republic* 394c. On evidence for Pindar's entry in the dithyrambic competitions at the City Dionysia in Athens at the beginning of the fifth century B.C., see *Oxyrhynchus Papyri* 2438, column ii, lines 9–10. On the total of fifty-six victories claimed for Simonides in various dithyrambic contests presumably held at various places, see *Palatine Anthology* 6.213 = EG 27.

120. This is not to say that there are no existing nonstanzaic types of Archaic lyric: see the general discussion at pp. 48 and following. The application of the word "genre" here seems to me too wide-ranging to be useful.

of the Alexandrians: the likes of Timotheus and Philoxenus, unlike the earlier masters of lyric, were already being excluded from the canon of traditional Athenian education in the "Classics," mainly on the grounds that the innovative virtuosity characteristic of such poets, and of the new genres that they represented, tended to restrict their oeuvre to performance by professionals and to defy the traditions of liberal education for nonprofessionals, that is, for the future citizens of the polis.[121]

With regard to this crucial era of the second half of the fifth century and thereafter, it is important to note that, alongside the emergence of new media of song as represented by the "new" **nomos** 'nome' and the "new" **dithurambos** 'dithyramb',[122] there is a concurrent obsolescence of the old media of song as represented by lyric poetry proper. In fact the traditions of composition in lyric poetry, as once practiced by Pindar, seem to be becoming extinct in this era of the "new" nome and the "new" dithyramb. Such a trend of extinction is most evident from the standpoint of traditions in performance. For example, in Eupolis F 366 Kock (= 398 KA; paraphrased by Athenaeus 3a) the complaint is made that the songs of Pindar have for some time been covered over in silence, ignored by the audiences of the day (Eupolis was a contemporary of Aristophanes). In Eupolis F 139 Kock (= 148 KA; quoted by Athenaeus 638e) we see a parallel theme: the speaker is complaining that the songs of Stesichorus, Alcman, and Simonides are considered out of date by contemporary audiences, who prefer the "modern" poetry of the likes of Gnesippus. The latter poet is ridiculed for his modernisms also by Cratinus (F 97 Kock = 104 KA), a pioneer of Old Comedy, who was an older contemporary of Eupolis and Aristophanes (Athenaeus 638ef).

121. From here on, I use the expression *liberal education* in the sense expressed here. For more on Athenian **paideiā** 'education', see in general p. 97. Any eventual patterns of exclusion in fifth-century Athens, however, need not have affected the adoption of these "new poets" as "Classics" at a later time, in the context of revivals of "old masters." For example, there is the report of Polybius 4.20.8 (quoted by Athenaeus 626b) concerning the choral education, in his own time, of Arcadian youths who were being brought up on the compositions of Timotheus and Philoxenus: for these Arcadians, at least, these poets represent the "Classics." The phenomenon of shifting perceptions, where a given style is perceived as "modernistic" by one generation and "Classical" by another, is illustrated by the attitudes dramatized in Plato *Laws* 802cd. As for Plato, when he rejects the modernisms of Timotheus and the like, he is rejecting trends that were by then some eighty or more years old (as Barker 1984.128n13 points out). Plato's tastes are a matter of nostalgic retrojection into the Classical period. Such prescriptions as three years of liberal education, starting with the age of thirteen, in the art of the lyre (*Laws* 810a) are surely a mere exercise in idealization from the standpoint of Plato's own era. In the fourth century, even in Athens, the rapidly increasing specialization of "music" had increasingly restricted it to the professionals: I cite the revealing discussion in Aristotle *Politics* 1341a9–36, 1341b8–18. The specialization is more pronounced in a place like Sparta: *Politics* 1339b1–4.

122. The new-style **nomos** and **dithurambos** are to be contrasted with earlier old-style attestations of these genres.

In Aristophanes *Clouds* 1353–1358, the figure of Strepsiades is taking an old-fashioned stance in berating his son Pheidippides, a new convert to the school of Socrates, representing modernist trends of education that have eroded the traditions of old-fashioned liberal education in the "Classics."[123] At a symposium Pheidippides refuses a request to take up the lyre and sing a famous lyric composition by Simonides (Aristophanes *Clouds* 1355–1356). The composition was an **epinīkion**, that is, a victory ode (Simonides PMG 507). Technically Pheidippides is refusing here to perform a **skolion**. This word **skolion**, as used in the time of Aristophanes, is an appropriate general designation for the performance, self-accompanied on the lyre, of compositions by the great lyric masters.[124] A notable example of this usage of **skolion** is Aristophanes F 223 Kock (= 235 KA), with reference to the performing of compositions by Alcaeus and Anacreon, which are here called **skolia**.[125] Such a general sense of **skolion** is lost later as the word becomes progressively restricted in meaning (as we see from Athenaeus 694f-695f).[126] The performances at symposia of the great lyric masters correspond to the monodic medium of the **kitharōidos**.[127] To engage in these performances was an old-fashioned convention at symposia, as we can see from such references as the present passage from the *Clouds* of Aristophanes, the scholia to Aristophanes *Wasps* 1222, and Eupolis F 139 Kock (by way of Athenaeus 638e).[128] According to "Plutarch" *On Music* 1140f, Pindar attributed the "invention" of the **skolion** to Terpander, who as we have seen is also the traditional "inventor" of the system of melodies used in **kitharōidiā** 'lyre singing' (*On Music* 1132d).[129]

As we see from the passage in the *Clouds*, Pheidippides ridicules the singing of Simonides' lyric poetry specifically because he considers it something that is passé (*Clouds* 1357–1358).[130] There is still, however, an important last stand of old-fashioned lyric poetry in the second half of the fifth

---

123. For more on Athenian **paideiā** 'education', see also p. 97.

124. Harvey 1955.162–163. That the **skolion** is not intrinsically monodic is made explicit in Athenaeus 694b, where we hear that older types of **skolia** could be choral. In this connection, we may note a report that Sophocles in his youth performed a dance, naked and anointed with oil, to the accompaniment of his lyre, around the trophy erected after the battle of Salamis (Athenaeus 20e-f); whatever we may think about the historicity of this account, its details point to a public choral setting. The "crookedness" implied by the word **skolion** is explained by Athenaeus (again 694b) as a metaphorical veering, by way of an individual's performance, from the "correctness" or "straightness" of collective performance in the singing and dancing of the chorus.

125. For the attestation of an actual **skolion** (PMG 891), composed in the Attic dialect, that closely corresponds in phraseology to a stanza in a larger poem composed in the Aeolic dialect and attributed to Alcaeus (F 249.6–9 V), see Nicosia 1976.73–74.

126. Harvey ibid.

127. Cf. p. 97.

128. Ibid.

129. Cf. p. 87.

130. On old-fashioned **paideiā** 'education' in lyric, see also pp. 406 and following.

century and thereafter, and it is to be found in the choral traditions of Athenian tragedy and comedy. The poets of Old Comedy, as we have seen, even ridicule the new poetry that purports to displace the old poetry. On another level Old Comedy could also ridicule the old poetry of lyric traditions, as in the parody of Pindar F 105 SM in Aristophanes *Birds* 926–930, 941–945 (note too the adjacent reference to Simonides in *Birds* 917–919).

The point remains that the old traditions of lyric are obsolescent by the time of Aristophanes, and in fact the *Birds*, presented in 414 B.C., is the last attested comedy of Aristophanes that mentions or parodies the compositions of Pindar.[131] We may note that Pindar F 105 SM is taken from a composition, known as a **huporkhēma**, intended for the tyrant Hieron of Syracuse.[132] The only other Aristophanic reference to a Pindaric composition where we know the identity of Pindar's intended audience is in *Acharnians* 637/639 and in *Knights* 1329/1323, both referring to Pindar F 76 SM, a passage from a famous **dithurambos** 'dithyramb' composed expressly for the glorification of Athens. Both these Aristophanic references to recognizable Pindaric passages, one the **huporkhēma** for Hieron and the other the **dithurambos** for the Athenians, focus on the beginning of a Pindaric composition. It seems that the allusion is being made to the most famous parts of famous compositions. Besides these two cases there seems to be only one more where we can be reasonably certain that the reference is to a well-known passage of Pindar: *Knights* 1264–1266, alluding to a **prosodion** 'processional song' (F 89a SM).[133] It has been observed that these three Aristophanic references to three passages apparently familiar to an Athenian audience can give us an indication of the kind of repertoire that was being taught to young Athenians in the years roughly between 450 and 420 B.C.[134] This repertoire is decidedly limited in scope, which converges with what we have observed about the canon of nine "Classics" of lyric poetry: given the vast variety of traditions that they represent, this canon is a relatively small corpus.

It seems likely that the evolving predominance of Athenian theater as a poetic medium played a major role in the obsolescence of lyric poetry in other media and by extension in other genres. From Plato's writings we hear of complaints about **theatrokratiā** (*Laws* 701a)[135] and about the intoxication of pleasure in the poetry of theater (*Laws* 700d), leading to 'transgressions' of genre (**paranomia**: *Laws* 700e).[136] To be contrasted are the good old days,

---

131. Irigoin takes note of this fact and adds (1952.15n3): "La lyrique chorale, qui passait déjà pour surannée, est désormais laissée de côté; c'est un genre littéraire dont la vogue est terminée, à Athènes tout au moins. Rares sont ceux qui en garderont le souvenir."

132. On the form of the **huporkhēma**, see p. 351.

133. Irigoin 1954.14.

134. Irigoin, p. 16.

135. Cf. Plato *Laws* 658a-659c, 669b-670b and the comments of Svenbro 1984.231n133.

136. Cf. Svenbro, p. 232n136.

as in the era of the Persian Wars (*Laws* 698b-700a),[137] when there were still distinct **eidē** 'types' and **skhēmata** 'figures' of song and dance (*Laws* 700a),[138] five of which are specified as examples: **humnos** 'hymn', **thrēnos** 'lament', **paiān** 'paean', **dithurambos** 'dithyramb', and **kitharōidikos nomos** 'citharodic nome' (*Laws* 700b). These genres,[139] as well as other genres left unspecified (ibid.),[140] are the structurally distinct aspects of **mousikē** 'music' (that is, for all practical purposes, lyric poetry), parallel to the structurally distinct aspects of **aristokratiā** in Plato's good old Athenian society (*Laws* 701a).[141] In contrast the progressive leveling by Athenian theater of generic distinctions in lyric poetry is for Plato parallel to the leveling by Athenian democracy of class distinctions in society.[142] What I have been describing as an infusion of lyric genres into theater, and their concomitant atrophy elsewhere, is seen by Plato as an illegitimate mixing of genres (*Laws* 700d), a degeneration into a superseding genre of lyric traditions in Athenian drama (ibid.). In contrast, as Svenbro points out,[143] Athenian drama is seen by Aristotle not as the product of degeneration but rather as a teleological organic development in the evolution of poetic traditions (*Poetics* 1449a14–15).[144]

From either point of view, the lyric poetry of Athenian theater would be considered the final productive phase of a medium that had otherwise become unproductive already by the second half of the fifth century. In Aristophanes *Clouds* 1361–1376, as we have seen, Pheidippides refuses to take up the lyre and sing a lyric composition by Simonides, on the grounds that the singing of lyric compositions at symposia is passé.[145] It is clear that Pheidippides is not well-versed in the art form of this kind of performance.[146]

137. Cf. Svenbro, p. 231n131. See at p. 97 and following for a parallel theme in Aristophanes, where the nostalgia for old-fashioned traditions in song making is linked with the good old days of Athenian **paideiā** 'education', the kind that purportedly produced the men who not only knew how to perform the traditional songs but also fought at the Battle of Marathon (*Clouds* 961).

138. For the notion of **skhēmata** as 'dance figures', postures and gestures that *represent,* see Barker 1984.119n10 on Xenophon *Symposium* 2.15. Cf. p. 38.

139. On the appropriateness of the term *genre* here, see again Svenbro 1984.225 and n135.

140. Cf. Plato *Ion* 534c, as discussed at p. 351, where the **dithurambos** 'dithyramb' is treated as parallel to the **huporkhēma** (for the meaning, see p. 351), the **enkōmion** 'encomium', the **epos**, and the **iambos** (all in the plural).

141. Cf. Svenbro 1984.225.

142. Ibid.

143. Svenbro, pp. 225–226.

144. Cf. Svenbro, p. 226 and n140 (where 1449b should be corrected to 1449a). As Lucas 1968.82 points out, this would imply "that there was no important change later than the early plays of Sophocles, and that no further development is to be looked for." This same attitude is already alive and well in Aristophanes, for whom anything after Sophocles is decadent (cf. *Frogs* 76–82, 787–794, 1515–1519).

145. See p. 107. See further Reitzenstein 1893.34 for a survey of illustrative passages.

146. Perhaps the most celebrated example of this theme is in Cicero *Tusculan Disputations*

Then he is asked at least to perform something from the compositions of Aeschylus, while holding a branch of myrtle (*Clouds* 1365).[147] The **aulos**, not the lyre, serves as the medium of accompaniment for the lyric compositions of Athenian drama.[148] Singing to the lyre implies potential self-accompaniment, whereas singing to the **aulos** does not. Thus a lower degree of education is required for performing in the chorus of an Aeschylean tragedy or for reperforming at a symposium selections from the choral songs of such a tragedy.[149] Even this kind of performance is refused by Pheidippides, who elects to recite a passage from a speech in Euripides (*Clouds* 1371). The word **rhēsis** 'speech' (ibid.) makes it clear that the modern Pheidippides opts for a medium that is devoid of the lyric element.[150]

Plato's portrait of nostalgia for those earlier days when lyric poetry had not yet been absorbed and ultimately usurped by Athenian theater returns us to the era of Pindar, last in the canon of lyric poets. Let us consider the genres in which Pindar composed. It is best to begin with the inventory of an Alexandrian edition of Pindar as reported in the *Vita Ambrosiana*, according to which Pindar's compositions are subdivided into seventeen books corresponding to specific genres of lyric poetry.[151] We are struck by the fact that of the distinct genres of lyric poetry mentioned in Plato's partial list, namely the **humnos**, the **thrēnos**, the **paiān**, the **dithurambos**, and the citharodic **nomos** (again *Laws* 700b), all but the last one are also represented in the *Vita Ambrosiana* inventory of Pindar's poems. The inventory of seventeen books attributed to Pindar contains ten distinct genres (an asterisk marks those genres that correspond to Plato's list):

1.4 on the embarrassment of Themistokles in being unable, at a symposium, to sing and accompany himself on the lyre; the traditions underlying this theme are examined by Reitzenstein 1893.33–34.

147. On the custom of substituting a myrtle branch for a lyre in performances at symposia: Dicaearchus F 89 Wehrli. Cf. the useful discussion of Barker 1984.103n16. On the earlier applications of **skolion** in a broader sense of a lyric song sung at a symposium (cf. Aristophanes F 223 Kock = 235 KA) and on the eventual semantic narrowing of this word to designate only such special Attic forms as the Harmodios-song, see Harvey 1955.162–163.

148. As Henderson 1957.339 puts it, a single **aulos** supports the tragic chorus.

149. Cf. the scholia to Aristophanes *Wasps* 1239. Cf. also Reitzenstein 1893.34. For further observations on Athenian **paideiā** 'education', see pp. 406 and following.

150. The supporting evidence is conscientiously surveyed and clearly discussed by Reitzenstein 1893.32–39; cf. Harvey 1955.162. On the interchangeability of **aeidō/āidō** 'sing' (as in *Clouds* 1371) and **legō** 'say' in referring to nonlyric as well as lyric delivery, see the discussion of Herington 1985.13 and 224–225n15; my interpretation of this interchangeability, however, differs from his.

151. Pindar scholia I, p. 3 Drachmann. I say *an* Alexandrian edition rather than *the* Alexandrian edition in light of observations made by Race 1987 concerning *Oxyrhynchus Papyri* 2438, c. 200 A.D., a papyrus life of Pindar: this document shows that the sequence of categories in the *Vita Ambrosiana* was hardly the only one.

* 1. **humnoi** 'hymns'
* 2. **paiānes** 'paeans'
* 3. **dithuramboi** 'dithyrambs'
* 4. same
  5. **prosodia**
  6. same
  7. **parthenia**
  8. same
  9. **parthenia** [distinct set]
  10. **huporkhēmata**[152]
  11. same
  12. **enkōmia**[153]
* 13. **thrēnoi** 'laments'
  14. **epinīkia** 'epinicians' or 'victory odes' [Olympians][154]
  15. same [Pythians]
  16. same [Isthmians]
  17. same [Nemeans][155]

It is difficult to be certain whether such an editorial organization of Pindar's poems goes further in time than the Alexandrian era—back to the time of Plato, for example.[156] But we do know for certain that Plato was familiar enough with Pindar's poems to refer to them at least sixteen times in the attested Platonic corpus.[157]

152. Mentioned by Plato in *Ion* 534c; see p. 109.

153. Mentioned by Plato in *Ion* 534c; see p. 109 above.

154. The notion of *epinician* will be discussed in detail at Ch.4.

155. This order of the epinician or victory odes seems to have been standard until the period when the text was transferred from papyrus roll to codex. When this transfer happened, the old sequence of *Isthmians-Nemeans* was reversed, perhaps accidentally, to become *Nemeans-Isthmians*: see Irigoin 1952.100. The fact that some of the genre categories of the Pindaric corpus take up more than one book has to do, of course, with the conventional space capacity of papyrus rolls. The expected maximum was roughly 2,400 lines, in that 2,400 is denoted by the terminal letter omega in the numbering system used by Alexandrian editors in counting the lines contained in a given roll (where each successive letter of the Ionic alphabet is 100 more than the previous one): see Irigoin 1952.40. The typical length of an Alexandrian roll is represented by the number of lines specified for Book 1 of Sappho in *Oxyrhynchus Papyri* 1231, which is 1,320 lines. Irigoin, p. 41, compares the length of the *Alexandra* of Lycophron (1,474 lines), the *Phaenomena* and *Prognostica* of Aratus (1,154 lines in all), the *Hymns* of Callimachus (1,083 lines), and the four books of the *Argonautica* of Apollonius of Rhodes (ranging from 1,288 lines for Book 2 to 1,779 lines for Book 4). Such a length for a roll would be just right for an Athenian tragedy or comedy (see Irigoin, p. 41n3). On the editorial arrangement of the epinicians of Simonides, with different rolls assigned to different athletic events, see Irigoin, p. 38; as for the epinicians of Bacchylides, they all could fit within one roll (ibid.).

156. For bits of evidence that may suggest Athenian editorial conventions predating the Alexandrian ones, see Irigoin 1952.39–40. Cf. also Young 1983.47–48.

157. See Irigoin 1952.16–18. No. 1: F 105a.1 SM, a passage from a **huporkhēma** (composed for Hieron of Syracuse), in *Meno* 76d. We have already noted (p. 109) that this passage

It remains to ask how exactly these references came about. One readily available explanation is that Plato was citing from a hypothetical edition of Pindar that was circulating in Athens.[158] Most likely such an edition would have been a school text going back to an earlier time when youths had still been well-educated in the actual performance of old-fashioned lyric compositions.[159] By Plato's time, however, it was becoming less and less likely that performers of **kitharōidiā** or **aulōidiā**, especially amateurs, could still have had in their repertoires selections from Pindar and other grand masters of lyric poetry. I quote from the summary of a musicologist:[160]

> The classic Athenian comedy had been made for a society which talked music as it talked politics or war. But in Aristophanes' post-war plays, a shrunken chorus gives us only a last flash or two of his musical parody; and his successors substituted *entr'actes* by variety artists. The Alexandrian era still has excellent stage gossip on performers, but a first-hand judgement on the style or quality of music is hardly to be found after the fourth century. Aristotle already prefers received opinions. His master Plato and his pupil Aristoxenus are the last who speak to us with the authority of musical understanding.

It must be kept in mind that the contemporary Athenian traditions of composing and performing lyric poetry had already outgrown, well before Plato's time, the traditions represented by Pindar.[161] I do not rule out the possibility that some of the better schools, even in Plato's time, insisted on extensive memorization of the libretti of the lyric masters, but it is clear that

---

was parodied in the *Birds* of Aristophanes. No. 2: same passage, in *Phaedrus* 236d. No. 3: F 169a.1–5 SM, a passage also cited in Herodotus 3.38.4, from a poem of undetermined genre, in *Gorgias* 484b. Nos. 4–6: same passage, in *Laws* 714e–715a as also in 690bc and 890a. No. 7: same passage, in *Protagoras* 337d. No. 8: F 133 SM, a passage apparently (but not necessarily) from a **thrēnos**, in *Meno* 81abc. Nos. 9–11: F 214, 213.1–2, 209 SM, passages from poems of undetermined genre, in *Republic* 331a, 365b, 457b. No. 12: F 292 SM, a passage from a poem of undetermined genre, in *Theaetetus* 173e. The rest are passages from the victory odes. No. 13: from *Olympian* 2.16 (composed for Theron of Akragas), in *Protagoras* 324b. No. 14: from *Isthmian* 1.2 (composed for Herodotus of Thebes), in *Phaedrus* 227b. No. 15: from *Olympian* 1.1 (composed for Hieron), in *Euthydemus* 304bc. No. 16: from *Pythian* 3.54–57 (composed for Hieron), in *Republic* 408b.

158. So Irigoin, pp. 19–20. Here is his summary of the major references: F 76 SM, a **dithurambos** for the Athenians, referred to by Aristophanes (*Knights* 1329/1323) and by Isocrates (*Antidosis* 15.166); F 89a SM, a **prosodion** 'processional song', apparently imitated by Aristophanes (*Knights* 1264–1266); F 105 SM, the **huporkhēma** for Hieron, mentioned in Aristophanes (*Birds* 926–930, 941–945) and two times in Plato (n157); F 169a.1–5 SM, cited in Herodotus 3.38.4, in Plato (five times, see n157), and apparently in Aristotle (*Rhetoric* 1406a). Aristotle also refers to Pindar F 96 SM (*Rhetoric* 1401a) and to *Olympian* 1.1 (*Rhetoric* 1364a).

159. Cf. pp. 107, 109. Cf. p. 408.

160. Henderson 1957.340.

161. See pp. 107, 109.

most schools limited their requirements to a small repertoire of selected passages to be memorized for recitation (cf. Plato *Laws* 810e).[162] As for professional musicians, there is evidence that they still had access, even at as late as the era of Aristotle, to the melodic traditions of Archaic masters like Pindar. I refer to a revealing report in "Plutarch" *On Music* 1142b attributed to the music theorist Aristoxenus, pupil of Aristotle: according to Aristoxenus, the son of a professional musician from Tarentum,[163] there was a composer, one of his own contemporaries, who in the course of his career reverted from the musical idiom of Timotheus and Philoxenus to that of the Archaic poets, among whom Pindar is mentioned first. Clearly the musical tradition of Pindar had survived until then. Still there would have been no chance for any major ongoing recomposition of Pindar's lyric poetry through performance in that contemporary traditions of choral lyric composition would have been sufficiently differentiated from Pindar's old-fashioned traditions. In fact the very traditions of performing Pindar's compositions had become obsolete.

In Pindar's own time, by contrast, his compositions could still be readily reperformed, ordinarily not by a chorus[164] but by individuals at symposia, simply as "Classics." As we have seen, Old Comedy represents the mode of reperforming an epinician composition of Simonides, at the symposium, in the format of a solo rendition with self-accompaniment to the lyre (Aristophanes *Clouds* 1355–1358). By implication there was a time when a choral composition, such as we see in the songs of Simonides or his contemporary Pindar, could be actively converted into a solo performance. Such interchangeability between choral and solo contexts is a clear indication, however indirect, of the flexibility of the choral lyric form as a still-living tradition in the era of Pindar.[165] This flexibility presupposes a solid education of nonprofessionals in the art of professionals known as **kitharōidoi** 'lyre singers'.[166] In the later era of Timotheus and Philoxenus, as we have also seen, such flexibility had broken down.

As "Classics" the compositions of a Pindar could be reperformed at will in the "good old days," but they would have to be grounded in an awareness of the situations and ideologies in which Pindar was commissioned to give public poetic testimony. These situations and ideologies, or *occasions*, may

---

162. Cf. also the discussion of Reitzenstein 1893.39n1. On the obsolescence of actual performance in song, see Reitzenstein, p. 42n1.

163. See again Henderson 1957.343.

164. There are exceptional cases where the Pindaric composition was apparently meant to be performed on more than one occasion. In Pindar *Olympian* 6.98–102, for example, the composition calls for its performance at two related but distinct occasions: both at Stymphalos in Arcadia, the native place of Hagesias, the immediate subject of praise, and at the court of the tyrant Hieron of Syracuse in Sicily. Cf. Mullen 1982.26.

165. The nature of choral lyric will be examined in detail at p. 339 and following.

166. Cf. pp. 98, 104, 107.

strike us at first as potential obstacles to the Panhellenization of such compositions. The very occasions of this lyric poetry, however, were of Panhellenic importance, with an impact lasting in prestige. Each of Pindar's compositions was originally commissioned for a specific occasion, to be performed ostensibly by a chorus assembled and trained for that one original occasion. But the prestige of such an occasion was meant to reverberate indefinitely in time and space.

This transcendent occasionality of Pindar's lyric poetry is most evident in the only genre of his compositions to survive almost intact: the four books of **epinīkia** 'victory odes'. These victory odes or *epinicians* were commissioned as ad hoc choral performances in celebration of victories won by athletes at the Panhellenic Games, and the four books of Pindar's epinicians match the four most prestigious Panhellenic athletic festivals: the Olympian, Pythian, Isthmian, and Nemean Games. Though each of Pindar's victory odes was an occasional composition, centering on a single performance, each containing details grounded in the historical realities of the time and place of performance, still each of these victory odes aimed at translating its occasion into a Panhellenic event, a thing of beauty that could be replayed by and for all Hellenes for all time to come.

The occasion of the poet's victory ode not only conferred Panhellenic prestige: it also received it since the athlete's victory itself was a Panhellenic event, the prestige of which depended on the relative Panhellenic prestige of the given games in which the victory occurred. Just as the concept of Panhellenism is relative in terms of poetry and song,[167] so also in terms of athletics: the older the athletic festival, the more Panhellenic was its prestige. Thus the Olympics of Elis (traditional founding date of 776 B.C.) were more Panhellenic than the Pythians of Delphi (582 B.C.), the Pythians more than the Isthmians near Corinth (581 B.C), the Isthmians more than the Nemeans near Argos (573 B.C.). The list could be extended, with such runner-up festivals as the Panathenaia of Athens (with athletic competitions instituted at 566/5 B.C.).[168]

It is clear that there would have been no rationale for recommissioning a chorus to reperform such a composition since the original occasion would have been archetypal from the standpoint of the lyric poetry. To put it another way, the original occasion would have been gone forever from the standpoint of us outsiders who are critics of this poetry. For us, any reperformance of such a composition in, say, Aristophanes' time seems at first sight to be just a performance of a canonical poet. From the internal point of view

167. Cf. p. 53.
168. The status of the *Nemeans* as originally the last book of epinician odes (see p. 111) helps explain why the last three of the odes in that book, *Nemean* 9, 10, and 11, celebrate victories won not at the Nemean Games. One of these, *Nemean* 10, celebrates a victory at the Heraia of Argos. *Nemean* 9 celebrates a victory in chariot-racing at Sikyon. Cf. Irigoin 1952.42.

represented by the poetic tradition, however, a reperformance in an old-fashioned symposium is a remaking of an original poetic event. There is no chorus, no chorus-leader present; instead a soloist performer must reconstitute their roles, while accompanying himself on the lyre.[169] The example of the young Pheidippides in the *Clouds* of Aristophanes, however, suggests an incipient failure of liberal education, even by the time of Old Comedy, to produce anyone to take up such a challenge.[170]

169. On the reperformance at symposia of choral passages from Old Comedy itself, see Aristophanes *Knights* 529–530, with references to the songs of Cratinus (F 69, 70 Kock = 70 KA).

170. Reitzenstein, p. 42n1, observes that by the time of New Comedy even the convention of referring to the performance of **skolion**, not just in the broader sense of lyric types associated with the likes of Pindar but also in the narrower sense of the lyric type known as the Harmodios-song (e.g., PMG 894), had become obsolete.

4 ▣▣ Pindar's *Olympian* 1 and the Aetiology of the Olympic Games

L et us begin a closer scrutiny of Pindar's traditions by examining an occasion that typifies the social context of his authorship. This occasion is memorialized in Pindar's *Olympian* 1, a composition commissioned by the tyrant Hieron of Syracuse to celebrate a Panhellenic victory in a horse race event of the Olympics of 476 B.C.[1] To begin, let us review the major themes of *Olympian* 1. In this composition the voice of the poet explicitly rejects the myth that told of the dismemberment of Pelops and his cannibalization at a feast of the gods. In its place is an explicit substitution of a myth that told of the young hero's abduction by the god Poseidon, who eventually repaid Pelops by helping him win a chariot race with Oinomaos. The telling of the second myth, however, is launched in *Olympian* 1 with a partial retelling of the first; the resulting juxtaposition of the two myths has led to major problems of interpretation. The focal point of these problems is the ongoing dispute over the meaning of ἐπεί at *Olympian* 1.26: was Pelops abducted 'after' or 'since' (in the causal sense) Klotho the Moira 'Fate' took him out of the 'purifying cauldron' (καθαροῦ λέβητος, 26), resplendent as he was with his shoulder of ivory (ἐλέφαντι φαίδιμον ὦμον κεκαδμένον, 27)? The bibliography for both alternatives, 'after' or 'since' (causal), is massive, and

1. See Köhnken 1974.205: Hieron won in the single-horse competition of the Olympics of 476 B.C., and the preoccupation of Pindar's *Olympian* 1 with the theme of chariot racing shows clearly that the tyrant is looking forward to winning a future Olympic victory in the more prestigious four-horse chariot competition. On the canonization of *Olympian* 1 as the lead poem of the corpus of Pindaric epinicians, see the arguments of Young 1983, especially pp. 47–48.

consensus is lacking.[2] In the course of my own investigation, I adopt the interpretation *after*.

In reaching this conclusion, however, I take an approach that differs from earlier attempts: instead of assuming that Pindar is literally substituting one myth for another, I argue that the substitution as represented in *Olympian* 1 is in fact a poetic expression of a preexisting fusion of two myths, where the earlier myth is officially subordinated to but acknowledged by the later myth. Furthermore I argue that the relative earliness and lateness of these two myths has to do not with any innovation by Pindar himself but rather with the historical sequence of the accretion of traditional myths officially associated with the complex institution of the Olympics. In other words both myths are traditional and in fact signal that they are traditional. As for the subordination of the myth that told of the dismemberment of Pelops to the myth that told of the abduction of Pelops by Poseidon and the hero's victory in the chariot race, I propose that this pattern corresponds to the subordination of the oldest athletic event of the Olympics, the single-course foot race, to the most prestigious athletic event of the Olympics in Pindar's time, the four-horse chariot race. In this sense Pindar's *Olympian* 1 may be said to reflect the evolving aetiology of the Olympics in the early fifth century.

Before we proceed, some definitions of terms are in order. By using the word *aetiology* here, I am implying that the relationship of given myths to given athletic events corresponds to the general relationship of myth to ritual.[3] Having noted in the previous discussion that the occasional nature of Pindar's songs or lyric poetry, especially as attested in his victory odes, seems at first a potential obstacle to Panhellenization, we have begun to explore, and later explore further, the transcendence of occasionality in this poetry. For now, however, we must concentrate on defining with greater precision the nature of the occasions for Pindar's victory odes, which will have a direct bearing on the nature of his poetry. The victory ode cannot be understood without coming to terms with the notion of victory from the standpoint of ancient Greek athletics. The most distinctive feature of this standpoint is that the essence of the ancient Greek athletic games, including the four great Panhellenic festivals known as the Olympian, Pythian, Nemean, and Isthmian Games, is fundamentally a matter of ritual. By *ritual* I mean a given set of formal actions that correspond to a given set of thought patterns that can take shape as a given myth.[4] The myth may refer to itself as the motivation, in

2. There is a useful inventory of opposing views in Köhnken 1983.66–67, who argues for the interpretation *since* (causal). Although I disagree with his conclusions, I have learned much from Köhnken's observations, as also from those of Slater 1979.63–70 and of Gerber 1982.55–56.

3. Cf. pp. 30–33.

4. This working definition of *ritual* can apply to the ritual foundations of tragedy as briefly discussed in p. 42. Further discussion at pp. 385 and following. My working definition of ritual is broad enough to accommodate much of the valuable comparative evidence on athletics assembled by Sansone 1988 (see especially pp. 129–130). Sansone's own formulation of ritual, how-

Greek, the **aition** 'cause', of the ritual. Such self-reference, commonly known as *aetiology*, should not be taken as evidence for the notion that myth exists in order to explain ritual. It would be more accurate to say that ritual motivates myth as much as myth motivates ritual. In another context I have offered the following additional observations on Greek **aition** 'cause' in the sense of "a myth that *traditionally* motivates an institution, such as a ritual": "I stress 'traditionally' because the myth may be a tradition *parallel to* the ritual, not *derivative from* it. Unless we have evidence otherwise, we cannot assume in any particular instance that an aetiological myth was an *untraditional* fabrication intended simply to explain a given ritual. The factor of *motivating* — as distinct from *explaining* — is itself a traditional function in religion, parallel to the traditional function of ritual. It is only when the traditions of religion become obsolescent that rituals may become so obscure as to invite explanations of a purely literary nature."[5]

For a most convenient introduction to the subject of the ritual essence of ancient Greek athletics, on which there is a considerable bibliography, I refer to the compressed summary in Walter Burkert's handbook on Greek religion, who concludes that the Archaic institutions of athletic activity evolved out of practices that could be described as (1) rituals of initiation into adulthood and (2) rituals of compensation for the catastrophe of death.[6] This is not to say that Greek athletics could be described synchronically as such rituals. Burkert says explicitly: "Of course, age groups and initiation were no longer part of the Panhellenic festival."[7] Still, a synchronic description reveals diachronic features of the two kinds of ritual just noted.[8] In fact such diachronic features can help us find a connection between these two kinds of ritual in the specific instance of Greek athletics.

A common characteristic of initiation is that it ritualizes or symbolizes death and rebirth from one given status to another: one must "die" to one's old self in order to be "reborn" to one's new self.[9] In this light we may note the following themes of symbolized death in the institutions of the Panhellenic Games:

---

ever, is narrower: for example, he assumes at p. 113 that a given society's procedures of fasting and purification in hunting "are by no means ritual matters" on the grounds that "they are rational and pragmatic measures designed to enhance the likelihood of success." There is no reason to assume that ritual cannot be "rational and pragmatic." Such narrowing leads to unnecessary complications in establishing a hermeneutic compatibility between ritual and athletics in Sansone's book (e.g., p. 19).

5. N 1979.279 §2n2. For further discussion of aetiology, see Calame 1977 I 44–45.
6. Burkert 1985.105–107.
7. Burkert 1983.101.
8. On the terms synchronic/diachronic: p. 4.
9. Cf., for example, Jeanmaire 1939.342–343. Cf. also Brelich 1969.

■ at the Olympics, the athletes' thirty-day period of separation, sexual abstinence, and fasting on a vegetarian diet[10]

■ the wearing of black garb by the judges at athletic events[11]

■ the crowning of the victor with garlands that bear funerary connotations.[12]

Such themes of symbolized death for the athlete on the level of ritual correspond to the themes of primordial death for a hero on the level of myth. Each founding of each Greek athletic festival was apparently motivated by at least one myth that told of a hero's death.[13] In the case of the four great Panhellenic Games, the main foundation myths are as follows:[14]

■ Olympian Games (Olympics), founded by the hero Pelops in compensation for the death of Oinomaos;[15] alternatively founded by the hero Herakles in compensation for the death of his great-grandfather, Pelops;[16] this foundation by Herakles can be treated as an act of refoun-

---

10. See Burkert 1985.106; fuller documentation in Burkert 1983.102n43. Also Sansone 1988.54.

11. Rohde 1898 I 152n1.

12. Ibid. Note too Rohde I 151n5 on the funerary symbolism of the myrtle and the use of this flower for victory garlands in the Theban Games known as the *Iolaia*.

13. There is a list of 20-odd examples collected by Pfister II 496–497, to be supplemented by the list of Brelich 1958.94–95. The variations in these myths reflect the political vicissitudes of the festivals themselves, in that different versions may represent the traditions of different groups, places, and times.

14. It is important to keep in mind the following formulation of Rohde 1898 I 151–152 (1925.117): "The greatest Games of all, to which all Greece assembled, the Pythian, Olympian, Nemean, and Isthmian, were during the historical period, it is true, celebrated in honor of the gods; but that they had been originally instituted as Funeral Games of Heroes and only subsequently transferred to higher guardianship was, at any rate, the general opinion of antiquity." Rohde's accompanying note at I 152n1 is particularly helpful.

15. Phlegon FGH 257 F 1: the Delphic Oracle is quoted as saying (lines 8–9) θῆκε δ' ἔπειτα ἔροτιν καὶ ἔπαθλα θανόντι | Οἰνομάῳ 'he [Pelops] established a festival and contests [ep-āthla] for the dead Oinomaos'. On the basis of observations to be presented below concerning the semantics of **epi** + dative of the person in funerary contexts, I infer that the collocation of **ep-āthla** 'contests' with the dative in this present passage conveys the notion, to be developed further below, that Pelops instituted the contests in compensation for the death of Oinomaos. In this particular case, furthermore, myth has it that Pelops actually caused, wittingly or unwittingly, the death of Oinomaos (cf., e.g., Apollodorus *Epitome* 2.7).

16. Phlegon ibid.: the Delphic Oracle is quoted as saying (lines 9–11): τρίτατος δ' ἐπὶ τοῖς πάις Ἀμφιτρύωνος | Ἡρακλέης ἐτέλεσσ' ἔροτιν καὶ ἀγῶνα ἐπὶ μήτρῳ | Τανταλίδῃ Πέλοπι φθιμένῳ 'after them, the third was Herakles, son of Amphitryon: he established the festival and the contest [agon] for the dead Pelops, son of Tantalos, a maternal relative' [the daughter of Pelops, myth has it, was the mother of Amphitryon, father of Herakles]. On the basis of the phraseology here, I am ready to argue that the collocation of **agōn** 'contest' with **epi** with the dative conveys the notion that Herakles instituted the festival in compensation for the death of Pelops (cf. Herodotus 5.8 on **agōn** as a response to death; cf. also p. 137 on the state-supported Athenian institution of the **agōn epi-taphios** in honor of the war-dead). From the standpoint of this oracular poem, Pelops and Herakles were respectively the second and the third founders of

dation[17] or more simply as the most definitive foundation (cf. Pindar *Olympian* 2.3–4)[18]

- Pythian Games, founded by the god Apollo in compensation for having killed the Python[19]
- Isthmian Games, founded by the hero Sisyphus in compensation for the death of the child-hero Melikertes = Palaimon[20]
- Nemean Games, founded by the heroes known as the Seven against Thebes in compensation for the death, by snakebite, of the child-hero Opheltes=Arkhemoros.[21]

Besides seasonally-recurring festivals of athletic events officially motivated by the death of heroes, there are early and rare traces in Archaic Greece of occasional or once-only festivals of athletic events motivated by the death of immediate ancestors or relatives. This evidence comes from dedicatory inscriptions that memorialize various prizes won at such events.[22] Just as the heroes of epic narrative can respond to the death of a fellow hero by instituting a once-only festival of athletic events 'for' this hero, a concept

---

the Olympics; the "first founder" was one Pisos (lines 6–7), the eponymous hero of Pisa, the site of the Olympics. For another version, see Pindar *Olympian* 10.43 and following, where Herakles founds the Olympics with the spoils taken from the dead Augeias (41–42). For a survey of versions about the foundation of the Olympics, with references, see Burkert 1983.95n7. On Herakles as the founder of the Olympics, there is a generalized reference in Pindar *Olympian* 2.3–4; see also Aristotle F 637 Rose (cf. Pausanias 5.13.12); overview in Brelich 1958.l03. According to the scholia to Pindar *Olympian* 1.149a Drachmann, Herakles is said to have instituted the practice of sacrificing first to Pelops and then to Zeus.

17. Cf. the note that immediately precedes.

18. Ibid.

19. Anonymous *Peplos* (quoted by scholia to Aristides *Panathenaicus* 189); Varro *De Lingua Latina* 7.17; Clement *Protrepticus* 1.2, 2.1. Besides Burkert 1985.105–107, see Brelich 1958.95–97, especially p. 96n70 on Python as a ritual hero. According to a variant, Diomedes was first to hold the Pythian Games in honor of Apollo: Pausanias 2.32.2 (Trozenian version).

20. Pindar F 5, F 6 SM (p. 3); Pausanias 2.1.3 (note the phraseology: ἀγῶνα ἐπ' αὐτῷ, with ἐπί + dative in the context of **agōn**); Hyginus *Fabulae* 273; Clement *Protrepticus* 2.29; *Hypotheses* to Pindar *Isthmians*. Cf. Brelich 1958.103. On infants as cult-heroes, see Brelich 1958.85, 121–122, 237.

21. Bacchylides 9.12 SM (note the phraseology: ἄθλησαν ἐπ' Ἀρχεμόρῳ, with ἐπί + dative in the context of **aethlos**); Aeschylus *Nemea* (TGF 149); Euripides *Hypsipyle* (ed. Bond) 97–103; Apollodorus 3.6.4 (note the phraseology: ἐπ' αὐτῷ . . . ἀγῶνα, with ἐπί + dative in the context of **agōn**); Hyginus *Fables* 273; Clement *Protrepticus* 2.29; and *Hypotheses* to Pindar *Nemeans*. This myth can function as a supplement to the myth of Herakles and the Nemean Lion: cf. Callimachus F 254–269 in the edition of Lloyd-Jones and Parsons 1983. W. Race points out to me that the myth involving the Seven may correspond to the chariot race specifically, as distinct from the myth involving Herakles.

22. There is a valuable collection of eight such inscriptions, ranging in date from the early seventh to the middle fifth centuries B.C., in Roller 1981.2–3. The author is helpful in addressing various questions raised about the geographical distribution of the evidence (p. 15n47).

that is regularly conveyed by the idiom of **epi** + dative of the hero's name,[23] so also the bereaved in real life could institute what appear to be once-only festivals 'for' the deceased, a concept again conveyed by the idiom of **epi** + dative of the name of the deceased.[24] This rarely attested custom of instituting once-only athletic events in honor of immediate ancestors was clearly obsolescent even by the time of the Archaic period,[25] and the custom that replaced it is clearly represented by the countless attestations of seasonally-recurring athletic events 'for' heroes, a concept yet again conveyed by the idiom of **epi** + dative of the given hero's name.[26] After the obsolescence of once-only athletic events instituted in honor of immediate ancestors, the way to institute funeral games for a person who had just died was for that person to be made a cult hero under the authority of the polis, so that seasonally-recurring athletic festivals could be held in his honor.[27]

The thought patterns that underlie both the once-only and the seasonally-recurring Greek athletic festivals are analogous to what Karl Meuli has found in various rituals of combat or mock combat in a wide range of societies throughout the world.[28] From Meuli's far-reaching survey, we find that in some specific instances of ritual combat a fundamental motive is to compensate for feelings of guilt — defined or undefined — about someone's death.[29] The dead person's anger can be assuaged — and the guilt

23. For example, *Odyssey* xxiv 91, where the idiom refers to Achilles as the dead hero in whose honor the Achaeans set up a once-only festival of athletic events. For a survey of the iconographic testimony on funeral games, see Roller 1981b.

24. The idiom is attested in seven of the eight inscriptions adduced by Roller 1981.2–3; the eighth is too fragmentary for us to be certain whether the idiom was used there as well.

25. See Roller, pp. 5–6, who ascribes the obsolescence of this custom to the progressive encroachment of the polis upon funerary practices and other such practices characteristic of powerful extended families. In the case of once-only athletic events in honor of immediate ancestors and the like, we must take note of the tendency toward Panhellenism even in this obsolescent custom: we know from the inscriptions that the athletes who competed in such events could come from other city-states (Roller, p. 3). Thus there must have been some degree of Panhellenic "advertisement."

26. For example, Hesychius s.v. ἐπ᾽ Εὐρυγύῃ ἀγών, with reference to the Athenian festival of the Panathenaia (cf. Amelesagoras FGH 330 F 2 and Jacoby's commentary). Also Hesychius s.v. Βαλλητύς· ἑορτὴ ᾽Αθήνησιν ἐπὶ Δημοφῶντι τῷ Κελεοῦ ἀγομένη, with reference to a seasonally-recurring ritual mock battle in compensation for the death of the child-hero Demophon (cf. *Homeric Hymn to Demeter* 262–267, with commentary by Richardson 1974.245–247); this mock battle seems to have been the ritual kernel of a whole complex of events known as the Eleusinian Games (cf. Richardson, p. 246). See also p. 119, with reference to the festival of the Olympics.

27. See, for example, the list in Rohde 1898 I 151n4: the Delphic Oracle orders hero cults, taking the form of seasonally-recurring athletic festivals, in honor of such historical figures as Miltiades (Herodotus 6.38), Brasidas (Thucydides 5.11), Leonidas (Pausanias 3.14.1: note the phraseology: ἐπ᾽ αὐτοῖς . . . [sc. for both Brasidas and Leonidas] ἀγῶνα). A comparable case is that of the murdered Phocaeans at Agylla/Caere (Herodotus 1.167.2).

28. Meuli 1968 (1926); 1975 (1941) 881–906.

29. There is no reason to assume that all instances of human ritual combat are built on any one

or pollution canceled — by a death or a mock death that serves as compensation for the original death.[30] More fundamentally, the combat in such instances is a special kind of ordeal — where you fight for your "life" or run for your "life" or struggle in whatever other form of competition for your "life." Thus a word more appropriate than *combat* might be *contest*.[31] Who is to "live" and who is to "die" is determined not by chance but by the given society's sense of cosmic order. In some societies, the real death of one person is compensated proportionately: one other person "dies" in a ritual contest, while the one or ones who competed with this other person "live." In other societies, however, including the Greek, the proportion is inverted: one person "lives" by winning in a ritual contest, while the one or ones who competed with this person "die" by losing. In this way the compensation for the pollution of a death takes the form of winning one other life rather than losing one.

From this point of view we can see how the diachronic features of initiation in the preliminary rituals of Greek athletic festivals are connected to the diachronic features of ritual contest in the actual athletic events: the athlete, like an initiate, undergoes a ritualized death in preparation for the new "life" that will be his if he wins in his contest. And as he engages in the contest, he is struggling for this "life" in order to compensate for the death that called for his own "death."

---

motivating principle. For a reassessment of Meuli's views, see Sansone 1988.38 and following. In considering the valuable comparative data adduced by Sansone, I distance myself from his notions of "common origin" (e.g., p. 52).

30. On the notion of compensation as owed by the living to the dead and more generally on the notion of a contract or pact between the living and their ancestors, see Lévi-Strauss 1984.245–248.

31. In this connection I found it helpful to read Ong 1981.104–107 on the custom of "land diving" as practiced on the New Hebrides island of Pentecost. In an annual ritual intended to promote a good yam crop, the men of the community compete with each other by diving "from tree-and-vine towers as high as eighty feet and more, headfirst, with lianas tied to their ankles, the woody vines just long enough to break the men's fall as they hit the bare ground below" (p. 104). For the participants, the aetiological motivation for the ritual is as follows: once "a man named Tamalie quarreled with his wife, who ran away and climbed a banyan tree. Tamalie followed to recapture her, she jumped down to escape him, and he jumped after her. But she had tied lianas around her ankles to break her fall, while he, without lianas, simply plunged to his death. The other men took up the practice of land diving so that no woman would trick them again" (p. 106). I infer that the mock death of the men engaged in the ritual, modeled on the mock death of the primordial woman in the myth, compensates for the "real" death of the primordial man in the myth. Note too that the setting for the stylized death in the ritual is a thing of culture, that is, a tower, while the setting for the "real" death in the myth was a thing of nature, a tree. Ong continues: "The threat of death is real enough, though accidents, which occur with fair frequency, are generally minor (pulled muscles, sprains, contusions, skinned shoulders), since even if the lianas break, they generally do so at a point where they have already notably decelerated the fall. But death is in the air, literally and figuratively, and it is meant to be" (p. 105).

Such a pattern of thought can be elicited from a rereading of Burkert's analysis of the chronologically oldest athletic event in the Olympics, the **stadion**, a single-course foot race in the stadium (the recording of victors in this race starts with 776 B.C.).[32] This event was as a rule inaugurated with the sacrifice of a black ram at the **Pelopion** 'precinct of Pelops',[33] to be followed by the corresponding sacrifice of a bull[34] at a heap of ash known as "the altar of Zeus," which was to serve as the finishing-point of the single-course foot race that came after these sacrifices (in fact the early stadium at Olympia ended at the altar of Zeus).[35] As Pausanias observes (5.13.1), the preeminence of Pelops among all the heroes involved in the sacrifices at Olympia corresponded to the preeminence of Zeus among all the gods. Thus the inaugural set of sacrifices to Pelops and to Zeus, before the foot race, unites the hero and god in a "polar tension,"[36] while the foot race itself "presupposes the bloody act of killing."[37] Moreover, from an aetiological point of view the foot race was actually part of the overall sacrifice, as we learn from the observation, made by Philostratus, that the sacrifice to Zeus was not complete until the foot race was won:

στάδιον δὲ ὧδε εὕρηται· θυσάντων Ἠλείων ὁπόσα νομίζουσι, διέκειντο μὲν ἐπὶ τοῦ βωμοῦ τὰ ἱερά, πῦρ δὲ αὐτοῖς οὔπω ἐνέκειτο. στάδιον δὲ οἱ δρομεῖς ἀπεῖχον τοῦ βωμοῦ καὶ εἱστήκει πρὸ αὐτοῦ ἱερεὺς λαμπαδίῳ βραβεύων· καὶ ὁ νικῶν ἐμπυρίσας τὰ ἱερὰ ὀλυμπιονίκης ἀπῄει.

Philostratus On Gymnastics 5

And the single-course foot race [**stadion**] was instituted in the following way.[38] After the Eleans had completed all their customary sacrifices [to Zeus], the consecrated parts would lie on the altar, though not as yet set on fire. The runners would stand at a distance of one stadium [**stadion**] from the altar, in front of which there was a priest signalling the start with a torch. And the winner would set fire to the consecrated parts and then depart as an Olympic victor.[39]

32. Burkert 1983.95–98. Datings for the introduction of various athletic events in the Olympics: Pausanias 5.8.6–7 (on which see Huxley 1975.38–39).

33. See Pausanias 5.13.1–2, and the comments of Burkert, p. 98.

34. Burkert, p. 98n25.

35. Burkert, p. 97. Such sacrifices in the context of the Olympics, as Burkert notes (p. 96), would have had smaller-scale analogues in the context of epichoric ritual practices at Olympia on occasions other than the Olympics.

36. Burkert, p. 97.

37. Burkert, p. 98.

38. The wording here indicates clearly that the author is concerned not so much with describing current athletic practice as with indicating the aetiology that accompanies athletic practice.

39. The translation follows Burkert, p. 97. Note the parallel wording adduced by Burkert, p. 97n22, from an inscription concerning institutional procedures at Delphi (as funded by

Another athletic event that counted as part of the overall scenario of sacrifice was the **diaulos**, a double-course foot race that followed the foot race of the **stadion** and was twice the **stadion** in length (this athletic event of the **diaulos** was apparently introduced in the Olympics at 724 B.C.).[40] Again, we turn to the description by Philostratus:

ἐπεὶ δὲ Ἠλεῖοι θύσειαν, ἔδει μὲν καὶ τοὺς ἀπαντῶντας Ἑλλήνων θύειν θεωρούς. ὡς δὲ μὴ ἀργῶς ἡ πρόσοδος αὐτῶν γίγνοιτο, ἔτρεχον οἱ δρομεῖς ἀπὸ τοῦ βωμοῦ στάδιον οἷον καλοῦντες τὸ Ἑλληνικὸν καὶ πάλιν εἰς ταὐτὸν ὑπέστρεφον οἷον ἀγγέλλοντες, ὅτι δὴ ἀφίξοιτο ἡ Ἑλλὰς χαίρουσα. ταῦτα μὲν οὖν περὶ διαύλου αἰτίας.

Philostratus On Gymnastics 6

When the Eleans made their sacrifice [i.e., the sacrifice to Zeus, where the winner of the **stadion** set fire to the consecrated parts], all the Greek envoys present had to sacrifice. But in order that their procession not be delayed,[41] the runners ran one stadium-length away from the altar [of Zeus], as if calling on the Greeks [= the envoys] to come, then turned and ran back as if to announce that all Greece was arriving to share in the joy. So much for the aetiology [**aitiā**] of the double course [**diaulos**].[42]

Burkert concludes about the foot race of the **stadion**:[43]

The end of the race, its goal, is the top of the ancient heap of ash [= the altar of Zeus], the place where fire must blaze and burn up the [thigh-portions].[44] The race marks the transition from blood to purifying fire,[45]

Eumenes II), LSS 44.15: ὁ δὲ δρόμος γινέσθω ... ἄχρι ποτὶ τὸν βωμόν, ὁ δὲ νικέων ὑφαπτέτω τὰ ἱερά 'the running is to extend up to the altar, and the winner is to set fire to the consecrated parts'. I am puzzled by the translation in LSJ s.v. ὑφάπτω: 'is to set the fire for lighting the sacred lamps'.

40. Datings for the introduction of various athletic events in the Olympics: Pausanias 5.8.6–7.

41. Note the translation of ὡς δὲ μὴ ἀργῶς ἡ πρόσοδος αὐτῶν γίγνοιτο by Jüthner 1909.139: "Damit aber deren Ankunft nicht ohne Zeremoniell vor sich gehe. . . ."

42. Translation after Burkert, p. 97, who notes (p. 100) that the portent recounted in Herodotus 1.59.1 about Hippokrates, father of the tyrant Peisistratos of Athens, must be understood as taking place immediately after the Olympic event of the **diaulos**, as the envoys were approaching the altar of Zeus. Hippokrates was one of these envoys, and as he approached, the water inside the sacrificial cauldrons (presumably at the altar of Zeus) started to boil before the application of fire. This portent seems to have conveyed the idea that the very presence of Hippokrates, as the future father of Peisistratos, was the equivalent of the Olympic victor's fire that was required to start the sacrifices at the altar of Zeus.

43. Burkert, p. 98.

44. I substitute 'thigh-portions' for 'thigh-bones', on the basis of the discussion in N 1979.216–217 (following Gill 1974).

45. On purification as transition, consider the semantics of Latin *pūrgō* 'purify', the etymology of which, according to Thurneysen 1912–1913, is *pūrigō* 'carry [verb *agō*] fire [*pūr*, as

from encountering death to the joyful satisfaction of surviving as manifested in the strength of the victor.[46] Thus, the most important [athletic event] at Olympia is part of a sacrificial act moving between the **Pelopion** and the altar of Zeus.

In other words the transition from the pollution of bloodshed to the purification of fire is a transition from participating in death to experiencing a life after death as manifested in the victory of the athlete and as symbolized by the sacrificial fire that he lights at the altar of Zeus.[47]

This foot race, then, framed by the set of sacrifices at the precinct of Pelops and at the altar of Zeus, is the ritual core of the Olympics. We can see the deeper significance of this ritual core as a diachronic feature of initiation by following through on Burkert's argument[48] that the very festival of the Olympics was from the earliest times onward correlated with a myth that told how the hero Pelops was killed, dismembered, and served up by his father Tantalos as sacrificial meat boiled inside a tripod cauldron, to be eaten by the gods — only to be reassembled and brought back to life inside the same sacrificial cauldron by the agency of these same gods.[49] Burkert adduces a crucial parallel:[50] the athletic festival of the Lykaia in Arcadia was aetiologically correlated with a myth that told how Arkas, the eponymous ancestor of all the Arcadians, was killed and served up by his grandfather Lykaon as

---

attested in Oscan *pūr*, Umbrian *pīr*, and Greek **pūr**]'. The context of **pūr agere* 'carry fire' is actually attested in a ritual recorded in the *Iguvine Tables* (Ib 12), where fire is being carried in a portable altar or brazier called an *ahti-* (from verb *agō*). See N 1974b.105.

46. Burkert's formulation can be more fully appreciated in light of the following observation on the typology of initiation: "Just as pollution is disease and disease is death, so purification is a renewal of life" (Thomson 1946.93).

47. On the symbolism of fire as victory, see p. 124 on the portent presaging the Panhellenic importance of the birth of Peisistratos: the fire of the victor is here made analogous to the begetting of the tyrant. Note too that the Greek word **kratos** designates not only political and military power but also athletic victory (cf. N 1979.90 §37n6). For a parallel thought pattern, consider the Roman aetiology for the games known as the *Compitālia*, a word derived from *com-pitum* 'crossroads', further derived from *com-petō* 'meet, come together; compete with others in pursuit of a given honor' (for the latter definition, see Nonius Marcellus 276.10 Lindsay). According to this aetiology, as reported by Pliny the Elder (*Natural History* 36.204), the games of the *Compitālia* were founded by Servius Tullius, a primaeval king of Rome who was begotten by a flaming phallus that appeared out of the royal hearth tended at the time by his mother; young Servius succeeded to the kingship when it was discovered that his head lit up while he slept (for more on this myth, see N 1974b.96–100). The aetiology specifically accounts for the foundation of the games as resulting from the belief that Servius Tullius had thus been begotten by the *Lār familiāris* 'the ancestral spirit of the family' of the previous king, Tarquinius Priscus (Pliny ibid.). Moreover, it is specified that Servius Tullius founded the games in honor of the *Lārēs* 'ancestral spirits' (ibid.).

48. Burkert 1983.100.

49. A survey of testimonia in Burkert, p. 99n32.

50. Burkert, p. 100.

sacrificial meat to be eaten by the gods — only to be brought back to life by Zeus.[51] It so happens that the pan-Arcadian athletic festival of the Lykaia, as Burkert has demonstrated, is a network of rituals and myths that are overtly characteristic of initiation into adulthood,[52] so that the very parallelism of the aetiological myth of Arkas with the myth of Pelops can be taken as a particularly telling point in support of Burkert's arguments concerning reflexes of initiation practices in the Olympics.

Specifically, as Burkert shows, the myth of the slaughter of Pelops must have been an **aition** correlated with the ritual of the slaughter of the black ram at the precinct of Pelops. In the myth the only part of the dismembered Pelops that was actually eaten by the gods was the hero's shoulder, consumed by Demeter, which was later replaced with an ivory piece in his reintegrated body.[53] Here we see a specific **aition** for the ritual reverence of the ivory shoulder blade of Pelops, a larger-than-life cult object on display at Olympia (Pausanias 5.13.4–6),[54] in that the shoulder blade of the slaughtered hero is analogous to the shoulder blade of slaughtered rams: in ancient Greece, as Burkert points out, "a ram's shoulder blade played a special part in the sacrifice of a ram."[55] Burkert notes that Demeter, who had eaten the hero's shoulder in the myth, also figures in the rituals of the Olympics: the priestess of Demeter occupied a special place at the Games (Pausanias 6.20.9).[56] Burkert concludes: "Thus, the Olympic ritual combines the very [figures] that went together in the myth — Pelops, Zeus, and Demeter. The cannibalistic myth of Pelops that so shocked Pindar clearly refers to the Olympic festival."[57]

I propose two qualifications. First, Pindar's "shock" is a poetic convention that allows the subordination of one myth, the dismemberment and reintegration of Pelops, to another myth. Second, the myth of Pelops' dismemberment and reintegration need not be viewed as an **aition** for the Olympic festival as a whole. True, it suits admirably the oldest aspect of the

51. On the dismemberment and eating of Lykaon by the gods, see Hesiod F 163 MW (and the comments by Burkert, pp. 86–87). On the revival of Lykaon, see [Eratosthenes] *Katasterismoi* (*Fragmenta Vaticana* ed. Rehm), p. 2 (and the comments by Burkert, p. 87n20).

52. Burkert, pp. 84–93. Note his discussion of age divisions at p. 90 and of expulsion/impulsion rituals at p. 92. I would draw special attention to this observation (p. 92): "The younger members of the rising generation had to be forced away into the wild 'outdoors' while the [older] twenty-five-year-olds, now marriageable, entered athletic competitions." In other words age classes could be differentiated by way of overt vs. stylized separation (i.e., rustication vs. athletics, respectively).

53. Sources in Burkert 1983.99n32: most notably Bacchylides F 42 SM, Euripides *Iphigeneia in Tauris* 386–388, Lycophron 152–155, Apollodorus *Epitome* 2.3.

54. Burkert, p. 99n30 cites further sources.

55. Burkert, p. 100, with documentation.

56. Burkert, p. 100 and n34.

57. Burkert, p. 100.

festival, the foot race of the **stadion** as framed by the sacrifices at the precinct of Pelops and at the altar of Zeus. But we must keep in mind that the Olympics kept evolving with later accretions of further and further athletic events, and that the ritual features of these events would have required a corresponding evolution in aetiology, with later accretions of myths.

For example, let us take the athletic event of the chariot race at the Olympics, supposedly introduced there in the year 680;[58] whether or not this date is exact,[59] until the introduction of the chariot race only the victors of the foot race had been consecutively recorded since the year 776.[60] Corresponding to the athletic event of the chariot race is an **aition**, the myth of the life-and-death chariot race of Pelops with Oinomaos. The death of Oinomaos, resulting from the race, led to the foundation of the Olympics by Pelops, according to one version of this myth.[61] As an **aition** for the foundation of the Olympics with special reference to the chariot race, the myth of the death of Oinomaos would at first seem to be at odds with the myth of the death of Pelops, an **aition** with special reference to the foot race. But in fact the two layers of myths are integrated into a sequence, just like the two layers of athletic events. Pelops had his chariot race with Oinomaos *after* he had been restored to life, as I argue on the basis of the narrative sequence in Pindar's *Olympian* 1.

The very activity of a chariot race, as an athletic event — which one would expect to be conceived in myth as a custom resulting from a hero's death—[62] is instead treated in the myth of Pelops as a preexisting institution. Oinomaos is represented as customarily challenging each of the suitors of his daughter, Hippodameia, to a chariot race to the death, where the loser had to forfeit his life; in a fragment from Hesiod (F 259a MW) we witness a reverse victory list of successive suitors who had in this way lost their lives to Oinomaos. The race between Pelops and Oinomaos, however, transforms the preexisting institution from the standpoint of the myth: with the death of Oinomaos the "old institution" with its consecutive series of losers *before Pelops* becomes a "new institution" with its consecutive series of winners *after Pelops*. The "new institution" clearly is based on the death of Oinomaos; but what about the "old institution"? We must keep in mind that the "new institution" of the chariot race, from an aetiological standpoint, is

58. Pausanias 5.8.7; this date seems to parallel the era when chariot fighting was becoming obsolescent in warfare. I owe this insight to J. L. Bentz.

59. Burkert 1983.95n9 gives bibliography on counterarguments in favor of an earlier date. On the role of chariots as a mark of aristocratic prestige, see Connor 1987.47–49, especially with reference to Strabo 10.1.10 C448 (p. 49).

60. Burkert, p. 95.

61. Cf. p. 119.

62. Consider the general aetiologies connected with the four Panhellenic Games, as discussed above.

also "new" by opposition to the genuinely older institution of the foot race, which is based on the death of Pelops. What is more, the chariot race of Pelops happens *after* this same death in the narrative. Thus the "old" institution of the life-and-death chariot race could be considered equivalent, in terms of the myth, to the genuinely older institution of the foot race on the level of ritual: in the chicken-and-egg pattern of myth making,[63] the death of Pelops could motivate the competition in which Pelops competes.[64] The death of Oinomaos in this competition could then motivate the successive competitions of the athletic event of the Olympic chariot race founded by Pelops.

Even in the later **aition** about the chariot race of Pelops and Oinomaos, however, there is a narrative connection with the earlier **aition** about the death of Pelops. The story has it that Oinomaos would sacrifice a ram before his chariot race with each suitor and let the suitor have a head start until the consecrated parts of the meat were consumed by fire; then he would chase after the suitor, catch up with him, and kill him.[65] This theme, by being parallel to the Olympic ritual of the ram's slaughter at the precinct of Pelops, is thereby also parallel to the Olympic myth about the slaughter of Pelops. In this way the older **aition** about the slaughter of Pelops leaves its signature on the newer **aition** about the chariot race of Pelops.[66]

The integration of an older **aition** that motivates the foot race with an expanded newer **aition** that motivates both the foot race and the chariot race leads to modifications or reshapings of the older **aition**. Thus, for example, the setting of the cannibalistic feast of the gods is shifted from Olympia in the Peloponnesus to Sipylos in Asia Minor;[67] this shift, as attested in Pindar's *Olympian* 1,[68] makes room for the chariot race of Pelops as the central **aition**, at Olympia, of the Olympics proper.[69] I see no reason to ascribe this shift to Pindar's invention[70] since it is in keeping with the Panhellenic prestige of the

---

63. On which see N 1974b.77.

64. Cf. N 1979.284 on the aetiological significance of the myth concerning the death of Aesop at Delphi: "The *Life of Aesop* tradition actually presents the death of Aesop as a *cause* of the First Sacred War, but the institutional reality that Aesop reproaches — namely, that the people of Delphi are sacred to Apollo — is a lasting *effect* of the First Sacred War. From the standpoint of the myth, the death of Aesop is the *effect* of his reproaching the institutions of Delphi; from the standpoint of these institutions, on the other hand, his death is their indirect *cause*. It is this sort of 'cause' that qualifies as an **aition**."

65. Diodorus 4.73.4; cf. Burkert 1983.98.

66. I note in passing the use of the word *signature* by Derrida 1972.393.

67. Burkert 1983.99n33.

68. Pindar *Olympian* 1.38.

69. Moreover the "new" setting in Asia Minor is perfectly in keeping with evolving patterns of myths about the origins of Peloponnesian dynasties. These patterns tend to augment the political prestige of Sparta and to diminish that of Argos: see pp. 294 and following.

70. *Pace* Burkert, p. 99.

chariot race as the central event of the Olympics in Pindar's time: I cite the testimonia of the Kypselos chest of about 570 B.C.[71] and the pedimental sculptures on the East side of the Temple of Zeus at Olympia.[72] In fact I prefer to think that the mythological rearrangements in *Olympian* 1 reflect the evolving aetiology of the Olympics.[73]

The most remarkable of these rearrangements in *Olympian* 1 is a narrative reordering, whereby the story about the dismemberment of Pelops is ostentatiously subordinated to a story that starts with his abduction by Poseidon, which leads into the story about the chariot race of Pelops. The key to this rearrangement is the detail about the ivory shoulder of Pelops in *Olympian* 1.27, which can be correlated with the cult object of the larger-than-life ivory shoulder blade of Pelops as described by Pausanias 5.13.4–6.

The story of the dismemberment of Pelops by Tantalos and the eating of his flesh by the gods is being ostentatiously rejected as a "false" substitute for the "true" story of the abduction and rape of Pelops by Poseidon (Pindar *Olympian* 1.28–29, 30–42, 46–53).[74] And yet, the "true" story turns out to be aetiologically equivalent to the rejected "false" story. In the "true" story as well, Pelops undergoes a process of symbolized "death" and "rebirth," since his being abducted and sexually forced by Poseidon is a scenario of initiation into adulthood.[75] As Jean-Pierre Vernant has observed,[76] there is a striking analogue attested in some legally sanctioned customs of Crete (Ephorus FGH

71. Burkert, p. 95; cf. Pausanias 5.17.7. For a slightly different dating, see Roller 1981b.109–110.

72. Burkert ibid.

73. My views here differ from what is found in the available commentaries on Pindar, which favor the idea that substantial parts of the myths related in *Olympian* 1 were the poet's own personal invention. For an example of this different view, see Lefkowitz 1976.81–82. For a systematic argumentation along these lines, see Köhnken 1974. I interpret σὲ δ' ἀντία προτέρων φθέγξομαι at *Olympian* 1.36 as 'I shall call upon you [= Pelops] in the presence of the predecessors', that is, with the past tradition as witness; for ἀντία in the juridical sense of 'in the presence of', cf. ἀντία σεῦ 'in your presence' in Herodotus 7.209.2; also καλίον ἀντὶ μαιτύρον 'summoning in the presence of witnesses' in the *Gortynian Code* (e.g., 1.41 [ed. Willetts], etc.). Others interpret ἀντία προτέρων in the sense of 'contrary to the predecessors' (e.g., Slater 1969.57), as if Pindar were contradicting the tradition that came before him. On **proteroi** 'predecessors, men of the past' as designating the tellers of the tradition (e.g., Pindar *Pythian* 3.80), see p. 200. Instead of 'contrary to the predecessors', I propose a slightly modified interpretation, 'in rivalry with the predecessors', which is compatible with 'in the presence of the predecessors' inasmuch as the present performance, in agonistic pride, calls to witness all past performances to validate its own truth. Further, this present truth is to be witnessed not only by the past but also by the future (*Olympian* 1.33–34).

74. On the contrast of **alēthea** 'true' versus **pseudea** 'false' at *Olympian* 1.28–32, see p. 65; there I argue that the version designated by **alēthea** is Panhellenic. As such, this version is appropriately the program of the Olympics.

75. This point is effectively argued by Calame 1977 I 421–427 and by Sergent 1984.75–84.

76. Vernant 1969.13–14. See also Sergent 1984.80–81.

70 F 149 by way of Strabo 10.4.21 C483–484),[77] where a boy can be abducted, sexually forced, and thereafter reintegrated with his society by an older citizen, who is then obliged to present the boy with various legally specified gifts (Ephorus ibid.). A final sacrifice, also legally specified (ibid.), underscores the institutional and even ritual nature of the proceedings. The diachronic features of initiation are perhaps most overt in the period of segregation, legally limited to two months in duration: after the boy is abducted, sexually forced, and taken away to the abductor's **andrōn** 'men's house', he is taken by his abductor into the wilderness, where men and boys spend their time hunting (ibid.). After this period of marginal activity, the boy is returned to his society as a man: one of the legally prescribed gifts that he then gets from his abductor is military equipment, as befits an adult warrior (ibid.).[78] Similarly with Pelops: after the boy is abducted, sexually forced, and taken to his divine abductor's home on Olympus,[79] the young hero receives from Poseidon the gift of a magnificent chariot team (Pindar *Olympian* 1.86–87). It is with this chariot team that Pelops wins his race against Oinomaos,[80] and the hand of Hippodameia, and thereby inaugurates a kingship that serves as a model of political power and sovereignty by virtue of being the ideological foundation for the royal Peloponnesian dynasties of Argos, Sparta, and Messene.[81] There is even an analogy with the Cretan boy's period of segregation: before Pelops gets his chariot team, he is expelled from his abductor's home on Olympus and banished to a place that is as yet foreign to him, the Peloponnesus.[82]

Pelops is expelled from Olympus because of a crime committed by his father Tantalos against the gods: according to Pindar's *Olympian* 1, Tantalos had stolen nectar and ambrosia from the gods and given some to his human

77. Cf. Brelich 1969.198–200. For evidence that these customs in Crete have antecedents reaching back into the second millennium B.C.: Koehl 1986.

78. For more on the Ephorus passage, see Sergent 1984.15–53.

79. On the topic of Poseidon's home on Olympus, as it figures in this story, see Köhnken 1974.204.

80. On the pertinence of this theme to Hieron in *Olympian* 1, see Köhnken, p. 205: after having won in the single-horse competition of 476 B.C., the tyrant is looking forward to winning a future Olympic victory in the chariot competition.

81. On the dynastic transition from Pelopidai to Herakleidai, representing the royal houses of Argos, Sparta, and Messene, see pp. 299 and following. The essence of Pelops as the archetype of political power and sovereignty in the Peloponnesus is clear from such indications as the passing of the **skēptron** 'scepter' from Zeus to Hermes to Pelops to Atreus to Thyestes to Agamemnon in *Iliad* II 100–108. The very name of the Peloponneus, the island of Pelops (cf. Tyrtaeus 2.15 W), bears out the status of Pelops as the prototypical king and authority (cf. West 1985.159); cf. Apollodorus *Epitome* 2.11, where the people of Mycenae install Atreus and Thyestes after being told by an oracle to choose a descendant of Pelops as their king.

82. In this "foreign" land, Poseidon helps Pelops succeed in his exploits. At *Olympian* 1.24 the Peloponnesus is described as the **apoikiā** 'settlement' of Pelops. After this ordeal in the chariot race, the Peloponnesus finally becomes his new home.

drinking companions (60–64).[83] Here we see the potential for a narrative substitution: the story about Tantalos' stealing of nectar and ambrosia serves as a functional equivalent of the story about his crime of creating a scene of cannibalism. In both cases Tantalos perverts the reciprocity of the feast by serving up inappropriate categories of food. In Pindar's retelling, however, the wording conveys a sense of both stories.[84] Having access to the ultimate food of nectar and ambrosia, the insatiable Tantalos is described as not being able literally to 'digest' his happiness:

> ἀλλὰ γὰρ καταπέψαι | μέγαν ὄλβον οὐκ ἐδυνάσθη, κόρῳ δ' ἕλεν | ἄταν ὑπέροπλον

> Pindar *Olympian* 1.55–57

He [Tantalos] could not digest his great bliss [**olbos**],[85] and, with his insatiability [**koros**],[86] he brought upon himself an overwhelming disaster [**atē**].

We are reminded of the witch who lived in the candy house in the story of Hänsel and Gretel: having access to the ultimate food, she lusts to eat the flesh of plump children.[87]

83. We may contrast the story of the abduction and rape of Ganymede by Zeus in *Homeric Hymn to Aphrodite* 200–217. In this case the boy never leaves Olympus (nor does he ever become a man), and the gift of a magnificent chariot team goes not to him but to his father — a fitting compensation for permanently losing the boy. I consider this story a variant, just as the story of the abduction and rape of Pelops by Poseidon must be considered a variant. It is methodologically unsound to insist that one variant is the exemplum and the other, the imitation.

84. I see no reason to argue that the story about Tantalos' perverted sharing of nectar and ambrosia was an invention of Pindar. That Tantalos had received the gift of nectar and ambrosia — a gift that he proceeded to misuse — can be analyzed as a traditional story pattern where (1) the gods wrong a mortal, (2) the mortal is given a divine gift in compensation for the wrong, (3) the mortal misuses the gift, thereby wronging the gods, and (4) the gods punish the mortal and take back the gift. It may be that Tantalos' gift of nectar and ambrosia from the gods was viewed as a payment in compensation for the gods' having taken Pelops to Olympus, just as the gift of a chariot team to the father of Ganymede was in compensation for the gods' having taken Ganymede to Olympus (see n83). Then, after Tantalos wrongs the gods, the gift is taken back and Pelops is expelled from Olympus. The compensation that was owed to Tantalos, so long as Pelops stayed on Olympus, now reverts to Pelops, once he is released, just as the abducted Cretan boy is compensated by his abductor upon being released. Thus Pelops gets the gift of a chariot team.

85. On the semantics of **olbos** 'good fortune, bliss' and **olbios** 'fortunate, blissful', see pp. 243 and following.

86. On **koros** as 'insatiability', see p. 292.

87. I owe this parallel to J. F. Nagy. It may well be that even the story of Tantalos' perverted feeding of human flesh to the gods — not just the story of his feeding nectar and ambrosia to mortals — presupposes that Tantalos had enjoyed the ultimate bliss of having access to nectar and ambrosia in the first place.

Thus the Pindaric retelling of the Tantalos story, though it steers away from the theme of cannibalism, still bears the signature of this theme. Besides the image of "digesting" just noted, there is also that of 'boiling' one's youthful vitality for an excessively long time, presumably just as fresh meat loses its vitality from overboiling. Pelops is pictured as using this image in the context of asking Poseidon for the gift of a chariot team and declaring to the god his desire to risk death in his quest for the hand of Hippodameia:

> ὁ μέγας δὲ κίνδυνος ἄναλκιν οὐ φῶτα λαμβάνει. | θανεῖν δ' οἷσιν ἀνάγκα, τά κέ τις ἀνώνυμον | γῆρας ἐν σκότῳ καθήμενος ἕψοι μάταν, | ἁπάντων καλῶν ἄμμορος ἀλλ' ἐμοὶ μὲν οὗτος ἄεθλος ὑποκείσεται.

> Pindar *Olympian* 1.81–85

Great risk does not take hold of any cowardly mortal. But if it is destined for humans to die, why should anyone sit around in the darkness and boil away his life to a futile old age without a name, having no share [**ammoros**] in all the beautiful things of the world?[88] I will undertake this ordeal [**aethlos**] at hand.

Clearly the crucial theme of death as an aetiological analogue of initiation into adulthood has been transferred from the story of Pelops in the cauldron to the story of Pelops in the chariot race, but the imagery of the cauldron has been ostentatiously retained. Even more remarkable is the incomplete replacement of the story of Pelops in the cauldron by the story of Pelops in the chariot race. Although the voice of Pindar rejects the first story as "false," the second and "true" story is begun with a detail from the first: Poseidon fell in love with Pelops as the young hero was taken 'out of a purifying cauldron' by the goddess of fate, the **Moira** called Klotho (καθαροῦ λέβητος *Olympian* 1.26).[89] Even more, Pelops is described in this same context as *having a shoulder of ivory* (*Olympian* 1.27: ἐλέφαντι φαίδιμον ὦμον κεκαδμένον). This detail presupposes the myth that tells how Demeter mis-

---

88. One of the anonymous referees for the earlier version of this presentation points out that the word **ammoros** 'having no share' in this passage may convey yet another image of eating; on the semantics of **moira** and related words in the sense of 'share, portion' of meat, see N 1979.134–135. I quote from the referee's incisive remarks: "Pelops, sitting by the cauldron of his stewing old age, cannot get a name for himself because he does not *reach* in and 'get his share'—the champion's portion." On the theme of the champion's portion of meat in Greek and Irish traditions, see N 1979.133§19n4.

89. On the purification in the cauldron, we may compare the formulation of Thomson quoted at p. 125. My interpretation of ἐπεί at line 26 as 'after' rather than 'since' is supported by the wording of Pindar *Olympian* 1.46–48, to be discussed further at p. 134. On the associations of Klotho with the theme of birth, see Köhnken 1983.70; I find it unnecessary, however, to deny the associations of Klotho with the theme of rebirth.

takenly ate the shoulder of the dismembered Pelops, which then had to be replaced with the artifact made of ivory.[90] Thus the aetiological sequence of the composite myth that motivates the Olympics is maintained, even though the aetiological emphasis is shifted.

The maintenance of the aetiological sequence of the Olympics in Pindar's *Olympian* 1 is at the cost of a narrative inconsistency in terms of the professed "true" story: the emergence of Pelops from the cauldron, ivory shoulder and all, just *before* his abduction by Poseidon (*Olympian* 1.25–27), gives the impression that, even from the standpoint of *Olympian* 1, there were two perverted feasts of Tantalos. It is as if Tantalos first fed human flesh to the immortals *before* the abduction of Pelops and then fed nectar and ambrosia to mortals *after* the abduction. This impression is "false" in terms of the professed "true" story of *Olympian* 1, but the sequence of two perverted feasts, one before and one after the abduction, may be valid in terms of the accretive aetiological program of the Olympics.[91] The full aetiological sequence is reinforced by the description of the feast at which Poseidon fell in love with Pelops as the youth emerged from the cauldron with his ivory shoulder, where the wording fits the context of the "first" feast (*Olympian* 1.37–40). In terms of the "true" story of *Olympian* 1, however, the two stories of the two perverted feasts must be alternatives, and Pindar's composition in fact treats them that way, explicitly rejecting one of the stories as "false" (= ABC) in favor of the other, which is "true" (= A′B′C′):

A Tantalos perverts feast by serving up inappropriate food
   (the flesh of Pelops) to immortals.
B Tantalos is punished by gods.
C Pelops survives cauldron.
   Pelops abducted by Poseidon.
   Tantalos gets nectar and ambrosia (as compensation?).

A′ Tantalos perverts feast by serving up inappropriate food
   (nectar and ambrosia) to mortals.
B′ Tantalos is punished by gods.
   Pelops is exiled from Olympus to Peloponnesus.
   Pelops calls on Poseidon for help.
C′ Pelops survives chariot race against Oinomaos.
   Pelops settles Peloponnesus.

In fact the rejection of the "false" story is already being introduced immediately after mention of the emergence of Pelops from the cauldron:

---

90. Cf. p. 126.
91. Cf. Hubbard 1987.9–11, who posits a parallel narrative sequence of two feasts in the Hesiodic treatment of the Prometheus myth.

ἦ θαύματα πολλά, καί πού τι καὶ βροτῶν | φάτις ὑπὲρ τὸν ἀλαθῆ
λόγον | δεδαιδαλμένοι ψεύδεσι ποικίλοις ἐξαπατῶντι μῦθοι

Pindar *Olympian* 1.27–29

Indeed there are many wondrous things. And the words that men tell,
myths [**mūthoi**] embellished by varied falsehoods, beyond wording
that is true [**alēthēs**], are deceptive.[92]

Still the details about the cauldron and the ivory shoulder, parts of the "false"
story, are linked with the details about the abduction of Pelops by Poseidon,
parts of the "true" story.[93] To paraphrase: "When the god saw you emerging
from the cauldron, with your shoulder of ivory, then it was that Poseidon
abducted you." The prominent details of the "false" story are but a momen-
tary flash: Poseidon abducts Pelops immediately after the young hero
emerges from the cauldron (ἐπεί at *Olympian* 1.26).[94]

With the *immediate* disappearance of Pelops, the "false" story about the
cannibalization can spread at the expense of the "true" story about the abduction:

ὡς δ' ἄφαντος ἔπελες, | . . . ἔννεπε κρυφᾷ τις αὐτίκα φθονερῶν
γειτόνων, | . . . ὅτι . . .

Pindar *Olympian* 1.46–48

As soon as you disappeared, immediately one of the envious
[**phthoneroi**][95] neighbors said stealthily that . . .

What 'steals' into the story is the rejected idea that Pelops had in fact never
emerged from the cauldron. At the same time, what 'steals' into Pindar's
own story is the ostentatiously rejected "false" story of Pelops in the cauldron. The aetiology of the Olympics amounts to a combination of the "false"
and the "true" stories, in the sequence ABCA′B′C′, with the subordination
of the "false" ABC to the "true" A′B′C′.

I stress again that Pindar's story even begins with a detail from the
"false" story, namely, the ivory shoulder of Pelops.[96] The detail of the ivory

92. On the connotations of **mūthoi** 'myths' in this passage, see p. 65.

93. Bundy 1972.70 writes: "Once [Pindar] has given his audience a familiar frame of reference, he can find this version not to his liking and dismiss it for another." Bundy's opinion is
that Pindar's preferred version is not one of his own making, and that it is less widely known
than the rejected version (ibid.). I agree with the first part of this opinion and disagree with the
second. Cf. p. 65.

94. My interpretation of ἐπεί here as 'after' rather than 'since' is supported by the wording of
Pindar *Olympian* 1.46–48, to be explained in what immediately follows.

95. On the programmatic use of the adjective **phthoneros** 'begrudging, envious' in the diction
of praise poetry to designate the generic opponent of praise poetry, see N 1979.223–232.

96. Bundy 1972.71n79 writes: "Although Pindar's purposes here require that he rejects this
version, yet the detail of the ivory shoulder is too good to spare, both for enhancing the beauty of

shoulder, which is out of joint with the "true" story of Pindar's *Olympian* 1, is also out of joint with the rest of Pelops' body. So too in the ritual dimension: we recall the larger-than-life size of the cult object venerated as Pelops' ivory shoulder at Olympia.[97] Yet just as the ivory shoulder of Pelops was on display as a centerpiece in the ritual complex of the Olympics, so it occupies primacy of place in the aetiological complex of Pindar's *Olympian* 1.

Pelops as inspirational to Poseidon's love and for making us aware of the power of art irrationally to persuade men's minds by directing them toward outward beauty and away from inner truth."

97. Cf. p. 126.

5 ▣▣ The Ordeal of the Athlete
and the Burden of the Poet

H aving contemplated the ritual ideology of athletic events in one particular festival from among the four seasonally recurring Panhellenic Games that produced the victors celebrated by the lyric poetry of Pindar, we may proceed to consider how this poetry formally relates itself to such ritual ideology.

A prominent word used in the lyric poetry of Pindar and elsewhere for the concept of athletic event is **agōn** (e.g., Pindar *Olympian* 1.7), apparently derived from the root **ag-** of **agō** as in **sun-agō** 'bring together, assemble, gather'.[1] The notion of 'assemble' is intrinsic to the general sense of **agōn**, that is, 'assembly' (e.g., Pindar *Pythian* 10.30). This meaning is still preserved in various contexts, from which we can see that there can be 'assemblies' of not just people but even, for example, ships (e.g., *Iliad* XV 428). But in numerous other contexts the word specifically means 'contest' (e.g., Pindar *Olympian* 9.90). Thus **agōn** conveys not only the social setting for an activity, namely, an assembly of people, but also the activity itself, namely, a contest. The implicitness of the notion of contest in the word for 'assembly' reflects a basic institutional reality about the ancient Greeks:[2] whenever they came together in whatever was called an **agōn**, they competed.[3] Using this word **agōn**, Nietzsche in fact characterized competitive-

---

1. Chantraine DELG 17.
2. I use *institution* in the sense adopted by Benveniste 1969.
3. For an institutional parallel as reflected by the Latin language, see p. 125 on the semantics of *com-petō*.

ness, this fundamental aspect of ancient Greek society, as *der agonale Geist*.[4] The notion of competition built into **agōn** is admirably reflected in the English borrowing *antagonism*.[5] To think of **agōn** as 'athletic contest', however, would be to understand but one aspect of the ancient Greek *agonale Geist*. The word applies not only to athletic but also to martial activity.[6] Moreover, it applies to poetic or rhetorical activity.[7] The ritual aspect of these activities is suggested by attestations of the derivative word **agōniā** in the sense of 'agony' (e.g., Demosthenes *On the Crown* 33, "Aristotle" *Problems* 869b6). Instead of the English borrowing *agony*, however, I prefer to use the word *ordeal*, which connotes not only the personal but also the ritual aspect of the **agōn** as a process diachronically characteristic of initiation into adulthood.[8]

The ritual aspect of the **agōn** is elucidated by another word, **aethlos** or **āthlos**,[9] which is likewise used in the sense of 'contest' in referring to the activities of athletics (e.g., Herodotus 5.22.2) and war (e.g., 1.67.1). A closely related word is **aethlon** or **āthlon**, meaning 'prize to be won in a contest';[10] a derivative is **āthlētēs**, meaning 'athlete' (the English word is a borrowing from the Greek). That this word **aethlos** carries with it the sense of ritual is already clear from the epithet that characterizes it: **hieros** 'sacred' (Pindar *Olympian* 8.64, 13.15). More than that: in Pindaric usage **aethlos** applies equally to the contests of athletes and to the life-and-death ordeals of heroes. We have already seen from the myth of the chariot race of Pelops that the ordeals of heroes on the level of myth correspond aetiologically to the contests of athletes on the level of ritual, in that the myths can motivate the rituals. Now we see that a word like **aethlos** can collapse the very distinction between the myth and the ritual. Thus when Pelops embarks upon

4. Background in Burkert 1985.105. See also Martin 1983.65–76 on the Greek notion of contest as a solution to problems.

5. Cf. **agōnismos** 'rivalry' in Thucydides 7.70.3.

6. See Brelich 1961 on the ritual parallelism of these two activities. Note especially the reference to war as **arēïos agōn** 'the **agōn** of Ares' in Herodotus 9.33.3. On the ritual dimensions of early Greek land warfare: Connor 1988, following Burkert 1985.169–170.

7. On **agōn** as a festival of contests in poetry, see *Homeric Hymn* 6.19–20. On **agōn** as a festival of contests in athletics *and* in poetry, song, and dance, see *Homeric Hymn to Apollo* 149–150 and Thucydides 3.10.3/5. On the state-supported Athenian institution of the **agōn epitaphios** in honor of the war-dead, featuring contests in athletics *and* in speeches praising the dead, see Demosthenes *On the Crown* 288 and Aristotle *Constitution of the Athenians* 58; cf. Roller 1977.26–30, especially p. 27 on the Funeral Oration of Pericles (Thucydides 2.35–46). Note too the following three subjects of the verb **agōnizomai** 'compete, engage in an **agōn**' in Herodotus: athletes (e.g., 2.160.3–4), warriors (e.g., 1.76.4), and **rhapsōidoi** 'rhapsodes' (5.67.1).

8. We may note the semantics of German *Urteil* 'judgment', cognate of English *ordeal*.

9. Note the combination ἐν . . . ἀγωνίοις ἀέθλοισι 'in **aethloi** [plural of **aethlos**] of the **agōn**' in Pindar *Isthmian* 5.7.

10. See Chantraine DELG 21; also Loraux 1982.187–188, especially nn84, 87.

the chariot race against Oinomaos with the understanding that he will live if he wins but die if he loses, he refers to the race as an **aethlos** (Pindar *Olympian* 1.84).[11] Elsewhere in Pindaric song, the word applies to the mortally dangerous tasks imposed by King Aietes on Jason as a precondition for the hero's possessing the Golden Fleece (Pindar *Pythian* 4.220)[12] — ordeals that include the ploughing of a large field with a pair of fire-breathing bronze bulls (4.224–227) and fighting to the death a monstrous dragon that was guarding the Fleece (4.243–246).[13] In yet another Pindaric context, **aethlos** applies to one of the Labors of Herakles, namely, the hero's life-and-death struggle with the Nemean Lion (Pindar *Isthmian* 6.48).[14] In the language of epic as well, **aethlos** applies either to an athletic competition, such as the Funeral Games of Patroklos (e.g., *Iliad* XXIII 646), or to a life-and-death struggle: as an example of the latter theme, I cite the Homeric application of the word in the plural to the Labors of Herakles, all considered together (*Iliad* VIII 363).[15] Finally, in the context of actual war, we find **aethlos** applying to the martial efforts, all considered together, of Achaeans and Trojans alike in the Trojan War (*Iliad* III 126), or, considered separately, to the efforts of the Achaeans in general (*Odyssey* iii 262) or of Odysseus in particular (iv 170).

For the athlete the ritual significance of these life-and-death struggles by heroes finds its expression in the occasional lyric poetry of Pindar. In order to introduce this topic, however, I choose a remarkably suggestive passage not from Pindar but from quite elsewhere, namely, the *Alcestis* of Euripides. Offstage, the quintessential hero Herakles has just wrestled with and defeated Thanatos, Death personified; then, on stage, he cryptically refers to this confrontation as an athletic event: ἀθληταῖσιν ἄξιον πόνον 'a worthy exertion [**ponos**] for athletes' (Euripides *Alcestis* 1027). In his speech Herakles does not reveal that he has struggled with Thanatos but prefers to represent his life-and-death ordeal as a wrestling match at a local athletic festival.[16] In the words of Herakles his 'exertion' in the wrestling match with Death was a

---

11. Quoted p. 132.

12. Cf. Pindar *Pythian* 4.165.

13. I interpret the word **ponos** at Pindar *Pythian* 4.243 as applying to the ordeal of slaying the dragon, not just to the feat of ploughing.

14. See also Bacchylides *Epinician* 9.8 SM. On **aethlos** as a generic designation of the Labors of Herakles, see Loraux 1982.186.

15. Also *Iliad* XIX 133; *Odyssey* xi 622, 624.

16. On the theme of wrestling with Death incarnate, common in latter-day Greek Demotic folklore, see Alexiou 1974.37–38. In view of the fact that Hades is the prevalent manifestation of the death god in Archaic Greek literature while Thanatos is rare, it is striking that the scholia to *Alcestis* 1 describe the myth of this drama as ἡ διὰ στόματος καὶ δημώδης ἱστορία 'the current and popular story'. See Alexiou, p. 5. As H. Pelliccia suggests to me, the expression διὰ στόματος 'orally, by word of mouth' conveys the idea that a given theme is current, in currency, as in Xenophon *Cyropaedia* 1.4.25 and Theocritus 12.21.

ponos (again *Alcestis* 1027).[17] This and another word for 'exertion', **kamatos**, are programmatically used in the diction of Pindar to designate the hardships of preparing for and engaging in athletic competition.[18] Moreover, both **ponos** and **kamatos** are used by the poet to designate the life-and-death struggles of heroes.[19] As with the word **aethlos** 'contest', with **ponos** and **kamatos** there is a collapsing of the distinction between the myth of the hero's struggle and the ritual of the athlete's competition. Accordingly, 'ordeal' may be more apt a translation than 'exertion' for both **ponos** and **kamatos** since it conveys not only a heroic but also a ritual experience.

This set of poetic words, as used in Pindar's diction, helps us understand more clearly the ritual ideology inherited by Greek athletics. As noted,[20] this ideology reveals diachronic features of two kinds of ritual: (1) initiation into adulthood and (2) compensation for the catastrophe of death. In the first case it is easy to see how the ordeal conveyed by words like **aethlos, ponos,** and **kamatos** is characteristic of initiation. In the second case, however, the connection between a hero's ordeal and the idea of compensating for a primordial death is more difficult to intuit. We must call to mind again the formulation of Karl Meuli: in various societies throughout the world, ritual combat can have the function of compensating for guilt about someone's death.[21] The guilt can be canceled by way of an ordeal that decides the guilty person, in that the guilty person is killed in the ordeal while any innocent person survives. Such an ordeal may take the form of either a life-and-death contest[22] or an attenuated form of competition where "living" and "dying" may be stylized as winning and losing, respectively.[23] As I have already proposed, however, the ancient Greek model of such an ordeal reflects a rearrangement in ideology: in contrast with other models where the ordeal instituted to compensate for the guilt of a given person's death requires that one contestant "die" by losing and thereby be proven guilty while the other contestant or

17. Cf. the parallel in Phrynichus TGF 2, where Herakles has a wrestling match with Hades (on which see Brelich 1958.102n90, 208).

18. For **ponos**, see, e.g., Pindar *Olympian* 5.15, *Isthmian* 5.25, etc. For **kamatos**, see, e.g., *Pythian* 5.47, *Nemean* 3.17, etc.

19. For **ponos**, see, e.g., Pindar *Pythian* 4.236 (ἐξεπόνησεν, applying to Jason's task of ploughing with the bronze bulls); *Pythian* 4.243 (the same); *Pythian* 4.178 (the voyage of the Argo). For **kamatos**, see, e.g., *Nemean* 1.70 (the Labors of Herakles). For more on **ponos** as a heroic struggle, see Loraux 1982.174nn13, 14. For **kamatos** as heroic 'fatigue', see the passages collected by Loraux, p. 183n61. Note too the expression **dus-ponos kamatos** at *Odyssey* v 493. On **mokhthos** 'struggle', another synonym of **ponos**, see Loraux, p. 185.

20. Cf. p. 118.

21. Cf. p. 121.

22. By *contest* I do not mean to exclude such events as a race to the death. In Plutarch *Sympotic Questions* 675c, there is a fascinating but all too brief reference to primordial combats to the death at Olympia.

23. Cf. p. 122.

contestants "live," the Greek model requires that one contestant "live" by winning.[24] This "survival" of one person is then pluralized, communalized by the **khoros** 'chorus', on the occasion of the epinician or victory celebration.[25] But the Greek model is still an ordeal, instituted to compensate for the guilt of a given person's death; to engage in the ordeal is to engage in the act of compensation. The ordeal, as part of an initiation, leads to a "winning" of life, a "rebirth" that compensates for death.

For an example, let us take the **Tlēpolemeia**, a seasonally recurring festival of athletic contests held on the island of Rhodes and named after Tlepolemos, son of Herakles and the founder of Rhodes.[26] In the words of Pindar this athletic festival was founded by Tlepolemos as a **lutron** 'compensation' for what the poet calls a 'pitiful misfortune' (λύτρον συμφορᾶς οἰκτρᾶς *Olympian* 7.77). The catastrophe to which Pindar's ode refers is the hero's deranged slaying, in anger, of his grandmother's half-brother (7.27–32).

The ideological pattern of these athletic games, compensating for the death of Tlepolemos' relative, is parallel to what we have seen in the Olympic foot race, supposedly compensating for the death of Pelops. The pattern can be summarized as follows. In the mythical past, some catastrophe occurs, typically but not necessarily entailing some form of guilt or pollution. Then a ritual is instituted to compensate for that one event. In contrast with the one event recounted in the myth, the events of the ritual are to take place seasonally and into perpetuity.[27] Finally, as we have seen from the diction of Pindar, the ritual ordeals of the athletes are ideologically equated, by way of concepts like **aethlos**, **ponos**, and **kamatos**, to the life-and-death ordeals of heroes in the past.[28]

The ritual ordeals of athletes need not correspond in detail to the life-and-death ordeals of heroes. Such correspondences as we find between the athletic event of chariot racing at the Olympics and the chariot race to the death between Pelops and Oinomaos are rare.[29] What is essential, rather, is

24. Cf. p. 122.

25. Note the formulation of Burnett 1985.42: "The numbers of the chorus generalized the singular success of the victor." She cites (ibid.) the expression of a collective possession of victory garlands at Bacchylides *Epinician* 6.8–9 SM (also at Pindar *Isthmian* 7.38).

26. See Nilsson 1906.462–463 on both the literary and the nonliterary evidence for this athletic festival; also Rohde 1898 I 151n1 (I draw attention to the particularly useful comments toward the end of this note).

27. Cf. Homeric *Hymn to Demeter* 262–267, with reference to a ritual mock-battle at Eleusis, a quasi-athletic event which was officially held on a seasonally-recurring basis to compensate for the death of the child-hero Demophon (N 1979.184); this mock-battle seems to have been the ritual kernel of a whole complex of events known as the Eleusinian Games (cf. Richardson 1974.246).

28. For more on **ponos** in such a context, see Loraux 1982.174n14.

29. In this instance I have even suggested at p. 123 and following that the quasi-athletic aspects of the ordeal of Pelops reflect the chronologically secondary nature of the Olympic

simply that the ordeals of heroes, as myths, are analogous to the ordeals of athletes, as rituals, in that the themes of living and dying in the myth are analogous to the themes of winning and losing in the ritual of athletics.[30] When athletes win or lose in an athletic event, they "live" or "die" like heroes, and their ordeal thus compensates for a primordial death stemming from the heroic age.

In the context of the athletic ordeal, however, the translation of winning into an actual winning of life is incomplete. From an anthropological point of view, the athletic ordeal proceeds from the phase of *segregation* in such rites of passage as an initiation into adulthood. Although the ideology of segregation presupposes reintegration, a new life after the death to one's old life, it is nevertheless preoccupied with the symbolism of death itself. Thus, for example, in the festival of the **Braurōnia**, an institution well-known for its overt features of initiation,[31] the young female initiates undergo a phase of segregation by ritually becoming "bears": this seasonally recurring event on the level of ritual (as attested for the cult of Artemis at Brauron) corresponds to a single event on the level of myth (as attested for the closely related cult of Artemis at nearby Mounychia), namely, the primordial killing of the bear of Artemis by an ancestor of the community.[32] In effect, then, the one primordial event of the bear's death is compensated by a perpetual series of seasonally recurring events where the young girls of the community must become "bears" and thus symbolically "die" before they are eligible to marry. In other words, the phase of segregation, where the girls become "bears" and thus prepare to "die," is a prerequisite for the phase of reintegration, where the girls become marriageable adults.

So also with the ritual athletics of males: as we have seen, the institution of a festival like the **Tlēpolemeia** is a **lutron** 'compensation' — to cite again the wording of Pindar — for a primordial death (*Olympian* 7.77), so that the athlete symbolically dies by participating in the ordeal of ritual athletics. Even though the one athlete who wins in a given athletic event thereby wins

---

chariot race and of the **aition** that motivates it: they are predicated on the Olympic foot race and on its respective **aition**.

30. When heroes themselves are represented as engaging in athletics, the narrative tends to treat the event overtly as athletics, not as a life-and-death struggle. I cite the story of the founding of the Nemean Games by the Seven against Thebes, who were the first to participate in the athletic events (e.g., Bacchylides *Epinician* 9.10–24 SM: see p. 120); also the Funeral Games of Patroklos in *Iliad* XXIII (in this case, however, the happenings in the athletic events at least latently mirror the life-and-death martial ordeals of the heroes who participate in these events: see Whitman 1958.169).

31. Brelich 1969.242–279; also Vidal-Naquet 1981.197–200 and Vernant 1982–1983.451–456. Cf. Henrichs 1981.198–208. Update in Kahil 1983.

32. The sources are conveniently assembled in Brelich 1969.248–249; cf. also Henrichs 1981.200n2. See Kahil, pp. 237–238 on the iconographic evidence for a sacred footrace, in which young girls run naked; also p. 238 on the sacred dance.

back "life," this winning is incomplete in terms of the ordeal itself: for the winning to be fully realized, the athlete must not only leave behind a ritual phase of segregation but also enter into a ritual phase of reintegration, which can happen only after the ordeal is completed. From the standpoint of ritual, what is needed after a victory in an athletic festival is a joyous return to the community—a reintegration or reincorporation symbolizing life after death. A formal realization of reintegration at home is the epinician or victory ode itself, performed at the victor's home city by a chorus of men or boys who are themselves natives of the city.[33]

The role of the chorus is essential. As the detailed investigations of Claude Calame have shown, the **khoros** 'chorus', a specially selected group of polis-dwellers whose sacred duty it is to sing and dance at a given ritual occasion,[34] amounts to a formal communalization of ritual experience by and for the community: the chorus represents, reenacts, the community of the polis.[35] In the case of an epinician performance, the ritual experience of a single person's athletic victory is being communalized through the chorus.[36]

What I am proposing, then, is that the epinician performance is the final realization, the final constitutive event, of the ritual process of athletics. In Pindar's own words the occasion of an epinician ode, stylized as **kōmos** '[occasion for a] band of revellers', is a **lutron** 'compensation' for the **kamatoi** 'ordeals' of the athlete (λύτρον ... καμάτων *Isthmian* 8.2). We had seen earlier that the ordeal of the athlete is a formal **lutron** 'compensation' for a primordial death (λύτρον συμφορᾶς οἰκτρᾶς 'lutron for the pitiful misfortune' *Olympian* 7.77). Now we see that the Pindaric victory ode is a formal 'compensation' for the athlete's ordeal.[37] The actual Greek word for 'victory ode', **epi-nīkion** 'epinician', literally means something like 'that which is in compensation for victory [nīkē]'.[38]

In sum, the choral lyric poetry of Pindar, specifically his epinician mode of speaking, refers to its own social function in terms of a final stage in the

33. This epinician theme of reintegration at home is explored at length by Crotty 1982.104–138 and Slater 1984. Cf. also Kurke 1988.

34. For an explicit reference to singing *and* dancing: Pindar *Pythian* 1.1–4; cf. p. 85.

35. Calame 1977; cf. Burnett 1985.50 and 175n6, who surveys a series of passages where the epinician poet equates the chorus with the polis. For a useful survey of festivals serving as contexts for choral performance in the Greek-speaking areas of Italy and Sicily, see Burnett 1988.129–147.

36. See p. 139. Cf. Hubbard 1987b.5–6. At p. 8 he writes: "The chorus in Pindar's epinicia is never an independent personality in its own right, but is significant mainly as a reflection of community spirit in celebration of the athletic victory or some other object of praise."

37. Just as the athlete's compensation is a **ponos** 'effort', so also the poet's: see Pindar *Pythian* 9.93 and *Paean* 7B.22. Also *Nemean* 7.74, as discussed by Segal 1967.437–439.

38. We may note that the **epi-** of this formation corresponds to the usage of the preposition **epi** with the dative case to designate the dead person for whom a given festival of funeral games was celebrated in compensation. See, for example, p. 119.

ritual program of the four great Panhellenic Games. This ritual program can be classified as belonging, in the most general of anthropological terms, to the categories of (1) initiation and (2) competition in honor of the dead. These categories, as we have seen, are appropriate to what we may call tribal society.[39] But we have had to move beyond the generalities of anthropology, toward the particularities of Greek civilization, where tribal institutions are reshaped by the twin phenomena of the emergence of the polis and the trend of Panhellenism. One clear symptom of the impact of these phenomena is the fact that the athletic contest leading to the athlete's victory is a competition not in honor of a dead relative, nor even of a distant ancestor—as we might expect from the standpoint of a tribal society—but of a hero. Now the Greek hero is a product of the polis, in that the cult of heroes is historically speaking a transformation of the worship of ancestors on the level of the polis. Furthermore, the Greek hero is a product also of Panhellenism, in that the epic of heroes as represented by Homeric poetry is an artistic and social synthesis on the level of Panhellenic diffusion.[40]

So much for the specific Greek variant of the general anthropological category of competition in honor of the dead. As for the other anthropological category that applies to the Panhellenic Games, the category of initiation, the athletic victory and the subsequent celebration of victory are not strictly speaking an initiation for the Greeks, in that the setting is not the tribe but, in the case of the victory, an assembly representing all Hellenes and, in the case of the subsequent celebration of victory, a chorus representing the victor's

39. Cf. p. 139. For a working definition of tribal society, see the discussion in N 1987.

40. Discussion in N 1979.5–9, 114–117. It may be that descriptions of the deaths of warriors in Homeric poetry serve as a compensation for the absence of ritual detail in descriptions of the deaths of sacrificial victims. Homeric poetry, as a medium that seems to have reached its synthetic Panhellenic status by virtue of avoiding the parochial concerns of specific locales, specific regions, tends to avoid realistic descriptions of ritual, including ritual sacrifice (N, pp. 118–141). This is to be expected, given that ritual sacrifice—as for that matter any ritual—tends to be a localized phenomenon in Archaic Greece. What sacrificial scenes we do find in Homer are highly stylized, devoid of the kind of details that characterize real sacrifices as documented in the epigraphical evidence (cf. N, pp. 132–134, 217). In real sacrifice the ritual dismemberment of the sacrificial victim corresponds to the ideological articulation of the body politic (cf. Detienne and Svenbro 1979). Moreover, the disarticulation of the body in sacrifice presupposes the rearticulation of the body in myths of immortalization (N, pp. 208–209). Given, then, that Homeric poetry avoids delving into the details of disarticulation as it applies to animals, in that it avoids the *Realien* of sacrificial practice, we may expect a parallel avoidance of the topic of immortalization for the hero. By contrast the local practices of hero cult, contemporaneous with the evolution of Homeric poetry as we know it, are clearly based on religious notions of heroic immortalization (N, pp. 151–210). While personal immortalization is a theme too localized in orientation for Homeric poetry, the hero's death in battle, in all its staggering varieties, is universally acceptable. Homeric poetry compensates for its avoidance of details concerning the sacrifices of animals by dwelling on details concerning the martial deaths of heroes. In this way, the epic poetry of the Greeks, in describing the deaths of heroes, seems to serve as a compensation for sacrifice.

polis. So, again, we are dealing with a product of the twin phenomena of Panhellenism and the polis.

I do not mean to say that these twin phenomena are antithetical to the tribal institutions that preceded them. Rather, they represent a set of differentiations emanating from tribal institutions. The polis, as not only heir to but also rival of the tribe, neutralizes the threat of rivalry derived from its own tribal heritage by absorbing the compatible aspects of this heritage and by internationalizing (that is, making inter-polis) the incompatible aspects.[41] I call *endoskeletal* those aspects of the tribe that are absorbed within the polis and *exoskeletal* those aspects that are generalized outside the polis.[42] In this line of thought, we may say that the institution of ordeal through competition, instead of surviving as the institution of initiation within the endoskeleton, has moved into the exoskeleton as the institution of the Panhellenic Games. Thus, there is a neutralization of a potential conflict between the institution of the polis and the ancestors, who represent the original focus of ordeal through competition and who are the very foundation of extended family structures that survive as institutions antithetical to the evolving polis. My formulation here dovetails with an observation made by Erwin Rohde, that the concept of ancestors in Archaic Greece becomes differentiated into two distinct categories: on the one hand there are the heroes, stylized remote ancestors, who are defined both by their cult in any given individual polis and by their being recognized as heroes by citizens of any other given polis, and on the other hand there are the immediate ancestors, who can be kept within the confines of the polis in the restricted context of families and extended families.[43]

Pursuing this line of thought, I also argue that epinician lyric poetry bridges the gap between the endoskeletal and exoskeletal heritage of tribal society. It preserves the ritual ideology of ordeal through competition, and it even presents itself as the final stage in the ritual process, where the victorious athlete is reintegrated into his community. But the community is no longer the family or tribe but the polis, and it is the polis that the chorus of the epinician ode ostensibly represents.[44] A notable example is Pindar F 194

---

41. Cf. N 1987.

42. These terms were inspired by a conversation with J. Wickersham.

43. See Rohde 1898.108–110; also Brelich 1958.144n202; N 1979.115. Cf. the distinction between the generation of Minos and ἀνθρωπηΐη γενεή 'human ancestry' in Herodotus 3.122.2, as discussed by Darbo-Peschanski 1987.25. The remote ancestors, as distinct from the immediate ancestors, tend to be absorbed into the political genealogies of the city-state's existing constitution. See, for example, Roussel 1976.68 and 76n21 on the Boutadai, named after the cult hero Boutes. The Reform of Kleisthenes led to the naming of one of the **dēmoi** 'demes', the new social subdivisions of Athens, as Boutadai, which in turn led to the designation Eteoboutadai 'genuine Boutadai' to distinguish the genuine lineage from the deme; only one of the two branches of the Eteoboutadai resided in the deme to be called Boutadai at the time of the Reform (ibid.).

44. On the chorus as representative of the polis, cf. again Burnett 1985.50 and 175n6, who

SM, where a chorus of Thebans is represented as if they were rebuilding the walls of Thebes, in that they are metaphorically 'building the walls' (τειχί-ζωμεν) of the **kosmos** 'arrangement' of the words of their song (lines 2–3).[45]

In these patterns of differentiation, it is clear that the concept of *local* in the opposition of *local* and *Panhellenic* is not to be equated with the concept of the polis itself. The polis is local only insofar as it absorbs the endoskeletal aspects of the tribe; but it is also Panhellenic in that it promotes the exoskeletal aspects. The ideology of the polis is not exclusively local, or epichoric: it is simultaneously Panhellenic. Thus whenever the chorus, as representative of the polis, speaks about things epichoric, it does so with a Panhellenic point of view.

---

surveys a series of passages where the epinician poet equates the chorus with the polis. Parallel to this function of the epinician poet, equating the chorus with the polis, is the function of the athlete himself within the ideology of epinician lyric poetry: as Hubbard 1986.44 notes, "the athletic victor too serves as a private man on a collective mission and [. . .] his victories are just as much an adornment of his city as to himself personally."

45. The polis of Thebes, myth has it, was founded when the sound of Amphion's lyre performance literally built the city walls (Hesiod F 182 MW; Pausanias 6.20.18). A related theme is apparent in the etymological connection of Latin *mūnus* 'token of reciprocity, duty' and *commūnis* 'communal' with *moenia* 'city walls'. The word **kosmos** can refer to (1) the 'arrangement' of beautiful adornment (*Iliad* XIV 187), (2) the beautiful 'arrangement' or adorned 'composition' of a song (as in Pindar F 194 SM; cf. *Odyssey* viii 489), (3) the 'arrangement' or 'constitution' of a polis (Herodotus 1.65.4), and later, by extension, (4) the 'arrangement' or 'order' of the universe (Xenophon *Memorabilia* 1.1.11). For the connection of this concept of **kosmos** with that of **harmoniā**, dramatized in Theognis 15–18 as the Wedding of Kadmos and Harmonia, an alternative myth about the foundation of Thebes, see N 1985.41 §25n2.

6 ▣▣ Epic, Praise, and the Possession of Poetry

I t has been argued that the athlete follows the ritual paradigm of the hero not only through an ordeal at the Games but also through a reintegration, by way of epinician lyric poetry, with the community at home. In what follows, I extend the argument: just as the Games, as ritual, momentarily collapse the distinction between hero and athlete, so too does epinician lyric poetry. For an effective demonstration, we must compare in detail the two different forms of poetry that are primarily associated with defining the hero and the athlete, namely, the epic of Homer and the epinician lyric poetry of Pindar. As the epinician is a kind of praise poetry, the distinction between epic and epinician can be traced back to a more fundamental opposition, between epic and praise poetry.[1]

In our initial survey of Archaic Greek literature from a broadened perspective of oral poetics, I started with the compositions attributed to Homer and ended with those of Pindar as the earliest and the latest examples respectively of Panhellenic traditions in poetry and song.[2] Before we set out to examine what else, besides a distinctly Panhellenic stance, is shared by these two traditions, let us observe the differences. For this purpose, we confront the question of occasionality in poetry and song, which helps explain the differentiation of epic and praise poetry. On this matter the testimony of Pindar's own wording is our most revealing source, and from it we learn not only about the nature of Pindar's traditions but also about the relationship of

1. In using the term *praise poetry* I consistently mean *poetry* in the broadest sense, to include the lyric poetry of *song*.
2. See also Ch.13 on Athenian Theater as heir to Panhellenic poetics.

these traditions to those of Homer in particular and to the other traditions of Greek poetry and song in general. The title of the whole book, *Pindar's Homer*, conveys the kind of relationship that I hope to demonstrate in the course of my presentation.[3]

The occasionality of Pindar's medium is reflected in a word used in Pindar's diction to designate this medium: the word is **ainos** or **ep-ainos**,[4] which may be translated primarily as 'praise' in view of Elroy Bundy's observation that Pindar's epinician poetic tradition has one overarching purpose, that of *praise*.[5] Hence the common designation of Pindar's medium is *praise poetry*. Another word used in Pindar's diction to designate his medium is **kleos** (plural **klea/kleea**), which can be interpreted to mean 'glory' or 'fame' — as conferred by song or poetry. An outstanding example is the declaration of Pindar:[6]

ξεῖνός εἰμι· σκοτεινὸν ἀπέχων ψόγον, | ὕδατος ὥτε ῥοὰς φίλον ἐς ἄνδρ᾽ ἄγων | κλέος ἐτήτυμον αἰνέσω

Pindar *Nemean* 7.61–63

I am a **xenos**.[7] Keeping away dark blame [**psogos**] and bringing genuine [**etētumon**][8] **kleos**, like streams of water,[9] to a man who is near and dear [**philos**], I will praise [= verb **aineō**] him.

From the epic poetry of Homer, we see that this medium too refers to

---

3. More at Ch.14. Cf. also p. 3.

4. Examples of **ainos**: Pindar *Olympian* 2.95, 6.12, 11.7; *Nemean* 1.6. An example of **epainos**: Pindar F 181 SM. Cf. Detienne 1973.21.

5. In examining the regularities typical of the Epinikion, the epinician poetic tradition shared by Pindar and Bacchylides, Bundy concludes that they are "not mannerisms of a given poet but conventions protecting the artistic integrity of a community of poets working within well-recognized rules of form and order" ([1986] 3). He goes on to say: "I have observed and catalogued a host of these conventions and find that they point uniformly, as far as concerns the Epinikion, to one master principle: there is no passage in Pindar and [Bacchylides] that is not in its primary intent en[c]omiastic — that is, designed to enhance the glory of a particular patron" (ibid.).

6. Commentary in N 1979.223; cf. also Steiner 1986.47–48.

7. A **xenos** is someone who is bound by the ties of reciprocity between guest and host. Such ties are presupposed to exist between poet and patron. For other Pindaric passages concerning the theme of poetic **xeniā** 'being **xenos**', see Woodbury 1968. 537n14. Fundamental discussion of **xeniā** in Benveniste 1969 I 341 = 1973.278; cf. N 1979.232–237, Watkins 1976c, Martin 1984.35. As Herodotus says expliticly at 7.228.4, the poetic tribute of Simonides to Megistes, one of the fallen at Thermopylae, is based on the relationship of **xeniā** between them.

8. On the use of **etumos/etētumos** 'genuine, noble' as a touchstone for the truth-value of poetic traditions, see pp. 422 and following.

9. On the traditional metaphor of **kleos** as an unfailing stream, primarily of water, see N 1974.244 on the expression **kleos aphthiton**, as in *Iliad* IX 413. The notion of *unfailing* is conveyed by **aphthito-** (ibid.; also Risch 1987.4–5); on the vegetal symbolism also inherent in this epithet, see N 1979 ch.10 and Steiner 1986.38.

itself as **kleos**.[10] More important for now, however, since we are considering the differences between praise and epic poetry, is the fact that epic does not refer to itself as **ainos**.[11]

In contrast with **kleos**, the word **ainos** is more exclusive in its applications. It is concerned with function more than form. Or, to put it another way, it stresses the occasion for which a given form is used. The **ainos** is an affirmation, a marked speech-act, made by and for a marked social group.[12] As we see from Pindar's traditional diction, the **ainos** restricts and is restricted by its audience. As a medium the **ainos** specifies listeners who have the following qualifications:

1. the **sophoi**, that is, those who are 'skilled' in decoding the message encoded by the poet in his poetry[13]
2. the **agathoi**, that is, those who are intrinsically 'noble' by virtue of having been raised on proper ethical standards, which are the message encoded in the poetry[14]
3. the **philoi**, that is, those who are 'near and dear' and who are thereby interconnected to the poet and to each other, so that the message that is encoded in the poetry may be transmitted to them and through them: communication through community.[15]

In this tripartite scheme, I have set up the distinction between *code* and *message*, with the terminology of the Prague School of Linguistics,[16] in order to drive home a point that the lyric poetry of Pindar's **ainos** consistently makes about itself: namely, that the **ainos** is a code that carries the right message for those who are qualified and the wrong message or messages for those who are unqualified. By way of its self-definition, the **ainos** is predicated on an ideal: an ideal audience listening to an ideal performance of an ideal composition. But at the same time it is also predicated on the reality of uncertainties in interaction between performer and audience in the context of the actual performance of a composition: the **ainos** of Pindar is by its very character ambiguous, both difficult in its form and enigmatic in its content.

---

10. See, for example, *Iliad* II 486, XI 227, as discussed in N 1979.15–18.

11. The fable of "The Hawk and the Nightingale" is explicitly designated as an **ainos** in Hesiod *Works and Days* 202 (quoted at pp. 255–56). This reference, however, applies to the whole discourse of the *Works and Days* only by extension. In any case, I see no compelling reason to assume that Hesiodic poetry is epic.

12. See p. 31.

13. For example, Pindar *Olympian* 2.83–86, *Isthmian* 2.12–13; note too the discussion in N 1979.236–238. I use *poetry* here in the broadest sense, to include *song*.

14. For example, Pindar *Pythian* 2.81–88; cf. further at the end of the same poem, lines 94–96; also *Pythian* 10.71–72, at the end of another poem.

15. For example (again), Pindar *Pythian* 2.81–88. Cf. Pindar *Nemean* 7.61–63, quoted immediately above. Note too the discussion in N 1979.238–242.

16. Cf., for example, Jakobson 1960.353.

As a difficult code that bears a difficult but correct message for the qualified and a wrong message or messages for the unqualified, the **ainos** communicates like an enigma — to use an English word that was borrowed from and serves as a translation for the Greek **ainigma** (as in Sophocles *Oedipus Tyrannus* 393, 1525), which in turn is an actual derivative of **ainos**. An important example of this usage occurs in the poetry of Theognis (667–682), where the voice of the poet finishes an extended metaphor, the image of the ship of state caught in a seastorm (671–680), with the following declaration about the meaning of the symbol:

ταῦτά μοι ᾐνίχθω κεκρυμμένα τοῖς ἀγαθοῖσιν.
γινώσκοι δ' ἄν τις καὶ κακὸν ἂν σοφὸς ᾖ.

Theognis 681–682

Let these things be riddling utterances [**ainigma** plural] hidden by me for the noble [**agathoi**].
One can be aware of even [future] misfortune, if one is skilled [= **sophos**].[17]

In contrast with the praise poetry of Pindar, the epic poetry of the Homeric *Iliad* and *Odyssey* makes no claims to exclusiveness and does not qualify as a form of **ainos**. Whereas both the epic poetry of Homer and the praise poetry of Pindar qualify as **kleos**, only praise poetry qualifies as **ainos**. On the other hand, whereas all praise poetry may qualify as **ainos**, not all examples of **ainos** are praise poetry. For example, the word **ainos** can also refer to the narrower concept of a speech of admonition, or **par-ain-esis** 'instructive speech'.[18] Or it can designate animal fables, such as those used by Archilochus to admonish his friends or blame his enemies.[19] As a double-edged mode of discourse, the **ainos** can admonish or blame as well as praise.[20] Moreover, the **ainos** can assume a variety of poetic forms. While it

17. For a defense of the manuscript reading κακόν — as opposed to the emendation κακός — and for general commentary on the entire passage: N 1985.22–26.

18. On **par-ain-esis** as an instructive and edifying speech that warns about proper moral behavior, see N 1979.238–239, with reference to Pindar *Pythian* 6.23 and *Isthmian* 6.68. See further at p. 196.

19. For example, Archilochus F 174 W.

20. Cf. pp. 392 and following. See also N 1979.250, 281–288. My interpretation, at p. 250, of Pindar F 181 SM ὁ γὰρ ἐξ οἴκου ποτὶ μῶμον ἔπαινος κίρναται 'for praise is by nature mixed with blame' is criticized by Kirkwood 1984.169–171, who argues that ἐξ οἴκου, bracketed by ὁ ... ἔπαινος, is attributive; his interpretation, however, does not account for ποτὶ μῶμον, which is likewise bracketed by ὁ ... ἔπαινος, and which is clearly nonattributive. I fail to see how Kirkwood's general argument, that Pindar's poetry praises the noble only and blames the base only (e.g., p. 179 on Pindar *Nemean* 8.39), goes beyond what I too have argued throughout my discussion in N, pp. 222–288. The difference between Kirkwood's position and mine is that I view this pattern of restriction on the range of blame as a specialization from earlier phases of **ainos**. For me, a passage like Pindar *Olympian* 6.74–76, where **mōmos** 'blame' looms over the

is sung and danced by choral groups in the Aeolic and dactylo-epitrite meters of Pindar, it is also recited by rhapsodes in such formats as the iambic meters of Archilochus[21] and the elegiac distichs of Theognis.[22] In other words it is better to think of the **ainos** as a mode of discourse, not as a genre. Still the point is that the genre of Homer's epic and the genre of Pindar's praise poetry are differentiated by the absence and presence respectively of self-definition in terms of **ainos**.

How then does the fact that the **kleos** of epic fails to define itself as **ainos** make this **kleos** different from the **kleos** of praise poetry? In order to comprehend the difference, we must first consider the implications of the word **kleos**. In the epic poetry of Homer just as in the praise poetry of Pindar, **kleos** denotes the act of praising,[23] but in epic the praise takes place by the very process of narrating the deeds of heroes, predominantly in the third person. In praise poetry the praise is more direct: here too **kleos** denotes the act of praising, but the praise in this case applies to the here and now, inviting narration in the second person. In the epinicians or victory odes of Pindar, for example, the praise applies to the victories of athletes who competed in the great Panhellenic Games. The victory would be celebrated on the occasion of the victor's return from the Games to his native polis. The praise poetry of Pindar, then, is occasional. Occasionality is the essence of **ainos**. The epic poetry of the Homeric *Iliad* and *Odyssey* on the other hand is distinctly not occasional: unlike the praise poem it does not praise anyone in the here and now of its own performance. The praise of Homeric poetry is restricted to the heroes of the distant past.[24]

Whereas the epic of Homeric poetry is restricted to heroes, the praise of Pindaric song is not restricted to the victorious men and boys who were subjects of the poet's here and now. The word **kleos** in Pindar's praise poetry applies equally to the man of the present and the hero of the past, as in the following example:

λέγεται μὰν Ἕκτορι μὲν κλέος ἀνθῆσαι Σκαμάνδρου χεύμασιν |
ἀγχοῦ, βαθυκρήμνοισι δ' ἀμφ' ἀκταῖς Ἑλώρου, | (. . .) δέδορκεν |

---

successful, is a self-reference to an earlier and less differentiated phase of the medium, where one man's praise proved to be another man's blame.

21. Note the self-reference to the given poem by way of the word **ainos** in Archilochus F 174 W. The recited meter of this particular composition is a combination of iambic trimeters and dimeters.

22. Note the self-reference to the given poem by way of the word **ainissō** in Theognis 681–682 (quoted immediately above).

23. Consider the use of the verb **kleiō**, derivative of **kleos**, at, for example, *Odyssey* i 338, *Homeric Hymn* 32.19. Cf. *Iliad* xi 227, as discussed in N 1979.15–18.

24. This is not the case with all poetry normally described as epic: cf., for example, Radloff 1885.xviii-xix (and Svenbro 1976.17–18). Cf. also Zumthor 1983.109 and Martin 1989.6–7.

παιδὶ τοῦθ᾽ Ἀγησιδάμου φέγγος ἐν ἁλικίᾳ πρώτᾳ

Pindar *Nemean* 9.39–42

It is said that **kleos** bloomed for Hektor near the streams of Skamandros. And near the steep cliffs that rise above Heloros, [. . .] this light shone upon the coming of age of the son of Hagesidamos.

Moreover, what is being praised about the man of the present, such as the athlete, is ideologically parallel to what is being praised about the hero. In the inherited diction of praise poetry, what an athlete undergoes in his pursuit of victory is denoted by **ponos** 'ordeal', also called **kamatos** or **aethlos**, and these very words apply also to the life-and-death struggles of heroes with their enemies, man and beast alike.[25]

In decidedly not making a distinction between the **kleos** due to an athlete of the present for his athletic event and the **kleos** due to a hero for his heroic deed, the ideology of Pindar's praise poetry is parallel to the ideology of the athletic games in which the athletes earned their **kleos**. As we have seen, the ideology of the games is fundamentally a religious one: each athletic festival, held on a seasonally recurring basis into perpetuity, is predicated on the death of a hero, on an eternally important proto-ordeal for which the seasonally recurring ordeals of athletes, in principle ongoing to eternity, serve as eternal compensation. This religious ideology, clearly attested in Pindar's praise poetry, is matched by the religious ideology of the poetry: each ordeal of each victorious athlete, compensating for the proto-ordeal of the hero who struggled and died, demands compensation of its own in the form of song offered as praise for the athlete. And the song in turn demands compensation from the victorious athlete and his family, to be offered to the composer of the song.

Such a concluding link in the chain of compensation is clearly articulated throughout the praise poetry of Pindar, whenever the voice of the poet says that he owes it to his patrons to create a song (e.g., *Olympian* 10.3, 8). This theme has been misunderstood by latter-day experts of Pindar as if it were a blatant illustration of Pindar's "mercenary Muse": when Pindar says that he owes the song to his patrons, critics misunderstand him as referring merely to a contract between patron and poet, entailing services to be performed and to be paid for.[26] This is to ignore the premonetary and in some respects sacral heritage of the very concept of value in Archaic Greek society.[27]

---

25. Cf. p. 138.

26. Woodbury 1968 gives a useful survey of the more extreme statements to the effect that Pindar is simply a poet for hire. Woodbury's own attitude is best reflected by what he says at p. 531 about Pindar *Isthmian* 2.1–13: "An obsession with fees is the least likely of themes for a Pindaric poem."

27. For a better appreciation of this concept, a good start is to read carefully the searching

Of course other contemporary deeds, besides those of athletics, could have demanded requital in song of praise. The most obvious category is victorious deeds in war, which are in fact denoted by the same terms that are used for victorious deeds in athletics: in the diction of Pindar and elsewhere, a man who fights in a war undergoes an ordeal as denoted by the words **ponos** (e.g., *Pythian* 1.54), **kamatos** (*Pythian* 2.19), and **aethlos** (e.g., *Iliad* III 126). Once again we see a collapsing of distinctions that affect the **kleos** due a hero and the **kleos** due a man. Only in the present case both hero and man are potentially getting **kleos** in return for the same activity, namely, a martial struggle. The internal evidence of poetic diction can be reinforced by external evidence: as we can observe from the facts collected by Angelo Brelich on the institution of warfare in Archaic Greece, fighting in wars was indeed a ritual activity, parallel to the ritual activity of engaging in athletic games.[28] Accordingly, the compensation for deeds of war through songs of praise, just like the compensation for deeds of athletics, can be considered a vital link of a ritual chain.

But the picture is drastically affected by other developments in the history of Archaic Greek civilization. With the evolution of the polis or city-state and the concurrent evolution of the **phalanx**, an army of citizen soldiers, the factor of communal effort in warfare tends to counteract the factor of individual aristocratic enterprise.[29] Thus the opportunity for individual feats of war, let alone the opportunity for celebrating them, is considerably reduced. The best chance for any individual distinction would have been afforded by being killed in war. (Pindar's *Isthmian* 7 gives us a vivid depiction.)

But even here the evolution of the polis produces a drastic effect. The emerging institution of the polis discourages, often by way of actual legislation, the glorification of aristocratic individuals or individual families in the context of funerary practices in general and funerary praise poetry in particular.[30] The very art form of the poetic epigram, where the written record becomes the equivalent of performance, is at least in part a reflex of the strictures imposed by the polis against the performance of elaborate songs of praise in the context of funerals.[31]

---

analysis in Gernet 1968.93–137; cf. also Laum 1924.

28. Brelich 1961; cf. Connor 1988. On the theme of **kratos** 'superior power' as it applies to both warrior *and* athlete: N 1979.90.

29. Burnett 1985.173n25 notes: "As an emblem of the new anonymity in battle note the disappearance of the shield design in the early classical period." She cites Beazley 1954.79; another discussion that could be cited is Lévêque and Vidal-Naquet 1964.57–61, especially p. 61 (cf. Roussel 1976.60n26). Burnett connects (ibid.) "the collectivity of hoplite war and the disappearance of recognized deeds of [**aristeiā**]," citing the discussion of Pritchett 1974.276–290.

30. Alexiou 1974.13, 18–19, 104, 106, 108; cf. N 1979.116.

31. Alexiou, pp. 104, 106. Cf. p. 18.

Such restrictions on the glorification of the aristocratic individual are a reflex of a much larger-scale phenomenon, where the institutions of the polis are in the process of being transformed from and then conflicting with the institutions of the tribal society that preceded it.[32] It is in this historical context that we must reconsider the social function of the **ainos**.

In the process of the detribalization of the polis, inherited ideologies and practices concerning ancestors — a key determinant of aristocratic individuality — were drastically curtailed. For one, the inherited ideologies about ancestors as encoded in genealogical traditions became differentiated into mythological genealogies of heroes and historical genealogies of immediate ancestors.[33] This process was of course intensified by a universal tendency to mythologize remote as opposed to immediate ancestry: in genealogical traditions the progressive distancing of a given ancestor from the here and now progressively reintegrates that person into the current patterns of myth making in the here and now. In any case, with the advent of the city-state heroes became differentiated from ancestors.[34] With this differentiation of inherited ideologies came a parallel differentiation of inherited practices: the institutional worship of ancestors became differentiated into two separate but related practices, the worship of heroes and the cult of immediate ancestors.[35]

In Archaic Greek history the gap produced by these differentiations between heroes and immediate ancestors could be bridged only by individuals who developed, or had already inherited, the wealth, power, and prestige to rise as individuals above the institutions of the city-state. A prime example of such bridging is the survival of inherited royal dynasties like the dual kingship at Sparta. It is said of the Spartans by Xenophon *Constitution of the Lacedaemonians* 15.9: οὐχ ὡς ἀνθρώπους ἀλλ' ὡς ἥρωας τοὺς Λακεδαιμονίων βασιλεῖς προτετιμήκασιν 'they have come to honor the [dead] kings of the Lacedaemonians [= Spartans] not as men but as heroes'.[36] Once dead, the kings of Sparta were exempt from distinctions between heroes and immediate ancestors because they tended to be exempt from the ongoing detribalization of the polis of Sparta.[37]

An equally important example of such bridging between heroes and immediate ancestors takes place in the so-called age of tyrants and thereafter, when personalities like Peisistratos of Athens, Periandros of Corinth,

32. Cf. pp. 142 and following.

33. See p. 144.

34. Cf. p. 144.

35. Ibid. On the parallelism in the formalities of worshipping heroes and immediate ancestors, see Rohde 1898 I 165.

36. Commentary on this passage by Cartledge 1988.

37. Cf. Hartog 1980.166–170 (especially p. 170), with reference to the customs connected with the funerals of Spartan kings. On patterns of gradual detribalization in the polis, cf. N 1987.

Polykrates of Samos, Thrasyboulos of Miletus, and Kleisthenes of Sikyon finally succeeded in making a breakthrough into our recorded history as real historical figures.[38] The public foundation of these personalities was the wealth, power, and prestige that they ideologically justified through their lineages, stretched all the way back to the age of heroes, as in the case of the Peisistratidai of Athens. Their dynasty claimed descent from the Neleidai, a lineage that extends forward in time to Melanthos and his son Kodros, two of the kings of Athens (Herodotus 5.65.3). The ancestor of the Neleidai is none other than Neleus, father of the Homeric Nestor (ibid.). The line extending all the way from Neleus down to king Kodros is given in full by Hellanicus FGH 4 F 125. The sons of Kodros are Medon and another Neleus. Myth has it that this second Neleus left Athens to become the founder of the Ionian constellation of the Twelve Cities (ibid.). In another report, Herodotus 9.97, Neleus, this younger son of Kodros, is specifically credited with the foundation of Miletus; here his name takes the form **Neileōs**. The ancient lineage of kings at Miletus traced themselves back to this Neileos (Aristotle F 556 Rose). As for Medon, the older son and heir of Kodros, myth has it that he remained in power at Athens, where he undergoes a transformation, according to some versions, from **basileus** 'king' to **arkhōn** 'archon' (Aristotle *Constitution of the Athenians* 3.3).[39] Such lineages represented not only relations in genealogy, both real and mythical: they also translated into relations in wealth, power, and prestige both within and beyond the polis.

The names of these aristocratic lineages took the form of plural patronymics, with suffixes in **-adai** and **-idai**, indicating a group that is linked by ties of common ancestry leading back to the cult of a given hero. This pattern corresponds to that of kings, as we see from the testimony of Ephorus FGH 70 F 118 (in Strabo 8.5.5 C366), who says that the two royal houses of Sparta were called Agiadai and Eurypontidai because it was the ancestors Agis and Eurypontos, not their respective fathers Eurysthenes and Prokles, whose hero cults constituted the basis of the lineage.[40] Another example, this time taken from Athens, is the powerful old lineage known as the Medontidai, who traced themselves back specifically to Medon, king of Athens (Pausanias 4.5.10), rather than to his father Kodros or to *his* father Melanthos (mentioned in Herodotus 5.65.3). A prominent descendant of this lineage of Medontidai is the Lawgiver par excellence of Athens, Solon (cf. Plutarch *Life of Solon* 1).[41] As yet another example, we may consider the Iamidai: in the

---

38. For background: Berve 1967 and Petre 1975.

39. Commentary by Rhodes 1981.100–101.

40. Cf. Brelich 1958.150. In this same context, Ephorus FGH 70 F 118, is a reference to the hero cult of the lawgiver Lycurgus. On the genealogies of the kings of Sparta, the prime testimony is Herodotus 7.204 and 8.131.2. Cf. Calame 1987. Cf. also p. 300.

41. The name of Medon, ancestor of Solon's lineage, is significant: see, for example, Benveniste 1973.404 on the participle **medōn** 'ruler' (e.g., *Iliad* II 79; singular in I 72), corresponding to

only instance where Pausanias ever refers to one of his 'guides' by name, citing 'Aristarchus, the guide at Olympia' at 5.20.4, the reference concerns a living descendant of the lineage of the Iamidai, "who are attested for almost one thousand years as the priests and seers of the Eleans."[42] Still other examples include the Bakkhiadai of Corinth, stemming from Bakkhis, the fifth king of Corinth (cf. Diodorus 7.9.4, Pausanias 2.4.4); the Penthilidai of Lesbos, stemming from the hero Penthilos, son of Orestes (Pausanias 2.18.5–6, Aristotle *Politics* 1311b27); and the aforementioned Neleidai of Miletus, stemming from Neleus/**Neileōs** (Aristotle F 556 Rose). Finally there is the outstanding example of the Peisistratidai at Athens. Herodotus (5.65.4) makes it explicit that Hippokrates, the father of Peisistratos, named his son after the hero Peisistratos, son of Nestor (cf. *Odyssey* iii 36). It is clear from this and other indications that the lineage of the Peisistratidai (Herodotus 5.62–63 et passim) was predicated on the ancestry of this Peisistratos, son of Nestor.[43] Even more, it can be argued that this lineage of the Peisistratidai was founded on the actual hero cult of this ancestor.[44] For a clear reference to hero cult as the basis for a given lineage, I cite "Aristotle" *On Marvellous Things Heard* 106, describing cult practices in Tarentum, where the Atreidai 'sons of Atreus' (as well as the Tydeidai, the Aiakidai, and the Laertiadai) are recipients of cult honors that are distinct from those of the Agamemnonidai, even though Agamemnon is of course the son of Atreus.[45]

References to such aristocratic lineages are conventionally made in terms of **oikos** (or **oikiā**) 'household' or 'family'.[46] A prominent example is the **oikiā** of Miltiades (Herodotus 6.35.1), of the lineage Philaidai, characterized as the steady producer of four-horse teams that win at chariot races (**tethrippotrophos**: Herodotus ibid.; cf. Pherecydes FGH 3 F 2); Philaios was son of Ajax, son of Telamon, son of Aiakos (Herodotus ibid.).[47] Another

---

the name **Medōn**: "in **medōn** we feel primarily the notion of authority and [secondarily . . .], the notion of a directing 'measure'."

42. Habicht 1985.146, with further discussion.

43. Shapiro 1983. See especially p. 89, where he argues that the Peisistratos who was archon in 669/668 B.C. was an ancestor of Peisistratos the tyrant. Note too the discussion (ibid.) of an early Archaic relief pithos with the figure of a warrior labeled 'Antilokhos', presumably identified with the son of Homeric Nestor (cf. *Odyssey* iii 112).

44. Cf. Mossé 1969.72 on the hero cult established in honor of the ancestors of the Peisistratidai.

45. Cf. Pfister II 469.

46. For a list of powerful **oikoi** or **oikiai**, 'families' whose influence extended beyond their native polis, see Roussel 1976.60n19. On the poetics of this concept of **oikoi** or **oikiai**, I cite the pathfinding work of Kurke 1988. On the sacral meaning of **oikos** as a cult place where a given hero is worshipped, see p. 269.

47. This passage in Herodotus 6.35.1 stresses that the genealogy of the Philaidai is to be localized at Aegina for the sequence of Aiakos to Telamon to Ajax to Philaios, from which point onward it is to be relocalized at Athens. In Pausanias 1.35.1–2 there is an intermediary stage in the genealogy, in that the son of Ajax is Eurysakes, whose son in turn is Philaios; it is made

example are the Alkmaionidai of Athens, the lineage of the celebrated Kleisthenes, Reformer of Athens, maternal grandson of the elder Kleisthenes, the tyrant of Sikyon (Herodotus 5.66–68).[48] One of the ancestors in this lineage of the Alkmaionidai, whose actual name was Alkmaion, was the very first Athenian to win the chariot race at the Olympics (Isocrates 16.25).[49]

Such rich and powerful families, one of whose primary means of demonstrating prestige was victory at the Panhellenic Games, could readily be perceived as a potential threat to the polis — as potential achievers of tyrannical power. A prime example is a figure called Kylon, an Olympic victor (probably 640 B.C.), who nearly succeeded in becoming tyrant of Athens in a coup d'état attempted at a time when the Olympics were in progress (possibly 632 B.C.; cf. Herodotus 5.71, Thucydides 1.126; Plutarch *Solon* 12.1–3). The men who were held responsible for the guilt of murdering some of the perpetrators, perhaps including Kylon, when that group sought asylum after the failed attempt (as we read in the same sources, with varying details), were members of the Alkmaionidai, the very lineage that has just been cited as a prime example of rich and powerful families who are perceived as a threat to the polis. The Alkmaionidai, as the lineage of one Megakles, who was held primarily responsible for the murders, were officially exiled in compensation for the pollution that they supposedly inflicted on the polis (Plutarch *Solon* 12.3).

This lineage of the Alkmaionidai was in any case notoriously suspect of potential tyranny. The son of this Megakles, Alkmaion, was the first Athenian to win the chariot race at the Olympics (again Isocrates 16.25). The chariot victory of Alkmaion is mentioned also by Herodotus, who describes him in this context as a **tethrippotrophos** 'producer of four-horse chariot teams' (6.125.5) and who links the Olympic victory with an anecdote about the fabulous wealth of this same Alkmaion, acquired from none other than the ultimate representative of tyranny, the tyrant Croesus of Lydia (6.125.1–4). This anecdote is pertinent to the conventional theme that stresses the corruption of aristocratic society by a surfeit of riches and the resulting dangers of tyranny.[50] A son of Alkmaion, another Megakles, mar-

---

explicit here that the colonization of Salamis by Telamon is an enterprise that must be credited to Aegina, and that the turning over of Salamis to Athens from Aegina is associated with the figure of Philaios, who thereby 'becomes Athenian' (γενόμενον ... Ἀθηναῖον ibid.). In the version recorded by Plutarch *Life of Solon* 10, Philaios and Eurysakes are brothers, and they both surrender Salamis to Athens; Philaios settles in the region of Brauron, where the **dēmos** 'deme' of the Philaidai is named after him (for a parallel naming of a **dēmos** 'deme', the new unit of social subdivision at Athens after the Reform of Kleisthenes, see p. 144 on the deme called Boutadai). On the concept of the Aiakidai at Aegina, as descended from Aiakos, see p. 176.

48. The Reform of Kleisthenes left traces of special privileges for the Alkmaionidai: cf. Lanza 1977.171n1.

49. Cf. Pausanias 2.18.8–9, where the Alkmaionidai are traced to an Alkmaion descended from Nestor of the Neleidai; on the Neleidai see p. 154.

50. Cf. pp. 286 and following.

ried the daughter of the tyrant of Sikyon, Kleisthenes (Herodotus 6.130.2).[51] As Herodotus concedes, it was for this reason (cf. 6.131.1), as well as many others (e.g., 1.59–61), that the Alkmaionidai throughout their history were perceived as potential tyrants.[52] In this context, we may note that another Megakles, whose father was a younger brother of Kleisthenes the Reformer and who won the chariot race at the Pythian Games in Delphi at 486 B.C., was ostracized from Athens in that same year, according to Aristotle *Constitution of the Athenians* 22.5;[53] this chariot victory by Megakles of the Alkmaionidai was celebrated by a victory ode of Pindar, *Pythian* 7, a composition in which the allusive use of **phthonos** 'envy' (19) apparently refers to the ostracism and exile of Megakles.[54] The mother of Alcibiades was descended from the Alkmaionidai (Isocrates ibid.); so too was the mother of Pericles of Athens (Thucydides 1.127.1; cf. Herodotus 6.131.2). Moreover, the tyrant Peisistratos had been married to the daughter of Megakles, son of the Olympic winner Alkmaion (Herodotus 1.61.1–2).

In the so-called age of tyrants, such personalities "represent a force for innovation in Greek political history and step upon its stage as Greece's first true individuals."[55] To overreach the polis is to become an individual, at least

51. Another of the descendants of Alkmaion may be the Athenian **Kroisos** = Croesus, memorialized in an inscription at the base of a *kouros*-statue, which refers to his death in battle and his **sēma** 'tomb' (CEG 27); this statue may have been carved sometime after 530 B.C., but the date of the battle in which this Athenian man died may be as early as 547 (Ridgway 1977.8). There is a possibility that our Athenian Croesus belonged to the lineage of the Alkmaionidai and may have been a direct descendant of the ancestor of this lineage, the Alkmaion who reputedly collaborated with Croesus, Tyrant of the Lydian Empire, in the story retold by Herodotus 6.125.2; see Jeffery 1962.144 (I owe this reference to M. J. Rein); cf. p. 266. This narrative in Herodotus concerning the alleged alliance of Alkmaion with Croesus of Lydia helps motivate the naming of a descendant of Alkmaion after the Tyrant of the Lydian Empire; cf. p. 266. T. J. Figueira draws my attention to the name of one of the descendants of the lineage of the Kypselidai at Corinth: **Psammētikhos** = Psammetichus, Tyrant of Corinth after the rule of Periandros, his paternal uncle (Aristotle *Politics* 1315b26; in the text of Nicolaus of Damascus FGH 90 F 60, his name is given as Kypselos). This name corresponds to **Psammētikhos** = Psammetichus, Pharaoh of Egypt, as in Herodotus 1.105.1, 2.2, and so on. For more on the Kypselidai of Corinth, see p. 183. On the political contacts of Psammetichus with the Greeks, cf. especially Herodotus 2.154.

52. As Roussel 1976.62 points out, there is an exceptional instance in the attested Athenian ostraka of the Archaic period where the candidate for ostracism is not only named but also specified as a member of a certain lineage; that lineage happens to be the Alkmaionidai ([Ἀλκ]μεον[ιδõν | Καλ]λίχσεν[ος | Ἀρ]ιστο[νύμο 'Kallixenos, son of Aristonymos, of the Alkmaionidai': Meiggs and Lewis 1975.40). The reference to the Alkmaionidai as **misoturannoi** 'tyrant-haters' at Herodotus 6.121.1 has to do with their well-known enmity with the Peisistratidai, who had in fact already achieved tyranny. The designation of tyrant-haters is a politically understandable stance for those who are themselves potential tyrants. On the partiality of Herodotus toward the Alkmaionidai, see Gillis 1969.

53. See Rhodes 1981.274–275.

54. Kirkwood 1984.178.

55. Most 1982.83; cf. Farenga 1981.

in public memory. Before the age of tyrants, such a pattern of standing out in the community could be achieved only by the likes of kings, who literally embodied the community through their status as the very incarnation of the body politic, and who maintained their status in public memory through the institution of dynasty, a continuum of power visibly expressed in the genetics of prestigious alliances through various strategies of intermarriage. In the age of tyrants, the royal patterns of embodying and thus potentially over-reaching the community were further extended, in line with the dictum of Aristotle that the way to maintain a tyranny is to make it ever 'more royal' (τυραννίδος σωτηρία ποιεῖν αὐτὴν βασιλικωτέραν *Politics* 1314a10). Whatever the policies of a tyrant may be, he must act the part of the king, says Aristotle (*Politics* 1314a39 and following). And the building of dynasties was energetically pursued: thus, for example, the tyrant Pittakos of Mytilene married into the royal house of the Penthilidai, descended from the Atreidai by way of Orestes (Diogenes Laertius 1.81).[56] Various tyrants claimed the title of king, as in the case of Periandros of Corinth (e.g., Herodotus 3.52.4) and Gelon of Syracuse (e.g., Herodotus 7.161.1).[57] Still more, the tyrant would claim a special relationship with the chief god of the community: thus, for example, Peisistratos of Athens, as personal protégé of the goddess Athena, was an occupant of the acropolis (Herodotus 1.59.6; Aristotle *Constitution of the Athenians* 14.1; Plutarch *Solon* 30), the traditional abode of the ancient kings of Athens (cf. *Iliad* II 547–549).[58]

Most important of all for the present argument, however, Peisistratos and the Peisistratidai, by virtue of controlling the acropolis of Athens, thereby controlled the central repository of oracular wisdom (Herodotus 5.90.2; cf. 5.72.3–4). Such oracular wisdom took the form of poetry (a fundamental passage is Herodotus 7.6.3–5).[59] And here we come to a point of central concern: the possession of poetry was a primary sign of the tyrant's wealth, power, and prestige.

When Kleomenes, king of Sparta, managed to penetrate the acropolis of Athens for a brief period after the expulsion of the Peisistratidai (Herodotus 5.90.2; 5.72.3–4), he expressly took possession of the **khrēsmoi** 'oracular utterances' that had been stored there by the family of tyrants in the **hieron** 'temple':

ἐκτήσατο δὲ ὁ Κλεομένης ἐκ τῆς Ἀθηναίων ἀκροπόλιος τοὺς χρησμούς, τοὺς ἔκτηντο μὲν πρότερον οἱ Πεισιστρατίδαι, ἐξελαυνό-

---

56. Cf. Page 1955.150. For these and other examples, see Petre 1975.564.
57. For these and other examples, see Petre, pp. 564–565.
58. Further discussion in Petre, p. 568.
59. Cf. also Herodotus 1.62.4, 8.96.2, and the remarks of Fontenrose 1978.157–159.

μενοι δὲ ἔλιπον ἐν τῷ ἱρῷ. καταλειφθέντας δὲ ὁ Κλεομένης ἀνέλαβε

Herodotus 5.90.2

Kleomenes had taken possession [= verb **kektēmai**] of these oracular utterances [**khrēsmoi**], taking them from the acropolis of the Athenians. Previously, the Peisistratidai had possession [= verb **kektēmai**] of them, but, when they were driven out of Athens, they left them in the temple. It was there that Kleomenes found them and took them.

It seems clear from the context that the poetry in question is private property: it is literally *possessed* (verb **kektēmai**), previously by the tyrants of Athens and subsequently by the king of Sparta.

I draw attention to a detail that explains what turns this poetry into private property: the words of such compositions have been written down. This detail, however, does not prove that writing was the actual key to the composition, let alone performance, of oracular poetry, the kind that we see here falling into the possession of tyrants and kings. In fact oracular poetry, like all the poetry of the Archaic era, was activated not through writing but through actual performance. Even as late as the second century A.D., the era of Plutarch, we can find indications of this inherited set of priorities:

καὶ γὰρ εἰ γράφειν ἔδει μὴ λέγειν τοὺς χρησμούς, οὐκ ἂν οἶμαι τοῦ θεοῦ τὰ γράμματα νομίζοντες ἐψέγομεν ὅτι λείπεται καλλιγραφίᾳ τῶν βασιλικῶν

Plutarch *The Oracles at Delphi No Longer Given in Verse* 397c

For if it were necessary to write the oracles, rather than say them, I do not think that we would consider the handwriting to be the god's and find fault with it as falling short of the calligraphic standards of royal scribes.

Turning to evidence from the earlier times, let us begin with an explicit reference by Herodotus to the *performance* of oracular poetry: a figure called Onomakritos, described as a **khrēsmologos** 'speaker of oracular utterances [**khrēsmoi**]' (7.6.3), is pictured in the act of 'singing oracular utterances [**khrēsmoi**]' for the purpose of persuading the Great King of Persia (χρησμῳδέων 7.6.5), with the active support of the now-exiled Peisistratidai of Athens and the Aleuadai of Thessaly,[60] who reinforce what he sings by presenting, through their own speeches, their supporting judgment (γνώμας ἀποδεικνύμενοι 'presenting judgments' ibid.).[61]

---

60. At Herodotus 7.6.2, the Aleuadai are described as **basilees** 'kings' of Thessaly.

61. The interactive presentation of poetry and bracketing speech by singers of oracular utterances and by tyrants respectively is a negative version of the medium inherited by Herodotus himself (in terms of this medium, we may equate *speech* with *prose*): see p. 328.

Even when the utterance of an oracle is written down, being written down does not make it private property. Throughout the narrative of Herodotus, it is normal procedure for the official emissaries who consult an oracle to write down the poetic utterances they hear (e.g., 1.47–48, 7.142.1, 8.135.2–3; cf. Aristophanes *Birds* 982). Still, the force of the oracular statement is not activated, the words do not become a completed speech-act, until they are performed before the audience for whom it was intended. Let us take for example the case of the Athenian emissaries who consulted the Delphic Oracle about their impending fate in the Persian War: having written down what the oracle told them, they returned to Athens and ἀπήγγελλον ἐς τὸν δῆμον 'announced it to the people' (Herodotus 7.142.1). In fact there are surviving reports of severe punishments visited upon an emissary who would reveal the message of the oracle, once transcribed, to anyone other than the intended audience (*Suda* s.v. τὰ τρία).[62]

With this added perspective let us return to the story of Herodotus about the oracular utterances kept by the Peisistratidai on top of the acropolis (5.90.2).[63] To repeat, the writing down of the oracular utterances makes it possible for the tyrants to possess this poetry as their private property. But this poetry is private property only because the tyrants, as Herodotus implies with the details about the storage of poetry on the acropolis, have the power *not* to make all such poetry public property, by withholding public performance.[64]

This negative attitude toward tyrants, as reflected in the story of Herodotus, contrasts with the positive attitude fostered by the tyrants themselves as the owners of poetry. It is a recurrent theme in the public image of the tyrant that he makes it possible for the community to possess, as its own public property, the poetic heritage that had been usurped for private gain by a degenerate aristocracy. A fundamental passage in this regard is "Plato" *Hipparchus*, where Socrates describes Hipparkhos, here presented as the oldest of the sons of Peisistratos, as wishing to educate the citizens of Athens (βουλόμενος παιδεύειν τοὺς πολίτας 228c) by introducing the public performance of the epics of Homer at the Feast of Panathenaia (228b), by sending a

62. Cf. Fontenrose 1978.217n27.

63. Cf. p. 158.

64. There is a story reported by Diogenes Laertius 9.6 (Heraclitus 22 A 1 DK) that Heraclitus deposited his writings in the temple of Artemis at Ephesus so that only the powerful might have access to it (ὅπως οἱ δυνάμενοι ⟨μόνοι⟩ προσίοιεν αὐτῷ καὶ μὴ ἐκ τοῦ δημώδους εὐκαταφρόνητον ᾖ); in the same context there is a report that Heraclitus belonged to the royal lineage of Ephesus, and that he at one point resigned his hereditary "kingship" in favor of his brother (Diogenes ibid.). Members of the royal lineage of Ephesus, descended from Androklos son of Kodros of Athens, were entitled to be called **basileis** 'kings', to occupy the front seats at the games, to wear purple robes as a sign of their royal descent, to carry a staff called a **skipōn** (as distinct from a **skēptron**), and to be in charge of the sacred rites of Eleusinian Demeter (Pherecydes FGH 3 F 155 by way of Strabo 14.1.3 C633 = Heraclitus 22 A 2 DK) .

ship to fetch the poet Anacreon from Teos (228c), and by keeping in his company the master of choral lyric poetry, Simonides of Keos (ibid.). In doing these things, Hipparkhos showed that he was generous in sharing his **sophiā**, his own understanding of poetry, with the community (οὐκ οἰόμενος δεῖν οὐδενὶ σοφίας φθονεῖν 228c).[65] After having 'educated' the people in the city proper, he turned his attention to the population of the countryside (228c-d), where he erected public inscriptions of poetry reflecting his **sophiā**:

> κἄπειτα τῆς σοφίας τῆς αὐτοῦ, ἥν τ' ἔμαθεν καὶ ἣν αὐτὸς ἐξηῦρεν,
> ἐκλεξάμενος ἃ ἡγεῖτο σοφώτατα εἶναι, ταῦτα αὐτὸς ἐντείνας εἰς ἐλε-
> γεῖον αὐτοῦ ποιήματα καὶ ἐπιδείγματα τῆς σοφίας ἐπέγραψεν

"Plato" *Hipparchus* 228d

He then selected what he considered to be the most skillful things [sopha] from his own understanding of poetry [= **sophiā**], both what he had learned [from others] and what he had invented for himself,[66] and personally put these things into the elegiac meter,[67] inscribing them as poems of his own [on the herm-statues] and as public displays [**epideigmata**] of his understanding of poetry [= **sophiā**].[68]

The language of the two epigrams that are quoted and attributed to Hipparkhos in "Plato" *Hipparchus* 229a-b matches that of an actual inscription on a herm-statue from the era of the Peisistratidai (CEG 304).[69]

It is made explicit in this Platonic passage that the poetic utterances of the tyrant were intended to rival those that are attributed to the Oracle of Apollo at Delphi (*Hipparchus* 228e). Moreover, it is implicit that the public display of these poetic utterances, by way of inscriptions set up in public, is the equivalent of public performance. Such equivalence is the essence of the epigram. I draw attention to the wording that introduces the accomplishments of Hipparkhos, starting with his organization of Homeric performances, continuing with his patronage of such figures as Anacreon and Simonides, and concluding with the public display of his epigrams: in doing all these things, Socrates is quoted as saying, Hipparkhos 'presented publicly the beautiful accomplishments connected with his understanding of poetry [**sophiā**]' (καλὰ ἔργα σοφίας ἀπεδείξατο 228b). Such a stance of sharing

---

65. Cf. Theognis 769–770 and the commentary of Ford 1985.92, Edmunds 1985.106–107.

66. In other words some poems are so ad hoc as to be considered Hipparkhos' own compositions while others are thought of as recompositions of the compositions of others.

67. By implication a composition can be switched from one meter to another in the process of recomposition in performance. The available epigraphical evidence suggests that the Peisistratidai played a major role in the evolution of the elegiac distich as the canonical meter of the epigram: see Wallace 1984, especially p. 315.

68. The translation here closely follows that of Ford 1985.90.

69. For parallelisms in diction with, for example, Theognis 753–756, see Ford 1985.91 §17n1.

with the public is what lies behind the public gesture recorded in Gorgon FGH 515 F 18 (by way of the scholia to Pindar *Olympian* 7, I, p. 195 Drachmann), where a victory ode of Pindar, *Olympian* 7, commissioned to celebrate the Olympic victory of Diagoras of Rhodes in 464 B.C., is inscribed in gold letters and dedicated in the temple of Athena Lindia in Rhodes. We are dealing here with a public gesture.[70] So also in the case of the poetry attributed to the tyrant Hipparchus, where the words are ostensibly written down as a public inscription, not as a private transcript of secret documents to be hoarded in some treasure chest.[71]

The notion of 'public presentation', as in the Platonic description of the poetry attributed to the tyrant Hipparchus, is expressed by way of the verb **apo-deik-numai** (ἀπεδείξατο *Hipparchus* 228b).[72] Similarly in the case of Onomakritos, described in the act of 'singing oracular utterances [**khrēsmoi**]' to persuade the Great King of Persia (χρησμῳδέων Herodotus 7.6.5): the narrative makes it clear that the performance of these oracular utterances is being authorized by the Peisistratidai (along with the Aleuadai), who in this instance even reinforce what Onomakritos sings by publicly presenting in their own speeches their supporting judgment (ibid.). Again, the notion of 'public presentation' is expressed here by the verb **apo-deik-numai** (ἀποδεικνύμενοι ibid.).[73]

That oracular poetry, in order to have effect, requires public performance is made clear by the semantics of the words **prophētēs** 'declarer' and **theōros** 'emissary'.[74] Let us begin with **prophētēs**, designating a figure in society whose hereditary role is to formalize in poetry the inspiration received by the **mantis** 'seer', as we see from the explicit wording of Plato: ὅθεν δὴ καὶ τὸ τῶν προφητῶν γένος ἐπὶ ταῖς ἐνθέοις μαντείαις κριτὰς ἐπικαθιστάναι νόμος 'and for this reason it is customary to appoint the lineage of declarers [**prophētēs** pl.] to be judges [**kritēs** pl.] over the inspired [**entheos** pl.] mantic utterances [**manteia** pl.]' (Plato *Timaeus* 72a). As such, the **prophētai** are **hupokritai** 'actors', in that they act out the mantic utterance, with its **ainigmoi** 'enigmatic words' (τῆς δι' αἰνιγμῶν οὗτοι φήμης καὶ φαντάσεως ὑποκριταί *Timaeus* 72b).[75] The prime example is the official

---

70. Cf. p. 174. We may contrast this gesture with that of Heraclitus, as described at p. 160, where the depositing of a transcript in the temple of Artemis at Ephesus is interpreted as a way of restricting access.

71. On the symbolism of hiding poetry away in a box, see p. 171 and p. 172.

72. Cf. the collocation of **apo-deik-numai** 'present publicly' with **sophiā** 'skill in discourse' at Herodotus 4.76.2. More on this verb **apo-deik-numai** at pp. 217, 218 and following, pp. 222 and following.

73. See the previous note.

74. More below on the meaning of **theōros**; for the moment, I find it useful to cite the working definition of Delcourt 1955.69: "chargé d'une mission religieuse."

75. For another such explicit definition, I cite the scholia A to *Iliad* XVI 235: προφήτας γὰρ λέγουσι τοὺς περὶ τὰ χρηστήρια ἀσχολουμένους καὶ τὰς μαντείας τὰς γινομένας ὑπὸ τῶν ἱερέων ἐκφέροντας 'declarers [**prophētēs** pl.] is the name for those who officiate at oracles and

prophētēs of the Oracle of Apollo at Delphi (cf. Herodotus 8.36, 37).[76] The **prophētēs** declares, formalizes as a speech-act, the words of the inspired **mantis**.[77] In the case of the Oracle at Delphi, the office of the inspired **mantis** was traditionally held by a priestess, known as the **Puthiā** 'Pythia' (cf. Plutarch *The Oracles in Delphi No Longer Given in Verse* 397b-c; Strabo 9.3.5 C419).[78] From stories about famous attempts to bribe the Pythia (e.g., Herodotus 6.66.3, 6.75.3),[79] we know that it was the Pythia, not the **prophētēs**, who controlled the *content* of the mantic utterance. I infer that the **prophētēs** controlled the *form*. The standard transmission of this form, as we see most clearly in the numerous quotations of the Delphic Oracle in Herodotus, was the poetic form of dactylic hexameter. Accordingly, I see no reason to doubt that the **prophētēs** was involved in the poetic formalization of prophecy.[80]

The **mantis**, then, is the middle man between the source of inspiration and the **prophētēs**, the recomposer of the inspired message in poetic form. Alternatively, in the realm of myth, there are situations where we see no middle man. Thus the seer par excellence, Teiresias, who declares the will of Zeus, is the '**prophētēs** of Zeus' (Pindar *Nemean* 1.60). Here we are witnessing a relic of an earlier and undifferentiated stage, in that Teiresias is generally known as a **mantis** (e.g., *Odyssey* xi 99). In other words the figure of Teiresias represents a stage where the **prophētēs** *is* the **mantis**.[81] The diction of poetry preserves further relics of such an undifferentiated stage, where the prophecy of the **mantis** and the poetry formulated by the **prophētēs** are as yet one: there are instances where the word **prophētēs** designates the poet as the one who declares the voice of the **Mousa** 'Muse' (Bacchylides *Epinician* 8.3). A particularly striking example is Pindar F 150 SM: μαντεύεο Μοῖσα προφατεύσω δ' ἐγώ 'be a **mantis**, Muse, and I shall be the **prophētēs**'.[82]

---

bring forth the mantic utterances [**manteia** pl.] that take place through the agency of the priests'.

76. Fontenrose 1978.218 argues that the official title of the **prophētēs** of the Oracle of Apollo at Delphi was not **prophētēs** but simply **hiereus** 'priest'.

77. Cf. p. 168. It is the fact that he is the actor of a speech-act that qualifies the **prophētēs** 'declarer' as a **hupokritēs** 'actor' (again Plato *Timaeus* 72b).

78. For a minimalist survey of the Pythia's role, see Fontenrose, pp. 196–228.

79. For a collection of such testimonia, see Fontenrose, p. 224, referring to entries Q137, Q124, and H7 in his Catalogue of Delphic Responses.

80. *Pace* Fontenrose, pp. 218–219.

81. It is this kind of undifferentiation that is being discussed in Plato *Timaeus* 72b.

82. The very form **Mousa/Moisa** (from *mont-ia; possibly *month-ia) may well be derived from the same root *men- as in **maniā**. This possibility, along with others, is discussed by Chantraine DELG 716. If this etymology is correct, then the very word for "Muse" reflects an earlier stage where not only the one who is inspired and the one who speaks the words of inspiration are the same, but even, further, the type of mental state marked by **maniā** is not yet differentiated

There is yet another pertinent use of **prophētēs**: this word also designates the herald who declares the winner at athletic games (e.g., Bacchylides
Epinician 9.28: in this case the reference is to the Isthmian Games). This
usage is crucial for our understanding of another word, **theōros** 'emissary',
meaning literally 'he who sees [root **hor-**] a vision [**theā**]', in the specific
sense of designating the official delegate of a given polis who is sent out to
observe the athletic games and to bring back the news of victory (Herodotus
1.59.1, 8.26: in this case the reference is to the Olympic Games). Thus the
prophētēs is the one who declares the message of victory at the Games,
while the **theōros** is the one who witnesses the message and takes it back to
the polis, where he declares it to the polis.

Similarly the **theōros** is the official delegate of a given polis who is to
bring back the message of the oracle: there are many examples, the most
famous of which is Kreon in Sophocles *Oedipus Tyrannus* 114. Thus the
prophētēs is the one who declares the message of the Oracle at Delphi, while
the **theōros** is the one who witnesses the message and takes it back to the
polis, where he declares it to the polis.[83]

After the consultation at Delphi, the **theōros** was to deliver to his community the communication of the Oracle, and there were severe sanctions
against any emissary who would divulge the message of the oracle to outsiders before returning home (again *Suda* s.v. τὰ τρία).[84] This message was a
privileged kind of communication. As Heraclitus declares (22 B 93 DK), the
god at Delphi neither **legei** 'speaks' nor **kruptei** 'conceals': rather he
sēmainei 'indicates'.[85] The verb **sēmainō** 'indicate' is derived from the noun
sēma, which means 'sign' or 'signal' and which derives from a concept of
inner vision (as attested in the Sanskrit cognate *dhyāma*, derived from the
verb *dhī-*).[86] Correspondingly the word **theōros** means literally 'he who sees
[root **hor-**] a vision [**theā**]'. Thus the god Apollo of the Oracle at Delphi,
when he **sēmainei** 'indicates', is conferring an inner vision upon the **theōros**,
the one who consults him. Both the encoder and the decoder are supposedly
operating on the basis of an inner vision. Greek usage makes it clear that the
prophētēs, who communicates the words of Apollo to those who consult the
god, likewise **sēmainei** 'indicates' (cf. Herodotus 8.37.2). In this relationship, where the god of inspiration **sēmainei** 'indicates' to the **theōros** the
inner vision of the poetry, we see the hermeneutic model for the processes of
encoding and decoding the **ainos**. Moreover, this relationship between the

---

from the type of mental state marked by formations with *men-t- and *men-h₂– 'remember, have
the mind connected with'.

83. For an overview of the function of the **theōros** as an official emissary of the polis, see
Delcourt 1955.68–70.

84. Cf. Delcourt 1955.68–70 and Fontenrose 1978.217n27.

85. Further details at p. 164.

86. Extensive discussion in N 1983.

words **sēmainō** 'make a sign [**sēma**]' and **theōros** 'he who observes the vision' is pertinent to the usage of the modern lexical creations *semantics/semiotics* and *theory*.

In Greek usage someone **sēmainei** 'indicates', that is, 'makes a sign [**sēma**]', when speaking from a superior vantage point, as when a scout goes to the top of a hill and then comes back down to indicate what he saw (Herodotus 7.192.1, 7.219.1).[87] By extension, someone **sēmainei** 'makes a sign [**sēma**]' when he or she speaks from a metaphorically superior vantage point, as when an authoritative person makes a pronouncement that arbitrates between contending points of view (Herodotus 1.5.3). But the ultimate voice of authority belongs to the god of the Oracle at Delphi, whose supreme vantage point confers upon him the knowledge of all things, even the precise number of all grains of sand in the universe (Herodotus 1.47.3; cf. Pindar *Pythian* 9.44–49).

Thus it is most appropriate for poets, when speaking with the voice of authority, to compare themselves to a **theōros**, one who consults the Oracle and to whom the Oracle **sēmainei** 'makes a sign [**sēma**]' through the intermediacy of the priestess of Apollo, the Pythia:[88]

τόρνου καὶ στάθμης καὶ γνώμονος ἄνδρα θεωρὸν
εὐθύτερον χρὴ ⟨ἔμεν⟩ Κύρνε φυλασσόμενον,
ᾧτινί κεν Πυθῶνι θεοῦ χρήσασ' ἱέρεια
ὀμφὴν σημήνῃ πίονος ἐξ ἀδύτου·
οὐτέ τι γὰρ προσθεὶς οὐδέν κ' ἔτι φάρμακον εὕροις
οὐδ' ἀφελὼν πρὸς θεῶν ἀμπλακίην προφύγοις

Theognis 805–810

A man who is **theōros** must be more straight, Kyrnos, being on his guard,
than a carpenter's pin and rule and square
— a man to whom the priestess [i.e., the Pythia] of the god at Delphi makes a response,
as she indicates [**sēmainei**] the Voice [= **omphē** 'sacred utterance']89 from the opulent shrine.
For you would not find any remedy if you add anything,
nor would you escape from veering, in the eyes of the gods, if you take anything away.

Just as the priestess, through her intermediacy, **sēmainei** 'indicates' the message of the god, so also the poet speaks authoritatively, as if a lawgiver.

87. See Hartog 1980.368–369.
88. Extensive commentary in N 1985.36–41.
89. Cognate with English *song*.

Again I quote from Theognis:[90]

χρή με παρὰ στάθμην καὶ γνώμονα τήνδε δικάσσαι
Κύρνε δίκην, ἰσόν τ᾽ ἀμφοτέροισι δόμεν,
μάντεσί τ᾽ οἰωνοῖς τε καὶ αἰθομένοις ἱεροῖσιν,
ὄφρα μὴ ἀμπλακίης αἰσχρὸν ὄνειδος ἔχω

Theognis 543–546

I must render this judgment, Kyrnos, along [the straight line of] a
carpenter's rule and square,
and I must give to both sides their equitable share,
with the help of seers, portents, and burning sacrifice,
so that I may not incur shameful reproach for veering.

By implication the poet is a **theōros** who **sēmainei** 'indicates' to the community what the god indicates to him. To be a **theōros**, as he declares, you may not change for your audience one iota of what the god had imparted to you, just as the man who consults the Oracle must report to the community exactly what the priestess had told. In these examples from Theognis, there is no middle man, no **prophētēs**, between the Pythia and the **theōros**, because the **theōros** is the **prophētēs** as well. The poetry here collapses the attested differentiation between the one who formulates the inspired word as poetry and the one who takes it back to the community.

That the poet is truly speaking here in the mode of a lawgiver is clear from the traditions reported by Herodotus 1.65.4 about Lycurgus, the lawgiver of Sparta: it is the Pythia of the Oracle of Apollo at Delphi who indicates (φράσαι) to Lycurgus the law code of Sparta.[91]

We have seen the following patterns of semantic differentiation in words that designate the transmitters of oracular poetry:

1. **mantis**: 'he who is in a special mental state', that is, 'he who is inspired [**entheos** = having the god within]' (cf. Plato *Timaeus* 72a), he who communicates in a sacred medium
2. **prophētēs**: either **mantis** (e.g., Teiresias) or more specifically one who communicates the message of the **mantis** in a poetic medium (e.g., the official who turns the inspired message of the Pythia into dactylic hexameters or the poet who turns the inspiring message of the Muse into a variety of meters)
3. **theōros**: either **prophētēs** (e.g., Lycurgus or Theognis in the stance of a lawgiver) or, more specifically, one who is officially delegated by the

90. Extensive commentary in N 1985.36–41.

91. In contrast with this particular Spartan version, Herodotus also gives the contemporary version, also ascribed by him to the Spartans, according to which Lycurgus got the code from Crete (again 1.65.4); more on this contemporary Spartan version in N 1985.31–32.

polis to communicate the message of the **mantis/prophētēs**[92] to the polis.[93]

The essence of oracular poetry is that it serves to uphold the existing social order; it derives its authority from such ultimate sources of authorization as Apollo's Oracle at Delphi. For this reason, the two kings of Sparta were the official safekeepers of oracular poetry (Herodotus 6.57.4), sharing their knowledge with four officials, two appointed by each of them, whose duty it was to be emissaries to the Oracle at Delphi and who were known as the **Puthioi** (6.57.2, 4). These **Puthioi** were public figures, taking their meals with the kings at the public expense (6.57.2). The existence of these officials at Sparta makes it clear that the poetry of oracular utterances, just like other poetry, was considered to be the possession of the polis.

In Sparta the use of poetry for private gain, even on the part of a king, was a symptom of tyrannical tendencies, of usurpation: thus, for example, in the story told by Thucydides concerning the downfall of the Spartan king Pausanias — whose meteoric rise in personal prestige as a result of the Persian War led to his eventual downfall — the charges brought against the king included the fact that he had an epigram inscribed on the victory tripod dedicated at Delphi celebrating the defeat of the Persians, an epigram commissioned 'for his private purposes' (ἰδίᾳ Thucydides 1.132.2). The poet who was commissioned to compose this epigram, as quoted by Thucydides (ibid.), was none other than Simonides of Keos (Simonides EG 17; on the authority of Pausanias 3.8.2), whom we have already seen described as a member of the inner circle of Hipparkhos, tyrant of Athens ("Plato" *Hipparchus* 228c).[94] In this case even the mention of a single person's name is enough to raise suspicions that the poetry in which the name is mentioned is being used for private purposes, though the dedication on which the epigram is inscribed happens to be a public offering at Delphi.

92. Or in the case of athletics the sacred message of the victory itself.

93. At Herodotus 1.29.1, Solon the lawgiver of Athens gives **theōriā** as the pretext (**prophasis**) for his travels, but his other motive, as made explicit in the narrative, is to prevent his being compelled to undo any aspect of his law code. At 1.30.1, it is made clear that **theōriā** was indeed also his motive. So there are two motives, but only one is made explicit by Solon to his audience; the other motive is kept implicit by Solon but made explicit by Herodotus to *his* "audience."

94. Cf. p. 161. After the fall of the Peisistratidai, Simonides did not become a persona non grata with the new democratic government at Athens. According to the anonymous *Life of Aeschylus* (8), prefixed to the corpus of Aeschylus, Simonides defeated Aeschylus for the state commission of composing an epigram in honor of those who fell at Marathon (doubts about the credibility of this tradition in Podlecki 1984.185–187). Also Simonides EG 75 is an epigram marking the **sēma** 'tomb' of Megakles of the Alkmaionidai, the same figure who is the subject of praise in Pindar's *Pythian* 7 (on whom see p. 157). On Simonides and Themistokles, see Bowra 1961.356.

In the story told by Herodotus about the possession of oracular poetry by the Peisistratidai, the misuse implied by the narration is analogous. Here the public possession of poetry to be performed is implicitly being diverted to private possession, the private gain of tyrants, by way of writing: when Herodotus says that the Peisistratidai of Athens ἔκτηντο 'had possession [= verb **kektēmai**]' of the oracles (5.90.2), he is in effect talking negatively about the private usurpation of public performance meant for the polis. But the force of an oracular statement is not activated, the words do not become a completed speech-act, until they are performed before the audience for whom it was intended, as in the story about the Athenian emissaries who consulted the Delphic Oracle about their impending fate in the Persian War: having written down what the Oracle told them, they returned to Athens and ἀπήγγελλον ἐς τὸν δῆμον 'announced it to the people' (Herodotus 7.142.1).[95]

This Herodotean outlook on tyrants, as reflected by his story about the Peisistratidai and their private possession of oracular poetry, may be con-

95. On **angeliā** 'announcement' as speech-act in the poetics of Pindar, cf. Nash 1976. Another particularly revealing passage is Herodotus 8.135.3, concerning the **prophētēs** 'declarer' of the oracular voice of Apollo at the shrine known as the Ptoön of the Thebans; the official who is actually inspired by Apollo has the title **pro-mantis** (8.135.2). The story has it that the **pro-mantis** on one particular occasion made utterances in a non-Greek language (ibid.; it is made explicit that the utterances were normally in Greek). These utterances were then declared by the **prophētēs** (τὰ λεγόμενα ὑπὸ τοῦ προφήτεω 8.135.3), but they were not understood by those present (ibid.). At this point, one Mys takes the initiative of writing the words down on a tablet that he impulsively seizes from the Thebans who officially accompanied him to consult the oracle (ibid.). The wording ἀπογραψομένους and συγγραψάμενον here at Herodotus 8.135.3, where the compound verbs of **graphō** 'write' are used in the middle voice, implies that those who consult the Oracle may not only take notes but also commission someone to write a definitive transcript, to be brought back home to their native city for "publication," through public performance. The written word, then, can serve as intermediary for that ultimate speech-act. It is clear from this passage that the **prophētēs** does not interpret the message of the **mantis**: he simply formalizes it. The **prophētēs** 'declarer' can be described as a **hupokritēs** 'actor' (Plato *Timaeus* 72b). The verb **hupokrīnomai**, from which **hupokritēs** 'actor' is derived, conveys a secondary formal speech-act, consistent and true, in response to a primary formal speech-act. For this reason, **hupokrīnomai** can be translated either as *answer* or in other contexts as *interpret*, where the object of the verb is a dream or omen (cf. Thomson 1946.181–182 and Svenbro 1987.37–39, with special reference to *Odyssey* xv 167–170). To *interpret* is really to formalize the speech-act that is radiating from the dream or the omen or, let us say, the **mantis**. As for the translation of **hupokrīnomai** as *answer*, it applies to situations where one speech-act is a formal answer to a preceding speech-act, which is a formal question. In one Archaic inscription (CEG 286) the voice of the inscribed letters promises that it 'answers' (ὑποκρίνομαι) the same thing to all men who ask their questions. My interpretation here of **hupokrīnomai** differs from that of Svenbro (1987.37–39), though I agree with his argument that this inscription illustrates the function of the written word as a substitute for the formalization of performance (p. 39): "The statuette is a 'speaking object' because of the vocal implications of **hupokrīnomai**. It is in fact our earliest clear example of an inscription using, with regard to itself, the metaphor of the voice." In such a case the inscription *is* the **hupokritēs**, the actor, and therefore it *is* the **prophētēs**, the formalizer of the speech-act.

trasted with the outlook of Thucydides, whose wording nevertheless reflects similar patterns of thought concerning the contrast of private and public possession of discourse. Let us consider the expression κτῆμα . . . ἐς αἰεί 'a possession [ktēma, derivative of verb kektēmai] for all time' used by Thucydides (1.22.4) in talking positively about his own private preservation of knowledge about affairs of state. Thucydides here is setting up a choice between a private possession of knowledge on the one hand, which is in his power to transmit to the one who possesses the text, and on the other hand the public display or performance of such knowledge, which would be conditioned by the vicissitudes of public performance in the polis, and which he describes as a 'competitive effort [agōnisma, derivative of agōn] meant for hearing in the here and now' (ἀγώνισμα ἐς τὸ παραχρῆμα ἀκούειν ibid.). This negative image of public performance, which is meant to serve as a foil for the work of Thucydides, is equivalent to the medium represented by Herodotus.[96] From the standpoint of Herodotus, by contrast, the possession of his own medium is open to the public: his medium is in fact presented as a public possession, so that whatever he writes can be equated with whatever he would say publicly.[97]

This positive notion, that a piece of writing can in fact become a public possession, brings us back to the corresponding negative notion, that writing had encouraged the private possession of the public media of singing or making speeches: for Herodotus, such private possession by way of writing is a characteristic of tyrants. In the *Histories* of Herodotus, the very act of writing letters is typical of tyrants and the kind of power that they exercise (e.g., Polykrates of Samos at 3.40.4 in the general context of 3.40–43; cf. 2.123.1).[98] The secretiveness of this kind of writing is best symbolized in the story about a stratagem contrived by the tyrant Histiaios of Miletus. He had a secret letter written on top of the shaven scalp of a faithful slave, whose hair was then allowed to grow back before he was finally sent off to deliver his message (Herodotus 5.35.2–4). The hair that grows over the letter — the cover that hides the message — must be removed for both the encoding and the decoding.[99]

To return to the story about the private possession of oracular poetry by the Peisistratidai (Herodotus 5.90.2): as long as private interests control the public medium, there is the ever-present danger of premeditated selective control over the content of poetry, leading to stealthy distortions or perver-

96. For more on the medium of Herodotus, see p. 328. Cf. Havelock 1963,54n8.

97. For more on *writing* as a performative substitution, in the medium of Herodotus, for *saying* publicly: pp. 217 and 219.

98. Hartog 1980.287–288.

99. What the message says under the cover of the hair is expressed by way of the verb **sēmainō** 'make signs, indicate' (σημαίνοντα 5.35.2; σημῆναι *bis*, ἐσήμαινε 5.35.3), on which see p. 233.

sions of the poetic truth. This is the point made by Herodotus when he narrates how Onomakritos was once 'caught red-handed, by Lasus of Hermione, in the act of putting his own poetry, an oracular utterance [khrēsmos], inside the wording of Musaeus' (ἐπ' αὐτοφώρῳ ἁλοὺς ὑπὸ Λάσου τοῦ Ἑρμιονέος ἐμποιέων ἐς τὰ Μουσαίου χρησμόν 7.6.3). The protection against such tampering can be visualized as a **sphrāgis** 'seal', such as the one that is figuratively placed on the poetry of Theognis (19–20), which prevents any stealthy changes to the genuine wording (21).[100] Similarly the words of the Oracle, as received from the Pythia (Theognis 807) and delivered by the **theōros** to his community (805), must resist any and all stealthy changes (809–810).[101] In the language of inscriptions, we can see that the literal placing of a **sphrāgis** on a ratified speech-act is tantamount to making it public:

λαβόντες τόδε τὸ ψάφισμα παρὰ τοῦ | γραμματέος διαπεμψάσθων
Κνιδίων προστά| [τ]αις καὶ [τῶ]ι δάμωι [σφ]ραγιξαμένων τῶν
ταμι| ἀν τᾶι [δαμ]οσίαι σφραγῖδι

DGE 226.3–6 (Thera iii/ii B.C.)

... taking this resolution from the scribe, let them send it to the presidents and **dēmos** of the Knidians, after the treasurers [**tamiai**] have sealed it with the public seal [**sphrāgis**].

The mention of Musaeus at Herodotus 7.6.3, where his oracular utterances are being stealthily reshaped by Onomakritos, should be compared with another passage, at 8.96.2, where Herodotus goes out of his way to stress the authority that he attaches to the oracular utterances of Musaeus and a figure called Bakis.[102] The inspiration of Bakis reportedly comes from the nymphs (Pausanias 4.27.4, 10.12.11; cf. Aristophanes *Peace* 1070–1071); he is reputed to have predicted many of the crucial moments of the Persian War (Herodotus 8.20.2, 8.77, 8.96.2, 9.43). According to the scholia to Aristophanes *Peace* 1071 and the *Suda* (s.v.), Bakis was a name assumed even by the tyrant Peisistratos himself. In the *Knights* of Aristophanes, the Kleon-figure possesses the oracles of Bakis in order to keep Demos under control (109–143, 195–210, 960–1096, 999 and following). It has been said about the "quotation," at *Knights* 1015–1016, of one of the oracles of Bakis, that "if Kleon had not said that his [oracles] were oracles of Bakis we would say that

100. For more on the seal of Theognis, see Ford 1985; cf. N 1985.33.
101. See p. 165. We may compare the tradition according to which the Pythia communicated to Lycurgus, lawgiver of Sparta, the law code of Sparta (Herodotus 1.65.4); cf. p. 166. On the ideology of unchangeability as affirmed by the law code itself, cf. N 1985.31–34, especially p. 32: "Inside the ideology of narrative traditions about a given lawgiver, his code is static, unchangeable; outside this ideology and in reality, however, the code is dynamic, subject to modifications and accretions that are occasioned by an evolving social order."
102. For more on Bakis, see Fontenrose 1978.158–162.

this purported to be a Delphic response."[103] In this oracle of Bakis, there is mention of the λογίων ὁδόν 'path of oracles [**logia**]' (again *Knights* 1015) that Apollo himself proclaimed from Delphi (1015–1016).

In this same passage from the *Knights* of Aristophanes, I draw attention to the challenge, issued by Demos, that the disguised Kleon-figure should 'read out loud' the oracles (ἀναγνώσεσθέ μοι 1011), which are contained in a **kibōtos** 'box' (1000). In this image we see a metaphor for the making public of what is potentially kept private by the tyrannical mentality. The word for 'read out loud' in *Knights* 1011, **ana-gignōskō**, means basically 'know again, recognize' (cf. also 118, 1065). To 'read' is to 'know again' by reperforming to oneself and potentially to others the last in a series of preexisting performances — this last one having been written down rather than spoken, whereas the previous ones had been spoken. The act of *reading* here is a metaphor for the activation, through public performance, of the composition. To *know again* the composition, that is, to *recognize* it, is to be performing it. Such a *recognition* takes place in the mind of both performer and audience as one hears the words being read out loud.[104] In Pindar's *Olympian* 10, the song starts with the command to 'read out loud' (verb **ana-gignōskō**: ἀνάγνωτε 10.1) the Olympic winner, who is 'written down' inside the **phrēn** 'mind' (πόθι φρενὸς ἐμᾶς γέγραπται 10.2–3). Thus the image of reading out loud can even serve as the metaphor for the public performance of a composition, and the image of writing, as the metaphor for the composition itself.[105] Moreover, the image of writing here conveys the fixity of the composition in the mind of the composer, with the implication that it will not be recomposed in the process of performance by the chorus. The notion of fixity in composition is also illustrated by the very essence of State Theater in Athens, where the public is not supposed to affect directly, and thereby recompose, the action ongoing in the drama as acted by the actors.[106] To this extent the image of writing is again appropriate in conveying the fixity of the composition: the composition of drama in Athenian State Theater is metaphorically a text, a script.[107] But the matching performance of drama is metaphorically

103. Fontenrose, p. 159.

104. This point is stressed by Svenbro 1987.32–33, who also points out that the Ionian word **epi-legesthai** 'read' (as at Herodotus 8.128.3) implies that the reader adds (hence **epi-**) the sounds of the words to the letters that he sees (p. 32). For more on the semiotics of reading as *recognizing*, see N 1983, especially p. 39; also Pucci 1987.87.

105. For other instances of the metaphor of writing as inscribed in the **phrēn** 'mind', see Svenbro, p. 46n27, who cites, for example, Aeschylus *Libation-Bearers* 450, *Eumenides* 273–275; Sophocles *Philoctetes* 1325. On the Platonic notion that ordinary writing is an **eidōlon** 'simulacrum' of metaphorical writing (*Phaedrus* 276a), see Svenbro, p. 46n26, following Derrida 1972b.172.

106. This point is elaborated by Svenbro, p. 35. On State Theater as the creation of tyrants, see pp. 384 and following.

107. It is pertinent to bring to mind again the frequent use in drama of the metaphor of writing

not just any kind of *reading* as we know it, but specifically *reading out loud:* in essence the process of reading out loud is a speech-act, like performance itself, and it is public, not private. We may note the expression δρᾶμα ἀνα-γιγνώσκειν 'to read out loud [**ana-gignōskō**] the drama', referring to the function of producing a drama, in the scholia to Aristophanes *Clouds* 510.[108]

In contrast with *reading out loud*, the process of *silent reading* is decidedly not a speech-act: thus for example in the *Hippolytus* of Euripides, the figure of Theseus, when he reads silently the tablet left behind by the dead Phaedra, does not activate the force of these words until he sums up their contents publicly to the chorus (856–886).[109] Similarly in the *Knights* of Aristophanes, we see the figure of Nikias engaged in the silent reading of the oracles of Bakis while conversing with the figure of Demosthenes, who comically misunderstands pieces of his interlocutor's conversation as if they were portions of the oracles being read out loud; instead of reading out loud, however, Nikias simply summarizes for Demosthenes what he had already grasped through an instantaneous silent reading (115–146).[110] Such silent reading is symptomatic of the tyrant's power to control the performance of a composition. We have already noted the image, occurring later in the *Knights*, of a **kibōtos** 'box' that stores the oracles of Bakis (1000). These oracles can be taken out by the Kleon-figure and 'read out loud' to Demos (1011), but we know that the reader of the oracles also has the power to read ahead, silently, and then interpret his reading, with a voice that is accepted as the authority of the oracles (again 115–146). In these images of storing oracles in a box and then taking them out either to be read out loud to Demos or, alternatively, merely to be interpreted, we see the ultimate metaphor for the control of performance by the State.[111]

With these considerations in mind, let us return to the story of confrontation between Onomakritos and the poet Lasus of Hermione: as a result of this

---

as inscribed in the **phrēn** 'mind', as cited at p. 171. Cf. also Svenbro, pp. 42–45 on Athenaeus 453c-454a.

108. As Pickard-Cambridge 1968.84n4 notes, such an expression cannot refer literally to the reading of a drama in the theater.

109. Svenbro, pp. 31, 40, following Knox 1968.433.

110. Svenbro, p. 31.

111. It does not necessarily follow, however, that the implicit metaphor for Athenian State Theater is an act of silent reading, as argued by Svenbro, p. 35 and following. Again I note the expression δρᾶμα ἀναγιγνώσκειν 'to read out loud [**ana-gignōskō**] the drama', referring to the function of producing a drama, in the scholia to Aristophanes *Clouds* 510. We may also compare Plato *Laws* 817d, a passage implying that each drama, in competition with other dramas, had to be approved by the archons, on the basis of some kind of audition, before a chorus could officially be constituted for its production (cf. Pickard-Cambridge 1968.84); I stress that there is no reference in this passage to a written text, a script. On the notion that the dialogues of Plato amount to an internalization of Theater inside the Book, see Svenbro, p. 41, following, for example, Derrida 1972b.264.

confrontation, Herodotus goes on to say, Onomakritos had been publicly exiled by his own patrons, the Peisistratidai themselves (7.6.4); yet in the here and now being narrated, we see him back in their good graces as he performs before the Great King of the Persian Empire, once again distorting the truth by way of premeditated selectivity (7.6.4–5). The context of this same passage (7.6.3–4), however, makes it apparent that Lasus of Hermione, as a rival of Onomakritos, was also under the patronage of the Peisistratidai. In fact we have explicit testimony that even a figure like Simonides, master of choral lyric poetry, had once been under the patronage of the Peisistratidai ("Plato" *Hipparchus* 228f, where Simonides is mentioned along with Anacreon).[112] From the standpoint of Herodotus it is clear that the patronage of tyrants discredits a poet. Yet, from the standpoint of the tyrants themselves, it seems just as clear that this same patronage must have been expected to serve as a public guarantee of the poet's truthfulness. Thus the discrediting of one rival poet by another could still have served to validate the tyrant's legitimacy, even if Herodotus can then reuse that same discrediting of the poet to expose the perceived illegitimacy of the tyrant. Such is the narrative strategy of Herodotus in his story about the public exposure of Onomakritos by Lasus of Hermione, who happens to be, like Simonides, a master of choral lyric poetry.[113] In fact, a passage in Aristophanes *Wasps* 1410–1411 alludes to a historical occasion where the poetic compositions of Lasus and of Simonides were entered in competition with each other, and where the medium of competition is clearly that of choral lyric poetry (ἀντεδίδασκε 1410). Similarly the Herodotean story about the exposure of Onomakritos by Lasus implies an occasion where the two poets are publicly competing in the performance of poetry, and where one poet can discredit another by making manifest what is incorrect, untrue, stealthily falsified: through the public performance of rival poets the truth can come to light. We may compare the comic competition between oracular poems assigned to Bakis and those of his mock rival, the "older brother" Glanis, in Aristophanes *Knights* 998 and following.

In sum, the story about the exposure of Onomakritos by Lasus illustrates a fundamental theme concerning tyrants and poetry. Both tyrants and antityrants can agree that the public performance of poetry is a possession of the polis, a forum where the truth is expected to come to light. In contrast the private possession of poetry by tyrants, despite their self-proclaimed status as public benefactors, can be perceived by antityrants as a threat to the truth of poetry, a threat that can be exposed by poetry itself in the light of public performance. As long as the tyrant possesses a poem before it is activated in performance, the danger of distortion is there. For Herodotus, who

112. Cf. p. 161.
113. Cf. p. 388.

represents an antityrannical attitude, the tyrant's possession of poetry is at issue in the story about the public discovery that Onomakritos tampered with the oracular utterances of Musaeus (7.6.3).[114] In the same context Onomakritos is described as a **diathetēs** 'arranger' of the **khrēsmoi** 'oracular utterances' of Musaeus in the era of the Peisistratidai (διαθέτην χρησμῶν τῶν Μουσαίου Herodotus ibid.). This possession of Musaeus by the Peisistratidai is parallel to their possession of Homer: there is a report that Onomakritos, along with three others, was commissioned in the reign of Peisistratos to supervise the 'arranging' of the Homeric poems, which were before then 'scattered about' (διέθηκαν οὑτωσὶ σποράδην οὔσας τὸ πρίν *Anecdota Graeca* 1.6 ed. Cramer).[115]

Toward the end of this Archaic phase of Greek civilization, the so-called age of tyrants, when important families were generating public personalities that could and did overreach the institutions of the polis, and when the public medium of poetry was coming under the threat of being possessed by the private power of tyrants, enters the figure of Pindar, master of choral lyric poetry. From here on I argue that Pindar and his contemporaries or near-contemporaries, figures like Simonides and Bacchylides, made their own breakthroughs as individuals, as historically verifiable persons whom we may call authors, by virtue of being protégés of powerful families of tyrants or quasityrants who forged their individuality through such public media as poetry itself. As a prime example of tyrants as patrons of Pindar, I cite the referent of Pindar's *Olympian* 1, Hieron of Syracuse,[116] whom Pindar addresses as **basileus** 'king' (e.g., *Olympian* 1.23) as well as **turannos** 'tyrant' (in a nonpejorative sense: *Pythian* 3.85).[117] As a telling example of quasityrants, I cite the pointed reference in Pindar *Pythian* 7.1–8 to the **oikos** 'house' and **patrā** 'lineage' of Megakles of Athens, of the **geneā** 'lineage' of the Alkmaionidai.[118] Another such example is the case of Diagoras of Rhodes, celebrated in *Olympian* 7: this composition is explicitly directed toward praising the island state of Rhodes, the native place of Diagoras, in the context of praising the lineage of this victor, the Eratidai:

Ἐρατιδᾶν τοι σὺν χαρίτεσσιν ἔχει | θαλίας καὶ πόλις

Pindar *Olympian* 7.93–94

Through the beautiful and pleasurable acts of reciprocity [= **kharis**

---

114. On Musaeus, see p. 170.

115. Quoted by Allen 1924.232–233. For a parallel myth concerning the reassembling of the Homeric poems by Lycurgus, lawgiver of Sparta, see p. 174.

116. See p. 116.

117. The latter passage is quoted at p. 280.

118. Cf. Roussel 1976.60n19; for more on this Megakles, see p. 157.

{plural}]][119] by the Eratidai, the city too is making merry with festivities.

This lineage of the Eratidai, descended from the royal line of Argos and extending all the way back to Herakles (20–24), had a history of dominating Ialysos, one of the three sectors of Rhodes, and in fact all of Rhodes.[120] And we have the explicit testimony of *Oxyrhynchus Papyri* 842 (x col. xi 1–34 and col. iii 23–26) that the family of Diagoras was eventually deposed as "tyrants." Certainly the importance of the family within the society at large is illustrated by the very words of Pindar, quoted immediately above, with the emphasis on the nobility and generosity of the Eratidai in sharing their epinician experience with the polis. We have historical evidence that this family considered the composition of Pindar that they commissioned, *Olympian* 7, as their precious personal possession, which they had generously shared with the public through the medium of public choral performance, in the public spirit described in the words of Pindar: according to Gorgon FGH 515 F 18, the words of this victory ode were inscribed in gold letters and dedicated in the temple of Athena Lindia in Rhodes.[121] The public sharing through the medium of public choral performance was in this case reinforced by another stage of public sharing, that is, public display through the medium of a lavish inscription, comparable to the public displays of inscribed poetry self-attributed to Hipparkhos, tyrant of Athens.[122]

My present line of interpretation, which connects Pindar's patronage with the political power of tyrants or quasityrants, may seem unsettling in light of the commonly-held and comforting assumption that poets like Pindar were simply protégés of aristocrats in general and that their association with tyrants like Hieron developed from their already-established prestige in smaller aristocratic circles. Such an assumption, glossing over the fact that many of Pindar's most famous compositions were commissioned by tyrants or tyrantlike personalities, is based on an implicit argument from silence: many other compositions, the reasoning goes, were commissioned by aristocratic figures about whom we have no explicit historical evidence pointing to anything specific like the power of tyrants. Yet the first impressions that one might have formed about these aristocratic figures are in the end deceiving.

I start with the most difficult case, the aristocratic families of victors from the island-polis of Aegina as celebrated in the victory odes of Pindar. There seems at first little evidence that would even suggest the presence of tyrants or tyrantlike personalities.[123] It is a daunting task indeed to find direct

119. On **kharis** as a 'beautiful and pleasurable compensation, through song or poetry, for a deed deserving of glory', see p. 65.

120. Details, with bibliography, in Bresson 1979.149–157.

121. Cf. p. 162.

122. Cf. p. 161.

123. Cf. Davison 1968.306.

evidence that would help us weigh their relative power. Even in the case of Aegina, however, there are indirect indications that the patrons of Pindar tend to be a closed and specially privileged group within their own aristocratic communities. Among these indications is the special use of **patrā** 'patriliny' in all attestations of the word as applied to the lineages of Aegina in the Aeginetan odes of Pindar. In each case there is a pointed mention of the Aiakidai 'descendants of Aiakos', or of the hero Aiakos himself, elsewhere in the same composition: the word **patrā** designates the Theandridai at *Nemean* 4.77 (Aiakidai at 11), the Bassidai at *Nemean* 6.35 (Aiakidai at 17), the Euxenidai at *Nemean* 7.70 (Aiakidai at 10), the Psalukhiadai at *Isthmian* 6.63 (Aiakidai at 19, 35), and the Meidulidai in *Pythian* 8.38 (Aiakos at 99). As for non-Aeginetan contexts, in contrast, **patrā** can take on the default meaning of 'homeland' (e.g., Pindar *Pythian* 11.23). This consistency in the pattern of referring to Aeginetan lineages, and in associating them with the Aiakidai, suggests a closed and specially privileged group. The very name **Aiakidai** may serve as implicit evidence in this regard. Such a patronymic formation suggests a group that is linked by ties of common ancestry leading back to the cult of a given hero.[124]

The cult of the hero Aiakos is native to Aegina, as we see most clearly from the explicit testimony of Pausanias (2.29.6–9). The relationship of Aiakos to the Aiakidai of Aegina is illuminated by one passage in particular, in Herodotus 8.64.2: at the battle of Salamis a ship is sent back to Aegina to fetch 'Aiakos and the other Aiakidai' (ἐπὶ δὲ Αἰακὸν καὶ τοὺς ἄλλους Αἰα-κίδας νέα ἀπέστελλον ἐς Αἴγιναν; cf. also Herodotus 8.83.2, 8.84.2). This mention of 'Aiakos and the other Aiakidai' is generally interpreted to mean some sort of sacred simulacra of the hero,[125] but decisive parallels are lacking, and the reference to 'the other Aiakidai' remains puzzling.[126] As an

124. See p. 154.
125. See Powell 1939.108.
126. Powell ibid. points to the remark of Pausanias 2.29.2 that the only king ever to rule Aegina was Aiakos himself, on the grounds that none of the three sons of Aiakos remained a resident of the island: one of the three, Phokos, was killed by the other two, and his sons went to Phokis, while the other two brothers, Peleus and Telamon, went into exile for the murder (Pausanias ibid.; cf. Pindar *Nemean* 5.14 and following, with scholia). Peleus went to Phthia (Apollodorus 3.13.1) and Telamon, to Salamis (Pausanias 2.29.10; Apollodorus 3.12.7). The assertion, however, that Telamon is not a hero of Aegina, with the implication that he had no Aeginetan descendants to claim him, seems to reflect a pro-Athenian and anti-Aeginetan version. The pro-Athenian slant becomes more clear in another passage, where Pausanias reports that Phi-laios of Salamis, son of Eurysakes son of Ajax son of Telamon, handed over the island of Salamis to the Athenians and was adopted by Athens as an Athenian (2.35.2); this Philaios is the ancestor of the Athenian Philaidai, on whom see p. 155. Which brings us back to the remark at Herodotus 8.64.2 about 'Aiakos and the other Aiakidai': the full context of this remark is that the Greeks at Salamis resolved, in their moment of crisis, to invoke the spirits of the cult heroes of Salamis, Telamon and Ajax (αὐτόθεν μὲν ἐκ Σαλαμῖνος Αἴαντα τε καὶ Τελαμῶνα ἐπεκα-λέοντο Herodotus 8.64.2), *while they sent a ship to Aegina to get Aiakos and the other Aiakidai* (ἐπὶ δὲ Αἰακὸν καὶ τοὺς ἄλλους Αἰακίδας νέα ἀπέστελλον ἐς Αἴγιναν). For Herodotus, then,

alternative explanation, the acceptance or rejection of which does not affect my overall argument about the significance of the Aiakidai, we may interpret 'Aiakos' here as the reputed bones of the hero, the centerpiece of his worship as a cult hero. In support of this possibility I cite a central feature of Archaic Greek hero cults, namely, the belief that the bones of a hero are a talisman of fertility and good fortune for the community that worships him, and of sterility and bad fortune for its enemies.[127] A clear example of this tradition is the story in Herodotus 1.67–68 about the bones of Orestes, the recovery of which by Sparta leads the Spartans to victory in their war with the Tegeans.[128] Another is the report by Plutarch (*Life of Kimon* 8, *Life of Theseus* 36) about the official transplanting of the bones of Theseus, in 476 B.C., from Skyros back to his "home" at Athens.[129] It is also in a parallel sense that we may possibly interpret the mention of Aiakidai in Herodotus 5.80.2: when the Aeginetans send the 'Aiakidai' to the Thebans, who had asked their allies for help in their war with Athens, they may be sending the bones of Aiakos, possibly accompanied by living representatives of the current lineage of Aiakidai, who would function as the ceremonial bearers of the ancestral relics. When the Thebans fail in their campaign against the Athenians, they send back the Aiakidai to the Aeginetans, saying that they would rather have as allies not the Aiakidai but **andres** 'men' (Herodotus ibid.). In other words, they request an army of fighting men, not cult objects.

The notion of Aiakidai as a totality consisting of the body of the ancestor Aiakos and an unbroken succession of descendants fits the pattern of a grammatical formation known as the elliptic plural, where plurality consists not of A+A+A+A . . . but of A+B+C+D . . ., and where A is the defining and dominant principle, while B+C+D . . . are extensions thereof.[130] As a vivid example I cite the singular **patēr** 'father' and the plural **pateres** 'ancestors' (as in Pindar *Pythian* 8.45), that is, a primordial father followed by an unbroken succession of fathers; or again, singular **toxon** 'bow' (e.g., *Iliad* IV 124) and elliptic plural **toxa** 'bow plus arrow plus arrow plus arrow . . .' = 'bow and arrows' (XXI 502). The ellipsis is made explicit in Herodotus 8.64.2: Αἰακὸν καὶ τοὺς ἄλλους Αἰακίδας 'Aiakos and the other Aiakidai'; elsewhere, as at 5.80.2, it is implicit: Αἰακίδας '[Aiakos and the other] Aiakidai'. We may

---

the designation of Aiakidai not only includes the heroes of Salamis, Telamon and Ajax: it also links them with Aegina, not Athens. This attitude is also apparent from the remarks of Herodotus at 6.35.1, on which see p. 155.

127. Fundamental discussion in Rohde 1898 I 159–166 (cf. II 242–245) and Pfister I 196–208; also Bérard 1982 and Snodgrass 1982. Cf. Hartog 1980.149–153; also Brelich 1958.129–131; Henrichs 1983.94.

128. Cf. Hartog 1980.151n6; also Calame 1987.177.

129. Rusten 1983.293n15 argues that if the bones of Themistokles were credited with heroic powers, "their public return to Athens [Pausanias 1.1.2] would be as effective politically as the stories of Orestes' and Theseus' returns."

130. See the discussion of elliptic plurals in N 1979.55–56§20n6; also Muellner 1976.70.

compare Sophocles *Philoctetes* 652, where **toxa** refers to the arrows, not the bow.

To return to the subject of hero cults: we may further speculate whether in the story of Herodotus the Thebans might have been using the bones of Aiakos against the Athenians much as the Athenians apparently used the bones of Oedipus against the Thebans. We are reminded of the myth about Oedipus at Colonus, as dramatized by Sophocles,[131] where Oedipus is exiled from Thebes on account of his blood guilt and is thereafter purified at Athens, in response to which the hero donates to the Athenians his own corpse as the talisman of his represented hero cult at Colonus.[132] In *Oedipus at Colonus* 1545–1546, 1761–1763, the precise location of the corpse of Oedipus in the precinct of the Eumenides at Colonus is represented as a sacred secret.[133] Similarly with the cult of the hero Aiakos on the island-polis of Aegina, it is specified in Pausanias 2.29.9 that the identification of a specific **bōmos** 'altar' with the tomb of Aiakos was a sacred secret. Just as Oedipus was a native Theban who turned against Thebes, Aiakos could have been perceived by the Thebans, though not by the Aeginetans, as a native "Athenian" who turned against Athens. We may note the testimony of Herodotus 5.89.2 on the existence of a **temenos** 'precinct' for the cult of Aiakos at Athens, instituted by the Athenians for the purpose of neutralizing Aeginetan power.[134]

To pursue the topic of the lineage known as the Aiakidai of Aegina: we may be witnessing a category of lineage that includes such specific patrilinies as the Theandridai, Bassidai, Euxenidai, Psalukhiadai, and Meidulidai.[135] Still I suggest that this category of Aiakidai, seemingly inclusive from the standpoint of an outsider, is in turn relatively exclusive from the standpoint of native Aeginetans.[136]

131. Cf. p. 32.

132. Cf. Edmunds 1981, especially p. 223n8; also Brelich 1958.40, 69–73.

133. Cf. p. 32.

134. Cf. Herodotus 5.66.2: Kleisthenes the Reformer considers Ajax, as cult hero, a **summakhos** 'ally'.

135. Perhaps we may compare the agglomerate lineage in Archaic Athens known as the Eupatridai, as it existed before the complex reshapings of the polis under the tyranny of the Peisistratidai and thereafter; in *Anecdota Graeca* 1.257 ed. Bekker, the Eupatridai of Athens are described as those who lived in the city proper, were of royal birth, and controlled the rituals of the polis. Cf. Roussel 1976.67–68.

136. Even if the entire population of Aegina may in certain contexts be designated as Aiakidai (cf. Slater 1969.15 s.v. Αἰακίδας category "c"), such a designation could still amount to an elliptic recognition of the power of one lineage. (On the question, whether the Aiakidai may be described as a ruling lineage, cf. Kirsten 1942.296, 303; for a related discussion that concentrates on distinctions between real and mythical genealogies in Aegina, see Figueira 1981.299–303.) In other words the term **Aiakidai** could serve to designate the whole community by way of a prominent part of the whole. To outsiders Aiakidai could represent an inclusive category designating all Aeginetans, while to insiders they could represent the exclusive lineage who trace themselves back to the hero Aiakos. Cf. Tyrtaeus F 11.1 W, where the sum total of Spartans is addressed as

We may compare the case of the Aigialeis in the polis of Sikyon. Although the political pattern here differs in many ways, the actual naming pattern of the Aigialeis seems parallel to that of the Aiakidai. Just as the Aiakidai are predicated on the hero Aiakos, the ancestry of the Aigialeis goes back ostensibly to the hero Aigialeus, who is son of the hero Adrastos of the Seven against Thebes tradition and who figures as the archetype of the old aristocracy of Sikyon (Herodotus 5.68.1–2).[137] The Aigialeis count as a **phūlē**, one of the four major subdivisions of Sikyonian society,[138] the other three **phūlai** being the traditional Dorian categories of Dymanes, Hylleis, and Pamphyloi (Herodotus ibid.). Of these four subdivisions, the **phūlē** of the Aigialeis represents ostensibly an aristocratic pre-Dorian lineage, integrated into the Dorian system of three **phūlai**.[139] In the account of Herodotus, the

---

Ἡρακλῆος . . . γένος 'the race of Herakles' (cf. Tyrtaeus F 2.12–15W). Clearly not all Spartans are in fact Herakleidai 'Heraclids'. On the concept of Herakleidai as the basic lineage of the Dorian royal dynasties, see Pindar *Pythian* 1.61–66, 5.69–72; also Apollodorus 2.8.4–5; cf. Herodotus 9.26, 27.1–2. I see another possible parallel in the case of the name **Spartē** 'Sparta', which is apparently connected with the Theban concept of **Spartoi**, warriors "sown" in the earth when Kadmos planted the dragon's teeth; the fully grown and armed Spartoi began killing each other as soon as they were generated from the earth, and the five Spartoi who survived this mutual slaughter became ancestors of the Theban aristocracy (e.g., Apollodorus 3.4.1, Pausanias 9.10.1; cf. Pausanias 8.11.8 on Epameinondas as a descendant of the Spartoi). The key to the connection between Spartoi and Sparta is a lineage at Sparta known as the **Aigeidai** (on which see Herodotus 4.149.1); tradition has it that they were connected by marriage to the royal line of the Herakleidai, in that Theras, an ancestor of the Aigeidai, whose father had fled in exile from Thebes to Sparta, was the maternal uncle of Eurysthenes and Prokles, the two Herakleidai who became the ancestors of the two royal houses of Sparta (Herodotus 6.52.2); cf. Vian 1963.218n4. Now these Aigeidai traced themselves to the Spartoi of Thebes (the mother and wife of Oedipus, Iokaste, is descended from Ekhion, one of the Spartoi who married Agaue, daughter of Kadmos), and, according to Timagoras FGH 381 F 3, the Spartoi who fled from Thebes to Sparta (these Spartoi were the Aigeidai: Vian, p. 223) actually gave their name to Sparta.

137. On Aigialeus and the Aigialeis, see Roussel 1976.252.

138. It is misleading to translate **phūlē** as 'tribe'. This word ordinarily designates the major subdivision of a given Archaic polis; the subdivision itself is a tribal heritage, but the functional heir of the tribe is not the **phūlē** but the entire polis itself. Full discussion in N 1987.

139. Roussel 1976.256n27. Cf. Herodotus 4.149.1–2, who uses the word **phūlē** in referring to the Aigeidai, an important lineage at Sparta that claimed pre-Dorian origins from a lineage by the same name at Thebes. See n136. The Aigeidai of Sparta traced themselves, by way of their ancestor Aigeus (Herodotus ibid.), all the way back to Polyneikes, son of Oedipus (4.147.1–2). That the Aigeidai of Sparta originate from Thebes is proudly proclaimed in the words of Pindar *Isthmian* 7.14–15. There is an argument to be made that Pindar himself was a descendant of the original Theban branch of the Aigeidai: see p. 380. On the restructuring of the family tree of the Aigeidai in the context of Spartan political history, see Vian 1963.219. Aside from the Herodotean mention of the Aigeidai as a **phūlē** at Sparta, this polis is known for its three standard Dorian **phūlai** of Dymanes, Hylleis, and Pamphyloi (e.g., Tyrtaeus F 19.8 W). In the account of a famous battle in the series of campaigns known as the Messenian Wars, Pausanias 4.7.8, there is a description of the battle line of the Spartans, where the left and the right wings are each commanded by one of the two Spartan kings, while the center is reserved for a descendant of the Aigeidai (4.7.8).

four **phūlai** of Sikyon were renamed by Kleisthenes, tyrant of the polis, in pursuit of his anti-Argos policy, and the name Aigialeis, establishing connections with Aigialeus and his Argive father, Adrastos, was at that point changed to Arkhelaoi (5.68.1–2).[140] This name reflects a closed and specially privileged group: **Arkhelāoi** means 'they who rule the host of fighting men [= **lāos**]'.[141]

140. The tyrant's model, featuring the primacy of the *phūlē* Arkhelaoi and suppressing the names Dymanes/Hylleis/Pamphyloi for the other three *phūlai*, was changed at around 500 B.C. to a model where the name Arkhelaoi was replaced by Aigialeis and where the names Dymanes/Hylleis/Pamphyloi for the other three *phūlai* were restored: see Herodotus 5.68.2 and the commentary of Roussel 1976.252, who argues that, by this time, Sparta rather than Argos was the Dorian city *par excellence*, and Sikyon would no longer be threatened by an Argive model of Dorian society. It is even possible that the fourth **phūlē** had been created by the tyrants as an addition to the Dymanes/Hylleis/Pamphyloi, and that the name of this fourth **phūlē**, Aigialeis, represents simply a reformation of the name given by the tyrants, Arkhelaoi. As for the Spartan model as a threat to other Dorian societies, we may note what happened after the Battle of Leuktra in 371 B.C.: the liberated Messenians rejected the **phūlē**-divisions of the Spartans, Dymanes/Hylleis/Pamphyloi, choosing instead Kresphontis/Daiphontis/Aristomakhis/Hyllis/Kleolaia (IG 5.1.1433). As Roussel argues (p. 256n29), all these Messenian designations are appropriate to the "Sons of Herakles," the Herakleidai, and they thus reaffirm the Dorian identity, however distinct, of the Messenians. On the concept of Herakleidai 'Heraclids' as the basic lineage of the Dorian royal dynasties, see again Tyrtaeus 2.12–15W; Pindar *Pythian* 1.61–66, 5.69–72; *Isthmian* 9.1–3; Apollodorus 2.8.4–5; cf. Herodotus 9.26, 27.1–2.

141. Herodotus 5.68.1 thinks that the meaning of the name **Arkhelāoi** 'they who rule the **lāos**' indicates that the **phūlē** to which Kleisthenes belonged was the lineage of the tyrant. I would argue further that the name also proclaims, in wording that avoids Argive connections, the inherited standing of this particular **phūlē** in relation to the others. On **lāos** 'host of fighting men' as a designation for the community at large, see N 1979.69§1n3 and 114§26n1 (following Benveniste 1969 II 91–95), with special reference to the derivative **lāiton**, native to the people of Achaea, which Herodotus 7.197.2 describes as a word meaning **prutaneion** 'presidential hall'. For a semantic parallel to **Arkhelāoi** 'they who rule the **lāos**', I cite the Messenian **phūlē** called **Kleolaiā** 'whose **lāos** has glory [**kleos**]', as mentioned in the note immediately above. Moreover, the meaning of **Arkhelāoi**, where the component **lāos** 'host' refers to the primordial society that was divided into **phūlai**, is comparable to the meaning of **stratos** 'host' in Pindar *Isthmian* 9.2–3, referring to the Dorian occupation of Aegina: Ὕλλου τε καὶ Αἰγιμιοῦ Δωριεὺς [. . .] στρατός 'the Dorian host [**stratos**] of Hyllos and Aigimios'. Hyllos, eponymous ancestor of the Hylleis, was the adopted son of Aigimios, son of Doros, the eponymous ancestor of the Dorians, while Aigimios had two sons of his own, Dyman and Pamphylos, eponymous ancestors of the Dymanes and Pamphyloi (Ephorus FGH 70 F 15; cf. Strabo 9.4.10 C427 and Apollodorus 2.8.3). This compressed Pindaric reference to the three basic Dorian **phūlai** of Dymanes/Hylleis/Pamphyloi in terms of a **stratos** 'host' at Aegina can be compared with the mention of a **startos** 'host' of the Aithaleis at Gortyn in the *Law Code of Gortyn* (5.5 Willetts), from which group the chief magistrates of the polis, the **kosmoi**, were to be selected at a given period (cf. DGE 185.1, again with mention of the Aithaleis as **kosmoi** at Gortyn). Gortyn, a polis on the island of Crete, is Dorian, like Aegina. As Aristotle points out, the **kosmoi** of Crete were traditionally chosen only from a few specially privileged lineages (*Politics* 1272a), and their rotation of political power was subject to the tyranny-prone dangers of factionalism among aristocrats vying for power (1272b). Since there is also evidence that the **kosmoi** of a specific period are in some instances designated as belonging to a specific **phūlē**, such as the Dymanes (*Inscriptiones Creticae* 182.21–22), it is possible that the members of a specially privileged lineage like the Aithaleis

Having merely raised the possibility that the Aiakidai of Aegina were a closed and specially privileged group, and that Pindar's references to their name reflect his acknowledgment of their patronage, let us leave this particularly difficult case behind and proceed toward firmer ground, following the main argument that such poets as Pindar ultimately achieved their definitive identities as authors through the authority and patronage of powerful families of tyrants or quasityrants. Here and in the chapters that follow, I rely not only on external evidence in making this argument but also the internal evidence of the traditional themes inherent in the medium of Pindar's self-expression, the **ainos**. This medium of ethical discourse, as an inherited instrument of social criticism, consistently warns against the emergence of tyranny from an aristocracy that it can blame for losing its ethical foundations. Since the **ainos** presupposes an idealized community of aristocrats with whom it can communicate, it is important to add that the historical reasons for the emergence of tyrants and quasityrants are indeed to be found in the social context of aristocratic circles.[142] In other words the social context of aristocracy in the polis is the breeding ground of would-be tyrants both from the external standpoint of history and from the internal standpoint of the **ainos** as an instrument of social criticism that warns against tyranny.

Let us consider in some detail the testimony of Pindar's choral lyric poetry, as a medium of **ainos**. In Pindar *Pythian* 2.87–88, the polis is represented as capable of three forms of government, described as a tyranny (τυραννίδι); a democracy, 'wherever there is a host of men intemperate' (χώπόταν ὁ λάβρος στρατός); or an aristocracy, 'when the wise [**sophoi**] watch over the city' (χ̄ῶταν πόλιν οἱ σοφοὶ τηρέοντι). Such a view of society reflects a poetic tradition, also attested in Theognis 39–52, where again we find an ideological representation of an aristocracy. Yet despite the ideological approval, this aristocracy is pictured as a potential breeding ground of degeneration, and the ethical teaching of the poem is to warn against such destruction of the aristocracy from within, which is said to be the harbinger of tyranny (39–40, 51–52).[143]

This tradition recurs, with a twist, in the celebrated Debate of the Constitutions, Herodotus 3.80–87, where the future Great King of the Persians is represented as cynically restating the poetic tradition: he too describes the Greek polis as capable of three forms of government, that is, democracy, oli-

---

tenuously shared power, through the rotating office of **kosmoi**, with representative lineages selected from the Dorian **phūlai**, that is, the Dymanes, Hylleis, and Pamphyloi (cf. Roussel p. 257). In any case the **startos Aithaleus** 'host of the Aithaleis' seems to be a specially privileged group in the polis of Gortyn (Roussel, p. 258). Such points of comparison from Crete suggest that the **stratos** of Dorian society at Aegina, as mentioned in the ode of Pindar, may be hierarchically integrated with a preeminent **stratos** of Aiakidai. See further at p. 183.

142. Cf. again Petre 1975; also Loraux 1986.282n24.

143. Commentary in N 1985.42–46.

garchy, and 'monarchy'.[144] The Persian king unrestrainedly refers to aristocracy as **oligarkhiā** 'oligarchy' (3.82.1). He is more restrained about
tyranny, which he calls **monarkhiā** 'monarchy' (3.82.1, 3), the superiority of
which over oligarchy is proved, he says, by the regular pattern of a gradual
shift from any oligarchy into a 'monarchy' (3.82.3). The Great King's
description of this shift, however, shows that this arch-villain of the Hellenes
has been tricked by the narrative of Herodotus into becoming a teacher of
ethics, in that he is in effect unwittingly warning the aristocracy against the
temptations of degeneracy and tyranny. In the Persian king's words the supposedly predictable shift from oligarchy to 'monarchy' stems from the quest
for personal advantage, which leads to a movement toward 'monarchy' in
three stages: (1) **stasis** (plural) 'social conflicts', (2) **phonoi** 'killings', and,
finally, (3) **monarkhiā** 'monarchy' (3.82.3). These categories mark the very
same concepts that are cited by the native traditions of Hellenic poetry as the
stages of degeneracy and incipient tyranny, as in Theognis 50–52.[145] In this
passage the notion of private or personal interest is expressed by way of **kerdos** 'gain, advantage, profit' (Theognis 50). Private gain that entails public
detriment leads to (1) **stasis** 'social conflict' (Theognis 51),[146] (2) **phonoi**
'killings' (51),[147] and finally (3) tyranny, a notion that is attenuated here
again as **monarkhoi** 'monarchs' (52). These three stages of degeneracy, as
the poetry makes clear, are symptomatic of **hubris** (Theognis 40, 44). In the
debate passage of Herodotus, the notion of tyranny that underlies monarchy
is made clear: the Great King's speech is preceded by an earlier speech containing a calculated equation of the attenuated word **monarkhos** 'monarch'
with the explicit **turannos** 'tyrant' (Herodotus 3.80.2/4).

There is a striking parallel to the theme of tyranny as generated by a
degenerate aristocracy in a myth retold by Herodotus about the powerful
lineage known as the Bakkhiadai of Corinth.[148] Herodotus stresses that the
Bakkhiadai were an **oligarkhiā** 'oligarchy' and that their exclusiveness was
manifested in their practice of endogamy (5.92β.1). The native Corinthian
myth has it that Labda, a female in the lineage of the Bakkhiadai, was born
lame and was consequently forced to marry outside the lineage; the outsider
husband, Eetion, is described as one of the Kaineidai, descendants of the
Lapith Kaineus (5.92β.1). This aberrant episode of exogamy within the
already aberrant endogamous lineage of the Bakkhiadai leads to the birth of

---

144. Further discussion at p. 304.

145. Commentary in N 1985.42–46.

146. Cf. N, pp. 22 §2n2, 36, 41, 46, 52, 59. Cf. the use of **stasis** at Xenophanes F 1.23 W =
21 B 1.23 DK, where the theme of social strife is represented as a poetic subject typical of the
here and now, as distinct from stories about Titans (1.21) or Centaurs (1.22), subjects typical of
the remote past.

147. An example of such 'killings' is the story of Kylon, on which see p. 156.

148. On whom see p. 155.

Kypselos and thus generates as it were the dynasty of tyrants at Corinth known as the Kypselidai (5.92 passim; 6.128.2).[149] The quasi-incest inherent in the practice of endogamy by the Bakkhiadai is a traditional poetic theme suggestive of tyranny.[150] So too are the lameness of Labda and the illegitimacy, from the standpoint of the Bakkhiadai, of the tyrant Kypselos. We may compare a theme recorded in Plutarch *Lysander* 22.6, where the statement is made that the royal house of Sparta will be lame if bastards are allowed to reign instead of the "Sons of Herakles," the Herakleidai.[151]

The theme of genuine Dorian kingship, as legitimated by the title *Sons of Herakles*, recurs as a central theme in the poetry of Theognis, that is, in the characterization of the boy called Kyrnos, the main recipient of advice in the "Mirror of Princes" tradition that distinguishes much of this poetry.[152] The very name **Kurnos** is identified by Servius (on Virgil *Eclogues* 9.30) as a son of Herakles.[153] On the other hand the word **kurnos** means 'bastard' (Hesychius s.v. κύρνοι· νόθοι), in line with a theme central to the poetry of Theognis: excessive wealth leads to degeneration and debasement (e.g., Theognis 183–192).[154] In other words the very concept of Kyrnos has a two-sided message, like an **ainos**: this fickle youth loved by Theognis is simultaneously a bastard and a prince of the lineage of the Herakleidai 'Heraclids'.

The Bakkhiadai are described in the utterance of the Delphic Oracle quoted at Herodotus 5.92β.2 as **monarkhoi** 'monarchs', an attenuated designation for tyrants. There is a clear parallel at Theognis 52, where it is claimed that a degenerate aristocracy will lead to such social ills as **monar-**

149. Pausanias 2.4.4 reports the tradition that one Melas, ancestor of Kypselos, had joined Aletes, first Dorian king of Corinth, in conquering Corinth and was accepted as their **sunoikos** 'co-inhabitant'. By implication the Kypselidai are understood to be non-Dorian or perhaps pre-Dorian. In contrast the Bakkhiadai trace themselves to Bakkhis, fifth in the lineage of kings starting with Aletes (ibid.). Eumelus of Corinth, to whom the fundamental poetry about the foundation of Corinth is ascribed, was one of the Bakkhiadai (Pausanias 2.1.1, who implies at 2.2.2 that he has read Eumelus). Similar to the pattern in Corinth is what we find in Aegina: the Dorians who conquered the island of Aegina are described as **sunoikoi** 'co-inhabitants' of the **arkhaioi** 'ancients' who were already there (Pausanias 2.29.5). By implication these **arkhaioi**, whom we may equate with the primordial Aiakidai, were the lineage of local rulers. That the Aiakidai, from the standpoint of the newcomer Dorians, supposedly never became a formal dynasty of kings is confirmed by the report that there were no kings of Aegina, except for Aiakos himself (Pausanias 2.29.2). Similarly there is a report that the Bakkhiadai were not kings but **prutaneis** 'presidents' (2.4.4).

150. This point is argued in detail by Vernant 1982, following Gernet 1953.

151. Cf. Vernant, p. 35n16a. On the concept of Herakleidai 'Heraclids' as the criterion of Dorian kingship, see p. 180. Further discussion of the Kypselidai of Corinth: Sourvinou-Inwood 1988.

152. On the "Mirror of Princes" tradition in the poetry of Theognis, in the Hesiodic *Works and Days*, and in the *Odyssey*, see the crucial article of Martin 1984.

153. Further discussion in N 1985.33.

154. Extensive examples and commentary in N, pp. 51–60.

khoi.[155] To repeat, the Bakkhiadai are described by Herodotus as an aristocratic **oligarkhiā** 'oligarchy' (5.92β.1). In the same utterance where the Bakkhiadai are described as **monarkhoi**, the Oracle, here addressing Eetion, describes the future tyrant Kypselos as someone who will make Corinth **dikaios** 'just' (ibid.). Again we can see a clear parallel in the same passage of Theognis (39–40): the degenerate aristocracy, as the voice of the poet prophesies, may one day yield to a man who will be an **euthuntēr** 'straightener' of the social ills caused by his predecessors. The theme of 'straightening' is a prime symbol of **dikē** 'justice' (e.g., Solon F 36.19 W).[156] This 'straightener' who brings justice is described as being literally born to the polis, pregnant in its degeneracy (κύει, Theognis 39), just as the future champion of **dikē** in Corinth is described by the Oracle as being born to the pregnant Labda (κύει, Herodotus 5.92β.2), whose very lameness symbolizes the tyrannical potential within her lineage.[157] In sum, according to this utterance by the Delphic Oracle, favorable to the Kypselidai, the Bakkhiadai are quasi-tyrants who will generate the ultimate rulers of Corinth, the Kypselidai. Similarly in Theognis 39–52, the passage that we have been comparing, the future tyrant is presented in attenuated terms as a potential reformer and champion of **dikē** (again Theognis 40).[158]

Another oracular utterance, however, where the Delphic Oracle is addressing the other party, the Bakkhiadai, describes the future tyrant Kypselos as a lion that is **ōmēstēs** 'eater of raw flesh' (Herodotus 5.92β.3). In this utterance, unlike the other, the tyrant generated by the degenerate aristocracy is treated negatively: the theme of eating raw flesh is a prime symbol of **hubris** 'outrage', the opposite of **dikē** 'justice' (e.g., Theognis 541–542).[159] Again we can see a clear parallel in the poetry of Theognis: in 1081–1082b, a passage closely similar in form but strikingly different in content from the passage that we have already considered concerning the birth of a future tyrant (39–52), the polis is again described as pregnant (κύει, Theognis 1081), but this time it generates a champion not of **dikē** but of **hubris** (1082).[160] Thus the response of the Delphic Oracle to the dynasty of tyrants at Corinth, the Kypselidai, is ambivalent. When it addresses the side of the Kypselidai, it stresses the potential **dikē** 'justice' that can come from this dynasty. When it addresses the side of the Bakkhiadai, it stresses the potential **hubris** 'outrage'. Herodotus in 5.92δ.1 takes this side, to the extent that

---

155. See the commentary in N 1985.42–46. For a calculated equation of the attenuated word **monarkhos** 'monarch' with the explicit **turannos**, see again Herodotus 3.80.2/4 as discussed at pp. 181 and following.

156. Commentary in N 1985.43.

157. This parallel is noted by Vernant 1982.35–36n22, following a suggestion by N. Loraux.

158. Commentary in N 1985.41–46.

159. Commentary in N 1985.51.

160. Commentary in N, p. 46.

he stresses the negative aspects of tyrants: bad things will 'sprout' (ἀνα-βλαστεῖν) for Corinth from Eetion. As the Oracle affirms in yet another utterance, quoted at Herodotus 5.92ε.2, the dynasty of the Kypselidai will be short-lived.[161]

Like the Delphic Oracle, the poetry of Theognis assumes the stance of predicting the advent of tyrants, as we have seen in the two poems about the pregnant polis, Theognis 39–52 and 1081–1082b.[162] Like the Oracle, the poetry of Theognis can be ambivalent about the tyrant, describing him as an exponent of either **dikē** 'justice' (cf. 39–40) or **hubris** 'outrage' (cf. 1082). In this light we may consider the meaning of **Theognis** 'he whose breeding [**genos**] is from the god(s)', which is parallel to the meaning of **Theāgenēs**, the name of the historical tyrant of Megara (on whom see Aristotle *Politics* 1305a24, *Rhetoric* 1357b33).[163] On the basis of Theognis 39–42, where the emerging tyrant is presented as a potential champion of **dikē** 'justice', I offer the following observation:[164]

> It is as if the words of Theognis could have been, in one phase of the poetic tradition, the words of Theagenes the tyrant. Verses 39–42 of Theognis would represent a later phase, of course, in that the poet and the tyrant are here distinct. Still, although the poet deplores the emergence of tyranny in these verses, the social corrections undertaken by the tyrant are described in words that could just as well have described the social corrections undertaken by Solon.

The social corrections of Solon the Reformer, as expressed in the poetry of Solon, have close parallels in the poetry of Theognis.[165] Both Lycurgus the lawgiver of Sparta and Kypselos the tyrant of Corinth take control of their respective cities after consulting the Oracle at Delphi (Herodotus 1.65.2–5 and 5.92ε.1–2, respectively).[166] We may note too the self-representation of Theognis as a **theōros** (805),[167] and the remark by Aristotle *Politics* 1310b that one of the ways to achieve tyranny in a polis was through occupying the office of **theōros**.

If indeed the figure of Theognis is ambivalently a tyrant or a lawgiver, depending on the political circumstances of Theognidean transmission, we may compare the figure of Pittakos, a lawgiver from the standpoint of the Seven Sages tradition but a tyrant from the standpoint of the lyric poetry of

---

161. Further discussion of this theme: Sourvinou-Inwood 1988.
162. Cf. p. 184.
163. Cf. the overview in N 1985.35–36.
164. N 1985.51 §39n1.
165. See N, pp. 43, 50. In this connection we may take note again of Solon's ancestry, the lineage of the Medontidai, as mentioned at p. 154.
166. I am grateful to S. Bartsch for pointing out this connection to me.
167. On which see p. 165.

Alcaeus (as in the explicit declaration of F 348 V). Given that the name of Alcaeus = Alkaios bears Heraclid connotations (e.g., Herodotus 1.7.2),[168] like that of Kyrnos (Servius on Virgil *Eclogues* 9.30),[169] I suggest that the attitude of Kyrnos toward Theognis, if the Heraclid prince were given a voice, would perhaps be parallel to the attitude of Alcaeus toward Pittakos in the lyric poetry of Alcaeus.

When it predicts or at least warns about future ills, the poetry of Theognis speaks in the language of **ainigma** 'enigma', as in Theognis 681, quoted above.[170] So too does the Delphic Oracle, as we see in Sophocles *Oedipus Tyrannus* 393, 1525. Moreover, the figure of Theognis can actually assume the stance of speaking like a **theōros**, that is, one who consults the Oracle (805).[171]

Like Theognis, Pindar speaks with a voice that can warn about the dangers that loom over the polis, not the least of which is tyranny. And the medium for Pindar's message, in Pindar's own words, is the **ainos**; it is from this word, to repeat, that **ainigma** is derived.

What then gives Pindar the occasion to warn against tyranny, if indeed the social circles of his patronage are the very breeding ground of tyranny? It can be argued that the epinician or victory odes of Pindar are indeed an appropriate occasion, in that there was a pervasive thematic parallelism between the reality of an athlete's victory and the potential of a tyrant's power, as dramatized by the Olympic victor Kylon when he chose the season of the Olympics for his attempt at a coup d'état in Athens.[172] The **ainos** of Pindaric choral lyric poetry has the built-in ideology of warning about this potential. If the potential has already become a reality, the poetry can shift to a stance of praising the **turannos** 'tyrant' as a **basileus** 'king' while all along maintaining a condemnation of tyranny. We have noted that the voice of Pindar can refer to the tyrant Hieron of Syracuse as **basileus** 'king' (e.g., *Olympian* 1.23) as well as **turannos** 'tyrant' (in a nonpejorative sense: *Pythian* 3.85).[173] We may note as well that the Oracle of Delphi, as quoted at

168. Cf. p. 301.
169. Cf. p. 183.
170. Cf. p. 149.
171. Cf. p. 165.
172. Cf. p. 156. In Thucydides 4.121.1 we read that the people of Skione enthusiastically greeted the Spartan general Brasidas as the liberator of Hellas, crowning him with a golden wreath and decorating him with a headband as though he were an **āthlētēs** 'athlete' (ἐταινίουν τε καὶ προσήρχοντο ὥσπερ ἀθλητῇ); there is a similar anecdote about Pericles on the occasion of his having delivered his Funeral Oration (Plutarch *Life of Pericles* 28.5). On the symbolism of headbands as decoration for victorious athletes, see Sansone 1988.80–81.

173. See p. 174. In this connection we may note the testimony of Timaeus FGH 566 F 133 (by way of Clement *Stromateis* 1.64.2), who was a historian of Sicily, that Xenophanes was a contemporary of Hieron of Syracuse (whose reign is dated from 478 to 467 B.C.). In the words of Xenophanes, the prestige of the athletic victor is but a foil for what is achieved through the poetic **sophiā** 'skill' of the poet himself (F 2.12, 14 W = 21 B 2.12, 14 DK); in a catalogue of various

Herodotus 5.92ε.2, refers to the tyrant Kypselos of Corinth as a **basileus** 'king', while the prose narrative that frames the poetry of the oracular utterance characterizes him as a **turannos** (ibid.).

My argument is not that we can point to actual tyrants in each and every case of Pindaric patronage; hence my use of the expression *tyrants or quasi-tyrants*. Rather the point is simply that there was a pervasive thematic parallelism between the reality of an athlete's victory and the potential of a tyrant's power. The function of Pindar's epinician lyric poetry was to praise the reality of victory and to warn against the potential of tyranny (cf. *Pythian* 11.52–53).[174] We can see that potential also in a later era, as when Alcibiades, in a speech of 415 B.C., is represented by Thucydides (6.16.2) as boasting of his seven entries in the Olympic chariot race of 416 B.C., where he won the first, second, and fourth prizes. Alcibiades goes on to say: καὶ τἆλλα ἀξίως τῆς νίκης παρεσκευασάμην 'and I made the rest of my arrangements worthy of my victory' (Thucydides ibid.); these arrangements included the commissioning of an epinician performance, with Euripides as composer (Plutarch *Alcibiades* 11.2).[175]

In sum, the songs that celebrated the figures who commissioned the likes of Pindar were occasional, potentially exempt from the process of ongoing recomposition in performance that would have characterized any composition transmitted solely through the ever-evolving polis. While the poets of such occasional songs owe their fame as historical individuals to their patrons, the tyrants owe their corresponding fame at least partly to these same poets, who enhance the breakthrough of their patrons into the remote past of the heroes. The poet Ibycus says this explicitly, as he tells the tyrant Polykrates of the everlasting **kleos** that is to be conferred on him by the poet's song, which is also called **kleos**:

> καὶ σύ, Πολύκρατες, κλέος ἄφθιτον ἑξεῖς
> ὡς κατ' ἀοιδὰν καὶ ἐμὸν κλέος

Ibycus SLG 151.47–48

You too [i.e., you as well as the heroes just mentioned in the song],
  Polykrates, will have **kleos** that is unfailing [**aphthiton**],
in accordance with my song, my **kleos**.[176]

The double use of **kleos** here reenacts the notion of reciprocity built into the

---

kinds of athletic accomplishments, the feat that is placed closest to that of the poet is a victory in chariot racing (2.12).

174. On the balance of praise and admonition in Pindar, see in general Ch.1 of Hubbard 1985.

175. Cf. Kirkwood 1982.7.

176. I read καί as marking apposition here; on the appositional usage of καί, see Denniston 1954.291. For a commentary, with extensive bibliography, on Ibycus SLG 151, see Woodbury 1985.

word: the patron gets fame from the praise of the poet, whose own fame depends on the fame of a patron in the here and now.[177] The Indo-European heritage of this convention is evident from a comparison with Old Irish traditions of reciprocity between poet and patron: "The Irish king is certified by the poet; reciprocally, the poet is maintained by the king and tribe."[178]

As long as the patronage of the audience is ideologically conferred by the community at large, a reciprocal relationship between poet and patron can be maintained. Thus even a tyrant like Polykrates can in theory fit the Indo-European model of poetic patronage, as long as he succeeds in being perceived as the embodiment of community, the body politic. This is the essence of kingship. If on the other hand the tyrant is perceived as overreaching the community, the polis, in his maintenance of power, then the very concept of tyranny sets off a crisis in the poetic ideology of reciprocity. We have seen that the notion of compensating a poet for the "ordeal" of composing a poem is part of a ritual chain of reciprocity, where the value of the compensation owed the poet, even if it takes the shape of material gifts, is still transcendent inasmuch as it is considered sacred. If, however, the community loses its trust in the powers that be, then the compensation owed to the poet sponsored by those powers stands to lose its sacral status. Thus the poet must not only praise the patron: the poet must maintain the trust of the community by reasserting the transcendent nature of his compensation as proof of links to the community as the audience. For such reassertion to be successful, the poet can set up, as a foil for the transcendent compensation, a negative value for the kind of compensation that is purely material in nature.

Granted, the notion of material compensation for the composition of a Pindaric song is generally treated as a positive value by the song, as in *Isthmian* 2.1–13 and elsewhere.[179] Still the picture of a Muse who is **philokerdēs** 'lover of profit [**kerdos**]' and **ergatis** 'working for wages' at *Isthmian* 2.6 is a negative value, serving as a foil for the positive value of a transcendent reciprocity between the poet and his subject.[180] For Pindaric song making, the true **misthos** 'wage' of compensation for song is equated with **kharis**, the beauty and pleasure of reciprocity between the poet and the subject of his praise:

---

177. Cf. N 1974.250–251 and Watkins 1976c; also Martin 1984.35.

178. Martin, p. 35.

179. Woodbury 1968; cf. also Descat 1981.25–27 and Hubbard 1985.158–162.

180. Cf. Kurke 1988.194–209, who argues that the contemporary model of a "mercenary Muse" at the beginning of *Isthmian* 2 is transformed by the end into a positive value through the appropriation of the idealized old-fashioned model of the nonprofessional Muse. For more on the idealization of the nonprofessional Muse in *Isthmian* 2, see pp. 340 and following.

ἀρέομαι | πὰρ μὲν Σαλαμῖνος Ἀθηναίων χάριν | μισθὸν, ἐν Σπάρτᾳ
δ' ⟨ἀπὸ⟩ τᾶν πρὸ Κιθαιρῶνος μαχᾶν

Pindar Pythian 1.75–77

I will earn, as my wage [**misthos**], the **kharis** of the Athenians concerning Salamis, and of Sparta, concerning the fighting at the foot of
Mount Kithairon [= Plataia].[181]

This more positive value of compensation is simultaneously materialistic and
transcendent for the simple reason that it is sacred: inside the framework of
Pindaric song, the notion of compensation for composition is sacred as long
as it stays within the sacred context of such occasions as an epinician celebration.

Outside the framework of Pindaric song, in the real world of Pindar,
compensation is becoming a purely monetary value.[182] It is this outside reality that makes it possible for Pindaric song to set up the "mercenary Muse" as
a foil for its own transcendence. In this real world the system of reciprocity
within the community at large, as represented by the polis, is breaking down.
It is an era when individuals can achieve the economic power to overreach
the polis itself, and the pattern of overreaching extends to the realm of song.
In this real world the craft of song is in danger of shifting from an expression
of community to an expression of the individual whose power potentially
threatens the community. This shift has been aptly described as a diverting
of the poetic art:[183]

> Before the end of the [fifth] century choral poetry was divested of its
> traditional connections with the festivals of cult, probably by Ibycus,
> certainly by Simonides, and diverted to the praise of the great. The
> change meant that the expense of the poet's fee and the choral produc-
> tion was assumed by a wealthy patron, with whom lay the power of
> decision in regard to all questions relating to the performance of the
> ode. The Muse, in Pindar's phrase, had grown fond of money and gone
> to work for a living.

In the real world, the "great" men who are being praised are the potential
tyrants and quasityrants that are being generated by the aristocracy. For the
ideological world of Pindar, in contrast, the aristocracy remains an ideal that
must resist the degeneration that breeds tyrants.[184] And it is the real world
that makes it possible for Pindaric song to set up the "mercenary Muse" as a
foil for its own transcendence.

181. On **kharis** as the beauty and the pleasure of reciprocity, see p. 65.
182. Cf. Descat 1981.26–27.
183. Woodbury 1968.535.
184. Cf. pp. 181 and following.

In this connection I cite Pindar *Isthmian* 1.47–51, with a brief catalogue of different kinds of work that earn different kinds of **misthos** 'wages' (47): in each case the worker is working in order to feed his hungry **gastēr** 'stomach' (49); such a **misthos** is a foil for the ultimate **kerdos** 'profit' of being praised by song (51). In Homeric and Hesiodic poetry as well, the hungry **gastēr** is a foil: it serves as a symbol for the dependence of the poet, as itinerant artisan, on the patronage of a localized audience (*Theogony* 26–28, in the context of *Odyssey* xiv 124–125 and vii 215–221).[185] The juxtaposed ideal, for which the **gastēr** 'stomach' serves as foil, is the ostensibly absolute truth of Panhellenic poetry.[186]

The Greek word **misthos** 'wages' is cognate with Indic *mīḍha-* 'competition' or 'prize won in competition', and its inherited meaning must be something like 'honorific compensation for deed performed'.[187] There is an important adjustment, however, to be made in the context of historical developments in Archaic Greece: even in the early evidence this sense is already becoming limited to the work of artisans, becoming ever less appropriate for designating any 'service' performed by a citizen for the polis.[188] This emerging split leads to the specialized notion of 'wages for an artisan' and tends to put **misthos** into a negative light from an aristocratic standpoint.[189] Hence the Pindaric use of **misthos** is a foil for the ultimate **kerdos** 'profit' of being praised by song (*Isthmian* 1.51).[190]

Since the praise inherent in poetry, as represented by Archaic poetry, is held to be a transcendent value, it follows that a deed worthy of praise by poetry is incompatible with wages suitable for artisans. Thus we read in Apollodorus 2.5.5 that the taskmaster Eurystheus tries to invalidate one of the Labors of Herakles, the cleaning of the stables of Augeias, on the grounds that the hero had performed it for a **misthos** 'wage'; conversely, Augeias refuses to pay Herakles when he learns that the hero's labor was at the behest of Eurystheus, in other words, that this labor was one of *the* Labors (ibid.).[191]

To return to the poem of Ibycus in praise of the tyrant Polykrates, we have noted that the poet effects the fame of his patron not merely by recording the subject's accomplishments or qualities in the here and now but also

185. See N 1982.47–49.

186. Ibid.

187. Benveniste 1969 I 163–169.

188. Will 1975.

189. See Will, p. 437, who also notes the efforts of Plato and Aristotle to rehabilitate the word. We may compare the contemporary semantics of *service*: besides such materialistic contexts as we see in phrases like *room service*, there are also transcendent usages, such as *unselfish service to the community*.

190. This transcendent kind of 'profit' from the praise of song is parallel to the theme of **olbos** 'bliss' in the sense of a simultaneously materialistic and transcendent kind of well-being, as captured by the discourse of the **ainos**: see the discussion at pp. 243 and following.

191. Commentary by Loraux 1982.190–191.

by linking him with the heroes of the past. This kind of linking can even be directly genealogical. Thus, for example, the praise poetry of Pindar confirms the political claim of the tyrant Theron of Akragas, to the effect that Theron is descended from Polyneikes, a hero of the Seven against Thebes epic tradition (Pindar *Olympian* 2.41–47).[192]

The situation is different with the poetry of epic. By the age of tyrants, the epic traditions of the Greeks, as represented by the *Iliad* and *Odyssey* of Homer, were reaching a Panhellenic and thereby canonical status, exempt from the political exigencies of tyrants. The universalism of the Homeric poems is the consequence not of a single event, such as the writing down of the poems, but rather of an evolutionary process whereby the Panhellenic diffusion of the Homeric traditions, concomitant with ongoing recomposition in performance at international (that is, inter-polis) festivals, led gradually to one convergent Panhellenic version at the expense of many divergent local versions. While the divergence of localized versions might be to the occasional advantage of the localized concerns of tyrants, the convergent Panhellenism of the Homeric performances could in the end become an obstacle to the tyrants' current political ideologies: we recall the testimony of Herodotus (5.67.1) to the effect that Kleisthenes, tyrant of Sikyon, banished the public performances of "Homer" in his city on the grounds that the contents were partial to Argos, a city that was at that point an enemy of Sikyon.[193] With its Panhellenic stature, then, the poetry of "Homer" would become ever less capable of accommodating the occasional and localized needs of the audience; we cannot expect it to be overtly responsive to such ad hoc considerations as the genealogies of powerful patrons.[194] In the epic poetry of Homer

192. More precisely the claim being made is that Theron is descended from Thersandros, son of Polyneikes. The process of derivation evidently starts with Thersandros rather than Polyneikes because the lineage is founded on the hero cult of Thersandros. See also Herodotus 2.43 on the genealogy of Herodotus' predecessor and rival, Hecataeus. For a list of other comparable claims of lineage, see Brelich 1958:148–150: Andocides as descended from Odysseus (Plutarch *Alcibiades* 21.1), Socrates from Daidalos (Plato *Alcibiades* 121a), Alcibiades from Eurysakes (Plato ibid.), and Peisistratos from Neleus (Herodotus 5.65.3). In the case of the descent of Alcibiades from Eurysakes, son of Ajax, we may note that it is Eurysakes, not Ajax, who has a cult in Athens (Pausanias 1.35.3). For a similar situation in the case of the Peisistratidai, the family of the tyrants at Athens, see p. 154.

193. On the contents of these "Homeric" performances at Sikyon, see p. 22.

194. The tendency to avoid genealogical connections between the characters of epic and the audience of the here and now is a characteristic of Homeric poetry, not necessarily of epic poetry in general: see p. 150. In this connection I note the observation of Roussel 1976.31 that names with the suffix -**adēs** and -**idēs**, conventionally used in the plural to express lineages (such as **Aiakidai**), are regularly confined to the singular in Homeric diction, designating persons and not groups (such as **Atreidēs** = Agamemnon, **Aiakidēs** = Achilles). Note too the campaign against family group-namings of the type -**adai** and -**idai** in the context of the reforms of Kleisthenes of Athens: cf. Aristotle *Constitution of the Athenians* 21.4 and the comments of Roussel 1976.56; also p. 62 concerning the fact that some Alkmaionidai had the personal name Alkmaionides (for the occurrence of which on ostraka indicating the ostracism of "tyrannophiles," see Meiggs and

the gap that separates the heroes of the past and the men of the present could not and would not be bridged.[195] Little wonder, then, that heroes could lift stones that not even two of us 'today' could even manage to budge (*Iliad* XII 445–449).

As for the praise poetry of Pindar, it does more than just confirm the extension of the genealogies of powerful families into the heroic past: the **kleos** of victorious athletes who come from such families is pointedly equated with the **kleos** of heroes as they are known from epic.[196] But the praise poetry of Pindar does not claim to be descended from the epic of Homer — a stance that would have matched the way in which his patrons may claim to be descended from heroes praised by the narration of epic poetry. The **kleos** of Pindar praises not only the victors of the present but also the heroes of the past, and this praise of heroes is treated as intrinsic to the medium of praise poetry. In the words of Pindar the medium of epinician praise poetry existed even before the Seven against Thebes: by implication, praise poetry was praising heroes even before the events recorded by epic (*Nemean* 8.50–51).[197] In the praise poetry of Pindar, Homer figures as but one in a long line of poets who are masters of **kleos**. In other words, the **kleos** of Homer is treated as an offshoot of the **kleos** that survives as the praise poetry of Pindar. Unlike the **kleos** of Homer, however, the **kleos** of Pindar extends into the here and now, linking the heroes of the past with the men of the present. In the diction of Pindar the very concept of **nea** or **neara** 'new things' applies not to poetic innovations but to poetic applications of the past glories of heroes to the present glories of men who are being praised in the here and now.[198]

The built-in conceit of Pindaric choral lyric poetry, that its praise collapses the distinction between heroes of the past and men of the here and now, accentuates the occasionality of his medium. This point brings us back to the self-definition of Pindar's medium as **ainos** — a self-definition not

---

Lewis 1975.41 on Ἱπποκράτες Ἀλκμεωνίδο Ἀλοπεκε̃θεν). In contrast, we note that Pindar in *Nemean* 2 celebrates Timodemos of Akharnai (Τιμόδημε 14) as one of the Timodemidai (Τιμο-δημίδαι 18).

195. The closest thing to such bridging in Homeric poetry is the survival of names, within the epic tradition, that are matched by historical personages. Shapiro 1983.89 notes: "Almost without exception, historical Athenians of the Archaic and Classical periods did not bear the names of epic heroes, as their descendants often do in Greece today; Peisistratos is the one exception." I interpret this exception as resulting from the nonerasure of the name and identity of the hero Peisistratos (e.g., *Odyssey* iii 36) from the Homeric tradition, *despite* the historical presence of the tyrant Peisistratos. In other words it could be argued that the prestige of the tyrant is what preserved a pattern of identification that is otherwise by and large erased by the Homeric tradition.

196. Pindar *Nemean* 9.39–42, as discussed at p. 150.

197. Cf. Köhnken 1971.34–35; N 1979.227–228.

198. Cf. p. 69.

shared by Homeric poetry. Contemporary feats of athletics are particularly appropriate for celebration by the **ainos** as a form of expression that purports to close the gap between the heroic past and the historic present, in that the very activity of athletics is from the standpoint of religious ideology a present-day ordeal that reenacts, in a perpetual series of seasonally recurring festivals, the primordial ordeal of the hero. We see the same ideology depicted in the Funeral Games of Patroklos in *Iliad* XXIII, where the Games are instituted as compensation for the death of the hero Patroklos and where, as Cedric Whitman has noticed, the athletic activity of each character in some way reenacts the martial activity appropriate to his own heroic character.[199]

Contemporary feats of war would have been equally appropriate for celebration by praise poetry, had it not been for the evolution of the polis. Moreover, even if we discount for the moment the emphasis that the polis placed on the communal effort as opposed to individual aristocratic enterprise, any celebration of martial feats still raises the problem of inter-polis politics: what counts as a success for one polis will be a failure for another, so that it becomes difficult for any military victory to achieve Panhellenic recognition in poetry or song. In contrast the victories of athletes at the four great Panhellenic Games are by definition recognized by all Hellenic city-states. It should come as no surprise, then, that in the case of military victories, the one notable exception meriting Panhellenic recognition in poetry and song was in fact a supposedly Panhellenic victory. I refer to the Greek victory over the Persians in 479 B.C., as, for example, celebrated by Pindar in *Isthmian* 8 alongside the supposedly central topic of that composition, an athletic victory by an Aeginetan in the Isthmian Games of 478 B.C.[200] The special appropriateness of athletics to praise poetry is best illustrated by Pindar's claim that epinician praise poetry had existed even before epic (*Nemean* 8.50–51).[201] The Seven against Thebes, in the same Pindaric context, are

199. Whitman 1959.169. Cf. p. 141. In Ch.7 I offer a detailed case in point, centering on the figure of Antilokhos in *Iliad* XXIII.

200. The theme of Panhellenic victory in Pindar's *Isthmian* 8 may be compared with the compositions of Simonides known as *The Sea-Battle of Artemisium* (PMG 532–535) and *The Sea-Battle at Salamis* (PMG 536). The second of these compositions was possibly commissioned to be sung and danced at the Feast of the Panathenaia (Bowra 1961.344). As for the first, it seems to have featured prominently the theme of the divine intervention of Boreas the North Wind and his consort Oreithyia in the Battle of Artemisium (cf. PMG 534). Herodotus reports explicitly that the Athenians on this occasion sacrificed and prayed to Boreas and Oreithyia to scatter the fleet of the Persians (7.189). Herodotus also reports that the same wind that scattered the fleet of the Persians was called the **Hellēspontiēs** 'the one from the Hellespont' by the natives of the locale (7.188.2). By implication the wind that thwarted the Persians came from the Hellespont, the site of the tomb of Achilles (e.g., *Odyssey* xxiv 80–84; cf. N 1979.344); their shipwreck at Cape Sepias, where Thetis had been abducted by Peleus (Herodotus 7.191.2), was interpreted as a sign of the anger of the mother of Achilles, Thetis, who was then supplicated by the Magi (ibid.). For more on Thetis, see Slatkin 1986.

201. Cf. p. 192.

represented as having engaged in an athletic contest specifically before they embarked on their famous war (e.g., Bacchylides *Epinician* 9.10–24 SM).[202] This athletic contest, serving as prototype for the Nemean Games, would have been celebrated by the prototype of Pindar's current Nemean Ode in honor of the current victor at the Nemean Games.[203]

The ideology of the athletic games, as expressed in the epinician praise poetry of Pindar, may even be said to be a sort of compensation for the historical differentiation between heroes and ancestors in that the **kleos** of the hero and the **kleos** of the ancestor converge precisely in the context of praising the athlete's immediate ancestors. By upholding the values of the epic heroes, the victor is represented as simultaneously upholding the values of his own immediate ancestors. In one particularly striking passage Pindar expresses this simultaneity in the actual words of a dead hero, who is represented as speaking from the dead about the martial victories of his son. The son, who from the standpoint of his father's words is still a living hero, is Alkmaion, one of the Epigonoi, the sons of the Seven against Thebes who succeeded in destroying Thebes. The father is Amphiaraos, son of Oikles, one of the original Seven against Thebes who had failed in what their sons were later to succeed. The theme of these heroes is introduced in the context of praising the athlete Aristomenes of Aegina for his victory in wrestling at the Pythian Games of 446 B.C. I begin the quotation with the words of the poet in praise of the victorious Aristomenes for the glory that this athlete has conferred upon his immediate ancestors, the lineage of the Meidulidai:

> αὔξων δὲ πάτραν Μειδυλιδᾶν λόγον φέρεις, | τὸν ὅνπερ ποτ' Ὀι-
> κλέος παῖς (...) αἰνίξατο (...)| (43) ὧδ' εἶπε μαρναμένων· | φυᾷ
> τὸ γενναῖον ἐπιπρέπει | ἐκ πατέρων παισὶ λῆμα ...| (55) τοιαῦτα
> μὲν| ἐφθέγξατ' Ἀμφιάρηος. χαίρων δὲ καὶ αὐτὸς| Ἀλκμᾶνα στεφά-
> νοισι βάλλω.
>
> Pindar *Pythian* 8.38–57

Making great the house of the Meidulidai, you win as a prize[204] the utterance that once the son of Oikles said [= said as an **ainos**]. [...] Thus he spoke about those who fought: "The will of the <u>fathers</u> [**pateres**] shines through from them, in the very thing that is inborn in the nature of their sons." Thus spoke Amphiaraos. And I also take joy in casting a garland at Alkmaion.

The gesture of casting a garland at the hero Alkmaion is a stylized act of

---

202. Cf. p. 120.

203. Cf. N 1979.227–228.

204. On **pherō** in the sense of 'win as a prize', see Kurke 1988.228 with n93 (following Gildersleeve 1899.330); cf. Pindar *Pythian* 4.278 (p. 202).

hero cult.[205] The voice of the poet, in saying that he "met" the hero on the way to Delphi (*Pythian* 8.56–60), is in effect saying that he experienced an epiphany of the hero, which is the inspiration, as it were, of Pindar's words.[206] The theme of epiphany is relevant to my interpretation of φυᾷ τὸ γενναῖον ἐπιπρέπει | ἐκ πατέρων παισὶ λῆμα 'the will of the fathers [**pateres**] shines through from them, in what is inborn in the nature of their sons' (43–44). The word **pateres** in this passage means not only 'fathers' but also 'ancestors'.[207] The latter meaning emerges more clearly as the ode progresses:

> ἐπάμεροι· τί δέ τις τί δ' οὔ τις σκιᾶς ὄναρ | ἄνθρωπος. ἀλλ' ὅταν αἴγλα διόσδοτος ἔλθῃ, | λαμπρὸν φέγγος ἔπεστιν ἀνδρῶν καὶ μείλι-
> χος αἰών.

Pindar *Pythian* 8.95–97

Creatures of a day.[208] What is a someone, what is a no one?[209] Man is the dream of a shade. But when the brightness given by Zeus comes, there is at hand the shining light of men, and the life-force [**aiōn**] gives pleasure.[210]

I interpret **skiās onar** 'dream of a shade' as a recapitulation of the earlier words of the dead Amphiaraos about his living son. In Homeric usage the word **skiā** 'shade' can designate a dead person.[211] I suggest that the shade of the dead person is literally dreaming—that is, realizing through its dreams—the living person. In other words the occasion of victory in a mortal's day-to-day lifetime is that singular moment when the dark insubstantiality of an ancestor's shade is translated, through its dreams, into the

205. This point is argued by Kurke, pp. 221–225.

206. On Pindar's mystical encounter with the epiphany of the hero in *Pythian* 8.58–60 as "both a transition and a source of inspiration for this song," see Kurke, p. 225n87. For an overview of the allusions to the hero cult of Alkmaion in this poem, see Rusten 1983; cf. also Pòrtulas 1985.213, 220. In a forthcoming work, T. K. Hubbard argues that the epiphanic hero in this context is Amphiaraos himself, not the hero's son, Alkmaion.

207. On **pateres** 'fathers' as 'ancestors', see p. 177.

208. Race 1986.100: "Men are creatures of a day, 'ephemeral' [. . .] We cannot know from day to day who we are, or if we will even continue to exist."

209. See Giannini 1982 for the arguments in favor of the interpretation given here and against the interpretation "What is man, what is not man?"

210. On **aiōn** 'life-force' as an expression of both material security and the transcendent concept of *eternal return*, see N 1981.114–116, following Benveniste 1937.110, 112.

211. This usage is stressed by Lefkowitz 1977.216, who translates "man is a shadow's dream," noting that **skiā** "means both shadow and shade of the dead, a partial reflection of a living being." She interprets the saying "man is a shadow's dream" as an expression of insubstantiality, "but at the same time it can be said to denote significant appearances that presage victory, Amphiaraus' vision of Alcmeon with his shield, Pindar's encounter with Alcmeon on his way to Delphi" (ibid.).

shining life-force of the victor in full possession of victory, radiant with the brightness of Zeus.[212] It is as if we the living were the realization of the dreams dreamt by our dead ancestors.[213] We may recall the words of Walt Whitman, in *Crossing Brooklyn Ferry*:[214]

> I am with you, you men and women of a generation, or ever so many
>   generations hence,
> Just as you feel when you look on the river and sky, so I felt,
> Just as any of you is one of a living crowd, I was one of a crowd,
> Just as you are refresh'd by the gladness of the river and the bright
>   flow, I was refresh'd,
> Just as you stand and lean on the rail, yet hurry with the swift current, I
>   stood yet was hurried
>
> . . .
>
> I too and many a time crossed the river of old
>
> . . .
>
> Closer yet I approach you,
> What thought you have of me now, I had as much of you — I laid in
>   my stores in advance,
> I consider'd long and seriously of you before you were born.
>
> . . .
>
> Who knows, for all the distance, but I am as good as looking at you
>   now, for all you cannot see me?

In Pindaric song the link of the victorious athlete to his ancestors is celebrated through the **kleos** of heroes. In this case the **kleos** of heroes is not epic but **ainos**. Alternatively, however, the **kleos** of heroes can even be **ainos** as represented by epic. I think of *Iliad* IX, when old Phoenix gives his admonition to Achilles in the format of an **ainos** (specifically the format qualifies as a **par-ain-esis** 'instructive speech'):[215] he refers here to his own discourse as

212. Kurke, p. 229, cites Gildersleeve 1899.191 on Pindar *Olympian* 7.91–93: "The oracle of Diagoras is the wisdom of his ancestors, which is personated in him." As Kurke points out (ibid.), the oracle of Diagoras in *Olympian* 7 is parallel to the oracle of Alkmaion in *Pythian* 8.60, which that hero had inherited from his father Amphiaraos. We may compare the Fijian notion that poet-seers have personal contact with the ancestors, from whom they receive their songs directly (Finnegan 1977.111). Perhaps these themes are pertinent to the expression **patria ossa** 'ancestral voice' in Pindar *Olympian* 6.62, applied to the words of Apollo as he speaks to his son Iamos, the primordial seer who is ancestor of the Iamidai. On the relationship between dead ancestors and the athletic victors whose deeds are witnessed by them, see Segal 1986, especially p. 207 on Pindar *Pythian* 5.94–103.

213. We may compare the Australian Aboriginal notion of the ancestral past as "dream time": see Clunies Ross 1986.244.

214. Whitman 1892 [1980] 144–147.

215. On the function of the expression οὕτω at *Iliad* IX 524 as a marker of the beginning of an **ainos**, see Fraenkel 1950 II 339. Cf. also Maehler 1963.47. On the **par-ain-esis** of Phoenix, see further at p. 205. For more on **par-ain-esis**, see p. 149.

tōn prosthen ... klea andrōn | hērōōn 'glories [**klea**] of men of the past, heroes' (IX 524–525). In the story of Phoenix a prime example of 'men of the past' is Meleager, a hero. The story is aimed at a man of the present, Achilles, whom the *Iliad* presents as a hero in the making. The actual message of the story told by Phoenix to Achilles turns out to be — from the standpoint of the *Iliad* — the very name of Patroklos, **Patro-kleēs** 'he who has the glories [**klea**] of the ancestors'.[216] In the Homeric theme of Patroklos the differentiation between heroes and ancestors has not yet happened. In this theme the praise of ancestors and the praise of heroes are as yet one. So too in the songs of Pindar in praise of athletes, the praise of their ancestors is realized in the praise of heroes.

The Iliadic theme of Patroklos, as conveyed by the **ainos** told by Phoenix to Achilles, is an instance where epic refers to the format of the **ainos** without actually identifying itself with it. We can find other instances as well, especially in the *Odyssey* (e.g., xiv 508),[217] and each time we may observe the same pattern: whereas epic can refer to the format of the **ainos**, it is not an **ainos** itself.

This point brings us back one more time to the self-references of **ainos** as praise poetry. Praise poetry both calls itself **kleos** and explicitly identifies itself with the **kleos** of epic. It is as if occasional poetry, particularly praise poetry, were the primordial form of epic.[218] This is what Aristotle says, that epic is descended from poetry praising gods and men (**humnoi** and **enkōmia**, respectively: *Poetics* 1448b27, 32–34).[219] It is also what epic itself seems to be saying in situations where one character, in praising another, predicts that this praise will become the **kleos** heard by future audiences (e.g., *Odyssey* xxiv 192–202).[220] Even the sporadic instances in Homeric poetry where a hero is addressed in the second person give the impression that the third-person narrative of epic is but a transformation of the second-person direct address of praise poetry (e.g., *Iliad* XVI 787). Still, however we may want to formulate the transformation of epic poetry *as a derivative form* from occasional poetry, including praise poetry — which would count *as a parent form* — we must keep in mind that while the derivative form was evolving into the generalized and universally accessible medium of Homeric poetry,

216. N 1979.111, 114–115. On **pateres** as 'ancestors', see p. 177.

217. Cf. N 1979.234–237.

218. There is no attempt in praise poetry, however, to describe itself explicitly by way of features that characterize the current performance of epic poetry. For example, when heroes are said to be getting **kleos** from praise poetry in *Isthmian* 5.24–28, it is specified that there is musical accompaniment by both lyre and reed. This detail suggests that the performance is along the lines of contemporary lyric poetry or song, not epic (on the nonmelodic recitation of epic, see pp. 20 and following).

219. At least in this context we find no mention by Aristotle of Pindar or of any other such poets of praise.

220. N 1979.36 (§13n1), 255–256.

the parent form was in the meantime evolving into the specialized and re-
strictively difficult medium attested in the epinician lyric poetry of Pindar.[221]

Earlier we had seen an idealized vision of compensation as conveyed by
the medium of the epinician or victory ode, where the athlete's deed literally
demands to be requited in song, and the realization of the song in turn
demands to be requited by way of a **kharis**, a beautiful and pleasurable
reciprocity that is simultaneously material and transcendent in nature. Such a
vision is also preserved in epic, where epic indirectly refers to its evolution
from occasional poetry and song. The idealized description in *Odyssey* ix
3–11 of the singer's performance at an evening's feast, with its programmatic
reference to the spirit of **euphrosunē** 'mirth, merriment' that holds sway on
such an occasion (ix 6), serves as a signature for the evolution of poetic performance from the occasionality of the **ainos** to the universalism of the epic
of Homeric poetry.[222] In the medium of Pindar, which calls itself **ainos**, the
word **euphrosunē** 'mirth' (as in *Nemean* 4.1) refers programmatically to the
actual occasion of performing poetry and song.[223] In the *Odyssey* it is said
about the **euphrosunē** generated by the singer's performance at the feast that
there is no **telos**, that is, no social act to be performed and duly completed,
with more beauty and pleasure in its reciprocity than such an occasion. And
the beauty and pleasure of this reciprocity finds expression in the concept of
kharis:[224]

οὐ γὰρ ἐγὼ γέ τί φημι τέλος χαριέστερον εἶναι

Odyssey ix 5

I say that there is no act to be performed and completed that has in it
more **kharis**.

The ideal of such **kharis** lives on in the **ainos** of Pindar.

221. It goes without saying that the evolution of the parent form, as represented by Pindaric
praise poetry, is crystalized much later than that of the derivative form, as represented by
Homeric poetry. For a valuable discussion of epic and praise poetry in early Indic society, see
Dillon 1975.54.

222. Cf. N 1979.18–19, 91–92, 236, 260. So also in Xenophanes F 1 W = 21 B 1 DK, the
occasion of performance (1.12 and following) is represented as a setting of **euphrosunē** 'mirth'
(B 1.4). I interpret αἰνεῖν at Xenophanes 1.19 as 'follow in the tradition of' (cf. N, pp. 98 §6n4,
260 §10n3).

223. Bundy 1986.2.

224. On **kharis** as a 'beautiful and pleasurable compensation, through song or poetry, for a
deed deserving of glory', see p. 65.

7 ▢▢ Pindar and Homer, Athlete and Hero

Having observed how epic and the **ainos** of praise poetry can converge as well as diverge, we have begun to appreciate how the convergent **kleos** of Pindar's epinician lyric poetry may momentarily collapse the distinction between hero and victorious athlete. Perhaps the clearest example that we have seen so far is *Nemean* 9.39–42, where the **kleos** of the hero Hektor and the **kleos** of the victorious athlete are drawn into an explicit parallel.[1] The link between hero and athlete can also be achieved by the formal mention of the athlete's immediate ancestors, who are treated by the **ainos** of epinician lyric poetry as if they were a logical extension from the world of heroes. The continuum of the ancestors is made conveniently open-ended by the epinician as it reaches back in time, extending far back to the world of heroes. We can see that same kind of open-endedness in the speech of Phoenix to Achilles, spoken in the mode of an **ainos** and introduced by the following phrase:[2]

οὕτω καὶ τῶν πρόσθεν ἐπευθόμεθα[3] κλέα ἀνδρῶν
ἡρώων

Iliad IX 524–525

1. Cf. p. 150.
2. On the speech of Phoenix as **ainos** or **par-ain-esis** 'instructive speech', cf. p. 196.
3. For the phraseology, compare Mimnermus F 14.2 W, as discussed at p. 200.

For thus[4] we have learned the **klea** of men who came before,[5]
heroes[6] . . .

In this Homeric case the **klea andrōn**, the 'glories of men' who came before,
does not have to reach very far back in time since the discourse is already
happening in the world of heroes. For heroes in the world of heroes, the 'men
who came before' *are* their ancestors. Still, the reference is open-ended in its
vagueness, and the vagueness helps emphasize the unbroken continuum of
the 'men who came before' for men of the present. And the name of the person who is the hidden subject of the **ainos** told by Phoenix, Patroklos or
Patro-kleēs 'he who has the **klea** of the ancestors', reinforces the notion that
the 'men of the past' are indeed the ancestors for men of the present.[7]

In the diction of Pindar's **ainos**, however, the 'men who came before'
are not only the heroes who receive the **kleos** but also those who give the
kleos to the heroes. Thus, for example, the **proteroi** 'men of the past' at Pindar *Pythian* 3.80 are clearly the actual tellers of the tradition, not its subject
matter: μανθάνων οἶσθα προτέρων 'you know, learning from men of the
past'.[8] The same sort of ambiguity is attested in other poets as well:

οὐ μὲν δὴ κείνου γε μένος καὶ ἀγήνορα θυμὸν
τοῖον ἐμεῦ προτέρων πεύθομαι, οἵ μιν ἴδον
Λυδῶν ἱππομάχων πυκινὰς κλονέοντα φάλαγγας
Ἕρμιον ἂμ πεδίον, φῶτα φερεμμελίην.

Mimnermus F 14.1–4 W

That one's strength [**menos**] and proud spirit [**thūmos**],
as I learn from men who came before me,
were not like *this* [= what I see in my own time]. They [= the men who
came before me] saw him

---

4. On the function of this expression οὕτω as a marker of the beginning of an **ainos**, see again
Fraenkel 1950 II 339. Also p. 196, and p. 205.

5. Compare τῶν πρόσθεν 'who came before' here at *Iliad* IX 524 with the word προτέρων in
κλέεα προτέρων ἀνθρώπων 'the **klea** of men who came before' at Hesiod *Theogony* 100, where
the **klea** refers to both epic and theogonic poetry.

6. Compare κλέεα προτέρων ἀνθρώπων | ἡρώων 'the **klea** of men who came before, heroes'
with κλέα φωτῶν | . . . ἡμιθέων 'the **klea** of men, demigods [**hēmitheoi**]' at *Homeric Hymn*
32.18–19 and γένος ἀνδρῶν | ἡμιθέων at *Homeric Hymn* 31.18–19, where the word γένος seems
to refer explicitly to genealogical poetry. On **hēmitheoi** 'demigods, heroes' as a word connoting
hero cult, see N 1979.159–161.

7. Cf. p. 196.

8. Cf. Pindar *Nemean* 3.52–53: λεγόμενον δὲ τοῦτο προτέρων ἔπος ἔχω 'I have this utterance [**epos**] as spoken by those that came before'. (On the possibility of translating 'spoken of'
instead of 'spoken by' here, see N 1979.325 §8n5 and Hubbard 1985.42–43n92.) On the
interpretation of σὲ δ' ἀντία προτέρων φθέγξομαι at *Olympian* 1.36 as 'I shall call upon you
[= Pelops] in the presence of the predecessors', that is, with the past tradition as witness, see p.
129.

rushing tempestuously at the strong battle-lines of the horse-riding
Lydian warriors,
along the Plain of the River Hermos.[9] A spear-carrying man was he.[10]

There is reason to think, then, that the phrase **klea andrōn** 'glories of men'
inherits a neutrality of active / passive diathesis in the genitive plural **andrōn**
'of men': in other words the genitive in this phrase seems to carry with it
both an objective and a subjective function. The glories are being told simultaneously about and by the men of the past. There is a presupposition of an
unbroken succession extending from the men of the past to the men of the
present, both those men who are the subjects of the glory and those men who
perpetuate the glory through song. These glories, these **klea**, are evidently
the shared property throughout time of both the patrons and the poets who
sing about them. As we have seen in the words of the poet Ibycus addressed
to his patron, the tyrant Polykrates, your glory, your **kleos**, is my **kleos**
(Ibycus SLG 151.47–48).[11]

The **kleos** that is given by the poet is ultimately given by the hero in the
sense that the hero is the source of inspiration to the poet. When the voice of
Pindar says that he experienced, on his way to Delphi, the epiphany of a hero
(*Pythian* 8.56–60), we are in effect witnessing an equation of the hero's message with the poet's message.[12] To the extent that the message belongs to the
hero as well as the poet, **klea andrōn** is potentially the glorification sung by
as well as about heroes. When Achilles is represented as singing the **klea
andrōn** in the *Iliad* (IX 189), he is a model for the hero's possession of **kleos**.
The possession of epic, as in the subtitle of this book, can be read as both an
objective and a subjective genitive construct: not only does the poet possess

9. On the possibility that **Mimn-ermos** 'Mimnermus' is a name commemorating the resistance (as conveyed by the verb **mimnō**), at the river Hermos (**Hermos**), of the Smyrnaeans
against the Lydians, see West 1974.73, who adduces the tradition that Hellanicus, **Hellanīkos**,
was born on the day of the Hellenic victory over the Persians at Salamis (Hellanicus FGH 4 T 6).

10. As I tentatively interpret this poem, it concerns the miraculous appearance of a hero from
the past at a decisive moment of battle in the recent history of a given polis; for a collection of
testimonia related to the subject of the epiphany of a hero who rescues, in some contemporary
crisis, the community in which he is traditionally worshipped, see Brelich 1958.91–92 on
Theseus at Marathon (Plutarch *Life of Theseus* 35.5), Phylakos and Autonoos at Delphi (Herodotus 8.34–39; Pausanias 10.8.7). For instances where a group prays to heroes for intervention in
moments of crisis, see Brelich ibid. on Ajax and Telamon at Salamis (Herodotus 8.64),
Idomeneus and Meriones in a Cretan war (Diodorus 5.79.4). The emphatic use of **keinos** 'that
one' at lines 1 / 9 of Mimnermus F 14 suggests, of and by itself, an epiphany: cf. Sappho F 31.1
V (where the collocation of φαίνεταί μοι κῆνος with ἴσος θέοισιν likewise suggests an epiphany, even if the following infinitive at line 2, on which see Race 1983.94n10, shifts the understanding of φαίνεται from 'is manifested' to 'seems'). The description of 'that one' as a man
who was by far the best man in his own time suggests a figure like Achilles.

11. Cf. p. 187.

12. Cf. p. 194. In a forthcoming work, T. K. Hubbard argues that the epiphanic hero in this
context is Amphiaraos himself, not his son Alkmaion.

the **kleos** of epic, but the **kleos** of the epic hero can possess the poet to sing it, just as the hero had once sung it.

There is comparative evidence for the objective / subjective neutrality of the genitive in **klea andrōn**: in the diction of the *Rig-Veda*, the expression *śámso narā́ṃ* 'glory of men' allows either an objective or a subjective function for the genitive plural *narā́ṃ* 'of men': the emphasis can thus shift back and forth from the glory due the patron of the sacrifice to the glory due the composer of the sacred hymn that activates the sacrifice.[13] The neutralization of objective / subjective diathesis is not clearly attested in the case of *śrávo* . . . *nṛṇā́ṃ* 'glory of men' at *Rig-Veda* 5.18.5, where we see a direct cognate of **klea andrōn**: here the genitive plural seems to be specialized in the objective sense. In this connection, however, I draw attention to the contrast between singular *śrávas-* in Indic and plural **klea** in Greek: the singular conveys the notion of a single given composition, while the plural seems to emphasize a given tradition of composition.[14] When Achilles is singing the **klea andrōn** in the *Iliad* (IX 189), Patroklos is described emphatically as the only one who is listening to him (190). Presumably Patroklos will take up where Achilles left off: δέγμενος Αἰακίδην, ὁπότε λήξειεν ἀείδων 'he was waiting for whatever moment the Aeacid would stop singing' (191). The name of Patroklos seems appropriate to this theme: it is only through **Patrokleēs** 'he who has the **klea** of the ancestors' that the plurality of performance, that is, the activation of tradition, can happen. As long as Achilles himself sings the **klea andrōn**, these glories cannot be heard by any audience except Patroklos.[15]

The theme of reciprocity between the **kleos** of heroes in the past or of patrons in the present on one hand and the **kleos** of poets from past to present on the other hand finds direct expression in Pindaric song, where the idealized poet of the past can be represented as "Homer" while the implicit poet of the present is Pindar:

> τῶν δ' Ὁμήρου καὶ τόδε συνθέμενος | ῥῆμα πόρσυν'. ἄγγελον
> ἐσλὸν ἔφα τιμὰν μεγίσταν πράγματι παντὶ <u>φέρειν</u>. | αὔξεται καὶ
> Μοῖσα δι' ἀγγελίας ὀρθᾶς
>
> Pindar *Pythian* 4.277–279

Of all the words of Homer, understand and apply the saying that I now tell you: the best messenger, he said, <u>wins as a prize</u> [= verb **pherō**][16]

---

13. See Geldner 1951 I 265–266; also Schmitt 1967.98.

14. Cf. Schmitt, p. 96.

15. On the Homeric device creating a sense of interchangeability between characters of epic and members of the audience, see Frontisi-Ducroux 1986; in particular I cite her persuasive argument that Patroklos as the audience of Achilles is interchangeable with the audience of the *Iliad*; cf. also Russo and Simon 1968.

16. On **pherō** in the sense of 'win as a prize', see p. 194.

the greatest honor [tīmē] for everything. And the Muse too becomes greater [= verb **auxō**][17] by way of the correct message.

In other words, just as the Muse of poetry and song gives the greatness of tīmē 'honor',[18] so also she receives it.[19] Just as the poet, whether it is the "Homer" of the past or the Pindar of the present, 'wins as prize' [= verb **pherō**] for his subject the honor [tīmē] as conferred by the words of poetry, thereby 'making great' [= verb **auxō**] both the subject of the poetry and the poetry itself,[20] so also the person who happens to be the subject of the poetry, as a man of the present who has performed a glorious deed, can 'win' the honor conferred by the words of poetry in an unbroken continuum extending from the world of heroes to the world of the here and now, thereby 'making great' the immediate ancestry that produced him. Such was the case of the victorious athlete Aristomenes of Aegina, glorified by Pindar in *Pythian 8*:

17. For the collocation of **tīmē** 'honor' and **auxō** 'make / become greater' here, we may compare Pindar *Nemean* 7.32: τιμὰ δὲ γίνεται ὧν θεὸς ἁβρὸν αὔξει λόγον τεθνακότων 'tīmē becomes the possession of those who get words [**logos**] told about them, when they are dead, that are made great [**auxō**] and luxuriant [**habros**] by the divinity'. (On the positive usage of **habros** 'luxuriant' see p. 281 and following.) On the collocation of **logos** 'word(s)' and the genitive designating the subject of the song, compare λόγον Ὀδυσσέος 'words [**logos**] about Odysseus' at *Nemean* 7.21, which are attributed to "Homer" (21). The notion that there are more 'words' [**logos**] *about* Odysseus than 'experiences' [**pathā**] *by* Odysseus, as expressed at 7.20–21, is correlated at 7.23 with the presence of supposedly misleading **mūthoi** 'myths' about Odysseus. On the semantics of **mūthoi** as a broader and relatively unreliable concept as opposed to **alētheia** 'truth' as the narrower and absolutely reliable one, see pp. 65 and following. In the *Odyssey*, we may note, the outnumbering of the actual experiences of Odysseus by the stories about Odysseus has to do with the telling of numerous adventures, most often by Odysseus himself, in the format of an **ainos**: pp. 236 and following.

18. See also Pindar *Isthmian* 4.37–38, where "Homer" is represented as giving **tīmē** to a subject, in this case the hero Ajax. I interpret δι᾽ ἀνθρώπων here as a functional variant of Homeric ἐπ᾽ ἀνθρώπους in the sense of 'throughout humankind', a phrase deployed in collocation with **kleos** 'glory' and other designations of song and its performance (as at *Iliad* x 213, xxiv 202; *Odyssey* i 299, xix 334, xxiv 94, 201). The variation of ἐπί + accusative and διά + genitive, where both the accusative and the genitive convey the diffusion of song, is attested in a single context at *Nemean* 6.48–49: πέταται δ᾽ ἐπί τε χθόνα καὶ διὰ θαλάσσας τηλόθεν ὄνυμ᾽ αὐτῶν 'their reputation spreads over land and sea' (with reference to the glory of the Aiakidai: 45–47, quoted at p. 222).

19. See also Pindar *Isthmian* 6.67, where "Hesiod" is represented as being given **tīmē** by virtue of having an audience that not only listens to his poetic words but also applies their inherent wisdom. In this case the audience is specified as Lampon, who passes on this wisdom to his sons, in the mode of **par-ain-esis** (υἱοῖσι τε φράζων παραινεῖ 'indicating to his sons, he makes **par-ain-esis**' 6.68; more on **par-ain-esis** 'instructive speech' at pp. 149, 196), and who even shares this wisdom with the community at large, thus bringing about **kosmos** 'orderliness' (6.69; more on **kosmos** at p. 145).

20. The underlined word καὶ makes clear that not only the poetry but also the subject of the poetry is meant: αὔξεται καὶ Μοῖσα (*Pythian* 4.279). I use the word *poetry* here in the broadest sense, to include *song*.

αὔξων δὲ πάτραν Μειδυλιδᾶν λόγον φέρεις, | τὸν ὅνπερ ποτ' Ὀι-
κλέος παῖς (...) αἰνίξατο (...) | (43) ὧδ' εἶπε μαρναμένων· | φυᾷ
τὸ γενναῖον ἐπιπρέπει | ἐκ πατέρων παισὶ λῆμα ... | (55) τοιαῦτα
μὲν | ἐφθέγξατ' Ἀμφιάρηος. χαίρων δὲ καὶ αὐτὸς | Ἀλκμᾶνα
στεφάνοισι βάλλω.

Pindar Pythian 8.38–57

Making great [= verb **auxō**] the house of the Meidulidai, you [= Aris-
tomenes] win as a prize [= verb **pherō**]²¹ the utterance [**logos**] that
once the son of Oikles said [= said as an **ainos**]. ... Thus he spoke
about those who fought: "The will of the fathers [**pateres**] shines
through from them, in the very thing that is inborn in the nature of their
sons." Thus spoke Amphiaraos. And I also take joy in casting a garland at Alkmaion.²²

To extend the stories of heroes into the present, with a contemporary deed
implicitly worthy of the **kleos** that the heroes had earned through the **klea
andrōn**, is to 'win as a prize [= verb **pherō**] the words [**logos**]', as in this
passage (*Pythian* 8.38). As we also see in this passage, such words take the
form of an **ainos** (8.40).

Conversely the past deeds of heroes, worthy as they are of **kleos**, may be
said to extend all the way to the present, if the contemporary deed is worthy
of **kleos**, and this too is to 'win as a prize [= verb **pherō**] the words [**logos**]',
as we see from the Pindaric description of the heroic legacy of Achilles:

τὸν μὲν οὐδὲ θανόντ' ἀοιδαὶ ⟨ἐπ⟩έλιπον, | ἀλλά οἱ παρά τε πυρὰν
τάφον θ' Ἑλικώνιαι παρθένοι στάν, ἐπὶ θρῆνόν τε πολύφαμον
ἔχεαν. | ἔδοξ' ἧρα καὶ ἀθανάτοις, | ἐσθλόν γε φῶτα καὶ φθίμενον
ὕμνοις θεᾶν διδόμεν. | τὸ καὶ νῦν φέρει λόγον, ἔσσυταί τε Μοισαῖον
ἄρμα Νικοκλέος | μνᾶμα πυγμάχου κελαδῆσαι

Pindar Isthmian 8.56a-62

Even when he [Achilles] died, the songs did not leave him, but the Hel-
iconian Maidens [= the Muses] stood by his pyre and his funeral
mound, pouring forth a song of lamentation [**thrēnos**] that is famed far
and wide. And so it was that the gods decided to hand over the worthy
man, dead [**phthi-menos**] as he was, to the songs of the goddesses [=
Muses].²³ And this, even now, wins as a prize [= verb **pherō**] the
words [**logos**], as the chariot team of the Muses starts moving on its
way to glorify the memory of Nikokles the boxer.

21. On **pherō** in the sense of 'win as a prize': p. 202.
22. Cf. p. 194.
23. As I argue in N 1979.176–177, the phraseology here implies that Achilles was destined to
have a **kleos** that is **a-phthi-ton** 'unfailing, unwilting', as explicitly formulated at *Iliad* IX 413.
Cf. Steiner 1986.38.

The thought expressed here has been paraphrased by one critic as follows: "This handing over of a brave man [= Achilles] and his achievements to poetry even today brings fame (as it formerly did with Achilles)."[24] In other words the death of Nikokles, by virtue of his deeds in the contemporary world, merits the same tradition of song that the death of Achilles had once merited and still merits in the here and now by virtue of his deeds in the heroic world. The name of Nikokles, **Nīkoklēs** 'he who has the glory [**kleos**] of victory [**nīkē**]', is made appropriate to the themes of Pindar's *Isthmian* 8 in that the death of this Nikokles, cousin of the Isthmian victor Kleandros who is the primary honorand of this composition, is said not to impede the glory that he merited as a victorious boxer: rather the death is said to be the key to the continuation of the boxer's glory, just as the death of Achilles was the key to the extension of the glory of heroes in the present. The name of Kleandros, **Kleandros** 'he who has the glories of men [**klea andrōn**]', is thus likewise made appropriate to the themes of *Isthmian* 8 in that the 'glories of men', the **klea andrōn**, are more specifically 'the glories of men who came before, heroes' (τῶν πρόσθεν ... κλέα ἀνδρῶν | ἡρώων (*Iliad* IX 524–525),[25] that is, the glories of dead men of the past, as we saw from the implicit **ainos** narrated by Phoenix to Achilles.[26] In that particular instance the message carried by the **ainos** of the old man Phoenix, from the overall standpoint of the *Iliad*, is also carried by the very name of Patroklos, **Patroklees** 'he who has the glory [**kleos**] of the ancestors'.[27] The thematic appropriateness of the honorand's name, **Kleandros**, as indicating the **klea andrōn** 'glories of men', is underlined by its placement as the first word of *Isthmian* 8. In all the attested epinician poems of Pindar, Kleandros stands out as the only victor whose name begins the composition.[28] Even the inherited reciprocity of the concept of **klea andrōn** 'glories of men', in that the 'men' may be either the poets or the subject of the poets, is recapitulated in the composition of *Isthmian* 8: the poet, Pindar of Thebes, and the subject, Kleandros of Aegina, are represented as mythological relatives in that the nymphs Thebe and Aegina are twin sisters, both sired by the river Asopos (*Isthmian* 8.15–23). The son of Zeus and Aegina is none other than Aiakos (8.21–22), ancestor of the Aiakidai, while the Aigeidai, who represent the patriliny of Pindar himself (*Pythian* 5.75),[29] are elsewhere described as the

---

24. Köhnken 1975.30; cf. Pòrtulas 1985.214.

25. Cf. p. 200.

26. Cf. 7.

27. Cf. p. 197.

28. This detail is noted by Köhnken 1975.32n3. For an analogous emphasis on an honorand's name by way of initial positioning in the composition, see Bacchylides *Epinician* 6.1 SM: here the theme of Λάχων, the honorand's name and the first word of the composition, is immediately picked up by λάχε at 6.2.

29. Cf. p. 380.

descendants of Thebe (*Isthmian* 7.15). In view of this relationship Pindar of Thebes offers the flower of the **Kharites** 'Graces', personifications of reciprocity,[30] to Aegina, the community of the honorand (8.16–16a).[31]

In *Iliad* IX, the **klea andrōn** 'glories of men' is dramatized both as an **ainos** told by Phoenix to Achilles (524) and as an epic sung by Achilles to his one-man audience (189).[32] The audience of the epic is also the hidden subject of the **ainos**: he is **Patro-kleēs** 'he who has the **kleos** of the ancestors', whose name conveys both the medium of the epic and the medium of the **ainos**. In *Iliad* IX the **kleos** of the **ainos** about the implicit subject of Patroklos is appropriated by the epic, which is a **kleos** that is **aphthiton** 'unfailing, unwilting' (413). The situation is the opposite in Pindar's *Isthmian* 8, where the **kleos** of the epic about the explicit subject of Achilles is appropriated by the **kleos** of the **ainos**, in that the never-ending **kleos** of Achilles is presented as extending all the way into the **kleos** of the victor.[33] Here too, as in *Iliad* IX, the **kleos** of the ancestors plays a role. This time, however, the **kleos** of the ancestors is realized not in the theme and the name of Patroklos but rather in the actual **kleos** of the victor's own ancestors as celebrated by the lyric poetry of Pindar. In this particular case, moreover, the **kleos** of the victor's ancestors is realized in the victor's own name, **Kleandros**. The victor Kleandros is living proof that the **kleos**, the very identity, of his family is predicated on the achievements of its members. The victor of *Isthmian* 8 was planned from the start, from the very time that he was named, to become what he, to his good fortune, became through his athletic victory. A person's name, which he is given at birth on the basis of his ancestry, commits him to his identity. In the case of Kleandros, we see that a historical person — and even his identity as defined by his name — can fit the themes of the epinician. This can happen because the family's prestige and their very identity depend on the traditional institution of glorification by way of poetry and because this institution is preserved by epinician lyric poetry.

Let us consider another example of the potential close relationship between a man's good name and his **kleos** as conferred by epinician lyric poetry. The name in question is to be found in Pindar's *Pythian* 6. This time, instead of withholding the name till the final stages of the argument, as in the case of Kleandros, I begin immediately with the given person's name and

---

30. On **kharis** (plural **kharites**) 'grace' as a designation of reciprocity, see, for example, p. 65.

31. This gesture of offering the flower of the **Kharites** is followed by οὕνεκα 'because', introducing the myth of the daughters of Asopos (Pindar *Isthmian* 8.17 and following; cf. *Nemean* 3.3–5). For another reference to this myth, which served to validate an alliance between Thebes and Aegina, see Herodotus 5.80; on the role of the Aiakidai in this passage, see p. 177. For yet another reference, cf. Bacchylides *Epinician* 9.53 and following. Cf. Hubbard 1987c.15–16.

32. On Patroklos as audience, see p. 202.

33. See again *Isthmian* 8.56a-62, as quoted at p. 204 above.

with the implications built into it. The man in question is called **Thrasu-boulos**. At first the two components of this compound strike us as an oxymoron: **thrasu-** implies rashness or impetuousness, while **-boulos** implies deliberation or wise counsel.[34] But such a combination represents a traditional theme, as we find it in a lesson given by Nestor. The lesson takes place in *Iliad* XXIII, where the old hero instructs his son Antilokhos how to win a prize in a chariot race. The chariot race in question happens to be the centerpiece of the Funeral Games for Patroklos. As we shall see, Nestor's lesson is appropriate to the specific theme of funeral games and even to the general theme announced by the very name of Patroklos.

As we unravel the story of Antilokhos in *Iliad* XXIII, I argue that the very identity of our victor, **Thrasuboulos** (henceforth spelled Thrasyboulos), has been planned, presumably from birth onward, by virtue of his name to participate in the epic themes of the Antilokhos story — though not necessarily the Antilokhos story of *Iliad* XXIII in particular. To put it another way, I argue that Thrasyboulos was named after the Antilokhos story, as an expression of the hopes and ambitions of his family — hopes and ambitions that centered on success in the Games and on a glorification of this success by way of poetry and song. It is as if Thrasyboulos, given the themes surrounding his name, had been bred not only for success at the Games but also by extension for immortalization by epinician lyric poetry, which is what formalizes such success.[35] Such hope and ambition should not surprise us, if indeed it was founded on the traditional belief that epinician poetry was so venerably ancient as to exist already when the Seven marched against Thebes.[36] We find this belief expressed in the epinician lyric poetry of Pindar, but surely Pindar did not privately invent it, any more than he privately invented the epinician tradition.

The connections between Antilokhos and Thrasyboulos are unmistakable.[37] Antilokhos, the focus of our attention in *Iliad* XXIII, enters the chariot race in the Funeral Games of Patroklos, driving his father's chariot in place of Nestor, who is too old to compete as an athlete (621–623, 627–645). So also the young Thrasyboulos, the victor in *Pythian* 6, is represented as driving the chariot for his father Xenokrates, the official victor (cf. *Olympian*

---

34. Cf. Aristotle *Rhetoric* 1400b21.

35. Another striking example is the name of a victor's father in *Pythian* 11.43, **Puthonīkos** 'he who has victory at the Pythian Games'. What goes for athletes goes for horses as well: consider the name of the prize horse of Hieron, **Pherenīkos** (*Olympian* 1.18, *Pythian* 3.74), which means 'he who carries off the victory [nīkē]'. Cf. Burnett 1985.179n7, who offers a list of "puns" in Pindar and Bacchylides; I suggest, however, that the term *pun* in this context is too narrow, implying as it does a playful attitude towards the names of the honorands. On the serious function of the name as a "micro-récit" in Archaic Greek traditions, see Calame 1986.155 and Loraux 1988b.

36. Cf. p. 192.

37. Cf. Farnell 1932.187.

2.14–20). According to one interpretation of line 19 of *Pythian* 6, Thrasyboulos is pictured as driving the victorious chariot while his father is riding on his right.[38] In the epic tradition Antilokhos not only drives the chariot for his father Nestor but also rescues the old man from death by giving up his own life. He is struck down by Memnon, after the father's chariot is immobilized when Paris shoots Nestor's horse with an arrow (Pindar *Pythian* 6.28–42; cf. *Odyssey* iv 186–188).[39] Given such a prominence of chariots in the epic career of Antilokhos, it would be well to look closely at the lesson on chariot driving given by Nestor to Antilokhos in *Iliad* XXIII. We find in this lesson a traditional theme corresponding to the oxymoron built into the name of Thrasyboulos.

Nestor's lesson on chariot driving amounts to a lesson on how to think for oneself in a moment of crisis. The key to the lesson, which Nestor calls a 'signal' or **sēma** (XXIII 326), is what Antilokhos should do when he reaches the **terma** 'turning point' in the parabola-shaped course of the chariot race. Let us picture the trajectory of the racecourse as a counterclockwise movement around the turning point (cf. XXIII 336), which is at the twelve-o'clock position: as the driver approaches the turning point, he prepares to round it as closely as possible by restraining with the reins his horse-team on the left side while impelling them with a goad on the right side (XXIII 336–341). As Douglas Frame has pointed out to me about this passage, the key to success here is a blend of opposites: impulsiveness on one side, restraint on the other.[40] The **noos** 'mind' of Antilokhos, which we may define for the moment as his ability to "read" a **sēma** 'sign, signal',[41] responds to this lesson (νοέοντι XXIII 305) by finding an occasion to apply the principle. The

38. This interpretation requires that νιν at *Pythian* 6.19 refer to πατρὶ τεῷ at 15: cf. Gildersleeve 1899.318.

39. There is a variation on this epic scene in *Iliad* VIII 80 and following, where it is Diomedes rather than Antilokhos who saves Nestor, this time from Hektor, after Nestor's chariot is immobilized as Paris shoots the old man's horse with an arrow (unlike Antilokhos, of course, Diomedes himself does not get killed in performing the rescue). On the pointed references to Diomedes as a stand-in, as it were, for Antilokhos, as in *Iliad* IX 57–58, see Schein 1987.247. It is the apparent Iliadic awareness of the story of Antilokhos' death that guarantees the epic pedigree of this story as Pindar alludes to it.

40. In this connection, Frame also draws my attention to the description of the Siamese twins known as the Aktorione Molione in Nestor's narrative about the chariot race at the Funeral Games of Amarynkeus in *Iliad* XXIII: in this contest, which is the only one that Nestor says that he did not win (XXIII 638), the twins were victorious by way of their combined efforts, where one twin was consistently guiding the horses as he held the reins while the other twin would urge them on with the whip (XXIII 641–642). Since the left hand is conventionally the bridle hand (see LSJ s.v. ἡνία I.3) and since this heroic pair were Siamese twins, I assume that the user of the reins, the twin of restraint, would have to be on the left side, and that the twin of impulse would have to be on the right.

41. On the semiotics of reading as 'recognizing', see N 1983, especially p. 39; also Pucci 1987.87. Cf. also pp. 171 and following.

occasion comes earlier than the situation described by Nestor, which is at the turning point. Before Antilokhos ever reaches the turning point, he impulsively seizes an opportunity to pass the chariot of Menelaos, thereby nearly "fishtailing" the older hero and thus nearly killing them both (XXIII 402–441). This seemingly reckless act of Antilokhos is in reality a rational application of the principle taught by Nestor, as we see at the moment that Antilokhos decides to take the risk: he does so by recourse to his **noos** (νοήσω at XXIII 415, picking up νοέοντι at XXIII 305).[42] What Menelaos thinks is a matter of reckless adolescent driving, an act lacking in **noos** (νῦν αὖτε νόον νίκησε νεοίη XXIII 604), is in reality a deliberate and rational move.[43] Though Antilokhos risks everything, his risk is a calculated one nevertheless, and the overarching principle of rational behavior is underscored by the restraint with which Antilokhos handles the angry Menelaos in the following scene: the two disputing contestants finally come to terms, with Menelaos generously allowing Antilokhos to keep the prize that should rightfully have been his own (XXIII 586–611).[44] This restraint of Antilokhos, which leads to his success in keeping the prize, complements the earlier impulsiveness when he nearly "fishtailed" Menelaos (XXIII 418–441).[45]

In the case of Antilokhos his **noos** enables him to win because he understands and can apply what Nestor had taught him, particularly through the **sēma** 'sign, signal' (XXIII 326) about what to do at the turning point. In other words Antilokhos "reads" the **sēma** 'sign' of Nestor, and this reading is a matter of **noos**.[46] The verb **noeō** 'recognize', derivative of **noos**, is practically synonymous with "read" in the sense of "read the sign." In view of Nestor's specifically saying that the **sēma** 'sign' of victory (XXIII 326) centers on the way in which Antilokhos is to make his turn around the turning point, and in view of Nestor's explicitly linking this **sēma** 'sign' and this **terma** 'turning point', it is noteworthy that the narrative goes on to indicate that the **terma** is itself a **sēma**. But now (XXIII 331) the word **sēma** has the specific meaning of 'tomb', which is conventionally visualized as a mound of earth, such as the tomb of Patroklos (at XXIII 45):

ἤ τευ <u>σῆμα</u> βροτοῖο πάλαι κατατεθνηῶτος,
ἢ τό γε νύσσα τέτυκτο ἐπὶ <u>προτέρων</u> ἀνθρώπων,

---

42. That Antilokhos is behaving here as an exponent of **mētis** 'cunning intelligence' is argued further in N 1983.53n37, extending the arguments presented by Detienne and Vernant 1974.22–24, 29–31.

43. Again, this point is argued in N 1983.53n37.

44. Cf. N, p. 48.

45. Ibid. Thus the act of balancing restraint and impulsiveness achieves in the end a dominant sense of restraint.

46. Cf. p. 208.

καὶ νῦν τέρματ' ἔθηκε ποδάρκης δῖος Ἀχιλλεύς.

XXIII 331–333

It is either the tomb [sēma] of a man who died a long time ago, or it
was a turning point [nussa; i.e, in racing] of men who came before[47]
Now swift-footed brilliant Achilles has set it up as the turning point
[= terma plural].

The two distinct alternatives set up by this Homeric passage, either a turning
point or a tomb, correspond to one and the same thing in the institution of
chariot races as attested in the Panhellenic Games, where the turning points
of chariot racecourses were conventionally identified with the tombs of
heroes.[48] According to Pausanias the spirit of such a hero, called **Taraxippos**
'he who disturbs the horses', often causes the racing chariots to crash as they
round the turning point (6.20.15–19). Similarly, in the chariot race in honor
of the dead hero Patroklos, it is the turning point where Antilokhos must take
care, according to Nestor, not to let his chariot crash (XXIII 341–345).

Despite the collapsing of distinctions between turning point and hero's
tomb in the institution of chariot racing within the framework of the Games,
the narrative of the *Iliad* overtly maintains their distinctness: the turning point
for the chariot race in honor of Patroklos had been in the past either just that,
a turning point, or else a **sēma** 'tomb' of a hero, of one who came before
(XXIII 331–332). But here too is a collapsing of distinctions, though this happens only latently, by way of the double use of **sēma** in the sense of both
'sign' (XXIII 326) and 'tomb' (XXIII 331).[49] The emphasis on one alternative
interpretation, that the object in question is the tomb of a hero, is expressed
by a word that points to the other alternative interpretation, that the object in
question is a turning point: the word is **sēma**, which conveys not only the
notion of 'tomb' (XXIII 331) but also the 'sign' of Nestor (XXIII 326) concerning precisely how to make a turn at a turning point (XXIII 334–348; cf. 309,
318–325). Thus the ostentatiously presented alternative of a **sēma** 'tomb'
(XXIII 331), in view of the **sēma** 'sign' of Nestor to his son only five verses
earlier (XXIII 326), bears its own message: not only the tomb is a sign but the
very mention of the tomb may be a sign. Thus the **sēma** is a *reminder*, and
the very use of the word is a *reminder*. In a more detailed study of **sēma**, I
have characterized the attitude of this narrative concerning Nestor's lesson as
one of take it or leave it: "If you reject the alternative that the turning point is

---

47. This usage of **proteroi** 'men who came before', as we have seen at p. 200, implies an
ainos (on which see pp. 147 and following). Like the **ainos**, the **sēma** here is one code conveying at least two messages.

48. See Rohde 1898 I 173 and n1 (= 1925.127 and n147n59); also Sinos 1980.53n6 and N
1983.46.

49. The **sēma** here is like the **ainos**: one code conveying two messages.

a **sēma** 'tomb' of a dead man, then the **sēma** 'sign' of Nestor to Antilokhos has a simplex message about how to make a turn; if you accept it, on the other hand, then the same **sēma** 'sign' has an additional message about the **sēma** 'tomb' as a reminder of **kleos**."[50]

Moreover, in the case of Antilokhos this **sēma** is a reminder not just of **kleos** in general but of **Patro-kleēs** 'he who has the **klea** of the ancestors' in particular. After the death of Patroklos, Antilokhos takes over from Patroklos the role of ritual substitute, so that the **sēma** 'sign' for Antilokhos is about a role model who will set the pattern, from the standpoint of the *Iliad*, of stories in the future epic career of Antilokhos.

As I have argued at length elsewhere, the role of Patroklos as ritual substitute of Achilles is conveyed by his characterization as **therapōn** of Achilles.[51] This word **therapōn**, normally translated as 'attendant' or 'companion in arms', is apparently a borrowing of an Anatolian word, attested in Hittite as *tarpašša-/tarp(an)alli-* 'ritual substitute'.[52] This sense of **therapōn** is latent in most Homeric contexts, but it comes to the surface in the application of the word to Patroklos in the context of his dying in place of Achilles. As long as Patroklos behaves as an attendant of Achilles, his identity is subsumed under that of Achilles and he is safe from harm; once he ventures on his own, however, he is doomed to die in place of Achilles. This two-way relationship of Patroklos to Achilles, passive as an understudy and active as a ritual substitute, is conveyed by the word **therapōn**.[53] A primary function of Patroklos, as an attendant of Achilles, was to be his **hēniokhos** 'chariot driver' (XXIII 280). One Automedon, who had served as chariot driver for Patroklos when Patroklos ventured off on his fatal quest, takes over from Patroklos as chariot fighter after Patroklos dies, while one Alkimedon takes over from Automedon as chariot driver (XVII 474–483). Both Automedon and Alkimedon are described as **therapontes** 'attendants' of Achilles (XXIV 573–574), whom the hero honored more than all his other **hetairoi** 'companions in arms' after the death of Patroklos (XXIV 574–575). Another **hetairos** 'companion in arms' who is very dear to Achilles is Antilokhos (XXIII 556), and he is described in this way specifically in the context of his winning a prize from Achilles as a result of his success as a chariot driver in the Funeral Games of Patroklos. In the *Odyssey*, when the spirits seen in Hades by the newly killed suitors are enumerated, Antilokhos ranks high enough to be the third hero mentioned, immediately after Achilles himself and Patroklos (xxiv 16). This parallelism of Antilokhos with Patroklos is

---

50. N 1983.47.

51. N 1979.292–295; Sinos 1980.29–38; Lowenstam 1981.126–177.

52. Van Brock 1959.119: "Le *tarpalli-* est un autre soi-même, une projection de l'individu sur laquelle sont transférées par la magie du verbe toutes les souillures dont on veut se débarasser."

53. Again, N 1979.292–295.

also to be found in the *Aithiopis*, where Achilles avenges the death of Antilokhos at the hands of Memnon (Proclus summary, p. 106 lines 4–6 Allen),
much as he avenges the death of Patroklos at the hands of Hektor in the *Iliad*.
Antilokhos, then, is a potential **therapōn** of Achilles in traditional epic narrative, and he is acknowledged as such in the *Iliad* (again XXIII 556).[54]

If indeed the **sēma** 'signal' given to Antilokhos by his father, Nestor,
conveys the name of **Patro-kleēs** 'he who has the **klea** of the ancestors', then
the relevance of the message may be that Antilokhos, like Patroklos, is to
become a **therapōn**, a ritual substitute. Yet Antilokhos dies not in place of
Achilles but rather in place of his own father. Antilokhos not only drives the
chariot for his father but also rescues the old man from death by giving up his
own life when Nestor's chariot is immobilized (cf. Pindar *Pythian*
6.28–42).[55]

Which brings us back to the name of Thrasyboulos, combining the
themes of rashness (**Thrasu-**) and prudence (**-boulos**). The same themes are
combined in the actions of Antilokhos when he rashly swerved past the
chariot of Menelaos and then, showing due restraint, prudently talked his
opponent out of a prize. The same themes are also combined in the instructions of Nestor, ostensibly concerning the proper way to make a turn around
the turning point in the chariot race: applying impulse on the right-hand or
dominant side of the horse-team must be counterbalanced by applying restraint on the left-hand or recessive side.[56] The key to understanding the synthesis of these themes is to have **noos** just as Antilokhos had **noos**.

In Pindar's *Pythian* 6, honoring the young charioteer Thrasyboulos, a
direct connection is established between the **noos** of Thrasyboulos and that of
Antilokhos. After a reference to the **par-ain-esis** 'instructive speech' of
Cheiron to Achilles (παραινεῖν 6.23), where the old Centaur instructs the
young hero that one must honor one's parents in the same way that one
honors Zeus most of all (6.23–27), the lesson for the present is applied
directly to Antilokhos, who had died on the battlefield as a substitute for his
father:

> ἔγεντο καὶ πρότερον ᾿Αντίλοχος βιατὰς | νόημα τοῦτο φέρων, | ὃς
> ὑπερέφθιτο πατρός, ἐναρίμβροτον | ἀναμείναις στράταρχον Αἰ-
> θιόπων | Μέμνονα. Νεστόρειον γὰρ ἵππος ἅρμ᾿ ἐπέδα | Πάριος ἐκ
> βελέων δαιχθείς· ὁ δ᾿ ἔφεπεν | κραταιὸν ἔγχος· Μεσσανίου δὲ γέ-
> ροντος | δονηθεῖσα φρὴν βόασε παῖδα ὅν, | χαμαιπετὲς δ᾿ ἄρ᾿ ἔπος
> οὐκ ἀπέριψεν· αὐτοῦ | μένων δ᾿ ὁ θεῖος ἀνὴρ | πρίατο μὲν θανάτοιο
> κομιδὰν πατρός, | ἐδόκησέν τε τῶν πάλαι γενεᾷ | ὁπλοτέροισιν

---

54. Sinos 1980.30 remarks: "It was Patroklos who succeeded in the competition with his
multiforms, Antilokhos, Automedon, and Alkimedon."

55. Cf. p. 208.

56. Cf. p. 208.

ἔργον πελώριον τελέσαις | ὕπατος ἀμφὶ τοκεῦσιν ἔμμεν πρὸς ἀρετάν.
| τὰ μὲν παρίκει· τῶν νῦν δὲ καὶ Θρασύβουλος | πατρῴαν μάλιστα
πρὸς στάθμαν ἔβα, | πάτρῳ τ' ἐπερχόμενος ἀγλαίαν {ἔδειξεν} ἅπα-
σαν. | νόῳ δὲ πλοῦτον ἄγει, | ἄδικον οὔθ' ὑπέροπλον ἥβαν δρέπων,
| σοφίαν δ' ἐν μυχοῖσι Πιερίδων· | τίν τ', Ἐλέλιχθον, ἄρχεις ὃς ἱπ-
πιᾶν ἐσόδων, | μάλα ἀδόντι νόῳ, Ποσειδάν, προσέχεται.

Pindar *Pythian* 6.28–51

In the past [**proteron**][57] as well, there was a man, Antilokhos, a man of
violent strength [**biē**], who won as his prize this thought [= this piece of
instruction: **noēma**, from **noos**].[58] | 30 He died for his father, standing
up to the man-killer, the war-lord of the Aethiopians, Memnon.
Nestor's horse, struck down by the arrows of Paris, got in the way of
his chariot, while Memnon was wielding his powerful spear. The mind
of Nestor, the old man from Messene, was stung, and he shouted for his
son. The word that he uttered did not fall, useless, to the ground. This
godlike man [= Antilokhos] made his stand, right there, and he paid the
price of death for the saving of his father. | 40 To the young people of
that time long gone, he was manifestly the foremost when it comes to
achievement [**aretē**] concerning parents. He had accomplished a
mighty deed. But those things are in the past. As for the present,
Thrasyboulos stands up to the standard of the ancestors [= adjective
patrōio-] better than anyone else. He has clearly measured up to his
uncle [= Theron of Akragas] in every manner of excellence. By way of
his thinking [**noos**] does he bring about wealth,[59] reaping the benefits of
a youth that is neither without d**i**kē nor overweening. Rather he reaps a
skill [**sophiā**] that is to be found in the recesses of Pieria [= the abode
of the Muses]. He is close to you, with a **noos** that is very pleasing to
you, O Earth-Shaking Poseidon, you who rule over the races of horses.

Here the linking of the present with the past of both the heroes and the ancestors is explicit: "But those things [= the deeds of the hero Antilokhos] are in
the past. As for the present, Thrasyboulos stands up to the standard of his

57. The use of the adverb **proteron** here should be compared with that of the adjective **pro-
teros** in indicating that an **ainos** is at work (cf. p. 200).

58. Compare νόημα τοῦτο φέρων 'who wins as a prize this thought' here at *Pythian* 6.29,
applying to Thrasyboulos as well as to his model Antilokhos, with λόγον φέρεις 'you win as a
prize the words' at *Pythian* 8.38, applying to Aristomenes as well as to his model Alkmaion (as
discussed at p. 194).

59. Compare πλοῦτον ἄγει 'does he bring about wealth' here with ψυχὰν κομίξαι ... δέρμα
τε κριοῦ ... ἄγειν 'to save the **psūkhē** and bring back the fleece of the ram' at Pindar *Pythian*
4.159. The materialism here is of the "otherworldly" sort (pp. 243 and following). Cf. Pindar
Pythian 6.5: ὀλβίοισιν Ἐμμενίδαις 'for the patriliny of the Emmenidai, who are **olbioi**'; again,
the materialism here is "otherworldly" (pp. 243 and following).

ancestors." As we have seen in another Pindaric passage, the victorious man of the present is said to be repeating the patterns of the ancestors by virtue of repeating the patterns of the heroes, in this case, of Antilokhos.[60] Just as Antilokhos had **noos** (νόημα: 6.29), with an emphasis on the impulsive side of the hero (**biātās**: 6.29),[61] so also does Thrasyboulos have **noos** as he enriches his family by winning (νόῳ 6.47) and as he pleases Poseidon, the lord of horse racing (νόῳ 6.51). In the meantime the theme of the ancestors, as conveyed by the name **Patrokleēs** for Antilokhos in the *Iliad*, is conveyed for Thrasyboulos by the model of Antilokhos in Pindar's *Pythian* 6.

We have seen three clear examples where the victorious man of the present is said by Pindar's lyric poetry to be repeating the patterns of the ancestors by virtue of repeating the patterns of the heroes: there was Aristomenes in *Pythian* 8, Kleandros in *Isthmian* 8, and now Thrasyboulos in *Pythian* 6. In each case, epic is represented as extending into the epinician **ainos** of Pindar, which in turn presents itself as the ultimate authority of tradition. More than that, the medium of the epinician **ainos**, as mastered by the likes of Pindar, is accepted as the ultimate authority by a society that can even name its children in accordance with the grand themes of the epinician tradition.

60. Compare again νόημα τοῦτο φέρων 'who wins as a prize this thought' here at *Pythian* 6.29, applying to Thrasyboulos as well as to his model Antilokhos, with λόγον φέρεις 'you win as a prize the words' at *Pythian* 8.38, applying to Aristomenes as well as to his model Alkmaion (p. 213).

61. On **noos** as a balance of impulsiveness and restraint, initially favoring the former and ultimately adopting the latter, see pp. 208 and following. The **noos** of Patroklos is described as **biātās** at Pindar *Olympian* 9.75, precisely in a context where Achilles warns him not to venture off on his own (9.76–79).

8 ▫▫ The Authoritative Speech of Prose, Poetry, and Song: Pindar and Herodotus I

The **historiā** 'inquiry' of Herodotus, like the **ainos** of epinician poets like Pindar, claims to extend from the epic of heroes. Like the **ainos** of Pindar, the **historiā** of Herodotus is a form of discourse that claims the authority to possess and control the epic of heroes. I propose to support these assertions by examining the structure of Herodotus' narrative, traditionally known as the *Histories*, and by arguing that the traditions underlying this structure are akin to those underlying the **ainos** of Pindar's epinician heritage.[1] With reference to my working definition, in Chapter 1, of *song, poetry,* and *prose,* I argue that the study of Herodotus, master of prose, will help further clarify our ongoing consideration of the relationship between song in Pindar and poetry in epic.

As in the songs of Pindar, the figure of Homer is treated as the ultimate representative of epic in the prose of Herodotus (e.g., 2.116–117).[2] In fact, the poetry of Homer along with that of Hesiod is acknowledged by Herodotus as the definitive source for the cultural values that all Hellenes hold in common:

> ὅθεν δὲ ἐγένοντο ἕκαστος τῶν θεῶν, εἴτε αἰεὶ ἦσαν πάντες, ὁκοῖοί τέ τινες τὰ εἴδεα, οὐκ ἠπιστέατο μέχρι οὗ πρώην τε καὶ χθὲς ὡς εἰπεῖν λόγῳ. Ἡσίοδον γὰρ καὶ Ὅμηρον ἡλικίην τετρακοσίοισι ἔτεσι δοκέω μευ πρεσβυτέρους γενέσθαι καὶ οὐ πλέοσι. οὗτοι δέ εἰσι οἱ ποιήσαντες θεογονίην Ἕλλησι καὶ τοῖσι θεοῖσι τὰς ἐπωνυμίας δόντες

---

1. In making this attempt, I reach an important turning point at p. 262.
2. Further commentary on this passage at p. 420.

καὶ τιμάς τε καὶ τέχνας διελόντες καὶ εἴδεα αὐτῶν σημήναντες. οἱ
δὲ πρότερον ποιηταὶ λεγόμενοι τούτων τῶν ἀνδρῶν γενέσθαι
ὕστερον, ἔμοιγε δοκέειν, ἐγένοντο τούτων. τὰ μὲν πρῶτα αἱ Δωδωνί-
δες ἱέρειαι λέγουσι, τὰ δὲ ὕστερα τὰ ἐς Ἡσίοδόν τε καὶ Ὅμηρον
ἔχοντα ἐγὼ λέγω.

Herodotus 2. 53.1–3

But it was only the day before yesterday, so to speak,[3] that they [= the
Hellenes] came to understand wherefrom[4] the gods originated [= root
gen-], whether they all existed always, and what they were like in their
visible forms [**eidos** plural]. For Hesiod and Homer, I think, lived not
more than four hundred years ago. These are the men who composed
[= verb **poieō**] a theogony [with root **gen-**] for the Hellenes, who gave
epithets [**epōnumiai**][5] to the gods, who distinguished their various
tīmai [= spheres of influence][6] and **tekhnai** [= spheres of activity],[7]
and who indicated [= verb **sēmainō**][8] their visible forms.[9] And I think
that those poets who are said to have come before these men really
came after them.[10] The first part of what precedes[11] is said by the
priestesses of Dodona.[12] The second part, concerning Hesiod and
Homer, is my opinion.[13]

Not only does Herodotus stress the Panhellenic importance of Homer

3. Herodotus here is contrasting the relatively recent fixing of the Hellenic heritage with that
of the Egyptian.

4. The relative pronoun ὅθεν 'wherefrom', used here as an indirect question, reflects the
"prooemium style," discussed in detail at pp. 218 and 220.

5. Cf. How and Wells 1928.193–194.

6. Cf. Hesiod *Theogony* 73–74 and the commentary of West 1966.180.

7. Cf. Herodotus 2.83 on **tekhnē** as 'system of operation'; on classification by way of **tekhnē**
as 'sphere of activity', cf. Herodotus 2.164.1.

8. On the pertinence of this word to the speech-activity of Herodotus, see pp. 229, 233, and
following.

9. On **eidos** as 'visible form', there is further elaboration at p. 261.

10. Such a ranking makes Hesiod and Homer more canonical, more Panhellenic: see p. 84. In
his allusion to the other poets, Herodotus probably means Orpheus and Musaeus; for the conventional ideology that presents them as predecessors of Homer and Hesiod, see Lloyd 1976.247,
251. Cf. Hippias 86 B 6 DK; Aristophanes *Frogs* 1032–1035; Plato *Apology* 41a; cf. also
Ephorus FGH 70 F 101, Plato *Republic* 363a, 377d, 612b. We may note with particular interest
the tradition that Homer was descended from Orpheus: Pherecydes FGH 3 F 167, Hellanicus 4 F
5, Damastes 5 F 11; or from Musaeus: Gorgias 82 B 25 DK. Cf. Lloyd 1975.177 on the Herodotean scheme of 3 generations = 100 years.

11. That is, the discussion at Herodotus 2.52.1 and following, not quoted here.

12. The priestesses are named later by Herodotus (2.55.3).

13. I stress that the discourse of Herodotus acknowledges at 2.53 the authority of Homer and
Hesiod (above) in the context of acknowledging at 2.52 and 2.53.3 the authority of the Oracle of
Zeus at Dodona.

and Hesiod. He takes both a Homeric and a Hesiodic stance. Let us begin with his Homeric stance,[14] which is evident at the beginning of the *Histories*, the so-called prooemium.[15] Although I have no doubt that Herodotus had Homer in mind when he composed the prooemium of the *Histories*, I plan to show in what follows that the prose narrative of the *Histories* is the product of an oral tradition in its own right, related to but not derived from the poetic narrative of the *Iliad*.[16]

I now quote the prooemium of Herodotus in its entirety:

Ἡροδότου Ἀλικαρνησσέος ἱστορίης ἀπόδεξις ἥδε, ὡς
    (a) μήτε τὰ γενόμενα ἐξ ἀνθρώπων τῷ χρόνῳ ἐξίτηλα γένηται
    (b) μήτε ἔργα μεγάλα τε καὶ θωμαστά, τὰ μὲν Ἕλλησι, τὰ δὲ
    βαρβάροισι ἀποδεχθέντα, ἀκλεᾶ γένηται,
τά τε ἄλλα καὶ δι' ἣν αἰτίην ἐπολέμησαν ἀλλήλοισι.[17]

Herodotus prooemium

This is the public presentation [= noun **apo-deixis**][18] of the inquiry [**historiā**][19] of Herodotus of Halikarnassos, with the purpose of bringing it about

---

14. The Hesiodic stance of Herodotus will be taken up at p. 255.

15. On the aptness of Latin *prooemium*, a word borrowed from Greek **prooimion** (on which see pp. 353 and following), as applied to the first sentence of the *Histories* of Herodotus, see Krischer 1965. Unlike Krischer, however, I do not think that the resemblances between the prooemium of the *Iliad* and the prooemium of the *Histories* (on which see p. 220) can be ascribed simply to the imitation of Homer by Herodotus.

16. This point is perhaps more simple than it seems at first sight: I mean that the rhetoric of Herodotus' prooemium in particular and his entire composition in general is predicated on the traditions of speaking before a public, not of writing for readers. To me, that in itself is enough to justify calling such traditions *oral*. See p. 169. To many others, however, this same word *oral* has a much more narrow meaning, restricted by our own cultural preconceptions about writing and reading. Cf. p. 8. On the important distinction between reading aloud and silent reading, see pp. 171 and following; cf. Svenbro 1987, following Knox 1968. On silent reading in the late medieval context, see Saenger 1982.

17. Following Krischer and others I have supplied indentations in order to delineate the syntax; I have also set off as (a) and (b) the two negative purpose clauses, coordinated not only by μήτε . . . / μήτε . . . but also by the *homoioteleuton* . . . γένηται / . . . γένηται.

18. The Ionic form **apodexis** in the usage of Herodotus, guaranteed by the testimony of inscriptions written in the Ionic dialect (see, for example, LSJ s.v. ἀποδείκνυμι), apparently reflects a conflation of **apo-deik-numai** 'present publicly, make public' and **apo-dek-omai** 'accept or approve a tradition'. Such a conflation seems to be at work in Herodotus 6.43.3; as M. Lang points out to me, the implication is not only that whatever is accepted is made public but also that whatever is made public is accepted. Such acceptance is the presupposition of a living tradition. On the syntax of what is introduced by ἀπόδεξις ἥδε, see p. 220. For an earlier mention of the contexts of **apo-deik-numai** 'present publicly', see p. 162.

19. For the semantics of **historiā** 'inquiry, investigation', see pp. 250 and following.

(a) that whatever results from men may not, with the passage of time, become evanescent,[20] and

(b) that great and wondrous deeds — some of them publicly performed [= verb **apo-deik-numai**][21] by Hellenes, others by barbarians — may not become **akleā** [= without **kleos**].

In particular[22] [this **apodeixis** of this **historiā** concerns] why (= on account of what cause [**aitiā**]) they entered into conflict with each other.[23]

It is important to pay careful attention here in the prooemium to the development of thought that links the noun **apodeixis** 'public presentation' with the verb from which it is derived, **apo-deik-numai**, to be found in the clause b that follows. We would expect this verb in the middle voice to mean 'make a public presentation of', that is, 'publicly demonstrate, make a public demonstration'; there are contexts where such a translation is indeed appropriate. Thus when Xerxes has a canal made in order to turn the isthmus of Mount Athos into an island, he is described as ἐθέλων τε δύναμιν ἀποδείκνυσθαι καὶ μνημόσυνα λιπέσθαι 'wishing to make a public demonstration of his power and to have a reminder of it left behind' (Herodotus 7.24; cf. 7.223.4). Combined with the direct object **gnōmēn/gnōmās** 'opinions, judgments', this verb in the middle voice is used in contexts where someone is presenting his views in public; the contexts include three specific

20. For more on the semantics of **exitēla** 'evanescent', see p. 225.

21. I discuss the translation 'performed' below.

22. The adverbial τά τε ἄλλα καὶ ... that precedes the relative construction ... δι' ἣν αἰτίην ... has the effect of throwing the emphasis forward from the general to the specific, to parallel the movement from general to specific in the negative purpose clauses (a) and (b). For more on Herodotean devices of shading over and highlighting, see p. 70.

23. This final clause, τά τε ἄλλα καὶ δι' ἣν αἰτίην ἐπολέμησαν ἀλλήλοισι, is difficult. I interpret it as an indirect question, thus disagreeing with Erbse 1956.211 and 219: he takes the whole construction as an elaborated direct object of a hypothetical ἱστορήσας in a hypothetical expression Ἡρόδοτος Ἁλικαρνησσεὺς ἱστορήσας ἀπέδεξε τάδε, which has supposedly been reshaped into the actual expression that we read in Herodotus, Ἡροδότου Ἁλικαρνησσέος ἱστορίης ἀπόδεξις ἥδε. I also disagree with Erbse's view (p. 215) that δι' ἣν αἰτίην ... is a relative construction as opposed to an indirect question (in other words that the construction is equivalent to τὴν αἰτίην δι' ἣν ...). Relative constructions can in fact be used for the purpose of indirect question: cf. Herodotus 2.2.2 Ψαμμήτιχος δὲ ὡς οὐκ ἐδύνατο πυνθανόμενος πόρον οὐδένα τούτου ἀνευρεῖν, οἳ γενοίατο πρῶτοι ἀνθρώπων 'when Psammetichus was unable to find, by way of inquiry, a method of discovering who were the first race of men ...'; Herodotus 1.56.1 μετὰ δὲ ταῦτα ἐφρόντιζε ἱστορέων, τοὺς ἂν Ἑλλήνων δυνατωτάτους ἐόντας προσκτήσαιτο φίλους 'after this, he took care to investigate which of the Hellenes were the most powerful, for him to win over as friends'; Thucydides 5.9.2 τὴν δὲ ἐπιχείρησιν, ᾧ τρόπῳ διανοοῦμαι ποιεῖσθαι, διδάξω 'I will inform you in what way the attempt that I have in mind is to be accomplished'. In most cases the relative clause is linked with verbs that express or connote the speech-act of narration: see p. 220.

instances of self-expression by Herodotus (2.146.1, 7.139.1, 8.8.3).[24] Yet in the context of the prooemium, and also in other Herodotean contexts where **apo-deik-numai** in the middle voice is combined, as here, with the direct object **ergon/erga** 'deed(s)', it is to be translated simply as 'perform' rather than 'make a public presentation or demonstration of'. Thus in Powell's *Lexicon to Herodotus* we can find 29 contexts where **apo-deik-numai**, in combination with direct objects like **ergon/erga**, is translated as 'perform'.[25] In the prooemium that we have just read, for example, the reference is to the **megala erga** 'great deeds' that have been **apodekhthenta** 'performed' by Hellenes and barbarians alike. If we translated **apodekhthenta** here as 'publicly presented' or 'demonstrated' instead of 'performed', the text would not make sense to us. So also 'performed' is suggested in a context like the following, where a dying Kallikrates expresses his deep regret

> ὅτι οὐδέν ἐστί οἱ ἀποδεδεγμένον ἔργον ἑωυτοῦ ἄξιον προθυμευ-
> μένου ἀποδέξασθαι

> Herodotus 9.72.2

that there was no deed performed by him that was worthy of him, though he had been eager to perform [one].

Clearly this young man's sorrow is not over the fact that he has not made a public display of a great deed but over the more basic fact that he does not have a great deed to display. The obvious explanation for these usages of **apo-deik-numai** in the sense of *performing* rather than *publicly presenting* or *demonstrating* or *displaying* a deed is that the actual medium for publicly presenting the given deed is in all these cases none other than the language of Herodotus. In other words, performing a deed is the equivalent of publicly presenting a deed because it is ultimately being displayed by the *Histories* of Herodotus.

Similarly *saying* something is in the case of Herodotus the equivalent of *writing* something because it is ultimately being written down in the *Histories* (e.g., 2.123.3, 4.195.2, 6.14.1, 7.214.3; cf. also Hecataeus FGH 1 F 1).[26] In other words saying and writing are treated as parallel speech-acts.[27] This sort of parallelism goes one step beyond what we have seen in the use of **ana-gignōskō** 'know again, recognize' in the sense of 'read out loud', as in Aris-

24. Comparable to these three instances of **apo-deik-numai** + **gnōmēn/gnōmās** as object is **apo-phain-omai** + **gnōmēn** as object at Herodotus 2.120.5: here again Herodotus is going publicly on record. On the synonymity of **apo-deik-numai** and **apo-phain-omai**, see the co-occurrence of these two words at Herodotus 5.45.1–2 (as discussed in p. 316).

25. Powell 1938.38 s.v. ἀποδείκνυμι B II (middle).

26. Cf. pp. 169 and 217.

27. Cf. Hartog 1980.292–297 for an extensive survey of Herodotean contexts. Cf. also Sven-bro 1987.39.

tophanes *Knights* 118, 1011, 1065.[28] This meaning of **ana-gignōskō** is a metaphorical extension of the notion of public performance, as we see in Pindar *Olympian* 10.1, where the corresponding notion of the actual composition by the poet is kept distinct through the metaphor of an inscription inside the **phrēn** 'mind' (10.2–3).[29] As for the language of Herodotus, in contrast, not only the composition but also the performance, as a public speech-act, can be conveyed by the single metaphor of writing. For Herodotus, the essential thing is that the *writing*, just like the *saying*, is a public, not a private, speech-act (again 7.214.3).[30] The **historiā** 'inquiry' that he says he is presenting in the prooemium of the *Histories* is not a public oral performance as such, but it is a public *demonstration* of an oral performance, by way of writing. Moreover, the very word **apodeixis**, referring to the 'presentation' of the **historiā** in the prooemium, can be translated as the 'demonstration' of such oral performance.

Whereas Herodotus represents his writings as a public presentation, Thucydides represents his as if they were private: they are a κτῆμα . . . ἐς αἰεί 'a possession for all time' (1.22.4), where the noun **ktēma**, derivative of the verb **kektēmai** 'possess', conveys the notion of private property.[31] Moreover, Thucydides avoids the words **historiā** and **historeō**,[32] as also **apodeixis** 'public presentation' (with only one exception, at 1.97.2).[33] In the *Histories* of Herodotus, by contrast, precisely such words designate the performative aspect of the words of Herodotus taken all together. To return to the first words in the prooemium to the *Histories* of Herodotus, this whole composition is in itself an act of **apodeixis** 'public presentation': Ἡροδότου Ἁλικαρνησσέος ἱστορίης ἀπόδεξις ἥδε 'this is the **apodeixis** of the **historiā** of Herodotus of Halikarnassos'.[34]

---

28. Cf. p. 171.

29. Ibid. Cf. the use of **ana-gignōskō** 'read out loud' in Diogenes Laertius 9.54, with reference to the "public première" of various compositions by Protagoras (80 A 1 DK); cf. also the anecdotes in Plutarch *On the Malice of Herodotus* 862a-b (Diyllus FGH 73 F 5) and in Lucian *Herodotus* 1–2 about public "readings" supposedly performed by Herodotus himself.

30. Hartog, p. 294, suggests that the *writing* of the name of Ephialtes at 7.214.3 is as if the words of Herodotus were emanating from "une stèle d´infamie." For more on Herodotus 7.214.3, see p. 235.

31. Cf. p. 169.

32. See Snell 1924.65.

33. Hartog 1980.285.

34. The noun **apodeixis** takes on the syntax of a verb designating narration, as is already indicated by the conjunction ὡς immediately following the clause . . . ἀπόδεξις ἥδε . . . and introducing the complex purpose clause that comes before the concluding clause of indirect question (on which see p. 218). Moreover, as Krischer 1965.162 points out, the indirect question in the prooemium of Herodotus, δι' ἣν αἰτίην ἐπολέμησαν ἀλλήλοισι 'on account of what cause they got into conflict with each other' in the prooemium of Herodotus is parallel to the indirect question in the prooemium of the *Iliad* (ι 6), ἐξ οὗ δὴ τὰ πρῶτα διαστήτην ἐρίσαντε '[narrate to me, Muse, . . .] starting with what time they first quarrelled, standing divided'. I stress that the relative clause 'on account of what cause they got into conflict with each other' is linked with 'This

Wherever **apo-deik-numai** designates the performance of a deed (or the execution of a monument, as in Herodotus 1.184, etc.), the *performance* (or *execution*) is tantamount to a *public presentation* as long as it can be sustained by a medium of public presentation.[35] As Herodotus declares in the prooemium, the **apodeixis** 'public presentation' of his *Histories* is for the purpose of ensuring that the great deeds performed by Hellenes and barbarians alike should not be **akleā** 'without **kleos**'. This purpose of sustaining **kleos** is a traditional one, already built into the inherited semantics of the verb **apo-deik-numai**: the great deeds are already being literally **apodekhthenta** 'publicly presented' because they are in the process of being retold in the medium of Herodotus — just as they had been retold earlier in the medium of his predecessors.[36] These predecessors of Herodotus, as the wording of the transition from the prooemium to the *Histories* proper makes clear, come under the designation of **logioi** (Herodotus 1.1.1). For reasons that become clear as the discussion proceeds, I consistently translate **logioi** as 'masters of speech'.

In order to grasp the concept of **logioi**, I draw attention to the word for the particular subject of the *Histories*, namely, the **aitiā** 'cause' of the conflict between Hellenes and barbarians: τά τε ἄλλα καὶ δι' ἣν αἰτίην ἐπολέμησαν ἀλλήλοισι 'in particular, [the **apodeixis** concerns] why (= on account of what cause [**aitiā**]) they entered into conflict with each other' (Herodotus *prooemium*). This word is immediately picked up in the first sentence of the *Histories* proper: Περσέων μέν νυν οἱ λόγιοι Φοίνικας αἰτίους φασὶ γενέσθαι τῆς διαφορῆς 'the **logioi** of the Persians say that it was the Phoenicians who were the cause of the conflict' (Herodotus 1.1.1). This transition reveals that Herodotus, in concerning himself with the **aitiā** 'cause' of the conflict, is implicitly a **logios** 'master of speech' like his pro-Persian counter-

---

is the **apodeixis** of the investigation of Herodotus . . .', just as 'starting with what time they first quarrelled . . .' is linked with 'Sing, goddess, the anger of Achilles . . .' (I 1). Note too the parallelism of wide syntactical gaps spanned by ἀπόδεξις ἥδε . . . δι' ἣν αἰτίην . . . 'making public . . . on account of what cause' in Herodotus and by ἄειδε . . . ἐξ οὗ δὴ τὰ πρῶτα . . . 'sing . . . starting with what time they first . . .' in the *Iliad* (Book I lines 1–6). Among the other Homeric attestations of both actual prooemia and indirectly retold prooemia (for a list of both types, see van Groningen 1946), there are other occurrences of relative clauses used as indirect questions (the clearest example is *Odyssey* viii 76 ὥς ποτε δηρίσαντο . . . 'how they once fought'; note too the frequent use of **prōta/prōtos/prōton**/etc. 'first' in the indirect questions of the prooemia, as at *Iliad* I 6/XI 217/XVI 113, to be compared with **prōtoi** 'first' at Herodotus 2.2.2, quoted at p. 218. Cf. also p. 216 above. On the parallelisms between the Homeric *Iliad* and the Herodotean *Histories* in the formal transition from prooemium to narrative proper, see n37.

35. A monument can be such a medium, as in the case of μνημόσυνα 'monument', direct object of **apo-deik-numai** (ἀποδέξασθαι), at Herodotus 1.101.2. Immerwahr 1960.266 remarks: "The conception of fame underlying both monuments and deeds is exactly the same." Cf. Hartog 1980.378n3.

36. It is from such contexts of **apo-deik-numai** that we begin to understand the basis of its apparent conflation with **apo-dek-omai** 'accept or approve a tradition', on which see p. 217.

parts, explicitly called **logioi**, who concern themselves with the question: who were the cause of the conflict?[37]

As we learn from the language of Pindar, it is the function of **logioi** 'masters of speech' to confer **kleos**:

> πλατεῖαι πάντοθεν <u>λογίοισιν</u> ἐντὶ πρόσοδοι | <u>νᾶσον εὐκλέα</u> τάνδε
> κοσμεῖν· ἐπεί σφιν Αἰακίδαι | ἔπορον ἔξοχον <u>αἶσαν ἀρετὰς</u>
> <u>ἀποδεικνύμενοι</u> μεγάλας

Pindar Nemean 6.45–47[38]

Wide are the approaching paths from all sides, for the **logioi** to adorn this island with glory [**kleos**]; for the Aiakidai have conferred upon this island an exceptional share [i.e., of glory],[39] presenting [**apo-deik-numai**] great achievements [**arete** plural].

Just as both Hellenes and barbarians can have their deeds **apodekhthenta** 'publicly presented' and thus not become **aklea** 'without **kleos**', by virtue of **apodeixis** 'public presentation' as explicitly conferred by Herodotus,[40] so also the lineage of Achilles, the Aiakidai, can go on 'publicly presenting', **apodeiknumenoi**, their achievements even after death — by virtue of the public display implicitly conferred by the **logioi**, who are described here in the language of Pindar as a source of **kleos**.[41]

Elsewhere the language of Pindar draws the **logioi** into an explicit parallelism with **aoidoi** 'poets', and the emphasis is on their enshrining the achievements of those who have long since died:

---

37. On the semantics of **aitiā** 'cause' and **aitioi** 'responsible ones' [= 'the cause'] as in Herodotus *prooemium* and in 1.1.1, see Krischer 1965.160–161; also p. 228. For a parallel transition from prooemium to narrative proper by way of repeating, with variation, a key word (in this case αἰτίην followed by ἐπολέμησαν 'cause . . . getting into conflict' picked up by αἰτίους followed by διαφορῆς 'cause . . . conflict'), see Krischer ibid., who points to the prooemium of the *Iliad* (ἐξ οὗ δὴ τὰ πρῶτα διαστήτην ἐρίσαντε 'starting with what time they first quarrelled, standing divided' at I 6) and the first line of the narrative proper (τίς τ' ἄρ σφωε θεῶν ἔριδι ξυνέηκε μάχεσθαι; 'who, then, of the gods set them off against each other, to fight in a quarrel?' at I 8). Krischer also adduces the prooemia to the *Catalogue of Ships* (ἀρχούς at *Iliad* II 493, picked up by ἦρχον at II 494), to the *Odyssey* (νόστιμον ἦμαρ at i 9, picked up by νόστου at i 13), and to the *Theogony* (ὅ τι πρῶτον γένετ' αὐτῶν at line 115, picked up by ἤ τοι μὲν πρώτιστα Χάος γένετ' at 116).

38. For the phraseology that immediately follows this passage, see p. 203.

39. For this interpretation, see Farnell 1932.285.

40. Cf. the remarks at p. 218 on the syntactical continuity of ἀπόδεξις . . . ἀποδεχθέντα.

41. The Aiakidai are not only the immediate lineage of Aiakos, including the sons Peleus and Telamon, the grandsons Achilles and Ajax, and so on, but also the ultimate lineage of Aiakos, extending into the here and now, into the population of Aegina in Pindar's time: see pp. 176 and following.

ὀπιθόμβροτον αὔχημα δόξας | οἷον ἀποιχομένων ἀνδρῶν δίαιταν
μανύει | καὶ λογίοις καὶ ἀοιδοῖς. οὐ φθίνει Κροίσου φιλόφρων
ἀρετά.

Pindar Pythian 1.92–94

The proud declaration of glory that comes in the future is the only thing
that attests, both for **logioi** and for singers [**aoidoi**], the life of men who
are now departed; the **philos**-minded achievement [**aretē**] of Croesus
fails[42] not.[43]

This explicit parallelism of **logioi** and **aoidoi** should be compared with that of
logoi 'words' and **aoidai** 'songs' in *Nemean* 6 (ἀοιδαὶ καὶ λόγοι 30),[44] the
same poem from which I have just quoted the only other attestation of **logioi**
in Pindar's epinician lyric poetry.[45] Let us turn back, then, to *Nemean* 6:

εὔθυν᾽ ἐπὶ τοῦτον, ἄγε Μοῖσα, οὖρον ἐπέων | εὐκλέα· παροιχομένων
γὰρ ἀνέρων, | ἀοιδαὶ καὶ λόγοι[46] τὰ καλά σφιν ἔργ᾽ ἐκόμισαν

Pindar Nemean 6.28–30

In the direction of this house, Muse, steer the breeze, bringing good
kleos, of these my words. For even when men are departed, **aoidai** and
logoi[47] bring back the beauty of their deeds.

In short the language of Pindar makes it explicit that **logioi** 'masters of
speech' are parallel to the masters of song, **aoidoi**, in their function of maintaining the **kleos** 'glory' of men even after death, and it implies that this
activity of both **logioi** and **aoidoi** is a matter of **apodeixis** 'public presentation'.

As for Herodotus, I have already argued that he is by implication
presented at the very beginning of his *Histories* as one in a long line of
logioi,[48] and he makes it explicit that his function of maintaining **kleos** is a

42. The Greek verb **phthi-** in the intransitive expresses various images of transience, most
notably the failing of liquid sources and the wilting of plants (for a survey of passages, see N
1979.174–189; also Risch 1987).

43. The song goes on to declare that the virtue of Croesus contrasts with the depravity of the
tyrant Phalaris (Pindar *Pythian* 1.95–98). Thus the **logioi**, like the **aoidoi**, have in their repertoire
such Hellenes as Phalaris, not just non-Hellenes like Croesus (cf. p. 224).

44. This emended reading is adopted in the edition of SM; the manuscript reading ἀοιδαὶ καὶ
λόγιοι, however, in conjunction with the papyrus reading αοιδοι και λο[(Π41), makes it possible to read instead ἀοιδοὶ καὶ λόγιοι, if λόγιοι may be scanned as a disyllable (on which see, for
example, Farnell 1932.284).

45. Cf. p. 222.

46. The quotation here follows the emended reading adopted in the edition of SM: see above.

47. Alternatively, if we follow the reading ἀοιδοὶ καὶ λόγιοι (above): **aoidoi** and **logioi**.

48. Cf. p. 221. Note too that the Egyptians as the most proficient **logioi** of all humans are
described as μνήμην ἐπασκέοντες 'engaging in the practice of memory' in Herodotus 2.77.1.

matter of **apodeixis**.[49] Accordingly I find it anachronistic to interpret **logioi** as 'historians'.[50]

The medium of **logioi**, as the contexts of **apodeixis** make clear, is at least ideologically that of performance, not of writing. Like the poets, the **logioi** can recreate with each performance the deeds of men. That is what Pindar's words have told us. Thus the **aretē** 'achievement' of a Croesus, for example, as we have just read in Pindar's *Pythian* 1,[51] does not 'fail' (verb **phthi-**)[52] because it is transmitted by **logioi** and **aoidoi**. In this particular case we even have actual attestations of parallel but mutually independent Croesus stories in the prose narrative of one who speaks in the mode of a **logios** (Herodotus 1.86–91) and in the poetic narrative of an **aoidos** (Bacchylides *Epinician* 3.23–62).[53] It would seem then that the **logios** is a master of oral traditions in prose, just as the **aoidos** is a master of oral traditions in poetry and song.[54]

The notion that a **logios**, just like an **aoidos**, can prevent the transience of a man's **aretē** 'achievement' is found not only in Pindar: we have seen it

49. Cf. p. 221.

50. *Pace* Farnell 1932.116.

51. Cf. p. 222.

52. Cf. p. 223.

53. See p. 275 and following. See also p. 277 for iconographical evidence on the story of Croesus that is even earlier than the testimony of Pindar and Bacchylides (500 B.C.: Beazley 1963.238 no. 1).

54. I use the word *prose* here in the sense of a mimesis of speech: p. 46. In the case of an opposition between **logioi**, masters of speech, and **aoidoi**, masters of song, we can say that *speech* or *speaking* is unmarked, while *song* is marked. On the terms *unmarked* and *marked*, see p. 5. One cannot define **logioi** in terms of **aoidoi**, in that **logioi** is the unmarked category in the usage of Herodotus. Herodotus is implicitly a **logios** even by virtue of not being an **aoidos**. Moreover, I have already argued (p. 221 above) that the syntax of the transition from the prooemium to the first sentence of the *Histories* proper is for us explicit evidence that Herodotus considered himself a **logios**. It is only for Herodotus that this consideration is implicit, not explicit. I would therefore disagree with the view that the use of the word **logios**, in the three attestations besides Herodotus 1.1.1, shows that it is appropriate only to non-Hellenes in Herodotus (2.3.1, 2.77.1, 4.46.1). In two of these attestations (2.77.1 and 4.46.1), non-Hellenes happen to be singled out within the category of **logioi**, but there is no indication that the category itself is foreign to Greek institutions. Even if we accepted the view that **logioi** implies non-Hellenes, we would still have to reckon with Herodotus' practice of referring explicitly to things foreign while at the same time referring implicitly to things Greek (cf. Hartog 1980). Finally **logios** is not the only word for the referent in question, that is, for the master of speaking before an audience. Besides the opposition of **logios** and **aoidos** in the diction of Herodotus, we find the parallel opposition of **logopoios** 'speechmaker, artisan of speech' and **mousopoios** 'songmaker, artisan of song', where the first referent is Aesop and the second referent is Sappho herself (Herodotus 2.134.3 . . . 135.1 Αἰσώπου τοῦ λογοποιοῦ . . . Σαπφοῦς τῆς μουσοποιοῦ). The significance of this application of **logopoios** to the figure of Aesop in particular will be discussed in p. 325. Elsewhere in Herodotus, the word **logopoios** applies to a predecessor of Herodotus, Hecataeus (Herodotus 2.143.1 Ἑκαταίῳ τῷ λογοποιῷ; also 5.36.2, 5.125); further discussion in p. 325. It is the likes of Hecataeus that Herodotus had in mind when he used the word **logioi** in the first sentence of the *Histories* proper (1.1.1).

conveyed twice in the prooemium of Herodotus. The first time around, it occurs in the negative purpose clause ὡς μήτε τὰ γενόμενα ἐξ ἀνθρώπων τῷ χρόνῳ ἐξίτηλα γένηται 'with the purpose of bringing it about that whatever results from men may not, with the passage of time, become **exitēla** [= evanescent]'. This clause is then coordinated with another negative purpose clause, this second one being more specific than the first: μήτε ἔργα μεγάλα τε καὶ θωμαστά, τὰ μὲν Ἕλλησι, τὰ δὲ βαρβάροισι ἀποδεχθέντα, ἀκλεᾶ γένηται 'and that great and wondrous deeds—some of them performed by Hellenes, others by barbarians—may not become **aklea** [= without **kleos**]'.[55]

In other attested contexts, the adjective **exitēlos** can designate such things as the fading of color in fabrics (Xenophon *Oeconomicus* 10.3) or in paintings (Pausanias 10.38.9), the loss of a seed's generative powers when sown in alien soil (Plato *Republic* 497b), and the extinction of a family line (Herodotus 5.39.2). The references to vegetal and human evanescence reveal this adjective to be semantically parallel to the verb **phthi-**, which I have been translating as 'fail' in its application to the transience of man's **aretē**.[56] Moreover, the adjective **aphthiton**, derived from **phthi-** and translatable as 'unfailing, unwilting',[57] is a traditional epithet of **kleos** in the inherited diction of praise poetry, as when the poet Ibycus makes the following pledge to his patron Polykrates:

καὶ σύ, Πολύκρατες, κλέος ἄφθιτον ἑξεῖς
ὡς κατ' ἀοιδὰν καὶ ἐμὸν κλέος

Ibycus SLG 151.47–48

You too [i.e., you as well as the heroes just mentioned in the song],
    Polykrates, will have **kleos** that is unfailing [**aphthiton**],
in accordance with my song, my **kleos**.[58]

What emerges then from this comparison of phraseology in song, poetry, and prose is that the two negative purpose clauses in the prose prooemium of Herodotus—the first one intending that human accomplishments should not be evanescent and the second, that they should not be without **kleos**—amount to a periphrasis of what is being said in the single poetic phrase **kleos aphthiton**.

In this regard we may compare various Platonic passages concerning the concept of collective memory as a force that preserves the extraordinary and

55. I disagree with the proposal of Krischer 1965.166 that the two negative clauses reflect different media.
56. On the references of **phthi-** to vegetal and human evanescence, see p. 223. Cf. Steiner 1986.38.
57. Cf. p. 3.
58. Cf. p. 187.

erases the ordinary.[59] To be noted especially is the expression τινα διαφοράν
... ἔχον 'that which has some distinctness to it' in designating that which
deserves to be recorded, at Plato *Timaeus* 23a. In this sense the memory of
oral tradition is at the same time a forgetting of the ordinary as well as a
remembering of the extraordinary (but exemplary). Such an orientation is
parallel to what is being expressed by τά τε ἄλλα καὶ 'in particular' in the
prooemium of Herodotus.[60] Also to be noted are the similarities between the
prooemium of Herodotus and the following Platonic passage:

> πρὸς δὲ Κριτίαν τὸν ἡμέτερον πάππον εἶπεν ... ὅτι μεγάλα καὶ θαυ-
> μαστὰ τῆσδ' εἴη παλαιὰ ἔργα τῆς πόλεως ὑπὸ χρόνου καὶ φθορᾶς
> ἀνθρώπων ἠφανισμένα, πάντων δὲ ἓν μέγιστον, οὗ νῦν ἐπιμνησθεῖ-
> σιν πρέπον ἂν ἡμῖν εἴη σοί τε ἀποδοῦναι χάριν καὶ τὴν θεὸν ἅμα ἐν
> τῇ πανηγύρει δικαίως τε καὶ ἀληθῶς οἷόνπερ ὑμνοῦντας
> ἐγκωμιάζειν.

> Plato *Timaeus* 20e-21a

He [= Solon] said to Critias my grandfather . . .[61] that there were, inherited by this city, ancient deeds, great and wondrous, that have disappeared through the passage of time and through destruction brought
about by human agency. He went on to say that of all these deeds,
there was one in particular that was the greatest, which it would be
fitting for us now to bring to mind, giving a delightful compensation
[**kharis**] to you [= Socrates] while at the same time rightly and truth-
fully praising [ἐγκωμιάζειν] the goddess on this the occasion of
her festival, just as if we were singing hymns to her [ὑμνοῦντας].

The emphasis in the phrase πάντων δὲ ἓν μέγιστον 'there was one in particular that was the greatest' is comparable with the emphasis in the phrase τά τε
ἄλλα καὶ δι' ἣν αἰτίην ἐπολέμησαν ἀλλήλοισι 'in particular, [this **apo-
deixis** of this **historiā** concerns] why (= on account of what cause [**aitiā**])
they entered into conflict with each other' in the prooemium of Herodotus.[62]

The reciprocal relation between the man whose accomplishments or
qualities are celebrated by **kleos aphthiton** and the man who sings that **kleos**

---

59. Survey in Brisson 1982.23–28.

60. As discussed at p. 218. On the Herodotean device of highlighting the extraordinary by
shading over the ordinary, see also p. 70.

61. Solon, explicitly designated here as the wisest of the Seven Sages (Plato *Timaeus* 20d; cf.
p. 243), is represented as a friend and possibly a relative of the father of Critias, Dropides, whose
name he mentions in several passages of his attested poetry (20e; also Plato *Charmides* 157e);
see Solon F 22 W. Another poet who mentions Dropides is Mimnermus (Plato *Charmides*
157e); see Mimnermus PMG 495.

62. Cf. p. 218.

is made explicit in the words quoted earlier from Ibycus. To paraphrase: "My **kleos** will be your **kleos**, because my song of praise for you will be your means to fame; conversely, since you merit permanent fame, my song praising you will be permanent, and consequently I the singer will have permanent fame as well."[63] A parallel relation exists between the man who presents an **apodeixis** 'public presentation' of his *Histories* on the one hand, and on the other the Hellenes and barbarians whose accomplishments are **apodekhthenta** 'publicly presented' and thereby not evanescent, not without **kleos**.

The self-expressive purpose of Herodotus, to maintain **kleos** about deeds triggered by conflict, brings to mind the *Iliad*. Besides the fact that Homeric poetry refers to itself as **kleos**,[64] Achilles himself specifically refers to the Iliadic tradition, which will glorify him forever, as **kleos aphthiton** (IX 413).[65] Moreover, this glorification is achieved in terms of a story that ostensibly tells of a conflict between Achilles and Agamemnon in the context of a larger conflict between Achaeans and Trojans, that is, the Trojan War. This larger conflict is subsumed by the even larger conflict between Hellenes and barbarians, subject of **historiā** 'inquiry' on the part of Herodotus.[66] Like the Homer of Pindar, the Homer of Herodotus is being subsumed by a form of communication that goes beyond epic.

The notion that the framework of the **historiā** of Herodotus subsumes the framework of the *Iliad* is implied by the prooemium of Herodotus as compared with that of the *Iliad*. The expression δι' ἥν αἰτίην 'on account of what cause . . .' in the prooemium of Herodotus,[67] which asks the question why the Hellenes and barbarians came into conflict with each other, is functionally analogous to the question posed in the prooemium of the *Iliad*: that is, why did Achilles and Agamemnon come into conflict with each other (*Iliad* I 7–12)?[68] The latter conflict results in the **mēnis** 'anger' of Achilles (*Iliad* I 1), which in turn results in the deaths of countless Achaeans and Trojans (I 2–5).[69] These heroes would not have died when they did, in the course of the *Iliad*, had it not been for the anger of Achilles; in other words the

---

63. Cf. p. 187.

64. See, for example, *Iliad* II 486, XI 227, as discussed in N 1979.15–18.

65. Further discussion at p. 244.

66. More below on this subject.

67. This phrase is picked up by αἰτίους in the next sentence, at Herodotus 1.1.1.

68. The question "who caused the conflict between them?" at line 7 of *Iliad* I is answered with "Apollo" at line 8, followed by an explanatory clause at lines 8–9 (introduced by γάρ) that tells why Apollo caused the conflict: he was angry. Then comes another explanatory clause at lines 11–12 (introduced by οὕνεκα) that tells why Apollo was angry: Agamemnon had dishonored Chryses, the priest of Apollo. Thus there is a complex answer to a simplex question, and the answer assumes that the intended question is also complex: it asks not only "who caused this conflict?" but also "why did this conflict happen?"

69. On the anger of Achilles as the self-expressive "plot" of the *Iliad*, see N 1979.73. Cf. Considine 1986.

prooemium of the *Iliad* assumes that the original conflict of Achilles and Agamemnon resulted in the *Iliad*. Similarly the prooemium of the *Histories* of Herodotus assumes that the original conflicts of Hellenes and barbarians resulted in the *Histories*. In both cases the search for original causes motivates not just the events being narrated but also the narration. From the standpoint of the prooemia of the *Iliad* and of the *Histories*, Herodotus is in effect implying that the events narrated by the *Iliad* are part of a larger scheme of events as narrated by himself.

For Herodotus, the question of the prooemium, δι' ἣν αἰτίην ἐπολέμησαν ἀλλήλοισι 'on account of what cause they came into conflict with each other', begins to be answered in the first sentence of the narrative proper: Περσέων μέν νυν οἱ λόγιοι Φοίνικας αἰτίους φασὶ γενέσθαι τῆς διαφορῆς 'the **logioi** of the Persians say that it was the Phoenicians who were the cause of the conflict' (Herodotus 1.1.1).[70] The semantic relationship here between the noun **aitiā** 'cause' and the subsequent adjective **aitios**, which I have just translated as 'the cause', can best be understood by considering the definition of **aitios** in the dictionary of Liddell and Scott as 'responsible for' in the sense of 'being the cause of a thing to a person'.[71] There is a juridical dimension of **aitios** in the sense of 'guilty' and **aitiā** in the sense of 'guilt', operative throughout the *Histories* of Herodotus.[72] We may compare the semantics of Latin *causa*, which means not only 'cause' but also 'case, trial', and the derivatives of which are *ac-cūs-āre* and *ex-cūs-āre*. In the case of Herodotus' main question, what was the **aitiā** 'cause' of the conflict between Hellenes and barbarians, the inquiry proceeds in terms of asking who was **aitios** 'responsible, guilty'. From the standpoint of the **logioi** who speak on behalf of the Persians, Herodotus says, the Phoenicians were first to be in the wrong, **aitioi** (1.1.1): they abducted Io, and 'this was the first beginning of wrongs committed' (τῶν ἀδικημάτων πρῶτον τοῦτο ἄρξαι 1.2.1). This wrong is then righted when the Hellenes abduct Europa, and 'this made things even for them' (ταῦτα μὲν δὴ ἴσα πρὸς ἴσα σφι γενέσθαι 1.2.1). But then the Hellenes reportedly committed a wrong, thereby becoming **aitioi** 'responsible' (μετὰ δὲ ταῦτα Ἕλληνας αἰτίους τῆς δευτέρης ἀδικίης γενέσθαι 1.2.1), when they abducted Medea. This wrong is in turn righted when Paris abducts Helen (1.2.3). Up to this time, from the standpoint of the Persian **logioi**, there have been two cycles of wrongs righted: first the barbarians were **aitioi**, and the Hellenes retaliated; then the Hellenes were **aitioi**, and the barbarians retaliated. From then on, however, according to the Persians, the degree of wrongdoing escalated when the Achaeans captured Troy:

70. For poetic parallels to the device of recapitulating a key concept of the prooemium in the first sentence of the narrative proper, see p. 222.

71. LSJ s.v. αἴτιος II (+ genitive of the thing and dative of the person).

72. See especially Pagel 1927, with adjustments by Immerwahr 1956; Krischer 1965.160–161 (disagreeing with Erbse 1956); Hohti 1976.

τὸ δὲ ἀπὸ τούτου Ἕλληνας δὴ μεγάλως <u>αἰτίους</u> γενέσθαι· προτέρους γὰρ ἄρξαι στρατεύεσθαι ἐς τὴν Ἀσίην ἢ σφέας ἐς τὴν Εὐρώπην.

Herodotus 1.3.4

From here on, [they say that] it was the Hellenes who were very much in the wrong [**aitioi**], because it was they who were the first to begin to undertake a military campaign into Asia, instead of their [= the Persians'] undertaking a military campaign into Europe.

According to this Persian scenario then, the third and greatest cycle of wrongs to be righted is completed when the Persians finally invade Hellas.

Against this backdrop of the Trojan and Persian Wars, the testimony of Herodotus links up with the ongoing inquiry into the **aitiā** 'cause' of the conflict between Hellenes and barbarians. We have heard from the barbarians. Now we hear from Herodotus:

ταῦτα μέν νυν Πέρσαι τε καὶ Φοίνικες λέγουσι. ἐγὼ δὲ περὶ μὲν τούτων οὐκ ἔρχομαι ἐρέων ὡς οὕτως ἢ ἄλλως κως ταῦτα ἐγένετο, τὸν δὲ <u>οἶδα</u> αὐτὸς πρῶτον ὑπάρξαντα ἀδίκων ἔργων ἐς τοὺς Ἕλληνας, τούτον <u>σημήνας</u> προβήσομαι ἐς τὸ πρόσω τοῦ λόγου, ὁμοίως σμικρὰ καὶ μεγάλα <u>ἄστεα</u> ἀνθρώπων <u>ἐπεξιών</u>. τὰ γὰρ τὸ πάλαι μεγάλα ἦν, τὰ πολλὰ αὐτῶν σμικρὰ γέγονε, τὰ δὲ ἐπ' ἐμεῦ ἦν μεγάλα, πρότερον ἦν σμικρά. τὴν ἀνθρωπηίην ὦν ἐπιστάμενος <u>εὐδαιμονίην</u> οὐδαμὰ ἐν τὠυτῷ μένουσαν ἐπιμνήσομαι ἀμφοτέρων ὁμοίως.

Herodotus 1.5.3–4

So that is what the Persians and Phoenicians say. But I will not go on to say whether those things really happened that way or some other way. Instead, relying on what I <u>know</u>, I will <u>indicate</u> [= verb **sēmainō**] who it was who first committed wrongdoing against the Hellenes. I will move thus ahead with what I have to say, as I <u>proceed through</u> great <u>cities</u> and small ones as well. For most of those that were great once are small today; and those that used to be small were great in my time. Understanding that the <u>good fortune</u> [**eudaimoniā**] of men never stays in the same place, I will keep in mind both alike.

The very next word brings into focus the cause that Herodotus gives for the conflicts between Hellenes and barbarians that he is about to narrate: it is Croesus the Lydian (1.6.1),[73] who is described as the **turannos** 'tyrant' (ibid.) of the mighty Lydian Empire that preceded and was then replaced by the Persian Empire. It was Croesus, says Herodotus, who first compelled

73. Note the asyndeton that highlights the introduction of this subject: Κροῖσος ἦν Λυδὸς μὲν γένος, παῖς δὲ Ἀλυάττεω, τύραννος δὲ ἐθνέων τῶν ἐντὸς Ἅλυος ποταμοῦ ... (Herodotus 1.6.1).

Hellenes to pay tribute to a barbarian (1.6.2);[74] 'before the rule of Croesus, all Hellenes were still free [**eleutheroi**]' (πρὸ δὲ τῆς Κροίσου ἀρχῆς πάντες Ἕλληνες ἦσαν ἐλεύθεροι 1.6.3).[75] Herodotus' overall narrative explains the cause of the Ionian Revolt, which ultimately provokes the Persian invasion of Hellas, as provoked in the first place by the 'enslavement' of the Hellenes of Asia (5.49.2–3).[76] At the time of the Ionian Revolt, the 'enslaved' Hellenes were subject to the Persians; but the very first man to have 'enslaved' them was Croesus, tyrant of the Lydian Empire.

It is important to notice that Herodotus qualifies his assertion that Croesus was the first man ever to 'enslave' free Greek cities:

οὗτος ὁ Κροῖσος βαρβάρων πρῶτος τῶν ἡμεῖς ἴδμεν τοὺς μὲν κατεστρέψατο Ἑλλήνων ἐς φόρου ἀπαγωγήν . . .

Herodotus 1.6.2

This Croesus was the first barbarian ever, within our knowledge, to reduce some Hellenes to the status of paying tribute . . .[77]

The expression τῶν ἡμεῖς ἴδμεν 'within our knowledge' picks up the earlier expression that leads to the identification of Croesus as the cause of the conflict between Hellenes and barbarians — or at least of that part of the conflict that is narrated by Herodotus:

τὸν δὲ οἶδα αὐτὸς πρῶτον ὑπάρξαντα ἀδίκων ἔργων ἐς τοὺς Ἕλληνας, τοῦτον σημήνας προβήσομαι ἐς τὸ πρόσω τοῦ λόγου, ὁμοίως
σμικρὰ καὶ μεγάλα ἄστεα ἀνθρώπων ἐπεξιών.

Herodotus 1.5.3

74. Cf. also the first sentence of Herodotus 1.27.1.

75. For the notion, as expressed here in Herodotus 1.6.3, that the Hellenic cities were **eleutheroi** 'free' before Croesus, see p. 309. The first Hellenic city that Croesus attacks is Ephesus (1.26.1–2). He then proceeds to attack each of the other cities of the Asiatic Ionians and Aeolians (1.26.3), in each case contriving an **aitiā** 'cause' to justify his actions (1.26.3 ἄλλοισι ἄλλας αἰτίας ἐπιφέρων, τῶν μὲν ἐδύνατο μέζονας παρευρίσκειν, μέζονα ἐπαιτιώμενος, τοῖσι δὲ αὐτῶν καὶ φαῦλα ἐπιφέρων). In no instance does Herodotus indicate the specific **aitiā**.

76. Cf. Hohti 1976.42–43. For Herodotus, the **ktisis** 'colonization' of Asia by Hellenes does not count as a provocation because he clearly does not accept the Persian premise that all Asia belongs to the Persians (see 1.4.4). In fact the Croesus narrative shows that Herodotus thinks of the Hellenes' cities in Asia as rightfully theirs: the enslavement of these cities by Croesus led to the mistaken Persian premise. Furthermore by implication the crime of Croesus is pertinent to the concept of the Athenian Empire: pp. 308 and following.

77. See p. 309 for a discussion of how the theme of 'enslavement', that is, of making free Greek cities pay tribute, is developed by the narrative of Herodotus; also, how the theme of Croesus the Tyrant is formulated in the mode of an **ainos**; finally, how the **ainos** applies to Athens and its Athenian Empire, the heir to the Persian Empire, in turn the heir to the Lydian Empire.

Relying on what I know, I will indicate [= verb **sēmainō**] who it was who first committed wrongdoing against the Hellenes. I will move thus ahead with what I have to say, as I proceed through great cities and small ones as well.

The wording of what we have just read is reminiscent not of the *Iliad*, prime epic of the Trojan War, but of the *Odyssey*. Thus we come to the second aspect of the Herodotean appropriation of Homer.[78] In the discussion that follows, the focus is on two particular passages in the *Odyssey* that serve to illuminate the wording of Herodotus.

Let us begin by considering the prooemium of the *Odyssey*. After a reference to the destruction of Troy by Odysseus (*Odyssey* i 2), the hero's many subsequent wanderings are described in the following words:

πολλῶν δ᾽ ἀνθρώπων ἴδεν ἄστεα καὶ νόον ἔγνω

Odyssey i 3

He saw the cities of many men, and he came to know their way of thinking [**noos**].

The correlation here of *seeing* (ἴδεν) with consequent *knowing* (καὶ νόον ἔγνω) recapitulates the semantics of perfect **oida**: "I have *seen*: therefore I *know*."[79] This general quest of Odysseus is parallel to a specific quest that was formulated for him by the seer Teiresias; this brings us to the second pertinent passage from the *Odyssey*. In this passage we find Odysseus himself saying to Penelope:

ἐπεὶ μάλα πολλὰ βροτῶν ἐπὶ ἄστε᾽ ἄνωγεν
ἐλθεῖν

Odyssey xxiii 267–268

since he [= Teiresias] ordered me to proceed through very many cities of men.

Teiresias had told Odysseus to undertake this quest after the hero has killed the suitors (xi 119–120);[80] specifically Odysseus is to go inland, with an oar

---

78. Still to come, at p. 255, is a discussion of the Herodotean appropriation of Hesiod.

79. See Snell 1924.61 for areas of semantic overlap between perfect **oida** 'I know' and aorist **eidon** 'I saw', therefore 'I witnessed, experienced'. For example, κακὰ πόλλ᾽ ἐπιδόντα at *Iliad* XXII 61 means 'having experienced many evil happenings'; compare the description of Herakles at *Odyssey* xxi 26 as μεγάλων ἐπιίστορα ἔργων 'the one who experienced deeds of enormity [that is, of evil]'. Cf. p. 250.

80. As for the instructions of Teiresias concerning the **nostos** 'safe homecoming' of Odysseus (xi 100–118; **nostos** is the first word, at xi 100), the themes that are emphasized—not to mention the wording itself—are strikingly parallel to what we find in the prooemium of the *Odyssey* (i 1–10).

on his shoulder, until it is mistaken for a winnowing shovel (xi 121–137; xxiii 265–284). This experience, says Teiresias, will be a **sēma** 'sign, signal' for Odysseus (xi 126; xxiii 273). In such contexts the coding of a **sēma** in the dimension of *seeing* is analogous to the coding of an **ainos** in the dimension of *hearing*.[81] The **sēma** of Teiresias bears a twofold message: what is an oar for seafarers is a winnowing shovel for inlanders. The message of this **sēma**, however, is twofold neither for the seafarers nor for the inlanders since the former can surely distinguish oars from winnowing shovels while the latter are presented as knowing only about winnowing shovels. Rather the message is twofold only for Odysseus as the traveler since he sees that the same signal has two distinct messages in two distinct places: what is an oar for the seafarers is a winnowing shovel for the inlanders.[82] In order to recognize that one **sēma** can have more than one message, Odysseus must travel — πολλὰ βροτῶν ἐπὶ ἄστεα ... ἐλθεῖν 'to proceed through many cities of men' (again xxiii 267–268).[83] The wording brings us back to Herodotus, who describes himself as ὁμοίως σμικρὰ καὶ μεγάλα ἄστεα ἀνθρώπων ἐπεξιών 'proceeding through great cities and small ones as well' (again 1.5.3), in his quest to investigate the cause of the conflict that he is to narrate.

81. This point is elaborated in N 1983.51. Cf. p. 164. On **ainos** as a code, see p. 148.

82. There are further levels of interpretation, as discussed in N 1983.45. Let us consider the gesture of Odysseus, prescribed by the seer Teiresias, where he plants into the ground the handle of what he is carrying, at the precise point where it is no longer recognized as an oar (*Odyssey* xi 129). The picture of the implement planted into the ground is a **sēma** 'sign' bearing a twofold message. On the one hand it can mean "the sailor is dead," as in the case of Odysseus' dead companion Elpenor, whose tomb is to be a mound of earth with the handle of his oar planted on top (xi 75–78, xii 13–15); in fact the tomb of Elpenor is designated as his **sēma** (xi 75). On the other hand it can mean "the harvest is finished": to plant the handle of a winnowing shovel in a heap of grain at a harvest festival is a stylized gesture indicating that the winnower's work is done (Theocritus 7.155–156; I infer that the time of the year is July or August: cf. Gow 1952 II 127.). Cf. Hansen 1977.38–39 (also p. 35 on the Feast of St. Elias, July 20th). The first meaning reflects the god-hero antagonism between Poseidon and Odysseus, on the level of **nostos** 'homecoming'; the second reflects the more complex god-hero antagonism between Athena and Odysseus, on the two levels of **nostos** 'homecoming' and **noos** 'way of thinking': this point is elaborated in N 1983.53n31. On the role of Athena as patroness of pilots, and the related themes of **noos** and **nostos**, see N 1985.74–81. The complexity of the gesture of Odysseus in planting his implement is reinforced by the inherent symbolism of the winnowing shovel: just as this implement separates the grain from the chaff, so also it separates true things from false things; I compare the discussion of **krisis** in the sense of *separating, discriminating, judging* at pp. 61 and following.

83. To decode the code of a **sēma**, one has to know the **noos** 'way of thinking' of the one who encoded it: hence the expression καὶ νόον ἔγνω 'and he came to know their **noos**' in *Odyssey* i 3. For a survey of contexts where the **sēma** *is* the code, see N 1983. It may be possible to take the interpretation further: by knowing the **noos** 'way of thinking' of many men in many cities (*Odyssey* i 3), the hero may in effect come to know his own **noos** through that of others. Cf. *Odyssey* v 274 and the commentary at N 1979.202 (also 1983.39): the stargazer may come to understand his own situation by gazing at the situation played out by the stars (note too that Orion is defined by the Bear Star as the Bear Star takes aim at Orion).

Figuratively Herodotus travels along the 'roads of **logoi**' from city to city, much as Odysseus travels in his heroic quest. This argument meshes with the larger argument that the Homeric stance of Herodotus engages not only the *Iliad* but also the *Odyssey*.

It would be a mistake, however, to explain this as well as other correspondences in the wording of Homer and Herodotus as a simple matter of borrowing by Herodotus. It is a built-in tradition in the diction of Herodotus to imagine the process of narration itself as if it were a process of traveling along a road: for example, when he is ready to investigate the replacement of the Lydian Empire of Croesus by the Persian Empire of Cyrus, Herodotus says that he is about to tell 'the true and real **logos** [= word]' (τὸν ἐόντα λόγον 1.95.1),[84] though he would be capable of revealing three other alternative 'roads of **logoi** [= words]' (ἐπιστάμενος . . . καὶ τριφασίας ἄλλας λόγων ὁδοὺς φῆναι 1.95.1).[85] Here we see a close parallelism between the traditions of Herodotus' **historiā** and Pindar's **ainos** in that the same image of narration as the process of traveling along a road is extensively used in the diction of epinician poetry.[86]

The ideological correspondence between the quest of Odysseus and the quest described by Herodotus runs even deeper. Matching the **sēma** 'signal' that Odysseus gets from Teiresias is a **sēma** given by Herodotus when he *indicates* who committed the wrongdoing that led to the conflict that he narrates while traveling down the road through cities large and small: as we have seen, the word that expresses the idea of 'indicate' is **sēmainō**, derivative of **sēma** (1.5.3). The choice of this word in indicating that the wrongdoer was Croesus is apt in that **sēmainō** denotes a mode of communication that is implicit as well as explicit. The narrative of Herodotus never says explicitly how the wrongdoing of Croesus is linked with the previous wrongdoings in the ongoing conflict between Hellenes and barbarians. Up to the point where Croesus is named, the series of wrongdoings had reached a

84. On τὸν ἐόντα λόγον here at 1.95.1 in the sense of 'the true and real **logos**', see Woodbury 1958.155–156 and n34.

85. Note the wording: ἐπιδίζηται δὲ δὴ τὸ ἐντεῦθεν ἡμῖν ὁ λόγος τόν τε Κῦρον ὅστις ἐὼν τὴν Κροίσου ἀρχὴν κατεῖλε, καὶ τοὺς Πέρσας ὅτεῳ τρόπῳ ἡγήσαντο τῆς Ἀσίης 'Next, I look for the **logos** that tells what kind of a man Cyrus was—to have conquered the empire of Croesus—and how the Persians achieved hegemony over Asia' (1.95.1). For other examples of **hodos** 'road' in the sense of 'alternative version', see Herodotus 1.117.2 (here the choice is between one true **logos** and one false one) and 2.20.1 (note the use of the word **sēmainō** 'indicate' here) in conjunction with 2.22.1.

86. For Pindar, see the list compiled by Slater 1969.373 s.v. ὁδός (b); also id. p. 275 s.v. κέλευθος. Cf. Becker 1937.50–85. Precisely in the context of saying that he knows three roads of song but will tell the "real" story, Herodotus uses the word **graphō** 'write' in referring to his authoritative version (1.95.1). By implication, writing can be for Herodotus the authoritative speech-act in that whatever he *writes* can be equated with whatever he would *say* publicly (cf. pp. 169, 217, 219).

climax in the Trojan War. In the version attributed to the **logioi** who speak
on behalf of the Persians, the Hellenes were in the wrong when they undertook the Trojan War, and the barbarians were in the right when they retaliated with the Persian War, about to be narrated in the *Histories*.[87] But the
narrator of the *Histories* never says explicitly that this version is false.
Instead he keeps saying it implicitly. Something else happened between the
Trojan War and the Persian War, and that was the 'enslavement' of the Hellenes of Asia by Croesus (1.5.3, in conjunction with 1.6.1–3).[88] Thus even if
the Hellenes had been in the wrong when they undertook the Trojan War, the
barbarians had already retaliated for that wrong. The Ionian Revolt, in reaction to the 'enslavement' of the Hellenes (Herodotus 5.49.2–3),[89] would not
count as a wrongdoing in the latest cycle of wrongdoing and retaliation, in
that Herodotus clearly does not accept the Persian premise that all Asia
belongs to the Persians (1.4.4). Thus the real wrong in the latest cycle of
wrongdoing and retaliation is the invasion of Europe by the barbarians in the
Persian War. Again, Herodotus does not say this explicitly but implicitly,
and the word that he uses to designate his mode of communication is
sēmainō (1.5.3). We are reminded of the mode in which the god Apollo
himself communicates:

ὁ ἄναξ, οὗ τὸ μαντεῖόν ἐστι τὸ ἐν Δελφοῖς, οὔτε λέγει οὔτε κρύπτει
ἀλλὰ σημαίνει

Heraclitus 22 B 93 DK

The Lord whose oracle is in Delphi neither says nor conceals: he indicates [= verb **sēmainō**].[90]

In his investigations of causes, Herodotus himself follows the convention
of communicating in this mode. For example, in discussing the cause alleged
by Croesus for his attack on Cyrus, namely, the usurpation of Median
hegemony by the Persians, Herodotus promises to indicate the original cause
of that usurpation:

. . . δι' αἰτίην τὴν ἐγὼ ἐν τοῖσι ὀπίσω λόγοισι σημανέω

Herodotus 1.75.1

---

87. Cf. pp. 228 and following.
88. On this attitude of Herodotus, see pp. 229 and following, above.
89. See again pp. 229 and following, above.
90. Cf. p. 164. Cf. also Herodotus 6.123.2, where the communication of the Pythia or
priestess of Apollo's Oracle is again denoted by this verb **sēmainō**, as well as Theognis 808 (the
only instance of **sēmainō** in the attested nonepigraphic elegiac and iambic poetry of the Archaic
period). In Herodotus 7.142.2, what the words of the oracle are actually supposed to mean is also
expressed by way of the word **sēmainō**.

... on account of a cause [aitiā] that I will indicate [= verb sēmainō] in later logoi.[91]

As François Hartog points out, he who sēmainei 'indicates' does so on the basis of some privileged position of knowledge, as when scouts, having their special vantage point by having ascended to an elevated place, can then run down to indicate to those below the movements of the enemy (Herodotus 7.192.1 ἐσήμαινον, 7.219.1 ἐσήμηναν).[92] The privileged position of Herodotus brings to mind the ultimately privileged position of the Delphic Oracle, with its all-encompassing knowledge, revealing mastery of such "facts" as the number of grains of sand in the universe (Herodotus 1.47.3).[93] When Herodotus sēmainei 'indicates', he seems to have comparable authority within the realm of what he indicates, revealing mastery of such "facts" as the full dimensions of Scythia as it stretches from the Istros to the sea (4.99.2), the precise length of the Royal Road leading from the Mediterranean seacoast all the way to Susa (5.54.1),[94] and, more figuratively, all the 'roads of logoi' along which his predecessors have traveled (2.20.1).[95] Most important, he also knows who is aitios 'responsible' for the all-encompassing conflict that he narrates as he sēmainei 'indicates' that it is Croesus (again 1.5.3).[96]

91. Cf. also Herodotus 7.213.3: ... δι' ἄλλην αἰτίην, τὴν ἐγὼ ἐν τοῖσι ὄπισθε λόγοισι σημανέω '... on account of another cause [aitiā] that I will indicate [= verb sēmainō] in later logoi'. Here the 'other cause' has to do with explaining why Ephialtes was killed—a cause that Herodotus says is not connected with the man's guilt in betraying the Hellenes at Thermopylae. For that betrayal, however, Herodotus does hold Ephialtes guilty: τοῦτον αἴτιον γράφω 'I declare him in writing to be responsible [aitios]' (7.214.3). On the use of graphō 'write' in denoting the discourse of Herodotus, see p. 220 above. But Herodotus does not think that the death of Ephialtes is causally related to his betrayal of the Hellenes. In fact Herodotus' promised account of the real cause of the death of Ephialtes is nowhere to be found in the Histories. Such an omission suggests that the phrases ἐν τοῖσι ὄπισθε λόγοισι and ἐν τοῖσι ὀπίσω λόγοισι denote simply 'in a later narration', as if the attested Histories were simply one in a potential series of narrations by Herodotus. This stance is typical not only of written works but also of oral performance, where the given composition being performed presupposes a limitless series of future performances in which new compositions may take place.

92. Hartog 1980.368f. Cf. the expression koruphē logōn 'summit of words', as discussed at ##303.

93. Ibid. The first word of this the very first oracular utterance quoted by Herodotus is oida 'I know'.

94. Note the wording of Herodotus 5.54.1: εἰ δέ τις τὸ ἀτρεκέστερον τούτων ἔτι δίζηται, ἐγὼ καὶ τοῦτο σημανέω 'but if anyone seeks even more accuracy than this, I shall indicate [sēmainō] that as well'.

95. Cf. p. 233.

96. Here and elsewhere I have interpreted 1.5.3 thus: Herodotus sēmainei 'indicates' that Croesus was aitios 'responsible' for the ultimate conflict between Hellenes and barbarians. It is to be understood that the word aitios in this passage is implied by what Herodotus has been saying in the prooemium (δι' ἣν αἰτίην) and thereafter as discussed at pp. 221 and 228; to be aitios is to be aitios of an adikiā 'wrong' (1.2.1), and Herodotus at 1.5.3 sēmainei 'indicates' that

Thus when Herodotus **sēmainei** 'indicates', he does so *on the basis of superior knowledge*. We now see that he is doing something more than simply qualifying his statement when he indicates that Croesus was **aitios** 'responsible' for the conflict that he will narrate:

οὗτος ὁ Κροῖσος βαρβάρων πρῶτος τῶν ἡμεῖς <u>ἴδμεν</u> τοὺς μὲν κατεστρέψατο Ἑλλήνων ἐς φόρου ἀπαγωγήν

Herodotus 1.6.2

This Croesus was the first barbarian ever, <u>within our knowledge</u>, to reduce some Hellenes to the status of paying tribute . . .

These words pick up the earlier wording:

τὸν δὲ <u>οἶδα</u> αὐτὸς πρῶτον ὑπάρξαντα ἀδίκων ἔργων ἐς τοὺς Ἑλληνας, τοῦτον <u>σημήνας</u> προβήσομαι ἐς τὸ πρόσω τοῦ λόγου, ὁμοίως σμικρὰ καὶ μεγάλα <u>ἄστεα</u> ἀνθρώπων <u>ἐπεξιών</u>.

Herodotus 1.5.3

Instead, relying on what I <u>know</u>, I will <u>indicate</u> [= verb **sēmainō**] who it was who first committed wrongdoing against the Hellenes. I will move thus ahead with what I have to say, as I <u>proceed through</u> great <u>cities</u> and small ones as well.

Figuratively Herodotus owes his privileged position of knowledge to the many roads of **logoi** 'words' that he travels (again 1.95.1)[97] as he proceeds through cities great and small.

This privileged position is analogous to that of Odysseus, who 'saw the cities of many men, and came to know their way of thinking [**noos**]' (*Odyssey* i 3), the same man who was ordered by the seer Teiresias 'to proceed through very many cities of men' (xxiii 267–268).[98] Moreover, the discourse used by Herodotus in expressing his superior knowledge is likewise Odyssean. To **sēmainein** 'indicate' is to speak in a code bearing more than one message. Messages can be immediate as well as ulterior, even about the central theme of the conflict between Hellenes and barbarians, presented as an extension of the Iliadic theme of the Trojan War. In this respect the discourse of Herodotus is akin to that of the **ainos** as represented in the *Odyssey*. When the disguised Odysseus tells his host Eumaios a story about the Trojan War, bearing both the immediate message that he needs a cloak and the ultimate message that he is to be identified as Odysseus (xiv 462–506),[99]

Croesus was the first, as far as Herodotus knows, to commit **adika erga** 'wrongdoings' against the Hellenes.

97. Cf. p. 233.

98. Cf. pp. 231 and following.

99. For a discussion of the immediate and ultimate messages in the "code" of what the dis-

he is complimented by Eumaios for telling a good **ainos** (xiv 508).[100] In fact Odysseus is traditionally represented as a master of the **ainos**, as evident from his particularized epithet **polu-ainos** 'he of many **ainoi**' (e.g., xii 184).[101]

Thus the Homeric stance of Herodotus, in reflecting both Iliadic and Odyssean themes, is analogous to the stance of the disguised Odysseus as he tells his **ainos**: the subject is Iliadic, but the context is Odyssean. The Homeric stance of Herodotus is also analogous to the stance of an epinician poet like Pindar, whose medium is likewise a type of **ainos**.[102] Like Herodotus, Pindar too conventionally represents himself as traveling along 'roads of **logoi**'.[103] Moreover, Pindar's diction reveals an ideology according to which he too has a lofty vantage point of knowledge. As a seer **sēmainei** 'indicates' by way of a **koruphē** 'culmination, summing up' of **logoi** 'words' (Pindar *Paean* 8a.13–14 καὶ τοιᾷδε κορυφᾷ σάμαινεν λόγων),[104] so also the man who gets praise from Pindaric song must understand the poet's **koruphē** of **logoi**:

εἰ δὲ λόγων συνέμεν κορυφάν, Ἱέρων, | ὀρθὰν ἐπίστα, μανθάνων
οἶσθα προτέρων

Pindar Pythian 3.80–81

If you understand, Hieron, the unerring culmination [**koruphē**] of words [**logoi**], you know, learning from those who have gone before, that . . .

How then are we to read the message of Herodotus, if indeed he stands in such a privileged position of knowledge? We must look for signs, and we come back to the **sēma** 'sign' given by Herodotus when he **sēmainei** 'indicates' that Croesus the Lydian was **aitios** 'responsible' for the conflict that is

---

guised Odysseus has to say, see N 1979.233–241. For a study of the word **khlaina** 'cloak' as a symbol of ambiguous discourse, I cite the unpublished work of R. Ingber.

100. See the arguments in N ibid. supporting the notion that the *Odyssey* is referring to the **ainos** as a distinctly poetic form of expression.

101. N, p. 240 §19n1, after Meuli 1975 (=1954) 742–743n2.

102. Cf. pp. 147 and following.

103. Cf. p. 233.

104. The seer represented in this Pindaric passage is probably Cassandra: see SM *ad loc*. Cf. also Pindar *Olympian* 7.68–69 τελεύταθεν δὲ λόγων κορυφαὶ ἐν ἀλαθείᾳ πετοῖσαι 'and the **koruphai** of **logoi** were accomplished, falling into place in truth [**alētheia**]' (this passage concerns an oath about the future, as sworn by Lachesis the **Moira** 'Fate', in conjunction with the Will of Zeus: *Olympian* 7.64–68). For **apo-koruphoō** in the sense of 'sum up' (note also the imagery of achieving a high vantage point in the English expression), see Herodotus 5.73.2. Bundy [1986] 18 paraphrases ὁ δὲ καιρὸς ὁμοίως παντὸς ἔχει κορυφάν at Pindar *Pythian* 9.78–79 as follows: "By judicious selection and treatment [**kairos**] I can convey the spirit [**koruphē**] of the whole just as well." Cf. Race 1979.254, 265n11.

narrated (1.5.3). The immediate message here is that even if the Persian **logioi** were correct in determining who was **aitios** 'responsible' for each wrongdoing up to the Trojan War — in which case the ancestors of the Hellenes would have been in the wrong — the Persian War nevertheless puts the Persians, not the Hellenes, in the wrong because of the intervening wrongs committed by Croesus.[105] But there is also an ulterior message here, one that we can best understand by first confronting the question: who was in the wrong in the *Iliad*?

The main theme of the *Iliad*, the **mēnis** 'anger' of Achilles, which leads to the deaths of countless Achaeans and Trojans,[106] is caused by the insult of Agamemnon, whom Achilles holds **aitios** 'responsible' (*Iliad* I 335; cf. XIII 111).[107] In the later reconciliation scene between the two heroes, however, when Achilles finally renounces his **mēnis** (XIX 35, 75), Agamemnon claims that he was not **aitios** (XIX 86), but that it was Zeus — along with **Moira** 'Fate' and an **Erīnūs** 'Fury' — who inflicted upon him a baneful **atē** 'derangement' (XIX 87–88). Even the other gods hold Zeus responsible for creating a new phase of conflict between Achaeans and Trojans (XI 78 ἠτιόωντο) — a phase triggered by the conflict between Achilles and Agamemnon in the *Iliad*.[108] As for the overall conflict between Achaeans and Trojans, triggered by the abduction of Helen, Priam can claim the same sort of exculpation: it was not Helen who was **aitiē** 'responsible' to him for all his woes, but rather all the gods (III 164). Such claims that the phase of the war narrated by the *Iliad* — or, for that matter, the entire Trojan War — was all part of a grand divine scheme is perfectly in accord with what the *Iliad* announces about its own plot: it *is* the Will of Zeus (I 5).[109] At the beginning of the *Cypria*, the entire potential narrative of the Trojan War is equated with the Will of Zeus (F 1 Allen).[110] King Alkinoos even tells a weeping Odysseus that the Trojan War was devised by the gods so that poets may have something to sing about for men of the future (viii 579–580).[111] In the same line of thinking Telemachus defends Phemios when this poet sings about the suffering of the Achaeans after the Trojan War, on the grounds that Phemios is not **aitios** for what he narrates (i 347–348; cf. xxii 356); rather it is Zeus himself who is **aitios** (i 348).

---

105. Cf. pp. 229 and following.

106. Cf. pp. 227 and following.

107. In contrast Achilles says that the Trojans are not personally **aitioi** 'responsible' to him (*Iliad* I 153); similarly Poseidon says that Aeneas is not personally **aitios** to the Achaeans (XX 297).

108. Cf. pp. 227 and following.

109. This point, that the traditional plot of an epic narrative is programmatically equated with the Will of Zeus, is elaborated in N 1979.82 §25n2.

110. N 1979.131 §17n1. Cf. also *Odyssey* xi 558–560: Odysseus is telling the shade of Ajax that no one else but Zeus was **aitios** 'responsible' for the tragic misfortune that befell Ajax.

111. Commentary on the element of self-reference in this passage: N 1979.100–101.

In contrast the overarching narrative of Herodotus about the conflict between Hellenes and barbarians, linked as it is with the epic conflict between Achaeans and Trojans, seems on the surface to be preoccupied with a different and nonpoetic perspective, inquiring into the question: who were *juridically* responsible? Here too, however, the word conveying responsibility is **aitioi.**

Let us for the moment examine the question from a juridical point of view: who then was in the wrong? The Persian view is that the Hellenes were in the wrong when the Achaeans undertook the war against the Trojans, though the Trojans had been in the wrong earlier when Paris abducted Helen. On the surface, then, it is a juridical matter of a series of retaliations for wrongs committed.

But another principle is at work whenever retaliation happens — a principle that is not made explicit at the beginning of Herodotus' inquiry. Accepting the authority of the Egyptians, whom he describes elsewhere as the supreme **logioi** among all men ever encountered by him (λογιώτατοι 2.77.1),[112] Herodotus says that he personally does not believe that Helen was at Troy when the city was destroyed by the Achaeans (2.120). At the same time he clearly accepts the premise that the destruction of Troy was in retaliation for the abduction of Helen (ibid.). In fact Herodotus reasons that the absence of Helen from Troy sealed the fate of the Trojans. It made it impossible for them to offer compensation to the Achaeans and thus avoid retaliation since the Achaeans refused to believe that Helen was not in Troy until they destroyed it (ibid.). The cause for the Trojans' predicament is made clear when Herodotus finally makes explicit something that had been kept implicit up to this point:

> ἀλλ' οὐ γὰρ εἶχον Ἑλένην ἀποδοῦναι οὐδὲ λέγουσι αὐτοῖσι τὴν ἀληθείην ἐπίστευον οἱ Ἕλληνες, ὡς μὲν ἐγὼ γνώμην ἀποφαίνομαι, τοῦ δαιμονίου παρασκευάζοντος ὅκως πανωλεθρίῃ ἀπολόμενοι καταφανὲς τοῦτο τοῖσι ἀνθρώποισι ποιήσωσι, ὡς τῶν μεγάλων ἀδικημάτων μεγάλαι εἰσὶ καὶ αἱ τιμωρίαι παρὰ τῶν θεῶν. καὶ ταῦτα μὲν τῇ ἐμοὶ δοκέει εἴρηται.

Herodotus 2.120.5

The fact is, they [= the Trojans] did not give back Helen because they did not have her. What they told the Hellenes was the truth, but they did not believe them. The reason is, and here I display [= verb **apophain-omai**] my judgment [**gnōmē**],[113] that the power of a superna-

---

112. If indeed Herodotus is implicitly a **logios**, on which subject see pp. 221 and 224, then his expressed opinion about the authority of the Egyptians as supreme **logioi** (2.77.1) is in line with the prominence of his narrative about his own journey to Egypt in Book II of the *Histories*.

113. For this expression, see p. 219.

tural force [**daimōn**] arranged it that they [= the Trojans] should be completely destroyed and thereby make it clear to mankind that the gods exact enormous retributions for enormous wrongdoings. I say this in accordance with what I have decided about the matter.

We begin to see that the narrative of Herodotus is describing implicitly the workings of the gods as it describes explicitly the deeds of men. I now argue that when Herodotus **sēmainei** 'indicates' that Croesus should be held **aitios** 'responsible' for the conflict that is being narrated (1.5.3),[114] he is also indicating, by way of his overall narration, that Croesus is destined to incur retribution from the gods—retribution that will take the form of some human action that can be explicitly narrated.

What we are about to see is a pattern of narration where a man who does wrong, who is **aitios**, pays for that wrong by suffering a great misfortune, for which he then holds a god responsible, **aitios**. Then the given god makes clear that it was really the wrongdoer who was juridically responsible for the wrong that he did, and that the god is 'responsible' only for the transcendent scheme of divine retribution for that wrong.

Croesus the Lydian suffers the great misfortune of losing his mighty empire at the hands of Cyrus the Persian, whose empire he had attacked. When Cyrus asks Croesus why he had taken up arms against him, Croesus replies:

ὦ βασιλεῦ, ἐγὼ ταῦτα ἔπρηξα τῇ σῇ μὲν εὐδαιμονίῃ τῇ ἐμεωυτοῦ δὲ κακοδαιμονίῃ· αἴτιος δὲ τούτων ἐγένετο ὁ Ἑλλήνων θεὸς ἐπάρας ἐμὲ στρατεύεσθαι

Herodotus 1.87.3

O king, I did it because of your good fortune [**eudaimoniā** = having a good **daimōn**] and my bad fortune [= having a bad **daimōn**]. But the one who is responsible [**aitios**] is the god of the Hellenes, who impelled me to take up arms.

This outcome, a violent shift from good to bad fortune, is the central theme already formulated in the initial words of Herodotus as he began his inquiry into the responsibility of Croesus:

τὸν δὲ οἶδα αὐτὸς πρῶτον ὑπάρξαντα ἀδίκων ἔργων ἐς τοὺς Ἕλληνας, τοῦτον σημήνας προβήσομαι ἐς τὸ πρόσω τοῦ λόγου, ὁμοίως σμικρὰ καὶ μεγάλα ἄστεα ἀνθρώπων ἐπεξιών. τὰ γὰρ τὸ πάλαι μεγάλα ἦν, τὰ πολλὰ αὐτῶν σμικρὰ γέγονε, τὰ δὲ ἐπ᾽ ἐμεῦ ἦν μεγάλα, πρότερον ἦν σμικρά. τὴν ἀνθρωπηίην ὦν ἐπιστάμενος

---

114. Cf. pp. 229 and following.

εὐδαιμονίην <u>οὐδαμὰ</u> ἐν τὠυτῷ μένουσαν ἐπιμνήσομαι ἀμφοτέρων ὁμοίως.

Herodotus 1.5.3–4

Relying on what I know, I will indicate [= verb **sēmainō**] who it was who first committed wrongdoing against the Hellenes. I will move thus ahead with what I have to say, as I proceed through great cities and small ones as well. For most of those that were great once are small today; and those that used to be small were great in my time. Understanding that the good fortune [**eudaimoniā** = having a good **daimōn**] of men never stays in the same place, I will keep in mind both alike.

Maintaining the implicitness of the divine scheme in his narrative, Herodotus tells how the Oracle of Apollo at Delphi rejects the accusation of Croesus that Apollo is responsible for the king's misfortune: Croesus is informed by the Oracle that he had read the wrong message into its ambiguous utterance, which had told him only that he would destroy a great empire if he attacked the empire of Cyrus (1.91.4; cf. 1.53.3). This ambiguity brings to mind once again the words of Heraclitus, describing how Apollo speaks through his Oracle: the god neither says nor conceals, but he **sēmainei** 'indicates' (22 B 93 DK).[115] Returning to the narrative of Herodotus, we note a particularly significant detail: the Oracle goes on to say that Croesus, in misunderstanding Apollo's message, has no one but himself to hold as responsible for the misfortune. The word used is **aitios**: ἑωυτὸν αἴτιον ἀποφαινέτω 'let him [= Croesus] publicly display himself as the one <u>responsible</u> [**aitios**]' (1.91.4).

There is an interesting juridical distinction here. The god Apollo is clearly the *cause* of the Lydian king's misfortunes, in that it was Apollo's Oracle that gave Croesus the opportunity to make his mistake, but Apollo is not legally responsible, **aitios**. Croesus made the mistake.[116] There is an analogous theme in Homeric poetry. We have seen how the gods are presented as the causes of human misfortunes and thus accused by mortals as **aitioi** 'responsible'. But here too the gods can disclaim legal responsibility, as when Zeus says:

ὢ πόποι οἷον δή νυ θεοὺς βροτοὶ <u>αἰτιόωνται</u>.
ἐξ ἡμέων γάρ φασι κάκ’ ἔμμεναι· οἱ δὲ καὶ αὐτοὶ
σφῇσιν ἀτασθαλίῃσιν ὑπὲρ μόρον ἄλγε’ ἔχουσιν

Odyssey i 32–34

---

115. See p. 234.
116. Croesus comes to admit this after hearing the Oracle's response to his recriminations: Herodotus 1.91.6.

> Alas, how mortals <u>hold</u> us gods <u>responsible</u> [= **aitioi**]!
> For they say that their misfortunes come from us. But they get their
>   sufferings,
> beyond what is fated, by way of their own acts of recklessness
>   [**atasthaliai**].

The notion that mortals are responsible for the misfortunes that they suffer as retribution for their wickedness is a prominent one in the *Odyssey*,[117] setting it apart from the *Iliad*, which stresses the Will of Zeus as the force that controls the plot of the epic.[118] In other words, whereas the *Iliad* stresses that a grand divine scheme is at work in all human actions, even when one mortal wrongs another, the *Odyssey* in contrast stresses the responsibility of mortals in committing any wrong. The difference, however, is not as great as it first seems. Even the *Iliad* acknowledges the legal responsibility of a wrongdoer, and even the *Odyssey* acknowledges a divine scheme in human actions. Thus when Agamemnon claims that not he but Zeus was **aitios** 'responsible' for his conflict with Achilles (XIX 86), as the gods inflicted **atē** 'derangement' upon him (XIX 87–88; 134–136), he nevertheless acknowledges that he is legally in the wrong and expresses his willingness to offer retribution for his wronging Achilles (XIX 137–138).[119] Conversely even the *Odyssey* acknowledges a grand divine scheme in the actual pattern of retribution for wrongdoing, most notably when Odysseus takes vengeance upon the reckless suitors through the active planning of the gods, especially of Athena.

At the risk of oversimplification, it could thus be said that the *Iliad* stresses the divine scheme in why a mortal commits a wrong, while the *Odyssey* stresses the divine scheme in how a mortal pays for that wrong. In light of what we have just observed concerning the usage of the word **atē** in the overall scheme of the *Iliad*, we may note with interest that the primary wrongdoers of the *Odyssey*, the suitors, are nowhere overtly described as being afflicted with **atē**.[120]

---

117. *Odyssey* i 33–34, as quoted immediately above, should be understood in conjunction with i 6–7.

118. Further discussion at N 1979.113 §24n3.

119. Dodds 1951.3 remarks: "Early Greek justice cared nothing for intent—it was the act that mattered." Dodds also points out (ibid.) that even Achilles as the aggrieved party accepts Agamemnon's premise, that he had not acted of his own volition (XIX 270–274; cf. I 412). Further observations on this point at p. 254.

120. I believe that this pattern of omission in the *Odyssey* is the reflex of an opposition in theme between the *Iliad* and *Odyssey* (above). In other words the divergences in the uses of **atē** in the *Iliad* and the *Odyssey* do not reflect divergences in the actual meaning of **atē**. See Francis 1983.97–99 for passages in the *Odyssey* where we can find latent implications of **atē** for the suitors in an Iliadic sense. Moreover, **atē** can apply in an Iliadic sense to other characters in the *Odyssey* (e.g., Helen at iv 261, who is afflicted by Aphrodite). Conversely in the *Iliad* **atē** applies at least once in an Odyssean sense, where Phoenix says that the **Litai**, goddesses of supplication personified (IX 502), afflict with **atē** a man who does wrong in cruelly rejecting supplications (IX 510–512). The message here is intended for Achilles, for whom **atē** would be a form

Applying these Homeric perspectives of human accountability to the narrative of Herodotus, we can see that the story of Croesus conveys both an Iliadic and an Odyssean moral perspective. The narrative dramatizes both why a mortal commits a wrong and how he pays for that wrong — all in accordance with an implicit divine scheme. Let us briefly reexamine the narrative with these themes in mind.

After Croesus subjugates the Hellenes of Asia — which is the very context in which he is marked as responsible for the overall conflict between Hellenes and barbarians from the standpoint of the *Histories* of Herodotus —[121] the Lydian king turns his attention to the Hellenic islands; and he is dissuaded from attacking them only through the ingenuity of one or another of the Seven Sages (the narrative leaves it open — either Pittakos of Mytilene or Bias of Priene, 1.27.2).[122] Turned away from attacking in this direction, Croesus thereupon resolves to attack the Persian Empire, and for this new acquisitive enterprise he seeks the alliance of what are characterized as the two foremost cities of Hellas, Athens and Sparta (1.53.1, 1.56.2–3). The stage is now set for the ultimate conflict between Hellas and Persia. The stage is also set, by way of highlighting Athens and Sparta, for the here and now of the **apodeixis** 'making public' of Herodotus' inquiry.

The narrative of Herodotus effectively dramatizes a divine scheme that accounts for both why Croesus is indeed in the wrong and how he pays for that wrong. Yet another of the Seven Sages, Solon of Athens, visits the court of Croesus when the Lydian king is at the height of his wealth (Herodotus

---

of punishment. See p. 254. Yet another dimension to consider is the meaning of **atē** in juridical discourse: in the *Law Code of Gortyn*, for example, **atā** actually means 'damage' (6.23, 43; 9.14 Willetts) and even 'obligation, indemnity, loss in a lawsuit' (e.g., 10.23–24; 11.34–35, 41); see Francis, p. 121n83. Thus **atē** can refer both to crime, that is, how someone commits a wrong, and to punishment, that is, how someone pays for a wrong. In terms of cause and effect, **atē** can be both. To quote Wyatt 1982.261n18 (following Stallmach 1968.88n160): "Indeed, this is the meaning of personification — taking the act (or state) and making it also the cause of the state. Or, put grammatically, placing in subject position what should be the object or the instrument of the action." For the imagery of **atē** as even reflected by its etymology (root *auē-, in the sense of 'being blown off course'), see in general the suggestive article of Francis 1983. For another possible etymology, see Wyatt 1982.

121. Cf. pp. 229 and following.

122. The basic testimony on the concept of the Seven Sages is conveniently assembled in DK no. 10 (pp. 61–66). The canonical list attributed to Demetrius of Phaleron in Stobaeus 3.1.172 is as follows: Kleoboulos of Lindos, Solon of Athens, Khilon of Sparta, Thales of Miletus, Pittakos of Mytilene, Bias of Priene, Periandros of Corinth. In Plato *Protagoras* 343a, Myson is in place of Periandros. In Ephorus FGH 70 F 182, it is Anacharsis the Thracian who is in place of Periandros; also in Plutarch *Banquet of the Seven Sages*. Diogenes Laertius also mentions Pythagoras as an optional variant in the grouping (1.41, 42). For other variations, see again Diogenes Laertius 1.40–42 and the references in DK, p. 61 (cf. also Privitera 1965.55–56). One particular variation, noted at p. 341, is the membership of Aristodemos in the grouping of the Seven Sages. On the theme of Solon as the wisest of the Seven Sages, see, for example, Plato *Timaeus* 20d (cf. p. 226).

1.29.1). In the dialogue between the Sage and the Tyrant, it becomes clear that Croesus thinks that he himself is the most 'fortunate' of all men, in that he is the richest, and the word used for the concept translated here as 'fortunate' is **olbios** (1.30.3, 1.34.1). In responding to the tyrant, however, the sage understands the same word **olbios** differently. Whereas the understanding of the tyrant is simplex, that of the sage is complex, corresponding to his privileged mode of communication. In the Herodotean narrative that dramatizes the encounter between Solon and Croesus, the sage communicates in the mode of an **ainos**, a code that carries the right message for those who are qualified and the wrong message or messages for those who are unqualified.[123]

The understanding of the word **olbios** by Croesus, as narrated by Herodotus, is symptomatic of the tyrant's derangement, or **atē**. Although the noun **olbos** denotes 'wealth',[124] it becomes clear from Solon's teachings to Croesus that the adjective **olbios** here means something more than simply 'wealthy' or even 'fortunate'. From Solon's represented vantage point, this word has an implicit meaning that transcends material wealth and good fortune: far from being a mere equivalent of **plousios** 'wealthy' (1.32.5–6), **olbios** applies especially to those who lived a righteous life and who are then rewarded with **tīmē** 'honor' after death (Tellos, 1.30.5; cf. Kleobis and Biton, 1.31.5).[125] Here and elsewhere in Archaic Greek thought, **olbios** conveys the image of material security, but it tends to restrict this image — in a way that **plousios** 'rich' does not — to ulterior contexts of bliss in an afterlife (it would not be inappropriate to translate **olbios** in such contexts as 'blissful').[126]

123. For this definition of **ainos**, see p. 148.

124. For example, Solon F 6.3W and F 34.2W; cf. Hesiod *Works and Days* 637 (where **olbos** is used synonymously with **ploutos** 'wealth' and **aphenos** 'riches') and *Theogony* 974 (**Ploutos**, son of Demeter, gives **olbos**).

125. On the use of **tīmē** in Herodotus and elsewhere to specify the 'honor' that a hero receives *in cult* after death, see N 1979.118 §1n2.

126. In other words, if we juxtapose **plousios** and **olbios**, we find that the second is the marked member in that it can specify concepts not specified by the first. On the terminology of *marked* and *unmarked*, see p. 5. For a survey of traditional Greek poetic designations for the concept of immortalization by way of images conveying the material security of wealth, see N 1981, especially with reference to the words **aiōn** 'vital force' and **aphthito-** 'unfailing, unwilting, inexhaustible'. Cf. also Risch 1987. The article N 1981 was written in response to that of Floyd 1980, who argues that the Indo-European heritage of the epithet **aphthito-** is semantically restricted to the notion of material wealth. There is a similar argument offered by Finkelberg 1986 (who cites Floyd 1980 but not N 1981). At p. 5 she asserts that the application of **aphthito-** to an "incorporeal entity" is a "semantic innovation"; at p. 4 she argues that, on the grounds that **aphthito-** applies mostly to "material objects," the "concrete associations of the term must have been the original ones." I question such a weighing of statistical predominance in determining what is "original." And I point out a salient feature, not noted by Finkelberg, in the contexts where **aphthito-** applies to "material objects": the concrete associations are otherworldly ones. In response to Finkelberg's argument that **kleos aphthiton** as used at *Iliad* IX 413 is not a

I cite here a striking example from Pindar:[127]

ὄλβιος ὅστις ἰδὼν κεῖν' εἶσ' ὑπὸ χθόν'· | οἶδε μὲν βίου τελευτάν, | οἶδεν δὲ διόσδοτον ἀρχάν.

Pindar F 137 SM

Blissful [**olbios**] is he who goes beneath the earth after having seen those things;[128] he knows the fulfillment [**teleutē**, = literally 'end'][129]

"self-contained unit," I point to the discussion in N 1974.104–109, where the relationships that link the phrase types κλέος ἄφθιτον ἔσται (as at IX 413), κλέος ἔσται (as at VII 458), and κλέος ἄφθιτον (as at Sappho F 44.4 V) are explored from the perspective of a less narrow understanding of *formula*. I agree with Finkelberg that κλέος ἄφθιτον ἔσται at IX 413 is coefficient with κλέος οὔποτ' ὀλεῖται as at II 325. I can also accept the possibility that κλέος οὔποτ' ὀλεῖται does not occur at IX 413 because ὤλετο is already present at the beginning of the line. But I disagree with her inference that the presence of κλέος ἄφθιτον ἔσται instead of κλέος οὔποτ' ὀλεῖται at IX 413 is an innovation; it could be an archaism that survives precisely for the stylistic purpose of avoiding word duplication. As a general approach to poetics, I suggest that allowance should always be made for the possibility that more archaic forms can be activated in situations where the more innovative device is inappropriate. For an illuminating discussion of the usage of relatively older and newer forms in poetics, see Meillet 1920. For another critique of Finkelberg's argumentation, see Edwards 1988.

127. This Pindaric passage is quoted by Clement of Alexandria (*Stromateis* 3.3.17), who says that it concerns the Eleusinian Mysteries. Whether or not this specific ascription may stand, the language is in any case mystical. The poem is apparently from a **thrēnos** 'lament' for Hippokrates (scholia to Pindar *Pythian* 7.18a). On the affinities of this genre of lamentation called **thrēnos** with mystical themes of immortalization, see N 1979.170–177.

128. Compare *Homeric Hymn to Demeter* 480: ὄλβιος ὃς τάδ' ὄπωπεν ἐπιχθονίων ἀνθρώπων 'blissful [**olbios**] is he who has seen these things [= the Eleusinian Mysteries]'; later the **olbios** man who is favored by Demeter and Persephone (*Hymn to Demeter* 486) is described as getting the gift of **Ploutos** 'Wealth' personified (488–489). Again we see that material wealth is but a physical manifestation of transcendent bliss.

129. In light of Solon's point that Tellos is most **olbios** of men (Herodotus 1.30), it is worth noting that this name **Tellos** seems to be a hypocoristic shortening of any one of a set of names built from the noun **telos** 'end, fulfillment, achievement', such as **Telesiphrōn** (on the morphology, see Immerwahr 1966.156–157n21). Whether or not Tellos was a historical figure (for bibliography, see Immerwahr ibid.), it is clear that the name has a bearing on the narrative of Herodotus, as we see from the profusion of **teleutē/teleutaō** in this Herodotean passage: this noun/verb is related to **telos** and means 'end, fulfill[ment]' (in the case of Tellos, τελευτή 1.30.4; in the case of Kleobis and Biton, τελευτή 1.31.3; in the case of Croesus, τελευτήσαντα and τελευτῆσαι 1.32.5; τελευτήσει and τελευτήσῃ 1.32.7; τελευτήσῃ and τελευτήν 1.32.9; τελευτήν 1.33; τελευτήσειν *bis* 1.39.2). (This interpretation of the significance attached to the name of Tellos has a bearing on the expression πάντα παραμείναντα at Herodotus 1.30.4, which I translate as 'all his possessions having lasted' in light of the parallel use of **paramenō** 'last, endure' at 3.57.3.) The form **telos** itself is used in the expression ἐν τέλεϊ τούτῳ ἔσχοντο 'they were held fast in this **telos**', which refers to the mystically dead state of Kleobis and Biton after they had performed their labors for the goddess Hera and had fallen asleep, never to be awakened again to this world (1.31.5). (On the use of ἔσχοντο 'were held fast' here in the sense of a ritualized pose, as in a dance, see p. 38.) I interpret **telos** here (*pace* Powell 1938.353: 'death') in the sense of 'service to a god' (LSJ, p. 1773 s.v. τέλος I.6). This same word in the plural is regularly

of life, and he <u>knows</u> its Zeus-given beginning.

When Herakles is immortalized on Olympus after performing his Labors, he too is described as **olbios** (Hesiod *Theogony* 954; cf. Pindar *Nemean* 1.71).[130] We may note too the following passage, where we find an analogous theme, with a twist in the sequence of events:

ἇ μάκαρ εὐδαίμων τε καὶ ὄλβιος, ὅστις ἄπειρος
ἄθλων εἰς Ἀΐδου δῶμα μέλαν κατέβη . . .

Theognis 1013–1014

Ah, blessed [**makar**], fortunate [**eudaimōn** = 'having a good
  daimōn'], and <u>blissful [**olbios**]</u> is he
who goes down to the dark house of Hades without having experienced
  <u>labors</u> [**āthloi** = **aethloi**] . . .[131]

Herodotus goes on to tell how the teachings of Solon fall on deaf ears and how Croesus is then marked for **nemesis** 'retribution' (1.34.1) precisely because he thought that he was the most **olbios** of men (ibid.). In Solon's teachings the word **atē** had come up twice in the context of describing how disastrous it is when it afflicts someone who is rich but **an-olbos**, that is, 'not **olbios**' (1.32.6). In all of Herodotus the noun **atē** occurs only here.[132] The **nemesis** 'retribution' against Croesus takes the immediate form of the accidental death of his son, whose name happens to be **Atus**.[133] And the man who killed him accidentally with a spear happens to be called **Adrāstos**, where the morphology of the adjectival **a-drāstos** suggests the interpretation 'he from whom one cannot run away'.[134] This interpretation is supported by the attestation of **Adrāsteia** as the epithet of the goddess **Nemesis** (Aeschylus *Prometheus* 936). Adrastos is then told by the grieving Croesus:

εἰς δὲ οὐ σύ μοι τοῦδε τοῦ κακοῦ <u>αἴτιος</u>, εἰ μὴ ὅσον ἀέκων ἐξερ-

---

applied to the Eleusinian Mysteries (LSJ ibid.); the derivative of **telos**, **teletē** (cf. **genos** and **genetē**), means primarily 'initiation [into the mysteries of a god]', for example, at Herodotus 4.79.1/2.

130. On the use of the word **aethlos** in designating the Labors of Herakles, see p. 138. In this connection we may note the word **aethlophoroi** 'prize-winners' describing Kleobis and Biton at Herodotus 1.31.2.

131. Cf. Bacchylides *Epinician* 5.50–55 SM. On the variations in themes of afterlife, with Hades on one side and Olympus/Elysium/Islands of the Blessed [**Makares**] on the other, see N 1979.164–210. In Hesiod *Works and Days* 172, the inhabitants of the Islands of the Blessed are called **olbioi hērōes** 'blissful heroes'. On the implications of **olbios** at *Odyssey* xi 137, see N 1981.116n22.

132. The accepted reading is ἄγη not ἄτη at Herodotus 6.61.1.

133. That this name is used in Herodotus as an evocation of **atē**: Immerwahr 1966.157–158.

134. Cf. Immerwahr, p. 158n25.

γάσαο, ἀλλὰ θεῶν κού τις, ὅς μοι καὶ πάλαι προεσήμαινε τὰ μέλλοντα ἔσεσθαι

Herodotus 1.45.2

You are not responsible [**aitios**] to me for this great disaster, except insofar as you were the unwilling agent, but someone of the gods is, who long ago indicated [= verb **sēmainō**] to me in advance what was going to happen.

Croesus is referring to a dream that had 'indicated' to him — and again the verb in question is **sēmainō** — that his son would die by the spear (1.34.2).[135] This pattern of accusing a god as **aitios** 'responsible' for a misfortune only proves that the accuser is the one who is **aitios**. In the course of his later and ultimate misfortune, the loss of his empire, Croesus again accuses a god — this time Apollo directly — as **aitios**, who in turn makes clear that Croesus was really **aitios** (Herodotus 1.91.4).[136] In this connection we may note the teaching of Hesiod in the *Works and Days*: **olbios** 'blissful' is the man who acts in a ritually and morally correct manner (ὄλβιος ὃς τάδε πάντα | εἰδὼς ἐργάζηται 826–827)[137] and who is therefore **an-aitios** 'not **aitios**' to the gods (ἀναίτιος ἀθανάτοισιν 827).

In both misfortunes of Croesus, which are linked by the narrative, we have seen the Odyssean theme of *how* a man pays for a wrong. In the story of the first misfortune, how the king lost his son, we may also recognize the Iliadic theme of *why* a man commits a wrong in the first place: it is because of the derangement of Croesus, explicit in the use of the word **atē** in Solon's speech to him and implicit in the names **Atus** and **Adrāstos**. This derangement, as realized in his faulty perception of himself as the most **olbios** 'blissful' of men, provokes a pattern of divine retribution against Croesus in the form of two successive misfortunes, the death of his son and the loss of his empire. In both cases Croesus manifestly reveals himself as **aitios** by making the additional mistake, both times, of accusing the god who had forewarned him with signs.[138]

Besides the teachings of Solon as dramatized by Herodotus, we get parallel insights about **atē** from the Sage's teachings in the actual poetry that is ascribed to him. We learn from this poetry that **atē** 'derangement' happens when a mortal seeks **ploutos** 'wealth' by espousing **hubris** 'outrage' and

135. The message is of course ambiguous, in that the notion of 'spear' would suggest primarily a context of war, not hunting.

136. The wording is quoted at p. 241.

137. On the parallelism established in the *Works and Days* between ritually and morally correct behavior, see N 1982.61.

138. A related topical convention: when men are afflicted by misfortune, they may say that the *cause* is the anger of a god, and the word for 'cause' in such contexts is, appropriately, **aition** in an aetiological sense. A striking example is Herodotus 9.93.4.

rejecting **dikē** 'justice' (Solon F 13.11–13 W); then Zeus punishes that mortal for his **hubris** (13.16–18).[139] In contrast Solon defines the transcendent concept of **olbos** 'bliss' (13.3) figuratively as the kind of **ploutos** 'wealth' that is given by the gods and is attended by **dikē** 'justice' (13.3–8).[140]

In the actual poetry of Solon, then, the teaching of the Sage about this topic is direct: **hubris** is a cause of **atē**. In the narrative of Herodotus, on the other hand, Solon's teaching about **hubris** is indirect. The attitude of Croesus at the time of his encounter with Solon is surely symptomatic of **atē**, but what the Lydian tyrant has actually done in attacking the Persian Empire is surely an act of **hubris**: Croesus is being irresistibly drawn into a pattern of unlimited expansion that will ultimately ruin him and set Hellas and Persia on a collision course. Still, the **atē** and **hubris** of Croesus are not confronted directly by Solon in the encounter dramatized by Herodotus. In his own poetry, Solon can speak in his juridical role as lawmaker. In his encounter with a tyrant, however, he is more diplomatic. The juridical point that Croesus is guilty, that is to say **aitios** 'responsible' for his misfortunes (Herodotus 1.91.4),[141] is established not by Solon directly but by the turn of events that bring to fulfillment the words of Solon. Without the narration of Herodotus, neither the guilt of Croesus the tyrant nor the meaning of Solon the sage could be manifest. The words of the Sage have been ambiguously spoken in the mode of an **ainos**, the true meaning of which can only be brought out by the turn of events as narrated by Herodotus. The narration itself underlines the universal applicability of its lesson at a later point, as we see Croesus, now a captive of the Persians and about to be burned to death on a funeral pyre, reminiscing about the wise words that Solon had once addressed to him and declaring his present realization that Solon had at that time been speak-

---

139. In that **atē** inevitably leads to retribution, it can be synonymous with retribution itself (cf. Solon F 13.75–76 W). For the semantics, see n120.

140. In other words, marked **olbos** is equivalent to unmarked **ploutos** *plus* divine sanction and **dikē** 'justice'. Previously at p. 244, we have seen an optional unmarked/marked opposition between **plousios** and **olbios**, where the latter is marked as a transcendent image of material security, in terms of afterlife. I say *optional* because the marked/unmarked opposition is not activated in every context: in some contexts **ploutos** and **olbos** are synonymous: see p. 244. In the present passage from Solon, we see the transcendence of **olbos** in terms of life in the here and now, not in the afterlife. For other instances where **olbos**, instead of being synonymous with **ploutos** 'wealth' (see p. 244), is restricted to convey the ethical notion of material security granted or taken away by the gods as a reward or punishment for righteous or unrighteous behavior, see Hesiod *Works and Days* 281, 321, 326. In the *Odyssey* the struggle of the righteous Odysseus against the unrighteous suitors is played out with many references to **olbos** and how it is dispensed by the gods (the perspective of Odysseus on this matter is the "correct" one: see, for example, *Odyssey* xviii 19). For the timeless image of material security as prevailing under the rule of a righteous king, see *Odyssey* xix 109–114 (cf. Hesiod *Works and Days* 225–237). On **dikē** as 'justice' or 'righteousness' long-range and 'judgment' short-range, see N 1982.58–60.

141. The wording is quoted at p. 241.

ing not so much to him as to the whole human race, especially 'to those who think that they are fortunate [**olbioi**]' (οὐδέν τι μᾶλλον ἐς ἑωυτὸν λέγων ἢ ἐς ἅπαν τὸ ἀνθρώπινον καὶ μάλιστα τοὺς παρὰ σφίσι αὐτοῖσι ὀλβίους δοκέοντας εἶναι Herodotus 1.86.5). I see in this detail from Herodotus an explicit formulation of a Classical ideal concerning the function of the **ainos**. On the surface the **ainos** is predicated on the reality of uncertainties in interaction between performer and audience; underneath the surface, however, it is predicated on the ideology of an ideal audience, listening to an ideal performance of an ideal composition, the message of which applies to all humanity.[142]

142. Cf. p. 148.

9 ▣▣ The Authority of *Historiā*
and the Sign of the Hero

The juridical aspect of Herodotean narrative — that it can establish who is **aitios** 'responsible' for the ultimate struggle between Hellenes and Persians — is articulated already in the prooemium of the *Histories*, in that the purpose of the entire narrative is said to be an inquiry into the **aitiā** 'cause' of that struggle.[1] Moreover, the word for 'inquiry' in the prooemium, **historiā**,[2] is a juridical concept, semantically distinct from later uses of the word and from the current use of *history*. As we can see clearly from Bruno Snell's doctoral dissertation, **historiā** is connected with the juridical words **histōr** 'witness, arbitrator' and **historeō** 'witness; inquire; conduct an inquiry'.[3] The noun **histōr**, derived from the verb represented by the aorist **uid-* of **idein** 'see' and the perfect **ueid-/*uoid-* of **eidenai/oida** 'know' (= "I have seen: therefore I know"),[4] is still attested in the sense of 'witness'

---

1. See p. 227 and following, with commentary on the relationship between **aitiā** 'cause' in the prooemium and **aitioi** 'responsible, guilty' in 1.1.1 of Herodotus.

2. See p. 217.

3. Snell 1924.59–71. On the word **histōr** see also Dewald 1987, especially p. 153n18, with further bibliography.

4. For the semantics of **histōr** as 'he who knows', Snell, p. 60n3, cites **eidotes** 'they who know' in the sense of 'witnesses' at Demosthenes 55.9, 11ff, 35, and at Isocrates 17.44. He also adduces (ibid.) the rare and apparently Solonian word **idūos/eidūos**, cited by Eustathius as a synonym of **histōr** in the context of *Iliad* XVIII 501. As an agent noun, **histōr** is not to be linked with **eidenai** 'know' only, to the exclusion of **idein** 'see': see Snell, p. 61, on the expression Ἡρακλῆα μεγάλων ἐπιίστορα ἔργων 'Herakles, the one who experienced deeds of enormity' at *Odyssey* xxi 26, where **epi-histōr** 'he who experiences' is to be derived from **ep-idein** (not **ep-eidenai**), as in κακὰ πόλλ' ἐπιδόντα 'having experienced many evil happenings' at *Iliad* XXII 61. Cf. p. 231.

in some contexts,[5] but in others the word has undergone semantic specialization, acquiring the sense of 'arbitrator'. A similar semantic specialization takes place in the Latin word *arbiter* 'arbitrator'.[6]

Snell draws our attention to one particular example of **histōr** in this sense of 'arbitrator': it occurs at *Iliad* XVIII 501, in the context of the description of the Shield of Achilles.[7] On the Shield is depicted a scene of litigation (XVIII 497–508),[8] specifically a **neikos** 'conflict' (νεῖκος 497, ἐνείκεον 498) over a **poinē** 'penalty, fine' (498) to be paid as compensation for the death of an anonymous man (499).[9] Our first impression is that the penalty is the equivalent of the Anglo-Saxon *wergild*, a fine payed by the kinsmen of the manslayer to the kinsmen of the slain (cf. the uses of **poinē** at *Iliad* IX 633, 636; XIII 659; XIV 483). But there is more to it. The anonymous defendant 'was making a claim' (**eukheto** 499)[10] that he paid the fine in full (**pant' apodounai** 499), but the anonymous plaintiff 'was refusing to accept anything' (**ho d' anaineto mēden helesthai** 500).[11] This case can be contrasted

5. In Boeotian inscriptions **histōr** seems to be used in contexts where other dialects would feature **martūs** 'witness' (e.g., DGE 491.18, 492.7, 503a.28, 511.7, 512.6, 523.64). In line with such oath-expressions as ἴστω νῦν Ζεύς 'may Zeus now be witness' (e.g., *Iliad* X 329), we may note that the gods are called upon as **histores** 'witnesses' and as **sun-(h)istores** in the sworn declaration quoted by Thucydides 2.74.3.

6. Snell, p. 60n4, who also adduces the entry **ep-ēkooi** in Hesychius s.v.

7. Snell, p. 60. The only other attestation of **histōr** in the *Iliad/Odyssey* is at XXIII 486, where Idomeneus suggests to Ajax that they call on Agamemnon as **histōr** to settle a dispute that they are having.

8. In my interpretation of this scene, I am guided primarily by the analysis of L. Muellner (1976.100–106).

9. The setting of the litigation is an **agorā** 'assembly': *Iliad* XVIII 497.

10. See Muellner, pp. 100–106 on the juridical sense of **eukheto** here, for which there is a striking parallel in the use of *e-u-ke-to* = **eukhetoi** 'makes a claim' in the Linear B texts (Pylos tablets Ep 704 and Eb 297). Muellner also points out (ibid.) that the defendant in the *Iliad* passage is addressing his claim to an entity called the **dēmos** (δήμῳ πιφαύσκων XVIII 500), the same word that is attested as *da-mo* = **dāmos** in the litigation recorded in one of the same Linear B texts that feature the verb *e-u-ke-to* = **eukhetoi** 'makes a claim' (Ep 704). In this context the **dāmos** actually figures as one of the parties involved in the litigation (the other party is a *i-je-re-ja* = **hiereia** 'priestess'). The role of the **dāmos** here is in line with the following definition of **dāmos** as used in the Linear B texts: "An administrative entity endowed with a juridical function" (formulation by Lejeune 1965.12). Similarly in Homeric diction **dēmos** can have the sense of 'district' (e.g., *Iliad* V 710; XVI 437, 514); in fact this sense may well be primary (cf. N 1979.149n6; also p. 56 above). In the context of an **agorā** 'assembly' (*Odyssey* ii 7, 10, 26; note again that the setting of the litigation depicted on the Shield takes place in an **agorā**: see n9) — which is the occasion for **agoreuein** 'speaking publicly' (*Odyssey* ii 15) — what a speaker says in public is technically **dēmion** 'of the **dēmos**' = public business for the **dēmos** (*Odyssey* ii 32, 44), as opposed to private business (ἐμὸν αὐτοῦ χρεῖος ii 45). The act of publicly saying what is **dēmion** is conveyed by the two verbs **piphausketai** 'declares' and **agoreuei** 'speaks publicly' (ii 32 and 44, respectively), the first of which is also found in collocation with **dēmos** at *Iliad* XVIII 500: **dēmōi piphauskōn** 'declaring to the **dēmos**'. What is being declared to/in the public, the **dēmos**, is being made public, that is, **dēmion**.

11. Here I am following the interpretation of Muellner 1976.105–106 ('but he said that he

with the pattern in a speech addressed by Ajax to Achilles (*Iliad* IX 632–636), where a defendant, charged with killing a plaintiff's brother or son, tries to assuage the plaintiff and offers a **poinē** 'fine' (IX 633, 636) that is then accepted by the assuaged plaintiff.[12] Thus the litigation depicted on the Shield is inconclusive,[13] and we find both parties in the process of submitting the case to arbitration:

ἄμφω δ' ἱέσθην ἐπὶ ἴστορι πεῖραρ ἑλέσθαι

Iliad XVIII 501

... and both were striving to come to terms in the presence of an arbitrator [**histōr**].

The process of arbitration is presented as a contest among a group of elders, where each takes his turn in offering, with **skēptron** 'scepter' in hand (XVIII 506),[14] a formula for resolution of the litigation (502–506); whoever pronounces the most equitable formula is to be awarded a given measure of gold (507–508).[15]

The pertinence of the **neikos** 'conflict' depicted on the Shield of Achilles goes far beyond the juridical issues of the litigation and subsequent arbitration narrated by the artifact. The narration has a dramatic as well as juridical dimension, and as such it has a bearing on the *Iliad* as a whole.[16] The refusal of the plaintiff to accept compensation is parallel to the refusal of Achilles to accept compensation (called **apoina**[17] at *Iliad* IX 20) from Agamemnon for the grievances that he suffered.[18] When Agamemnon, through his ambassadors, announces to Achilles an offer of compensation, one of these ambassadors, Ajax, actually contrasts the refusal on the part of Achilles with the acceptance on the part of a hypothetical plaintiff who is being offered

---

would accept nothing'), who notes the modal implication of negative **mēden** as opposed to **ouden**.

12. This passage figures prominently in the discussion that follows. Note the expression καί ῥ' ὁ μὲν ἐν δήμῳ μένει αὐτοῦ πόλλ' ἀποτείσας 'and he stays in the **dēmos**, making a big payment' here at *Iliad* IX 634, in light of the discussion at p. 251.

13. Another sign that it is inconclusive: the defendant rather than the plaintiff is represented as speaking first.

14. For a parallel collocation of **skēptron** with the verb aïssō, see *Iliad* III 216.

15. The process whereby a formula is offered for resolution is designated by the verb **dikazō** 'render judgment' (δίκαζον XVIII 506); the notion of pronouncing the most equitable formula is equated with pronouncing **dikē** 'judgment' in the most correct way, that is, 'in the straightest manner' (ὃς μετὰ τοῖσι δίκην ἰθύντατα εἴποι 508).

16. Muellner 1976.101, following the grammatical analysis of *Iliad* XVIII 500 by Corlu 1966.331–336, remarks that the interpretation of ἀναίνετο μηδὲν ἑλέσθαι as 'he [= the plaintiff] said that he would accept nothing' makes the conflict "dramatic."

17. On the formulaic parallelism of **apoina** and **poinē**, see Muellner, p. 102n11.

18. See Muellner, p. 106.

compensation, **poinē**, for the death of his brother or son (*Iliad* IX 632–636).[19]

The point made by Ajax is that the heart of a man can be assuaged by compensation even if he has lost someone as close as a brother or father, whereas Achilles is supposedly heartless in refusing compensation for the loss of someone who is surely far less close, the girl Briseis (*Iliad* IX 636–638).[20] Ajax is in effect accusing Achilles of ranking Briseis ahead of his own **hetairoi** 'comrades-in-arms' by failing to be swayed by the comrades' **philotēs**—the mutual state of being **philoi** 'near and dear' to each other (IX 628–632).[21] From the vantage point of the ambassadors, they as comrades-in-arms of Achilles should be closest to him—that is, most **philoi** 'near and dear' to him (so says Phoenix at IX 522).[22] From the superior vantage point of the overall narrative, however, someone is more **philos** 'near and dear' to Achilles than Briseis or the **hetairoi**—someone who is in fact so close to him as to be his other self, Patroklos.[23] For Achilles, Patroklos is πολὺ φίλτατος ... ἑταῖρος—the '**hetairos** who is the most **philos** by far' (*Iliad* XVII 411, 655). When Achilles gets the news that Patroklos has been killed, he mourns him as the **philos hetairos** whom he ranked above all other **hetairoi** (XVIII 80–81). For a man other than Achilles, as the god Apollo remarks, a brother or a son would be more **philos** than a comrade-in-arms (XXIV 46–49). For a man other than Achilles, then, the compensation for the death of a brother or a son would have to be greater than any compensation for the death of a comrade-in-arms, and yet even such a man comes to terms with death, whereas Achilles does not (ibid.). Apollo makes this remark in the context of blaming the heartlessness of Achilles (XXIV 39–45). Earlier, in the same context of blaming the heartlessness of Achilles (IX 628–632), we have seen that Ajax had contrasted the willingness of a hypothetical plaintiff to accept compensation for the death of someone who is even as close as a brother or a son (IX 632–636). In the first case the paradigm of accepting compensation is being applied to the hero's refusal of compensation offered by Agamemnon for the taking of Briseis; in the second case it is being applied to his refusal of any compensation offered by Priam for returning the corpse of Hektor (witness the use of **apoina** 'compensation' at XXII 349).[24] Thus in neither case is anyone intending compensation for the death of

19. See p. 252.

20. On the definition of the identity of a person by way of identifying with others, that is, by way of measuring the relative closeness of this person to others in a group, where the notion of closeness is expressed by way of the word **philos** 'near and dear', see N 1979.102–111.

21. This argument is undercut by the **par-ainesis** of Phoenix (on which see p. 196), as understood by Achilles: see N pp. 105–111.

22. The argument of Phoenix is in turn undercut by his own story: see ibid.

23. The topic of Patroklos as the ritual substitute and thereby the other self of Achilles has been examined extensively in N 1979.32–34, 292–294; also Sinos 1980 and Lowenstam 1981.

24. Cf. also *Iliad* XXIV 137, 139, 276, 502, 555, 579, 594, 686.

Patroklos. Yet the paradigms applied to the hero's refusal of compensation indicate that, from the superior vantage point of the overall narrative, what is really at stake for Achilles is coming to terms with his own death by accepting compensation for the death of someone who is more **philos** 'near and dear' to him than anyone else — his other self, Patroklos.

Which brings us back to the litigation depicted on the Shield of Achilles, a scene that reflects in microcosm the vantage point of the overall narrative.[25] By the time this scene is unveiled, Patroklos is already dead and Achilles has just been mourned by his mother as if he too were dead (at XVIII 54–60).[26] The anonymous little plaintiff pictured on the Shield is frozen in his inflexible position of refusing compensation for the death of a victim — a victim who is none other than the plaintiff himself from the overarching standpoint of the *Iliad*.[27] Soon after this scene, however, Achilles in the end accepts compensation from Agamemnon, who declares publicly that he was not **aitios** 'responsible' for causing the anger of Achilles — that it was really Zeus who inflicted **atē** 'aberration, derangement' (*Iliad* XIX 86–88, 134–136).[28] If Agamemnon really was **aitios**, of course, he would also be **aitios** for the death of Patroklos, which had resulted from the withdrawal of Achilles from his comrades-in-arms on account of his anger. But the situation is more complicated. Achilles too had incurred **atē** by refusing the entreaties of those who were near and dear to him.[29] As a reflection then of

25. In this connection I draw attention to the use of the word **sēma** to denote the device on a shield, that is, the images on a warrior's shield that convey his identity: see Euripides *Electra* 456, with reference to the Shield of Achilles. On the various **sēmata** in the *Seven against Thebes* of Aeschylus (e.g., 643), see Zeitlin 1982.

26. See N 1979.113, 183.

27. Cf. Muellner 1976.105–106; also N, pp. 109–110, 312.

28. See p. 242. That the dishonoring of Achilles by Agamemnon is a matter of Agamemnon's **atē** is already indicated by Achilles at *Iliad* I 412. That this **atē** was inflicted by Zeus is admitted by Achilles at XIX 270–274. In this same passage it is also made clear that the **atē** of Agamemnon caused the anger of Achilles.

29. The **atē** that is to befall Achilles is indicated at *Iliad* IX 502–512, where Phoenix tells of the **atē** that is to befall those who reject the **Litai**, goddesses of supplication personified (502–512). See p. 242. The **Litai** are said to heal the **atē** committed by wrongdoers when these wrongdoers offer compensation for such **atē** (502–507) — a reference to the **atē** that Agamemnon admits having committed and for which he stands ready to offer **apoina** 'compensation' (115–120, **apoina** at 120). In rejecting the **Litai**, one is rejecting the process whereby compensation can be awarded for damage suffered — and the word for 'damage' here is **Atē** personified (504, 505); compare the juridical attestations of **atē** in this sense, as discussed at p. 243. The punishment for such refusal is another round of **atē** — this time suffered by the one who rejects the **Litai** (510–512). For Achilles, this **atē** would be the death of Patroklos, who personally experiences **atē**, at the moment of his death, in the form of an aberration of the senses (XVI 685–687; 804–806; **atē** at 805). At XIX 270–274, Achilles seems to realize that both he and Agamemnon have been afflicted with **atē**. On this passage Michel 1983.298–299 comments: "Achilles now realizes to his horror that what had seemed to be his own intention and resolve was really the mysterious will of the god working through him. That sickening sense of the temporary alienation of one's will is what the realization of one's own **atē** always involves."

the **neikos** between Achilles and Agamemnon, the **neikos** between the anonymous plaintiff and the anonymous defendant on the Shield of Achilles presents the ultimate juridical problem. Who in the end is **aitios** 'responsible': is it one of the two heroes, or both, or, as one of them claims, the god himself, who is explicitly accused of inflicting **atē**?

The *Iliad* does not address such a problem directly; instead it refers the case to a **histōr** 'arbitrator' (XVIII 501). In the separate world of the Shield of Achilles, a group of arbitrators must compete with each other in rendering justice, until one winning solution can at last be found. Such a winning solution is also needed for the *Iliad* as a whole, which does not formally take a position on who is **aitios** in its narrative. The question is left up to a figure who is beyond the *Iliad*, that is, to the **histōr**, whose function it is to render **dikē** 'judgment'.[30]

At this juncture we may shift our emphasis from a preoccupation with the Homeric stance of Herodotus. It is time to consider his Hesiodic stance, as reflected in the concept of **historiā**. As one who pronounces **dikē** 'judgment', the **histōr** 'arbitrator' of the Shield of Achilles fits a pattern that is clearly visible in the portrait of the ideal king in the Hesiodic *Theogony* (80–93). The ideal king is one who has the moral authority to arbitrate and thus bring to an end 'even a great **neikos** [= conflict]' (αἶψα τε καὶ μέγα νεῖκος ἐπισταμένως κατέπαυσεν *Theogony* 87).[31] The ideal king stops the **neikos** 'conflict' in the setting of an **agorā** 'public assembly' (ἀγορεύων/ἀγορῆφι/ἀγρομένοισιν *Theogony* 86/89/92), which is also the setting for the **neikos** that is to be stopped by the **histōr** (both words **neikos** and **agorā** at *Iliad* XVIII 497).[32] To be able to arbitrate, Hesiod explains, kings must be **ekhephrones** 'sound of mind' (*Theogony* 88).[33] This quality is the same one that is required of the kings who are to understand the **ainos**—here we may translate the word as 'fable'—told by Hesiod in the *Works and Days*:

---

30. *Iliad* XVIII 506: ἀμοιβηδὶς δὲ δίκαζον 'they took turns in rendering **dikē** [= judgment]'; the prize is to go to ὃς μετὰ τοῖσι δίκην ἰθύντατα εἴποι 'the one among them who pronounces **dikē** in the straightest way' (508).

31. The ideal king is described as 'sorting out the divine laws [= themis in the plural]' (διακρίνοντα θέμιστας *Theogony* 85) by way of his 'straight judgments [**dikē** in the plural]' (ἰθείῃσι δίκῃσιν *Theogony* 86). We may compare the depiction of the ideal **histōr** 'arbitrator' on the Shield of Achilles as 'the one among them who pronounces **dikē** in the straightest way' (*Iliad* XVIII 508); see n30.

32. See p. 251.

33. Note the wording of *Theogony* 88–90: τοὔνεκα γὰρ βασιλῆες ἐχέφρονες, οὕνεκα λαοῖς | βλαπτομένοις ἀγορῆφι μετάτροπα ἔργα τελεῦσι | ῥηϊδίως, μαλακοῖσι παραιφάμενοι ἐπέεσσιν 'It is for this reason that there are kings, sound of mind, namely, because they can easily turn right around the [wrong] things | that are done to people who are wronged in the public assembly [**agorā**]. | They can do it by persuasion, using soft words.'

νῦν δ' αἶνον βασιλεῦσιν ἐρέω³⁴ φρονέουσι καὶ αὐτοῖς

Hesiod Works and Days 202

Now I will tell the kings a fable [**ainos**] — sound of mind [**phroneontes**] as they are.

Hesiod's presupposition of the kings' soundness of mind is really a condition here: if the kings do not understand the **ainos**, then they are not sound of mind.³⁵ These same kings have so far in the *Works and Days* displayed just the opposite of soundness, in that they have earlier been described as ready to pronounce a **dikē** 'judgment' that is unsound (οἱ τήνδε δίκην ἐθέλουσι δικάσσαι *Works and Days* 39). This unsound **dikē** was pronounced by the kings in the context of their arbitrating a **neikos** 'conflict' between Hesiod and his brother Perses (*Works and Days* 35);³⁶ it is in this light that Hesiod seeks to instruct them, by way of his **ainos** (202) of "The Hawk and the Nightingale,"³⁷ in how to pronounce a sound **dikē**. If the kings understand the **ainos**, then they will have learned the lesson that **dikē**, in its ultimate sense of 'justice', is superior to its opposite, **hubris** 'outrage';³⁸ if they do not understand, however, then their very *raison d'être*, which is to pronounce **dikē** 'judgment', is undermined, and they are left without any authority.

In fact the *Works and Days* claims an authority of its own, not dependent on that of any earthly king. It is founded on the higher authority of Zeus as a model for kings. When a king pronounces **dikē** 'judgment' (as at *Theogony* 86), he is in effect 'sorting out' (= verb **dia-krīnō**: διακρίνοντα *Theogony*

---

34. I have not followed the reading βασιλεῦσ' ἐρέω of West 1978.205.

35. Cf. West, pp. 205–206.

36. This unsound **dikē** at *Works and Days* 39, pronounced by kings who are described as **dōrophagoi** 'those who devour gifts' (ibid.; also 264), is mentioned again at *Works and Days* 249 and 269 (cf. also 264); cf. N 1982.58–60.

37. The **ainos** 'fable' of "The Hawk and the Nightingale" is told at *Works and Days* 202–212. The hawk seizes the nightingale, described as an **aoidos** 'singer' (that is, 'poet': see *Works and Days* 208), on the premise that might makes right (I paraphrase 206, 207, 210), and he boasts of having the ultimate power of either releasing or devouring his victim (209). On the importance of this **ainos**, *as a bird omen*, in the overall structure of the *Works and Days*, see p. 65.

38. The "moral" of the fable becomes clear at *Works and Days* 274–285: Perses is urged to espouse **dikē** in the ultimate sense of 'justice' (275, 278, 279, 283), for those without it will devour each other like wild beasts (276–278). The parallel with the hawk, whose stance of might makes right corresponds to the stance of kings (n37), imposes itself. As for **dikē** in the ultimate sense of 'justice', I argue in N 1982.57–61 that **dikē** is 'judgment' in an immediate sense, as at *Works and Days* 39, 249, 269 (n36), and that this 'judgment' becomes 'justice' (personified as the goddess **Dikē**, *Works and Days* 256) only with the passage of time, under the supervision of the gods (*Works and Days* 217–218; cf. Solon F 4.14–16 W). Further, I argue (ibid.) that the *Works and Days* dramatizes the actual passage of time required for the workings of **Dikē** to take effect, so that the faulty 'judgment' of the kings (**dikē** at *Works and Days* 39, 249, 269) may be transformed eventually into the 'justice' of Zeus (**dikē** at *Works and Days* 256, 275, etc.).

85) what is **themis** 'divine law' and what is not (that is, διακρίνοντα θέμιστας ibid.). Still, as we see from the *Works and Days*, the **dikē** 'judgment' of a king may not always be the same thing as 'justice'.[39] For the equation of 'judgment' and 'justice', the model of Zeus must come into play: at the beginning of the *Works and Days*, Hesiod invokes Zeus to keep **themis** [plural] 'divine laws' straight by way of his divine **dikē** — where the 'judgment' of Zeus is tantamount to the 'justice' of Zeus.[40] This action of Zeus, the pronouncing of **dikē**, is explicitly made parallel to the words of Hesiod as he speaks to Perses (*Works and Days* 10),[41] and we must keep in mind that the words of Hesiod as addressed to Perses are in fact the *Works and Days* as a poem. Thus the justice of Zeus and the *Works and Days* are treated as coefficients in the context of a **neikos** 'conflict' that Hesiod and Perses must 'sort out' *for themselves* (again, = verb **dia-krīnō**: διακρινώμεθα νεῖκος 'let us sort out for ourselves this **neikos**' *Works and Days* 35).[42] Since Hesiod is here saying that he and Perses should resolve their conflict themselves, it is clear that their **neikos** — and the whole poem for that matter — will not in the end require the authority of a king as arbitrator. In fact after the last admonition of Hesiod to the kings, at *Works and Days* 263–264, the kings are never to be heard of again in the poem. From a dramatic point of view, it is as if the poem were eliminating the authority of kings while maintaining the ultimate authority of Zeus as king; I interpret this state of affairs as a poetic reflex of the historical fact that the institution of kingship was obsolescent in most Greek cities by the time of the Archaic period.[43]

Thus the *Works and Days* of Hesiod, a poem founded on the authority of Zeus as king, can teach the citizens of cities that are no longer ruled by kings. In fact it can teach all citizens of all cities. The structure of the poem, which a comparative study can relate to the cognate juridical traditions of India as embedded in the body of wise sayings known as the *Law Code of Manu*, reflects a moral authority that could in theory serve as foundation for a law code.[44] But the laws of Greek cities in the Archaic and Classical periods are a local affair, with each law code reflecting the idiosyncratic history and politics of each city. Thus the *Works and Days*, by stopping short of formulating laws, can communicate a Panhellenic authority for the diverse law codes of all cities — whether the city's government be an oligarchy, a tyranny, or even

39. See p. 256.

40. N 1982.58.

41. N, pp. 58–60.

42. This time the verb **dia-krīnō** is in the middle voice, whence the translation 'let us sort out *for ourselves*'; contrast the active voice of **dia-krīnō** at *Theogony* 85 (διακρίνοντα θέμιστας), where the agent is the ideal king.

43. Cf. N, p. 60; this view differs from that of West 1978.151, who tentatively retrojects to the life and times of Hesiod the testimony of Diodorus Siculus 4.29.4 about the rulers of Thespiai.

44. On the correlation of ritual and ethical correctness, see N, p. 61.

a democracy. Even in a democracy, the ideological basis of authority is the **dikē** 'justice' of Zeus, just as it is elaborated in the *Works and Days:* thus, for example, the laws of Athens, as the poetry of the city's lawgiver Solon proclaims, are founded on the authority of Zeus *as king* (Solon F 31W).[45]

The juridical authority of earthly kings is eliminated not only in the *Works and Days*. Even in the *Iliad*, an epic about warriors who are simultaneously represented as kings,[46] the scene of litigation on the Shield of Achilles leaves out any mention of kings; the group of men taking turns at standing with **skēptron** 'scepter' in hand and arbitrating the litigation by pronouncing **dikē** (XVIII 503–508) are described not as kings, but merely as **gerontes** 'elders' (503). This omission is remarkable in view of the fact that the **skēptron** is the visible sign of a king's authority in the *Iliad* (e.g., IX 97–99).[47] Another such omission in the Hesiodic *Theogony* is even more remarkable in view of the fact that a theogony is by nature a formal confirmation of royal authority.[48] In the *Theogony* we find a significant omission in the detailed portrait of the ideal king (80–93), that man who can arbitrate the ultimate **neikos** 'conflict' (87): the ideal king is not pictured as wielding a **skēptron**. Instead the man who is given a **skēptron** is Hesiod himself, who gets it from the Muses (*Theogony* 30). Thus the man who tells the **ainos** in the *Works and Days* is the same man who holds the symbol of ultimate juridical authority in the *Theogony*.[49]

Let us try to sum up what we know about the **histōr** 'arbitrator'. From the comparative evidence to be found in Homeric and Hesiodic poetry, we see that a **histōr** is a man who has the authority, derived from the kingship of Zeus, to solve conflicts, even by deciding who is **aitios** 'responsible' for what. His mode of discourse, based on privileged information, is that of the **ainos**.

In the mode of a **histōr**, the **historiā** 'inquiry' of Herodotus likewise takes a position on who is **aitios**. When Croesus, like Agamemnon, declares publicly that a god was **aitios** for the misfortunes that have been narrated, the **historiā** represents the god Apollo as having the last word: Croesus himself is manifestly **aitios** (Herodotus 1.91.4).[50] Moreover, the man who conducts the **historiā**, Herodotus, publicly takes the same position, and the word that

45. N, p. 60. For a comparative study of the theme of "ruler's truth," see Watkins 1979; cf. also Martin 1984.

46. On this subject, cf. N 1983.198–203; cf. N 1979.120 §3n3.

47. Further details in N 1982.52–53.

48. This point about the nature of any theogony is argued in N, p. 56. A survey of theogonic traditions native to diverse societies of the world reveals that a basic function of a theogony is to confirm the authority that regulates a given social group. The authority figure of the king symbolically incorporates society in that the king embodies the community through his status as the very incarnation of the body politic. Cf. p. 158.

49. On the Panhellenism of the Hesiodic *Theogony*: N 1982.51–57.

50. Cf. p. 241.

he uses in this context to designate his privileged mode of communication is sēmainō (1.5.3)[51] —a word that is characteristic of the discourse of the ainos.[52]

By now we see more clearly how the **historiā** of Herodotus, in seeking to establish who was responsible for the ultimate conflict between Hellenes and barbarians, is analogous to the task of the **histōr** depicted on the Shield of Achilles. In the microcosm of the Shield, an ideal **histōr** must seek the most equitable solution of a conflict between two litigants; in the macrocosm of the *Iliad* this same conflict recapitulates the ultimate conflict that leads off the entire narrative, the **neikos** of Achilles and Agamemnon.

But the question still remains: what is the semantic relationship of the word **histōr** in the sense of 'arbitrator' with the verb **historeō** 'inquire, conduct an inquiry' and the noun **historiā** 'inquiry' as used in Herodotus? The derivation of **histōr** from **oida** ("I have seen: therefore I know")[53] and its primary sense of 'witness'[54] can be misleading as we examine the usages of **historeō** and **historiā**: although the process of inquiry conveyed by these two words is primarily on the level of seeing (e.g., Herodotus 2.99.1),[55] it can also be on the level of hearing but not seeing (e.g., 2.29.1).[56] So also with the word **oida** itself: after all, knowledge may at times be founded on hearing only (cf., e.g., Herodotus 1.5). The semantic evolution of **histōr** from 'one who sees' = 'eyewitness'[57] to something like 'he who sees beyond what others see' (where the vision may be figurative as well as real) is comparable to what we find in the French word *voyant:* literally this word means 'one who is endowed with sight', but the *voyant* is in fact endowed not with normal sight but "something that goes beyond it, 'second sight'."[58] It seems to me no

51. Cf. pp. 229, 233, and following.

52. Ibid.

53. Cf. p. 250.

54. Ibid.

55. The wording of Herodotus 2.99.1 is worth scrutiny: μέχρι μὲν τούτου ὄψις τε ἐμὴ καὶ γνώμη καὶ ἱστορίη ταῦτα λέγουσά ἐστι, τὸ δὲ ἀπὸ τοῦδε Αἰγυπτίους ἔρχομαι λόγους ἐρέων κατὰ τὰ ἤκουον· προσέσται δέ τι αὐτοῖσι καὶ τῆς ἐμῆς ὄψιος 'up to this point it is my **opsis** [= seeing] and **gnōmē** [= judgment] and **historiā** that is saying these things, but from this point onward I am going to tell the Egyptian accounts according to what I heard; to which will be added a portion that will be my own **opsis**'.

56. Note again the wording of this passage, Herodotus 2.29.1: ἄλλου δὲ οὐδενὸς οὐδὲν ἐδυνάμην πυθέσθαι, ἀλλὰ τοσόνδε μὲν ἄλλο ἐπὶ μακρότατον ἐπυθόμην, μέχρι μὲν Ἐλεφαντίνης πόλιος αὐτόπτης ἐλθών, τὸ δ' ἀπὸ τούτου ἀκοῇ ἤδη ἱστορέων 'I was unable to ascertain anything from any other person [except the aforementioned], having gone as **autoptēs** [= eyewitness] as far as the polis of Elephantine, but from there on conducting the **historiā** by way of **akoē** [= hearing]'. Cf. Herodotus 2.123.1.

57. Cf. pp. 250 and following.

58. Benveniste 1973.527 = 1969 II 278; this example is cited in the context of Benveniste's discussion of Latin *superstes* as a witness "who has his being beyond," one "who stands over the matter" (p. 526 = 1969 II 276).

accident that the first word of the first oracle directly quoted by Herodotus, where the voice of Apollo declares that it knows the number of every grain of sand and the full dimensions of the sea, is **oida** 'I know' (1.47.3).

In this light we may also consider the semantic specialization of Latin *arbiter*. From the survey by Emile Benveniste of this word's usage in the diction of Plautus,[59] it becomes clear that the *arbiter*, unlike the *testis*, is a 'witness' only in a special sense: whereas the *testis* is known to the parties in a given case or situation, the *arbiter* may or may not be known and may or may not even be seen:

> *secede huc nunciam si videtur, procul,*
> *ne arbitri dicta nostra arbitrari queant*

Plautus Captivi 219–220

Come over here, please, a way off,
so that *arbitrī* may not *arbitrārī* what we say.

> *eamus intro, non utibilest hic locus factis tuis*
> *dum memoramus, arbitri ut sint qui praetereant per vias*

Plautus Mercator 1005–1006

Let's go inside. This is not a suitable place for us to talk about what you've done.
Those who pass by on the streets may be *arbitrī*.

> *miquidem iam arbitri vicini sunt, meae quid fiat domi,*
> *ita per impluvium intro spectant*

Plautus Miles 158–159

The neighbors are now *arbitrī* of whatever happens in my house:
they peer through the impluvium.

In explaining how such a "clandestine witness" as an *arbiter* evolves into an arbitrator, a judge, Benveniste adduces the semantics of *iūdex*:[60]

---

59. Benveniste, pp. 396–397 = 1969 II 119–122.

60. Benveniste, pp. 397–398 = 1969 II 121–122. See also Benveniste, pp. 389–392 = 1969 II 111–113 on this same word *iūdex*, a compound built from *iūs* in the sense of 'juridical formula' and from the root *deik-/*dik- as in *dīcō* 'say' (note the collocation *iūs dīcere*) or in the *dic-* of *dicis causā* 'for the sake of proper form'. I should draw special attention to a derivative of *dic-*, *in-dic-āre*, the English borrowing of which, *indicate*, I have been using to translate Greek **sēmainō**. The Latin *dīcō* is cognate with Greek **deik-nu-mi** 'show, indicate, make manifest'; moreover, Latin *dic-* as in *dicis causā* and *in-dic-āre* is cognate with Greek **dikē** 'judgment, justice'. In this light ἱστορίης ἀπόδεξις 'the **apo-deixis** of the **historiā**' in the prooemium of Herodotus becomes all the more pertinent.

We must recall that in the most ancient sense of the word the name *iūdex* was given to every authoritative person charged with passing judgment in a disputed case. In principle it was the king, the consul, the holder of all powers. But for practical reasons this power was delegated to a private judge who, according to the nature of the cases, was called *iūdex* or *iūdex privātus*, or *iūdex selectus* or *arbiter*. The last was empowered to decide in all cases which were not foreseen by the law. [. . .] In effect, the *arbiter* makes his decision not according to formulae and the laws but by a personal assessment and in the name of equity. The *arbiter* is in fact a *iūdex* who acts as an *arbiter*; he judges by coming between the two parties from outside like someone who has been present at the affair without being seen, who can therefore give judgment on the facts freely and with authority, regardless of all precedent in the light of the circumstances.

Although Benveniste does not directly adduce **histōr** or **historiā** in this connection, we can see that his working definition of *arbiter* is pertinent to the meanings of both these Greek words.[61] The **histōr**, whose authority is derived from Zeus as king, can be understood as thereby having the privileged vantage point of the gods themselves, who can see without being seen.[62] The same goes for the **historiā** 'inquiry' of Herodotus: when he **sēmainei** 'indicates' that Croesus is **aitios** 'responsible' for the ultimate conflict between Hellenes and barbarians (Herodotus 1.5.3),[63] he is in effect speaking from a privileged vantage point similar to that of the god Apollo himself, who **sēmainei** 'indicates' by way of his Oracle (Heraclitus 22 B 93 DK)[64] — and who likewise declares that Croesus is **aitios** (Herodotus 1.91.4).[65]

In this connection, now that we are reaching the end of our inquiry into both the Homeric and the Hesiodic stances of Herodotus, it is fitting to reiterate what Herodotus had said about the Panhellenic contributions of Homer and Hesiod: these are the poets 'who indicated the visible forms [**eidos** plural][66] of the gods'. Again the word translated by 'indicate' here is

61. The pertinence of *arbiter* to **histōr** is brought up at a later point in Benveniste's discussion, 1973.442 = 1969 II 174–175, in another connection.

62. I have in mind the oath expressions cited at p. 251. We may also compare the invisible **phulakes** 'guardians' of **Dikē** 'justice' at Hesiod *Works and Days* 124–126, as discussed in N 1979.153; also the theme of the Eye of Zeus at *Works and Days* 267–269, as discussed in N 1983.42–43.

63. Cf. pp. 229, 233 and following.

64. See p. 234.

65. Cf. p. 241.

66. The derivation of **eidos** 'visible form' from the verb represented by the aorist **uid- of **idein** 'see' is pertinent to the semantics of **historiā** as discussed at pp. 250 and following.

sēmainō (εἴδεα αὐτῶν σημήναντες Herodotus 2.53.2).[67] In other words Homer and Hesiod are represented by Herodotus as communicating in the same mode in which Herodotus himself communicates. We have seen that this is in fact not so, that the discourse of Herodotus in fact makes the sort of judgments that are avoided in a poem like the *Iliad*. Still the discourse of Herodotus, by implicitly claiming identity with the discourse of Homer, is appropriating it. Similarly we have seen that the discourse of Pindar, distinct as it is from the discourse of Homer, nonetheless claims identity with it and thus appropriates it, possesses it. Such parallelism of appropriation is yet another indication that the discourse of Herodotus has close connections with the **ainos**, which is the essence of Pindar's lyric poetry in contexts of appropriating epic.[68]

Such parallelism between Herodotus and Pindar has been our concern since the beginning of Chapter 8, with the assertion that the **historiā** 'inquiry' of Herodotus, like the **ainos** of epinician poets like Pindar, is a form of discourse that claims the authority to possess and control the epic of heroes.[69] I had then proposed to support this assertion by arguing that the traditions underlying the **historiā** are akin to those underlying the **ainos** of epinician lyric poetry. It is time to take stock of all that we have observed so far about the **historiā** of Herodotus.

The very word **historiā**, as used by Herodotus in his prooemium, indicates the juridical aspect of what Herodotus has to say. In finding Croesus guilty or **aitios** 'responsible' for the ultimate conflict between Hellenes and barbarians, Herodotus is taking a stance similar to that of the **histōr** on the Shield of Achilles. Earlier we saw that Croesus proves himself to be guilty even by way of his behavior, which the narrative of Herodotus represents as a paradigm of **atē** 'derangement'. This representation is achieved in a quasi-juridical framework insofar as **atē** is defined through the teachings of the lawgiver Solon. But the **atē** of Croesus, as we have noticed, is not confronted directly by Solon in the encounter dramatized by Herodotus.[70] Moreover, Solon in Herodotus' *Histories* does not tell Croesus directly what we find him teaching in his own poetry, that **atē** is brought about by **hubris**.[71] This indirectness is not just a matter of diplomacy on Solon's part. Rather it can best be explained by considering the medium of Herodotus, **historiā**. With his privileged position of knowledge, the master of **historiā** is implicitly narrating divine actions as he explicitly narrates human actions.[72]

---

67. The passage is quoted at p. 215. Note again the etymological pertinence of Latin *in-dic-āre*, as discussed at p. 260.

68. Ch.6, Ch.7.

69. Cf. pp. 215 and following.

70. Cf. p. 248.

71. Ibid.

72. Cf. pp. 239 and following.

The divine pattern of **atē** as brought about by **hubris** is for Herodotus an implicit message as he **sēmainei** 'indicates' that Croesus was in the wrong. The task still at hand is to show how the implicitness of Herodotus, and even his dramatization of Solon as a sage who formulates implicit messages about the dangers of **hubris** and **atē**, is akin to the communication of Pindar through the **ainos**.

The implicit **hubris** of Croesus the Lydian is indicated by the context of the story of Croesus and Solon in the *Histories* of Herodotus. This story makes it clear that the Persians acquired the characteristic of being **habroi** 'luxuriant', which as we shall see is a basic feature of **hubris**, from the Lydians, whom they had conquered: before the conquest, in the words of Herodotus, the Persians had nothing that was **habron** 'luxuriant' (ἦν οὔτε ἁβρὸν οὔτε ἀγαθὸν οὐδέν 1.71.4; cf. also the context of οὐκ ἄλλο ἀγαθὸν οὐδέν at 1.70.3).[73] Before the Lydians, the story goes, the Persians had a 'harsh' life, living in a 'harsh' country.[74]

In order to understand the traditional theme that being **habros** 'luxuriant' is a basic feature of **hubris**, let us turn to the traditions about the **ktisis** 'foundation' of the Greek city of Colophon, as reported by Phylarchus: in the beginning the colonizers of Colophon led a harsh life (Phylarchus FGH 81 F 66 in Athenaeus 526a), but eventually they turned to **truphē** 'luxuriance' when they came into contact with the Lydians (ibid.).[75] At this point Phy-

---

73. That the Lydians are characterized by what is **habron** 'luxuriant' is a theme also reflected in the epithet **pod-(h)abros** 'with a footstep that is luxuriant [**habros**]' applied to Croesus the Lydian in the oracular pronouncement at Delphi as quoted at Herodotus 1.55.2 (ποδαβρέ). I suggest that the notion of *foot* in this epithet can refer not only to a graceful step but even to its corresponding mimesis, a graceful *dance*-step, as conveyed, for example, by the use of ἁβροβάται in Aeschylus *Persians* 1073 (for the diction, cf. ἁβρὸν βαίνουσα παλλεύκῳ ποδί in Euripides *Medea* 1164; cf. also 830). For a possible reference to an *ungraceful* dance-step, as a mimesis of **hubris**, cf. Sophocles *Oedipus Tyrannus* 878.

74. To quote from Herodotus 1.71.2: χώρην ἔχοντες τρηχέαν 'having a harsh country'. On the detail of the leather clothing worn by the Persians before they became contaminated by the Lydians, at 1.71.2, cf. p. 389.

75. Phylarchus uses the expression εἰς τρυφὴν ἐξώκειλαν 'they [= the Colophonians] ran aground on **truphē** [= luxuriance]' (FGH 81 F 66). Elsewhere he uses the expression ἐξοκείλαντες εἰς τρυφήν 'running aground on **truphē**' in describing the luxuriance of the people of Sybaris (Phylarchus 81 F 45 in Athenaeus 521c). After this description Phylarchus uses the expression ἐξοκείλαντες εἰς ὕβριν 'running aground on **hubris**' in describing the savage behavior of the people of Sybaris (81 F 45 in Athenaeus 521d): they had murdered the ambassadors of the people of Croton and cast out their corpses to be devoured by wild animals. That was the beginning of the misfortunes of Sybaris, reports Phylarchus, μηνίσαντος τοῦ δαιμονίου 'because of the anger [**mēnis**] of the **daimonion** [= power of the **daimōn**]' (ibid.); the anger is manifested by portents: the statue of Hera vomits bile and a fountain of blood erupts in her shrine. In this story, as elsewhere, the luxuriance of a society goes hand in hand with a propensity to savage behavior. For the nautical image of 'running aground on **truphē/hubris**', compare Theognis 855–856: the city often runs aground, like a veering ship, because of the degeneration of its élite. On the equivalence of **habrosunē** and **truphē** as 'luxuriance', see Knox 1984.

larchus (F 66 in Athenaeus 526a-b) quotes the following words of Xenophanes about the Colophonians:

ἁβροσύνας δὲ μαθόντες ἀνωφελέας παρὰ Λυδῶν,
ὄφρα τυραννίης ἦσαν ἄνευ στυγερῆς . . .

Xenophanes F 3.1–2 W = 21 B 3 DK

Learning the useless ways of luxuriance [= being **habros**] from the
   Lydians,
while they [= the Colophonians] were still free of hateful tyranny . . .[76]

The Colophonians are ultimately ruined by their own **hubris**:

ὕβρις καὶ Μάγνητας ἀπώλεσε καὶ Κολοφῶνα
καὶ Σμύρνην· πάντως Κύρνε καὶ ὕμμ' ἀπολεῖ

Theognis 1103–1104

Hubris ruined the Magnesians, and Colophon
and Smyrna; and it will assuredly ruin you [plural] too, Kyrnos!

The expression Κολοφωνία ὕβρις 'Colophonian **hubris**' is in fact proverbial
(*Corpus Paroemiographorum Graecorum* I p. 266.6–7).[77]

   In the passage just quoted from Xenophanes, the ruin of Colophon is
linked with **turanniē** 'tyranny', and we get further thematic details from
Theopompus (FGH 115 F 117 in Athenaeus 526c): the luxuriance of the
Colophonians resulted in **turannis** 'tyranny' and **stasis** [plural] 'discord', so
that the city and its people were 'destroyed'. In this case 'tyranny' is probably to be understood as some form of political domination by Lydia: Herodotus, for example, refers to the capture of the lower city of Colophon by
Gyges the Lydian (1.14.4), parallel to the capture of Smyrna by Alyattes, the
great-grandson of Gyges (1.16.2).[78] But the point of this traditional story
about Colophon seems to be that the misfortune of tyranny was caused primarily from within, not from without: the luxuriance of the Colophonians
brought about their defeat at the hands of their external enemies. A parallel

76. The whole passage of Xenophanes as quoted by Phylarchus FGH 81 F 66 should be compared with a passage about the luxuriance of the Samians, ascribed to Asius and quoted by Duris
of Samos FGH 76 F 60 in Athenaeus 525e-f.

77. That this theme is linked ultimately with the **ktisis** 'foundation'/'colonization' of Colophon is suggested by another text, Mimnermus F 9.3–4 W, where the actual colonizers of Colophon, the speaker included, are characterized as βίην ὑπέροπλον ἔχοντες 'men of overweening
violence [**biē**]' and ὕβριος ἡγεμόνες 'leaders of **hubris**'. Further discussion in N 1985.52–53.

78. On the eventual domination of Colophon and Smyrna by Lydia, see Jeffery
1976.224–225. In his own narrative Herodotus chooses not to present these instances of the
domination of Hellenes by previous tyrants of Lydia as equivalent to the later domination by
Croesus. The effect is to sharpen the parallelism between the Lydian Empire of Croesus and the
Athenian Empire, on which theme see pp. 229, 308 and following.

point is made in the story about the ruin of the Magnesians, whose luxuriance brought about their defeat at the hands of the Ephesians (Callinus F 3 W; Archilochus F 20 W; cf. Theognis 603–604).[79] The ruin of the Magnesians is mentioned alongside that of the Colophonians and that of the Smyrnaeans in the poem of Theognis quoted above (1103–1104).

For Theognis, such stories are made applicable to the **hubris** that the poet finds in his own city of Megara (ibid.; also Theognis 603–604). In another poem, Theognis 1081–1082b, the voice of the poet goes so far as to say that Megara is pregnant with a future tyrant, a man of **hubris**.[80] From this image of the pregnant city we see most clearly that tyranny can be generated from within. That the man of **hubris** in this poem is indeed a tyrant becomes evident from another poem, Theognis 39–52, a variant in which the emphasis shifts from the **hubris** represented by the future tyrant to the **hubris** that could bring forth the tyrant in the first place. Again the poet says that his city is pregnant (Theognis 39), but this time he fears that it will give birth to a man who will be 'a corrector of our base **hubris**' (εὐθυντῆρα κακῆς ὕβριος ἡμετέρης Theognis 40).[81] He goes on to say that the unjust behavior of his city's élite leads to **stasis** [plural] 'discord', intrasocietal **phonos** [plural] 'killings', and **monarkhoi** 'monarchs' (Theognis 51–52).[82] This triad of misfortunes matches closely the one found in the celebrated Herodotean passage known as the Debate about the Constitutions,[83] where the Persian king Darius is dramatized as praising tyranny and blaming oligarchy: in an oligarchy, says Darius, the behavior of the élite leads to **stasis** [plural], from which arises **phonos** 'killing', from which arises **monarkhiā** 'monarchy' — so that monarchy, he reasons, *must* be superior to oligarchy (Herodotus 3.83.3).[84] As

---

79. The sources that make this story explicit are Strabo 14.1.40 C647 and Athenaeus 525c. The disasters befalling Magnesia are compounded: apparently after their capture by the Ephesians, Magnesia was destroyed by the invading Cimmerians (Strabo ibid.). On the grounds that Callinus (F 3 W) mentions the Magnesians as still flourishing while Archilochus (F 20 W) refers to their misfortunes at the hands of their enemies, Strabo (ibid.) and Clement (*Stromateis* 1.131.7–8) reason that Callinus is an earlier poet than Archilochus. Such reasoning, perpetuated in latter-day scholarship on the Greek lyric poets, should be subject to doubt in view of the poetic device where the poet is presented as foreseeing a disaster that is yet to befall a community (on this theme see, for example, Solon F 9 W and the commentary in N 1985.45; also Theognis 39–52 and 1081–1082b, to be discussed immediately below).

80. An important variant, Theognis 39–52, is taken up in the discussion that immediately follows.

81. On **euthunō** 'straighten, correct' in the sense of 'check the growth of a plant, prune' as a metaphor for **dikē** 'justice', see N 1985.61; cf. Michelini 1978.

82. See pp. 181–82; 368.

83. Ibid.

84. The élite behave as follows: each of them strives eagerly for **aretē** 'excellence', and great hatreds break out as a result (again Herodotus 3.83.3). Compare Theognis 401–406: the man who is too eager for **aretē** and seeks **kerdos** 'personal gain' commits a grave error: his divine punishment is that he thinks that **kaka** 'bad things' are **agatha** 'good' and the other way around. On **kerdos** as a potential aspect of **hubris**, see Theognis 46 and 50; also 835, discussed at p. 275.

this particular passage makes clear, the word **monarkhos** 'monarch' is the attenuated equivalent of **turannos** 'tyrant' (Herodotus 3.80.2 in conjunction with 3.80.4).[85]

The point of this traditional topic is that whether tyranny afflicts a community from without or from within, its causes are from within. Granted, the Hellenes apparently learned the word **turannos** from the Lydians, as we may infer from its early attestation, applied to Gyges the Lydian, in Archilochus F 19 W (cf. Hippias of Elis FGH 6 F 6).[86] Still the experience of tyranny and of its causes is a native Hellenic tradition. While it is a matter of history that Colophon was culturally influenced and then politically subjugated by the Lydians, it is a matter of myth making that the stories of what happened in Colophon and elsewhere became paradigms for analogous patterns of happenings in other Hellenic city-states. The analogies vary considerably, but the language that expresses the analogous patterns follows closely the language of the paradigms. For example, whatever happened in Colophon or Smyrna or Magnesia is surely different from the ongoing events in mainland Megara, seemingly far beyond the reach of luxuriant Lydians or savage Cimmerians.[87] And yet, for Theognis, the same **hubris** that destroyed those three luxuriating cities from within 'now' threatens to destroy Megara as well (Theognis 1103–1104; cf. 603–604). This kind of warning by the figure of Theognis is typical of the mode of discourse that we have already identified as the **ainos**.[88]

In the Croesus story of Herodotus, a similar warning is ostensibly being made — not about any Hellenic city but about the Lydians themselves. Their ultimate luxuriance, manifested in the material over-acquisitiveness of their king Croesus as he tries to conquer the Persian Empire, leads to their own

85. See pp. 181 and following.

86. Cf. the testimonia collected at Archilochus F 19 W, most notably *Etymologicum Gudianum* s.v. τύραννος, where we learn that the word **turannos** is derived from an epithet of Gyges as King of Lydia — a piece of information inferred apparently from the actual poetry of Archilochus. Also, I draw attention to the use of the word **turannos** for the title of Croesus as King of the Lydian Empire (e.g., Herodotus 1.6.1; cf. especially the use of **turannis** in the context of 1.14.1). As we shall see in detail later at pp. 275 and following, the supreme generosity of Croesus in his public display of material offerings to Apollo at Delphi (Herodotus 1.50.1–1.53–2) is a traditional theme in the epinician lyric poetry of Pindar and Bacchylides, directly compared to the generosity of Hieron as Tyrant of Syracuse. It is in this context that we can understand the nonpejorative application of the word **turannos** to Hieron, as in Pindar *Pythian* 3.85, discussed in pp. 174 and following. It is also in this context that we can understand the naming of an otherwise unknown Athenian as **Kroisos** = Croesus, memorialized in an inscription at the base of a *kouros*-statue, on which see p. 157.

87. I say *seemingly* because we have to reckon with the political relations of Megara as mother city with its daughter cities, on which subject see p. 71.

88. In the context of Theognis 681–682: pp. 148 and following; also pp. 181, 183, and following.

defeat. In this case, however, the conquerors learn the ways of luxuriance from the defeated, and not the other way around: the Persians, who had previously led a harsh life, acquire the quality of being **habros** 'luxuriant' from the Lydians (Herodotus 1.71.2).[89] Ominously, however, the harsh life of the Persians before Croesus is different from that of men like the early settlers of Colophon. As the captured king Croesus observes, in reaction to the sight of Persians looting the captured Lydian city of Sardis, the Persians are 'by nature men of **hubris**' (Πέρσαι φύσιν ἐόντες ὑβρισταί ... Herodotus 1.89.2). As we are about to see, **hubris** can have an aspect other than luxuriance, the aspect of savagery.[90]

The two aspects of **hubris**, luxuriance and savagery, tend to alternate in poetic treatments. In the poetry of Theognis, for example, the **hubris** that threatens to destroy Megara is *either* the same **hubris** that destroyed the luxuriant Hellenes, as we have read in the passages cited, *or* the same **hubris** that destroyed the Centaurs, 'eaters of raw flesh' (Theognis 541–542; ὠμοφά-γους at 542).[91] The eventual destruction of Megara can be visualized as happening *either* from the inside, with the degeneration of the élite (again Theognis 39–52)[92] *or* from the outside, with the influx and subsequent ascendancy of savages (Theognis 53–68), who are described as 'formerly' living outside the city like grazing deer, wearing the hides of goats for clothing (54–56).[93] There is a similar description of the Persians in Herodotus, before they conquered the Lydians: as an advisor points out to Croesus, the Persians still wear leather for their trousers and indeed for all their clothing (οἱ σκυτί-νας μὲν ἀναξυρίδας, σκυτίνην δὲ τὴν ἄλλην ἐσθῆτα φορέουσι 1.71.2). 'Once they taste of our good things', says this Lydian advisor, 'they will cling to them and we will be unable to push them away' (γευσάμενοι γὰρ τῶν ἡμετέρων ἀγαθῶν περιέξονται οὐδὲ ἀπωστοὶ ἔσονται 1.71.3). Thus the Persians of Herodotus are a combination of the worst: already savage, they then become luxuriant as well.[94]

89. Cf. p. 263.

90. This other aspect has already emerged in the discussion at p. 263 of Phylarchus 81 F 45, where the savagery of the people of Sybaris is parallel to their luxuriance.

91. Cf. Apollodorus 2.5.4 (Pholos the Centaur eats his own portions of meat raw) and the comments at N 1985.51 §39n2.

92. Cf. p. 265.

93. This image of savages seems to be a reflex of poetic traditions describing colonization, where the polis of transplanted Hellenes is surrounded by local barbarians: see p. 71. In Theognis 53–68, the equation of ethically inferior citizens with sociopolitically inferior savages who threaten the polis from the outside (cf. N 1985.44 §29n4, 51 §39n2, 54) may convey a colonial point of view adopted from a daughter city on the coast of the Black Sea: see Figueira 1985.129.

94. The luxuriance of the Persians is a dominant theme in the *Persians* of Aeschylus; cf. the use of **habros** and its derivatives at lines 41, 135, 1072.

For Herodotus, the ultimate exponent of the luxuriance and savagery of **hubris** is Xerxes, the Great King of the Persians, leader of the "Asian" hordes massed against Hellas. Even more interesting for my present purposes, however, is another Persian exponent of **hubris**, whose story pointedly brings to a close the *Histories* of Herodotus. He is Artauktes, descendant of a man who had advised Cyrus, founder of the Persian Empire, to move from the 'harsh' land of Persia (γῆν ... τρηχέαν Herodotus 9.122.2) to some milder place (ibid.). Cyrus had rejected this advice on the grounds that men become 'soft' and slavelike when they live in 'soft' places (φιλέειν γὰρ ἐκ τῶν μαλακῶν χώρων μαλακοὺς ἄνδρας γίνεσθαι Herodotus 9.122.3). With this thought, along with the observation that the Persians at that former time had heeded the advice of Cyrus, Herodotus ends his narrative in the last sentence of the *Histories*. Obviously the Persians of later times, under the kingship of Xerxes, failed to heed the advice of Cyrus as they sought to occupy a new European homeland in the wake of Xerxes' invasion of Hellas. From the standpoint of the *Histories*, the Persians had already been corrupted by the Lydians: they had acquired from these fellow Asians the characteristic of being **habroi** 'luxuriant' (1.71.4), abandoning the harsh life that went hand in hand with living in a harsh country (1.71.2).[95] The topic of corruption is picked up again at the end of the *Histories*, where Cyrus is seen arguing against the advice given by the ancestor of Artauktes, who had argued that the Persians should move from the harsh land of Persia (9.122.2). With this background we come to the story of Artauktes—a story that realizes the advice given by his ancestor and that serves as a negative paradigm for the advice given by Cyrus.

Described as an underling of Xerxes, Artauktes was put in charge of administering a region on the "Greek" side of the Hellespont, which he ruled in the style of a **turannos** 'tyrant' (ἐτυράννευε Herodotus 9.116.1). The story has it that Artauktes was a dreadful and **atasthalos** 'wanton' man (9.116.1)—and the word **atasthalos** in Archaic Greek poetry regularly characterizes a man of **hubris**[96] —who contrived to occupy as his own property the **oikos** 'house' of 'a Greek man' (ἔστι οἶκος ἀνδρὸς Ἕλληνος ἐν-θαῦτα 9.116.3). At least Xerxes was led to believe that Artauktes was to occupy the house of 'a Greek man'. The story is actually being told by Herodotus in a mode analogous to that of an **ainos**, in that double meanings abound.[97] To begin with, the 'house' of the 'Greek man' is really the sacred precinct of the hero Protesilaos, a cult center filled with riches supplied by the hero's worshippers (9.116.2).[98] Lusting to possess these riches, Artauktes

95. Cf. p. 263.

96. A survey of passages in N 1979:163. Cf. also, for example, Herodotus 3.80.4.

97. On the **ainos** as a discourse with one code that bears at least two messages: p. 148.

98. For a detailed discussion of the hero cult of Protesilaos, see Boedeker 1988; some of her conclusions, reached independently, concerning the deployment of the Protesilaos story in the

had deceived Xerxes by asking the king to grant him the ownership of an **oikos** 'house' of 'a Greek man' who had died while attacking the land of Xerxes:

δέσποτα, ἔστι οἶκος ἀνδρὸς Ἕλληνος ἐνθαῦτα, ὃς ἐπὶ γῆν τὴν σὴν στρατευσάμενος δίκης κυρήσας ἀπέθανε, τούτου μοι δὸς τὸν οἶκον, ἵνα καί τις μάθῃ ἐπὶ γῆν τὴν σὴν μὴ στρατεύεσθαι.

Herodotus 9.116.3

Master, there is here a house [**oikos**] belonging to a Greek man who had made war against your land. Getting his just deserts, he had died. Give me this man's house [**oikos**], so that everyone may learn not to make war against your land.

What Artauktes had said actually conveys an ulterior meaning: in Greek epic tradition Protesilaos was the first Achaean to die fighting the Trojans (*Iliad* II 698–702). Moreover, **oikos** is a word that can designate the sacred precinct of a hero (e.g., Sophocles *Oedipus at Colonus* 627).[99] For Xerxes, the **oikos** requested by Artauktes is the 'house' of a Greek; for Artauktes, it is the precinct of Protesilaos. Once he is granted ownership of the precinct, Artauktes proceeds to rob it of its riches, to which the narrative refers as the **khrēmata** of Protesilaos (9.116.1, 3; 9.120.3). The personalized tone reminds us of the same word **khrēmata** in a poem of Theognis (667, 677), describing the loss of possessions on the part of a figure who is presented as an exponent of **dikē** 'righteousness' and who speaks in the mode of the **ainos** (ἠνίχθω 681).[100] Artauktes commits the further outrage of farming the lands of the precinct for his own profit and having sexual intercourse with women within the shrine (9.116.3). From a Hellenic standpoint Artauktes is clearly an exponent of **hubris**.

Sometime after the Greek victories over the Persians at Salamis and Plataea, Artauktes is captured by the advancing Greeks as they push the Persians back to Asia, and a miracle supposedly happens just as Artauktes is about to be executed in retribution for the wrongs that he had committed. As one of his Greek captors is roasting **tarīkhoi** 'preserved fish' for a meal (Herodotus 9.120.1),[101] the dead fish suddenly come alive. Artauktes reacts as follows:

---

narrative of Herodotus coincide with those presented in N 1987c; the main points of the latter article are recast in what follows.

99. See N 1985.76–77, 81 §79n1, especially with reference to the riddle in Theognis 1209–1210; see also Edmunds 1981, especially p. 223n8, with reference to Sophocles *Oedipus at Colonus* 627 and other related passages involving **oikos** and its derivatives.

100. Cf. pp. 149, 183, and following. Cf. N 1985.22–24, 76–78. On **ainigma** 'riddle' as a derivative of **ainos**: N 1979.240–241.

101. I translate **tarīkhos** generally as 'preserved' rather than specifically as 'dried', 'smoked',

ξεῖνε Ἀθηναῖε, μηδὲν φοβέο τὸ τέρας τοῦτο. οὐ γὰρ σοὶ πέφηνε, ἀλλ' ἐμοὶ σημαίνει ὁ ἐν Ἐλαιοῦντι Πρωτεσίλεως ὅτι καὶ τάριχος ἐὼν δύναμιν πρὸς θεῶν ἔχει τὸν ἀδικέοντα τίνεσθαι.

Herodotus 9.120.2

Athenian stranger, do not be frightened of this portent. For it was manifested not for you. Rather, the Protesilaos who abides in Elaious is indicating [= verb **sēmainō**] to me that, even though he is dead — and a **tarīkhos**— he has the power from the gods to exact retribution from the one who commits wrongdoing [= does deeds without **dikē**].

The word **tarīkhos**, possibly of Anatolian provenience,[102] has two meanings: either 'preserved fish', as from the standpoint of the man who was roasting the preserved fish, or 'mummy', as from the standpoint of Herodotus in describing the funerary practices of the Egyptians.[103] What the two meanings seem to have in common is the idea of *preservation*. In an everyday sense, rotting is negated by *preservation* through the drying or salting of fish; in a hieratic sense, rotting *and death itself* are negated by *preservation* through mummification, which is from the standpoint of Egyptian religion the ritual phase of the mystical process of immortalization.[104]

In the Egyptian ritual of mummification, the ideology of immortalization is evident in the relationship between the corpse and the *wt* 'bandager', which is made analogous to the relationship between Osiris, the first person to be mummified, and Anubis, the inventor of mummification. It has been observed that "each ritual was a re-enactment of the prototype, the deceased, as throughout the cult, being regarded as Osiris while the *wt* could be addressed as Anubis, take his epithets and occasionally, from the New Kingdom onwards, even wear the Anubis-mask."[105] When Herodotus discusses the most expensive procedure of mummification, he remarks ostentatiously that he does not wish to give away the name of the procedure (2.86.2), and

---

'salted', or 'pickled'; that brine or salt is used for the process of **tarīkheusis** 'preservation' is evident from Herodotus 4.53.3 (also 2.77.4).

102. Chantraine DELG 1094 s.v. **tarīkhos** allows for the possibility that this word is connected with **tarkhuō**. At p. 1095 s.v. **tarkhuō**, where he follows the evidence presented by Laroche 1958.98–99 and Heubeck 1959.32–35, Chantraine concedes that **tarkhuō** was a borrowing from an Indo-European language of Anatolia—whether that language be Hittite, Luvian, or Lycian. But here (p. 1095) he goes on to deny the connection that he mentioned as a possibility at p. 1094. On the meaning of **tarkhuō**, see N 1983b and Schein 1984.48. Cf. also Boedeker 1988.40–41.

103. For **tarīkhos/tarīkheuō** as 'mummy/mummify', see especially Herodotus 2.85–2.89, with a detailed description of the process of mummification. Cf. also Plato *Phaedo* 80c.

104. We may compare the everyday and the hieratic or mystical sense of **olbios**, as discussed at p. 244.

105. Lloyd 1976.354–355.

his stance here is typical of his general stance toward mysteries.[106]

In the image of a dead fish that mystically comes back to life, we see a convergence of the everyday and the hieratic senses of *preservation*. This image in the story of Herodotus, where Protesilaos **sēmainei** 'indicates' (9.120.2) the power that he has from the gods to exact retribution from the wrongdoer, amounts to a **sēma** or 'sign' of the revenant, the spirit that returns from the dead.[107] The hero Protesilaos himself is represented as giving the **sēma**, the 'sign' of his power as a revenant from the heroic past.

This theme recurs in the anonymous *Alexander Romance,* conventionally dated to the third century A.D.[108] After conquering the Persian Empire, Alexander pushes on further east till he reaches the edge of the world (τὸ τέλος τῆς γῆς 2.39.4), and he finds himself in the Land of the **Makares** 'Blessed' (2.39.1). There his **mageiros** 'cook' discovers a spring of immortalizing water when he washes a **tarīkhos** 'preserved fish' in the spring and the dead fish ἐψυχώθη 'recovered its **psūkhē**', that is, came back to life (2.39.12). Alexander is not told of this water, and he fails to drink of it. Later, when he comes to a place that is described as 'where the gods dwell' (3.24.1), a place where he has visions of lightning (ibid.), he asks the apparition of the **kosmokratōr** Sesonchosis, who now dwells in this realm, this question: how long will I live (3.24.2–3)? The apparition refuses to answer this question, which implicitly acknowledges Alexander's mortality, and indicates instead that the city founded by Alexander, Alexandria, is suitable compensation for mortality (3.24.3–4). The apparition even implies that Alexander will not really be dead, in that his corpse will have Alexandria as its **oikos** 'abode': οἰκήσεις δὲ αὐτὴν καὶ θανὼν καὶ μὴ θανών. τάφον γὰρ αὐτὴν ἕξεις ἣν κτίζεις πόλιν 'you will have it [= Alexandria] as your **oikos** both as one who is dead and yet also as one who is undead, for you will have as your tomb the very city that you founded' (3.24.4). What Alexander is being told at the edge of the world corresponds closely to what he had read inscribed in the shrine of Sarapis, back home in Alexandria, before he had begun his expedition to the East; the text here reads: σὺ δὲ ἀποθεωθεὶς προσκυνηθήσῃ νεκρὸς καὶ δῶρα λήψῃ ἐκ πολλῶν βασιλέων πάντοτε, οἰκήσεις δὲ αὐτὴν καὶ θανὼν καὶ μὴ θανών. τάφον γὰρ ἕξεις αὐτὴν ἣν κτίζεις πόλιν 'you will become a god and you will be worshipped, as a corpse, receiving gifts from many kings for all time, and you will have it [= Alexandria] as your **oikos** both as one who is dead and yet also as one who is undead, for you will have as your tomb the very city that you founded' (1.33.9). It has been argued that

---

106. Lloyd, p. 18, cites Herodotus 2.61, 2.86, 2.132, 2.170, and 2.171. It seems that this mystical procedure was named after Osiris, the prototype of immortalization (ibid.).

107. For more on this theme, see N 1985.68–81; also 1983.54n55. Again we may compare the everyday and the mystical meanings of **olbios** as discussed at p. 244.

108. I follow the edition of van Thiel 1974. In using this source, I have benefited from the advice of M. N. Nagler.

the enigmatic description of Alexander as dead and yet not dead refers to his status as founder and cult hero of Alexandria.[109] In becoming the cult hero of Alexandria, Alexander's corpse was to be transformed from a thing of nature into a thing of culture — a mummy.[110] The paradox of Alexander's being both dead and immortalized is comparable to the ideology of Archaic Greek hero cults, where the hero's abode is visualized simultaneously as (1) a cult place where his corpse is buried and (2) a paradise-like setting at the edge of the world, where he has been immortalized. The names for the two kinds of abode may even converge, as in the case of **Ēlusion** 'Elysium' and the **Nēsoi Makarōn** 'Islands of the Blessed': both names designate either a cult place or a paradisiacal setting.[111]

Let us return to the story of Herodotus. The hapless Artauktes attempts to offer compensation for the wrongs that he had committed (9.120.3), but his offer is refused by his captors; he is executed at a spot near the place, as Herodotus emphasizes, where Xerxes had committed the ultimate outrage of bridging the Hellespont (9.120.4). On the surface Artauktes is paying retribution that is being exacted by human agency, that is, by his Athenian captors. Under the surface, however, retribution is being exacted by divine agency, through the hero Protesilaos.

The role of Protesilaos is significant. By virtue of being the first Achaean to die in the Trojan War (*Iliad* II 698–702), he is described by Artauktes as a prominent Hellene who dared to attack Asians (again Herodotus 9.116.3). The narrative makes a point of drawing attention to the Persian assumption that underlies this description: the Persians take it for granted that all Asia belongs to them (9.116.3). With this theme the **historiā** of Herodotus comes full circle in that the same assumption is cited at the beginning of the narrative (1.4.4) in the context of explaining why the **logioi** of the Persians find the Hellenes **aitioi** 'responsible' for the ultimate conflict (1.4.1): that the Hellenes were in the wrong when they attacked Troy (ibid.). Even if this Persian assumption — that all Asia is theirs — were valid, the Persians would have been in the wrong when Xerxes bridged the Hellespont separating Asia from Europe in that even the assumption of the Persians implicitly cedes Europe to the Hellenes. Besides, the **historiā** of Herodotus

---

109. See van Thiel 1974.178.

110. On the mummy of Alexander, see Pfister II 422n33; also I 178, 192, 296; II 434–436, and 584. The tomb of Alexander at Alexandria was officially known as the **Sēma** 'Tomb': Strabo 17.1.8 C794. Also as **Sōma** 'Body': *Alexander Romance* 3.34.5. On the relationship of **sēma** 'tomb' and **sōma** 'body' in the context of Alexander's place of entombment in Alexandria, see van Thiel 1974.195.

111. See N 1979.189–192 for documentation; note too that both of these names are associated with the mystical theme of being struck by lightning. On the association, at Hesiod *Works and Days* 172, of the word **olbioi** with the heroes who inhabit the Islands of the Blessed, see N 1979.170 §30n2.

had already established at the beginning who is **aitios** for the present conflict as Herodotus **sēmainei** 'indicates' that Croesus had initiated the wrongdoing (1.5.3). Now, at the end of the **historiā**, the first of the Hellenes whom the Persians hold responsible for the present conflict is vindicated: he is really the party wronged by the Persians, just as all Hellenes are wronged when the Persians cross over to Europe, and it is he who exacts retribution from the offending Persians. As he does so, he **sēmainei** 'indicates' his power, which is equated here with the efficacy of the gods (again Herodotus 9.120.2).

Protesilaos is thus giving a **sēma** 'sign'. The 'sign' is intended not only for Artauktes but also for those to whom Herodotus is offering his narrative. At the same time that the hero Protesilaos **sēmainei** 'indicates' to Artauktes the power of the divine apparatus in bringing about justice (Herodotus 9.120.2), the narrative of Herodotus is conveying the same message, a message that is saying to the Hellenes that they were in the right. Thus not only Protesilaos gives a **sēma** here. So too does Herodotus, the narrator of this **sēma**, who at the beginning of his **historiā** 'indicates', **sēmainei**, that the Asians started it all (again Herodotus 1.5.3).[112] When Herodotus 'indicates', **sēmainei**, he is indirectly narrating the actions of the gods by directly narrating the actions of men. The most powerful 'indication' is the **sēma** of the hero, whose message is also his medium, the tomb. The double meaning of **sēma** as both 'tomb' and 'indication, sign'[113] is itself a monument to the power of the ideology inherent in the ancient Greek institution of hero cults — an ideology that appropriated the very concept of meaning to the tomb of the hero. Moreover, this ideology is inherent in the poetic form that can both celebrate the institution of hero cults and make it apply to a given situation in the present. That poetic form is the **ainos**.[114]

112. Yet even if the Hellenes were in the right, the way in which the Asians were in the wrong corresponds to the way in which the Athenian Empire was in the wrong: on this point see pp. 308 and following.

113. For more on this double meaning, see Sinos 1980:48–49 on *Iliad* XXIII 326/331; also N 1983:45–48.

114. For the intervention of the hero into the present, through the medium of the **ainos**, see pp. 194 and following.

10 ▫▫ The Charms of Tyranny:
Pindar and Herodotus II

T he paradigm of the tyrant in Herodotus is clearly a negative concept, serving as a foil for the moral message of **historiā**. Yet in the case of the archetypal tyrant figure, Croesus the Lydian, the perspective is not exclusively negative. There are positive sides to the traditional concept of Croesus the Tyrant, and the balancing of his negative and positive sides in the **historiā** of Herodotus has a striking parallel in the **ainos** of Pindar and Bacchylides. The parallel treatment of tyranny in **ainos** and **historiā** illuminates the comparison of these two forms of discourse.

Let us review the negative side. In the **historiā** of Herodotus the **hubris** of Croesus the Lydian is implied even by his being the prototype of the Persians in wronging the Hellenes. Moreover, the luxuriance exhibited by Persians like Artauktes is supposed to be clearly a consequence of the Lydian heritage, and the testimony of Archaic Greek poetry and song leaves no doubt that luxuriance is an aspect of **hubris**.

But we have also seen that luxuriance does not by itself constitute **hubris**. True **hubris** is also marked by savagery,[1] as is clearly evident in the behavior of the Persians.[2] Here we can pause to consider a point in defense of Croesus: at least he is not characterized in the *Histories* as an exponent of savagery. Croesus and his Lydians are characterized by Herodotus as indeed luxuriant but not necessarily savage. Moreover, Croesus is nowhere in Herodotus described directly as a man of **hubris**, although the Lydian blames the god Apollo as **aitios** 'responsible' for his own calamities (1.87.3) in a manner

---

1. Cf. pp. 263, 267, and following.
2. Cf. pp. 267 and following.

that is characteristic of someone who has indeed committed deeds of **hubris**.³ So too in the poetry of Theognis, men of **hubris** are apt to blame some god as **aitios** for the calamities they suffer, and the poet has to point out their error:

πάντα τάδ' ἐν κοράκεσσι καὶ ἐν φθόρῳ· οὐδέ τις ἥμιν
αἴτιος ἀθανάτων Κύρνε θεῶν μακάρων,
ἀλλ' ἀνδρῶν τε βίη καὶ κέρδεα δειλὰ καὶ ὕβρις
πολλῶν ἐξ ἀγαθῶν ἐς κακότητ' ἔβαλεν

Theognis 833–836

Everything here has gone to the ravens and perdition. And not one of the immortal and blessed gods is
responsible [**aitios**] to us for this, Kyrnos,
but the violence [**biē**] of men and their baneful personal gains [**kerdos** plural] and their **hubris**⁴
have plummeted them from their many good things into debasement.⁵

Such a poetic teaching, with its tragic ring, is surely appropriate to Croesus. In fact the Croesus story of Herodotus has often been compared with actual tragedy.⁶ In this light the absence of any explicit characterization of Croesus as a man of **hubris** may remind us of the prerequisite formulated by Aristotle for an appropriate figure in tragedy as someone who is "intermediate" in a field of conflict between **dikaiosunē** 'righteousness' and its opposite (*Poetics* 1453a7–12).

But there is yet another reason for the attenuation of any charge of **hubris** in the case of Croesus. The **historiā** of Herodotus is following a pattern of indirectness that is strikingly parallel to the pattern found in the **ainos**, as exemplified by the epinician songs of Pindar and Bacchylides. We see already from the internal evidence of Herodotus' *Histories* a motivation for the indirectness in conveying the **hubris** of Croesus. With his untold wealth, Croesus is not only the most luxuriant of men: he is also the most generous. Specifically he outdoes everyone in his public display of material offerings to Apollo at Delphi (Herodotus 1.50.1–1.53–2); he reminds the god of this generosity when he is about to be incinerated by the flames of a funeral pyre that he had mounted for his public execution by the Persians (1.87.1). Then, as

---

3. Cf. pp. 241 and following.

4. Note the diminishing tricolon (cf. Mimnermus F 1.3 W), ending with the general category of **hubris**. The aspects of **hubris** that I have been calling luxuriance and savagery are conveyed by the words **kerdos** and **biē** respectively. For more on **kerdos**, see pp. 265–266. On **biē** as a symptom of **hubris**, in Hesiod *Works and Days* 143–155 and elsewhere, see N 1979.156–157.

5. The 'good things' are both wealth and nobility, while 'debasement' is both poverty and degeneration. On the semantic shift from the socioeconomic to the purely ethical sense of **agathos** 'noble' and its synonyms, cf. N 1985.51–60; also p. 44 §29n4 and p. 45 §30n1.

6. Stambler 1982.219, Waters 1985.21; cf. Immerwahr 1966.70.

Croesus invokes the god, a sudden storm extinguishes the flames, and his captor Cyrus, recognizing that this prisoner is a man **agathos** 'noble' and **philos** 'dear' to the gods, spares his life (1.87.2).

We have arrived at a specific point of thematic contact between the **historiā** of Herodotus and the **ainos** of epinician poets like Pindar and Bacchylides. The generosity of Croesus is a traditional theme of epinician song, worthy of direct comparison with the generosity of the given patron who has commissioned the given epinician poem and who is destined to be praised in that poem. In *Epinician* 3 of Bacchylides,[7] for example, where the tyrant Hieron of Syracuse, the **olbios** 'blissful' son of Deinomenes (3.8),[8] is being praised as winner in the chariot race at the Olympic Games of 468 B.C., a special point is made about praising Hieron as **tris-eu-daimōn** 'thrice-fortunate' (3.10) for knowing how to display his wealth, which is greater than that of any other Hellene (3.10–14).[9] There follows a description of lavish offerings of gold made by Hieron to Apollo at Delphi (3.15–21),[10] concluding with the following thought:

θεὸν θ[εό]ν τις | ἀγλαιζέθω· γὰρ ἄριστος ὄλβων

Bacchylides 3.21–22

It is the god, yes, the god that everyone should glorify, for *he* is the best bliss [**olbos**] of them all.

The transcendence of the god is being applied to a man's material wealth, making it transcendent as well: hence my translation of **olbos** here as 'bliss' rather than 'wealth'.[11] Immediately following this thought, the conjunction ἐπεί 'since' abruptly introduces the story of Croesus as if to validate the thought that **olbos** is indeed transcendent: Apollo is the very essence of **olbos**, the poem says, and the reason given is simply that once upon a time Apollo saved Croesus (ἐπεί ποτε καὶ Λυδίας ἀρχαγέταν ... φύλαξ' Ἀπόλλων Bacchylides 3.23– 28).[12]

What follows is a detailed narrative that closely parallels that of Herodotus — up to a point. As in the narrative of Herodotus, the poem of Bacchylides likewise has Croesus about to be incinerated by the flames of the

7. For an evaluation of this poem, see Carson 1984; also Burnett 1985.61–76, who disagrees with previous works that stress the "pessimism" of the ode.

8. On the transcendent semantics of **olbios**, see pp. 243 and following.

9. For pertinent contexts of **eudaimoniā** 'good fortune', see p. 240.

10. The wording λάμπει ... ὁ χρυσός 'the gold [**khrūsos**] gleams' at Bacchylides *Epinician* 3.17 here is crucial for understanding the poetic equation of **khrūsos** and **euphrosunē** 'merriment', to be discussed at p. 277.

11. On the transcendence of **olbos** as well-being that is material from the outside and mystical from the inside, see p. 243 and following.

12. The phrase φύλαξ' Ἀπόλλων 'Apollo saved ...' is syntactically carried over from stanza Β' and emphatically begins stanza Γ'.

funeral pyre (3.29–35, 48–51).[13] Here too Croesus invokes Apollo (3.35–48), reminding him of his offerings at Delphi (3.38, in conjunction with 3.61–62).[14] Here too a sudden storm extinguishes the flames (3.53–56; in this version Zeus himself is pictured as sending the storm). After the rescue, however, we find an important additional theme in Bacchylides: Apollo **kat[en]asse** 'transported' Croesus, daughters and all, to the Land of the Hyperboreans (3.58–60).[15] This transporting of Croesus by Apollo formalizes the transcendence of **olbos** from the 'wealth' of this life to the 'bliss' of a timeless existence beyond death. In support of this interpretation, let us consider a striking analogue: when Zeus **katenasse** 'transported' the warriors who fought in the Theban and the Trojan War (Hesiod *Works and Days* 168), he took them to the Islands of the Blessed (170–173), to be immortalized there as **olbioi hērōes** 'blissful heroes' (172).[16]

The reward of Croesus, in being transported to the Land of the Hyperboreans, is on account of his **eusebeia** 'piety' (Bacchylides 3.61)[17] in that he gave the greatest offerings of all mankind to the Temple of Apollo at Delphi (3.61–62). The stage is set for the juxtaposition with Hieron: this tyrant in turn has given the most gold *of all Hellenes* to the Temple of Apollo at Delphi (3.63–66). Already in the initial description of Hieron's offerings at Delphi, the focus had been on the gleam of gold (3.17),[18] and it was this description that led directly to the thought that Apollo himself is the best **olbos** 'bliss' of them all (again 3.21–22).[19]

Later, gold is equated with the poetic celebration of Hieron's victory, as designated by the programmatic word **euphrosunē** 'mirth' (εὐφροσύνα δ' ὁ

---

13. There is also an attested iconographical variation on the story, a Red Figure amphora dated around 500 B.C. (Beazley 1963.238 no. 1) showing Croesus calmly seated on the pyre while an attendant labeled **Euthumos** is apparently getting ready to set fire to it.

14. At Bacchylides 3.38, the expected reciprocity of the gods in return for all the generosity of Croesus is expressed as **kharis**; cf. Herodotus 1.90.4.

15. On the Land of the Hyperboreans as a multiform analogous to Elysium, the Islands of the Blessed, the White Island, and so forth, cf. Hesiod F 150.21 MW, *Epigonoi* F 3 Kinkel, scholia to Pindar *Pythian* 3.28, and so on.

16. See N 1979.164. My understanding of Hesiod *Works and Days* 158–168 is that the heroes of the Theban as well as the Trojan War are eligible for immortalization. I take the μέν at *Works and Days* 166 as parallel to the instances of μέν at 122, 137, 141, 161 (*pace* West 1978.192): in other words, I argue that this μέν at 166, like the others here listed, is continuative, and that it does not set up a contrast with the δέ of 167. In line with this interpretation, the heroes who are transported by Zeus had to die before they could be transported to a state of immortalization. Compare the transportation of the dead Achilles from the funeral pyre to the White Island, where he is immortalized: *Aithiopis*/Proclus p. 106.14–15 Allen.

17. Compare Herodotus 1.86.2: Cyrus makes Croesus ascend the pyre for various possible reasons, one of which is to find out if any **daimōn** 'supernatural force' would save a man so **theosebēs** 'pious'.

18. Cf. p. 276.

19. Cf. ibid.

χρυσός 3.87).[20] Gold is the visible sign of Hieron's own **olbos** (3.92), which is displayed in public by way of his consecrated offerings and by way of the poetic celebration (3.88–98). The piety of consecrating gold offerings to the god makes the wealth of Hieron a transcendent thing, **olbos** 'bliss', raising hopes that he will be immortalized like Croesus. Gold, as an imperishable substance, is an ideal symbol for **olbos** as immortalization.[21] But the juxtaposition of Hieron and Croesus raises fears as well. At the moment when Hieron is called **megainētos** 'he who receives great **ainos**' (3.64) in the context of being praised for giving more gold to Apollo than any other Hellene (3.63–66), we may be reminded that the poetic medium of the **ainos** has the power to convey implicit as well as explicit messages.[22] The juxtaposition with Croesus, who is being praised for giving more riches to Apollo than any other human in general (3.61–62), seems to warn implicitly as well as to praise explicitly.[23] We have learned from Herodotus that the **olbos** 'wealth' of Croesus, meant to be consecrated by way of magnificent offerings to Apollo, was instead destroyed because of the tyrant's implicit **hubris**. This part of the story is left unspoken in Bacchylides.

20. For more on the programmatic function of the word **euphrosunē** 'mirth', see p. 198.

21. Gold is also a symbol of culture as distinct from nature: in the myth of the Golden Age, for example, as in Hesiod *Works and Days* 117–118, gold signifies the suspension of the natural, of the cycles and rhythms of vegetation, by way of the artificial (extensive discussion in N 1979.179–190; at *Works and Days* 172, the immortalized heroes on the Islands of the Blessed are called **olbioi** 'blissful'). In *Iliad* II 268, it is gold that makes the scepter a thing of culture, of artifice, not of nature, since it is **aphthiton aiei** 'unfailing forever' (II 46, 186; commentary in N, pp. 179–180). In Bacchylides 3.85–87, there is a tripartite crescendo of imperishable elements, where the first is the **aithēr** 'aether', described as 'incorruptible' (ἀμίαντος 86), which separates sky and earth; the second is the water of the sea, which 'does not disintegrate' (ὕδωρ ... οὐ σάπεται 86–87); and the third is the **khrūsos** 'gold' that is **euphrosunē** (εὐφροσύνα δ᾽ ὁ χρυσός 87). The two foils for gold here are things of nature, while gold itself is a thing of culture. As for Pindar's *Olympian* 1, in contrast, the hierarchy is different: here the element of water is said to be best (ἄριστον μὲν ὕδωρ 1), juxtaposed with **khrūsos** 'gold' as the best display of wealth (1–2; cf. *Olympian* 3.42), but the greatest of **aethla** 'prizes' (3) to be sought is the sun itself (5), as it shines through the **aithēr** (6), preeminent among celestial bodies just as the Olympics are preeminent among athletic contests (5–7). It is as if gold were just a reflection of the sun itself, so that gold, like water, is in truth a thing of nature, not culture. Since water is a symbol for the **kleos** of song, as in Pindar *Nemean* 7.62–63 (p. 147), it is as if song were a thing of nature, not a thing of culture, of artifice. In the poetics of Pindar, the genius of song is presented as natural, not artificial. To the extent that the natural is perceived as "realistic," unlike the artificial, we may again apply the dictum: the more the realism, the greater the artifice (p. 36). On the traditional poetics of **aphthito-** 'unfailing' as applicable to **kleos** and to water, see N 1974.229–244; also Risch 1987.4–5. On the vegetal symbolism of **aphthito-**: N 1979 ch.10 and Steiner 1986.38.

22. Cf. p. 148 and following.

23. On the **ainos** as an instrument of social criticism that can warn as well as praise, see pp. 181 and following.

We learn from Bacchylides on the other hand that the **olbos** of Croesus was indeed ultimately consecrated by an act of Apollo, but that this **olbos** was not material wealth: instead it took the form of the tyrant's being saved from the funeral pyre and being transported by Apollo to the Land of the Hyperboreans. The latter part of the story is in turn left unspoken in Herodotus: the good fortune of Croesus does not go beyond his being saved from the funeral pyre. Such an attenuated salvation of Croesus is still enough to vindicate him after all his sufferings as at least a man who is **agathos** 'good' and **philos** 'dear' to the gods (again Herodotus 1.87.2), but it is not enough to confer upon him the epithet of **olbios** in the transcendent sense of 'blissful'. For Herodotus, Solon's injunction—that one may call no one **olbios** until he is dead (1.32.7; 1.86.3)—deprives Croesus of the title altogether: since he has lost all his wealth and since his salvation from the pyre does not transcend his mortal life, he is represented in the *Histories* as a man who is **olbios** 'wealthy'/'blissful' in neither the material nor the transcendent sense.[24] This is as it should be in the narrative of Herodotus, who 'indicates' (= verb **sēmainō**: 1.5.3), in the mode of an **ainos**,[25] that Croesus was the first barbarian, within the span of knowledge ostensibly achieved by Herodotus, to have committed wrongdoing against Hellenes (1.5.3 in conjunction with 1.6.1–3).

Conversely it is also as it should be that wherever Croesus is mentioned in the praise song of Bacchylides and Pindar—praise that is called **ainos** by the song—the stress is on the Lydian tyrant's positive side whenever he is being directly compared with the given patrons of the praise song. For example, when Bacchylides praises the tyrant Hieron of Syracuse, we hear of the **aretē** 'achievement' of Croesus (Bacchylides 3.90) in the context of that earlier tyrant's **olbos** (3.92). So also in Pindar's praise of Hieron, the **aretē** of Croesus is given due emphasis:

ὀπιθόμβροτον αὔχημα δόξας | οἶον ἀποιχομένων ἀνδρῶν δίαιταν μανύει | καὶ λογίοις καὶ ἀοιδοῖς. οὐ φθίνει Κροίσου φιλόφρων ἀρετά.

Pindar Pythian 1.92–94

The proud declaration of glory that comes in the future is the only thing that reveals, both for **logioi** and for singers [**aoidoi**],[26] the life of men

---

24. Note the frequent use of **olbos/olbios** as a term that is specifically inapplicable to Croesus: Herodotus 1.86.3, 5 (two times), 6; note also the use of **an-olbos** 'without **olbos**' in the response of the Delphic Oracle to Croesus (1.85.2).

25. See pp. 229, 233, and following.

26. On the **apodeixis** 'public display' of **aretē** 'achievement' by way of **logioi** and **aoidoi**, masters of oral tradition in prose and song respectively, see pp. 222 and following.

who are now departed; the **philos**-minded achievement [**aretē**] of Croesus fails [= root **phthi-**] not.[27]

Still the very suppression of the obviously well-known negative aspect of Croesus is in itself a sign or signal, an implicit warning of what can happen when **olbos** is perverted.

Not only for Croesus but even for the very concept of **turannos** 'tyrant', praise song can stress the positive aspects whenever the song is actually praising a tyrant. In Pindar's *Pythian 3*, for example, the poem has this to say to Hieron, Tyrant of Syracuse:

τὶν δὲ μοῖρ᾽ εὐδαιμονίας ἕπεται. | λαγέταν γάρ τοι τύραννον δέρ-κεται, | εἴ τιν᾽ ἀνθρώπων, ὁ μέγας πότμος.

Pindar *Pythian* 3.84–86

A portion of good fortune [**eudaimoniā**] is attracted to [= verb **hepomai**] you. Great destiny looks at the **turannos**, if at any man, as the leader of the people [**lāos**].

Yet the very next thought is negative: even heroes like Peleus and Kadmos, who had the ultimate **olbos** in the immediate sense of 'material prosperity' (ὄλβον ὑπέρτατον 3.89), could not achieve an **aiōn** in the immediate sense of 'lifetime' that was **asphalēs** 'secure' (3.86–87).[28] After a quick glimpse of these heroes' subsequent misfortunes (3.88–105), there follows another implicit warning of what can happen when **olbos**, in the sense of 'material prosperity', is perverted:

ὄλβος {δ᾽} οὐκ ἐς μακρὸν ἀνδρῶν ἔρχεται | σάος, πολὺς εὖτ᾽ ἂν ἐπιβρίσαις ἕπηται

Pindar *Pythian* 3.105–106

The prosperity [**olbos**] of humans does not go ahead, safe and sound, for a very long time, when it gets attracted [= verb **hepomai**] to them, with its full weight [ἐπιβρίσαις].

In this context of material possessions, we must pay special attention to

27. The description of the **aretē** of Croesus as 'unfailing', by way of the root **phthi-**, draws the theme of the tyrant's generosity into a symbolic parallelism with imperishable substances like gold, which is also the symbol for the medium of poetry and song that glorifies such generosity and which is associated with the quality of being **aphthito-** 'unfailing, imperishable': see p. 278. The 'unfailing' **aretē** of Croesus at Pindar *Pythian* 1.94 is then contrasted with the savagery of the tyrant Phalaris of Akragas, who was reputed to roast his victims alive within the brazen simulacrum of a bull (*Pythian* 1.95–96).

28. Besides the immediate sense of **olbos** as 'material prosperity' and of **aiōn** as 'lifetime', there is an ulterior sense built into both words: on **olbos** in the ulterior sense of 'bliss', see pp. 243 and following; on **aiōn** in the ulterior sense of 'vital force', see N 1981.

the last word of this passage, ἐπιβρίσαις from the verb **epi-brīthō** 'weigh heavily'. This verb is semantically parallel to the noun **hubris**, the etymology of which is recapitulated in these quoted words of Pindar concerning material prosperity, **olbos**, described as coming down with its full weight upon its owner: in the standard etymological dictionary[29] **hubris** is segmented etymologically as **hu-/u-** (ὑ-/ὐ-) in the sense of **epi-** (ἐπί-) 'on, on top of'[30] plus root **bri-** (βρι-) as in **briaros** (βριαρός) 'heavy, massive, solid, strong'.[31] The built-in connotations of **hubris** in this quoted Pindaric passage are reinforced by the following two parallels:

τίκτει γὰρ κόρος ὕβριν, ὅταν πολὺς ὄλβος ἕπηται
ἀνθρώποις ὁπόσοις μὴ νόος ἄρτιος ᾖ

Solon F 6.3–4 W

For insatiability [**koros**] gives birth to **hubris** when much prosperity
[**olbos**] gets attracted [= verb **hepomai**]
to men whose intent [**noos**] is not fit.[32]

τίκτει τοι κόρος ὕβριν, ὅταν κακῷ ὄλβος ἕπηται
ἀνθρώπῳ καὶ ὅτῳ μὴ νόος ἄρτιος ᾖ

Theognis 153–154

Insatiability [**koros**] gives birth to **hubris** when prosperity [**olbos**] gets
attracted [= verb **hepomai**]
to a man who is base [**kakos**] and whose intent [**noos**] is not fit.[33]

The implicit warning about **hubris** in *Pythian* 3 conveys the negative potential of any tyrant. But the use of the word **turannos** in this poem is clearly not negative, only ambivalent. In the poetic medium of Pindar, the word **turannos** is like the figure of Croesus, conveying overt positive aspects as well as latent negative ones.[34]

The positive aspects of **turannos**, as with the Lydian Croesus, have to do with the material security that allows the tyrant to be a paragon of generosity. But this material security, as we have seen, is at the same time an ambivalent

---

29. Chantraine DELG 1150.

30. For documentation of **hu-/u-** (ὑ-/ὐ-) in the sense of **epi-** (ἐπί-), see Perpillou 1987.

31. Cf. Perpillou, pp. 197–199. On the relationship of **briaros** and **brīthō**, see DELG 196.

32. Commentary at N 1985.48–49, 60–61.

33. Again, commentary at N 1985.48–49, 60–61. Cf. Pindar *Olympian* 13.10, where the relationship is expressed in reverse: **hubris** gives birth to **koros**. Gildersleeve 1899.229–230 observes about the reverse order in Solon and Theognis: "But that makes little difference, as, according to Greek custom, grandmother and granddaughter often bore the same name. It is a mere matter of **Hubris - Koros - Hubris**."

34. On the use of the word **turannis** 'tyranny' at Pindar *Pythian* 11.53, see p. 290.

conceit, conveyed by words like **habros/habrotēs** 'luxuriant'/'luxuriance'.[35] These words certainly apply to Croesus, who is actually called **pod-(h)abros** 'with luxuriant [= adjective **habros**] footsteps' by the Oracle of Apollo in the context of the god's implicitly foretelling the tyrant's doom (Herodotus 1.55.2).[36] We have already noted some other implicitly negative contexts of **habros** and its derivatives,[37] but we have yet to examine how these words too, like the themes of Croesus in particular and **turannos** in general, have an explicitly positive aspect as well. Turning back to Pindar's *Pythian* 3, we note the following example in a passage that immediately follows the warning, quoted just now, about the perversion of **olbos**:

> σμικρὸς ἐν σμικροῖς, μέγας ἐν μεγάλοις | ἔσσομαι, τὸν δ' ἀμφέποντ' αἰεὶ φρασὶν | δαίμον' ἀσκήσω κατ' ἐμὰν θεραπεύων μαχανάν. | εἰ δέ μοι πλοῦτον θεὸς ἁβρὸν ὀρέξαι, | ἐλπίδ' ἔχω κλέος εὑρέσθαι κεν ὑψηλὸν πρόσω

> Pindar *Pythian* 3.107–111

I will be small among the small, great among the great.[38] I shall practice my craft on the **daimōn** that occupies my mind, tending it in accordance with my abilities. And if the god should give me wealth [**ploutos**] that is luxuriant [**habros**], then I have the hope [**elpis**] of finding lofty **kleos** in the future.

Here then is yet another variation on a theme that we have already witnessed many times before: the song of the poem is making the admittedly pleasurable material security of the tyrant into a transcendent thing. There follows a quick glance at epic heroes like Nestor and Sarpedon, made famous by song (3.112–114), and then a coda about the transcendence of **aretē** 'achievement' through the efficacy of the poem:

> ἁ δ' ἀρετὰ κλειναῖς ἀοιδαῖς | χρονία τελέθει

> Pindar *Pythian* 3.114–115

And achievement [**aretē**] becomes enduring through songs of **kleos**.

---

35. Cf. pp. 263 and following.

36. Cf. p. 263, with a discussion of the possibility that **pod-(h)abros** 'with a footstep that is luxuriant [**habros**]' at Herodotus 1.55.2 connotes specifically *dancing* steps. Cf. also Bacchylides 3.48, where the funeral pyre that Croesus voluntarily ascends is called a **habro-batēs domos** (ἁβροβάταν δόμον) 'construction for luxuriant [**habros**] footsteps'. I interpret this expression to refer to the luxuriant manner in which Croesus walked up the constructed pyre, headed for certain doom (*pace* SM, apparatus ad loc.). For a different interpretation, where ἁβροβάταν is read as **Habrobatās**, the name of a page, see, for example, Burnett 1985.180.

37. Cf. pp. 263 and following.

38. On the theme of variations in human fortunes from mighty to slight, slight to mighty, cf. Herodotus 1.5.3–4 and the discussion at p. 240.

In epinician song the word **habros** and its derivatives can in fact be so positive as to characterize the luxuriance that a victor earns and deserves as the fruit of his struggles, either in athletics or in war. It is in such a context that the **kūdos** 'emblem of victory' won by the victor is described as **habron** 'luxuriant':

ὃς δ' ἀμφ' ἀέθλοις ἢ πολεμίζων ἄρηται κῦδος ἁβρόν . . .

Pindar Isthmian 1.50

. . . but whoever, engaged in struggles for athletic prizes [**aethloi**] or fighting in a war, strives for and achieves [= verb **ar-numai**][39] an emblem of victory [= **kūdos**] that is luxuriant [**habron**], . . .[40]

Also, **habros** applies to the garland of myrtle won by the athlete Kleandros (Pindar *Isthmian* 8.66). The words of praise spoken about victors who are already dead qualify for the same sort of description:

τιμὰ δὲ γίνεται | ὧν θεὸς ἁβρὸν αὔξει λόγον τεθνακότων

Pindar Nemean 7.31–32

Honor [**tīmē**] comes into the possession of those about whom the god magnifies the word [**logos**] of repute, so as to be **habros**, on the occasion of their death.

As for the living, we have just seen that the luxuriance deserved by the victor is manifested as **ploutos**, material security, which is likewise described as **habros** (again Pindar *Pythian* 3.110) and which is to be followed up by **kleos**, fame by way of song, in the future (3.111)—even after death, as in the case of heroes (3.112–115). It is specifically the **elpis** 'aspiration' of the victor that he will gain **kleos** on the basis of **ploutos** that is **habros** (3.110–111). Thus the luxuriance conveyed by **habros** can apply not only to the victor's **ploutos**, which is transient, but also to the praise that he gets from song, which is transcendent. In the context of such transcendent luxuriance, **elpis** 'aspiration' makes the victor's thoughts soar beyond mere **ploutos**:

ὁ δὲ καλόν τι νέον λαχὼν | ἁβρότατος ἔπι μεγάλας | ἐξ ἐλπίδος
πέταται | ὑποπτέροις ἀνορέαις, ἔχων | κρέσσονα πλούτου μέριμναν.
ἐν δ' ὀλίγῳ βροτῶν, | τὸ τερπνὸν αὔξεται· οὕτω δὲ καὶ πίτνει χαμαί,

---

39. The traditional themes associated with the verb **ar-numai** 'strive to achieve' here correspond to those of the noun **aretē** 'achievement', which is in fact etymologically derived from it: see Francis 1983.82–87.

40. Cf. Pindar *Olympian* 5.7.

| ἀποτρόπῳ γνώμᾳ σεσεισμένον

Pindar Pythian 8.88–94

But if one gets as his lot some beautiful new thing, in this time of great luxuriance [**habrotēs**],[41] he soars at the impulse of aspiration [**elpis**], lifted high in the air by his acts of manliness, with his ambition [**merimna**] beyond material wealth [**ploutos**].[42] The pleasure [**terpnon**] that mortals get waxes in a short space of time. And, just as quickly, it falls to the ground, shaken by adverse opinion.[43]

In other words **ploutos** 'wealth' becomes a transcendent thing when it is enhanced by the luxuriance earned through victory at the Games:

ὁ μὰν πλοῦτος ἀρεταῖς δεδαιδαλμένος φέρει τῶν τε καὶ τῶν | καιρὸν βαθεῖαν ὑπέχων μέριμναν ἀβροτέραν,[44] | ἀστὴρ ἀρίζηλος, ἐτυμώτατον | ἀνδρὶ φέγγος

Pindar Olympian 2.53–56

Embellished with achievements [**aretē** plural], wealth [**ploutos**] gives scope for actions of every kind,[45] supporting an ambition [**merimna**] that is more luxuriant [**habros**].[46] It [= the **ploutos** 'wealth'] is a preeminent star, the most genuine light for man.

A quality inherent in the concept of **habros** 'luxuriant' that makes it transcend mere **ploutos** 'wealth' is that of sensuality. We see it in the application of **habros** to the beautiful body of Iamos (Pindar *Olympian* 6.55) or to

---

41. I interpret ἀβρότατος ἔπι μεγάλας 'in [this] time of great **habrotēs**' as referring to the time after, not before or during, the victory (*pace* Gildersleeve 1899.333, who interprets **habrotēs** here as the luxuriance that tempts the athlete in the austere period of his training).

42. Compare Bacchylides *Encomium* 20B.8–16: Κύπριδος ἐλπίς 'aspiration [**elpis**] for Aphrodite' (line 8), in the context of intoxication at a symposium, seems to be the subject of ἀνδράσι δ' ὑψοτάτω πέμπει μερίμνας· | αὐτίκα μὲν πολίων κράδεμνα λύει, | πᾶσι δ' ἀνθρώποις μοναρχήσειν δοκεῖ 'sends ambitions [**merimna** plural] to the uppermost heights for men; straightaway it undoes the protective headbands of cities, and it thinks that it will be monarch [**monarkhos**] over all mortals' (lines 10–13). On **monarkhos** 'monarch' as the attenuated synonym of **turannos** 'tyrant', see pp. 182, 184. This passage, Bacchylides *Encomium* 20B.8–16, is treated at greater length below, at pp. 287 and following.

43. This second clause, where the theme concerns soaring *and* falling, contrasts with the first clause, where the theme concerns soaring only.

44. I accept this emendation of the manuscript reading ἀγροτέραν, deemed corrupt in the edition of SM.

45. So Nisetich 1980.89.

46. Compare πλοῦτος ... ὑπέχων μέριμναν ἀβροτέραν here with ἔχων κρέσσονα πλούτου μέριμναν at *Pythian* 8.91–92, quoted immediately above. Note too that **merimna** 'concern' has been interpreted here throughout in the sense of 'ambition' rather than 'worry'; cf. Slater 1969.329.

the seductive Hippolyta (*Nemean* 5.26), who is described by this adjective in the specific context of a "Potiphar's Wife" story (having tried and failed to seduce Peleus, she then slanders him to her husband: 5.26–36; cf. *Nemean* 4.54–65). We may even note a trace of this quality in the application of **habros** to the garland of myrtle blossoms won by the athlete Kleandros (*Isthmian* 8.66).[47]

This inherent sensuality, even eroticism, of **habros** and its derivatives is most vividly attested in the compositions of Sappho. For Sappho, the adjective **habros** is the epithet of Adonis (F 140.1 V)[48] and of the attendants of Aphrodite, the **Kharites** (F 128 V),[49] while the adverb **(h)abrōs** describes the scene as Aphrodite is requested to pour nectar (F 2.13–16 V). For Sappho, **(h)abrosunā** 'luxuriance' is a theme connected with 'lust for the sun':

ἐγὼ δὲ φίλημμ᾽ ἀβροσύναν, [. . .] τοῦτο, καί μοι
τὸ λάₗμπρον ἔρως⁵⁰ ἀελίω καὶ τὸ κάˌλον λέₗλˌογχε

Sappho F 58.25–26 V

But I love luxuriance [**(h)abrosunā**]. . . . this,
and lust for the sun has won me brightness and beauty.[51]

Sappho's theme of luxuriance is also connected with the concept of Lydia as a touchstone of sensuality. Contemplating the beauty of the girl Kleis, Sappho says that she would not exchange her even for all of Lydia (F 132.3 V). Of another girl she says that she would rather contemplate the sight of her lovely footsteps and her radiant face than the magnificence of the Lydian army in full array (F 16.17–20 V). The attractiveness of yet another girl, now turned woman, stands out amidst a bevy of Lydian women, much as the moon stands out amid surrounding stars (F 96.6–9 V).[52]

---

47. Cf. p. 283.

48. There is an implicit danger in the application of this epithet **habros** to Adonis: we may note that the luxuriant Adonis is an exponent of **hubris** in a botanical sense, on which see the full discussion in N 1985.60–63.

49. Compare Sappho F 194 V for the image of Aphrodite riding on the chariot of the **Kharites**.

50. Cf. Hamm 1957 §241.

51. Cf. Pindar *Pythian* 11.50, as discussed at p. 290. This interpretation of the Sappho passage differs from that of, for example, Campbell 1982.101, who reads τώελίω (τὸ ἀελίω), agreeing with τὸ λάμπρον. Even if we were to accept the reading τώελίω, we could theoretically interpret the crasis along the lines of τῶ ἀελίω = τώελίω (cf. e.g. πω ἔσλον = πῶσλον at Alcaeus 69.5 V; cf. Hamm, p. §91e). The theme of 'lust for the sun' is to be connected with that of Sappho's love of Phaon/Adonis: cf. N 1973.177 in connection with the theme of crossing the strait with Phaon.

52. On the reference to women as distinct from girls here, cf. Rissman 1983.95.

The Lydian connection brings us back to the negative theme: the quality of being **habros**, for all its attractiveness, has its built-in dangers. We have seen this negative theme in the story of the Colophonians: these men, in the words of Xenophanes, learned **habrosunē** 'luxuriance' from the Lydians (F 3.1–2 W),[53] and the misfortune of the **turanniā** 'tyranny' that befell them was because of this (ibid.).[54] The luxuriance of the Colophonians, as we have also seen, was a manifestation of their **hubris**, which led to their utter ruin (Theognis 1103–1104),[55] as was also the case with such other formerly great cities as Magnesia and Smyrna (ibid.).[56] Even for Sappho, who declares that she loves **(h)abrosunā** 'luxuriance' (F 58.25–26 V), the attractions of sensuality are not only foreign, as typified by the Lydians, but also dangerous: the Lydian army in full array may be a beautiful thing to behold, but it is also a threat—more overtly so than the lovely footsteps and radiant face of a pretty girl (F 16.17 V).[57] As recently argued,[58] the theme of luxuriance and its dangers must have figured in the lost final stanza of the celebrated ode by Sappho describing her reactions to a girl whose attention is being held by a godlike young man (F 31 V), and this theme is still to be found in the final stanza of the version by Catullus:

> otium, Catulle, tibi molestum est,
> otio exsultas nimiumque gestis,
> otium et reges prius et beatas
> perdidit urbes

Catullus 51.13–16

> Luxuriance,[59] Catullus, is distressing to you.
> In luxuriance you exult and are elated to excess.
> It is luxuriance that in times past caused the ruin
> of kings and wealthy cities.[60]

---

53. Cf. pp. 263 and following. The Lydians are characterized as **habro-diaitoi** 'living luxuriantly' in Aeschylus *Persians* 41; cf. the context of the same epithet in Thucydides 1.6.3, as applied to the "Ionian" style among old-fashioned aristocratic Athenians.

54. The evidence for this theme is supplemented by the testimony of Theopompus FGH 115 F 117 in Athenaeus 526c. See p. 264. Cf. also the Sybaris theme as discussed at p. 263.

55. The passage is quoted at p. 264. The evidence for this corollary theme is supplemented by the testimony of Phylarchus FGH 81 F 66 in Athenaeus 526a. See pp. 263 and following.

56. Cf. p. 264. On the theme of variations in human fortunes from mighty to slight, slight to mighty, cf. Herodotus 1.5.3–4 and the discussion at p. 240.

57. Cf. perhaps Archilochus F 23.17–20 W.

58. Knox 1984.

59. Fraenkel 1957.211–213 notes that Latin *otium* is used to convey the traditional Greek topic of **truphē** 'luxuriance' as resulting in the ruin of cities; see Knox 1984.98n5 for a sample of passages. This is not to say that *otium* is the exact equivalent of **truphē**.

60. Cf. also Lattimore 1944, who adduces Theognis 1103–1104, quoted above at p. 264.

The dangers of luxuriance apply also to that quintessentially sensuous center-piece of the Sapphic repertoire, the **(h)abros** Adonis (for the epithet, see again Sappho F 140.1 V). In the ideology of his cult the botanical luxuriance of Adonis leads to his own sterility and even doom.[61]

Dangerous as it is, however, luxuriance is a thing appreciated and cele-brated by the transcending medium of song—even if the luxuriance makes a man's thoughts turn to tyranny. This theme is evident in *Encomium* 20B (SM) of Bacchylides, where the voice of the poet declares that no mortal has ever had access to complete **olbos** 'bliss' in his lifetime (20B.23–24).[62] With this thought in mind, the poet visualizes in the same poem the intoxicated lightheartedness of a symposium at the very moment when the singing and dancing get under way; it is in this setting that the poet's thoughts can con-verge on wealth, sensuality, and tyranny:

ὦ βάρβιτε, μηκέτι πάσσαλον φυλάσ[σων] | ἑπτάτονον λ[ι]γυρὰν
κάππαυε γᾶρυν· | δεῦρ' ἐς ἐμὰς χέρας· ὁρμαίνω τι πέμπ[ειν] | χρύ-
σεον Μουσᾶν Ἀλεξάνδρῳ πτερὸν συμπος[ίαι]σιν ἄγαλμ' [ἐν] εἰκά-
δεσ[σιν], | εὖτε νέων ἁ[παλὸν] γλυκεῖ' ἀνάγκα | σευομενᾶν κυλί-
κων θάλπησι θυμόν, | Κύπριδός τ' ἐλπὶς <δι>αιθύσσῃ φρένας, | ἀμ-
μειγνυμένα Διονυσίοισι δώροις· | ἀνδράσι δ' ὑψοτάτω πέμπει
μερίμνας· | αὐτίκα μὲν πολίων κράδεμνα λύει, | πᾶσι δ' ἀνθρώποις
μοναρχήσειν δοκεῖ. | χρυσῷ δ' ἐλέφαντί τε μαρμαίρουσιν οἶκοι, |
πυροφόροι δὲ κατ' αἰγλάεντα πόντον | νᾶες ἄγουσιν ἀπ' Αἰγύπτου
μέγιστον | πλοῦτον· ὣς πίνοντος ὁρμαίνει κέαρ.

Bacchylides *Encomium* 20B 1–16 SM

Lyre, do not stay hanging on the peg, holding back your resonant seven-stringed sound. Come into my hands as I ponder what to send from the Muses to Alexander—something golden and winged—an adornment for symposia, in the last ten days of the month, when the sweet compulsion of jostling drinking-cups warms the heart of the young and makes it delicate, and when the <u>aspiration</u> for Aphrodite rushes through one's inner feelings, mixed with the gifts of Dionysus. It sends ambitions [**merimna** plural][63] to the uppermost heights for men; straightaway it undoes the protective headbands of cities, and it thinks that it will be monarch [**monarkhos**] over all mortals.[64] Build-

---

61. On the theme of the luxuriant Adonis as an exponent of **hubris** in a botanical sense, I cite again the full discussion in N 1985.60–63.

62. See the apparatus of SM, p. 98, for Snell's tentative reconstruction: ὄλβ[ον δ' ἔσχε πάντα οὔτις] ἀνθρώπων.

63. At Pindar F 124(ab).5 SM (on this poem cf. p. 288), **merimnai** is more easily translated in the general sense of 'concerns'.

64. Cf. p. 284.

ings gleam with gold and ivory, and throughout the shining sea there are wheat-bearing ships carrying the greatest wealth [**ploutos**] from Egypt. Such things it is that the heart of the drinking man ponders.[65]

Elsewhere too thoughts of sensuality and tyranny converge. Let us consider the following words of Simonides, in light of the well-known verse of Mimnermus in praise of sensuality, quoted immediately thereafter:

τίς γὰρ ἁδονᾶς ἄτερ θνατῶν βίος ποθεινὸς ἢ ποία τυραννίς | τᾶσδ᾽
ἄτερ οὐδὲ θεῶν ζηλωτὸς αἰών

Simonides PMG 584

What life of mortals, or what tyranny [**turannis**], is to be yearned for, if it is to be without pleasure [**hēdonē**]? Without it, even the lifetime [**aiōn**] of the gods is not to be envied.[66]

τίς δὲ βίος, τί δὲ τερπνὸν ἄτερ χρυσῆς ᾿Αφροδίτης·

Mimnermus F 1.1 W

What is life, what is pleasurable, without golden Aphrodite?

In the poetry of Archilochus we can detect an analogous theme: luxuriance and sensuality are attributes of not just any tyranny but Lydian tyranny in particular. The poet quotes a speaker as saying:

οὔ μοι τὰ Γύγεω τοῦ πολυχρύσου μέλει,
οὐδ᾽ εἷλέ πω με ζῆλος, οὐδ᾽ ἀγαίομαι
θεῶν ἔργα, μεγάλης δ᾽ οὐκ ἐρέω τυραννίδος·
ἀπόπροθεν γάρ ἐστιν ὀφθαλμῶν ἐμῶν

Archilochus F 19 W

I do not care about the possessions of Gyges rich in gold.
Envy has not yet taken hold of me. And I am not indignant
about what the gods do. Nor do I lust after great tyranny [**turannis**].
For it is far away from my eyes.[67]

65. Note the ring composition achieved with the placement of ὁρμαίνω/ὁρμαίνει 'ponder(s)' at lines 3/16. See van Groningen 1960.100–101 for a word-by-word comparison of Bacchylides F 20B 1–16 SM with Pindar F 124ab SM. The striking parallelisms lead van Groningen to worry about which of the two poems was imitated by the other.

66. Cf. the use of **terpnos aiōn** 'pleasurable lifetime' at Pindar F 126 SM, words addressed to Hieron, Tyrant of Syracuse, as quoted by Heraclides Ponticus F 55 Wehrli by way of Athenaeus 512d; this quotation from Pindar comes immediately after the quotation in Athenaeus 512c of the present passage from Simonides. Cf. Young 1968.

67. The last part of this statement, spoken by a character identified as Charon the Carpenter in Aristotle *Rhetoric* 1418b30, is analogous to a theme in the Gyges story as retold in Herodotus 1.7.2: the king of the Lydian Empire, Kandaules, tries to persuade his trusted bodyguard Gyges, who was later to become king himself by overthrowing Kandaules, to view the queen naked, on

In connection with Gyges, Tyrant of Lydia, Herodotus in fact testifies that Archilochus 'continued the memory [= root **mnē-**]' of a story told about Gyges (ἐπεμνήσθη 1.12.2) — presumably the same story that is narrated with such sensual gusto in the *Histories* of Herodotus: how Gyges acquired the **basileia** 'kingship'[68] of Lydia by winning the sexual favors of the Queen of Lydia (1.8.1–1.12.2).[69] This poetic theme, the memory of which is continued by Archilochus and, after him, by Herodotus, is made directly pertinent to the story of Croesus' misfortunes, which as we have seen is central to the *Histories* of Herodotus: the Oracle of Apollo at Delphi says that the usurpation committed by Gyges, that is, his political acquisition of the Lydian Empire and his sexual acquisition of the Lydian queen, calls for a **tisis** 'retribution' that will befall the fifth tyrant in the dynasty started by Gyges (1.13.1–2). This fifth tyrant turns out to be Croesus (1.15.1–1.16.1; 1.26.1).[70] For Herodotus, the continuity from Gyges to Croesus is a matter of thematic development, not just genealogy, in that Gyges serves to prefigure Croesus. This earlier Tyrant of Lydia, like Croesus, makes generous offerings to Apollo at Delphi (1.14.1–2);[71] moreover, he too attacks the cities of the Hellenes in Asia Minor — in this case Miletus, Smyrna, and Colophon (1.14.4).[72] Most important of all, the story of Gyges, like that of Croesus, manifests signs of **hubris** that set the theme for the overall narrative of the *Histories*. In the story of the tyrant Gyges, the **hubris** is manifested in an unrestrained sensuality that goes hand in hand with unrestrained political power. To repeat the essence of the tale: Kandaules, the tyrant whose queen and empire Gyges acquired, had a lust so great — ostensibly for the queen — that thinking her to be the most beautiful of all women, he was seized by a compulsion to reveal her naked to his trusted bodyguard, Gyges (1.8.1). Such is the legacy of tyrants, usurped by Gyges. It should come as no surprise then that the word **erōs** is used in the *Histories* of Herodotus only in two senses: sexual desire

---

the grounds that the queen's beauty can be witnessed by the eyes more reliably than by the ears. The answer given by Gyges to Kandaules at Herodotus 1.7.3–4 (on which see Benardete 1969.11–12) resembles in tone the quoted statement of Charon the Carpenter in Archilochus F 19 W.

68. On the semantic overlap of **basileus** 'king'/**monarkhos** 'sole ruler'/**turannos** 'tyrant', see pp. 174, 182, 184.

69. That the mention of Archilochus in Herodotus 1.12.2 refers to an integral narrative about Gyges and the Queen in the poetry of Archilochus, not just to the naming of Gyges as Tyrant of the Lydians, is argued by Clay 1986.11–12, who also raises the possibility that Archilochus F 23 W contains a dialogue between Gyges and the Queen.

70. On the symbolism of the number 5 in conveying the notion of coming full circle, see N 1979.169.

71. In fact Herodotus asserts that Gyges was the first barbarian to make offerings to Apollo at Delphi, except for Midas of Phrygia (1.14.2–3).

72. The distinction that Herodotus makes between the aggression of Croesus against the Hellenes on the one hand and that of this tyrant's predecessors on the other is made clear at 1.5.3, in conjunction with 1.6.1–3, on which passages see pp. 229 and following.

and the desire for tyranny.[73] Tyranny, as the daughter of the tyrant Periandros of Corinth observes in the *Histories*, has many **erastai** 'lovers' (3.53.4).[74]

Having seen that epinician song has the capacity both to appreciate the sensuality of the wealth inherent in victory and to warn against its perversion, we should not be surprised that, in the one attested Pindaric instance where the song explicitly warns against tyranny, it does so while all along promoting the ideals of moderation in a language that clearly espouses sensuality:

> θεόθεν ἐραίμαν καλῶν,| δυνατὰ μαιόμενος ἐν ἁλικίᾳ. τῶν γὰρ ἀνὰ
> πόλιν εὑρίσκων τὰ μέσα μακροτέρῳ| {σὺν} ὄλβῳ τεθαλότα, μέμ-
> φομ' αἶσαν τυραννίδων·| ξυναῖσι δ' ἀμφ' ἀρεταῖς τέταμαι· (...)[75]
> εἴ τις ἄκρον ἑλὼν ἡσυχᾷ τε νεμόμενος αἰνὰν ὕβριν| ἀπέφυγεν,
> μέλανος {δ'} ἂν ἐσχατιὰν καλλίονα θανάτου ⟨στείχοι⟩ γλυκυτάτᾳ
> γενεᾷ| εὐώνυμον κτεάνων κρατίσταν χάριν πορών

Pindar *Pythian* 11.50–58

May I lust for beauty that comes from the gods,[76] as I seek out in my own age that which is possible. As I search throughout the city, I find that the middle way flourishes with bliss [**olbos**], which is far more lasting than anything else. I find fault with the lot of tyrannies [**turannis** plural]. Instead, I exert myself by aiming for achievements [**aretē** plural] that are for the common benefit. (...) Whoever attains the highest point and abides serenely, escaping terrible outrage [**hubris**], such a man attains an ultimate goal that surpasses black death with its beauty, leaving behind for his beloved descendants a gratification [**kharis**] that confers a good name — a **kharis** that is the most precious of possessions.[77]

I may add in passing that this same poem of Pindar makes a fleeting mention of Troy, in the context of its ultimate doom, with words that convey the sensuality of both the city and the woman on whose account it was destroyed:

> ἐπεὶ ἀμφ' Ἑλένᾳ πυρωθέντας| Τρώων ἔλυσε δόμους ἁβρότατος

Pindar *Pythian* 11.33–34

... after he [= Agamemnon] destroyed Troy's edifice of luxuriance [**habrotēs**], incinerated because of Helen.[78]

---

73. Documentation in Benardete 1969.137.

74. For a most useful survey of this theme, see Hartog 1980.335–336. Note especially the expression ἐρασθεὶς τυραννίδος 'lusting after tyranny [**turannis**]' at Herodotus 1.96.2.

75. I omit here a stretch of the text where the testimony of the manuscripts is garbled.

76. Cf. ἔρος τὠελίω at Sappho F 58.26, which I interpret as 'lust for the sun' at p. 285.

77. So the **kharis** transcends the material possessions [**kteana**] that were won in the contest. On **kharis** as a 'beautiful and pleasurable compensation, through song or poetry, for a deed deserving of glory', see p. 65. More on Pindar *Pythian* 11 in Young 1968.

78. Compare *Iliad* XIII 631–639, a passage with a parallel theme — but with a martial twist.

Figures of myth, such as Helen of Troy, provide unambiguously negative paradigms for warning against the perversion of **olbos** 'bliss'. Let us take the specific example of Ixion:

ἔμαθε δὲ σαφές. εὐμενέσσι γὰρ παρὰ Κρονίδαις | γλυκὺν ἑλὼν βίοτον, μακρὸν οὐχ ὑπέμεινεν ὄλβον, μαινομέναις φρασὶν | Ἥρας ὅτ᾿ ἐράσσατο, τὰν Διὸς εὐναὶ λάχον | πολυγαθέες· ἀλλά νιν ὕβρις εἰς ἀυάταν ὑπεράφανον | ὦρσεν· τάχα δὲ παθὼν ἐοικότ᾿ ἀνὴρ | ἐξαίρετον ἕλε μόχθον

Pindar Pythian 2.25–29

He [= Ixion] learned his lesson, and a clear one it was. For, receiving a life of pleasure from the kindly disposed children of Kronos [= Zeus and his siblings], he did not, in his crazed mind, await expectantly his great bliss [**olbos**], as he conceived a lustful passion for Hera, whose bed of delights was for Zeus alone to share. But outrage [**hubris**] propelled him into conspicuous derangement [**atē**]. The man quickly got his just deserts, suffering exceptional distress.

In this case man's perversion of **olbos** is manifested in sensual extravagance, the violation of sexual norms. For an analogous case of crime and punishment, we may compare the example of Tantalos:

εἰ δὲ δή τιν᾿ ἄνδρα θνατὸν Ὀλύμπου σκοποὶ | ἐτίμασαν, ἦν Τάνταλος οὗτος· ἀλλὰ γὰρ καταπέψαι | μέγαν ὄλβον οὐκ ἐδυνάσθη, κόρῳ δ᾿ ἕλεν | ἄταν ὑπέροπλον, ἄν τοι πατὴρ ὕπερ | κρέμασε καρτερὸν αὐτῷ λίθον, | τὸν αἰεὶ μενοινῶν κεφαλᾶς βαλεῖν εὐφροσύνας ἀλᾶται. | ἔχει δ᾿ ἀπάλαμον βίον τοῦτον ἐμπεδόμοχθον

Pindar Olympian 1.54–59

If ever there was a mortal man who was honored by the guardians of Olympus [= Zeus and his gods], it was this one, Tantalos. But he was not able to digest his great bliss [**olbos**], and, with his insatiability [**koros**], he got an overwhelming derangement [**atē**],[79] which the

---

Menelaos is blaming the Trojans as **hubristai** 'perpetrators of outrage [**hubris**]' (633), with a **menos** 'disposition' that is **atasthalon** 'reckless' (634). In this context the Trojans are described as insatiable in war (634–635), with the notion of satiation expressed by the verb **kor-ennumi** (κορέσασθαι 635). Menelaos goes on to say that all pleasures reach a point of satiety, **koros** (πάντων μὲν κόρος ἐστί 636) — namely, the pleasures of sleep, sex, song, dance (636–637) — and that he would expect a man to take his fill of these pleasures, not of war (638–639). But, he concludes, the Trojans are **akorētoi** 'insatiable' in war (639). As C. Cowherd points out to me, Menelaos does not mention the pleasures of food and drink, though the expression ἐξ ἔρον εἶναι 'take one's fill' (638: noun **eros**!) is conventionally applied to satiation in food and drink.

79. On **atē** 'derangement' as punishment (consequence) as well as crime (cause), see p. 243.

Father hung over his head in the form of an unyielding rock, which he [= Tantalos] forever seeks to dodge, as he keeps missing out on <u>mirth</u> [**euphrosunē**].[80] And he has this irremediable life of everlasting distress.

Having given the general reason for the punishment of Tantalos, his failure 'to digest his great bliss [**olbos**]', the poem proceeds to give the specific reasons: Tantalos stole and distributed to the other members of his symposium the nectar and ambrosia that the gods had given to him alone (Pindar *Olympian* 1.60–64). Earlier the poem had entertained and then denied another possible version, according to which Tantalos had given the unsuspecting gods the flesh of his own son, Pelops, to eat (47–53). The expression κατα-πέψαι μέγαν ὄλβον οὐκ ἐδυνάσθη 'he was not able to digest his great **olbos**' (55) covers both versions in that the perversion of **olbos** by Tantalos entails in either case a violation of dietary norms,[81] just as the perversion of **olbos** by Ixion entails a violation of sexual norms (again *Pythian* 2.26–29).[82]

The story of Tantalos, attested already in such early traditions as the Cycle (e.g., *Nostoi* F 10 Allen in Athenaeus 281b), is especially important for this entire presentation because it helps us understand how the story of Croesus, as applied both in epinician song and in the *Histories* of Herodotus, is closer to home than we may at first have imagined. The initial impression of Croesus the Lydian as the quintessential foreigner, an oriental potentate who is supposedly the antithesis of what it means to be a Hellene, comes into question as we begin to consider in more detail the myth of Tantalos, the earliest Lydian of them all. Son of the god Zeus himself and of a mortal woman called **Ploutō**, wealth incarnate (Pausanias 2.22.3),[83] Tantalos ruled over a land rich in gold, stretching from Lydia to Phrygia and the Troad (Aeschylus *Niobe* TGF 158, 162, 163). The Lydian dynasty of Tantalos was short-lived, however: his son, Pelops, was deposed and driven out by 'Ilos the Phrygian' (Pausanias 2.22.3). This Ilos, son of Tros and brother of Ganymede, had gone to Phrygia and founded Ilion—that is, Troy—at a spot known as the Hill of **Atē** (Apollodorus 3.12.2–3);[84] he is the same Ilos reported to be

---

80. In the words of Bacchylides gold as the symbol of good and genuine **olbos** 'bliss' is the same thing as **euphrosunē** (εὐφροσύνα δ' ὁ χρυσός 3.87); whoever perverts **olbos**, as Tantalos did, is punished by a failure ever again to achieve **euphrosunē**.

81. Cf. pp. 133 and following.

82. The parallelism of dietary and sexual violations is pertinent to the semantics of **koros** 'satiety, point at which satiety is reached, insatiability' (as at *Olympian* 1.56). Although **koros** applies primarily to food and drink, it can also apply to sex (*Iliad* XIII 636–637, as discussed at p. 291). Note too the collocation of **koros** at *Olympian* 2.95 with **margos**, an adjective conveying both dietary and sexual excess (on which see N 1979.229–231).

83. On Tantalos as son of Zeus, cf. also Euripides *Orestes* 5.

84. On the Hill of **Atē**, see also Stephanus of Byzantium s.v. **Ilion**. This theme is pertinent to another, the **habrotēs** 'luxuriance' of Troy: see p. 290.

worshipped by the Trojans as their cult hero in the *Iliad* (e.g., X 415).[85] As for Pelops, Herodotus has the Persian king Xerxes referring to him as a mere vassal of the mighty empire inherited by the Persians, and Xerxes even calls him 'Pelops the Phrygian' (Πέλοπος τοῦ Φρυγός Herodotus 7.8γ.1, Πέλοψ ὁ Φρύξ 7.11.4). From the Persian point of view, then, Pelops is an antecedent of such figures as Midas the Phrygian (named, for example, in Herodotus 1.14.2) — not to mention Croesus the Lydian.

But Xerxes also takes note that this same Pelops, this 'slave' of the predecessors of Xerxes (δοῦλος Herodotus 7.11.4), had conquered the Peloponnesus, which was named after him (again 7.11.4). Moreover, the Persian king's arrogant appropriation of Pelops and hence of the Peloponnesus is actually based on a Hellenic myth to the effect that Pelops was indeed a Lydian (Λυδοῦ Πέλοπος, Pindar *Olympian* 1.24, Λυδὸς ἥρως Πέλοψ, *Olympian* 9.9), who was ousted from his homeland and emigrated to the Peloponnesus (in Pindar's words the Peloponnesus is the **apoikiā** 'colony' of Pelops: *Olympian* 1.24).[86] This myth, from the vantage point of the *Histories* of Herodotus, is particularly suited to Sparta, the Hellenic city-state that came to dominate the Peloponnesus and was the foremost of all Hellenic states on the Mainland to establish an alliance with Lydia. As Herodotus observes, most of the Peloponnesus was under the domination of Sparta at the time when Croesus sought the alliance of this city-state (ἤδη δέ σφι καὶ ἡ πολλὴ τῆς Πελοποννήσου ἦν κατεστραμμένη 1.68.6), and in fact the narrative of Herodotus attributes the alliance to the premise, accepted by Croesus, that Sparta was decidedly the foremost city of all Hellas (1.69.2 and 1.70.1).[87] Whether or not we may view this premise as a historical fact, it is certainly presented as such in the *Histories* of Herodotus.[88] In any case, it is indeed a

85. On this passage, cf. N 1979.145 §8n2.
86. Cf. p. 130.
87. Elsewhere in Herodotus, Sparta and Athens are presented as sharing in the honor of being the foremost city-states of Hellas, to be sought out by Croesus as allies (1.56.2–3, following up on 1.53.1). The inclusion of Athens, however, is more by hindsight: it sets the stage for the central roles to be played by Sparta and Athens in the rest of the *Histories*, and it provides an opportunity for a brief sketch, at the outset of the narrative, of the importance of both cities (Athens: 1.56.3–1.64.3; Sparta: 1.65.1–1.68.6). We may note that from the ostensible standpoint of Croesus the initial importance of Athens is viewed almost exclusively in terms of the achievements of the tyrant Peisistratos (1.59–1.64.3).
88. Let us consider again the ostensible standpoint of Croesus: the importance of Sparta is viewed in terms of its military successes in dominating the Peloponnesus, but there is also mention of the city's political successes in developing an outstanding constitution, thanks to the achievements of the lawgiver Lycurgus (1.65.2–1.66.1). Note the vegetal imagery inherent in the expression ἀνά τε ἔδραμον . . . καὶ εὐθενήθησαν 'they shot up and flourished' (1.66.1), applied to the Spartans in their state of **eunomiā** 'good government' (μετέβαλον δὲ ὧδε ἐς εὐνομίην 1.65.2; οὕτω μὲν μεταβαλόντες εὐνομήθησαν 1.66.1). For parallel uses of the verb **ana-trekhō** 'shoot up' in describing the growth of plantlife, see *Iliad* XVIII 56, 437; also Herodotus 7.156.2, 8.55; for a parallel use of **eutheneō** 'flourish' in the context of **eunomiā** 'good government', see Herodotus 2.124.1. Note too the vegetal imagery in Solon F 4.32–35 W: **eunomiā** (personified)

historical given that the Lydian connection was formalized politically in the alliance between Sparta and Lydia (as also in earlier contacts: Herodotus 1.69.3–4). Moreover, the same Lydian connection was formalized ideologically in the myth about the colonization of the Peloponnesus by Pelops the Lydian.

This is not to say that the myth about a Lydian founder of the Peloponnesus was invented out of nothing by the Spartans in order to justify their Lydian policy. The alien — that is to say, Lydian — identity of Pelops was a theme appropriated by the Spartans as validation of their Lydian contacts: if Sparta's self-image is to be glorious, then its Lydian contacts are also glorious. But the actual theme of a Lydian Pelops was not invented ad hoc for the Lydian policy of Sparta: rather it was inherited from an earlier phase of Hellenic history and myth making — the era of the colonization of Asia Minor and the transplanting of native myths and rituals from the Mainland.[89]

From the standpoint of the Greek cities of Asia Minor, the tomb of Tantalos is on Mount Sipylos, overlooking the city of Smyrna (Pausanias 2.22.3; cf. 5.13.7, 7.24.13, 8.17.3).[90] Already in the *Iliad*, the realm of Tantalos is visualized in the environs of Mount Sipylos, as we see from the details of the reference to his daughter Niobe (XXIV 615).[91] Yet other evidence suggests that these figures of Tantalos and his family were originally native to the Peloponnesus; one version, for example, locates his place of origin as Argos (Hyginus *Fables* 124).[92] There was a tradition native to the city of Argos, a tradition reported but not accepted by Pausanias, to the effect that the bones

---

'withers the burgeoning blossoms of derangement [atē]' (αὐαίνει δ' ἄτης ἄνθεα φυόμενα).

89. On the reflexes of such patterns of transplanting in the **ktisis** ('foundation, colonization') poetic traditions of various city-states, see N 1979.8 §14n1 (with cross-references) and especially pp. 139–141; also N 1982.63–64 and 1985.51 §38n1 and 63 §51n2. I stress that these patterns are a reflex not of colonization itself but rather of the poetic traditions about colonization.

90. The testimony of Pausanias associating Tantalos with the region of Mount Sipylos is particularly valuable in light of this author's background. As Habicht 1985.13–15 has convincingly argued, Pausanias is probably native to the Sipylos region ("everything points to Magnesia on the Sipylos as his place of origin": p. 14). Habicht, p. 15n66, draws attention to ten passages where Pausanias gives revealing specific details about this region, one of which concerns an epichoric dance (6.22.1). On the unrelenting emphasis given by Pausanias to the perspectives of the Archaic and Classical periods of Greece, to the disadvantage of the Hellenistic and later periods, see Habicht, pp. 23, 134, 149.

91. The river **Akhelōios**, mentioned at *Iliad* XXIV 616 as a landmark in the same environs as Mount Sipylos, is thought by Pausanias to be distinct from the river of the same name that flows through Acarnania and Aetolia (8.28.9–10) or the one in Arcadia (8.28.10).

92. Survey in Sakellariou 1958.227n2 of versions indicating the Peloponnesian provenience of Tantalos; see in general pp. 409 and 226–227 on the transplanting of the Tantalos figure from regions of the Mainland to the region of Smyrna in Asia Minor. Sakellariou also surveys the evidence for maintaining that Greeks were established in the region of Smyrna before the Lydians (pp. 408–410; cf. also pp. 391–392).

of Tantalos were actually kept in Argos (2.22.2).[93] The Argives had another tradition, again reported but not accepted by Pausanias, that not all the children of Niobe died at the hands of Apollo and Artemis: two of them, Chloris and Amyklas, had been saved by Leto, and the statue of Chloris was housed in the sanctuary of Leto at Argos (2.21.9–10).[94] It seems that from the Argive point of view Tantalos and his family never left the Peloponnesus.[95] Since the location of a hero's bones was the ultimate test of his authentic affinities to any given place,[96] this native Argive tradition, in claiming the bones of Tantalos, father of Pelops, was in effect asserting the right of Argos to dominion over the Peloponnesus. Thus the Spartan adoption of an alternative tradition, appropriate to the Hellenic colonizations of Asia Minor, serves a dual purpose. First, the localization of Tantalos and his tomb at Sipylos, a region associated with the Lydian Empire, would negate any direct Argive claim to dominion over the Peloponnesus, which would have been based on the notion that Tantalos as father of Pelops is the symbolic progenitor of political power, of dynasty itself, in the Peloponnesus. Second, such a localization serves the interests of Sparta, the rival of Argos, in drawing attention to the alliance of the Lydian Empire with Sparta.[97]

The fact remains, however, that Lydia is a foreign concept to all Hellenes, and that the founder of the Peloponnesus, Pelops, is also conceived as foreign. This aspect of the myth of Pelops, that he is a foreigner, serves to illustrate an important lesson of myth: it is the paradox that whatever is alien is also native. The message of such a paradox is at the same time reassuring and disquieting. Let us consider the positive aspect first. It is surely reassuring to think that whatever is threatening, alien, can really be understood as familiar, native. To be ethnocentric is to explain, rationalize, and motivate the alien or the Other in terms of the native or the Self, and the ethnocentrism

93. Pausanias accepts a version that makes this Tantalos prosopographically distinct (2.22.3). The main reason for the rejection of the Argive version by Pausanias has to do with his own close ties to the region of Sipylos, as discussed at p. 294. Pausanias is openly hostile to Argive versions: 2.23.6.

94. Pausanias 2.21.9–10 accepts the Homeric version, which does not draw attention to any local variation: according to the *Iliad* all the children of Niobe were killed (xxiv 609). In the tradition of Argos the first man and first king is Phoroneus (Acusilaus FGH 2 F 23) — a version followed by Plato *Timaeus* 22a4–b3, who mentions Niobe in the same context without specifying her relationship to Phoroneus. If Tantalos is father of Niobe, I infer that he is son of Phoroneus in this Argive version. Such a construct would dovetail with the claim, rejected by Pausanias 2.22.2–3, that the bones of Tantalos were the possession of Argos.

95. Note too the prominent mention of Tantalos in the prologue of the *Orestes* of Euripides (1–10), the setting of which is Argos. The punishment of Tantalos is the same in the *Orestes* (5–7) as in Pindar's *Olympian* 1 (57–60). The crime of Tantalos is described, obliquely, at *Orestes* 8–10.

96. See p. 177.

97. See p. 293.

of the Hellenes is no exception to this general anthropological pattern.[98] When Hellenes come into contact with cultures that appear more prestigious by reason of greater antiquity or greater achievement, a typical response of their Hellenocentrism is to establish links with such cultures genealogically.[99] Thus the city-state of Argos, for example, claims as its founder an "Egyptian" named Danaos, twin brother of **Aiguptos**, who emigrated from Egypt on the first ship ever built (Apollodorus 2.1.4; Hesiod F 129 MW; cf. Aeschylus *Suppliants* 318 and following; also Herodotus 2.91.5).[100] Also, the city-state of Thebes claims as its founder a "Phoenician" named Kadmos, brother of **Phoinix** and of Europa (Apollodorus 3.1.1; cf. Herodotus 2.49.3, 5.57.1).[101] In both these cases the prestige of civilizations that are considered by the Hellenes to be older and superior is being appropriated by city-states in rivalry with each other for the sake of their own self-advancement and self-reassurance. In these particular cases the myths of Argos and Thebes can be contrasted with the claim of Athens that its population is so ancient as to be autochthonous (e.g., Euripides *Ion* 20–21, 29–30; Plato *Menexenus* 245d; cf. Herodotus 1.56.3).[102] We may compare the claim, compatible with Sparta, that Pelops, founder of the Peloponnesus, migrated there from Lydia (e.g., Pindar *Olympian* 1.24)[103] or from Phrygia (Herodotus 7.8γ.1, 7.11.4).[104] So much for the positive side of the equation "alien is native." On the negative side, however, this equation raises anxieties about whatever is native, familiar, just as it lowers them about whatever is alien. The threats that come from without can, according to this equation, really come from within.

The negative lesson inherent in the equation "alien is native" is illustrated by the Dionysus myth, as dramatized in the *Bacchae* of Euripides.[105] In this myth the newcomer Dionysus is perceived by the Hellenic citizens of Thebes as if he were the ultimate foreigner, and yet he turns out to be a native son: he is on his mother's side a grandson of Kadmos, founder of

98. This insight is thoroughly examined and illustrated by Hartog 1980; cf. also Redfield 1985.

99. Cf. Bickerman 1952.71.

100. Overview of the genealogy in West 1985.78.

101. See How and Wells 1912 I 349–350. On the variant that claims Europa as the daughter rather than sister of Phoinix: Apollodorus ibid. (already in *Iliad* XIV 321). Overview of variations in West 1985.82–83. For the Indo-European foundations of the Kadmos myth, cf. Vian 1963 and the discussion of Boedeker 1974.5.

102. On autochthony as a measure of the nobility of a polis: Aristotle *Rhetoric* 1360b31–32. On the ideology of Athenian autochthony in its various political phases, see Loraux 1982b, 1987b.

103. Cf. p. 293.

104. Cf. p. 293.

105. Overview of the Dionysus myth in the *Bacchae*: Segal 1982 (cf. Henrichs 1979). Cf. also pp. 385 and following.

Thebes. As the myth of Dionysus evolves through the ages, it keeps attracting features that characterize what is perceived as foreign to each passing age of Hellenism; what remains a constant is simply the foreignness of the figure, and it is this foreignness that is paradoxically native to him. Moreover, it is an old theme that he is always new: the structure keeps asserting that it is very new, when it is in reality very old. When the foreign is negative, it is perceived as very new; when the foreign is positive, it is recognized as very old. Since the myth of Dionysus keeps stressing the god's newness, experts in the history of Greek religion were used to thinking of him as a new import — until the name of Dionysus was discovered on a Linear B tablet dating back to the second millennium.[106] The delusions about the god go all the way back to Pentheus himself, a grandson of Kadmos on his father's side: this hero commits the ultimate mistake in not recognizing a fundamental message of the myth, that whatever he thought was alien to himself was really part of himself.[107] Dionysus seems to be new, not old, but he is in fact both old and new from the standpoint of the myth; similarly he seems to be alien, not native, but he is in fact both native and alien from the standpoint of the myth.

Wine, a primary feature of Dionysus, brings together the outsider and the insider. As we have just read in a poem of Bacchylides (*Encomium* 20B.1–16),[108] the intoxication of symposiasts — which is the gift of Dionysus — induces an **elpis** 'aspiration' for Aphrodite that sends the mind soaring with sensual reveries of tyranny, of gold and ivory, of ships sailing home with all manner of riches from foreign lands (in this case from Egypt).[109]

Another example of the negative lesson inherent in the equation "alien is native" is to be found in the myth of Adonis. The name itself, a Semitic borrowing,[110] has encouraged historians of Greek religion to think of the entire myth of Adonis as a borrowing — a transformation of the myths of the Phoenician Eshmun, the Syrian Tammuz, and the Sumerian Dumuzi.[111] Yet the myths of these related figures do not correspond closely to the Greek myth of Adonis, and Marcel Detienne has made a good case for the proposition that the structure of the Greek story is in fact autonomous.[112] It is simply that the story requires for its central character a figure who counts as an outsider. Thus the role of the outsider, a role that is really inside the tradition, attracts genuinely foreign features to reinforce itself. It even absorbs a

---

106. Cf. Boedeker 1974.4–5.
107. Boedeker ibid.
108. Cf. pp. 284, 287.
109. Cf. ibid.
110. Chantraine DELG 21.
111. Overview in Detienne 1972. 237–238.
112. Ibid.

foreign name to highlight its "foreign" identity.[113] I cite the formulation of Detienne in his attempt to grasp the essence of Adonis:[114]

> His quality of being oriental is linked to the way in which the Greeks represented the Orient — an Orient so close and yet so far away. Here was a world where the refinements of civilization and the enjoyment of the most dissolute pleasures promoted a style of life characterized by softness and sensuality. To take on the role of seducer and effeminate lover, to bring to life the persona of a young boy whom the search for pleasure ultimately condemned to a premature old age, what was needed was a **daimōn** whose traits were vague enough to get lost in this image of the Orient which the Greeks had made for themselves. Besides, only a foreign **daimōn** could represent the Other so overtly within the Greek system of thought. Only an oriental force-field could assume, to such an extent, a radical negation of the values represented by Demeter on both the religious and the political levels.

Let us sum up then the impact of the message "alien is native" in the myth of Pelops. A threatening connection with Lydians, with the Other, is really not so threatening at all for Sparta, since the first Lydian sired Pelops, founder of the homeland, who in turn was paternal grandfather of Menelaos, local hero of Sparta. On the other hand the threat itself is not neutralized: the converse of "alien is native" is that the reassurance to be found in things native can lead to self-deception since the threats associated with things foreign, such as luxuriance, can in fact come from within.

This two-way Spartan view of Lydia extends to other aspects of their institutions. A prominent example can be found in the traditions of singing and dancing at Sparta, as represented by the poet Alcman. The compositions attributed to such a figure are integral to the ritual complex of Spartan festivals.[115] The tradition specifies, in the case of Alcman, that this poet's provenience is Lydia (PMG 13a; also PMG 1 Scholion B; Velleius Paterculus 1.18.2; Aelian *Varia Historia* 12.50), and this detail can be correlated with the fact that there were Spartan rituals that centered on Lydian themes, such as the event known as τῶν Λυδῶν πομπή 'Procession of the Lydians' in connection with the cult of Artemis Orthia (Plutarch *Life of Aristides* 17.10). We may compare an event known as the 'Dance of the Lydian Maidens' at a festival of Artemis at Ephesus (Autocrates F 1 Kock, KA, by way of Aelian *De natura animalium* 12.9; Aristophanes *Clouds* 599–600).[116] In this case, it

113. On one of the "native" names of Adonis, Ἄωος (Hesychius s.v., *Etymologicum Magnum* s.v.), see Boedeker, p. 67.

114. Detienne, pp. 237–238. The translation is mine. For "god" I substitute **daimōn**, to accommodate 'hero' as well as 'god'.

115. Cf. pp. 343 and following; Calame 1977 II 34–35.

116. Cf. Calame I 178–185. For an overview of the contacts between Lydia and Ephesus, see Sakellariou 1958.392, 427–430.

seems clear that the term 'Lydian Maidens' designates a ritual role played by the local girls of Ephesus.[117] To return to the subject of Alcman: the pattern "alien is native" operates not only in terms of the official Spartan characterization of Alcman as a Lydian but also within his songs: luxuriance, for example, is represented by the songs of Alcman as a characteristically Lydian thing.[118] Indeed the songs themselves are well known for their characteristic luxuriance. We may apply here what we already know from other attestations that we have just surveyed: the luxuriance typified by the Lydians is an implicit threat from within, not just an explicit threat from without.

Which leads us to a question: was the theme of affinity between Hellenes and Lydians initiated by the Hellenes of Asia Minor as an ideological justification of their Lydian contacts or by the Lydians to legitimize their eventual hegemony over the Hellenes of Asia Minor and their alliance with other Hellenes, especially the Spartans? The answer cuts both ways.

To begin, let us take one more look at the story of Herodotus about Croesus the Lydian: we have already noted that this foreigner is in fact part of a Hellenic story pattern, bearing an implicit message of admonition for all Hellenes. We have also noted that for the Hellenic audience of Herodotus the affinities of Pelops the Founder with the Lydians make Croesus a figure as familiar as he is foreign.

In the *Histories* of Herodotus, however, we can see the pattern of familiarity extended even further to include the Persians themselves. To understand how this is done, let us consider the genealogical background. Tradition has it that the dynasty of Pelops was preceded by the dynasty of Perseus, father of Alkaios, grandfather of Amphitryon, and thus nominally great-grandfather of Herakles (e.g., Apollodorus 2.4.5). Since Alkaios had married a daughter of Pelops (Hesiod F 190.6–8 MW), this genealogy has Herakles as great-grandson of both Perseus and Pelops. Perseus was also father of Sthenelos, grandfather of Eurystheus (F 190.11–12);[119] the dynasty of Perseus ended with this Eurystheus, the infamous figure who stood in the way of any eventual kingship for Herakles (*Iliad* XIX 95–133).[120] After Eurystheus, the dynasty of Perseus is replaced by the dynasty of Pelops, father of Atreus and Thyestes, grandfather of Agamemnon and Menelaos. In the actual sequence of ruling kings, the rule of Eurystheus is followed by that of Atreus and Thyestes (e.g., Apollodorus *Epitome* 2.11).[121] The dynasty of Pelops is in

117. For more on ritual role playing, see Ch.12.

118. Cf., for example, p. 347.

119. Like Alkaios, Sthenelos too married a daughter of Pelops (Hesiod F 190.9 and following).

120. On the theme of Herakles as kingmaker but never king, see Davidson 1980.

121. Further details and commentary in West 1985.159n75. In the *Iliad*, however, the field of vision is restricted to the sequence of Pelopidai: the scepter goes from Pelops to Atreus to Thyestes to Agamemnon (II 101–108).

turn replaced by the **Hērakleidai** 'sons of Herakles', who represent the ancestors of the Dorian dynasties who took over the major political centers of the Peloponnesus in the Dark Age (Tyrtaeus 2.12–15W; Pindar *Pythian* 1.61–66, 5.69–72; *Isthmian* 9.1–3; cf. Herodotus 9.26, 27.1–2). The two most prominent Herakleidai, great-grandsons of Hyllos, the son of Herakles who killed Eurystheus (e.g., Apollodorus 2.8.1), are Temenos, founder of the royal dynasty of Argos (Theopompus FGH 115 F 393), and Aristodemos, whose two sons Eurysthenes and Prokles are co-founders of the dual royal dynasty of Sparta (Herodotus 6.52.1, Pausanias 2.18.7).[122] Eurysthenes is the forefather of the royal line of the Agiadai (Herodotus 4.147, 6.52, 7.204; Pausanias 3.1.7), while his twin Prokles is the forefather of the royal line of the Eurypontidai (Herodotus 6.52.1, 8.131.2). Thus in the case of Sparta a historical figure like King Leonidas can trace his genealogy all the way back to Herakles: he is thirteen generations removed from Agis, son of Eurysthenes, son of Aristodemos, great-grandson of Hyllos, son of Herakles (Herodotus 7.204). Likewise in the case of Argos, the dynasty of the Herakleidai was still a concept to be reckoned with in the early fifth century, at the time of the Persian War, as we see from an explicit comparison in Herodotus 7.149.2 of the two kings of Sparta with the one king of Argos.[123] From the standpoint of either Sparta or Argos, then, the Herakleidai or "Sons of Herakles" represent a reestablishment of the dynasty of Perseus. In other words both Sparta and Argos have legitimate genealogical claims to dominion over the Peloponnesus by way of their respective dynasties in that both cities can trace their kings back to Hyllos, son of Herakles and descendant of the House of Perseus.

With this genealogical background we come finally to the myth of a Persian affinity with Hellenes. In seeking the cooperation of the city-state of Argos, the Persian king Xerxes sends the Argives a messenger promising to treat them as superior to all others and claiming as the basis of the Persians'

---

122. Variations in Apollodorus 2.8.2 and following; convenient summary in West 1985.113. Another brother of Temenos and Aristodemos is Kresphontes, founder of the dynasty of Messenia (Pausanias 4.3.3–4).

123. Pausanias 2.19.2 reports that the royal authority of Medon, the grandson of Temenos the Heraclid, was already in that era checked by the polis of Argos so that the political power of the descendants of Medon was diminished; also that Meltas, the tenth descendant of Medon, was deposed altogether. The testimony of Pausanias about the removal of Meltas need not be interpreted to mean that kingship was abolished altogether. Meltas was the descendant of King Pheidon of Argos, who is described as a **turannos** 'tyrant' in Herodotus 6.127.3 (on his genealogy, see Theopompus FGH 115 F 393; cf. Jeffery 1976.135–136 on the political ideology of the "Heritage" of Temenos, as pursued by King Pheidon). How and Wells 1928 II 189 remark that Pheidon's reassertion of royal power was an exceptional phase, analogous to a tyranny, and that "presumably the monarch only retained the old royal right to priesthood and other formal honours, perhaps presidency of the Boule." On the problems of dating the genealogical sequence of the Argive dynasty, see Kelly 1976.105–111.

offered friendship the common ancestry of Argives and Persians: they both can trace themselves all the way back to Perseus, he claims, in that Perseus had yet another son, named Perses, who was ancestor of all Persians (Herodotus 7.150.1–2 in conjunction with 7.61.3). The Persians could have said the same thing to the Spartans in that Sparta, just like Argos, preserved a dynasty of Herakleidai, but the enmity of Persia and Sparta was at this point already set, even serving as the actual premise for the Persian overture to Argos.

The Lydians, under the dynasty that preceded the reign of Gyges, might have said something very similar to what the Persians are saying here to the Argives: from the standpoint of their foreign relations with Hellenes, the dynasty of Kandaules, Tyrant of Lydia, was a dynasty of Herakleidai 'Heraclids' ('Ηρακλειδέων Herodotus 1.7.1) in that Kandaules claimed to be the descendant of one Alkaios, son of Herakles (Herodotus 1.7.2).[124] This dynasty of Herakleidai was overthrown later by Gyges, ancestor of Croesus (Herodotus 1.7.2–1.14.4).

It would be simplistic to suppose that such a genealogy was invented in a vacuum. Instead it would make more sense to infer that the Lydians were in this case drawing upon the ethnocentric thought patterns of their Hellenic neighbors. This is not to say that the Lydians could not or did not effect changes, even radical ones, in contemporary Greek thought patterns. In that myth making is a social phenomenon, the domination of a given society by, say, Lydian dynasts can be expected to have an effect on the myths of that society. The process of reshaping myths must take place in terms of the myths themselves.

To pursue the argument that the Lydian dynasts, by way of calling themselves Herakleidai, were drawing upon the ethnocentric thought patterns of their Hellenic neighbors, let us consider a myth ascribed by Herodotus to the Greeks who settled the regions of the Pontos ('Ελλήνων . . . οἱ τὸν Πόντον οἰκέοντες 4.8.1): according to this myth the barbarian natives of these regions, the Scythians, can be traced back genealogically to the sexual union of Herakles himself with a half-woman, half-snake (4.8–10). No doubt this myth contains native Scythian elements,[125] but it has been appropriated and reshaped by and for Hellenes. It need not matter whether or not we know which side initiated the appropriation, the Hellenes or the Scythians. After all, myth is a matter of communication, and it is more important to recognize that we are dealing with a dialogue between two distinct societies than to

124. This particular model of Alkaios the Heraclid may be attested indirectly at least in the native Greek context of the Lesbian traditions about Alkaios = Alcaeus, if we accept the argument that the Alcaeus figure, as contrasted with Pittakos in the poetry of Alcaeus, is thematically parallel to the Kyrnos figure, as contrasted with Theognis in the poetry of Theognis: see p. 186. On the possibility that the Kyrnos of Theognis represents a Heraclid prince, see p. 183.

125. How and Wells 1928 I 305. On Herodotus 4.5–7, see Dumézil 1978.171 and following.

ascertain which society initiated the dialogue. Moreover, if a given myth serves as dialogue between two distinct societies, it can speak to both even when it is expressed from the standpoint of one. For a Scythian to accept the Hellenic standpoint of the myth under consideration is the same thing as accepting — or offering — a token of some level of relationship with Hellenes. In this case we cannot be specific about the nature of the relationship. In the case of the Lydians, however, the situation is more clear. The Lydians, in asserting their hegemony over neighboring Hellenes, adopt a Hellenocentric viewpoint to establish this relationship. The earlier dynasty of Lydia does this by claiming descent from Herakles, thus appropriating a prestige that is commensurate with that of dynasties of the Peloponnesus that are direct heirs to the heroic age of Hellas. As for the Lydian dynasty after the Herakleidai, starting with Gyges and ending with Croesus, it seems to have taken an ethnocentric stance in its own right by claiming as the very first king of Lydia the figure of Tantalos, who is seemingly native to Argos.[126] This appropriation of Tantalos as a Lydian serves the purposes of the Lydians in that Tantalos is the father of Pelops, revered by Hellenes as founder of the Olympics and as an emblem of the political power implicit in the concept of the Peloponnesus, the "Island of Pelops." This appropriation also serves the purposes of the Spartans in their rivalry with Argos, if indeed the Argives considered Tantalos their own native son.[127] Thus the Lydian version of the Tantalos myth affords a dialogue, so to speak, between Lydia and Sparta at the ideological and political expense of Argos.

This theme brings us back to the Persian overtures to Argos, expressed in terms of a myth that tells how Perseus was the father of Perses, ancestor of the Persians (again Herodotus 7.150.1–2).[128] In this case the Persian version of the Perseus myth affords a dialogue between Persia and Argos in the con-

126. Cf. p. 294.

127. Cf. p. 294.

128. Although this "dialogue," from the Persian point of view, is at the political expense of Sparta, there is nothing in the myth of Perses, son of Perseus, that would directly undercut the Spartan kingship's genealogical derivation from Perseus. Herodotus elsewhere records another aspect of the myth, this one clearly congenial to the Persians from their ethnocentric point of view and just as clearly less appropriate for any overture to Argos: according to the Persians, Herodotus says, Perseus was originally an Assyrian who, *unlike his ancestors*, became a Hellene (6.54). Besides, continues Herodotus, both Persians and Hellenes agree that Perseus was an Egyptian on his mother's side (ibid.). Herodotus says that he chooses to say no more about the Egyptian connection on the grounds that the subject has already been treated by others (6.55; note the implication of textuality in this statement). The mother of Perseus is Danae — who represents a point that is as far back as the general Hellenic vision of the genealogy of Dorian kings goes, according to Herodotus (6.53.1). But we know that the genealogy can in fact be taken further back in the Argive version of the myth: Danae was the daughter of Akrisios, who was son of Abas, who was son of Hypermestra, who was daughter of Danaos, the founder of Argos (Apollodorus 2.1.4; Hesiod F 129 MW; cf. Aeschylus *Suppliants* 318 and following; also Herodotus 2.91.5). Cf. West 1985.78.

text of Persia's ostensible support for the hegemony of Argos over the Peloponnesus. This theme in turn brings us back to the subject of the rivalry of
Argos and Sparta. At the time of the Persian invasion, when Persia was making overtures to Argos, the contest seemed to have been already won by
Sparta. The Argives had been decisively defeated by the Spartans at Sepeia
in 494 B.C. (Herodotus 6.76–83, 92) — a defeat that can be described as "the
logical culmination of events that began more than a half a century earlier
with the Spartan conquest of and alliance with Tegea and the subsequent victory over Argos in the Battle of Champions [546 B.C.]."[129] Even in the context of this earlier period, when Sparta defeated Tegea and overtures were
being made to the Spartans by Croesus the Lydian, Herodotus observes that
much of the Peloponnesus was already under Spartan domination (1.68.6).[130]

It seems then that the preeminence assigned by Herodotus to Sparta at
the time of the overtures made by Croesus the Lydian is at least in part a
matter of hindsight on the part of the *Histories*. From the hindsight of the
Spartan victories over Argos in 546 B.C. and in 494 B.C., both predating the
overtures of Croesus,[131] Sparta did indeed become the preeminent power in
the Peloponnesus. The hindsight extends further: it can be argued that the
preeminence assigned by Herodotus to the two states of Athens and Sparta at
the dramatic juncture of Croesus' overtures, as also throughout the *Histories*,
is a direct function of the successes achieved by these two particular states in
the War with the Persians.

This is not to say that in the *Histories* the motive for dramatizing the
theme that Athens and Sparta were the preeminent city-states of Hellas was a
bias on the part of Herodotus in favor of these states. True, it has often been
claimed that Herodotus takes sides,[132] especially in favor of the Athenians,[133]
but in fact the various statements in the *Histories* that work to the advantage
or disadvantage of any city-state cannot be understood without first coming
to terms with the traditional stance of Herodotus. As one who conducts a
historiā 'inquiry', he is assuming an overarching position of authority that
entails emphasizing the point of view that he deems the most just. At least in
theory he must not associate himself with the interests of any one city-state.
He will not even associate himself consistently with the Greeks in that the
Hellenes are for him sometimes "we," sometimes "they."[134] From such a

129. Kelly 1976.140. On the Battle of Champions, see Herodotus 1.82 (cf. Kelly, p. 116). Cf.
also Calame 1987.177.

130. See p. 293.

131. From the standpoint of Herodotus 1.82–83, Sardis was already being besieged by the
Persians when the Spartans were preoccupied with the events culminating in the Battle of the
Champions.

132. For example, How and Wells 1928 I 37–43.

133. How and Wells I 41–43.

134. Survey and analysis in Hartog 1980.371–372, 376.

privileged position, he proceeds to narrate and thereby to adjudicate the ultimate conflict between Hellenes and Persians; the fact that the Hellenes are treated partially is motivated by the principle that the Persians in particular and the Asiatics in general are found to be guilty, in the wrong, by way of the narrative itself. It is as if Herodotus merely must have a good sense of judgment in his narration so that the patterns of divine justice could implicitly work their way through this narration.

Yet since the principle "alien is native" is so ingrained in the traditions of the Greek city-states, the voice of **historiā** has much to teach the Hellenes by way of a grand juxtaposition of the foreign with the native in the narrative of Herodotus. Whenever Greeks and barbarians interact in the overall conflict recorded by the *Histories*, the barbarian point of view becomes an intellectual exercise in Hellenic introspection through the overarching perspective of **historiā**.

This intellectual exercise can perhaps be seen most clearly in the so-called Debate of the Constitutions (Herodotus 3.80–87), where the leaders of the Persian Empire are represented as debating the relative merits of three possible forms of government: democracy, oligarchy, and 'monarchy' (3.82.3).[135] While this debate is, of course, an absurdity from the standpoint of our own notions of history—and Herodotus is defensive about the lack of verisimilitude in this part of his narrative—it nevertheless serves as an ideal focus for the entire narrative from the standpoint of **historiā**. These three forms of government correspond to the three protagonists of the *Histories*: the democracy of Athens, the oligarchy of Sparta, and the 'monarchy' of Persia. At first blush the 'monarchy' of Persia seems an institution foreign to the Greeks, but the word **monarkhos** 'monarch' is ostentatiously equated in the Debate passage with **turannos** 'tyrant' (Herodotus 3.80.2/4)—the same word that the *Histories* of Herodotus and all Archaic Greek poetry and song consistently associate with both the attractions and the pitfalls of the wealth and the power that goes with tyranny. The pitfalls, moreover, as manifested in **hubris**, are not confined to tyranny. As the Debate passage makes clear, **hubris** proves to be the negative trait of men in a democracy as well (Herodotus 3.81.1–2); as for an oligarchy, the three symptoms of its shift toward 'monarchy' in the Debate passage (3.82.2) correspond to the three symptoms of **hubris** that lead from aristocracy to tyranny in the poetic traditions that warn against tyranny (Theognis 51–52; **hubris** at 40, 44).[136] The Persian king-to-be argues not only that oligarchies evolve into 'monarchy' (again Herodotus 3.82.3); so do democracies (3.82.4). Such patterns are supposed to prove the supremacy of tyranny (3.82.4–5). Thus the threat of tyranny is

135. Cf. p. 181. On the Indo-Iranian themes disguised underneath these Greek categories of democracy, oligarchy, and 'monarchy', see Dumézil 1985.246–253.

136. Cf. pp. 182, 265, 369.

in fact posed not just from without, by the Great King of the Persians, but also from within, by the wrongdoings of the Hellenes themselves.

In this regard it is important to keep in mind the historical context — and I am using *historical* here in the conventional sense of the word in our own time — for the composition of the *Histories* of Herodotus. It is a well-known fact that the *Histories* were composed at a time when the Peloponnesian War, the two main antagonists of which were the democracy of Athens and the oligarchy of Sparta, was under way.[137] That even the narrative of Herodotus can be perceived as functionally a prelude to the Peloponnesian War is clear from the narrative strategy of Thucydides (cf., e.g., 1.89.1–2), whose account of the events leading to the Peloponnesian War starts where Herodotus' account of the Persian War left off.

Given such a historical context for the composition of Herodotus' *Histories*, and that Herodotus "is interpreting the past by the present,"[138] we may ask ourselves what the message of his narrative might have been for the Hellenes of his time. In terms of the Debate passage the outward subject of the *Histories* is the struggle of Hellenes — primarily the democracy of Athens and the oligarchy of Sparta — against the tyranny of the Persians; the inward subject, however, is the struggle of the Hellenes against each other or, to put it another way, against themselves. In terms of the Peloponnesian War it can be said that this struggle takes the external form of the overall Hellenic conflict between the democracy of Athens and the oligarchy of Sparta; in terms of the Peloponnesian War the third main character of the *Histories*, that ultimate exponent of **hubris**, the Great King of the Persians, is in the background. In terms of the *Histories*, on the other hand, he is in the foreground. The intention of the *Histories* is to narrate the conflict of the Great King, exponent of **hubris**, with the Hellenes — and thereby to render a judgment about who was in the right and who was in the wrong. Such is the juridical function of **historiā**: to speak as a **histōr** 'arbitrator'.

Which brings to mind a suggestion: perhaps the implicit intention of the **historiā** of Herodotus is to "arbitrate" the ongoing conflict between the democracy of Athens and the oligarchy of Sparta — corresponding to the explicit intention of "arbitrating" the past conflict between tyrannical and anti-tyrannical ways of life.[139] In support of this suggestion, we may look to the traditions about the life of Herodotus: he is said to have settled, died, and been buried in Thourioi (Stephanus of Byzantium s.v. Θούριοι),[140] a city

---

137. Opinions differ about *termini post quem* for the final text fixation of the *Histories*. For a balanced discussion of evidence for a late dating, possibly even as late as 415 B.C., see Raaflaub 1987.236–237 (cf. also Fornara 1971b).

138. So Fornara 1971.88.

139. For details about the traditions of international (that is, inter-polis) arbitration, see Ch.11.

140. Commenting on the testimony of Duris of Samos FGH 76 F 64 and others to the effect that Herodotus is the Θούριος 'the man from Thourioi', How and Wells 1928 I 3 remark: "It is

founded ostensibly as a Panhellenic venture, with the involvement of both Athens and Sparta (Diodorus 12.10–11).[141] The city of Thourioi, founded in 444/3 B.C.,[142] was built at a site where once stood the city of Sybaris, that ultimate symbol of luxuriance and the **hubris** that goes with it.[143] The setting of Thourioi as a reborn and reformed Sybaris would have been an ideal context for a reaffirmation of the values that bind Hellenes together in an ultimate conflict against **hubris**. The **historiā** of Herodotus would have been an apt realization of such a Panhellenic goal. While I do not insist that the city of Thourioi was the actual setting for the composition of the *Histories* of Herodotus, I at least reaffirm the possibility.[144] Moreover, the **stasis** 'conflict' between Ionians and Dorians that reportedly developed in the city of Thourioi in the year 434/3, ten years after its foundation (Diodorus 12.35.2),[145] may well have appeared to Herodotus as a smaller-scale prefiguration of the larger-scale misfortune of the Peloponnesian War itself.[146]

It seems clear in any case that Herodotus thought of the Peloponnesian War as a misfortune for all Hellenes. In commenting on the earthquake that shook Delos in 490 B.C., Herodotus has this to say:

> καὶ τοῦτο μέν κου τέρας ἀνθρώποισι τῶν μελλόντων ἔσεσθαι κακῶν
> ἔφηνε ὁ θεός. ἐπὶ γὰρ Δαρείου τοῦ Ὑστάσπεος καὶ Ξέρξεω τοῦ Δα-
> ρείου καὶ Ἀρτοξέρξεω τοῦ Ξέρξεω, τριῶν τουτέων ἐπεξῆς γενεέων,
> ἐγένετο πλέω κακὰ τῇ Ἑλλάδι ἢ ἐπὶ εἴκοσι ἄλλας γενεὰς τὰς πρὸ Δα-
> ρείου γενομένας, τὰ μὲν ἀπὸ τῶν Περσέων αὐτῇ γενόμενα, τὰ δὲ ἀπ᾽
> αὐτῶν τῶν <u>κορυφαίων</u> περὶ τῆς ἀρχῆς πολεμεόντων.

Herodotus 6.98.2

And this was, I suppose, a portent whereby the god revealed to men the misfortunes that were to be. For in the reigns of Darius son of Hystaspes, Xerxes son of Darius, and Artaxerxes son of Xerxes, in the space of these three successive generations, more misfortunes befell Hellas than in the twenty generations before Darius. These misfortunes befell Hellas in part from the Persians, in part from its <u>leading figures</u> [**koruphaioi**][147] as they fought each other for supremacy.

Mention of the rule of Artaxerxes indicates that the era before and during the

---

141. A brief survey of known facts about the foundation of Thourioi in Graham 1983.35–37.
142. See Graham, p. 36.
143. On the Sybaris theme, see p. 263.
144. Discussion in Stambler 1982.226.
145. Graham, pp. 36–37.
146. Cf. Stambler 1982.226.
147. On the significance of this word **koruphaioi** 'leading figures': p. 368.

Peloponnesian War is meant as one chronological extreme; as for the other extreme, "twenty generations before the accession of Darius, at Herodotus' normal equivalence of three generations to the century, is 1189 B.C., the period of the Trojan War."[148] Thus the **historiā** of Herodotus associates its narrative, extending into the Peloponnesian War, with an epic theme, "the beginning of misfortunes,"[149] from the vantage point of the Trojan War.

Even the ending of the *Histories* seems to indicate — albeit indirectly — an association that stretches all the way from the Trojan War to the Peloponnesian War. The man who refused the compensation offered by the Persian Artauktes in return for wronging Protesilaos, the first "Hellene" to die in the Trojan War, was Xanthippos, father of Pericles of Athens (Herodotus 9.120.3–4).[150] At this point the Athenians led by Xanthippos were already acting on their own at the Hellespont, no longer assisted by their Hellenic allies from the Peloponnesus who had earlier fought on their side against the Persians and who had by now gone back home (Herodotus 9.114.2). Moreover, the behavior of the Athenian leader Xanthippos in executing Artauktes by crucifixion (Herodotus 9.120.4) stands in pointed contrast with that of the Spartan king Pausanias, who had rejected the suggestion that he impale the body of the Persian general Mardonios, in return for the Persians' having mutilated the body of the Spartan king Leonidas: Pausanias says simply that the mutilation of the enemy's corpse would be a deed that suits barbarians, not Hellenes (Herodotus 9.79.1).[151] This characterization of Pausanias by Herodotus undercuts the position taken by the Athenians, that this Spartan king was a man of **hubris** (Herodotus 8.3.2). The Athenians took this position, as Herodotus pointedly observes, in order to gain for themselves sole hegemony over the Hellenic alliance against Persia (8.3.2).

At an earlier time, as Herodotus observes in the same context, the Athenians had renounced sole hegemony, thereby avoiding **stasis emphūlos** 'intrasocietal conflict' that would have destroyed Hellas (8.3.2). The word **em-phūl-os**, which I translate here as 'intrasocietal', is clearly being used by Herodotus in the sense of 'Hellene against Hellene'. We find in a poem of

148. Stambler 1982.229.

149. For another important attestation of this theme in Herodotus, see 5.97.3: the ships sent by Athens to aid the Ionian Revolt are described as the **arkhē kakōn** 'beginning of misfortunes' for Hellenes and barbarians alike (at this point Athens is described as the most powerful of Hellenic city-states with the exception of Sparta: 5.97.1). Compare the epithet **arkhekakoi** 'beginners of misfortune' at *Iliad* v 63, describing the ships used by Paris for the abduction of Helen — the act that precipitated the Trojan War. Compare also the expression **kakou . . . arkhē** 'beginning of misfortune' at xi 604, marking the beginning of Patroklos' fatal involvement as ritual substitute for Achilles (commentary in N 1979.33–34, 88 §34n4).

150. The word used in the sense of 'compensation' here at Herodotus 9.120.3 is **apoina**, and the word for the 'possessions' of the hero Protesilaos in his hero shrine is **khrēmata** (ibid.).

151. At Herodotus 9.79.2, Pausanias goes on to say that Leonidas is getting adequate compensation through the deaths of all those who were killed at Plataea.

Theognis a parallel use of the word **stasis** 'conflict' in a Panhellenic sense: contemplating the Persian threat to his city (Theognis 773–779, 781–782), the poet declares that he fears the heedlessness and **stasis** of the Hellenes (781) — a **stasis** that destroys the **lāos** 'people' (ἦ γὰρ ἔγωγε δέδοικ' ἀφραδίην ἐσορῶν | καὶ στάσιν Ἑλλήνων λαοφθόρον 780–781). As in Herodotus, the external threat is represented here as meshing with the internal one. In another poem of Theognis is a parallel use of the word **em-phūl-os** 'intrasocietal', this time in the specific sense of 'citizen against citizen': in declaring his fear that a tyrant is about to emerge in his city, the voice of the poet blames the situation on the **hubris** of the city's leaders (39–50, ὕβρις/ὑβρίζειν at 40/44), the three symptoms of which are **stasis** [plural] 'conflict', **emphūloi phonoi andrōn** 'intrasocietal killings of men',[152] and **monarkhoi** 'monarchs' (51–51).[153] The same three misfortunes figure in the Debate of the Constitutions, where the Persian king Darius describes an oligarchy as a situation where everyone vies to be the **koruphaios** 'leading figure' and where this rivalry results in **stasis** [plural] 'conflicts', the **stasis** results in **phonos** 'killing', and the **phonos** results in **monarkhiā** 'monarchy' — which Darius himself equates with 'tyranny'.[154] The same word **koruphaios** 'leading figure' was used by Herodotus in describing the Athenians and the Spartans 'as they fought each other for supremacy'.[155]

When the Athenians had at first renounced sole hegemony of the Hellenic states allied against Persia, Herodotus says, they avoided **stasis emphūlos** 'intrasocietal conflict' that would have destroyed all Hellas (8.3.2). Herodotus is at least implying, then, that the Athenians then caused precisely such a disaster by seizing sole hegemony later, with the emergence of the Athenian Empire. In this light the final action of the *Histories*, an implicitly barbaric deed committed by the father of Pericles in the context of an Athenian initiative taken without the acquiescence of the Peloponnesian allies, signals for the Athenians the threat of **hubris** from within, not from without. In this light even the initial guilty act of the *Histories*, the aggression of the Lydian "tyrant" Croesus against Hellenic cities, figures as an implicit warning to the Athenians. What made the aggression of Croesus distinct from that of his barbarian predecessors, as Herodotus makes clear, is that he was the first barbarian to reduce Hellenic cities to the status of tributaries:

---

152. Cf. Loraux 1987c.8–11.
153. See pp. 182, 265, 369.
154. Cf. ibid.
155. Cf. p. 306.

οὗτος ὁ Κροῖσος βαρβάρων πρῶτος τῶν ἡμεῖς ἴδμεν τοὺς μὲν κατεστρέψατο Ἑλλήνων ἐς φόρου ἀπαγωγήν . . .

Herodotus 1.6.2

This Croesus was the first barbarian ever, within our knowledge, to
reduce some Hellenes to the status of paying tribute . . .[156]

Reducing Hellenic cities to the status of tributaries is also what the Athenians
themselves did in the context of the Athenian Empire. To be a tributary, for
Herodotus, is to be no longer **eleutheros** 'free', as we see from what he adds
pointedly after his observation that Croesus the **turannos** 'tyrant' (1.6.1) was
the first barbarian to make tributaries out of Hellenic cities:

πρὸ δὲ τῆς Κροίσου ἀρχῆς πάντες Ἕλληνες ἦσαν ἐλεύθεροι

Herodotus 1.6.3

Before the rule of Croesus, all Hellenes were still free [**eleutheroi**].[157]

The theme of Croesus the Tyrant is formulated in the mode of an **ainos**,
which applies to Athens with its Athenian Empire, the heir to the Persian
Empire, in turn the heir to the Lydian Empire. That the Athenian Empire is a
turannis 'tyranny' is acknowledged by none other than the figure of Pericles
of Athens in his last oration (Thucydides 2.63.2).[158]

All this is not to say that Herodotus in his **historiā** took sides against the
Athenians. He takes pains to give credit where credit is due, even allowing
that Hellas would never have remained **eleutherā** 'free' without the initiative
of Athens (7.139.5 in the context of 7.139.2–6). He goes so far as to say that
the Athenians became **sōtēres** 'saviors' of Hellas by successfully resisting
the Great King of Persia (7.139.5).[159] This judgment of Herodotus, however,
that Athenians are **sōtēres** 'saviors' of Hellas,[160] is expressed against the
backdrop of the Athenian Empire, which had obviously made the Athenians
unpopular among the Hellenes:

---

156. See p. 230.

157. Cf. ibid.

158. On the theme of Athens as **polis turannos**, "familiar to all Greeks since roughly the middle of the [fifth] century," see Raaflaub 1987.224. On the pertinence of the characterization of
Oedipus as **turannos** 'tyrant' in the *Oedipus Tyrannus* of Sophocles, see Knox 1954.

159. It is added that it was μετά γε θεούς 'next in order to the gods' that the Athenians drove
back the Great King (Herodotus 7.139.5). In other words the gods must be given a major share
in the credit.

160. In light of the reference above, we may take note of the epithet **sōtēr** 'savior' as applied
to Oedipus in the *Oedipus Tyrannus* of Sophocles (e.g., 48).

ἐνθαῦτα ἀναγκαίη ἐξέργομαι γνώμην ἀποδέξασθαι ἐπίφθονον μὲν
πρὸς τῶν πλεόνων ἀνθρώπων, ὅμως δέ, τῇ γέ μοι φαίνεται εἶναι
ἀληθές, οὐκ ἐπισχήσω

Herodotus 7.139.1

And here I am constrained by necessity to make public [= make an
apodeixis of] an opinion [**gnōmē**] that is invidious from the standpoint
of most men. Still, inasmuch as it seems to me at least to be true
[**alēthēs**], I shall not hold back.

The hesitation of Herodotus is motivated by the ambiguity that is being set up
by his **historiā**: the city that once freed the Greeks from tyranny now
threatens to enslave them. The city that became great by overthrowing the
tyranny of the Peisistratidai (Herodotus 5.78) stands to lose all by imposing
tyranny on other Hellenes. The contrast is made all the more effective in that
the continuous narrative of the *Histories* stops at 479 B.C. — just before the
Athenian Empire begins to take shape.[161]

The power of the **historiā** of Herodotus to instruct, even to warn, is
analogous to what we find in a specialized aspect of the **ainos**, the **par-ain-
esis**.[162] At times, moreover, the stories of Herodotus take on not only the
function of a **parainesis** but also the actual form of an **ainos**. There is, for
example, the story of Agariste, granddaughter of Kleisthenes the Athenian:
she dreamed that she gave birth to a lion, and a few days later she gave birth
to a son, Pericles (6.131.2).[163] Besides the obviously positive associations of
this image, there are negative ones. In the *Agamemnon* of Aeschylus
(717–736) is a similar story that has long been recognized as an **ainos**: it is
about a lion cub that was raised in a household to become the bane of its
inhabitants.[164] In Herodotus as well, there is a parallel to this sinister image

161. If Herodotus were to have continued narrating the Persian Wars to their formal end at
448 B.C. or thereabouts, with the Peace of Kallias, the contrast between the old Athens as liberator
of Hellas from the Persians and the new Athens as the supreme power of a new empire would
have been blurred.

162. Cf. pp. 149, 196. For an ideal example of a represented **parainesis** in Herodotus, I cite
1.59.3, where the wise words of Khilon of Sparta, one of the Seven Sages, who is warning the
father of Peisistratos of Athens, are designated by the verb **paraineō**.

163. On this passage see Fornara 1971.53; also Raaflaub 1987.225n10. The theme of a
woman's giving birth to a lion is parodied by Aristophanes *Knights* 1037–1040 in the form of a
quoted oracular utterance emanating from Bakis (on this figure, see p. 170); this mock oracle is
strikingly similar to the oracular utterance quoted at Herodotus 5.92β.3 concerning the birth of
Kypselos, future tyrant of Corinth (on which see p. 184).

164. See Fraenkel 1950 II 338–339, who collects valuable parallels for the two formal characteristics of the **ainos** in this passage from the *Agamemnon* of Aeschylus, namely, the usage of
ἀνήρ at line 719 and of οὕτως at 718. For a parallel usage of οὕτως at *Iliad* IX 524, in the **ainos**
addressed by Phoenix to Achilles, see p. 196. For an interpretation of the **ainos** at *Agamemnon*
717–736 in the context of the entire *Oresteia* trilogy, see Knox 1952, who interprets the lion cub
as a symbol of the new **hubris** that grows out of the old (φιλεῖ δὲ τίκτειν ὕβρις μὲν παλαιὰ

of a lion cub that became the 'priest of Derangement [Atē]' for the household that had raised him (Aeschylus *Agamemnon* 735–736): in describing the gestation of lions, Herodotus says that the embryonic lion cub claws away at the insides of its mother so that the womb is destroyed by the time of the cub's birth (3.108.4). Herodotus offers this description in the context of arguing that limited fertility is the compensation paid by predatory animals for their predatory nature (3.108.1–3).

This kind of reasoning illustrates the affinity of Herodotus' **historiā** with the traditions of what we know as natural history, that is, **historiā** 'inquiry' into the **phusis** 'nature' of the universe.[165] Natural history can equate the principles that operate in the realm of human events with those in the realm of natural phenomena, as we see from a celebrated observation of Anaximander about natural change:

ἐξ ὧν δὲ ἡ γένεσίς ἐστι τοῖς οὖσι, καὶ τὴν φθορὰν εἰς ταῦτα γίνεσθαι κατὰ τὸ χρεών· διδόναι γὰρ αὐτὰ <u>δίκην</u> καὶ <u>τίσιν</u> ἀλλήλοις τῆς <u>ἀδικίας</u> κατὰ τὴν τοῦ χρόνου τάξιν

Anaximander 12 B 1 DK

And the source of coming-to-be for existing things is that into which destruction, too, happens, in accordance with necessity; for they pay penalty [**dikē**] and retribution [**tisis**] to each other for their <u>wrongdoing</u> [**a-dik-iā**][166] in accordance with the assessment of time.[167]

The underlying assumption in such examples of natural history is that the course of human events follows a cosmic order, with the emergence of **dikē** 'justice' in the due course of time.[168] The same sort of assumption operates in the *Works and Days* of Hesiod, where it is also made clear that the cosmic order is an expression of the divine apparatus.[169] The workings of the divine

νεάζουσαν ἐν κακοῖς βροτῶν ὕβριν *Agamemnon* 764–766). As Knox points out, the lion cub of this **ainos** refers not just to Paris but also to Agamemnon, Clytemnestra, even Orestes. Cf. also Goldhill 1984.63.

165. Stambler 1982.221–222, following Snell 1924.

166. Kirk, Raven, and Schofield 1983.120 make note of the "legalistic" metaphor, adding: "The prevalence of one substance at the expense of its contrary is 'injustice' [= **a-dik-iā**], and a reaction takes place through the infliction of punishment by the restoration of equality — of more than equality, since the wrong-doer is deprived of his original substance, too. This is given to the victim in addition to what was his own, and in turn leads (it might be inferred) to **koros**, surfeit, on the part of the former victim, who now commits injustice on the former aggressor."

167. This translation is based on Kirk, Raven, and Schofield 1983.118. On **taxis** as 'assessment', they write (p. 120) that the word "suggests the ordaining of punishment by a judge or, more aptly, the assessment of tribute as in the Athenian tribute-lists."

168. Cf. Kirk, Raven, and Schofield, pp. 120–121, with reference to a comparable text in Solon (F 36 W).

169. Cf. pp. 255 and following.

apparatus emerge also from the **historiā** of Herodotus, as we have seen.[170] For Herodotus too, "natural history" and "moral history" overlap: assuming that natural phenomena and the course of human events do indeed follow the same cosmic order, he can make such pronouncements as we see in the case at hand, that lions pay compensation for their savage and predatory nature by way of their limited fertility. Conversely, natural phenomena can be correlated with human events in the grand old tradition that we see in Hesiod when the voice of the poet says that the city of **dikē** 'justice' will be fertile while the city of its opposite, **hubris** 'outrage', will be sterile (*Works and Days* 225–247).[171] In making such an implicit equation between the course of human events and natural phenomena, Herodotus too is following the thought patterns of the **ainos** as 'fable'. We may compare the **ainos** of the Hawk and the Nightingale in the *Works and Days* of Hesiod (202–212; **ainos** at 202), where the predatory nature of the hawk is an *exemplum* of the ways of **hubris** as opposed to the ways of **dikē**.[172] By associating the birth of Pericles with that of the lion cub, Herodotus has exploited the ambiguity of the **ainos** as a form of discourse: the child Pericles will become either the savior or the predator, the destroyer, of the Hellenic community at large that will raise him.

This is not to say that Pericles is being subjected to blame. The **ainos** is simply an edifying discourse that bears implicit warnings of potential blame built into it. I see a similar sort of message in the **ainos** of the lion cub at Aeschylus *Agamemnon* 717–736.[173] In the symbol of the lion cub who is brought home to a palace and raised as a pet, as if he were native to human society, only to grow into an alien menace, bent on carnage, on destroying the very benefactors who had treated him as their own, we see a reference that extends not only to various characters of the *Oresteia*[174] but even to the audience itself as the embodiment of the Athenian Empire. The *Oresteia* was produced in 458 B.C.; already in 472 B.C., the **khorēgos** for the *Persians* of Aeschylus was none other than Pericles. All this is not to imply that Athens in general or Pericles in particular was being subjected to blame. Rather it is to say only that the **ainos**, true to its moral purpose, instructs as it implicitly warns. We may compare the characterization of Oedipus in the *Oedipus Tyrannus*, which can be interpreted as an implicit characterization of the city of Athens in its role as leader of the Athenian Empire.[175] The Empire *is* **turannos**, in the dramatized words of Pericles (Thucydides 2.63), and the

---

170. Cf. p. 239 on Herodotus 2.120.5: the power of a **daimōn** preordained the destruction of Troy in order to teach humans about the patterns of divine retribution for **a-dik-ēmata** 'wrongdoings, injustice'. This interpretation is expressed as the **gnōmē** 'judgment' of Herodotus (ibid.).

171. Commentary in N 1982.58–60, 63–64.

172. The "moral" of the fable becomes clear at *Works and Days* 274–285: see p. 256.

173. On οὕτως at *Agamemnon* 718 as a performative marker of **ainos**, see p. 310.

174. Ibid.

175. Knox 1954.

notion of an Athenian Empire is already presupposed in the *Histories* of Herodotus (e.g., 5.97). For Herodotus too, the Empire *is* **turannos**. In this sense the theme of "alien is native," with a focus on the concept of **turannos**, is a mark not only of the **ainos** but of the very master plan of Herodotean narrative.

11 ▣▣ The *Ainos* as Song or Speech: Pindar and Herodotus III

O n the level of content, we have seen some striking similarities between Pindaric song and Herodotean prose in conveying a moral message about the realities of wealth, power, and prestige. The actual tradition of such a moral message can be summed up in one word, **ainos**, a premier term of self-reference in the epinician medium of Pindar. Though we find no attestations of this term in the *Histories* of Herodotus, it is by now clear that this work is shaped by the principles of the **ainos**. Moreover, these principles are cognate with those of **historiā** 'inquiry', the medium of Herodotus. The authority of Herodotus is based on the traditional thought patterns of **historiā**, just as the authority of Pindar is based on those of the **ainos**. This relationship of **historiā** and **ainos** can best be seen wherever the prose of Herodotus, in order to demonstrate its authority, makes direct use of song, poetry, and other kinds of prose.

I begin with an example where Herodotus deploys an actual **ainos**, in the specific sense of 'fable'. We find it in Herodotus' narrative of the overtures made by Persia to Argos, a passage that we have already considered in connection with the Persian manipulation of an Argive myth that would entitle Argos to hegemony over the Peloponnesus (7.150.1–2).[1] In this narrative Herodotus leaves open the possibility that Argos, in its ambition to achieve hegemony and gain the upper hand over its rival, Sparta, cooperated with the Persians and thus betrayed the Hellenes allied against Persia. After giving

---

1. Cf. p. 300.

the Argive version of what really happened (7.148.2–149.3), Herodotus reports three opposing versions.

The first and least damaging of these versions is that Argos, in order to remain neutral toward Persia, deliberately set impossible terms for cooperation with Sparta (7.150.3). Second, Herodotus reports a version derived from Athenian sources, to the effect that the Persian king Artaxerxes, around the time of the Peace of Kallias, declared that no city was more dear to him than Argos (Herodotus 7.151). Then, after declaring that he is not certain whether these two versions are true, he exculpates the Argives by saying that even if these reports were true, the Argives would not thereby be guilty of the very worst deeds imaginable. In support of this thought Herodotus now speaks in a mode of **ainos** that is characteristic of Aesop's Fables:[2] if all men, he says, were to bring to one place all their **kaka** 'evils', they would surely, upon seeing what the other man has, take back home whatever they had brought (Herodotus 7.152.2).[3] This formulation is strikingly similar to the attested fable of Aesop known as "The Two Packs," likewise concerning the topic of one man's perception of another man's **kaka** 'evils' (Aesop *Fable* 266 Perry, Πῆραι δύο). Immediately after speaking in the mode of an **ainos**, Herodotus continues in the mode of one who conducts a **historiā**:

> ἐγὼ δὲ ὀφείλω λέγειν τὰ λεγόμενα, πείθεσθαί γε μὲν οὐ παντάπασιν ὀφείλω, καί μοι τοῦτο τὸ ἔπος ἐχέτω ἐς πάντα λόγον

> Herodotus 7.152.3

> I owe [**opheilō**] it to tell what is being told, but I by no means owe [**opheilō**] it to believe it, and what I say here should go for everything I say.

It is only after exculpating the Argives in the mode of an **ainos** and after making this all-inclusive statement about his procedures in **historiā** that Herodotus gets around to the third and final negative version about the Argives: that they themselves, in their rivalry with the Spartans, had invited the Persians to invade Hellas (7.152.3).

Having thus cushioned his negative reports about Argos, Herodotus assumes the stance of a fair and impartial arbitrator. This stance is obviously no longer evident to Greeks of later times, as when Plutarch, in his essay *On the Malice of Herodotus,* singles out this particular passage of Herodotus about Argos as a prime example of the author's malicious disposition (Plutarch *On the Malice of Herodotus* 863b–864a). The equitable but always diplomatic approach of Herodotus to the varied interests and prejudices of the city-states in the period after the Persian Wars is lost on Plutarch, who

2. On **ainos** as a 'fable' of Aesop: sources in N 1979.239 §18n2.
3. For the juridical implications, see Detienne 1973.88–89.

fails to observe the juridical dimension of what Herodotus has to say in the capacity of conducting a **historiā** 'inquiry'. In order to appreciate this dimension, we would do well to compare the surviving Greek texts of international, that is, inter-polis arbitration.

Let us consider, for example, an inscription recording the arbitration by King Lysimachus of Thrace, shortly before 281 B.C., of a territorial dispute between the states of Samos and Priene.[4] We may note in particular the phraseology that describes how the people of Priene presented their arguments:

> οἱ μὲν οὖν Πριηνεῖς τὴν μὲν ἐξ ἀρχῆς γεγενημένην α[ὐ]τ[οῖς] |
> [κτῆσι]ν τῆς Βατινήτιδος χώρας ἐπεδείκνυον ἔκ τε τῶν ἱστοριῶν
> κ[αὶ] | [τῶν ἄλ]λων μαρτυριῶν καὶ δικαιωμάτων [με]τὰ τῶν ἑξετῶν
> [σπον]δῶ[ν

> Inschriften von Priene no. 500.11–13[5]

The people of Priene were seeking to demonstrate [= make an **epi-deixis**] that the territory called Batinetis belonged to them on the basis of inquiries [**historiai**],[6] other evidence [**marturiai**], and documents, including[7] the six-year truce.

We may compare the phraseology used by Herodotus in describing a conflict of claims between the people of Sybaris and the people of Kroton:

> μαρτύρια δὲ τούτων ἑκάτεροι ἀποδεικνύουσι τάδε· (. . .) ταῦτα μέν
> νυν ἑκάτεροι αὐτῶν μαρτύρια ἀποφαίνονται· καὶ πάρεστι, ὁκοτέ-
> ροισί τις πείθεται αὐτῶν, τούτοισι προσχωρέειν

> Herodotus 5.45.1–2

Both parties make a public display [= verb of **apo-deixis**][8] of evidence [**marturia**] for their claims, as follows: [. . .] The above, then, are the evidence [**marturia**] that each of the two parties makes public [= verb **apo-phainomai**].[9] It is possible to agree with whichever side one believes.

In this case, as in his account of the policies of Argos at the time of the Persian Wars, Herodotus goes so far in his impartiality as not even to express his

---

4. Hiller von Gaertringen 1906 no. 500. Also Piccirilli 1973.17, no. 4. On the dating, see Tod 1931.41.

5. Hiller von Gaertringen ibid.

6. In what follows, I shall attempt to demonstrate why the juridical sense of 'inquiries' is more appropriate here for the word **historiai** than the literary sense of 'histories'.

7. I am following here the interpretation of Piccirilli ibid.

8. On the semantics of **apo-deixis**: pp. 217 and following.

9. Cf. pp. 219, 239.

own opinion.[10] It suffices for him merely to conduct his **historiā** 'inquiry'. Technically the **historiā** of Herodotus corresponds to the process of arbitration, not to the actual outcome.

Even in actual cases of juridical arbitration, the procedures do not necessarily lead to a juridical outcome: the given dispute may in the end be settled out of court if the arbitrator finds a successful formula for mediation, that is, if he can induce the two parties to agree mutually to an out-of-court settlement.[11] Otherwise the arbitrator must resort to a juridical verdict as he pronounces a final assessment or award. As one expert puts it, "An arbitrator may mediate, but a mediator as such has no arbitral authority, and in the cases before us, where a solution could not be reached by mutual agreement, the court had the right and the duty of pronouncing an award which was binding upon both parties."[12] In the dispute between Priene and Samos the verdict of the arbitrator, King Lysimachus, has aptly been described as follows:

> Note, first, the time and trouble devoted to the settlement of this difference by the ruler of a wide empire, the fair and dispassionate tone which characterizes his rescript, and his evident desire to justify his award to the reason and the conscience of the states directly concerned and of the world at large. And, in the second place, note that, so far as our knowledge goes, this arbitration of Lysimachus closed forever a dispute which had lasted, in varying degrees of intensity, for four centuries at least.[13]

The status of the arbitrator may vary considerably, as we see from this description of a verdict rendered in yet another dispute between Priene and Samos:[14]

> This time it is no powerful monarch who arbitrates, nor yet a large popular tribunal, embodying the democratic ideal of justice, like that court of six hundred Milesians who . . . adjudicated on the Spartan and Messenian claims to the *ager Dentheliates*. The matter is referred to the Rhodian state, and from its members a panel of five arbitrators is selected, a small body of men chosen, we may assume, for their character and ability. At the close of their proceedings, they drew up a report upon the whole case, and this reflects credit upon the clarity of their

10. For a dramatic example of a case where Herodotus does indeed express his own opinion, I cite the case of Croesus, as discussed at pp. 229 and following.

11. For such cases, see Tod 1913.123–127.

12. Tod 1913.127.

13. Tod 1932.56.

14. For the inscription, see Hiller von Gaertringen 1906, Inschriften von Priene no. 37. See Tod 1913.41 (early second century B.C.).

thought and expression, the thoroughness with which they carried out the task entrusted to them and the equitable nature of their final judgement.[15]

The evidence used by the arbitrator also varies. In the case of the latter dispute between Priene and Samos, the records show that the arbitrators heard testimony in neutral territory, as also at the disputed territory,[16] whereupon, as they declare, 'we arrived at our decision in accordance with what we have seen' (ἐπο[ιησάμεθα τὰγ] κρίσιν κατὰ τὰ ὑφ' | [ἁμῶν ἐφ]εοραμέ[να).[17] This figurative sense of 'seeing', clearly attested here in its juridical context of 'knowing', corresponds closely to the etymology of **oida** 'know' as 'have seen' and of **histōr** 'witness, arbitrator' as 'he who has seen'.[18] The arbitrator is a superwitness who builds an all-encompassing knowledge of a situation by bringing together the knowledge of all those who bear witness, no matter what their status may be. The crucial factor is the witness's knowledge of the facts, as we see strikingly illustrated in an inscription recording the arbitration of a dispute between Condaea and an unknown state,[19] where we are fortunate enough to have the actual deposition of an elderly shepherd who has known the disputed territory from boyhood:

... καὶ Λάδικος ὁ Ἀσκυριεὺς ἐμαρ| [τ]ύρησεν μαρτυρίαν τήνδε·
μαρτ[υ]| ρεῖ Λάδικος Ἀρμ[οδ]ίου Ἀσκυριεὺς | Κονδαιεῦσιν·
ἐπ[ίσ]ταμαι τὴν χώρα[ν], | [ἣ]ν καὶ παρὼν ἐνεφάνιζον τοῖς κριταῖς
ἀπὸ τῆς κορυφῆς τοῦ Ν[υ]σείου | [κ]αταβαίνων τὸν ἔν[γι]ον πρὸς
ἡμᾶ[ς] | [τ]όπον ἄχρι τῆ[ς] φάραγγος, ἧς καὶ Κον[δαι]| εῖς
ἐπεδείκ[ν]υον τοῖς κριταῖς, κ[αὶ] | τῶν πρεσβυτέρων ἤκουον προσ-
χω[ρεῖν] | [Κ]ονδαιεῦσι κατὰ το[ῦ]τον τὸν τόπον κ[αὶ μό]| νος
ἐπίσταμαι νομεύων ἐν τῇ χώρα[ι] | πλείω χρόνον καὶ [Κ]ονδαιεῖς
τηροῦντα[ς]| τὸ παραγώγιον ἐν τούτῳ τῷ τόπω[ι]·

IG 9.2.521.5–18

And Ladikos of Askyris <u>testified</u> as follows: "Ladikos, son of Harmodios, of Askyris, bears <u>witness</u> [= is a **martus**] to the Condaeans. I <u>know</u> [= verb **epistamai**] the land, which I also showed to the judges as I came down from the summit of Nyseion, the place nearer to us, as far as the defile, which the Condaeans too <u>pointed out</u> [= verb of **epideixis**] to the judges; and I used to <u>hear</u> from the older men that at this spot the land belongs to the Condaeans; and I <u>know</u> [= verb **epistamai**] of myself that I have been pasturing my flocks in the territory for a con-

---

15. Tod 1932.56–57.
16. Inschriften von Priene no. 37.20–24.
17. Inschriften von Priene no. 37.24–25.
18. Cf. Benveniste 1969 II 173–175.
19. IG 9.2.521, early third century B.C., found at Larisa.

siderable time and that the Condaeans keep the passage-duty at this spot."[20]

The juridical sense of 'seeing'/'knowing' as the foundation of evidence in the process of inquiry must be kept in mind as we consider references to the use of **historiā** as evidence in inscriptions recording arbitrations. In some cases such **historiai** can be identified as known literary works, such as the *Histories* of Duris of Samos.[21] Even here, however, the juridical heritage of the word **historiā** comes through: in the eyes of the law, **historiā** as 'inquiry' — even if it also happens to be a literary achievement — is a juridical process. This is as it should be, if indeed the concept of **historiā** is derived from the juridical concept of arbitration, as still reflected in the noun **histōr** 'witness, arbitrator'. This legal point of view, that **historiā** even as "history" is still a juridical process, can best be seen in the phraseological combination of **apo-deixis** 'public display' with **historiographoi** 'writers of histories' in an inscription recording admissible evidence for an arbitration.[22] We are reminded that the **historiā** of Herodotus is technically the **apodeixis** of his **historiā** (Herodotus *prooemium*). As for the inscription that we are now considering, there is more to the interesting phraseological combination of **apo-deixis** 'public display' with **historiographoi** 'writers of histories': besides 'writers of history', we see **poiētai** 'poets' also mentioned in the same context, so that the **apo-deixis** of historians is parallel to that of poets in the eyes of the law.

In this context we may recall the explicit association of the concept of **apo-deixis** with both **logioi** 'masters of speech' and **aoidoi** 'masters of song' in the traditional phraseology of Pindar.[23] For another interesting illustration of such parallelism, I cite the report of Tacitus on the arbitration of a territorial dispute between Sparta and Messenia by the Roman Senate in A.D. 25: the envoys of the Spartans had used as evidence the *annalium memoria vatumque carmina* 'records of annals and the songs of poets' (*Annals* 4.43), while the Messenians countered by pointing to the presence of certain ancient statues as evidence for the division of the Peloponnesus among the Herakleidai, the Sons of Herakles (ibid.), and added that *si vatum, annalium ad testimonia vocentur, plures sibi ac locupletiores esse* 'if they were to cite the evidence of poets and annals, they would have at their disposal more and richer sources' (ibid.).

It is clear that the juridical value of **historiā**, as something parallel to poetry, is not confined to the furnishing of factual evidence in our narrowest

---

20. Translation after Tod 1913.148–149. See also lines 19–38 of the same inscription, IG 9.2.521, for similar depositions given by local fishermen.

21. Duris of Samos FGH 76 F 25. See Piccirilli 1973.21.

22. SIG 685.93 (Crete, second century B.C.): [ποιη]τῶν καὶ ἱστοριογράφων ἀπόδειξεις.

23. Cf. pp. 221 and following, especially p. 224.

sense of the word: the admissible evidence to be used in the process of arbitration can include traditional myths as attested by both **historiā** and poetry. So also in the *Oratio Deliaca* of Hyperides, a speech delivered on behalf of Athens' claim to the administration of the Delian Sanctuary in a case of international (again in the sense of inter-polis) arbitration: here the author's copious treatment of myths about the wanderings of Leto and the birth of Apollo and Artemis can be connected with the remark of Maximus Planudes to the effect that Hyperides, 'desirous of proving that the Delian sanctuaries belonged of old time to the Athenians, has made great use of mythology' (Maximus Planudes *ad h.l.t.* V, p. 481 Walz, = *Oratores Attici* ii, p. 392 ed. Didot).

For further examples of the use of myths as evidence in cases of arbitration, we have not only the testimony of inscriptions (e.g., SIG 665.35–36) but also such specific anecdotes as the one about Solon's citing two verses from the Homeric *Catalogue of Ships* (*Iliad* II 557–558) to the Spartan arbitrators of a territorial dispute between Athens and Megara over the island of Salamis in 519/518 B.C. (Plutarch *Life of Solon* 10).[24] In Plutarch's account the specific word that designates Solon's actual citing of the given verses is **apo-deik-numai**, the verb of **apo-deixis** 'public display' (*Solon* 10.3). Again we see that poetry, the voice of myth, is a source of authority compatible with the juridical process of arbitration.

There is even an instance where the poetic voice can become the vehicle of arbitration. Thucydides reports that the Corcyraeans, in their dispute with the Corinthians, were willing to submit this dispute to arbitration by the Delphic Oracle (1.28).[25] The choice of the Delphic Oracle as an arbitrator was entertained as a course of action only by the Corcyraeans, not by the Corinthians, and the Corcyraeans did so only as a last resort, so that the choice was in fact unusual.[26] This distinctness of the Delphic Oracle as arbitrator is a function of its poetic mode of communication. In a standard book that surveys the attestations of arbitrations, we find only one instance where the Delphic Oracle actually served as arbitrator, in a dispute between Klazomenai and Kyme over the territory of Leuke,[27] and we can see immediately the distinctness of the situation: "no board of judges is appointed, no inquiry is held, no witnesses are heard."[28] Instead the Oracle simply issues a poetic

24. The testimony of Plutarch is to be supplemented by Strabo 9.1.10 C394; cf. Aristotle *Rhetoric* 1375b and Quintilian *Institutio oratoria* 5.11.40. Cf. Tod 1913.134n2; also Piccirilli 1973.46–56.

25. For a commentary on this passage of Thucydides, see Piccirilli 1973.112–116.

26. Tod 1913.95.

27. Tod ibid. This instance is recorded by Diodorus 15.18 (date: sometime after 383 B.C.). See also Piccirilli 1973.164–165; also pp. 11–16, citing one other exceptional instance where the Delphic Oracle reportedly served as arbitrator; in this case the dispute concerned the possession of a golden tripod fished from the sea.

28. Tod ibid.

utterance: in the paraphrase of Diodorus, the Oracle says that it awards Leuke to 'whichever state is the first to sacrifice at Leuke, but each must start out from their own territory at sunrise on the same day, which should be fixed by common agreement' (15.18.2). The utterance left considerable room for interpretation: the citizens of Klazomenai quickly founded a settlement that was closer to Leuke and thereby gained the necessary head start to arrive at this destination before the citizens of Kyme (Diodorus 15.18.3).

Despite its authority, then, the utterance of the Delphic Oracle is ambiguous even in cases of arbitration: like the **ainos**, the spoken word of the Oracle here again functions as a code containing at least two messages, as the citizens of Kyme must have discovered to their distress.[29] The ambiguity of the Oracle may account for its apparently limited use as a court of last resort, but it diminishes in no way its actual authority in upholding the process and even the ideology of arbitration: in fact the sanctuary of the Delphic Oracle was a traditional site for inscribing the records of awards in cases of inter-polis arbitration.[30]

I have gone into all this detail in considering the Hellenic institution of inter-polis arbitration because its juridical procedures match so closely the methods used by Herodotus in conducting his **historiā** 'inquiry'. As in a case of arbitration, he consistently records divergent as well as convergent testimony and declares his duty to report whatever is being said. A particularly striking illustration is the stance that he takes in considering charges of collaboration between Argos and Persia.[31] As in a typical case of arbitration, moreover, Herodotus too admits as evidence the testimony of historians and poets. We see him, for example, critically examining the findings of his predecessor, Hecataeus of Miletus (e.g., Herodotus 2.143.1, 6.137.1).[32] Also, we see him frequently referring to poetry and song: besides Homer (2.23, 2.53.2, 3; 2.116, etc.) and Hesiod (2.53.2, 3; 4.32), he manages to mention in one context or another such figures as Archilochus (1.12.2), Anacreon (3.121.1), Sappho (2.135), Alcaeus (5.95), Simonides (5.102.3, 7.228.4), Pindar (3.38.4) — whom he explicitly paraphrases (= Pindar F 169.1 SM) — and Aeschylus (2.156.6). Even more frequently Herodotus refers to and quotes the poetic utterances of oracles, especially of the Delphic Oracle.

In view of the established authority of the Delphic Oracle as the repository for recording awards in actual cases of arbitration, it is important to note again the function of the Oracle in the *Histories* of Herodotus as the ultimate

---

29. As for the winners, the people of Klazomenai established a festival, called the **prophthasia** 'anticipation', to commemorate their victory (Diodorus 15.18.3).

30. For an inventory of inscriptions recording awards in cases of inter-polis arbitration, see Tod 1913.95n2.

31. Cf. p. 314; cf. also the earlier discussion at p. 305.

32. Survey of Herodotean references to Hecataeus in How and Wells 1928 I 24–25. On Hecataeus as **logopoios** 'artisan of speech', see p. 224.

authority in assessing who was **aitios** 'responsible, guilty' in the ultimate conflict that he narrates. The guilt of the tyrant Croesus is determined immediately by the authority of Herodotus, who 'indicates' (verb **sēmainō**) who is guilty as he conducts a **historiā** 'inquiry', and ultimately by the authority of Apollo, who is described by Heraclitus as 'indicating' (again, verb **sēmainō**) his messages through his ambiguous but authoritative Oracle, and whose true message becomes in the end manifest through the narration of Herodotus.[33] In the end the ambiguous code of Apollo arbitrates the conflict between Europeans and Asiatics through the **historiā** of Herodotus.

Though Plutarch does not recognize the juridical stance inherent in the narrative of Herodotus,[34] he does observe condescendingly that this narrative is delivered in a mode that resembles that of Aesop's fables. Moreover, Plutarch is making this specific observation in the context of condemning what he deems to be the malice of Herodotus in his use of the utterances of the Delphic Oracle. After quoting a passage in the *Histories* where Herodotus is paraphrasing an utterance of the Oracle in favor of the Aeginetans and at the expense of the Athenians (Herodotus 8.122–123), Plutarch goes on to say:

> οὐκέτι Σκύθαις οὐδὲ Πέρσαις οὐδ' Αἰγυπτίοις τοὺς ἑαυτοῦ λόγους ἀνατίθησι πλάττων, ὥσπερ Αἴσωπος κόραξι καὶ πιθήκοις, ἀλλὰ τῷ τοῦ Πυθίου προσώπῳ χρώμενος ἀπωθεῖ τῶν ἐν Σαλαμῖνι πρωτείων τὰς Ἀθήνας

Plutarch *On the Malice of Herodotus* 871d

> He [= Herodotus] no longer assigns his words, as he makes them up, to Scythians or Persians or Egyptians, in the way that Aesop assigns his to ravens and monkeys, but he uses the persona of the Pythian god [= Apollo at Delphi] in order to prevent the Athenians from receiving the first prize at Salamis.[35]

This observation about Herodotus, pejorative though it is, hits the mark in calling our attention to an affinity between his form of discourse and that of Aesop. Technically a fable of Aesop is an **ainos**,[36] and the *Life of Aesop* tradition shows that fables of Aesop, as he is said to have told them, were

33. Cf. pp. 240 and following.
34. Cf. p. 315.
35. Plutarch is taking Herodotus to task for what he deems to be malice against Themistokles and the Athenians. Herodotus reports that the Delphic Oracle had pronounced Aegina and not Athens as worthy of the first prize for valor publicly displayed at the Battle of Salamis. We know that according to local Athenian traditions as reflected by Isocrates (*Panegyric* 72), Athens supposedly got the first prize. It surely seems ironic to us, at least, that Herodotus' account here, especially in the subsequent section that is neither quoted nor even mentioned by Plutarch (Herodotus 8.124.1), is in fact diplomatically complimentary to Themistokles.
36. Sources in N 1979.239 §18n2.

delivered in the ambiguous manner of the **ainos**, where whatever he says has both an explicit and an implicit meaning — the implication to be derived from the context in which he speaks.[37]

For example, Aesop tells his fable of "The Wolves, the Dogs, and the Sheep"[38] to the citizens of Samos, with the implicit meaning that the Lydian king Croesus is like the wolves, that he is like the dogs, and that the Samians are like the sheep.[39] At the moment Croesus is demanding that the Samians extradite Aesop, who had saved them as a dog saves sheep from the wolf, by having already told them another fable, "The Path of Freedom and the Path of Slavery."[40] According to this fable the path of freedom is harsh[41] at the beginning and pleasant at the end, while the path of slavery is the opposite. The path of slavery is characterized specifically by its initial **truphē** 'luxuriance', to be followed later by harshness.[42] In response to this fable the Samians had decided to accept the path of freedom[43] and had rejected the earlier demand of Croesus that they pay him tribute.[44] We are reminded of the lessons to be learned from the Croesus story of Herodotus, who authoritatively accuses the Lydian tyrant of being **aitios** 'responsible' for the ultimate conflict between Hellenes and Asiatics (1.5.3 in the context of 1.1.1, 1.2.1, and 1.3.4) precisely because he was the first barbarian, according to Herodotus, who reduced Hellenic cities to the status of tributaries (1.6.2).[45]

Later on in the same *Life of Aesop* narrative, Aesop voluntarily visits the court of Croesus and warns the king not to kill him, on account of the blame that would be incurred through such a deed; he reinforces this warning by telling the Lydian tyrant the fable of "The Poor Man and the Cicada":[46] a poor man, who resorts to eating locusts in order to stay alive, happens to catch a cicada, who pleads for his life on the grounds that he does not harm

37. For an introduction to the *Life of Aesop* tradition, see N, pp. 279–316. The implicit meaning of a fable may also be derived from the context in which one *does* something: see Karadagli 1981.75–76 on Herodotus 5.92.

38. *Life of Aesop* 97 and Aesop *Fable* no. 153 Perry.

39. Aesop wants the Samians to inscribe this fable on a **mnēma** 'monument' that is to be dedicated to him after his death (*Life of Aesop* G 96). See N 1979.286n1: "This narrative device of a self-fulfilling prophecy implies that the *Life of Aesop* tradition had once been suitable for an inscription in a precinct of Aesop as cult-hero." Note the reference in *Life of Aesop* W 100 to a **temenos** 'precinct' set aside in honor of Aesop by the citizens of Samos; at G 100, this precinct is called the **Aisōpeion**. For further discussion, including a comparison with the cult precinct of Archilochus at Paros known as the **Arkhilokheion**, see N, pp. 285–286n1.

40. *Life of Aesop* 94 and Aesop *Fable* no. 383 Perry.

41. In *Life of Aesop* 94, the word for 'harsh' (path) is **trākheia**, the same word used in a comparable context by Herodotus 9.122.2. See p. 268.

42. *Life of Aesop* G 94.

43. *Life of Aesop* 95.

44. For the wording about the tribute, see *Life of Aesop* 92.

45. Cf. p. 308.

46. *Life of Aesop* 99 and Aesop *Fable* no. 387 Perry.

men by robbing them of their possessions, as locusts do, but instead benefits them through his song, 'and you will find nothing more in me than my voice'.[47] The last phrase amounts to a warning: in a fragment of an earlier master of the **ainos**, Archilochus,[48] we see that the cicada is a master of blame whenever he is wronged (F 223 W).[49] Croesus responds to the warning by sparing the life of Aesop and offering to grant him a favor; Aesop then asks for and is granted a peaceful settlement between the Lydians and the Samians.[50]

In this way further meaning comes to light from the **sēmeion** 'sign'[51] that Aesop had partially interpreted at the beginning of his dealings with the citizens of Samos.[52] At a meeting of the Samian assembly, an eagle had seized and flown away with a ring to be worn by whoever was to be newly elected as 'guardian' of the city's laws.[53] Then the eagle had returned and dropped the ring in the lap of a slave. At the beginning Aesop had interpreted the **sēmeion** 'sign'[54] by drawing a parallel connecting the eagle with Croesus and the transfer of the ring to the slave with the shift from autonomy to tributary status for Samos.[55] As a reward for his interpretation, however, Aesop demands and is granted emancipation from his own status as slave.[56] In the end, then, the chain of events leads to the further interpretation that Aesop himself has effectively become the true guardian of the laws of the Samians. This quasi-juridical stance of Aesop should be kept in mind as we approach the topic of parallelisms between Aesop and Solon in the stories of their encounters with Croesus of Lydia.[57]

With these examples of Aesop's fables in mind, we return to the proposition that Plutarch's pejorative comparison of Herodotus with Aesop is apt. Herodotus too, as we have seen, can speak in the manner of the **ainos**, occasionally even telling an outright fable[58] and frequently manipulating the Hel-

---

47. *Life of Aesop* W 99; in version G 99 the distinction between locust (**akris**) and cicada (**tettix**) is garbled.

48. On self-references in Archilochean poetry to **ainos** (e.g., F 174 W), see N 1979.283.

49. Cf. N 1979.283, 302.

50. *Life of Aesop* 100.

51. The word is related to **sēma** 'sign', as discussed at pp. 229, 233, and following.

52. *Life of Aesop* 81.

53. *Life of Aesop* G 81. Aesop refers to this ring as **stratēgikos** 'belonging to the **stratēgos**' (G 91). Since the word **stratēgos** 'general' designates 'lawgiver' at Aesop *Fable* 348 Perry, a story that reveals striking parallels with the Samian story of Maiandrios, successor to the tyrant Polykrates (Herodotus 3.142–143; see n58), it may be pertinent also to compare the story of the Ring of Polykrates (Herodotus 3.41–42).

54. Again *Life of Aesop* 81.

55. *Life of Aesop* 91.

56. *Life of Aesop* 90.

57. Cf. pp. 332 and following. Note too the preoccupation of Aesopic fables with the juridical theme of guilt (as expressed by **aitiā** 'responsibility' and its derivatives): survey by Karadagli 1981.108–109.

58. See also p. 315. For a survey of instances where Herodotus tells fables, see Karadagli

lenic perspective, as Plutarch charges, by applying to Scythians, Persians, or Egyptians what really applies to Hellenes (*On the Malice of Herodotus* 871d).[59] In fact the language of Herodotus himself provides testimony that his own tradition of discourse and that of Aesop are related: in an incidental mention of Aesop, Herodotus refers to him as a **logopoios** 'artisan of speech' (Αἰσώπου τοῦ λογοποιοῦ Herodotus 2.134.3).[60] This word **logopoios** is used by Herodotus to refer to his own predecessor, Hecataeus of Miletus (e.g., Ἑκαταίῳ τῷ λογοποιῷ Herodotus 2.143.1).[61] Moreover, in the same context where Herodotus incidentally mentions Aesop as a **logopoios** 'artisan of speech', he mentions the poet Sappho as a **mousopoios** 'artisan of song' (Σαπφοῦς τῆς μουσοποιοῦ Herodotus 2.135.1), and the juxtaposition here of **logopoios/mousopoios** in the language of Herodotus seems perfectly parallel to the juxtapositon of **logios/aoidos** 'master of speech/song' in the language of Pindar.[62] In fact we have seen that Herodotus is by implication a **logios**, a 'master of speech' whose function is parallel to that of a Pindar as **aoidos**, a 'master of song'.[63]

Mention of this juxtaposition not only brings us back to the starting point of our discussion, where we had considered the comparative evidence of

---

1981 on Herodotus 1.25 (p. 77), 1.41 (pp. 23, 65), 1.158–159 (pp. 78–79), 3.46 (pp. 84–85), 4.131–132 (p. 91), 5.92 (pp. 75–76), 6.86 (pp. 35–37). Note too the close correspondence between the story of Maiandrios of Samos, Herodotus 3.142–143, and the fable of "The Wolf as Lawgiver and the Ass," Aesop *Fable* no. 348 Perry, as discussed by Detienne and Svenbro 1979.218–221. In this Aesopic fable the title of **stratēgos** 'general' is applied to the status of a lawgiver.

59. Cf. p. 322. Note, for example, the fable of "The Aulos-Player and the Fish," as told by the Persian king Cyrus (Herodotus 1.141). This kind of manipulation is not limited to fables in the strict sense of the word. I cite the celebrated passage known as the Debate of the Constitutions, Herodotus 3.80–88. I cite also the distinction, made by the scholia to Aristophanes *Birds* 471, between Aesopic and 'Sybaritic' fables: the latter supposedly concentrate on humans while the former concentrate on animals. Compare the reference in Aristophanes *Wasps* 1258–1260 to two kinds of discourse appropriate for learned merriment, the Aesopic and the 'Sybaritic' (**Subari-tikoi**), both of which are to be learned at the symposium.

60. Aesop gets the same title in Aristotle *Constitution of the Samians*, F 573 Rose. The context of Herodotus' mention of Aesop suggests that he was aware of the narrative traditions about Aesop in Samos, as attested in the passages of the *Life of Aesop* (81–95; see p. 324). Herodotus says that both a Thracian woman called Rhodopis and Aesop himself (also referred to as a Thracian in, e.g., Aristotle *Constitution of the Samians*, F 573 Rose) were slaves of one Iadmon, and that Rhodopis was taken to Egypt by 'Xanthes the Samian', from where she was later ransomed by the brother of Sappho (Herodotus 2.134–135). In the *Life of Aesop*, a Samian called Xanthos is the last of three masters who own Aesop as slave; in the end Xanthos frees Aesop (90). The first of the three masters, who is not named in the *Life*, may very well be the same character as the 'Iadmon' of Herodotus. (It should be clear from my choice of the word *character* that I think of *sameness* here not in terms of prosopography but rather in terms of story types.)

61. Cf. p. 321.

62. Cf. p. 224.

63. Ibid.

Pindar's language in investigating the essence of Herodotus' **historiā**. It also brings us to a confrontation with a crucial difference between Aesop and Herodotus, Plutarch notwithstanding: whereas the **ainos** of Aesop the slave, in line with Aesop's own social position, is lowly,[64] that of Herodotus is elevated. As such, the implicit **ainos** of Herodotus as **logios** has more in common with the **ainos** of a figure like Pindar, whose epinician lyric poetry overtly refers to itself as **ainos**.[65] Though Plutarch may begrudge Herodotus the quoting of oracles as a way of conveying a message (again *On the Malice of Herodotus* 871d), such a procedure seems perfectly in keeping with the lofty stance of a man who himself **sēmainei** 'indicates' from a superior position of knowledge akin to that of the oracles.[66] In fact the prose of Herodotus can combine with the poetry of oracles to convey the same sort of message that is conveyed by the uninterrupted lyric poetry of Pindar.

I close this part of the presentation with an illustration of this principle, where we juxtapose a given Herodotean passage with a corresponding Pindaric one. It seems fitting that the message of both the Herodotean and the Pindaric passages about to be quoted concerns an admonition about the evils of **hubris**. First, let us look at the passage taken from Herodotus, where the sequence of thought runs through a stretch of prose/poetry/back to prose:

χρησμοῖσι δὲ οὐκ ἔχω ἀντιλέγειν ὡς οὐκ εἰσὶ ἀληθέες, οὐ βουλόμενος ἐναργέως λέγοντας πειρᾶσθαι καταβάλλειν, ἐς τοιάδε πρήγ-
ματα ἐσβλέψας·

ἀλλ' ὅταν Ἀρτέμιδος χρυσαόρου ἱερὸν ἀκτὴν
νηυσὶ γεφυρώσωσι καὶ εἰναλίην Κυνόσουραν,
ἐλπίδι μαινομένῃ λιπαρὰς πέρσαντες Ἀθήνας,
δῖα Δίκη σβέσσει κρατερὸν Κόρον, Ὕβριος υἱόν,
δεινὸν μαιμώοντα, δοκεῦντ' ἀνὰ πάντα πίεσθαι.[67]
χαλκὸς γὰρ χαλκῷ συμμίξεται, αἵματι δ' Ἄρης
πόντον φοινίξει. τότ' ἐλεύθερον Ἑλλάδος ἦμαρ
εὐρύοπα Κρονίδης ἐπάγει καὶ πότνια Νίκη.

ἐς τοιαῦτα μὲν καὶ οὕτω ἐναργέως λέγοντι Βάκιδι ἀντιλογίας

---

64. For a striking illustration of this social perspective, consider the image of Aesop in Plutarch *Banquet of the Seven Sages* 150a: at the banquet Aesop is given a place next to Solon, but he sits on a **diphros** 'low chair' (it is in this context that Aesop tells the fable of "The Lydian Mule"). We may note the parallelism between Aesop and Solon as sages who visit the court of Croesus the Lydian: *Life of Aesop* 99 and Herodotus 1.29.1 (p. 243).

65. Cf. p. 147 and following.

66. Cf. pp. 229, 233, and following.

67. An emendation for the manuscript reading πιθέσθαι: discussion in Powell 1939.117. Retaining the manuscript reading, Fontenrose 1978.185 translates δοκεῦντ' ἀνὰ πάντα πιθέσθαι as 'thinking to subdue the world'.

χρησμῶν πέρι οὔτε αὐτὸς λέγειν <u>τολμέω</u> οὔτε παρ' ἄλλων ἐνδέκομαι

Herodotus 8.77

I cannot speak against the oracles, claiming that they are not <u>true</u> [**alēthees**]. I do not wish to try to discredit them, when they speak manifestly, as when I consider what follows:

> When they bridge the sea from the sacred headland of golden-
>   sworded Artemis,
> with ships, all the way to seaside Kynosoura,
> with frenzied <u>ambition</u> [**elpis**], after having destroyed shining
>   Athens,
> then shall bright <u>Justice</u> [**Dikē**] quench powerful <u>Insatiability</u>
>   [**Koros**], son of <u>Outrage</u> [**Hubris**],
> who rages terribly, thinking to swallow up the world.
> Bronze shall mingle with bronze, and with blood shall Ares
> make red the sea. Then will the day of freedom that belongs to
>   Greece
> be brought about by wide-seeing Zeus and Lady **Nīkē** [Victory].

So, looking at what precedes, I do <u>not have the daring</u> [= verb of **tolma**] to say things that would contradict what Bakis says so manifestly.[68] And I would not stand for it if anyone else would say anything contradictory either.

Now let us examine the analogous passage taken from Pindar, where the sequence of thought runs through a stretch of uninterrupted lyric poetry:

> ἐν τᾷ γὰρ Εὐνομία ναίει κασιγνήτα τε, βάθρον πολίων ἀσφαλές, |
> Δίκα καὶ ὁμότροφος Εἰρήνα, τάμι' ἀνδράσι πλούτου, | χρύσεαι παῖ-
> δες εὐβούλου Θέμιτος. | ἐθέλοντι δ' ἀλέξειν | Ὕβριν, Κόρου ματέρα
> θρασύμυθον. | ἔχω καλά τε φράσαι, <u>τόλμα</u> τέ μοι | εὐθεῖα γλῶσσαν
> ὀρνύει λέγειν

Pindar *Olympian* 13.6–12

There [= in Corinth], **Eunomiā**,[69] sure foundation-stone of cities, dwells with <u>Justice</u> [**Dikē**] and Peace, dispenser of wealth to man, her sisters, golden daughters of Lawfulness [**Themis**], lady of good counsel. They accede to warding off <u>Outrage</u> [**Hubris**], <u>the one with the rash words</u> [**mūthoi**], the mother of <u>Insatiability</u> [**Koros**]. I have fair

---

68. On the figure of Bakis, see p. 170.
69. On the metaphorical associations of **Eunomiā**, a word that conveys the notion of good government achieved through good laws, cf. N 1985.43, 61.

things to say, and straightforward daring [**tolma**] impels my tongue to speak.[70]

This juxtaposition of passages from Herodotus and Pindar, revealing important convergences in theme as well as divergences in style, leads to a fundamental observation about both the **logioi** 'masters of speech' and the **aoidoi** 'masters of song', who are both treated as conveyors of **kleos** 'glory' in the words of Pindar.[71] We can see from these juxtaposed passages that the **logios** and the **aoidos** are parallel not only as masters of **kleos**: they are parallel also in what they have to say, that is, in the message that they impart. As for the code of this message, it is explicitly designated as **ainos** in the diction of the **aoidos** 'master of song' as exemplified by Pindar.[72] In the diction of the **logios** as exemplified by Herodotus, however, the corresponding designation is reserved for only one aspect of the code, and that is the poetry, not the prose. In the code of the **logios**, the explicit message is in prose, while the implicit message is to be found in the poetry as bracketed or paraphrased by the prose. A positive example of this code, as presented by Herodotus, is the sum total of his own *Histories*, which consistently bear out the messages of the Delphic Oracle and other such sources of authority. A typical negative example on the other hand is evident in the narrative of Herodotus about the collaboration of Onomakritos, singer of oracular utterances, with the Peisistratidai and Aleuadai, tyrants respectively of Athens and Thessaly: Onomakritos is pictured in the act of 'singing oracular utterances [**khrēsmoi**]' for the purpose of persuading the Great King of Persia (χρησμῳδέων 7.6.5), with the active support of the Peisistratidai and the Aleuadai, who reinforce what he sings by publicly presenting their own supporting judgment (γνώμας ἀποδεικνύμενοι ibid.).[73] The kind of poetry that is bracketed or paraphrased by the prose of the **logios** qualifies as **ainigma**, derivative of **ainos**, as we see in the use of **ainissomai** 'utter riddles' in the expression αἰνίσσεσθαι τάδε τὰ ἔπεα 'to utter in a riddling way the following words' at Herodotus 5.56.1, the end of a prose sequence introducing the quotation of an utterance, in dactylic hexameters, of an oracular dream.[74] Once the poetry of the **ainigma** is

---

70. In this passage the emphasis is on having the **tolma** 'boldness' to say good things, whereas in the previous passage the emphasis is on not having the **tolma** to say bad things. Cf. Hubbard 1986.37–38.

71. Cf. pp. 222 and following.

72. Cf. pp. 147 and following.

73. See p. 159. Combined with the direct object **gnōmēn/gnōmās** 'opinions, judgments', the verb **apo-deik-numai** 'make a public presentation of' is used in contexts where someone is presenting his views in public, and the contexts include three specific instances of self-expression by Herodotus (2.146.1, 7.139.1, 8.8.3). See p. 219.

74. Cf. also the use of the same verb in Aristophanes *Birds* 970, where the subject is the oracular Bakis. On the figure of Bakis, see again p. 170.

quoted, Herodotus can return to a mode of explicit communication; he therefore reverts to prose.

Herodotus then is like Pindar not only in his self-professed intent to convey **kleos**.[75] He is also like Pindar in his mastery of the **ainos**, though his medium is not **ainos**: rather, it contains **ainos**. For Herodotus, the heritage of **ainos** is to be found in the traditions of poetry and song making as they are contained and applied in his *Histories* by way of quotation, paraphrase, or mere reference.

Even if the medium of Herodotus cannot be called **ainos** in form, it is parallel to the **ainos** of a poet like Pindar in both function and content. Just as the songs of Pindar profess the function of upholding **kleos**, bringing the values of the heroic past into the present,[76] so too the *Histories* of Herodotus, as he declares in his prooemium.[77]

This observation about the function of the traditional forms represented by Pindar and Herodotus can be extended to the level of content as well: just as Pindaric song dwells on the mystical possession of the lyric moment by the epic past of heroes, so too the narrative of Herodotean inquiry falls under the spell of active interventions by the heroes of cult and epic. Let us begin with Pindar: in his songs the heroic past is at times represented as literally intervening into the present through the epiphany of a hero, as when the voice of the poet says that he "met" the hero Alkmaion on the way to Delphi (*Pythian* 8.56–60).[78] In such a context the poet is possessed by the epiphany, in that the intent of his words is controlled by the spirit of the hero. Thus the subtitle of this book, *The Lyric Possession of an Epic Past*, cuts two ways: while lyric possesses epic as its property, as we have seen from the programmatic assertions of lyric authority to appropriate the content of epic,[79] lyric is also mystically possessed by epic, in that the heroes of epic assert their will, which becomes the content of lyric.[80] So too with Herodotus: the content of his *Histories*, the narrative, is allowed to be controlled, or at least affected, by the will of heroes. The outcome of a given narrative is frequently marked by an intervention, perceived by the characters within the narrative, of a hero who mystically manifests himself on the scene, as when Herodotus narrates the reports about an epiphany by the local heroes Phylakos and Autonoos in defense of Delphi from the invading Persians (8.34–39). At the very end of the *Histories*, the first hero who died in the primary epic setting of the Trojan War, Protesilaos, figuratively comes back from the dead to exact retribution

75. Cf. pp. 222 and following.
76. Cf. pp. 150, 192, and following.
77. Cf. pp. 221 and following.
78. See p. 195.
79. Cf. p. 192 and following. By extension, whatever private individual possesses the lyric performance as his property is thereby also possessing the heroic heritage.
80. Cf. p. 201.

and gives meaning to the portent of the preserved fish that come back to life: with this portent the hero Protesilaos literally **sēmainei** 'indicates' the power of the divine apparatus in bringing about an ultimately just outcome (Herodotus 9.120.2). Meanwhile, the narrative of Herodotus is conveying the same message, that the Hellenes were in the right when they struggled with the common enemy in the Persian War: thus not only the hero gives a **sēma** 'sign' here, but Herodotus too, as the narrator of this **sēma**, who already at the very beginning of his inquiry **sēmainei** or 'indicates' that the Asians started it all (again Herodotus 1.5.3).[81]

Although Herodotus veils the divine apparatus that is at work in his narrative, habitually distancing himself from expressing his own adherence to a world view that is predicated on the gods and heroes of the Hellenes, he nevertheless allows that divine apparatus to work its will in the narrative so that the program of themes in his *Histories* matches what we find in actual poetry and song. Thus, for example, in his narrative of the sea battle at Artemisium, Herodotus notes that the wind that scattered the Persian fleet before the battle was known to the local Greek population as the **Hellēspontiēs** 'the one from the Hellespont' (1.188.2), a detail that conjures up the idea that the divine apparatus was at work in this event. This idea can be reconstructed from two interconnected themes. First, from the standpoint of epic, the Hellespont is associated with Achilles, whose tomb is prominently located there (e.g., *Odyssey* xxiv 80–84; called **sēma** at *Iliad* XXIII 257).[82] Second, the Persians react to this detail of the name **Hellēspontiēs** by associating it with Achilles, by way of his mother Thetis: after the naval disaster they supplicated Thetis for fear that they had angered her since Thetis had been abducted by Peleus—and thus Achilles had been conceived—near the very locale where their fleet had been scattered by the wind (7.191.2).[83] The linking of the wind that scattered the Persian fleet before the sea battle at Artemisium with the divine apparatus of poetic traditions is reinforced by another detail reported by Herodotus, namely, that the Athenians on this occasion sacrificed and prayed to Boreas the North Wind and his consort Oreithyia to scatter the fleet of the Persians (7.189). This detail in the narrative program of Herodotus links it with the narrative program of a composition by Simonides, *The Sea Battle of Artemisium* (PMG 532–535), which seems to have featured prominently the theme of the divine intervention of Boreas and Oreithyia in the Battle of Artemisium (cf. PMG 534).[84]

---

81. See p. 273.
82. N 1979.341, 344–345.
83. Cf. p. 193; also N, pp. 344–345.
84. Cf. p. 193. For more on the theme of winds as "divine equalizers," cf. Hohti 1976.46, citing Herodotus 8.12–13; 7.178, 189.

The similarities between Herodotus and a master of choral lyric like Simonides extend beyond such parallel treatments of themes linked with the divine apparatus of gods and heroes: even the modes of treating these themes are parallel. As in the songs of figures like Simonides and Pindar, we can see in the prose of Herodotus an approach to myth that shades over local features while it highlights the Panhellenic ones. Even on the level of diction, we have already noted the common pattern of avoidance, in both Pindar and Herodotus, of the word **mūthos** 'myth' with its connotations of surviving links between local myth and local ritual.[85] In dismissing the authority of a tradition that happens to have been accepted by his predecessor, Hecataeus of Miletus, Herodotus refers to this particular tradition as a **mūthos** (2.23.1).[86] Just as Hecataeus asserts the Panhellenism of his own discourse by simultaneously claiming control of **alēthea** 'truth' and dismissing the reports of his predecessors as localized myths tied to localized rituals (FGH 1 F 1), so also Herodotus aims at an ever higher degree of universalism by undermining his own predecessor, Hecataeus.[87]

Like Pindar, Herodotus not only dissociates himself from **mūthos**: he also consistently highlights the more Panhellenic aspects of the Greek mythmaking traditions, while shading over the more localized ones. For example, he mentions at 5.94.2–95.2 a conflict between Athens and Mytilene over a disputed territory in the region of Troy, where the focal points are the "Trojan" Sigeion (cf. Herodotus 4.38.2), an outpost of Athenian power, and the Akhilleion, a rival outpost controlled by Mytilene (Herodotus 5.94.1–2), but he avoids in this context a local narrative tradition, native to Lesbos, concerning a victory of Mytilene over Athens in the form of a duel to the death between Phrynon of Athens, an Olympic winner, and Pittakos of Mytilene, tyrant and lawgiver, as recorded in Diogenes Laertius 1.74 and Strabo 13.1.38 C599–600, where Pittakos succeeded in slaying Phrynon (cf. Plutarch *On the Malice of Herodotus* 858ab). In their reports of the tradition, Diogenes Laertius and Strabo agree that the Mytilenaeans won in this particular conflict, only to lose later in an arbitration undertaken by Periandros, Tyrant of Corinth (this aspect of the tradition is not omitted in Herodotus 5.95.2).[88] While omitting the story about the victory of Pittakos, as a representative of Mytilene, over the Athenians, Herodotus includes a story that he says he knows from a poem of Alcaeus: the speaker of the poem declares that he has abandoned his armor when he fled after a battle between Mytilene and Athens, a battle won by the Athenians, and that this armor is now hanging as a trophy in the precinct of Athena at the Athenian outpost of

85. Cf. p. 66.
86. Ibid. Cf. again How and Wells 1928 I 170.
87. Ibid.
88. Cf. p. 75.

Sigeion (Herodotus 5.95.1–2; see Alcaeus F 401B V). Instead of using a story about the defeat of Athens by Pittakos of Mytilene, Herodotus chooses a story about the defeat of Mytilene by Athens, as experienced by Alcaeus of Mytilene, who happens to be the self-declared enemy of Pittakos (e.g., Alcaeus F 70, 348, 429 V).

In fact one aspect of the Panhellenic stance of Herodotus is the frequency of his cross references to poets who had become or were becoming canonical by the fifth century B.C. Besides Alcaeus (5.95), Herodotus also mentions Archilochus (1.12.2),[89] Anacreon (3.121.1),[90] Sappho (2.135), Simonides (5.102.3, 7.228.4), and even Pindar (3.38.4), whom he explicitly paraphrases (= Pindar F 169.1 SM).[91] To this list we may add figures like Arion, master of the dithyramb at Corinth (1.23),[92] and Aeschylus, master of the medium of tragedy at Athens (2.156.6). The *Histories* also include cross references to Homer (2.23, 2.53.2, 3; 2.116) and Hesiod (2.53.2, 3; 4.32).[93]

Besides the numerous cross references to canonical poets, we have observed another Panhellenic trend in Herodotus, that is, the even more numerous cross references to the poetry of oracles, especially the Oracle of Apollo at Delphi.[94] The oracular poetry that is bracketed or paraphrased by the *Histories* of Herodotus qualifies as **ainigma**, derivative of **ainos**: we have seen this in the use of **ainissomai** 'utter riddles' in the expression αἰνίσσεσθαι τάδε τὰ ἔπεα 'to utter in a riddling way the following words' at Herodotus 5.56.1, the end of a prose sequence that introduces the quotation of an utterance, in dactylic hexameters, of an oracular dream.[95] To repeat: once the poetry of the **ainigma** is quoted, Herodotus can return to a mode of explicit communication, and he therefore reverts to prose. Alternatively Herodotus may stay within the medium of prose as he paraphrases the messages that can elsewhere be found in poetic wisdom, as we see in his central story of the encounter between Solon the Sage and Croesus the Tyrant.[96] Even in such situations, however, the direct quotations of Solon as he addresses Croesus, though in prose, function as the equivalent of the direct quotations of Solon in the poetic tradition that is attributed to him.[97]

---

89. Cf. p. 289.

90. Note the context of Herodotus 3.121.1: the tyrant Polycrates of Samos is pictured as reclining in the men's quarters in the company of Anacreon of Teos.

91. Of the nine canonical poets of lyric poetry proper (cf. p. 82), only four are missing in Herodotus: Alcman, Stesichorus, Ibycus, and Bacchylides.

92. Herodotus 1.24.1 draws attention to the association of Arion with Periandros, Tyrant of Corinth.

93. Cf. p. 321.

94. Cf. pp. 322 and following.

95. Cf. also p. 328.

96. Cf. p. 248.

97. Cf. ibid.

The use of traditions in oracular poetry and wisdom poetry in the *Histories* of Herodotus, where the form of prose coexists and interacts with forms of poetry,[98] is analogous to such forms of expression as represented by the *Lives of the Seven Sages* tradition.[99] The traditions about Solon, described as the wisest of the Seven Sages in Plato (*Timaeus* 20d),[100] follow this pattern of *ad hoc* poetry bracketed by prose that situates the supposedly historical contexts of the Sage's advice, as reflected for example in Diogenes Laertius 1.49, with the reworked prose narrative bracketing the poetry of Solon F 10 W.[101]

The Panhellenic character of the very concept of the Seven Sages is reflected not only by their canonical status but even by the collectivization of their sayings: as we know from the testimony of Plato, it was believed that they were collectively responsible for such sayings as γνῶθι σεαυτόν 'know yourself' and μηδὲν ἄγαν 'nothing in excess', which were inscribed on the temple of Apollo at Delphi (*Protagoras* 343a-b). In light of such Panhellenism inherent in the Seven Sages theme, it is worthy of note that the cross references in Herodotus to figures eligible for inclusion in the canonical grouping of the Seven Sages are even more frequent than his cross references to the canonical grouping of lyric poets:[102]

- Thales of Miletus: 1.74.2, 75.3, 170.3
- Solon of Athens: 1.29.1, 30.1, 31.1, 32.1, 34.1, 86.3, 5; 2.177.2; 5.113.2
- Khilon of Sparta: 1.59.2, 3 (as warner about Peisistratos the Tyrant), 7.235.2
- Pittakos, Tyrant of Mytilene: 1.27.2 (as foil for Solon)
- Bias of Priene: 1.27.2 (as foil for Solon), 170.1, 3
- Anacharsis the Thracian: 4.46.1, 76.1–6 (γῆν πολλὴν θεωρήσας καὶ

---

98. Cf. the discussion of *chantefable* at p. 47.

99. On this tradition, see Snell 1966 [1954], especially p. 118. On the canonical membership of the grouping known as the Seven Sages, see p. 243. See especially Diogenes Laertius 1.35, 61, 71, 78, 85, 91, quoting poetry attributed respectively to Thales, Solon, Khilon, Pittakos, Bias, Kleoboulos (missing here from the group of seven is any repertoire for Periandros); the meter and diction of this poetry point to the fifth century B.C. or earlier (cf. Snell, p. 118).

100. Cf. p. 226.

101. Cf. also Plutarch *Life of Solon* 25.6, bracketing Solon F 7 W, and the commentary in N 1985.31, comparing Solon F 7 with Theognis 24. Besides the format of poetry bracketed by prose, there is also evidence for the format of poetry bracketed by poetry, such as PSI IX no. 1093, where the sayings of Khilon of Sparta are introduced by a hexameter narrative. The sayings include μηδὲν ἄγαν 'nothing in excess' (lines 21–22) and ἐγγύα, πάρα δ' ἄτα 'a pledge, and already there is perdition' (line 22); cf. Plato *Charmides* 165a and *Protagoras* 343a-b. Commentary by Snell 1966 [1955] 117–118.

102. The listing that I give here corresponds closely to the canonical membership of the Seven Sages as discussed in p. 243. We have already noted in that discussion that such figures as Pythagoras of Samos/Kroton are also eligible for inclusion as variants. There are cross references to him as well in Herodotus (2.81.2; 4.95.1, 2; 96).

ἀποδεξάμενος κατ' αὐτὴν σοφίην πολλὴν ἐκομίζετο ἐς ἤθεα τὰ Σκυ-
θέων 'having made a **theōriā**[103] over many lands and having publicly
presented [= verb **apo-deik-numai**] throughout these lands much skill in
discourse [= **sophiā**], he brought it back [i.e., the **sophiā**] to the tribes of
the Scythians' 1.76.2)[104]

- Periandros, Tyrant of Corinth: 5.95.2 (as arbitrator between Athens and
  Mytilene; omission, in this context, of Pittakos, Tyrant of Mytilene); also
  1.20, 23, 24.1, 24.7; 3.48.2, 49.1, 50.1, 50.3, 51.1–3, 52.1, 3, 6, 7, 53.1,
  2, 6, 7; 5.92ζ1, 2, 3; η1, 2, 3, 95.2.

The close association of the sayings of the Seven Sages with the sayings
of the Delphic Oracle, as emphasized in Plato's *Protagoras* (again 343a-b), is
parallel to the association of Solon's message with the message of the Oracle
in the Croesus narrative of Herodotus. The warnings of Solon the Sage to
Croesus the Tyrant combine with the warnings of the Oracle of Apollo in
conveying the overall ethical message of the Croesus story in Herodotus,
which is encoded in the mode of an **ainos**.[105] The use of oracular poetry in
the prose of Herodotus was condemned by Plutarch as akin to the fable making of Aesop (*On the Malice of Herodotus* 871d),[106] and in fact the utterances
of Aesop as framed by the *Life of Aesop* tradition function in the mode of
ainos.[107] Plutarch's pejorative comparison of Herodotus with Aesop is
justified to the extent that Herodotus too can speak in the manner of the
ainos, occasionally even telling an outright fable.[108] In this connection I cite
again the distinction, made by the scholia to Aristophanes *Birds* 471, between
Aesopic and 'Sybaritic' fables: whereas the Aesopic discourse concentrates
on animals, the 'Sybaritic' concentrates on humans.[109] Inasmuch as Herodotus is said to have settled, died, and been buried in Thourioi (Stephanus of
Byzantium s.v. Θούριοι), a polis founded ostensibly as a Panhellenic venture, with the involvement of both Athens and Sparta (Diodorus 12.10–11), at
a site where once stood the city of Sybaris, that ultimate symbol of luxuriance and the **hubris** that goes with it,[110] I have argued that the setting of
Thourioi as a reborn and reformed Sybaris would have been an ideal context
for a reaffirmation of the values that bind Hellenes together in an ultimate

---

103. On the semantics of **theōros** as 'he who sees [root **hor-**] a vision [**theā**]', see p. 164. On
Solon as **theōros**, see Herodotus 1.30.2; also 1.29.1 and the commentary at p. 167.

104. Cf. "Plato" *Hipparchus* 228b: καλὰ ἔργα σοφίας ἀπεδείξατο '[Hipparkhos] presented
publicly the beautiful accomplishments connected with his understanding of poetry [**sophiā**]',
with commentary at p. 161.

105. Cf. pp. 243 and following, especially p. 247.

106. Cf. p. 322.

107. Cf. pp. 323 and following.

108. Cf. p. 324.

109. Cf. p. 325.

110. On the Sybaris theme, see p. 263.

conflict against **hubris**.[111] In this kind of context, the composition of 'Sybaritic' discourse could serve the purpose of ethical instruction for the body politic in an exalted sense of including all Hellenes, and we may note again that the reference in Aristophanes *Wasps* 1258–1260 to two kinds of discourse appropriate for learned merriment, the Aesopic and the 'Sybaritic' (**Subaritikoi**), includes the specific point that both kinds are to be learned at the symposium.[112]

The language of Herodotus provides indirect testimony that his own tradition of discourse and that of Aesop are related: in an incidental mention of Aesop, Herodotus refers to him as a **logopoios** 'artisan of speech' (Αἰσώπου τοῦ λογοποιοῦ Herodotus 2.134.3), and this same word **logopoios** is used by Herodotus to refer to his own predecessor, Hecataeus of Miletus (e.g., Ἑκαταίῳ τῷ λογοποιῷ Herodotus 2.143.1).[113] Moreover, in the same context where Herodotus mentions Aesop as a **logopoios** 'artisan of speech', he mentions the poet Sappho as a **mousopoios** 'artisan of song' (Σαπφοῦς τῆς μουσοποιοῦ Herodotus 2.135.1), and this juxtaposition parallels that of **logios/aoidos** 'master of speech/song' in the language of Pindar.[114]

The parallelisms between the discourse of Herodotus and that of such masters of **ainos** as Aesop on one extreme and Pindar on the other bring to mind yet another example of the Herodotean use of **ainos**, that is, the frequent references throughout the *Histories* to the symbol of the **hēmionos** 'mule', as introduced in an oracular utterance of Apollo, addressed to the tyrant Croesus of Lydia, concerning the birth of Cyrus, the once and future founder of the Persian Empire: like a mule — born of a socially superior mother, the horse, and of an inferior father, the donkey — so also Cyrus is born of a mother who is a Mede and a father who is a Persian (Herodotus 1.55.2, 1.91.5).

I have saved for last this particular example of **ainos**-making in Herodotus because it resonates simultaneously with the social loftiness of Pindar and the lowliness of Aesop. Let us consider Aesop as he is represented in Plutarch's *Banquet of the Seven Sages* (150a): at the banquet held in the banquet hall of the Tyrant-Sage Periandros of Corinth, Aesop is given a place next to Solon, but he is seated on a **diphros** 'low chair'; it is in this context that Aesop tells the fable of "The Lydian Mule": a mule, seeing his own image reflected in a river, is struck with self-admiration and starts galloping like a horse, proudly tossing his mane, but then, suddenly realizing that he is the son of an ass, he stops running, and his spirit is broken for good (ibid.).[115]

---

111. Cf. p. 305.
112. Cf. p. 325.
113. Cf. p. 325.
114. Cf. p. 224.
115. Cf. p. 326. In this context, Plutarch *Banquet of the Seven Sages* 150a, it is made explicit that Aesop has been sent by Croesus of Lydia as an emissary both to Periandros and to the Oracle of Apollo at Delphi.

The symbol of the mule in Greek traditions of myth and ritual serves to define, as a negative foil, the very essence of political power and legitimacy. Let us consider again the ideology of the Olympic Games, that ultimate symbol of power and sovereignty.[116] In line with this ideology, it is tabu to breed mules within the territory that serves as the setting for the Games, the region of Elis, and in fact it is said to be impossible to do so (Herodotus 4.30.1); for that reason, during the season when the female horses of that region are in heat, they are herded outside Elis to be mated with male donkeys (4.30.2; Pausanias 5.5.2; Plutarch *Greek Questions* 52, 303b). The breeding of mules outside Elis, setting for the Olympics, is a foil for the implied breeding of thoroughbred horses inside Elis, as conveyed by the name of Hippodameia, containing the theme of *horses* and their *taming* or *domination*. The marriage of this figure Hippodameia to Pelops constitutes the archetype of political domination in the Peloponnesus.[117] By extension, the symbol of the mule as applied to Cyrus, founder of the Persian Empire and archetypal threat to Greek civilization, serves as a foil for the purebred legitimacy of Pelops as the dynastic prototype of the Hellenes and, in that capacity, as the preeminent hero of the Olympic Games.[118]

Such a foil of illegitimacy does not have to be foreign: the symbol of the mule is a traditional theme for testing the essence of sovereignty in Hellenic myths native to the Peloponnesus. There is, for example, a story native to Elis about one Oxylos, described as the driver of a mule, whose advice to the Herakleidai was the key to their occupation of the Peloponnesus (Pausanias 5.3.5–6). In return for his advice Oxylos was awarded possession of Elis (ibid.), which is the setting of the Olympic Games. This same Oxylos is credited with the invention of the **astrabē** 'mule saddle' (scholia to Pindar *Pythian* 5.10b Drachmann). In view of the Spartan connections of Oxylos (Pausanias 5.4.1–2), we may note the riddling story in Herodotus 6.67–69 about the Spartan hero **Astrabakos** , whose name means something like 'the one with the mule saddle'.[119] In this complex story as reported by Herodotus,

116. Cf. pp. 123 and following on the aetiological centering of the Olympics on the hero Pelops; also p. 130 on Pelops as the inaugurator of a kingship that serves as the model of political power and sovereignty in the Peloponnesus. In the narrative at Herodotus 1.59.1 concerning the portent of the boiling cauldron, presaging the birth of the tyrant Peisistratos of Athens, there is an implied ideological equation of the fire of Olympic victory with the essence of political power: pp. 124–25.

117. On the dynasty of Pelops as the model of political power and sovereignty in the Peloponnesus, see again p. 130.

118. Cf. pp. 123 and following. I disagree with the view that the myth of Pelops and Hippodameia may have conveyed some sort of aetiological analogy to the breeding of mules outside of Elis, where the Elian Hippodameia is to a horse as the non-Elian Pelops is to a donkey (bibliography in Calame 1977 I 418–419). In this connection I stress that the **Pelopion** 'Precinct of Pelops' anchors this figure to Olympia in Elis (p. 123).

119. Burkert 1965.173n23.

the hero Astrabakos took the place of King Ariston of Sparta in impregnating the queen, begetting King Demaratos, according to the story within a story told to Demaratos by his mother (6.69.1–5); according to the detractors of King Demaratos of Sparta, in contrast, he was begotten not by Ariston, nor by the hero Astrabakos, but by some **onophorbos**, a 'stableboy who tends donkeys' (6.68.2, 69.5). Now **hēmionoi** 'mules' are known to be sterile, and they are said to give birth only by miracle (e.g., Herodotus 3.151.2–153.2). Moreover, before King Ariston married the queen who gave birth to Demaratos, he had two previous wives with whom he had failed to produce children (Herodotus 6.61.1–2). It seems then that the theme of the stableboy who tends donkeys is linked with the meaning of 'mule' implicit in the name of Astrabakos. There is an air of illegitimacy conjured up by this name.[120] There is also an air of illegitimacy about Demaratos, which seems connected with the themes of his formal disqualification as king (Herodotus 6.65.3–67.3), his subsequent escape from Sparta (6.70.1–2), and, most important, his role as a prominent advisor of Xerxes when the Persians invade Hellas (e.g., 7.101–104).[121] There is room for speculation that had Xerxes succeeded in conquering the Greeks, Demaratos would have been installed by the Persians as an unconstitutional tyrant of the Peloponnesus.[122] Since Astrabakos belongs to the royal patriliny of the Agiadai (Pausanias 3.16.9), while Ariston stems from the Eurypontidai, it has even been suggested that "a Eurypontid king with an Agiad divine father would seem ideally suited for replacing the Spartan dual kingship by a monarchy."[123] In this connection we may note the remark of Herodotus that Demaratos was the only Spartan king up to that time ever to have won in the chariot races at the Olympic Games (6.70.5). Such a feat promotes the kind of legitimation that is sought by tyrants.[124] While giving such feats their due, the narrative of Herodotus, consistently inimical as it is to the institution of tyranny, undercuts the legitimation that goes with it.

This theme brings us finally to the glorification of such legitimation, as conferred by the epinician themes inherited through the songmaking traditions of Pindar. Just as Herodotus parallels the lowly Aesop with themes of **ainos** reminiscent of the fable, so also he parallels the lofty Pindar, again

120. We may note that **astrabikon** is the name of a type of bucolic song supposedly initiated at Karyai by rustic folk as a displacement, after the devastation of the Persian War, of choral performances by aristocratic girls (Probus by way of Servius 3.2, p. 324.8ff Thilo-Hagen; cf. Calame 1977 I 267n182 and 274n194, where further references are given; the pertinent texts are quoted in Nilsson 1906.198n1). On the traditional theme of rustic outsiders, formerly excluded from the city as illegitimate, whose institutions become subsequently included and thereby legitimated, see pp. 389 and following.

121. On Demaratos as a "warner" of Xerxes, cf. Boedeker 1987.195–196.

122. Burkert, p. 175n30, with bibliography.

123. Seeberg 1966.74.

124. Cf. pp. 156 and following.

with themes of **ainos**, this time reminiscent of the epinician ode. But these themes are used by Herodotus not to promote the legitimation of those who seek or already possess power. Rather they are there to undercut such legitimation; thus the themes are consistently historicized and therefore demystified. Let us take, for example, the exalted theme of **phuē** 'nature', which is contrasted with the foil of artificial glorification in order to convey "a natural and spontaneous enthusiasm that is divinely inspired" in epinician songmaking (as in Pindar *Olympian* 2.86, *Nemean* 1.25).[125] In contrast, the concept of **phuē** in Herodotus is presented in an ambiguous context, where the resources of culture, of artifice, are being used by the tyrant in order to manipulate nature. In a celebrated story of Herodotus about the seizure of political power by Peisistratos of Athens, **Phuē** is the name of a stunningly beautiful woman, three finger-lengths short of four cubits in stature, whom Peisistratos dresses up in full armor and with whom he then rides from the countryside into the city of Athens (1.60.4). Heralds have prepared the way, announcing the news that Athena herself is installing Peisistratos as the supreme power; the populace, when they see **Phuē** on the chariot, recognize her as Athena and accept the domination of Peisistratos (1.60.5).[126] The natural endowments of a beautiful woman have been manipulated by the artifice of a tyrant—an artifice comparable to the strategies of epinician **ainos**. In his public presentation of **Phuē**, Peisistratos has brought to life a central metaphor of the epinician tradition.[127] In the ideology of epinician songmaking, **phuē** 'nature' represents those spontaneous occasions when "the subject must speak for itself."[128] In the ideology of Herodotean **ainos**, such a spontaneous occasion is in fact an illusion created through artistry, through the artifice of the tyrant.[129]

125. Bundy [1986] 16; cf. also Bundy 1972.90n113.

126. For a valuable analysis of this episode, with important comparative observations concerning the politics of festivals and festive events in general, see Connor 1987.

127. Cf. Slater 1984.260–263.

128. Bundy [1986] 16.

129. For more on the Pindaric themes of spontaneity and artistry, nature and art, cf. Hubbard 1985.107–124.

12 ▣▣ Authority and Authorship in the Lyric Tradition

H aving compared the authority of Pindar's traditions in song with the authority of traditions in poetry and prose, we are ready to consider the actual medium of Pindaric song as a key to understanding the concept of authorship in lyric poetry. So far we have concentrated on the epinician tradition represented by Pindar. But now we must situate this tradition within the broader framework of Archaic Greek lyric poetry.

Let us begin with the concept of choral lyric poetry, which is the specific medium of Pindar. The **khoros** 'chorus' of choral lyric is a group that represents, by way of singing and dancing, a given community.[1] In Archaic choral lyric poetry, the community can be represented as the city-state, the polis itself.[2] This is not to say, however, that the representation of the polis by the chorus does not aim at Panhellenic prestige.[3]

As a representative of the polis, the chorus is concerned partly with local interests, and it can therefore serve as a formal vehicle of ritual, as in the case of the epinicians of Pindar, which constitute part of the ritual chain of athletics.[4] The range, however, of choral self-expression in matters of ritual is certainly not limited to the Games. Besides epinician odes, a given chorus in a given polis may perform a wide variety of other kinds of compositions related to various local or civic rituals. The range of this variety is apparent from the book titles in the Alexandrian editions of Pindar.[5] There are, for

1. Cf. p. 142.
2. Cf. p. 144.
3. Cf. p. 145.
4. See Ch.4, Ch.5.
5. See p. 111.

example, the maiden songs or **parthenia**, related ultimately to local/civic rituals of coming of age.[6] This type of song is also attested in compositions from earlier times, as we see in the upcoming discussion of Alcman and the choral traditions of Sparta. There are also, of course, choral odes connected directly with cults of the gods, such as Pindar's **paiānes** 'paeans' in honor of Apollo.[7] The list could be extended, but the point has already been made: choral lyric is public, a thing of the polis.[8]

Within the general category of song or lyric poetry, however, we have also had occasion to take note of another medium besides choral lyric: monody, that is, solo singing.[9] In studying the traditions of Archaic Greek monody, we have already examined the eventual differentiation of a composer/performer into a mythical protocomposer on the one hand and a contemporary professional performer, the **kitharōidos** 'lyre singer' or **aulōidos** 'reed singer' on the other.[10] But this type of differentiation in monody is just one of many possible patterns of evolution.

So also with choral lyric, there are many different patterns of evolution in the traditions of composition and performance. The basic difference between monody and choral lyric is on the level of performance. Whereas monody accommodates a single professional or nonprofessional performer, choral lyric requires a group of strictly nonprofessional polis dwellers as represented by the **khoros** 'chorus', who both sang and danced the song.[11] So much for distinctions between monodic and choral modes of *performance*.

Let us turn our attention to distinctions between monody and choral lyric on the level of *composition*. In the choral medium of Pindar the composer of the performances was clearly a professional, as we see explicitly in Pindar's own words, *Isthmian* 2.1–13.[12] In this sense, Pindar's medium was in fact professional, and it contrasts itself with the good old days when love songs were sung to the lyre, spontaneously and without pay, in the setting of symposia (*Isthmian* 2.1–5). Pindar's diction, describing the lyric poetry of the good old days, is suggestive of monody, in particular the grand old masters of sympotic love lyric, such as Alcaeus, Anacreon, and Ibycus (cf. Aristophanes *Women at the Thesmophoria* 160–163; Athenaeus 600d on Anacreon).[13] But the spontaneity of nonprofessional performance by these figures of the past

6. Cf. Calame 1977 I 18–20, 117, 249.

7. Cf. p. 111.

8. Cf. p. 142. For a useful survey of city festivals serving as contexts for choral performance in the Greek-speaking areas of Italy and Sicily, see Burnett 1988.129–147.

9. Cf. p. 85. For a cross cultural view of the maintenance of a distinction between solo and chorus, see Schneider 1957.4–5.

10. Cf. pp. 86, 90.

11. Cf. p. 85.

12. Cf. p. 151.

13. Woodbury 1968.532–533.

turns out to be an idealization, once we take fully into consideration the special skills needed for the traditions of performing this and other kinds of monodic poetry. These skills were transmitted professionally, through the medium of professional **kitharōidiā** 'lyre singing', either directly in performance or indirectly in the professional teaching of performance.

As a premier example of professional performance in monodic lyre singing, I cite the story of Arion in Herodotus 1.23–24.[14] This figure Arion, who is described as the most prestigious **kitharōidos** 'lyre singer' of his era (Herodotus 1.23), is represented as giving a monodic performance of lyre singing, in a ploy to save his life, for an audience of greedy sailors who had captured him in order to rob him of his great wealth (1.24.5); it is specified that Arion had amassed his riches, designated as **khrēmata** 'property', on a musical tour through Italy and Sicily (1.24.1–2).

In Pindar's *Isthmian* 2, this same word **khrēmata** 'property, possessions' is used in a context where one of the Seven Sages, in reaction to his personal loss of both property and friends (11) exclaims bitterly: χρήματα χρήματ' ἀνήρ 'Man is nothing more than **khrēmata**! Yes, **khrēmata**!' (ibid.).[15] Another variation on this bitter reaction is quoted in the monodic poetry of Alcaeus (F 360 V), again in a context where the Sage is bewailing the equation of self-worth with purely material value.[16] In other words the ethic of sympotic monody, as presented by Alcaeus and represented by Pindar, is the transcendence of purely material value. But the anecdote about Arion suggests that the art of sympotic monody is nevertheless founded on the dynamics of material value. So too with choral lyric poetry, as dramatized in Pindar's *Isthmian* 2: the poem is admitting that its art is founded on the dynamics of material value, but it proclaims the intent of transcending the purely material, claiming the ethic of old-fashioned sympotic monody as a model. Pindaric song fuses the contemporary art of monody, which is professional, into the transcendent ethic of monody, which rejects the superficial equation of **khrēmata** 'possessions' with self-worth. Pindar's fusion of the professional with the ethical — so that the professional aspect of monody is no longer evident — is itself an ethical gesture, corresponding to a parallel fusion that is ongoing within his own choral medium. This ideology of

14. Cf. p. 87.

15. That this figure is one of the Seven Sages, at least in one particular variant of the Seven Sages theme, is made explicit in the scholia to the passage (iii pp. 215–216 Drachmann: the authority is Andron of Ephesus). See also the following note.

16. In Alcaeus the name of the Sage is specified as Aristodemos, and his saying is localized in Sparta (F 360.1–2 V); in Pindar, by contrast, the Sage is called 'the Argive' (τὦργείου *Isthmian* 2.9). In Diogenes Laertius 1.41, where the traditions about alternative membership in the flexible theme of the Seven Sages are being discussed, Aristodemos is named as one of the Seven. For more on the theme of the poet as a righteous man who is bereft of his possessions and betrayed by his friends, see p. 429.

fusion should not lead to our own confusion about professionalism and nonprofessionalism in monody.

Having recovered the reality of professional performance in the art of lyre singing, we may turn to the professional teaching of performance in lyre singing. Again I cite the explicit reference in Aristophanes *Clouds* 961–989 to the schooling of young boys by professionals in the art of lyre singing, back in those "good old days" of the generation that had fought at Marathon.[17] The comic allusions in this passage to an atmosphere of aristocratic pederasty that pervades such schooling (e.g., 966) is indicative of a common theme, typical of not only monodic song but also elegiac poetry, linking aristocratic **paideiā** 'education' and aristocratic **paiderastiā** 'love of boys' in the context of the symposium.[18] In the comic vision of Aristophanes, even the schooling of the boys is pervaded by this dominant theme. In Pindar's idealized vision of nonprofessional monodic performance at the symposium, the songs being sung are called **paideioi humnoi** 'songs of boyhood' (παιδείους ... ὕμνους *Isthmian* 2.3), an expression that suggests **paideiā** and **paiderastiā** simultaneously.[19] The passage from Aristophanes about the old-fashioned schooling of nonprofessionals by professionals in this art helps put the spontaneity of the monodic moment into perspective.

The most we can say for nonprofessionalism in Archaic Greek songmaking is that the monodic medium, in contexts like the symposium, may at least allow for composition on a nonprofessional as well as professional level, whereas the choral medium of a figure like Pindar, according to his own words, has become restricted to the composition of professionals. Also, the monodic medium allows for performance on a nonprofessional as well as professional level, whereas the choral medium, as performed by the **khoros** 'chorus', is restricted to performance by nonprofessionals. Moreover, even choral compositions can be reperformed by nonprofessionals at symposia as solo pieces, but then these nonprofessionals are expected to accompany themselves on the lyre, and that in turn requires professional education in the specialized art of **kitharōidiā** 'lyre singing'.[20] In fact such solo performance was the ultimate sign of education, of direct access to the old traditions of song.[21]

In a word the symposium was a last stand for nonprofessional performance of both monodic and choral compositions. Still the choral medium was already professionalized in the dimension of composition, and the monodic, in the dimension of transmission through such specialized skills as **kitharōidiā** 'lyre singing'.

17. Cf. p. 97.
18. On which see Lewis 1985; cf. N 1982.61–62, 1985.51–56.
19. Kurke 1988.204–207; cf. Burnett 1988.139.
20. Cf. pp. 113 and following.
21. Ibid.

Given these patterns of differentiation between the choral and monodic media, we may ask about their diachronic relationship to each other. As the discussion proceeds, we encounter a series of indications that the direction of long-range development proceeded from choral lyric to monody as a differentiated offshoot. Further, monody can be seen as a midstage in the differentiation of song into poetry.

Let us observe more closely the patterns of restriction, in the Archaic choral lyric form, to performance by nonprofessionals, for whom such performance was a ritual act of community. This restriction is a fundamental indication that we are dealing with a less differentiated institution.[22] From the standpoint of later standards in the more differentiated world of poetic and musical professionalism, the inherited necessity of performance by a chorus of nonprofessionals imposed limitations on the virtuosity of both performance and composition (cf. "Aristotle" *Problems* 19.15). Moreover, as we shall now see, the references to nonprofessional choral performance in Homeric and Hesiodic poetry, combined with cross cultural comparative evidence, make it clear that the social institution of what we call the chorus even antedates the institution of the polis.[23]

In the songmaking traditions of choral lyric poetry, one of several possible patterns of evolution results in the attested differentiation between a protocomposer who is grounded in myth and a succession of contemporary nonprofessional performers, selected by age groupings, who sing and dance a protocomposition grounded in the ritual of seasonally recurring festivals. Such a protocomposition would be subject to potential ongoing recomposition with each seasonally recurring performance. Striking examples of this pattern of evolution can be found in the available testimony about the festivals of Sparta, which were the occasion for seasonal reperformances, in a ritual setting, of the lyric "protocompositions" of Terpander, Thaletas, Alcman, and others.[24]

The first **katastasis** 'establishment', that is, the ostensibly first phase of lyric traditions at Sparta, is traditionally attributed to Terpander ("Plutarch"

---

22. In this connection I cite Schneider 1957 for a useful cross cultural survey of collective performance. Although this work is in some respects outdated, many of its formulations have a lasting value, such as the following: "But the participation of a [chorus] not only helps the regularity of the rhythmic movement: it also contributes materially to the unification of the melodic line" (p. 4). As an example, he cites the following observation about collective performance in African pygmy society, which normally begins "with a wild cry for all the singers out of which a comparative union gradually emerges. The melodic line and the various rhythms of the opening gradually adjust themselves to one another and in the end there emerges a completely regular community chant" (ibid.). As Schneider notes further on, "the powerful influence of collective performance on the development of primitive music can be seen from the fact that even funeral music and love-songs are also very largely choral" (ibid.).

23. A pathfinding work in this regard is Calame 1977.

24. On the strict preservation of performance traditions in song at Sparta, see Athenaeus 633f.

On Music 1134b). This composer of the so-called 'first **katastasis**' was reputedly a singer from Lesbos who moved to Sparta, where he was the first of all winners at the reputedly oldest festival of Sparta, the Feast of **Karneia** (Hellanicus FGH 4 F 85 by way of Athenaeus 635e).[25] The second **katastasis** is attributed to Thaletas of Gortyn, Xenocritus of Locri, Polymnestus of Colophon (*On Music* 1134bc).[26] These composers of the so-called second **katastasis** are associated with the Feast of the **Gumnopaidiai** at Sparta, as well as the Feast of the **Apodeixeis** in Arcadia and the Feast of the **Endumatia** at Argos (*On Music* 1134c).[27] I draw attention to the opposite notions of ritual undressing and dressing inherent in the names **Gumnopaidiai** (henceforth "Gymnopaidiai") and **Endumatia** native to the traditions of Sparta and Argos, respectively. As for the Arcadian **Apodeixeis**, plural of the noun **apo-deixis** 'public presentation', we shall appreciate the significance of this name better at a later point, when we consider the related verb **apo-deiknumai** 'make a public presentation' in the context of a report by Herodotus about a local festival where female choral groups perform (5.83.3).[28] Earlier, we have seen the same word in a different but ultimately related context, the first sentence of the *Histories* of Herodotus, in referring to the 'public presentation', **apo-deixis**, of his **historiā** 'inquiry'.[29] For now, however, it is enough to stress that such festivals are a key to our upcoming consideration of the process of ongoing choral recomposition. There is a striking description, in Sosibius FGH 595 F 5 by way of Athenaeus 678bc, of choral events at the Spartan Feast of the Gymnopaidiai, featuring reperformances of compositions attributed to Thaletas, Alcman, and Dionysodotus.

It has been observed, on the basis of this and similar testimony, that "some at least of Alcman's compositions were still being reperformed well into the Hellenistic era."[30] What I argue, further, is that such patterns of sustained seasonal reperformance entail parallel patterns of sustained seasonal recomposition, affecting not only the content of the compositions but also the very personification of the archetypal composer.

In order to understand the progressive reshaping over time of the persona who claims the composition of a choral lyric performance in societies like that of Archaic Sparta, we must explore in greater detail the fundamental characteristics of the Archaic Greek **khoros**, the singing and dancing ensem-

25. See p. 86.

26. Cf. Barker 1984.214. On Xenocritus of Locri, as an exponent of *Aeolian* **harmoniā**, see p. 96.

27. This passage is the only extant reference to either the Arcadian **Apodeixeis** or the Argive **Endumatia**. On the Feast of the **Gumnopaidiai** at Sparta, see also Pausanias 3.11.9, and other passages surveyed by Nilsson 1906.140–142.

28. Cf. p. 364.

29. Ch.8.

30. Herington 1985.25–26.

ble or chorus. To begin, I stress that the **khoros** is by nature a microcosm of society.[31] The Spartans, for example, actually referred to the interior of their civic space as the **Khoros** (Pausanias 3.11.9).[32] As a microcosm of society, it is equally important to note, the **khoros** is also a microcosm of social hierarchy. Within the hierarchy that is the chorus, as the detailed investigation of Claude Calame has shown, a majority of younger members act out a pattern of subordination to a minority of older leaders; this acting out conforms to the role of the chorus as an educational collectivization of experience, including various forms of institutionalized or stylized homosexual experience serving as an initiation into the heterosexual status of marriage.[33] The concept of older leaders, within the hierarchy of the chorus, is in most instances embodied in the central persona of the **khorēgos** 'chorus leader'. There is a pervasive choral convention of emphasizing the superiority of the **khorēgos** and the subordination of the "I" that speaks for the choral aggregate; while the collectivity of the choral aggregate is egalitarian, the superiority of the **khorēgos** is a fundamental model of hierarchy.[34] In this connection Calame has observed in detail how various patterns of institutionalized homosexual sentiment as expressed by the choral "I" tend to center on the person who occupies superior status in the choral group.[35]

As a particularly striking example of the choral form as a hierarchical construct, I cite the Spartan song that is sung and danced by the chorus of Spartan girls as dramatized in Alcman PMG 1, where a chorus leader called Hagesikhora (verses 53, 57, 77, 79, 90), focal point of admiration for the aggregate (e.g., 45–57),[36] is described as **khorēgos** (44);[37] her very name, **Hāgēsikhorā**, recapitulates the meaning 'leader of the chorus'.[38] Similarly in Aristophanes *Lysistrata* 1296–1321, a choral song of the Spartan women, Helen in her role as major cult figure of Sparta is pictured by the chorus as the leader of their group, as the ultimate **khorēgos** (1315). Likewise in Theocritus 18, a composition known as the *Epithalamium for Helen*, a chorus of Spartan girls pictures Helen as a resplendent chorus leader, in terms that resemble strikingly the description of Hagesikhora in Alcman PMG 1.[39] It is clear from such evidence that a figure like Hagesikhora, as leader of the

31. See p. 142.
32. Cf. Calame 1977 ɪ 277. The choral performances at the Feast of Gymnopaidiai (on which see p. 344) took place within this space: Pausanias 3.11.9.
33. Cf. Calame 1977 ɪ 437–439.
34. Cf. Calame ibid.
35. Ibid.
36. That the αὔτα of verse 45 refers to Hagesikhora is argued by Calame 1977 ɪɪ 47n3; cf. also Calame 1983.326.
37. That the mention of **khorēgos** at Alcman PMG 1.44 refers to Hagesikhora: Calame 1977 ɪɪ 46–47; also Calame 1983.326.
38. Calame ɪɪ 46–47. Cf. Griffiths 1972.24–26.
39. Detailed comparison in Calame ɪɪ 123–126.

chorus, is represented as performing a reenactment, a mimesis,[40] of a given divinity in a given role.[41]

Although the specific divinity that matches the choral figure of Hagesi-khora seems at first sight to be the local Spartan version of Helen, a strong argument can be made for a variant identification. The real referent for Hagesikhora seems to be one of two less well-known cult figures native to Sparta, that is, a female pair known from other reports as the **Leukippides** (Pausanias 3.16.1), where the component **leuko-** means 'radiant, white' while **hippo-** means 'horse'; these Leukippides are themselves associated with the cult of Helen (Euripides *Helen* 1465–1466).[42] In the same composition the other of the two Leukippides may possibly be equated with another dominant choral personality, called Agido (Alcman PMG 1.40, 42, 58, 80), who is dramatized as the rival of Hagesikhora (e.g., PMG 1.50–59).[43]

It seems then that the two characters of two choral leaders in Alcman PMG 1, Agido and Hagesikhora, are acting out, on the level of the ritual presented by the chorus, the roles of the two Leukippides, who are cult figures that exist on the level of myth.[44] There is in fact independent evidence for such acting out: there is a report about an institution, at Sparta, where girls 'serve as priestesses' (ἱερῶνται) to the Leukippides and are in that capacity explicitly called Leukippides themselves (Pausanias 3.16.1).[45] It is crucial to stress this explicit identification here, by name, of distinct human and superhuman characters. The human characters are acted out by 'priestesses' who are the variable element in the identification, in that they are continually being replaced by upcoming generations, in the progression of time, while the immortal superhuman characters are the constant, with an unchanging identity that provides the ultimate model.[46] Just as the human Leukippides

40. I am using here the word *mimesis* in the sense outlined in the discussion of **mīmēsis** at p. 42 and following.

41. That the Hagesikhora figure is not divine is clear from the comparison with those quasi-Muses, the Sirens, to whom she is said to be inferior because *they* are goddesses (σιαὶ γάρ Alcman PMG 1.98); cf. Calame 1983.346–347.

42. On Helen and the Leukippides, see Kannicht 1969 II 381–382. Also Calame 1977 I 326–330, who shows that the theme of radiant horses is a sacred symbol for the dawn, a cult topic shared by the figure of Helen with the Leukippides, who in turn are consorts of the Dioskouroi, brothers of Helen. On the traditional association of Helen and the Dioskouroi with the symbolism of the dawn, see N 1973.172–173n94; note too N 1979.200 for a discussion of the epithet of Helen, **Dios thugatēr** 'daughter of Sky/Zeus' (*Odyssey* iv 227), which is inherited from the figure of Eos, the dawn goddess par excellence. It is important to note that the chorus of Alcman PMG 1 seems to be worshipping a dawn goddess, **Aōtis** (verse 87): see Calame II 124–125.

43. Calame 1977 II 126–133. The possible rivalry of Agido and Hagesikhora is to be noted for a later stage in the discussion.

44. Calame I 323–333.

45. Ibid.

46. In Polyaenus 8.59, we read of the appearance of a priestess of Athena who is dressed in full armor, like the goddess; cf. Connor 1987.46.

are not, from our standpoint, real people but instead characters filled by different real people at the different times of seasonally recurring ritual events, so also the figures named as Agido and Hagesikhora in Alcman PMG 1 are for me not real people per se but choral characters. Specifically I suggest that Agido and Hagesikhora are characters in a sacred mimesis, through the ritual of choral performance, of the cult figures known to Pausanias as the Leukippides (3.16.1).[47]

The actual forms of the names given to these characters, Agido and Hagesikhora, may have been subject to changes over time, but the function of these names, that is, identification with sacred models in the process of mimesis, can be expected to have remained a constant.[48] Such cult names are variables, and the constant element is to be sought in the context of the mimesis, the actual identification of the human character with the sacred model. There is a particularly striking illustration of such an ideology in a passage from Xenophon of Ephesus (1.2.2–7), a narrative describing a local festival of Artemis at Ephesus (ἤγετο δὲ τῆς Ἀρτέμιδος ἐπιχώριος ἑορτή 2), where the leader of a procession of marriageable maidens, a girl of fourteen called Antheia (5), is viewed by the festive crowd as the incarnation of the goddess Artemis (7).[49]

Like **Hāgēsikhorā**, the feminine name **Agidō** seems to be generic: in this case it fits into the naming pattern owned by the Spartan royal lineage of the Agiadai, as best known from the name of a particularly distinguished member of this lineage, **Agēsilāos**.[50] From this example we can see that the role model defined by a choral leader can be expressed in terms of royalty as well as divinity. An analogous case is to be found in Alcman PMG 10(b), where the figure of a yet-beardless youth (19–20) called **Agēsidāmos** (3), meaning 'leader of the local population [**dēmos**]',[51] is addressed specifically as **khorēgos** 'chorus leader' (11; cf. 15). There is a striking semantic parallel in the case of the choral leader **Astumeloisa** at Alcman PMG 3 (64, 73), where this generic name is actually translated in the song itself (74) as μέλημα δάμῳ 'an object of care and affection [**melēma**] to the local com-

47. The association of the Leukippides with the theme of radiant horses can be correlated with the comparison of Agido and Hagesikhora to two resplendent racehorses in Alcman PMG 1.50–59. For the choral application of racehorse imagery, see Calame II 83 on the equation of **khorēgos** and *cheval conducteur*. Calame II 70 shows that these horses in the Alcman passage are represented as *Scythian* and *Lydian*. Such foreign associations assert the Panhellenic prestige of Spartan traditions, in that they reflect the widespread contacts enjoyed by the polis; they also reinforce the theme of "foreign is native," on which see Ch.10, especially p. 298 and following.

48. Pausanias 3.16.1 gives the names of the Spartan Leukippides as **Hilaeira** and **Phoibē**, and Calame I 325 provides indications that they were considered daughters of Apollo.

49. Cf. Calame I 69, 181–182 and II 124; also Connor 1987.44.

50. Calame II 140–141, with n3. For more on the Agiadai, see p. 154.

51. On the reading **Agēsidāmos** as distinct from **Hāgēsidāmos**, see Calame 1983.457. On **dēmos** as 'local population', see p. 56.

munity [**dēmos**]' — which is exactly what the name means.[52] As with the feminine name **Agidō**, designating the counterpart of the Hagesikhora figure, the masculine name **Agēsidāmos**, by way of its semantic components, seems to fit into the naming pattern of the Spartan royal lineage of the Agiadai.[53]

That the roles of choral leadership indicated by names such as Agido or Agesidamos demand to be filled, in performance, by real royalty or aspiring royalty is shown indirectly: narrative traditions tell of aberrant situations where an individual Spartan of genuine royalty is denied a prominent position in a choral group, thus affording him the opportunity to assert a wise saying to the effect that it is after all the man in question who determines the status, not the status the man. In one such story, Plutarch *Sayings of Spartans* 208de, the focus of the story is none other than King **Agēsilāos** of Sparta, of the royal lineage of the Agiadai, who is pictured as still a boy when, one day at the Spartan Feast of Gymnopaidiai,[54] he is assigned an inconspicuous (**a-sēmos**) choral position.[55] The narrative emphasizes that, at this moment, as Agesilaos utters the wise saying about man and status, it is not yet clear that he will indeed become the king of Sparta; as Plutarch notes elsewhere, the young Agesilaos was brought up as a private citizen before he became king (*Life of Agesilaos* 596a, 597b).[56] The fact that other variants of this story are

52. Commentary in Calame 1983.414–415; also Calame 1977 II 106.

53. Calame II 141–142. Note too the naming of the father of **Agēsidāmos**, mentioned in the same composition, Alcman PMG 10(b).12: **Dāmotīmos** 'he who has the honor [**tīmē**] of the local population [**dēmos**]'. Specifically the father is named here by way of a patronymic adjective applied to Agesidamos: **Dāmotīmidās**. The use of the patronymic form here in Alcman PMG 10(b).12 seems parallel to the generic application of **Polupāidēs** 'son of the one who possesses much' to the figure of Kyrnos in Theognis 191 et passim, as discussed in N 1985.55–56. For more on expressive patronymics, see the references in N 1979.17 §4n1.

54. On the Gymnopaidiai, see p. 344; as we shall see later, n56, this Spartan festival plays a significant role in the narrative strategy at Herodotus 6.67.2.

55. For more on the semantics of **sēma** 'sign, symbol, distinguishing feature', from which **a-sēmos** 'without distinction' is derived, see pp. 208 and following.

56. Cf. also Plutarch *Banquet of the Seven Sages* 149a: in this retelling of the story, the person in charge of organizing the choral event, presumably again the Feast of Gymnopaidiai, is specified as the **arkhōn** 'leader' of the festival. We may compare a passage in Herodotus 6.67.2, where Demaratos, who at this point has been deposed as king of Sparta, is pictured as attending the Gymnopaidiai, and where he is insulted by Leotychides, the king who replaced him. Leotychides addresses to Demaratos the insulting question: how does it feel 'to be *leader*' [verb **arkhō**] after having been *king* [verb **basileuō**]? By implication Demaratos was an **arkhōn** 'leader' at the festival. In light of the Spartan lore about king and status at the Gymnopaidiai, the insult here has special pertinence. When Demaratos answers that at least he has experienced both positions, that is, both leadership at the Gymnopaidiai and kingship, whereas Leotychides has occupied only the second of the two (Herodotus 6.67.3), the pointed implication is that the present status of Demaratos as **arkhōn** at the Gymnopaidiai may have more to do with the question of real political power than does his former status as king of Sparta. Reinforcing such an implication, Demaratos adds that the mocking question of Leotychides will have enormous consequences, either great misfortune or good fortune, for the Spartans, whereupon he leaves the polis and defects to the Persians (Herodotus ibid.). The overall narrative of Herodotus further

assigned to other kings of Sparta[57] is yet another indication that kingship could and did determine preeminence of status in the choral groups of Sparta.

In short I infer that whoever performs the role of a choral leader in a given seasonally recurring Spartan festival would be performing a mimesis of a mimesis. The performers in the here and now would be experiencing a personal mimesis of choral characters with choral names like Hagesikhora and Agesidamos. Such characters or characterizations would be in turn part of a seasonally recurring institutional mimesis of authoritative role models like divinities or royal ancestors.[58] I see no justification for treating a text like Alcman PMG 1 as if it were a composition intended for a given group of historically verifiable persons at one and only one occasion in time.[59]

The more generic and impersonal the content of such a composition, in the eyes of the local Spartan community, the more Panhellenic prestige the presentation of this composition can have in the eyes of whatever Hellenes from the outside may be looking in, as it were, on Sparta. The local community's public self-esteem, in order to live up to the proper degree of admiration from both outside and consequently from within, must seek the least occasional and most catholic aspects of its seasonally recomposed choral self-presentation. The impulse of Panhellenism in Archaic Greece begins at home.[60]

---

reinforces this whole set of implications when, at a later point, Demaratos is pictured as returning to threaten all Hellas as chief advisor of the invading Persians.

57. Cf. Plutarch *Sayings of Spartans* 219e (King Damonidas) and Diogenes Laertius 2.73 (Aristippos). In the former case the King addresses the organizer of the choral event as **khorēgos**. The usage of **khorēgos** here may be parallel to what we see in Herodotus 6.67.2, on which see n56. Or it may reflect, anachronistically, the Classical Athenian meaning, on which see p. 378.

58. For a metaphorical perversion of such institutional mimesis by a Spartan king, at least from a Spartan point of view, see Thucydides 1.95.3, where the suspicions of the Spartans against their king Pausanias are described as follows: τυραννίδος μᾶλλον ἐφαίνετο μίμησις ἢ στρατηγία 'there was an appearance more of a mimesis of tyranny than a generalship'. As Nehamas 1982.57 points out, it is not that Pausanias is *counterfeiting* a tyrant: rather that he is *emulating* one. I agree with Nehamas that "even in the latter half of the fifth century, [the term **mīmēsis** and its cognates] did not go hand in hand with the Platonic notions of the counterfeit, the merely apparent, the deceitful, and the fake" (ibid.). For instances of **mīmēsis** as an *emulation* of forerunners, Nehamas, p. 75n49, adduces passages like Herodotus 5.67.1, where Kleisthenes the Reformer of Athens is said to have 'made a mimesis' (ἐμιμέετο) of his maternal grandfather, Kleisthenes the Tyrant of Sikyon. In this connection we may note the etymological links in Latin between the adjective *aemulus* 'striving to equal' and the verb *imitārī* 'follow the actions or conduct of, imitate'; related to *imitārī* is the noun *imāgō* 'representation; death mask of ancestor' (cf. Pliny *Natural History* 35.6).

59. Here I part company with previous commentators, who seek to find single historical occasions for compositions like Alcman PMG 1.

60. On the poetics of the **oikos** 'home, homestead, household' as the centripetal focus of Panhellenic prestige, especially as attested in the words of Pindar, see Kurke 1988.45–65; also Hubbard 1985.12–15.

The preceding sketch of Spartan choral performances is not without interesting ethnographic parallels. Among the Tiv of Nigeria, for example, there is a strong tradition of formal acceptance or rejection, by society, of choral compositions in the context of their performance:[61] "The most important type of song is called the Icham; this is sung by a soloist with chorus, frequently the soloist being the composer. A new song is submitted to the tribe by its composer for approval, even new words to an old setting can prompt a 'Royal Academy Sitting'!"

It remains to ask what relationship exists between the authority of the role model who is represented as leading the choral group and the authority of the composer who is credited with the representation. To put it another way: how does the authority of the **khorēgos** 'choral leader', as the focus of potential Panhellenic prestige for the local community, relate to the authority of the composer, real or re-created, who speaks through this persona? The answer should help define the concept of authorship that emanates from such authority.

To begin, it is important to notice that, in a choral composition like Alcman PMG 1, the two chorus leaders represented, Agido and Hagesikhora, seem not to have speaking parts: rather it is the aggregate that speaks *about* them, represents them, in all admiration. It is as if the chorus leaders were mainly dancing, while the choral group was all along singing and dancing.

The potential differentiation of the chorus leader, the **khorēgos**, from the singers and dancers, the **khoros**, can in fact proceed in various different directions. The **khorēgos** may become specialized as a virtuoso singer, a virtuoso dancer, or a virtuoso player of a musical instrument. The ultimate model is the god Apollo himself, who is conventionally represented by poetry as the leader of the choral group as he performs, *in his capacity as leader,* various combinations of the three components of choral lyric, that is, song, dance, and instrumental music. Perhaps the most undifferentiated picture can be found in the Homeric *Hymn to Hermes* (475–476), where Apollo is represented as simultaneously singing, dancing, and playing the lyre.[62] Elsewhere the specialties become clear. In the Homeric *Hymn to Apollo* (182–206), Apollo dances and plays the lyre (201–203), while the Muses sing

---

61. Lane 1954.13; cf. Merriam 1964.174.

62. The verb **melpomai**, as at *Hymn to Hermes* 476, covers both singing and dancing. On the undifferentiated designation of both components by this verb, see Calame 1977 I 163–165. In *Hymn to Hermes* 425–433, Hermes is represented as performing the first song ever performed, a theogony that represents an undifferentiated type of singing; commentary in N 1982.56–57. But when Hermes gives his lyre to Apollo (434–512), a differentiation in their roles happens in the process, on which see N ibid. Given that Hermes is a model for an undifferentiated and prototypical form of SONG, we may note with interest that the most undifferentiated representation of Apollo as master of song is presented in the words of Hermes himself (again *Hymn to Hermes* 475–476).

(189–193) and the rest of the gods dance (194–201), most notably the **Kharites** 'Graces' (194).[63] The emphasis here is on Apollo's specialty, the lyre. In other references, as in *Iliad* I (603–604), only the specialties are mentioned: Apollo plays the lyre and the Muses sing. A similar situation holds in the Hesiodic *Shield of Herakles* (201–206), where again Apollo plays the lyre while the Muses are described as choral leaders in song, by way of the verb **exarkhō** 'lead the chorus' in combination with **aoidē** 'song' (205).[64]

These different patterns of specialization are indirectly reflected in the semantic vicissitudes of a form of choral lyric that is classified in later times as the **huporkhēma**, where the component of dancing is specified as an accompaniment to the component of song, as indicated by the elements **hupo-** in the sense of 'in support' and **orkh-** meaning 'dance'.[65] The supporting role of a given component of choral lyric can entail an intensification of virtuosity for the performer of the supporting component. In Lucian *On Dance* 16, for example, it is specified that the **huporkhēma** is composed for a stratified type of chorus where the group in general executes one level of dancing while some of the best dancers stand out from the rest in executing a higher level of dancing to the words being sung. There is similar testimony from Polycrates FGH 588 F 1 by way of Athenaeus 139e on the dancing at the Spartan Feast of **Huakinthia**: it is specified that dancers who stand out from among the singing **khoroi** 'choruses' of youths perform an ancient form of dance that is **hupo-** 'in support' to the playing of the **aulos** 'reed' and to the singing of the song.[66] We may compare the picture on a Corinthian aryballos where a virtuoso dancer leaps ahead of four other boys and is labeled προχορευόμενος 'dancing in the forefront' (CEG 452).[67] A stylized

63. On **kharis** as 'pleasurable compensation, through song or poetry, for a deed deserving of glory', see p. 65.

64. The specialty of the Muses, song, in this case overlaps with dance by way of the verb **melpomai** at *Shield of Herakles* 206. On **melpomai** as 'sing and dance', see p. 350. For a rare glimpse of the Muses in their less differentiated role as singers *and* dancers, I cite Hesiod *Theogony* 1–21. Note that the Muses in this less differentiated role are pictured as local, living on Mount Helikon, whereas they become more differentiated as they move up to Panhellenic status at their new home on Mount Olympus (*Theogony* 22 and following); discussion in N 1982.55–57.

65. The earliest attestation of **huporkhēma** is in Plato *Ion* 534c, where it is treated as parallel to **dithurambos** 'dithyramb', **enkōmion** 'encomium', **epos**, and **iambos** (all forms occurring in the plural here). Note the usage of **huporkhēma** in Athenaeus 617b-f, who then quotes as illustration the text of Pratinas PMG 708; for an informative discussion of why Athenaeus refers to this particular composition of Pratinas as a **huporkhēma**, with special attention to the prescriptive self-references, at lines 6–7 of PMG 708, concerning the traditional subordination of dance to song, see Seaford 1977–1978.87–88. Seaford (pp. 92–94) argues convincingly that this passage from Pratinas, PMG 708, deliberately mocks, by parody, the style of **dithurambos** 'dithyramb' as perfected by the likes of Lasus of Hermione. On the semantics of **huporkhēma**, I have also benefited from the discussion of Mullen 1982.13–17.

66. Cf. Pickard-Cambridge 1968.255n2.

67. Cf. Mullen 1982.16.

example occurs in *Odyssey* viii 256–265, with a description of a performance of dancing that leads into the description of a song that the blind singer Demodokos sings about Ares and Aphrodite (266–366), followed by yet another description of virtuoso performance, this time, of "ball dancing" by soloists (367–380). It has been observed that "the seated blind bard in all this seems to be a leader with voice and lyre presiding over some kind of elaborate mime."[68] There is a compressed version of such choral lyric performance in *Iliad* XVIII 603–606, where the group dancing by the chorus is a backdrop to a higher level of dancing by two virtuosi, described as **exarkhontes** 'leaders' (606); also at *Odyssey* iv 17–19, where again there are two virtuosi described as **exarkhontes** (17). In the world of post-Classical scholarship, the description of the virtuoso dancers as **exarkhontes** was considered incongruous, in that the singer/lyre player was expected to be the leader (Athenaeus 180de).[69] Still, the application of **exarkhōn** 'leader' could be legitimately reassigned to a lead dancer so long as the singer/lyre player continued to be the real leader, in that his singing or lyre playing controlled the enactment performed center stage, as it were, by the dancers.

This topic brings us back to the choral lyric traditions of Archaic Sparta. In a composition like Alcman PMG 1, the figures of the choral leaders Agido and Hagesikhora may not necessarily have a speaking part, that is, singing part, in the song (to be contrasted with the reference at line 99 to singing by an ensemble of ten). Even if they do not have a speaking part, they are in the forefront of the dancing. Meanwhile, it is explicitly the choral aggregate who speaks for the chorus leaders, and it is implicitly the composer who speaks through the chorus members. In another example, Alcman PMG 39, the chorus members actually identify the composer of their song: they refer to the figure of Alcman by name, *in the third person,* as the one who composed what they sing. Further, in Alcman PMG 38, the chorus members praise the **kitharistēs** 'lyre player', a performer on the musical instrument who may or may not be visualized as distinct from the composer.

There are, however, other situations where the singer/lyre player may differentiate himself from the choral group by speaking in his own persona instead of theirs, as most dramatically illustrated by the declaration in Alcman PMG 26, where the singer says that he is too old and weak to dance with the chorus.[70] Such conventions of stylized separation and self-introduction may help explain the distribution of roles in *Iliad* XVIII 567–572, the description of a lyre playing boy who sings the Linus song in the midst of a festive chorus of boys and girls: here the singing is apparently in accompaniment to the lyre playing and dancing, as we see from the expression λίνον δ' ὑπὸ

---

68. Mullen, p. 13.
69. I agree with West 1971.309 in adducing the full text of *Iliad* XVIII 604–605.
70. Cf. Calame 1977 I 394–395.

καλὸν ἄειδε 'he sang, in accompaniment [**hupo-**], the Linus song' (570). So also in *Hymn to Hermes* 499–502: Apollo first struck up the lyre, and then ὑπὸ καλὸν ἄεισεν 'he sang beautifully, in accompaniment [**hupo-**]' (502). Just as dancing in accompaniment required heightened virtuosity and could be described in terms of choral leadership, so also here the singing of Apollo in support, in accompaniment, is a virtuoso performance. The distinction between the patterns of accompaniment in *Iliad* XVIII 567–572, where the boy's song responds to the lyre, and in *Odyssey* viii 256–265/367–380, where the dancing responds to the song, seems to be missed by later generations in the post-Classical era, as, for example, in Athenaeus 15d (though his explanation of **huporkhēma** at 628d takes note of the actual fact of support or accompaniment implied by **hupo-** in this word).[71]

The archetypal virtuoso performance of Apollo, where he first struck up the lyre and then ὑπὸ καλὸν ἄεισεν 'sang beautifully, in accompaniment [**hupo-**]' (*Hymn to Hermes* 502), is morphologically a **prooimion**, which can be translated roughly as 'prelude' but which I prefer to render with the more neutral Latin borrowing, 'prooemium'.[72] The **prooimion** is a framework for differentiated virtuoso singing by the individual **kitharōidos** 'lyre [**kitharā**] singer', and it literally means 'the front part of the song [**oimē**]' (just as **pronāos** means 'the front part of the temple [**nāos**]').[73] The **prooimion** or prooemium took the form of a prayer sung to a given god who presided over the occasion of a given seasonally recurring festival where the song was performed in competition with other songs. A clear reflex of this form can be found in the actual structure of the *Homeric Hymns*.[74] In fact Thucydides (3.104.3–4) uses the word **prooimion** in referring to the version of the Homeric *Hymn to Apollo* that he knew.[75] That the dramatized context of these *Hymns* is one of seasonally recurring festivals where contests in song are held is clear from the use of **hōrā** 'seasonal time' in *Hymn* 26.12–13 and of **agōn** 'contest' in *Hymn* 6.19.[76] That these *Hymns* are morphologically *preludes*, with the inherited function of introducing the main part of the performance, is illustrated by references indicating a shift to the performance proper, such as μεταβήσομαι ἄλλον ἐς ὕμνον 'I will shift to the rest of the song [**humnos**]' at *Homeric Hymns* 5 (verse 293), 9 (verse 9), and 18 (verse 11).[77] To sum up the essence of the **prooimion**, I quote the wording of Quin-

71. For more on the **huporkhēma**, see also Seaford 1977–1978.87–88: it seems clear that the semantics of **huporkhēma** progressed over time from more general to more specific. So also in the case of **skolion**, as discussed at p. 107.

72. Cf. pp. 216 and following, with reference to the mechanics of the **prooimion** in Archaic Greek poetry as compared with the first sentence of the *Histories* of Herodotus.

73. Koller 1956.191.

74. Detailed demonstration by Koller, pp. 174–182, 195–206.

75. Definitive discussion by Koller, pp. 173–174.

76. The latter passage is quoted at p. 77.

77. Full repertoire of examples, along with detailed interpretation, discussion, and commen-

tilian (*Institutio oratoria* 4.1.2): *quod* οἴμη *cantus est, et citharoedi pauca illa, quae antequam legitimum certamen inchoent, emerendi favoris gratia canunt, prooemium cognominaverunt* . . . 'that **oimē** is song and that the **kitharōidoi** refer to those few words that they sing before their contest proper, for the sake of winning favor, as **prooimion** . . .'.[78]

Quintilian's reference to 'those few words' sung by the **kitharōidoi** 'lyre [**kitharā**] singers' is belied by the proportions of some of the larger *Homeric Hymns*, which had evolved into magnificent extravaganzas that rival epic in narrative power, as in the case of the *Hymn to Apollo*. It is in fact legitimate to ask whether the *Homeric Hymns*, especially the larger ones, were *functional* preludes.[79] For now, however, it is enough to stress that they were *formally* just that, preludes. As we have seen, Thucydides refers to the *Hymn to Apollo* as a **prooimion** (3.104.4–5). Even the Hesiodic *Theogony*, with its even more imposing proportions, is morphologically a **prooimion**.[80] So also is the representation of the first theogony ever sung, an archetypal performance of lyre singing by the god Hermes, as described and paraphrased in *Hymn to Hermes* 425–433.[81] The crucial concept here is **anabolē** 'prelude', closely parallel to the concept of **prooimion**. Hermes sings his theogony ἀμβολάδην 'in the manner of a prelude [**anabolē**]' (426), just as the song started by Apollo's lyre is elsewhere described in terms of ἀγησιχόρων (. . .) προοιμίων ἀμβολάς 'the preludes [**anabolē** plural] of chorus leading [**hāgēsikhora**] prooemia [**prooimion** plural]' in Pindar *Pythian* 1.4.[82]

Still, the medium of the *Homeric Hymns*, which is poetry recited in dactylic hexameter, is several stages removed from the medium of **kitharōidiā**, that is, song. We have to step back and ask what form the **prooimion** 'prelude' would have had in the context of **kitharōidiā** 'lyre singing' and, further, what kind of performance can be expected to have followed the **prooimion** in this same context of **kitharōidiā**.

---

tary, in Koller 1956.174–182. More on **humnos** as 'song' in the discussion that follows. Koller, p. 177, stresses that **humnos** is the totality of performance; cf. ἀοιδῆς ὕμνον '**humnos** of the song' at *Odyssey* viii 429. We explore further below whether the 'rest of the song' that supposedly follows each of the *Homeric Hymns* may be a stylized formal convention rather than an actual sequel.

78. Commentary by Koller, p. 193, who shows that the *certamen* 'contest' of the **kitharōidoi**, that is, what the Greeks would call their **agōn**, corresponds to the **agōn** 'contest' of the rhetoricians, as in the beginning of Demosthenes *On the Crown*: πρῶτον μὲν, [. . .] τοῖς θεοῖς εὔχομαι πᾶσι καὶ πάσαις, [. . .] τοσαύτην [sc. εὔνοιαν] ὑπάρξαι μοι παρ' ὑμῶν εἰς τουτονὶ τὸν ἀγῶνα 'First of all, I pray to all the gods and goddesses that as much good will [as I have accorded to the community] will also be accorded to me from you, for this present contest [**agōn**]'.

79. Cf. N 1982.53–55.

80. Argued at length in N ibid.; cf. Koller, pp. 181–182.

81. On which see p. 350.

82. The adjective **hāgēsikhoros** 'chorus-leading' here is identical with the name **Hāgēsikhorā** 'she who leads the chorus', as in Alcman PMG 1.

Part of the answer is to be found in the lyric traditions ascribed to Terpander, reputedly the founder of the first **katastasis** 'establishment' of traditions in songmaking at Sparta (again "Plutarch" *On Music* 1134b).[83] We have seen that the figure of Terpander is credited with "inventing" the melodic patterns of **kitharōidiā**, which were called **nomoi** in this context (*On Music* 1132d).[84] Moreover, we have seen that a figure like Arion, the archetypal **kitharōidos** 'lyre singer' for the polis of Corinth (Herodotus 1.23), is specifically represented as performing a **nomos** when he sings a monodic performance to the accompaniment of his lyre (Herodotus 1.24.5).[85] The traditional association of **kitharōidiā** with the concept of **nomos**, which we may interpret most generally as a lyric composition that followed a set mode or melodic pattern,[86] must be compared with a traditional saying, variations of which are strikingly attested in the idiom of Plato, that a **prooimion** 'prelude' presupposes a **nomos** (Plato *Timaeus* 29d; *Republic* 531d, 532d).[87] This association is made explicit in Plato *Laws* 722d and following: the **prooimion** is a 'prelude' to the **nomos** in the specific context of **kitharōidiā**.[88]

Another part of the answer to the question about the actual form of the **prooimion** can be found in the diction of Pindar. So far we have examined the association of **prooimion** and **nomos** in the general context of **kitharōidiā**, but we have yet to see a reference to this association in a specifically *choral* context of **kitharōidiā**. The references in Plato clearly presuppose a *monodic* rather than *choral* context. Turning to the choral context, however, let us examine two passages taken from Pindar, *Nemean* 5.21–26 and *Pythian* 1.1–4. In *Nemean* 5, we see the representation of a **khoros** 'chorus' of Muses (23) who are specifically *singing* (ἄειδ' 22), and in their midst is the god Apollo himself, taking control as he strikes up a lyre that is **heptaglōssos** 'having seven languages' (24), leading the choral performance of 'all sorts of **nomoi**' (παντοίων νόμων *Nemean* 5.25). We have seen that the seven-string lyre, supposedly the "invention" of Terpander, could fit a wide variety of set melodic patterns, called **nomoi**, within a new interrelated system reflecting Panhellenic synthesis.[89] Here too, in the passage from Pindar, these melodic patterns are explicitly called **nomoi**. But in this case the **nomoi** that are represented as being performed are not monodic, which was the case when Arion sang his **nomos** (again Herodotus 1.24.5), but clearly choral: it is the **khoros** 'chorus' of Muses who are actually sing-

83. Cf. p. 343.
84. Cf. p. 87.
85. Cf. ibid.
86. Cf. ibid.
87. Cf. Koller 1956.183.
88. Koller, pp. 183, 188.
89. Cf. p. 89.

ing the **nomoi** (again *Nemean* 5.21–26). Moreover, this ensemble of Muses is represented here as actually singing the words of the **prooimion**. Although the word **prooimion** is not used in this passage, the phraseology of the Muses' paraphrased words (*Nemean* 5.25–26) is perfectly in accordance with the proper syntax and rhetorical strategy of attested prooemia.[90] The chorus of Muses is represented as performing not just the subsequent **nomoi** but also the **prooimion** that is expected to introduce a **nomos**, with Apollo's overall control being represented simply by his act of striking up the lyre.

We may now supplement the testimony of Pindar *Nemean* 5.21–26 with that of *Pythian* 1.1–4.[91] This passage, another *tour de force* in descriptive compression, pictures the lyre of Apollo, as the player strikes up a tune (4), straightaway being heard by the chorus, which starts dancing (2), as soon as the lyre gives off its **sēmata** 'signals' that are heeded by **aoidoi** 'singers' (3), thus creating the **anabolai** 'preludes' (4) of **prooimia** 'prooemia' (4) that are described as **hāgēsikhora** 'chorus-leading' (4). In short the diction of Pindar gives indications that even in terms of choral performance the **prooimion** 'prooemium' precedes what is being consistently called the **nomos**.

This Pindaric picture, however, of a **prooimion** *as if* performed by the chorus is idealized. Another example of such idealization is Pindar *Nemean* 3.1–12, where the chorus members are described, five lines into the composition, *as if* waiting for the voice of the Muse, which is to be their cue to start their performance; then, at lines 10–11 of the composition, the Muse is invoked to start (ἄρχε 10) the **humnos** 'song' (11), while the "I" of the lyre player, the persona of the composer, distributes the song to the chorus members and to the lyre (11–12).[92] The word for "lyre" here is twelve lines into the composition, and yet the context itself presupposes that it had started the whole performance, just as the chorus has been presumably performing the entire composition ever since the first line. Still another example is Pindar *Nemean* 2.1–3,[93] where the beginning of the composition *describes* the prooemium of a performance *without being a prooemium itself*, in that no

90. For ὕμνησαν Διὸς ἀρχόμεναι 'made a song [**humnos**], starting with Zeus' at *Nemean* 5.25, cf. Ἥλιον ὑμνεῖν ... ἄρχεο Μοῦσα 'start to make a song [**humnos**], Muse, about Helios ...'; also ὅθεν περ καὶ Ὁμηρίδαι | ῥαπτῶν ἐπέων τὰ πόλλ' ἀοιδοὶ | ἄρχονται 'from which point the Homeridai, singers [**aoidoi**] of stitched-together words, most often take their start, from Zeus **Prooimios** [= "Zeus of prooemia"]' at *Nemean* 2.1–3 (where "Zeus **prooimios**" = "Zeus of the prooemium"); further details below. For πρώτιστον μὲν ... ὥς 'at the very beginning, how it happened that ...' at *Nemean* 5.25–26, cf. ὡς τὰ πρῶτα (same translation) at *Hymn to Hermes* 427, where a paraphrase begins to recap the contents of the prooemium sung by Hermes (cf. p. 354 above).

91. Cf. p. 354.

92. I use the word "line" here simply as a visual reference to the text as printed. For an interpretation of Pindar *Nemean* 3.11–12 that differs from the paraphrase just presented, see Hubbard 1987b.

93. On which see also n90.

divinity has been directly invoked to start the performance. The prooemium being represented in *Nemean* 2.1–3 is specifically the prelude of a Homeric performance: the **Homēridai** 'Sons of Homer' (2.1), who are described as the **aoidoi** 'singers' (2.2.) of 'stitched-together words' (ῥαπτῶν ἐπέων 2.2), are said to 'start' (ἄρχονται) their performance by invoking Zeus **Prooimios**, the "Zeus of prooemia" (2.3).[94] The first word of *Nemean* 2, ὅθεν 'starting at the point where . . .', is *transitional*, to be expected *after* the given divinity has already been invoked. Then, at the very end of the composition, the chorus as **polītai** 'polis-dwellers' (24) are called upon to 'lead', as conveyed by the verb **exarkhō** (25), in celebration. In a functional prooemium this verb could be expected at the beginning of the performance.[95]

The stylized prooemia in Pindar then are idealizations. It is as if the traditions of differentiated monodic composition and performance had never happened. Yet the context of monody had already developed the form of the **prooimion** far beyond its native choral context of striking up the lyre for the chorus. There is evidence that what we call the **prooimion** had already undergone, by Pindar's time, a vast stretch of evolution in traditions of composition and performance in monodic song and even in poetry. This evolution serves as backdrop for the use, in Thucydides (3.104.4–5), of the word **prooimion** in referring to the Homeric *Hymn to Apollo*. The entire tradition of **kitharōidikoi nomoi** 'citharodic nomes', as attributed to the "invention" of Terpander, presupposes a corresponding tradition of monodic **prooimia** or "preludes" that literally led into these "nomes," and it was within the framework of these "preludes" that the **kitharōidos** 'lyre singer', set apart from the chorus, could speak about himself in his own persona. We have already noted the declaration in Alcman PMG 26, where the singer says that he is too old and weak to dance with the chorus. Elsewhere too, although it may well be the chorus itself that is speaking in the persona of the chorus leader, we can still see that this persona is set apart from the rest of the chorus in the context of self-introduction, the prooemium:

Μῶσ' ἄγε Καλλιόπα, θύγατερ Διός, | ἄρχ' ἐρατῶν ἐπέων, ἐπὶ δ' ἵμερον | ὕμνῳ καὶ χαρίεντα τίθη χορόν

Alcman PMG 27

Come, Muse Kalliope, daughter of Zeus! Make a start of your lovely

94. Commentary by Koller 1956.190–192.
95. Cf. Mullen 1982.27. Mullen, p. 234n36, cites, with reservations, Fränkel [1975] 429n6, who thinks that Pindar's *Nemean* 2, with its concluding sentence calling upon the chorus to start, was composed "so as to be repeated *da capo* as often as necessary, so that all the spectators lining the streets along the route might hear it in its entirety." Shifting the emphasis from performance to composition, Kurke 1988.29 offers compelling observations about the "looping effect" of an ending that proceeds into the beginning. I would observe, in addition, that it is a lyric ending that comes full circle to a Homeric beginning.

words, [put] desire [**hīmeros**][96] in my song [**humnos**], and set up a **kharis**-filled[97] chorus [**khoros**].[98]

In the case of Terpander, however, the **nomoi** with which he is credited are no longer a choral medium. We have seen that he is the traditional "inventor" of these **nomoi** in the specific context of **kitharōidiā** 'lyre singing' ("Plutarch" *On Music* 1132d), and that he likewise "invented" the genre known as the **kitharōidikos nomos** 'citharodic nome' (1132c).[99] This genre is monodic, as we have seen in the anecdote about the **nomos orthios** performed by Arion (Herodotus 1.24.5).[100] In this connection I cite a rare surviving quotation from Terpander: in *Suda* s.v. ἀμφιανακτίζειν, it is reported that Terpander 'sang' a **nomos**, specified as **orthios**, with a **prooimion** that began as follows:

ἀμφί μοι αὐτὸν ἄναχθ' ἑκατηβόλον ἀειδέτω φρήν

Terpander PMG 697

About[101] the far-shooting Lord himself let my mind sing forth.[102]

Moreover, according to "Plutarch" *On Music* 1140f, Pindar himself attributed the "invention" of the **skolion** to Terpander,[103] and we have already seen that the word **skolion**, as used in the time of Aristophanes, is an appropriate general designation for the specifically monodic performance, self-accompanied on the lyre, of compositions by the great lyric masters (as in Aristophanes F 223 Kock = 325 KA, with reference to the performing of compositions by Alcaeus and Anacreon).[104]

From the standpoint of a later source, the compositions attributed to Terpander are not just monodic but simply a collection of monodic preludes: it is reported in "Plutarch" *On Music* 1133bc that the compositions of Terpander were **prooimia**, supposedly serving as preludes simply to poetry, including specifically the poetry of Homer and the like. This formulation, though it has

96. Note the prayer in *Homeric Hymn* 10.5 that the god who presides over the occasion of performance may grant an **aoidē** 'song' that is **hīmeroessa** 'full of desire'.

97. On **kharis** as 'pleasurable compensation, through song or poetry, for a deed deserving of glory', see p. 65.

98. The verb **tithēmi** has two objects here; with the first I translate this verb as 'put'; with the second, as 'set up'.

99. Cf. p. 87.

100. Cf. p. 355.

101. The usage of ἀμφί 'about' here in Terpander PMG 697 is morphologically parallel to what we find in the prooemium framework of *Homeric Hymn* 7.1 and 19.1. Cf. Aristophanes *Clouds* 595; also Euripides *Trojan Women* 511–513.

102. In Photius s.v. ἀμφιανακτίζειν, it is said that this introductory phraseology can fit three possible **nomoi** of Terpander: the Boeotian, the Aeolian, or the **Orthios** (cf. p. 87).

103. Cf. p. 107.

104. Cf. ibid.

a validity with respect to etymology, is false with respect to function, as I now argue.[105] We have observed that the *Homeric Hymns*, as they have come down to us, are indeed **prooimia** with respect to etymology in that they presuppose, with such phrases as μεταβήσομαι ἄλλον ἐς ὕμνον 'I will switch [from the **prooimion**] to the rest of the song [**humnos**]', that the performance proper is to follow.[106] This performance to follow is to be imagined as Homeric poetry itself, as we see from the internal evidence of the Homeric *Hymn to Apollo*: here the self-characterization of the speaker, within the framework of a **prooimion**, as a blind singer from Chios whose songs will win over all others in the future (172–173) corresponds to the idealized character of Homer himself.[107] Similarly with Terpander: in a relatively late source like the one that we are considering, "Plutarch" *On Music* 1133bc, the corpus of Terpander could legitimately be considered a collection of monodic **prooimia**, composed predominantly in dactylic hexameter and therefore deemed suitable as preludes to Homeric poetry. From the standpoint of such a late source, it is as if the **nomoi** of Terpander, as introduced by the **prooimia**, had never existed.[108] Further, it is as if all the **prooimia** of Terpander had been composed in dactylic hexameter, as suggested in "Plutarch" *On Music* 1133c and more explicitly in 1132d. Such fragments as Terpander PMG 697 contradict this distorted view.[109] True, the meter of this fragment is closely related to the dactylic hexameter, and there may indeed have been a majority of hexametric **prooimia** in the Terpander tradition. Still the point is that the medium of **kitharōidiā** 'lyre singing' attributed to Terpander is not necessarily a functional prelude, as it is understood in "Plutarch" *On Music* 1133c. Rather it is a monodic form of lyric composition that evolved out of the morphology of the **prooimion**.

The solo performance of quasi-lyric monody, as in the case of Terpander, and the solo performance of nonlyric poetry, as in the case of the *Homeric Hymns*, are not the only media that evolved out of the **prooimion** 'prooemium' of the **kitharōidos** 'lyre singer'. The same could be said of the Hesiodic *Theogony*, which displays all the signposts of a **prooimion**.[110] The first theogony ever sung, as archetypally performed by Hermes in the *Hymn to Hermes* 425–433, is likewise a **prooimion**: Hermes sings his theogony ἀμβολάδην 'in the manner of a prelude [**anabolē**]' (426), just as the song started by Apollo's lyre is described in terms of ἀγησιχόρων (. . .) προ-

---

105. Perhaps it is this kind of formulation that led Cicero to think it typical of *citharoedi* (= **kitharōidoi** 'lyre singers') to sing a *prooemium* (= **prooimion**) that tends to be disconnected thematically from the *corpus* of the whole performance (*De oratore* 2.80).

106. Cf. p. 353.

107. Cf. N 1979.5, 8–9.

108. Koller 1956.183–184.

109. On this meter, cf. West 1982.130; also Gentili and Giannini 1977.35–36.

110. Cf. p. 354.

οἰμίων ἀμβολάς 'the preludes [**anabolē** plural] of chorus-leading prooemia [**prooimion** plural]' in Pindar *Pythian* 1.4.[111] There are even traces of the **prooimion** in the solo performance of epic, nonlyric poetry par excellence. Aside from such examples as the second performance of the blind singer Demodokos in *Odyssey* viii, where the singer assumes a choral personality[112] and where his performance starts with an **anabolē** 'prelude' (ἀνεβάλλετο viii 266),[113] there are such clearly monodic scenes as the first performance of the singer Phemios, where he too starts his performance with an **anabolē** 'prelude' (*Odyssey* i 155; cf. xvii 262).[114]

We can perhaps go one step further. It has been argued persuasively that the entire body of Archaic poetry as composed in dactylic hexameter, including Homeric and Hesiodic poetry, evolved out of the monodic medium of the **prooimion** in **kitharōidiā** 'lyre singing'.[115] For such an argument to be taken further, we would have to look back to the close formal affinities between the Homeric and Hesiodic hexameter on one hand and on the other the meters of such figures as Stesichorus, Sappho, and Alcaeus.[116] It so happens that these figures are in fact forerunners of the medium of **kitharōidiā** 'lyre singing'. Before we can turn to Stesichorus and the others, however, it is important to explore still further the question of the chorus and the relationship between choral and monodic forms. In particular we must ask how *poetry* may have become differentiated from monodic *song*, much as monody had earlier become differentiated from choral performance.

We started our survey of the prooemium with the vision of Apollo as he struck up the lyre for the very first time and then ὑπὸ καλὸν ἄεισεν 'sang beautifully, in accompaniment [**hupo-**]' (*Hymn to Hermes* 502).[117] Yet singing in response to the musical instrument of Apollo is a feature not only of Apollo himself as archetypal player of preludes. There are also specialists in the art of the prelude. I mean those supreme experts in song, the Muses, as they execute their special skills: as we have seen in the Hesiodic *Shield of Herakles* (201–206), the Muses are described as choral leaders in song (**exarkhō** 'lead the chorus' in combination with **aoidē** 'song': 205) by virtue of their responsiveness to the lyre of Apollo.[118] Paradoxically the subordination of the Muses to the choral leadership of Apollo in the overall domain of

111. Ibid.

112. Cf. p. 352.

113. Note too the details of usage characteristic of the prooemium: ἀμφί 'about' at viii 267, on which see the parallels at p. 358, and ὡς τὰ πρῶτα 'at the very beginning, how it happened that . . .', on which see the parallels at p. 356.

114. Cf. also *Odyssey* viii 499 and the commentary of Koller 1956.190n1.

115. Koller 1956.203–206.

116. See the Appendix.

117. Cf. p. 353.

118. Cf. p. 351.

choral performance, where Apollo controls all three components of song, dance, and musical instrumentation, is a key to the choral leadership of the Muses in the specific domain of song. Apollo generally dances and plays the lyre, while the Muses' function is more specifically that of singing or reciting. It is after all a Muse, not Apollo, who inspires the "song" of the *Iliad* (I 1), the "song" of the *Odyssey* (i 1). To put it another way: the specialization of the Muses as experts in the words of song, as differentiated from Apollo, who is overall master of all the components of song, is comparable to the specialization of Greek *song* as differentiated from a general category that I have been calling SONG.[119] As the generalist of SONG, Apollo is the ultimate chorus leader of the Muses, their authority in the choral integration of singing, dancing, and instrumentation.[120] As for the Muses, they are specialized chorus leaders of *song*, in stylized descriptions such as we have seen in the *Shield of Herakles* (205).

These divine models for the role of chorus leader are formalized, to repeat, in the noun **khorēgos** 'chorus leader': in the case of Alcman PMG 1, for example, we have seen that the character **Hāgēsikhorā** 'she who leads the chorus' is described as a **khorēgos** 'chorus leader' (44) and that, as such, she functions on the level of ritual as a substitute for a cult figure on the level of myth. There is a corresponding verb-plus-object combination that expresses the same model: it consists of verb **histēmi** 'set up, establish' plus the object of **khoros**, as in the expression θεῶν | ἵστησι χορούς 'he sets up [= verb **histēmi**] the choruses [**khoros** {plural}] of the gods' at Aristophanes *Birds* 219–220, with a lyre-playing Apollo as subject.[121] This combination recurs as the compound formation **stēsi-khoros** 'he or she who sets up the chorus', as in the expression στησίχορον ὕμνον ἄγοισαι 'introducing a **stēsikhoros** song [**humnos**]' inscribed on a kylix found at Naukratis (PMG 938[c]), where the understood subject of ἄγοισαι is apparently "Muses," in the context of a choral presentation.[122] The same compound **stēsikhoros** recurs on the François Vase, where one of the Muses, whose name elsewhere is **Terpsikhorē** 'she who delights in the chorus' (e.g., Hesiod *Theogony* 78), is instead labeled **Stēsikhorē** 'she who sets up the chorus'.[123] Finally, the

119. I am using here the schematic notions of SONG and *song* as developed in Ch.1.

120. The testimony of Archaic iconography on this theme is neatly articulated in Pausanias 5.18.4, who describes the image, on the Chest of Kypselos, of a lyre-playing Apollo in the midst of the chorus of Muses.

121. Cf. also [χο]ροστάτις = **khorostatis** 'she who sets up the chorus', applied to Hagesikhora at Alcman PMG 1.84; commentary by Calame 1983.342. For a collection of other passages showing the same traditional combination of verb **histēmi** 'set up, establish' plus the object of **khoros**, see Calame I 88–87n91; also p. 61n23.

122. Calame I 107n131.

123. Stewart 1983.56.

name of the poet Stesichorus is identical with this epithet **stēsikhoros**, the mark of divine choral leaders (cf. *Suda* s.v. Στησίχορος).[124]

Another way of expressing the divine model of choral leadership is the verb **exarkhō** 'lead, lead off, lead the chorus' and its derivatives. We have seen it applied to the Muses in their role as specialists in singing at a choral performance (Hesiodic *Shield of Herakles* 205). The word conveys the fundamental theme of a differentiated individual initiative, followed by an undifferentiated response or reinforcement by the group that joins in.[125] This theme helps explain the choral metaphor built into the extended meaning of the Greek verb **hēgeomai**, which means not only 'take the lead' (e.g., *Iliad* IX 168) but also 'think, have an opinion', in the sense of 'think authoritatively' (e.g., Herodotus passim); it is from this verb that the name **Hāgēsikhorā** 'she who leads the chorus' is derived. The verb **exarkhō** can take as its object the given genre in which the performance is happening, as in *Iliad* XVIII 51, where Thetis begins her **goos** 'lament'.[126] In such instances of spontaneous individual initiative as dramatized by the narrative, we can see an ultimate model for the **khorēgos** as the organizer of the spontaneous occasion, the one who gives it a form, a format, for the group to follow and join. To the extent that the **khorēgos** gives the occasion its form, the occasion *is* the genre.[127]

124. Calame I 96n114. We may note the prelude in Stesichorus PMG 278, where a single Muse is invoked to sing, accompanied by a lyre. For an argument against the notion, as proposed, for example, by West 1971, that Stesichorean performance is monodic, essentially the performance of a **kitharōidos** 'lyre singer', see Burkert 1987.51–55, who proposes that it is instead choral. Burkert, p. 52, points to a reference by the "Old Oligarch," pseudo-Xenophon *Constitution of Athens* 1.13, concerning a lavish type of song-performance that became obsolescent in Athens under the democracy: "Stripped of its polemical overtones, this remains an interesting account of musical events before the democratic revolutions." Burkert associates such "musical events" with Stesichorean performances; I do not agree, however, with his proposal (pp. 51–52) that such events were performed by chorus members who were itinerant *professionals*. It would be enough to say instead that the scale and the virtuosity of choral performance at festivals and other such events would be different in aristocratic and democratic settings, and that Stesichorus represents a decidedly aristocratic setting. Cf. Burnett 1988.129–147. As a description of the kind of musical event represented by Stesichorus, Burkert adduces the passage in the Homeric *Hymn to Apollo* where the figure of "Homer" meets the chorus of Deliades at a festival on the island of Delos; he interprets lines 162–165 as a reference to the "performance of choral lyrics" (p. 54). On this passage, see further at pp. 375 and following.

125. Cf. *Iliad* XXIV 721–722, where specialized singers of a differentiated form of lament, **thrēnoi**, are the **exarkhoi** 'starters' of the performance; then the women respond (ἐπί . . . 722) as a group, in a less differentiated form of lament, the **goos**. Cf. p. 36.

126. The **goos** is a less differentiated form of lament than the **thrēnos**. Still the **goos** too has a built-in hierarchy where someone has to lead off in performance, as designated by the verb **exarkhō** in the case of Andromache at *Iliad* XXIV 723, Hekabe at 747, and finally Helen at 761.

127. In this context, we may observe that the very concept of *genre* becomes necessary only when the *occasion* for a given speech-act, that is, for a given poem or song, is lost. Such is the case of the Hellenistic poets, as described by Williams 1968.35: "so they composed hymns to the gods, without any idea of performing them, or they wrote epitaphs, without any idea of inscribing

With these divine models of individual initiative in mind, it is now time to extend the proposal, articulated in the specific case of Alcman PMG 1, that a lead character like **Hāgēsikhorā** 'she who leads the chorus' is a substitute on the level of ritual for a corresponding cult figure who exists on the level of myth. The analogous name of a figure like Stesichorus, **Stēsikhoros** 'he who sets up the chorus', implies that a poet, like a lead character in a chorus, may somehow function as a ritual stand-in for the divine models of choral lyric poetry, Apollo and the Muses. As I have argued in another work, the generic poet in Archaic Greek traditions is by definition a ritual substitute, as conveyed by the word **therapōn**, in relation to the Muses explicitly and to their leader Apollo implicitly.[128] Further, the concept of ritual substitute is closely associated with that of cult hero.[129] Since this subject has been treated at length in the work just cited, I mention here only the essentials: that there is a pervasive symmetrical pattern of god-hero antagonism on the level of myth and of god-hero symbiosis on the level of cult.[130]

A premier example is the figure of Archilochus. The compositions ascribed to Archilochus take the form of a specialized kind of poetry that is differentiated from song: he belongs to the repertoire of a **rhapsōidos** 'rhapsode', not a **kitharōidos** 'lyre singer'.[131] Still the figure of Archilochus retains a choral personality, as evidenced by his self-description as an **exarkhōn** 'choral leader' of the specific genres known as the **dithurambos** 'dithyramb' (Archilochus F 120 W) and the **paiēōn** [= **paiān**] 'paean' (F 121 W).[132] Again we see that the genre *is* the occasion in such instances of dramatized individual initiative. The choral personality of Archilochus is also evident in the *Life of Archilochus* tradition as preserved by the Mnesiepes Inscription (Archilochus T 4 Tarditi). This inscription, of a relatively late date (ca. third century B.C.), is highly Archaic in theme: it narrates the life of Archilochus, giving context to "quotations" of the transmitted compositions that were attributed to him. The *Life of Archilochus* tradition, as memorialized by the Mnesiepes Inscription, motivates the hero-cult of Archilochus; in fact the setting for the Mnesiepes Inscription was the **Arkhilokheion**, the sacred precinct at Paros where Archilochus was worshipped as a cult hero.[133] The Mnesiepes Inscription gives explicit testimony about a tra-

---

them on a gravestone, or they wrote symposiastic poetry, without any real drinking-party in mind." Cf. also Rossi 1971.75.

128. N 1979.279–316.

129. Ibid.

130. Ibid.

131. Cf. pp. 20, 25, 26, 27, 393, and following.

132. Cf. pp. 20, 394, and following. For a stylized representation of Apollo as choral leader of the **paiēōn** [= **paiān**] 'paean', see *Hymn to Apollo* 514–519.

133. Details in N 1979.303–308. Note especially my argument at p. 304 §4n3 about the name of **Mnēsiepēs**, 'he who remembers the words [as in **epos** 'word']': "As the figure to whom

ditional myth, native to the island of Paros, that represented Archilochus as a chorus teacher of his community (T4 III 16–57).[134] Given that the figure of the poet Archilochus remains a choral personality, we may now move on to observe the tradition that represents Archilochus as a ritual substitute of his divine choral models: the story has it that Archilochus is killed through the indirect agency of Apollo, who at the same time promotes his status as cult hero, pronouncing the dead poet to be the '**therapōn** of the Muses' (Delphic Oracle 4 PW).[135]

The theme of the poet as ritual substitute could be pursued further, but we must stay on track with the topic at hand, which is, the role that the poet — let us call him or her the author — actually plays in the chorus. What needs to be shown is that the authority of Apollo over song, as formalized by his function as **khorēgos**, is the fundamental model for the concept of author-ship in choral lyric, as embodied in figures like the poet Alcman. A crucial passage in this regard is Herodotus 5.83, a precious glimpse of a local festival on the island of Aegina, where female choral groups perform in worship of two **daimones** 'spirits' (5.83.3),[136] called Damia and Auxesia (5.83.2), whose wooden statues or **agalmata** 'cult representations' (5.82, 5.83.2) are the centerpieces of the ritual event. From independent evidence, we know that both these names reflect epithets applied in the cults of the goddess Deme-ter.[137] We may compare in this regard the name **Hāgēsikhorā** in Alcman PMG 1, which is an appropriate epithet for visualizing, through a choral sub-stitute, a cult figure as the focal point of a choral group. Even more impor-tant, we must take note of a significant detail in the description of the Aegine-tan festival concerning the nature of the leadership over the female choral groups who perform at the Feast of Damia and Auxesia: χορηγῶν ἀπο-δεικνυμένων ἑκατέρῃ τῶν δαιμόνων δέκα ἀνδρῶν 'and there are ten men who are chorus leaders [**khorēgoi**], making public presentation [= verb **apo-deiknumai**] for each of the **daimones** [= Damia and Auxesia]' (Herodotus 5.83.3). The noun that corresponds to the verb **apo-deiknumai** 'make a pub-lic presentation' is **apo-deixis**, which we have seen is the name of a premier festival of choral song in Arcadia.[138] I infer that this seasonally recurring fes-tival featured the public presentation of ten presumably competing female choral performances, each one being 'presented' by a male **khorēgos** whose relationship to the female group corresponds to the stylized relationship of

---

Apollo ordains the cult of Archilochus in the **Arkhilokheion**, Mnesiepes bears a name that seems to correspond to his own function."

134. Details at pp. 395 and following.

135. Detailed commentary in N, pp. 301–302.

136. On the appropriateness of this word **daimōn** in designating either a god or a hero in the realm of cult: N 1979.128–129, 154.

137. The sources are collected by Nilsson 1906.414.

138. Cf. p. 343 and following.

Apollo to the Muses.[139] Such a relationship also corresponds to the relationship of the male figure Alcman to the female choral groups at Spartan festivals who sing and dance "his" compositions.[140] In the description of the Aeginetan festival, it is specified that the worship of the cult figures takes the form of ritual strife, where the characters in the chorus engage in mutual mockery (cf. κερτόμοισι: Herodotus 5.83.3).[141]

It seems that each of the ten choral performances at this local festival on the island of Aegina entailed two rival choral subdivisions, assigned to each of the two figures Damia and Auxesia: I draw attention to the force of ἑκατέρῃ 'to each' in Herodotus 5.83.3. We may compare the internal dramatized rivalry of Agido and Hagesikhora in Alcman PMG 1. We may also compare the "setting up" (verb **histēmi** 'set up, establish' plus the object **khoros**) of two choruses in worship of two distinct female cult heroes, Hippodameia and Physkoa, by a collegium of sixteen women at the Feast of Heraia at Olympia in Elis, as reported by Pausanias (5.16.6–7).[142] Tradition has it that this feast in worship of the goddess Hera, along with the collegium of sixteen women who organize it season after season, was established by Hippodameia to celebrate her marriage to Pelops (Pausanias 5.16.4).[143]

Another detail in this tradition bears special emphasis: the number sixteen here stems from the fact that two women are chosen from each of the eight **phūlai** 'tribal divisions' of Elis (Pausanias 5.16.7). Perhaps we are to understand that each of the two representatives of each **phūlē** 'tribal division'

---

139. As Calame 1977 ɪ 141 points out, there are attestations of female choruses with male **khorēgoi**, but not of male choruses with female **khorēgoi**. For an ethnographic parallel, see p. 377.

140. Note the first-person feminine in Alcman PMG 3.81, 83 (on the latter, cf. the commentary of Herington 1985.21–22). In light of the internal references to choral competition in Alcman PMG 1, I draw special attention to the use of **agōn** 'contest, place of contest' in Alcman PMG 3.8.

141. I infer that the expression **epikhōriai gunaikes** 'local women' in Herodotus 5.83.3 refers to the members of the choruses; the point being made here by Herodotus is that only 'local women' are mocked in these choral performances, and not men. We may compare the scene in the *Life of Archilochus* tradition where a youthful Archilochus, as he is driving his cow in the countryside, meets a group of females whom he proceeds to mock, thinking that they are farmworkers who are leaving their work behind and heading for the city (Mnesiepes Inscription, Archilochus T 4.27–30 Tarditi). These country women, as it turns out, are the Muses themselves (T 4.37). See N 1979.303. The juxtaposed picture of a mocking Archilochus is analogous to his persona as an **exarkhōn** 'choral leader', on which see p. 363. At p. 397, we see that the theme of Archilochus as a master of mockery is connected with the figure of Demeter; moreover, there are distinct parallelisms between Demeter and the figures of Damia and Auxesia (again Nilsson 1906.414–416). The theme of Archilochus and the Rustic Muses may be compared with the traditions about the **astrabikon**, where choral performance is visualized as shifting from the polis to the countryside: p. 337.

142. Commentary by Calame 1977 ɪ 60–62.

143. On the marriage of Pelops and Hippodameia as a fundamental model of power and political authority: Ch.4 above.

was assigned to one or the other of the two cult figures, Hippodameia and Physkoa. It may well be then that there were eight choral performances entailing two rival choral subdivisions, assigned to each of the two figures Hippodameia and Physkoa, with each of the sixteen women assigned as **khorēgos** to each of the sixteen choral subdivisions. Whatever the precise nature of these configurations may have been, I draw attention to the actual patterns of *division,* modeled on the patterns of *division* that make up the whole society, that is, the eight **phūlai.**[144] Such patterns of *division* in the *setting up* of the rival choral performances, where the notion of "setting up" is expressed by the traditional combination of verb **histēmi** 'set up' plus the object **khoros** 'chorus', can be connected with the attested negative meanings of **stasis** as 'conflict'. This noun **stasis,** derivative of **histēmi** 'set up, establish, take a stand', means not only 'setting up, establishment, standing, station, status' both in general applications (e.g., Herodotus 9.21.2, Euripides *Bacchae* 925) and in more specific applications to the chorus (e.g., *Suda* s.v. χοροδέκτης)[145] but also 'division, conflict, strife' in general applications to the community at large (Theognis 51, 781; Herodotus 3.82.3). The negative theme of conflict is associated with **stasis** in the navigational sense that we see in the expression ἀνέμων στάσιν '**stasis** of the winds' at Alcaeus F 208.1 V, where the ship's pilot must *contend* with the *contrary* 'lie' or 'setting' of the winds.[146] I would argue that **stasis** in the negative sense of 'conflict' is a

144. On **phūlē** 'tribal division' as a model of simultaneous integration and differentiation, see N 1987. We may compare the latter-day bureaucratic and military usage of *division* in the sense of a large functioning unit.

145. In the *Suda* entry, a χοροδέκτης = **khorodektēs** 'chorus receiver' is described as a **proexarkhōn** who 'receives' the '**stasis**' of the chorus. I take it that his function is to approve, by receiving, the constitution or constituency of a given choral group. Cf. Aristophanes *Wealth* 954, where **stasis** 'station, position' is found in collocation with **koruphaios** 'chorus leader' (953, used here in a figurative sense; more on this word at p. 368). Cf. also the usage of the compound **katastasis** 'establishment' in the traditions about the institution of Spartan choral festivals, as discussed at p. 343. As for **stasis** in the expression στάσιν μελῶν at Aristophanes *Frogs* 1281, see Cingano 1986, who shows that the first interpretation offered by the scholia for this line, claiming that the word denotes a stationary position for the chorus, does not square with the facts of choral performance. Cingano argues for the validity of the second interpretation offered by the scholia, that **stasis** here means **sunodos** (σύνοδον, scholia to 1281), where the word **sunodos** is to be interpreted in the sense of 'the *coming together* resulting from juxtaposition' (Plato *Phaedo* 97a, as translated in LSJ s.v.; cf. "Longinus" 10.3). Further, Cingano, p. 143, compares the relationship of **stasis** and **sustasis** (as in λόγων σύστασιν Plato *Republic* 457e) with that of **thesis** and **sunthesis** (as in τῶν ἐπῶν σύνθεσιν Diodorus Siculus 5.74.1). The meaning of **thesis,** as in the expression ἐπέων . . . θέσιν at Pindar *Olympian* 3.8, is *composition,* which helps explain the gloss in Hesychius s.v. στάσις: here the first three definitions of **stasis** are θέσις. χορός. συνέδρα 'composition [thesis], chorus [khoros], conference [sunedrā]' (Cingano ibid.). I agree with Pickard-Cambridge 1968.251 that the derivative **stasimon** means not that the chorus was standing "but that they had reached their station (στάσις) in the orchestra (they had not yet done this in the parodos; in the exodos they were leaving it)."

146. Cf. N 1985.24 §2n2. A neutral context for this sense of the 'lie' or 'setting' of the winds is evident in, for example, Herodotus 2.26.2.

metaphor, within the larger metaphor complex of the Ship of State in the crisis of a seastorm (as in Theognis 667–682),[147] for the ritualized interpersonal *divisions* that are acted out in the process of establishing or constituting choral performance; this constitution is in turn achieved through the literal *divisions* into which chorus members are systematically assigned when the chorus is organized.[148]

In this context we may note a variant tradition, again recorded by Pausanias (5.16.5–6), that the same collegium of sixteen women who are charged with organizing the Feast of Heraia at Elis was "originally" selected to settle the internal conflicts of Elis after the tyranny of one Damophon of Pisa in Elis; by extension the prototypical collegium of sixteen women took charge of a female athletic contest, as well as other rituals associated with the Heraia, including the choral events (5.16.6).[149] We may note also a variant tradition, native to Trozen,[150] about Damia and Auxesia: these figures were stoned to death in a setting that is described in terms of **stasis** 'social conflict' (στασιασάντων, ἀντιστασιωτῶν: Pausanias 2.32.2). This myth is cited as background for a festival that is named after its central event of ritualized conflict, the **Lithobolia** 'stone throwing' (ibid.).[151]

In sum, the ritual essence of the choral lyric performance is that it is *constitutive* of society in the very process of *dividing* it. For this reason, the concept of **stasis** is simultaneously *constitution* and *division*.[152] The notion of *constitution* is the unmarked member of the opposition, in that it includes and integrates *division*, which is the marked member.[153] *Constitution* is *integration*, and this unmarked-marked opposition can be rephrased in terms of unmarked *integration* and marked *division*. The inclusiveness of the unmarked category is the key to understanding the etymology of **stasis**. The etymology can in turn be correlated with the normal dynamics of collective performance, which is characterized by a gradual progression from dissonance at the beginning to relative consonance at the end.[154]

The very constitution of society, as visualized in the traditions of a polis like Sparta, is choral performance. We have already seen that the name for "civic space" in Sparta is in fact **Khoros** (Pausanias 3.11.5).[155] Moreover,

147. Extensive commentary in N 1985.22–36, 53, 64–68, 71, 76, 80–81.

148. Cf. Gluckman 1965.165 on the concept of multiple ties that bind, hence "divided loyalties," as an ideological foundation of society.

149. There is a description of the female **agōn** 'contest' in running by Pausanias 5.16.2–6 (note especially the specific use of **agōn** at 5.16.2 and 5.16.4 in referring to the race).

150. Trozen, not "Troizen": Barrett 1966.12.

151. More at Ch.4 above on such formalized relationships between myth and ritual.

152. Cf. Loraux 1987.108–112, 1987d.50–55, with reference primarily to the political aspects of **stasis**.

153. On the terms *unmarked* and *marked*: p. 5.

154. This formulation is pertinent to the discussion at p. 343.

155. Cf. p. 345.

Spartan myth insists that Chorus had to precede Constitution: in Plutarch's *Life of Lycurgus* (4.2–3), we see that Lycurgus, the lawgiver of Sparta, who is the culture hero credited with the institutional totality that is the Constitution of Sparta, brought his laws from Crete to Sparta only after he had already sent ahead the lyric poet Thales/Thaletas, whose songs had in them the qualities of **kosmos** 'order' (τὸ κόσμιον 4.3) and **katastasis** 'establishment' (καταστατικόν ibid.).[156] This same Thaletas figures in the so-called second **katastasis** of Spartan traditions in songmaking ("Plutarch" *On Music* 1134bc).[157] The Spartan tradition stresses that the social effects of the lyric poet are like those of the most powerful **nomothetēs** 'lawgiver' (Plutarch *Life of Lycurgus* 4.2). In this particular tradition, poet and lawgiver are differentiated as Thaletas and Lycurgus respectively. But in other traditions, the two roles are represented by one persona, as in the case of Theognis: he speaks not only as a choral lyric personality, singing and dancing to the lyre (Theognis 791)[158] or singing to the lyre and reed (531–534),[159] but also as a lawgiver (Theognis 543–546, 805–810).[160] In the case of a differentiated choral lyric personality like Thaletas, his affinities with the constitution of his community are made explicit.

The metaphor of the chorus, as conveyed by the concept of **stasis**, helps explain the use of the word **koruphaios** 'top person, leading figure' in the Debate of the Constitutions, Herodotus 3.82.3, where the Great King of the Persians is represented as cynically restating the poetic tradition, according to which the unmistakable mark of **oligarkhiā** 'oligarchy' is the spontaneous generation of **stasis**, which in turn leads to **phonos** 'killing', which in turn

156. More detailed discussion, with further comparative data, in N 1985.40–41.

157. Cf. p. 344. There is a similar story about Terpander under the entry μετὰ Λέσβιον ᾠδόν in the *Suda*: when the polis of Sparta was in disorder, an oracle told them to send for the singer from Lesbos; when Terpander arrived at Sparta, he put an end to the **stasis** 'social strife' (ibid.). Finally, in a fragment of a story reported by Philodemus *On Music*, p. 18 Kemke, Stesichorus is pictured as putting a stop to discord among the people of a city, by singing in their midst, just as Terpander had reputedly done in Sparta (ibid.); in another mention of this parallelism between Stesichorus and Terpander, Philodemus describes the social discord as **stasis** (*On Music*, p. 87).

158. The reference at Theognis 791 to singing and dancing accompanied by the lyre is to be supplemented by 776–779, an explicitly choral scene.

159. The reference to the performance of song accompanied by lyre and reed in Theognis 531–534 does not explicitly differentiate the choral element, as in Theognis 791 (cf. 776–779), from the monodic. Elsewhere, as at Theognis 759–764, the singing accompanied by lyre and reed is dramatized in the context of a symposium (cf. also the references to the reed at 825–830, 943–944, 1055–1058, 1065–1068). Such sympotic contexts indicate the differentiated forms of monody. In general the figure of Theognis speaks less as a generalized choral personality and more as a specialized sympotic personality (cf. especially Theognis 239–243).

160. Commentary in N 1985.36–41. Although the figure of Theognis seems to be more differentiated than that of Thaletas in the form of his poetry (p. 24), he is less differentiated in function: the point remains that his personality as poet is undifferentiated from his personality as lawgiver.

leads to **monarkhiā** 'monarchy', that is, tyranny. The same sequence is attested in Theognis 51–52, where **stàsis** (plural, 51) leads to **phonoi** 'killings' (51), which lead to **monarkhoi** 'monarchs' (52).[161] In the description of the oligarchy that generates **stasis**, it is pointed out that each and every member of the society, in his private pursuit of **aretē** 'excellence', is in effect competing to become the **koruphaios**, the 'top person' or 'leading figure' (Herodotus 3.82.3); this same word, **koruphaios**, is the technical term for 'leader of the chorus' as used by Aristotle *Politics* 1277a11, in the context of arguing that not every citizen of a polis has the same degree of **aretē** 'excellence', just as a **koruphaios** in a chorus has more **aretē** than the other members.[162] This vision of **stasis** can be compared with the description, in Herodotus 1.59.3, of the division of early Athenian society into three constituencies, each called a **stasis** and each having a prominent Athenian 'standing in the front' (cf. προεστῶτος). These three are Peisistratos, the once and future tyrant of Athens; Megakles of the lineage of the Alkmaionidai; and one Lykourgos (ibid.). In such a context the word **stasis** is conventionally translated as 'faction', and the story as retold by Herodotus reinforces the initial impression that these three "factions" were spontaneously generated by the society of Athens in the era that preceded the tyranny of the Peisistratidai. It can be argued, however, that the three constituencies described here are a reflex of a preexisting institution, a constitutional mechanism of tripartition where the principle of rotating power is expressed by the concept of **trittus** 'third'.[163]

The key to choral performance, then, as we have seen primarily with the help of the description of an Aeginetan festival by Herodotus, is the public presentation of the **khorēgos**, where the notion of 'public presentation' is conveyed by the verb corresponding to the noun **apo-deixis** (5.83.3).[164] With further help from such actual compositions as Alcman PMG 1, we have also seen that the authority of the **khorēgos** is *presented* through the performance of the "I" that is the chorus. It is from this authority that the authorship of the **khorēgos** emanates. The presentation through the chorus is the representation that is mimesis. The "I" of the choral ensemble is not just the collectivization of persons who are singing and dancing at the ritual: it is also the impersonation of characters that belong to whatever myth is being represented in the ritual.[165]

---

161. See pp. 181, 182; also N 1985.42–46.

162. Cf. the use of **koruphaios** 'leading figure' at Herodotus 6.98.2, quoted at p. 306.

163. N 1987.255.

164. Cf. p. 364.

165. Calame 1977 ɪɪ 126–127 makes a plausible argument that, while the characters Agido and Hagesikhora in Alcman PMG 1 represent the Leukippides, the chorus as a group represent a set of eleven cult figures known as the Dionysiades (on whom see Pausanias 3.13.6–7, Athenaeus 574d; also Calame ɪ 323–333).

We have seen how, in compositions like Alcman PMG 1, a differentiated **khorēgos** who is composer and who is offstage, as it were, makes the collectivized "I" of the chorus speak *about* another differentiated **khorēgos**, the alter ego of the composer, who is the mute virtuoso dancer and who is center stage, the focus of collectivized experience, either male or female. But there are other kinds of "I" besides the collectivized "I" of the chorus. Given that the **khorēgos** is the choral expression of the individual who momentarily stands out from among the collective, we have yet to see how the persona of the **khorēgos** itself would speak if it found a voice to go with the role of chorus leader *as a composer and performer*, on the model of Apollo as he simultaneously sings, dances, and plays the lyre.

One way for such a voice to be present can be found in the "I" of a **khorēgos** who engages in a dialogue with the rest of the chorus. I cite Bacchylides 18 SM, which represents a dialogue between Aigeus, the father of Theseus, and the chorus. It seems that it is the **khorēgos** here who represents Aigeus.

Another way for the voice of the **khorēgos** to be activated can be found in the "I" of a personality like Sappho, whose persona speaks as a **khorēgos** both *to* and *about* members of an aggregate of female characters who are bound together by ties that correspond to the ties that bind a chorus together.[166] In such a reversed situation, the "I" is not the group through whom the authority of the **khorēgos** finds a voice: rather the "I" who now speaks is the individual whom we have seen in another situation, at center stage, as the mute virtuoso dancer. In that other kind of choral situation, as illustrated in Alcman PMG 1, the "I" is spoken by the aggregate while the "I" of the **khorēgos** as individual and as composer is potentially mute. But as soon as the "I" of the **khorēgos** as individual starts singing, as it were, this same figure stops dancing and, even more, the aggregate stops both singing and dancing. This figurative and diachronic scheme of reassigned parts is the essence, I submit, of what we have been calling *monody*.

Even in choral performance, the singer/lyre player may differentiate himself from the choral group whenever the chorus speaks through his own persona instead of theirs, as most dramatically illustrated by the declaration in Alcman PMG 26 where the singer says that he is too old and weak to dance with the chorus.[167] Such an image reflects what I would call the tradi-

---

166. See Calame 1977 ı 367–372 (also 126–127) for a detailed and persuasive discussion.

167. Cf. p. 352. In this connection I note the following observation of Mullen 1982.34: "What is most noticeable about instances of Pindar's going out of his way to *distinguish* himself from the dancers is that he ususally does so only by way of foil, that is, only in brief passages where he is relinquishing his role as leader to someone else." According to Mullen (ibid.), this pattern of relinquishing choral leadership is simply a rhetorical strategy in *Isthmian* 8.1–4 (let someone other than me start the **kōmos** 'revel') and in *Nemean* 4.13–16 (if the victor's father were still alive, *he* would be the choral lyric poet for this occasion), while it may be literally happening in other compositions where others are specified as having taken Pindar's place in train-

tion of diachronic teaching, in that the tired old persona of the protopoet, as seasonally re-created in the here and now of choral performance, is visualized as ever-returning, albeit in a stylized and distanced manner, to teach yet another crop of new choral ensembles as the season of the festival comes round yet again.[168] There is an analogous tradition as evidenced in the poetry of Theognis. The poet is dramatized as being present at crucial stages in the history of his city, Megara, though the local color is consistently screened out in favor of a generalized Panhellenic highlighting.[169] "By implication the undying **noos** ['consciousness'] of Theognis the poet is ever testing, by way of a timeless poetry that keeps adapting itself through the ages, the intrinsic worth of the citizens of Megara."[170]

It should be clear then that I understand the monodic form to be not antithetical to the choral but rather predicated on it. A figure like Sappho speaks as a choral personality, even though the elements of dancing and the very presence of a choral group are evidently missing from her compositions. Still, these compositions presuppose or represent an interaction, offstage, as it were, with a choral aggregate.

As for the corpus of Stesichorus, it has been argued that it too is representative of monodic rather than choral performance.[171] There is a strong counterargument, however, in the triadic structure of Stesichorean compositions, which points to a persisting choral medium.[172] Moreover, even the name **Stēsikhoros** 'he who sets up the chorus' projects a choral personality.[173] True, such a characterization is not in itself decisive, as we see from the example of Archilochus, where the poet refers to himself as an **exarkhōn** 'chorus leader' in a medium that is apparently not even sung but recited.[174] It may also be true that the compositions that are credited to Stesichorus are of such enormous dimensions that we might expect them to defy any sustained singing and dancing by a choral aggregate.[175] Still our expectations may well

---

ing and leading the chorus (Aineias in *Olympian* 6.88 and Nikasippos in *Isthmian* 2.47).

168. On Alcman as **didaskalos** 'teacher' of the daughters of the Spartans, as also of their **ephēboi** 'citizen-initiates', in the activity of **patrioi khoroi** 'ancestral choruses', see lines 30–37 of the commentary in PMG, p. 30 (*Oxyrhynchus Papyri* 2506); cf. Herington 1985.24. Note too the vivid description of choral performances at the Spartan festival of the **Huakinthia**, Polycrates FGH 588 F 1 by way of Athenaeus 139e, where the compositions of Alcman were most likely at least part of the repertory (cf. the papyrus commentary to Alcman, PMG 10[a].5).

169. N 1985.30–36.

170. N, pp. 76; cf. 41–46, 74–76. In this case, however, the figure of the poet is less of a choral personality and more of a sympotic one: p. 368.

171. West 1971.

172. Burkert 1987.51; Burnett 1988.129–147, especially pp. 133–135.

173. See p. 362.

174. Cf. p. 363.

175. Cf. West 1971.302, 309, 313. On the basis of *Oxyrhynchus Papyri* 2617, it has been calculated that the *Geryoneis* of Stesichorus "contained at least 1,300 verses, the total being perhaps closer to two thousand" (West, p. 302). West concludes (ibid.): "Indeed, these *were* epic poems,

have to shift, especially if we consider the varying conditions of aristocratic as distinct from democratic settings for choral performance.[176] It is safer to say, then, that the corpus of Stesichorus represents the medium of choral performance, though we may make allowances for the evolution of a derivative medium that entails the monodic mimesis of choral performance. In fact we have already examined a reference to a tradition of monodic performance of Stesichorus, in the *Clouds* of Aristophanes (967).[177]

The repertoire of Stesichorus, as also most of the repertoire attributed to Ibycus, Sappho, Alcaeus, and Anacreon, can find expression in the monodic medium of **kitharōidiā** 'lyre [**kitharā**] singing'.[178] Alternatively the monodic medium of lyric is **aulōidiā** 'reed [**aulos**] singing'.[179] Just as the protocomposer of a choral performance can be impersonated by the chorus leader (e.g., in Alcman PMG 26), so also the protocomposer in nonchoral lyric is impersonated by a contemporary performer such as the **kitharōidos**.

The varieties of mimesis in monody correspond to what we have already seen in the choral form. To begin, the monodic form can have the performer impersonate individual figures other than the composer or protocomposer. A clear example is the first-person feminine in Alcaeus F 10 V. As for cases of direct self-presentation, there are particularly arresting examples in Sappho and Alcaeus. Alternatively, self-presentation in the form of first-person interaction and narrative can step backstage, as it were, while the self simply tells a third-person narrative, as in numerous examples from Stesichorus. Moreover, the lyric poetry or *song* of monody is not far removed from the ultimately differentiated forms of *poetry*, as in the compositions attributed to Archilochus or Theognis. Here singing is replaced by stylized speaking, but the choral personalities persist. We may note again that the characterization of a **khorēgos** 'chorus leader', which persists even in *poetry*, fits the pattern of ritual substitution. Just as the chorus leader in the *song* of choral performance enters a forcefield of antagonism with the divinity who is being represented in choral performance, so also the author in *poetry* is ultimately locked into a forcefield of antagonism with the god Apollo himself.[180]

There are traces even in Homer and Hesiod of choral personalities. The very name of Hesiod, **Hēsi-odos** 'he who emits the voice',[181] corresponds to the characterization of the Muses as **ossan hieisai** 'emitting the voice' (*Theogony* 10, 43, 65, 67), which applies to them in a choral context (7–8, 63). So

---

in subject and style as well as in length: epics to be sung instead of recited." Such calculations have been challenged by Burnett 1988.129–133.

176. On this point see p. 362.
177. Cf. p. 97.
178. On which see pp. 86, 97, 104.
179. Cf. p. 104.
180. Cf. N 1979.279–308.
181. N 1979.296–297.

also the name of Homer, **Hom-ēros** 'he who fits the song together', corresponds to the characterization of the Muses as **arti-epeiai** 'having words [**epea**] fitted together' (*Theogony* 29) and **phōnēi homēreusai** 'fitting [the song] together with their voice' (*Theogony* 39), again in the same choral context.[182] We have already considered the quasi-choral performance of Demodokos in *Odyssey* viii. Further, the contest won by the figure of Hesiod at the Funeral Games of Amphidamas, described in Hesiod *Works and Days* 654–658, is presented as if it were a choral competition.[183] The performance with which Hesiod won is actually called a **humnos** (*Works and Days* 655).

Alternatively the self-characterization of the poet in Homer and Hesiod can suit the more differentiated figure of the **kitharōidos** 'lyre [**kithara**] singer', appropriate to the differentiated format of *poetry*. Such is the description of generic poets at Hesiod *Theogony* 94–95.[184] Another example is the image of Hesiod holding a lyre, as attested by a statue seen by Pausanias at Helikon (9.30.3).[185]

Earlier, we had examined various possible stages of distinction between performer and composer in poetry.[186] Now we may add that once the performer and the composer become distinct in poetry, as also in both monodic and choral song, the persona of the composer can be reenacted by the performer. In other words the performer may impersonate the poet. The word for such reenactment or impersonation, as we have seen, is **mīmēsis**.[187] By extension, as we have also seen, **mīmēsis** can designate not only the reenacting of the myth but also the present reenacting of previous reenactments.[188] In that the newest instance of reenacting has as its model cumulatively all the older instances of performing the myth as well as the "original" instance of the myth itself, **mīmēsis** is a current 'imitation' of earlier reenactments.[189]

The concept of **mīmēsis**, in conveying a reenactment of the realities of myth, is a concept of authority as long as society assents to the genuineness of the values contained by the framework of myth. Correspondingly the speaker who frames the myth, or whose existence is reenacted as framing the myth, is an *author* so long as he or she speaks with the authority of myth, which is supposedly timeless and unchanging. The author has to insist on the

182. Ibid.
183. Koller 1956.166–167.
184. Koller, p. 167.
185. Pausanias ibid. worries about this visual association, in light of the laurel wand that the Muses give to Hesiod as a **skēptron** 'scepter' at *Theogony* 30. But there exist iconographical attestations of poetic figures who are pictured simultaneously with laurel branch and lyre, as in the case of Musaeus (documentation in Koller 1956.165n4).
186. See pp. 79 and following.
187. See p. 42.
188. Such is the case of Hagesikhora, as discussed at pp. 345 and following.
189. This is the sense of **mīmēsis** in the Homeric *Hymn to Apollo* 163, as discussed at pp. 43 and following.

timelessness and unchangeability of such authority, which resists the pressures of pleasing the interests of the immediate audience by preferring the pleasure of timeless and unchanging values transmitted to an endless succession of audiences by way of **mīmēsis**.

These thought patterns are particularly evident in two passages from Theognis of Megara. In the first the persona of Theognis declares that only the one who is **sophos**, that is, 'skilled' in the decoding and encoding of poetry,[190] can execute a **mīmēsis** 'reenactment' of Theognis:

οὐ δύναμαι γνῶναι νόον ἀστῶν ὅντιν' ἔχουσιν·
οὔτε γὰρ εὖ ἔρδων ἁνδάνω οὔτε κακῶς·
μωμεῦνται δέ με πολλοί, ὁμῶς κακοὶ ἠδὲ καὶ ἐσθλοί·
μιμεῖσθαι δ' οὐδεὶς τῶν ἀσόφων δύναται.

Theognis 367–370

I am unable to decide what disposition it is that the townspeople [**astoi**][191] have towards me.

For I do not please [= verb **handanō**] them, either when I do for them things that are advantageous or when I do things that are disadvantageous.[192]

There are many who find blame with me, base and noble men alike.

But no one who is not skilled [**sophos**] can reenact [**mīmeisthai**] me.[193]

In the second and related passage, we see that the notion of **mīmēsis** is an implicit promise that no change shall occur to accommodate the interests of any local audience in the here and now, that is, of the **astoi** 'townspeople'. The reperformance of a composition, if it is a true reenactment or **mīmēsis**, can guarantee the authenticity of the "original" composition. In the second passage, where the persona of Theognis actually identifies himself by name, thereby *authorizing* himself, there is an explicit self-description of the *author* as someone who practices **sophiā**, the 'skill' of decoding or encoding poetry,

---

190. On **sophos** 'skilled' as a programmatic word used by poetry to designate the 'skill' of a poet in encoding the message of the poetry, see p. 148. A successful encoder, that is, poet, is by necessity a successful decoder, that is, someone who has understood the inherited message and can therefore pass it on. Not all decoders, however, are necessarily encoders: both poet and audience are decoders, but only the poet has the authority of the encoder. On the terms *code* and *message* as applied to general poetics, see p. 148.

191. In this and related contexts, **astoi** 'townspeople' seems to be the programmatic designation of local audiences, associated with the special interests of their own here and now.

192. The "doing," of course, may amount simply to the performative level of "saying" *by way of poetry*.

193. The translation here may have veered too far from English idiom, which resists the notion of reenacting a person; accordingly we may choose to paraphrase thus: "But no one who is not skilled can reenact my existence."

and as one who therefore possesses the authority of timeless and unchanging value, resisting the necessity of having to please merely the audience of the here and now:

Κύρνε σοφιζομένῳ μὲν ἐμοὶ σφρηγὶς ἐπικείσθω
    τοῖσδ' ἔπεσιν, λήσει δ' οὔποτε κλεπτόμενα,
οὐδέ τις ἀλλάξει κάκιον τοὐσθλοῦ παρεόντος,
    ὧδε δὲ πᾶς τις ἐρεῖ· Θεύγνιδός ἐστιν ἔπη
τοῦ Μεγαρέως· πάντας δὲ κατ' ἀνθρώπους ὀνομαστός·
    ἀστοῖσιν δ' οὔπω πᾶσιν ἁδεῖν δύναμαι.

Theognis 19–24

Kyrnos, let a seal [**sphrāgis**] be placed by me, as I practice my skill [**sophiā**],
upon these my words. This way, it will never be undetected if they are stolen,
and no one can substitute something inferior for the genuine thing that is there.
And this is what everyone will say: "These are the words of Theognis of Megara, whose name is known among all mortals."
But I am not yet able to please [= verb **handanō**] all the townspeople [**astoi**].

The composer must risk alienation in his own here and now in order to attain the supposedly universal acceptance of the ultimate audience, which is the cumulative response of Panhellenic fame,[194] achieved through the authority and authenticity of **mīmēsis**. Implicitly, only the pleasure of exact reperformance, the ongoing achievement of **mīmēsis**, is truly lasting.[195] The pleasure elicited through changes in response to an immediate audience is ephemeral.

Before we leave the topic of solo singers or poets who speak as choral personalities even though their persona has become detached from the chorus, I draw attention to a remarkable case where the solo singer is represented as potentially becoming attached to a chorus as their **khorēgos**, only to stay detached in the end. In the Homeric *Hymn to Apollo* 150, there is a description of a festival on the island of Delos where contests in choral performance take place.[196] In this context, the figure of Homer describes a choral ensemble on the island of Delos, known as the Deliades, who can **mīmeisthai** 'make a mimesis' (*Hymn to Apollo* 163) of anyone who comes

194. This theme of the alienated poet is examined at length in N 1985.30 and following.

195. On the reenactment, through poetry, of both choral and sympotic settings in the compositions attributed to Theognis, see p. 368.

196. Thucydides refers to these contests as **agōn** (3.104 passim), comparing the festival, as he reconstructs it from the *Hymn to Apollo*, to the contemporary pan-Ionian festival of the Ephesia, on which see Nilsson 1906.243–247.

to the festival where they perform (162–164).[197] By implication they could make a mimesis of Homer as well. By performing Homer they could represent Homer. That is, *they* could be the speakers, the "I" of the performance, with Homer as their **khorēgos** and speaking through *their identity.* They would be like the girls in Alcman PMG 1, through whom Alcman speaks when they sing his words in choral ensemble. More fundamentally they would be like the Muses, through whom Apollo speaks when they sing the words of choral performance. But the figure of Homer indirectly declines the occasion, calling on the good will of the Deliades in the same way that the performer of a prelude calls on the good will of the god who is the subject and occasion of the prelude, so that the same performer may go on to the rest of the performance (*Hymn to Apollo* 166). He promises to sing *about* them as he proceeds on his way to give performances throughout the various cities of the Hellenic world (174–175).[198] Instead of staying in Delos as a choral personality who finds expression through the local quasi-Muses, the Deliades, he will be a Panhellenic personality whose "I" speaks for itself, and it will be through him that the Panhellenic Muse of the *Iliad* and *Odyssey* finds her own self-expression.[199]

Although the "I" of Homer is not taken over by the Deliades, it is their voice that is quoted in the glorification of Homer. Asking the Deliades to keep him in mind even as he moves on (*Hymn to Apollo* 166–167), the figure of Homer instructs them about what to say to anyone who comes to Delos and should ask the question: of the **aoidoi** 'singers' who have come to the island, which one has delighted you the most (169–170)? What the Deliades should 'answer' in this hypothetical dialogue is expressed as a direct quotation of what they would indeed say: he is a blind man, from Chios, whose songs will win universal approval in the future (172–173). The word here for 'answer' is **hupokrīnomai** (ὑποκρίνασθ': 171), from which the agent-noun **hupokritēs** 'actor' is derived.[200] In this way the Deliades are true to their choral function of serving as speakers, mouthpieces, as it were, of the composer, even though the composer declines in this case to stay as their chorus teacher.

Similarly with the figure of Hesiod, it is through him that the Panhellenic Olympian Muses find expression, transforming themselves from the local Helikonian Muses that they had once been at the beginning of the *Theo-*

197. Cf. p. 43 and following.

198. Commentary in N 1979.8.

199. To be contrasted is *Iliad* II 594–600, with the elliptic description of a negative encounter between the Muses and a figure called Thamyris (on the meaning of **thamuris** as 'assembly', synonymous with **agōn**, see N 1979.311 §2n6). This figure Thamyris fits the description of a **kitharōidos** (*Iliad* II 599–600, with the commentary of Koller 1956.160).

200. The **hupokritēs** is ordinarily the second actor, as distinct from the **prōtagōnistēs** 'protagonist' (cf. Pickard-Cambridge 1968.127).

gony.[201] It is through the encounter of Hesiod with the Helikonian Muses that he gets his power to speak **alēthea** 'true things', that is, to speak with a Panhellenic authority that reciprocally transforms the Helikonian into the Olympian Muses.[202] Similarly it may be that Homer gets his own Panhellenic authority through his encounter with the Deliades, who can represent anyone who comes to Delos. The centripetal model of the Deliades, who assimilate all the different languages that come their way from all the Hellenes converging at their festival at Delos, is the foundation for the centrifugal model of Homer, who leaves the island to spread *their* fame, their **kleos**. The **kleos** of the Deliades is not only what Homer sings about them but also, reciprocally, what they themselves say through Homer about Homer, which turns into the **kleos** of Homer. Their repertoire is that of all the Hellenes, who have come to Delos and who have all been represented by these most versatile Muses.

It is time to sum up what we have observed so far about the **khoros** 'chorus' as a formal expression of the simultaneity of hierarchy and egalitarianism in the polis. It is implicit that the **khorēgos** 'chorus leader' is diachronically a combination of composer and leading performer, while the rest of the **khoreutai** 'chorus members' are performers. The key to choral performance is the public presentation, the **apo-deixis**, of the **khorēgos**. The authority of the **khorēgos** is *presented* through the performance of the "I" that is the chorus, and it is from this authority that his authorship emanates. It is useful to cite a particularly interesting ethnographic parallel, taken from the following description of choral composition and performance in Andamanese society:[203]

> Every man composes songs, and the boys begin to practise themselves in the art of composition when they are still young. A man composes his song as he cuts a canoe or a bow or as he paddles a canoe, singing it over softly to himself, until he is satisfied with it. He then waits for an opportunity to sing it in public, and for this he has to wait for a dance. Before the dance he takes care to teach the chorus to one or two of his female relatives so that they can lead the chorus of women. He sings his song, and if it is successful he repeats it several times, and thereafter it becomes part of his repertory, for every man has a repertory of songs that he is prepared to repeat at any time. If the song is not successful [. . .] the composer abandons it and does not repeat it. Some men are recognized as being more skillful song-makers than others.

In what precedes, I have also stressed that the presentation through the

---

201. N 1982.53–57.
202. Ibid.
203. Radcliffe-Brown 1948.132; cf. Merriam 1964.175.

chorus is the representation that is mimesis. The "I" of the choral ensemble is not just the collectivization of persons who are singing and dancing at the ritual: it is also the impersonation of characters that belong to whatever myth is being represented in the ritual. We have seen in compositions like Alcman PMG 1 how a differentiated **khorēgos** who is composer and who is offstage, as it were, makes the collectivized "I" of the chorus speak *about* another differentiated **khorēgos**, the alter ego of the composer, who is the mute virtuoso dancer and who is center stage, the focus of collectivized experience, either male or female.

With these observations in mind, let us move away from the patterns of evolution in choral lyric as attested in a polis like Sparta and shift the emphasis to another possible pattern of evolution, within the highly complex institution of the dramatic festivals, especially the Feast of the City Dionysia, in the polis of Athens.[204] Here, to begin, the **khorēgos** 'chorus leader' has become ultimately differentiated as a contemporary nonperformer, who organizes and subsidizes both the composition and the performance.[205] Meanwhile, the differentiated function of a *performing* chorus leader is further differentiated by another split in functions, with a marked "first actor" on one hand and an unmarked chorus leader on the other. This further differentiation is represented in the story that tells of Thespis' "invention" of the first actor (Aristotle in Themistius *Orations* 26.316d; Charon of Lampsacus FGH 262 F 15).[206] A dialogue between the differentiated "first actor" and the undifferentiated chorus leader would be a further differentiation of a dialogue between the **khorēgos** and the chorus (cf. Aristotle *Poetics* 1456a25).[207] Finally, there are yet further stages of differentiation with the "invention" of the "second actor," attributed to Aeschylus (Aristotle *Poetics* 1449a15), and of a "third actor," attributed to Sophocles (ibid.).[208] The first actor, of course, is diachronically the composer. Such was the situation with Aeschylus,[209] whereas with Sophocles there is further differentiation between composer and actor, in that Sophocles, tradition has it, ceased to act in the later stages of his career.[210] It is in the interaction between first and second actor, I sug-

204. For a synopsis of the evolution of Athenian dramatic forms, see p. 384 and following.

205. For a review of the facts, see Calame 1977 I 92–93. There is an explicit formulation in Athenaeus 633b, to the effect that the Spartans use the word **khorēgos** not as 'the one who hires the chorus' but as 'the one who leads the chorus'. The differentiation of the **khorēgos** as one who sponsors instead of performs is for me schematically parallel to the differentiation of an "athletic" victor in the Panhellenic festivals who has sponsored a four-horse chariot team instead of having driven it himself.

206. Pickard-Cambridge 1968.130–131.

207. See also Pickard-Cambridge, p. 131n3. For an example of dialogue between **khorēgos** and chorus, I cite again Bacchylides 18 SM, as discussed at p. 370.

208. For another version, see Pickard-Cambridge, p. 131.

209. Cf., for example, Athenaeus 21e–22a and the comments of Mullen 1982.20; also Pickard-Cambridge, pp. 250–251.

210. Testimonia in Pickard-Cambridge, p. 130 and n4. In earlier stages of his career, Sopho-

gest, that the singular form of poetry in dialogue, iambic trimeter, probably becomes differentiated out of the plurality of various different forms of song in choral presentation.[211]

After this overview of complex patterns of differentiation, in Athenian drama, of the traditional interaction of **khorēgos** 'chorus leader' and **khoreutai** 'chorus members', we may turn back to the simple point of departure, that is, the fundamental component of performance by the chorus. As is still evident in the idiom of Attic Greek, the words **tragōidoi** 'performers of tragedy' and **kōmōidoi** 'performers of comedy' refer not only to the choruses but also to the actual performances of tragedy and comedy respectively.[212] These terms, in all their categorical inclusiveness, are parallel to **kitharōidoi** and **aulōidoi** as well as **rhapsōidoi**.[213]

Turning from this most differentiated and complex pattern of developments in choral traditions at Athens, I shift to my last example, a less differentiated but comparably complex pattern of choral tradition, as best represented by Pindar. In this case the **khorēgos** as protocomposer/performer remains a contemporary composer: he is a professional whose compositions are occasional, ostensibly performed by a chorus consisting of contemporary nonprofessionals. Here again the chorus as a group serves as the impersonator, the actor, of the **khorēgos**. Such is the case with the epinician or victory odes of Pindar, commissioned as choral compositions/performances that celebrate the victories of athletes in Panhellenic Games, notably, the Olympian, the Pythian, the Nemean, and the Isthmian Games.[214] In this case, as in other examples, the composer is no longer necessarily a performer, although his persona keeps speaking of himself as not only a composer but also a group of performers, maintaining the impersonation of his choral function as **khorēgos**. In this way the "I" of Pindar speaks in a diachronic mode that reflects in content the evolution of the **khorēgos** from "protocomposer"/performer into a differentiated contemporary composer.

In Pindaric as in other choral poetry, it is the chorus who performs the "I," but this "I" can at will refer to the composer. For example, since the

---

cles himself reportedly played the lyre when he played the role of Thamyris in the *Thamyris*, and he played ball with great skill when he played the role of Nausikaa in the *Nausikaa* (Athenaeus 20e-f; commentary in Pickard-Cambridge, p. 251). Mullen, p. 20, remarks: "In Sophocles the unity of poet, dancer, and musician reaches its *akmē* among dramatists."

211. Cf. pp. 20 and following.

212. Pickard-Cambridge, pp. 127–132. Note the phrasing at p. 127: "Without any conscious differentiation of actors and chorus"; for the tendency to apply the words **tragōidoi** and **kōmōidoi** to the protagonists in old plays, while the other actors are called **hupokritai** or **sunagōnistai**, see p. 129.

213. Plato *Laws* 658b, as discussed at p. 104.

214. For case-by-case refutations of various theories that various poems in the epinician corpus of Pindar are not really epinicians, see Young 1983.

chorus at any given epinician occasion consists of local polis dwellers, the references in Pindaric song to an "I" who comes to the polis from afar must be the mark of the poet.[215] Moreover, there are six Pindaric compositions addressed to non-Thebans that bear clear "signatures" of Thebes as the poet's native polis,[216] just as Bacchylides of Keos is surely referring to himself in attributing one of his choral compositions to 'the nightingale from Keos' (Bacchylides *Epinician* 3.96 SM).[217]

Such references to the self in the compositions of Pindar and Bacchylides should help solve the problem of a reference in Pindar *Pythian* 5.75 to the Aigeidai, a lineage orginating in Thebes and extending into important offshoots at Sparta and its colonies.[218] In the case of *Pythian* 5, a composition in honor of a chariot race victory of Arkesilas, king of Cyrene, the Aigeidai are described as participating in the colonization of Thera, from where the polis of Cyrene was in turn colonized (76 and following). In this context, the Aigeidai are described as ἐμοὶ πατέρες 'my ancestors [**pateres**]', and the problem is whether the word ἐμοὶ 'my' here refers to Pindar or to the chorus.[219] The second choice is unlikely if the body politic of Cyrene, as ostensibly represented by the chorus, is not ideologically derivable from the single lineage of the Aigeidai, even by way of ellipsis. And it would be special pleading to posit a Cyrenaean chorus consisting exclusively of members of the Aigeidai. It seems more plausible, then, to interpret ἐμοὶ πατέρες 'my ancestors' as a proud reference by the poet Pindar to his own lineage.[220] From the standpoint of Panhellenic prestige, the lineage of the Aigeidai can rival in distinction the corresponding lineage of any of the historical personages whom Pindar praises. If we can take Pindar's pride in his own Theban ancestry as a given, we can better understand the ideology of a Pindaric composition like *Isthmian* 8, which extends the symmetry in the reciprocal

215. See Mullen 1982.28, who cites Pindar *Olympian* 7.13–14; *Pythian* 2.3–4; *Isthmian* 5.21–22 and 6.20–21 as illustrations. This is not to go so far as to say that the poet of choral lyric should be considered a soloist (for arguments in that direction, see Lefkowitz 1985.47–49; also Lefkowitz 1988).

216. See again Mullen ibid., who cites Pindar *Olympian* 6.84–86, 10.85; *Pythian* 2.3–4, 4.299; *Isthmian* 6.74–75, 8.16.

217. Ibid. For further discussion of the Pindaric "I," see Lefkowitz 1963, Slater 1969b.89, and Hamilton 1974.113–115, where we see that the "I" of an epinician gravitates toward the **khorēgos**, while that of, say, a paean gravitates toward the **khoros**.

218. On the Aigeidai, see p. 179. On the Aigeidai as Thebans, see the reference in Pindar *Isthmian* 7 (14–15), a composition celebrating the victory of a Theban athlete.

219. Cf. Kirkwood 1982.3; cf. Lefkowitz 1985.45–47.

220. Cf. Farnell 1932.178–179; also Hubbard 1985.129n83, in disagreement with Bornemann 1891, who argues that the designation of the Aigeidai applies to Thebans in general. In Pindar *Isthmian* 7.14–15, the Aigeidai are indeed acknowledged as the Thebans; still, even if the poet were to say that the Aigeidai are the Thebans, such a vaunt could serve to acknowledge the prestige of an exclusive family by way of ellipsis, that is, the definition of the whole by way of a prominent part of the whole. Cf. the remarks on the Aiakidai at p. 178.

relation between the giver of praise, the poet, and the receiver of praise, the victor, to an overarching symmetry between their respective cities, Thebes and Aegina: since the nymphs Thebe and Aegina were twin sisters, as myth has it, the noble populations that were generated from them are in turn related to each other (*Isthmian* 8.15–23).[221] The metaphor of a genetic affinity between poet and victor has force, I suggest, if Pindar's lineage is comparable in status to that of the athletic victor from Aegina.

In Pindaric song, as a choral medium, not only the references to the "I" of the occasion reveal the control of the figure who is diachronically the **khorēgos** and synchronically the poet. Even the references to the occasion itself reveal that control, in that they all are orchestrated to convey what has been called the *absolute present* of the performance.[222] We have seen, for example, a self-reference, at the end of Pindar's *Nemean* 2, to the prelude that is supposedly getting under way at the poem's beginning.[223] This kind of time warp absolutizes the occasion, as also in general the numerous conventional futures and imperatives in Pindaric diction, the purpose of which is "to collapse into themselves the whole temporal sequence of the epinician occasion."[224]

At the end of this rapid survey of different patterns in the development of traditions in the composition and performance of song, it is time to recapitulate. These different patterns reveal different models for the distinction or potential distinction of performer and poet. We have noted not only the model of the **rhapsōidoi** in the realm of poetry but also the various different models of **kitharōidoi**, **aulōidoi**, **tragōidoi**, and **kōmōidoi** in the realm of song.[225] In all these models, the common point of departure is that the persona of the composer can be reenacted by the performer or performers. In other words the performer may impersonate the composer as well as the characters represented as speaking within the composition. Such reenactment or impersonation is the essence of **mīmēsis**.[226]

221. Cf. p. 205.
222. Mullen 1982.27.
223. Cf. p. 356.
224. Mullen, p. 27; cf. Slater 1969b.
225. Cf. p. 379.
226. Cf. pp. 42 and following.

13 ▣▣ The Genesis of Athenian State Theater and the Survival of Pindar's Poetry

I n the roughly defined chronological span of 650 to 450 B.C. covering the era of the nine canonical lyric poets,[1] Pindar is not only the latest but also the best known for what we have been calling *occasional* poetry and song. Close behind him are his near contemporaries, Simonides and Bacchylides, the two other poets whose lyric poetry is most easily identifiable with historically verified times and places. These three figures are prominently linked with the patronage of individuals whose political power transcends that of the polis.[2] As we move further back in time, by contrast, we find increasingly fewer instances of lyric poetry suited for single occasions. This pattern corresponds to increasingly fewer instances of individual patronage. In earlier lyric, details that may at first strike us as traces of a single occasion usually turn out to be, upon further scrutiny, more generic than historical. Even self-references tend to say more about a generic composer than about a historically situated poet, as we have seen in the case of a figure like Alcman.[3]

Having noted that the lyric compositions of Pindar were occasional in the strict sense that they were grounded in the historical circumstances of their performance, we now come to the basic question: how then did they ever even survive in the first place? Throughout this book I have resisted the option of seeking a be-all and end-all explanation in the actual writing down of Pindaric song. True, it seems at first an attractive solution to attribute the survival of occasional lyric poetry by Pindar, Simonides, and Bacchylides to

1. I am using the term *lyric* here without including iambic and elegiac.
2. Cf. p. 174.
3. Cf. pp. 350 and following.

the factor of literacy. After all, Pindar and these two near-contemporaries come closest of all the nine canonical lyric poets to what we conceive as the historical period, where the continuous re-creation of knowledge through oral tradition was being replaced by the episodic recording of knowledge through writing. As the closest to the historical period, Pindar could be expected to be the poet whose compositions are most likely to have been affected by the medium of writing. Even in this instance, however, there is no evidence that writing was a factor in the actual composition of Pindaric song; I have already argued that writing need not be posited as an indispensable factor in at least the earlier phases of transmission.[4] If writing had been the sole original means of transmission for compositions by the likes of Pindar, Simonides, and Bacchylides, why is it that while these "old lyric" poets ultimately became canonical, the later "new lyric" poets of the second half of the fifth century, in a period when literacy was becoming ever more pronounced, did not? Granted, there is no doubt that occasional "old lyric" would need to be recorded ultimately in writing if it were to survive, but there remains the more fundamental question: how did the occasional as well as nonoccasional compositions of "old lyric" actually become Panhellenic in prestige, and thereby canonical?

As long as Pindar's medium of song making depended on the prestige of public performance, we cannot assume that a written record could have maintained, of and by itself, such prestige. Rather we should be asking the question the other way around: what was it about the public prestige of Pindar's lyric poetry, *as it was once performed*, that made it possible in the first place for a written record to evolve and to be preserved for later generations?

This question takes us back to the problem inherent in the occasional nature of Pindar's lyric poetry. It is to be expected that occasional poetry is the least likely kind of oral tradition to become a synthetic canonical tradition, in that the Panhellenization of Greek oral traditions in song and poetry entails the gradual elimination of features and details that would tie down a composition to any specific time and place. How, then, did the occasional compositions of Pindar survive?

Part of the answer has to do with the realities of political power in the time of Pindar, which allowed occasional poetry and song to assert the interests of the individual, both patron and poet, in a grand Classical manner characteristic of the older kind of seasonally reperformed poetry and song serving the interests of the polis.[5] Another part of the answer, yet to be formulated, has to do with concepts of Classicism in the time after Pindar, especially at Athens, when the various distinctions between a poet like Pindar

---

4. Cf. p. 84.
5. Cf. pp. 174 and following.

and, say, a poet of the polis like Alcman were already becoming blurred. To appreciate these concepts, we have to consider at some length the role of the State Theater at Athens. In examining the traditions of Athenian Theater, it is crucial to keep in mind at all times that the medium of drama in general and tragedy in particular was the central context for the evolution of traditions in song and poetry at Athens.

The primary setting of Athenian State Theater, and by extension of Athenian traditions in song and poetry, was a synthetic festival known as the City Dionysia (or Great Dionysia), the significance of which is captured in the following brief description:[6]

> The importance of the festival was derived not only from the performances of dramatic and lyric poetry but from the fact that it was open to the whole Hellenic world and was an effective advertisement of the wealth and power and public spirit of Athens, no less than of the artistic and literary leadership of her sons. By the end of March the winter was over, the seas were navigable, and strangers came to Athens from all parts for business or pleasure.

From the text of Aristophanes *Birds* 786–789, we witness the central program of the City Dionysia in a given year, 414 B.C.: three days, each taken up with three tragedies, one satyric drama, and one comedy.[7]

Athenian tradition has it that the Feast of the City Dionysia was the occasion for the "first" contest in tragedy, won by Thespis, at around 534 B.C., under the tyrant Peisistratos (*Parian Marble* FGH 239 A 43).[8] The institution of contests in comedy at the City Dionysia was formalized by the State at a much later date, around 486 B.C.[9] Athenian tradition also has it that satyric drama was established at the City Dionysia in order to compensate for the loss of Dionysiac elements in the development of tragedy (Chamaeleon F 38 Wehrli, *On Thespis*; Zenobius 5.40); the introduction of satyric drama at the City Dionysia is particularly associated with Pratinas of Phleious, a city close to Corinth,[10] who is said to have competed in Athens during the seventieth Olympiad, 499–496 B.C. (*Suda* s.v. Pratinas; *Palatine Anthology* 7.707).

It can be argued that satyric drama amounts to a compensation for the elements lost by tragedy in a process whereby comedy became differentiated from tragedy *in the context of the City Dionysia*.[11] There are noteworthy

---

6. Pickard-Cambridge 1968.58.

7. Pickard-Cambridge, p. 64.

8. See Pickard-Cambridge, pp. 57–101; also Herington 1985.87.

9. Pickard-Cambridge, p. 82. As for the Feast of Lenaia, comedy is formalized there at around 442 B.C.

10. Cf. Seaford 1984.14. The provenience of Pratinas will become more significant as the discussion proceeds.

11. Seaford 1984.10–16.

typological parallels, such as the Japanese *Kyogen*, farcical interludes performed between the serious *Nō* plays and preserving aspects of an earlier and less differentiated form, *Sarugaku*, from which the serious *Nō* evolved;[12] a similar point can be made about the English Court Masque and Antimasque.[13] This argument helps explain Aristotle's derivation of tragedy from the satyric medium (**saturikon**, *Poetics* 1449a20–21). We could say that this satyric medium represents an undifferentiated form of tragedy/comedy; then comedy and the satyric drama become differentiated from tragedy, with comedy becoming detached from tragedy while the satyric drama stays attached as an ongoing compensation for the nonserious Dionysiac elements that tragedy gives up in its gradual evolution toward seriousness (cf. ἀπεσεμνύνθη, *Poetics* 1449a20–21).[14]

In trying to envisage an undifferentiated form of tragedy/comedy, we may look for important reflexes in the functioning parts of attested comedy, most notably the two aspects of "entrance" known as **parodos** and **parabasis** and the central aspect of a major contest or **agōn**.[15] Other functioning parts of comedy that reveal features of undifferentiated drama include "the size of the chorus (twice that of tragedy), the persistence of their hostility from **parodos** to **agōn**, the **antikhoria** [= rival choral groups] implied by the epirrhematic structure of the **agōn**,[16] [and] the extant examples of antagonistic **antikhoria**."[17]

Given that the Theater of Dionysus at Athens is the primary context for the evolution of drama, specifically for the eventual differentiation of choral dramatic contests into the separate categories of tragedy, comedy, dithyramb, and satyr drama, we may look for references to such evolution within drama itself. The ritual essence of Greek drama as a choral performance that takes place at a seasonally recurring festival is highlighted by the *Bacchae* of Euripides, a tragedy performed some time shortly after the death of the poet in 406 B.C., which represents the actions concerning the god Dionysus and the hero Pentheus as a sort of protofestival, a primitive version of the Feast of the City Dionysia in Athens.[18] "If," it has been argued, "the tradition that Thespis

12. Seaford, p. 12.

13. Ibid.

14. Lucas 1968.85 associates this evolution primarily with Aeschylus, who is hailed in Aristophanes *Frogs* 1004–1005 as the creator of tragedy (cf. ῥήματα σεμνά 1004). "Tragedy must have ceased to be satyric at latest by 492 B.C.," the reputed date of the staging of the *Capture of Miletus* by Phrynichus (Lucas ibid.).

15. Seaford 1984.16. On **parabasis** as a differentiated "entrance," see also Seaford 1977–1978.85.

16. The term *epirrhematic* refers to the format of a recited address to the audience, following a sung and danced strophe.

17. Seaford 1977–1978.86. We may compare the Aeginetan example of choruses subdivided into rival halves, as discussed at pp. 365 and following.

18. Cf. Foley 1985.205–258. Note Seaford 1984.43 on the affinities of the *Bacchae* with the Dionysiac theme of the captivity and liberation of satyrs.

produced a *Pentheus* as one of the earliest Greek dramas was current in Euripides' time, the choice of subject of Dionysus' introduction of a primitive drama into Thebes would be particularly appropriate."[19]

In *Bacchae* 714–716 and thereabouts, the herdsman is telling how he and his companions, **boukoloi** 'cowherds' and **poimenes** 'shepherds', had come together for a contest of words in describing the wondrous things being performed by the devotees of Bacchus. Concerning later traditions of dancing by **boukoloi** 'cowherds' in worship of Dionysus, it has been observed that such dances "may well have had their **aition** in such stories as the herdsman tells here."[20] In other words the myth of Dionysus and Pentheus is referring to itself as the motivation or, to put it in Greek, the **aition** 'cause', of the ritual complex known as the Feast of the City Dionysia, as represented by the *Bacchae*.[21] Moreover, this **aition**, telling of **boukoloi** 'cowherds' and **poimenes** 'shepherds' who *come together* (*Bacchae* 714) to compete in describing the wonders of Bacchus, reenacts the very etymology of the crucial word **agōn**, apparently derived from the root **ag-** of **agō** as in **sun-agō** 'bring together, assemble, gather'.[22] The notion of 'assemble', as we have seen, is intrinsic to the general sense of **agōn**, that is, 'assembly' (e.g., Pindar *Pythian* 10.30).[23] But the word can also specifically mean 'contest' (e.g., Pindar *Olympian* 9.90). Thus **agōn** conveys not only the social setting for an activity, namely, an *assembly* of people, but also the activity itself, namely, a *contest*.[24] Moreover, **agōn** can designate a festival of contests in poetry, as in *Homeric Hymn* 6.19–20.[25] The ritual aspect of these activities is suggested by attestations of the derivative word **agōniā** in the sense of 'agony' (e.g., Demosthenes *On the Crown* 33). A semantic parallel is the English usage of *trial* in the sense of *ordeal*, and we may also note that the cognate of English *ordeal* in German is *Urteil*, meaning 'trial'. In the *Bacchae* of Euripides, Dionysus himself describes the upcoming ordeal of Pentheus, where he will be dismembered by the god's devotees, as a great **agōn** (975). At the moment Pentheus may interpret **agōn** on the surface, in the mere sense of a "contest" with adversaries against whom he expects to win (cf. 964, 975), but the real winner will be Dionysus, while Pentheus will undergo an **agōn** in the deeper sense of the ultimate "agony" of an ultimate "ordeal" (again 964, 975). To that extent the

19. Foley, p. 215.

20. Dodds 1960.159.

21. On the semiotics of myth as the **aition** 'cause' of ritual, see p. 118.

22. Chantraine DELG 17. See p. 365. Note the usage of **sun-agō** in Euripides *Bacchae* 563 and 564 in the context of Orpheus as he plays the **kitharā**..

23. Cf. p. 136.

24. Ibid. Again cf. **agōnismos** 'rivalry' in Thucydides 7.70.

25. Cf. p. 137. On **agōn** as a festival of contests in athletics *and* in poetry, song, and dance, see *Homeric Hymn to Apollo* 149–150 and Thucydides 3.10.3/5. Note too the following three subjects of the verb **agōnizomai** 'compete, engage in an **agōn**' in Herodotus: athletes (e.g., 2.160.3–4), warriors (e.g., 1.76.4), and **rhapsōidoi** 'rhapsodes' (5.67.1).

competition of the herdsmen who come together to tell of the wonders of Dionysus *is* the ordeal of Pentheus.

The name of **Pentheus** is apt in this regard: it is derived from the noun **penthos** 'sorrow, lamentation' (as at *Bacchae* 1244), a word that expresses, in the diction of epic poetry, the actual expression or performance of lamentation in the form of song.[26] The noun **penthos** is in turn derived from the verb **paskhō** 'suffer, experience'. Another derivative of **paskhō** is **pathos** 'suffering, experience', which is applied specifically, in the plural **pathea**, to the ultimate agony that awaits Pentheus (*Bacchae* 971). The theme of the **pathos** of **Pentheus**, as dramatized by the verb **paskhō**, pervades the *Bacchae* (786, 788),[27] and it should be compared with the context of **pathos** at Herodotus 5.67.5, describing the dancing by **tragikoi khoroi** 'tragic choruses', at Sikyon in the time of the tyrant Kleisthenes, in reenactment of the **pathea** 'sufferings' of the hero Adrastos.[28]

The sufferings of Pentheus, as expressed by way of **paskhō** 'suffer, experience', can be juxtaposed with the activities of the god Dionysus: at that primordial festival conjured up by the *Bacchae* of Euripides as a prefiguration of the City Dionysia, these activities are described by cowherds and shepherds who have come together to compete in retelling the wondrous things performed by the devotees of the god (*Bacchae* 714–716).[29] In this context the performance of Dionysiac wonders is designated by the verb **draō** (716), which means 'do, perform' within the world of tragedy but also 'sacrifice, perform ritual' within the "real world," the outer world that frames the world of tragedy.[30] There is a grammatical logic built into the antithesis of **paskhō** and **draō**: the verb **paskhō** in the sense of 'experience things done to oneself' is the functional passive of the verb **draō**, synonym of **poieō** in the sense of 'do things to someone'. This antithesis of **paskhō** and **draō**, which is played out in other tragedies as well (e.g., Sophocles *Oedipus at Colonus* 538–539, 1644), is also reflected in the nouns that are derived from these verbs: whereas the derivative of passive **paskhō** is **pathos**, the deriva-

---

26. N 1979.94–102.

27. At *Bacchae* 846 the future form **peisomai** is ambiguously 'I will be persuaded' (verb **peithō**) or 'I will suffer' (verb **paskhō**), in the context of the juxtaposition of **peisomestha** with **paskhomen** at 786. See Segal 1982.249–254.

28. This passage has been discussed at p. 43 as an illustration of the concept of **mīmēsis** as reenactment. That **tragikoi** here refers to the medium of tragedy is supported by the testimony of Themistius *Orations* 27.377b on the perfecting of tragedy by the Sikyonians: cf. Gentili 1986.32–33.

29. The countryside setting of this protofestival, this proto-**agōn**, as it were, is juxtaposed with the urban characteristics of the man who tries to subvert the festival (καί τις πλάνης κατ' ἄστυ καὶ τρίβων 'and then, a town-wanderer, one experienced in words . . .' *Bacchae* 717). We may note the story, preserved in Diogenes Laertius 1.60, that Solon condemned tragedy as a source for the ruses of the tyrant Peisistratos (cf. Petre 1975.570).

30. Burkert 1966. Cf. p. 32.

tive of active **draō** is **drāma**, which survives as the English word *drama*. What is **pathos** or *action experienced* by the hero within the world of tragedy is **drāma**, that is, *sacrifice and the performance of ritual*, from the standpoint of the outer world that frames it. This outer world is constituted by the audience of the theater, who become engaged in the **drāma** and who thereby participate in the inner world that is the **pathos** of the hero.

It is symptomatic of structures that have lost their elasticity, becoming too rigid to accommodate further development, to intensify the semantics of self-reference as a sort of final act of self-reassurance. The patterns of self-reference by drama to drama as we see them in the *Bacchae* of Euripides reflect a crisis in the very genre of tragedy, in the context of drastic changes in Athenian society toward the end of the fifth century; the prospect is one of abrupt confrontation and loss.[31]

This is not the place to search for a formula that accounts for all the differentiations of poetic forms evolving out of the vast and complex institution of the City Dionysia. Still, a general outline has emerged from what precedes. In brief the City Dionysia is the context for the eventual differentiation of choral dramatic contests into the separate categories of tragedy, comedy, dithyramb, and satyr drama. We must add that the earlier phase of differentiation is followed by a later phase of mutual assimilation.[32]

Besides deriving the *form* of tragedy from the satyric medium (*Poetics* 1449a20–21), Aristotle derives the *performers* of tragedy from the **exarkhontes** 'choral leaders' of the **dithurambos** 'dithyramb' (1449a10–11).[33] This formulation is useful to the extent that the evolution of tragedy at Athens does become assimilated with the evolution of the dithyramb, an alternative Dionysiac form of Peloponnesian provenience. A key figure in this process of assimilation is Lasus of Hermione, whom tradition credits with the original institution of dithyrambic contests at the City Dionysia (*Suda* s.v. Lasos).[34] From Herodotus (7.6.3–4), we learn that Lasus was asso-

31. On this concept of confrontation and loss, see p. 60.

32. This point is highlighted in the discussion by Seaford 1984.16–21, who follows up his observation that "satyric drama was instituted in the Dionysia to preserve something of what tragedy had ceased to be" with this converse: "But this does not mean that it was itself immune to change" (p. 16). Eventually satyric drama loses its compensatory function and becomes obsolescent. By 438 B.C., Euripides can substitute the *Alcestis* in place of a satyr drama as the fourth element of a tetralogy (Seaford, pp. 24–25). In the same decade competitions in tragedy are instituted at the Lenaia, without satyric drama at all (Pickard-Cambridge 1968.40–41; cf. Seaford, p. 25). On the assimilation of satyric elements by Euripidean tragedy, see Seaford, pp. 31–32, with bibliography. On a larger scale we may note the early assimilation of tragedy at the City Dionysia in the direction of the major themes of epic as performed at the Great Panathenaia: a worthy case in point is the "Homeric" repertoire of Aeschylus, as discussed by Herington 1985.138–144.

33. Cf. Seaford, p. 13n39, on the role of satyrs in Arion's dithyrambs.

34. Cf. Pickard-Cambridge 1962.13–15. See Seaford 1984.15 on the introduction, by Lasus, of actual dithyrambic *style* at the City Dionysia.

ciated with the dynasty of tyrants at Athens, the Peisistratidai. The definitive formalization, however, by the State, of contests in dithyrambs at the Feast of the City Dionysia can be dated at ca. 509/8 B.C., *after* the expulsion of the Peisistratidai (*Parian Marble* FGH 239 A 46). It seems reasonable to infer that this tradition "refers to the first victory at the Dionysia as organized under the democracy, and as distinct from such contests as may have been arranged by the tyrants with the assistance of Lasos."[35] This is not to say that the stature of figures like Lasus did not survive the transition from the era of tyranny to that of democracy. In fact Lasus may well have been involved in the reformalization of the dithyramb in the era of democracy. Another such figure, compatible with both eras, is Simonides of Keos, rival of Lasus (Aristophanes *Wasps* 1410–1411), and a contemporary of Pindar.[36]

The Peloponnesian provenience of the dithyramb is made explicit in Herodotus 1.23, where the **kitharōidos** 'citharode' Arion of Methymna in Lesbos is credited with being the first to institute choral performances of the dithyramb in the city of Corinth during the reign of the tyrant Periandros (cf. *Suda* s.v. Arion).[37] In Solon (F 30a W) this same Arion is credited with introducing the first performance of tragedy in Athens, in contrast with the alternative tradition that credits Thespis (again *Parian Marble* FGH 239 A 43; *Suda* s.v. Thespis).[38] The Solonian version seems older in that Arion is represented as an introducer of tragedy, as if it were not yet differentiated from dithyramb. Thespis in contrast represents the differentiated form of tragedy.

The very name of *tragedy*, however, implies an earlier, undifferentiated phase of drama, compatible with the attested forms of tragedy, comedy, and satyr drama, all three. It appears that the form **tragōidoi** means 'goat singers' in the sense of 'singers who compete for the prize of a sacrificial goat'.[39] This meaning is not incompatible with the conventional theme of associating rustic folk with the wearing of goatskin, if we assume that the goatskin worn in performance of song represents the prize won in a continuum of earlier performances, each with its own sacrifice of goats. A key passage illustrating this theme of rustics wearing goatskin is Theognis 53–58, where a crisis within the polis is being described: values are being turned

---

35. Pickard-Cambridge 1962.15. On the tradition claiming Lasus of Hermione as the teacher of Pindar, see the *Vita* in Drachmann I, p. 4.12 and following (cf. Privitera 1965.60–61).

36. Cf. pp. 167, 172, and following, 193; also pp. 160, 161, 174, 189. On the tradition claiming Lasus of Hermione as the teacher of Pindar, see the *Vita* in Drachmann I, p. 4.12 and following (cf. Privitera 1965.60–61).

37. T. K. Hubbard draws my attention to the words of Pindar *Olympian* 13.18–19, referring to the Corinthian origins of the dithyramb and to its affinities with Dionysus.

38. Commentary on Solon F 30a W (= F 39 GP) by Gentili 1986.32–33; cf. Seaford 1984.13n38.

39. Burkert 1966.97–102, 115–121.

upside-down because the 'base' are now on the top of the social order while
the 'noble' are at the bottom, and all this because the 'base' population,
explicitly described as wearing goatskins (55), *moved inside the city from the
outside*, where they had lived previously, aware of neither 'justice' (**dikai**)
nor 'customary laws' (**nomoi**). This description is making an ethical point
about social degeneration,[40] but its central image corresponds to an aetiology
for an undifferentiated form of drama, functioning as a ritual inversion of
social values.[41] We may note that the chorus of satyrs in the *Cyclops*, a
satyr-drama of Euripides, are wearing goatskin (80).[42] The theme of formerly
excluded rustic outsiders is suggestive of a fundamental aetiology of comedy:
Aristotle pictures the primordial performers of comedy as wandering through
the **kōmai** 'countryside districts', deprived of rights and honor within the
polis (*Poetics* 1448a36–b1).[43] This aetiology accepts as a given that comedy,
in the present, is a thing of the polis.[44] In contrast the very concept of satyr is
a thing of the countryside (e.g., Horace *Ars Poetica* 236–247; *agrestes
satyros* at 221).[45]

The key transformation for the history of drama at Athens is the urbanization of the Feast of Dionysus by the tyrant Peisistratos, as we can observe
most clearly from the contrast between the Anthesteria, the oldest of the festivals of Dionysus at Athens (Thucydides 2.15.4 calls it the ἀρχαιότερα Διο-
νύσια 'older Dionysia'),[46] and the City Dionysia (Thucydides 5.20: Διο-
νύσια τὰ ἀστικά), which took shape under the rule of the Peisistratidai.[47]

40. Cf. N 1985.44 §29n4.

41. Cf. Figueira 1985.141. There will be more to say about ritual inversion when the discussion turns to the topic of carnival, p. 397.

42. Cf. Seaford 1984.118 for other such references.

43. We do not have to agree with Aristotle (ibid.) that such an etymological connection of
kōmōidiā to **kōmē** 'countryside district' is incompatible with another connection, to the word
kōmos 'group of revelers' and its derivatives. It appears that **kōmē** and **kōmos** are cognate:
Levine 1985.177 §2n1.

44. In the case of Athenian comedy, we may add, comedy articulates the authority of the
Demos, on which topic I cite the forthcoming work of J. Henderson.

45. Cf. Seaford 1984.32–33.

46. On the Anthesteria as the oldest Dionysiac festival, see Pickard- Cambridge 1968.1–25.

47. On the City Dionysia and the Peisistratidai, see Pickard-Cambridge p. 58. Seaford,
p. 31n81, observes: "The urbanization, probably of a preexisting celebration, may have consisted
partly in the transference of emergent drama to the city-centre." We may recall the dictum of
Aristotle *Politics* 1319b that the way to achieve democracy is to centralize the cults. Such a policy was already being practiced by the tyrants. In this connection, we should note that the democratic restructuring that resulted in the **dēmoi** 'demes' of Attica presupposes the existence of the
polis of Athens. This fact about the demes affects the very concept of "Rural Dionysia," a transitional stage of development between the Anthesteria and the City Dionysia: these "Rural
Dionysia," as celebrated in the demes of Attica, were "closer to the earth than the great festivals
of the city, and may have retained their religious content in greater strength and longer," but they
are already a thing of the polis, in that they are extensions of the demes and "mimic the city"
(Pickard-Cambridge, p. 51).

Whereas satyrs were apparently a traditional feature of the Anthesteria,[48] the satyric element was reduced to a subordinated attachment of tragedy in the City Dionysia.

A central point, then, can be made about all the dramatic competitions originating in the context of the City Dionysia: the differentiations into the distinct forms of tragedy, comedy, dithyramb, and satyric drama must have started in the era of the tyrants, the Peisistratidai, who played a major role in the shaping of the City Dionysia.[49] The dynasty of the Peisistratidai also played a major role in the shaping of the Panathenaia, the context for perfor-mance of epic (scholia to Aristides *Panathenaicus* 3.123; "Plato" *Hipparchus* 228b).[50] The close association of the Peisistratidai of Athens with the City Dionysia, context for performance of drama, and with the Panathenaia, con-text for performance of epic, is analogous to the association of the tyrant Kleisthenes of Sikyon with innovations in the performance of both epic (Herodotus 5.67.1)[51] and drama (5.67.5).[52] In sum, I stress the role of the tyrants in the shaping of urbanized festivals of Panhellenic repute, which pro-vided the actual context for the differentiation of major poetic genres, attract-ing masters of song from all over the Hellenic world. Moreover, even after the democracy replaced the tyrants in Athens, the leading citizens of the democracy, aristocrats that they were, continued to play a major role in the shaping of the dramatic festivals: thus, for example, the man who financed in 472 B.C. the production of a dramatic trilogy of Aeschylus that included the *Persians*, celebrating the great naval victory at Salamis in 480 B.C., was none other than Pericles of Athens,[53] serving in the official capacity of **khorēgos** 'chorus leader' (IG II² 2318 i.4).[54] We may note in this connection the report that Hieron, Tyrant of Syracuse, commissioned Aeschylus to train a chorus for a reperformance of the *Persians* when Aeschylus was summoned to his realm in Sicily (*Life of Aeschylus*, p. 333.24–25).[55]

This survey of the Athenian heritage in song making, as shaped by the City Dionysia, can serve as a foundation for the task at hand, which is to define Athenian notions of the Classical forms of song and to correlate these notions with the survival of Pindaric song. It is best to start with a recon-sideration of the fundamental nature of Pindar's song-making tradition, and

48. Seaford, pp. 7–9, 30, 39–40, 96–97.

49. Cf. p. 390.

50. Cf. Herington 1985.85–86. For more on the Panathenaia, see pp. 21 and following.

51. Cf. p. 22.

52. Cf. p. 43.

53. More on Pericles at pp. 157, 308, and following, p. 310.

54. Pickard-Cambridge 1968.104; see p. 90 on parallelisms in the relationship of Pericles and Aeschylus, Themistokles and Phrynichus. On the Classical Athenian usage of the word **khorēgos** 'chorus leader' to designate a contemporary nonperformer, who organizes and subsi-dizes both the composition and the performance, see p. 378.

55. In the Aeschylus edition of Page 1972.

how it may be related to the form of drama at a stage preceding the differentiations that took place in the context of the City Dionysia. An ideal point of comparison is Archilochus, who represents an undifferentiated tradition that is not only cognate with the differentiated and more specialized tradition of Pindar but also parallels in some striking ways the undifferentiated stages of Athenian drama.

We may begin to explore the undifferentiated nature of Archilochean tradition by considering two instances of fable telling in the poetry of Archilochus, where the fable refers to itself as **ainos** (F 174 and 185 W). This same word is used in the epinician lyric poetry of Pindar and Bacchylides in referring to the function of this medium.[56] What then does fable telling have in common with epinician lyric poetry? We find a clue in the fables of Aesop, as dramatized in the *Life of Aesop* tradition. The *Life* represents various contexts in which the fables of Aesop, traditionally recognized as **ainoi**, are being told to various audiences. In these contexts we see that the social function of the Aesopic **ainos** is either praise or blame.[57]

Thus one form, the **ainos**, has two potential social functions, praise or blame, as attested in the praise of epinician and the blame of Archilochean poetics. These two functions of praise and blame are an inherited feature of Archaic Greek poetry and song, as we see from the evidence collected by Marcel Detienne.[58] Among other sources Detienne cites Plutarch's *Lycurgus* (8.2, 21.1, 25.2; also 14.3, 26.3), where the essence of social regulation in Sparta is described as a matter of counterbalancing praise and blame, primarily through poetry and song. There is much to be said about the way in which these functions of praise and blame are described by poetry or song in general.[59] Also we have seen that there is a heritage of *one form* for both.[60] Perhaps the clearest testimony about the two-sidedness of the **ainos** is in Homeric poetry. The poet is represented as respectively praising and blaming what is right and wrong; in this capacity he is the watchdog of ritual and ethical correctness, as we see in the example of the poet whom Agamemnon had left behind to watch over Clytemnestra (*Odyssey* iii 267–271).[61]

---

56. Cf. p. 147.
57. N 1979.279–316.
58. Detienne 1973.18–27; cf. Dumézil 1969.103–124.
59. N 1979.222–242.
60. Cf. p. 149.
61. Cf. N 1979.37–38 §13n5: when Aigisthos persuades Clytemnestra to commit adultery and thus betray Agamemnon, he takes the poet to a deserted island (iii 270–271) so that the poet may not *see* the adultery; still the shameful behavior of Clytemnestra is *heard* by the audience of epic since the poet of epic does not depend on *seeing* (N, p. 16). The blind **kleos** of epic *hears* what the poet of **ainos** needs to *see*. On the metaphor of *seeing* in the songs of Stesichorus, in line with the ideology of the applied **ainos** as distinct from the generalized epic, see pp. 419 and following, especially p. 422.

But Pindaric song, and Archilochean poetry as represented by Pindar's tradition, reveal specialization. Pindaric song tends to praise more than blame.[62] Archilochus in contrast has at first blush the reputation of blaming only. This is the impression that we get from, say, the **ainos** in Archilochus F 174 W: this fable about the fox and the eagle is apparently being narrated *within* a poem of blame against Lykambes.[63] Our impression is reinforced by Horace: Archilochus is seen one-sidedly as a composer of diatribes against the family of Lykambes (e.g., *Epodes* 6.11–13; *Epistles* 1.19.23–25, 28–31). There is further reinforcement from one of the two direct references to Archilochus in Pindar *Pythian* 2.52–56, where Archilochus is described as the exponent of blame and therefore the enemy of praise.[64]

Yet, in the other Pindaric passage, *Olympian* 9.1–5, Archilochus is presented not only as a poet of praise but even as the primordial poet of praise.[65] He is being represented as a protopoet of epinician lyric poetry, as if he were some primitive forerunner of Pindar himself. Moreover, as a proto-laudator of the Olympics, Archilochus has as his proto-laudandus none other than a hero who figures as a founder of the Olympics, Herakles (the testimonia are collected in Archilochus F 324 W; the clearest account is in the scholia to Aristophanes *Birds* 1762).[66]

The tradition behind *Olympian* 9.1–4 stresses that Archilochus has no musical instrument (again I refer to the testimonia collected in Archilochus F 324 W, especially the scholia to Aristophanes *Birds* 1762). By implication then this primordial mode of epinician composition is not *lyric* in the strict sense. Such a characterization corresponds to the formal status of Archilochus' poetry, which is composed in meters that are asynartetic, that is, roughly half-way between strophic and stichic.[67]

---

62. In Simonides we may still see earlier and less specialized stages of epinician etiquette: in PMG 507.1 (cf. Aristophanes *Clouds* 1355–1356), for example, the name of the athlete **Krios**, which means literally 'Ram', is turned into a joke in that his defeat in a wrestling contest is described as a 'fleecing' (ἐπέξαθ').

63. Cf. West 1971.62. I cite the wording of Philostratus *Imagines* 3 (II, p. 298 Kayser): φοιτῶσιν οἱ μῦθοι παρὰ τὸν Αἴσωπον, ἀγαπῶντες αὐτὸν ὅτι αὐτῶν ἐπιμελεῖται. ἐμέλησε μὲν γὰρ καὶ Ὁμήρῳ μύθου καὶ Ἡσιόδῳ, ἔτι δὲ καὶ Ἀρχιλόχῳ πρὸς Λυκάμβην 'myths [**mûthoi**] are attracted to Aesop, loving him because he practices the art [of myth]; myth was also the practice of Homer and Hesiod; and even of Archilochus, in the context of his addressing Lykambes'.

64. Further discussion in N 1979.224–225.

65. There is an analogue on the level of metrics: the epinician lyric poetry of Pindar is *either* "Doric" (dactylo-epitrite) *or* Aeolic, whereas the hexameter of epic is both. So also on the level of function: Pindar must *either* praise *or* blame, whereas epic does both.

66. Cf. Miller 1981.140n21; also Simpson 1969.119, who argues that the Herakles myth was part of the καλλίνικος ὕμνος 'victory song' of Archilochus, which the voice of Pindar represents as having been sung spontaneously by the friends of the victor immediately after the victory that is now being praised again by Pindar in *Olympian* 9.1–4.

67. On the terms *synartetic* and *asynartetic*, see pp. 48 and following.

To be more precise about the metrical form of Archilochean poetry: Bruno Snell, in the metrical appendix to his edition of Pindar, offers the view that asynartetic meters of Archilochus are a metrical prototype of one of the two major metrical systems, which are both synartetic, used by Pindar (and Bacchylides), namely, the so-called dactylo-epitrite meters.[68] According to this view the nonlyric asynartetic meters that characterize Archilochus developed into lyric synartetic meters that characterize, say, Pindar. We have, however, already had reason to formulate the progression differently: the nonlyric asynartetic meters are in fact derived from the lyric asynartetic, while there is another line of progression from lyric asynartetic to lyric synartetic.[69]

Still we must account for the fact that Archilochean poetry refers to itself as a lyric medium: the persona of Archilochus describes himself as capable of being an **exarkhōn** 'choral leader' (F 120 and 121 W), that is, the leader of a chorus, a group of singers/dancers; in this description, he is accompanied by the **aulos** (F 121 W). Such self-reference seems to be an example of what I have called *diachronic skewing*, that is, where the medium refers to itself in terms of earlier stages of its own existence.[70] As I have argued, the medium of Archilochus was originally undifferentiated lyric, that is, sung and danced, and it developed eventually into differentiated nonlyric recitative in a complex and lengthy process of Panhellenization.[71] It appears that Pindar's medium, which remains lyric all along, takes note of the *eventual* nonlyric medium of Archilochus aetiologically, by implying a nonlyric *origin* for epinician (*Olympian* 9.1–5).[72]

More pertinent and important for us at this point, Pindar's medium also takes note of an aspect of the original function of Archilochean poetry that seems to have eluded Aristotle: the poetic tradition of Archilochus is suitable for epinician praise. Pindar's *Olympian* 9 is asserting that Archilochus is a protopoet of praise. We see here what amounts to the other side of the coin, matching the testimony of Aristotle *Poetics* 1449a and 1448b23, who evidently considered Archilochus exclusively as a protopoet of blame.

In the *Poetics* 1449a9ff, Aristotle says that both tragedy and comedy had a beginning that is **autoskhediastikē** 'improvisational' (ἀπ' ἀρχῆς αὐτοσχε-διαστικῆς),[73] and that tragedy was derived from the **exarkhontes** 'choral

68. SM vol. 2., p. 162.

69. Cf. pp. 48 and following.

70. Cf. p. 21. The use of οἶδα 'I know how' at Archilochus F 120.2 W suggests a potential situation for performance, not actual performance. Cf. West 1974.131 on the possibility that Archilochus F 120 is a continuation of F 118.

71. Cf. pp. 20, 25, 26, 27, 363. The transition from sung to recited may be a reflex of the transition from an earlier stage where each performance entails recomposition to a later stage where such recomposition no longer takes place. Cf. p. 54.

72. Again the sequence of myth reverses the sequence of diachrony: cf. p. 101.

73. Cf. Else 1957.149.

leaders' of the **dithurambos** 'dithyramb' (ἀπὸ τῶν ἐξαρχόντων τὸν διθύ-ραμβον).[74] Aristotle may have had Archilochus' passage in mind.[75] In Archilochus F 120 W, the persona of the composer declares that he knows how to be the **exarkhōn** 'choral leader' of the dithyramb, while his mind is thunder-struck with wine.[76] Else remarks: "Archilochus' impromptu, drunken dithyramb is closer than any other dithyramb we know of to being **autoskhediastikē** [improvisational]."[77] Else notes that Archilochus' meter in F 120 W is indeed trochaic tetrameter catalectic.[78] According to Aristotle the meter of dialogue in early tragedy, before it was replaced by iambic trimeter, was trochaic tetrameter catalectic (*Poetics* 1449a22ff). In short what Aristotle says about the evolution of comedy and tragedy implies that he thought that Archilochus was a typical **exarkhōn** of dithyramb, which he understood as characterized by trochaic tetrameter catalectic, typical of both comedy and tragedy.

What Aristotle might not have seen is that the "blaming" side of Archilochus was part of this poet's overall function as a socially redeeming exponent of **ainos**, one who blames what is ostensibly bad while he praises what is good. This socially redeeming function is a traditional civic function, viewed as integrating the community.

From the testimony of the Mnesiepes Inscription (Archilochus T 4 Tarditi),[79] we learn of a traditional myth, native to the island of Paros, that represented Archilochus as a chorus teacher of his community (T4 III 16–57). I propose to consider in some detail how this myth, preserved in the context of the poet's hero cult in Paros, dramatizes the social function of Archilochean poetry in the civic life of the polis.

In the wording of the Mnesiepes Inscription, it can be argued, we are witnessing a cognate of the source of Aristotle *Poetics* 1449a and 1448b23, who considered Archilochus an exponent of primitive blame poetry. Let us examine the pertinent passage from the Mnesiepes Inscription, Archilochus T4 III 16–57 Tarditi.[80] The story has it that Archilochus improvises ([αὐ-το]| σχεδιασ[19–20) a composition, which he teaches (διδάξαντα 22) to some of the citizens of Paros.[81] From the standpoint of the narrative, Archi-

74. Cf. Else, pp. 155 and following.

75. Else, pp. 157–158.

76. Cf. N 1979.252

77. Else, p. 158.

78. Ibid. Cf. pp. 20, 39.

79. For more on the Mnesiepes Inscription, a prime document of the *Life of Archilochus* tradition, see p. 363.

80. The full text is not given in Archilochus F 251 W; but see West 1974.25.

81. The text is too fragmentary for me to be certain, but the expressions παραδεδομ[ένα 'transmitted' at line 23 and κεκοσμημέ] 'arranged [derivative of **kosmos**]' at 24 suggest that a contrast is being made between the "impromptu" effusions of the protopoet and the "deliberate" arrangements of those charged with the transmission of the poetry. Note too the context of

lochus seems to be represented here as a "chorus teacher."[82] The Mnesiepes Inscription then proceeds to quote the words of the composition (F 251 W = 219 Tarditi): the text is fragmentary, but we can see clearly that Dionysus figures prominently (251.1), in the context of the epithet **Oipholios** (251.5), a derivative of the obscene verb **oiphō** 'have intercourse [male subject]'. The **polis** finds this composition 'too iambic' (ἰαμβικώτερο[Mnesiepes Inscription T4 III 38).[83] Archilochus is put on trial (ἐν τεῖ κρίσει T4 III 42) and apparently condemned. But then the polis is afflicted with a plague that affects the genitalia (42–44). Emissaries of the polis consult Delphi (45–46), and the Oracle tells them that the plague will not abate until the polis honors Archilochus (47–50). The connection here of Archilochus with Dionysus and the notion of **Oipholios** institutionalizes the 'iambic' composition of Archilochus. I should stress the explicit testimony of the Mnesiepes Inscription concerning the practice of worshipping various gods, along with the cult hero Archilochus, in the sacred precinct of Archilochus, the **Arkhilokheion** (T 4 II 14–19 Tarditi): among the gods listed (1–13), Dionysus is accorded a position of particular prominence (10).

The narrative pattern of the story of Archilochus and the punishment of the Parians is typical of aetiologies concerning the founding of a hero cult: (1) some hero is dishonored, sometimes even killed, by a community; (2) the community is then beset by some plague; and (3) the Oracle is consulted and prescribes the hero cult of the given hero as the remedy.[84] In such aetiologies the well-being of the community, as threatened by the plague, is visualized as fertility of crops and inhabitants alike — a fertility that is then restored and guaranteed to continue through the proper maintenance of the hero cult.[85] In the Archilochus story as well, the fertility of the polis is connected in general with the hero cult of Archilochus, which is after all the context for the telling of the story, and in particular with the institutionalization of Archilochus as

---

μιμνησκομ['remember' at line 52, which seems to be pertinent to the concept of **Mnēsiepēs** 'he who remembers the words [as in **epos** 'word']' as discussed at p. 363.

82. Cf. West 1974.25.

83. On the notion of *iambic*, I cite the succinct formulation of West 1974.22 (following Aristotle *Poetics* 1448b31): "iambic metre got its name from being particularly characteristic of ἴαμβοι [iamboi], not vice versa." I have explored the conventions of the 'iambic' tradition in N 1979.243–252, where I record my indebtedness to the observation of Dover 1964.189 that the word **iambos** refers basically to the type of occasion for which this form was appropriate. On the choral connotations of the word **iambos**, revealing a stage when the iambic form could be danced, see N 1979.242–243.

84. Cf. N 1979.285, with the focus on the aetiology for the hero cult of Aesop. For a collection of such narrative patterns, see Fontenrose 1968.73–79. The hero, at the time that he is being dishonored, may be represented by the narrative as either still alive (e.g., Oibotas of Dyme, Pausanias 7.17.13–14) or already dead (e.g., Theogenes of Thasos, Pausanias 6.11.6–8). If he is still alive, the dishonoring may lead directly to his death, as in the story of Aesop.

85. Fertility of crops: e.g., Pausanias 6.11.6–8; fertility of humans: e.g., Pausanias 2.3.6–7.

'chorus teacher'. Here we have the nucleus of the civic function of Archilochean poetry in that the chorus is the traditional medium for the self-expression of the polis.[86]

The theme of fertility is explicit in the story of Archilochus in his stylized role as chorus teacher, which is connected with the cult of Dionysus (cf. T 4 II 10 Tarditi and F 251 W; also F 120 W). The same theme of fertility is implicit in the connection of Archilochus with the cult of Demeter, in his stylized role as a participant in the **panēguris** 'festival' of the goddess and her daughter, **Korē** (F 322 W).[87] The given festival is that of the **Iobakkhoi**; the name expresses the complementarity, in terms of the festival, of Demeter with Bacchus, that is, Dionysus (Hephaestion *Encheiridion* 15.16).[88] Moreover, the fertility of the polis is connected with the 'iambic' nature of what Archilochus teaches to the community (again Archilochus T 4 II 38 Tarditi).[89] We are reminded that the notion of *iambic* is associated with the cults of both Dionysus and Demeter.[90] Moreover, according to Aristotle *Poetics* 1449b8, the notion of *iambic* is inherited by the synthetic genre of Athenian comedy.

The 'iambic' nature of comedy, and Aristotle's claims about the evolution of tragedy from the medium of **exarkhontes** 'chorus leaders' ostensibly like Archilochus, whose message was too 'iambic' for the people of his own time, reinforce the general notion that comedy and tragedy were once undifferentiated, becoming distinct in the specific context of the City Dionysia. Which brings us to the **aition** that motivates the City Dionysia, closely parallel to the **aition** that motivates Archilochean poetry. According to Athenian tradition the Feast of the City Dionysia was instituted in honor of Dionysus Eleuthereus, whose image had been brought over from Eleutherai in Boeotia to the theater precinct of Athens; there the god was not given his due honors, and the men of Athens were accordingly punished with some sexual affliction, from which they were freed only on the condition that they make ritual **phalloi** for Dionysus (scholia to Aristophanes *Acharnians* 243). Just as the Archilochean 'iambic' tradition participates in a symbiotic relationship with a cult of Dionysus, so does the undifferentiated tradition represented by the entire complex of dramatic contests at the City Dionysia.

This notion of *iambic*, with its emphasis on fertility, is analogous to the concept of *carnival* as applied by M. M. Bakhtin to the traditions inherited by

86. Cf. pp. 142, 144; also pp. 363 and following.

87. On the authenticity of Archilochus F 322 W, I agree with Miralles and Pòrtulas 1983.113 (*pace* West 1974.24). In the Mnesiepes Inscription (T 4 Tarditi), I note the apparent reference to vegetal fertility (καρπῶν II 40) in the general context of human fertility in the story of the punishment of the Parians (II 42–46).

88. See again Archilochus F 322 W.

89. For more on the notion of *iambic*, see N 1979.243.

90. See West 1974.23–25; also Richardson 1974.213–217, especially with reference to the passage about **Iambē** in *Hymn to Demeter* 192–205.

François Rabelais in the sixteenth century.[91] For Bakhtin, *carnival* is a synthetic description that accommodates a wide range of actually attested European carnivals celebrated on a seasonally recurring basis at various times of the year at various places. The synthetic description is particularly apt in view of the synthetic nature of carnivals: "This word combined in a single concept a number of local feasts of different origin and scheduled at different dates but bearing the common traits of popular merriment."[92] It is not inaccurate to say that the very concept of carnival is a synthesis: "These celebrations became a reservoir into which obsolete genres were emptied."[93] For Bakhtin, carnival is not a safety valve that helps prevent revolution, as was held to be political dogma at the time that his work on Rabelais was taking shape; rather carnival is revolution itself.[94] Its target is whatever happens to be current, the here and now, the differentiated, and it professes nostalgia for the past, the Golden Age, the undifferentiated. The very themes of carnival recapitulate the undifferentiated structures of the past and temporarily overthrow the differentiated structures of the present.[95] The feast of Saturnalia yearns for the ancien régime of Saturn and resists *whatever* régime is current.[96] Bakhtin argues that carnival attacks the differentiated present by

91. Bakhtin [1984b]. Cf. Rösler 1986. In the generations that followed the time of Rabelais, that is, in the preclassic times of the seventeenth century in the period preceding the reign of Louis XIV, "Rabelais did not as yet appear exceptional" (Bakhtin, p. 107). Soon thereafter, however, "the atmosphere in which Rabelais was understood vanished almost entirely, and he became a strange and solitary author who needed special interpretation and commentary" (ibid.). To an author like La Bruyère, writing in 1690, Rabelais is to be condemned for his crude obscenity and vulgarity, though he is to be praised for his exquisite genius and originality in the use of language; Bakhtin comments that La Bruyère sees the work of Rabelais as "two-faced" because "he has lost the key that could have locked together its two heterogeneous aspects" (p. 108). That key, in Bakhtin's terms, is carnival. Without insisting on the term, which lends itself to overextended use, I see here a striking analogy with the figure of Archilochus. Else's reference to Archilochus F 120 W as "Archilochus' impromptu, drunken dithyramb" (Else 1957.158) reminds me of the discussion by Bakhtin, pp. 265–266 of the expression "faire courir les personnages des diables," in a document from Amiens dated 1500, referring to the custom of letting characters who are chosen to represent the devils in a passion play *run loose*.

92. Bakhtin, p. 218.

93. Ibid.

94. On the political and ideological orthodoxies that were prevalent at the time that Bakhtin was formulating his vision of the carnival element in Rabelais, see Holquist in Bakhtin [1984b] xviii. We should note that in the sixteenth century, the time of Rabelais, "folk merriment had not as yet been concentrated in carnival season, in any of the towns of France" (p. 220). In other words the synthesis under the institutional heading of *carnival* had not yet reached the stage corresponding to Bakhtin's broadened sense of carnival. Later, when "the carnival [. . .] became the center of all popular forms of amusement, it diminished all the other feasts and deprived them of almost every free and utopian folk element" (Bakhtin, p. 220). "The other feasts faded away; their popular character was reduced, especially because of their connection with ecclesiastic or political rituals" (ibid.).

95. Cf. Bakhtin, pp. 334–336.

96. On the carnival as heir to the Roman Saturnalia, see Bakhtin, pp. 8, 81. On the tradition of nostalgia for the Golden Age, as implicit in the Saturnalia, see his p. 48. I should add that the

recapitulating the undifferentiated past, with an emphasis on the grotesque, and thus celebrating the renewal of fertility.[97] To this extent I find the notion of *carnival* useful for the present purposes. Carnival, however, cannot be viewed as independent of the society that frames it. It is not apolitical but just the opposite: a highly political and politicized celebration of the community as a whole. With this proviso in mind, we may return to the subject of the iambic tradition: like the carnival, it attacks whatever happens to be current, the here and now, while all along celebrating the theme of fertility.

The theme of fertility in the story of Archilochus and the punishment of the Parians is pertinent to the implicit relationship between him and Hera. To make this point, I begin with the so-called Cologne Epode of Archilochus (F 196A W), where boy meets girl and boy seduces girl in a beautiful setting, a *locus amoenus*. There are suggestive points of comparison to be found in the Provençal genre of the *pastorela* and its Old French equivalent, the *pastourelle*.[98] In connection with the typical setting of the *pastourelle*, that is, a *locus amoenus* of a garden or of the countryside, I draw attention to scraps of evidence, some dating to as early as the eighth century A.D., for countryside rituals that dramatize themes that are analogous to some of the central themes found in the pastourelle, in the form of dances miming chthonic powers of fertility.[99] I would compare the *locus amoenus* of the Cologne Epode of Archilochus: the setting for the seduction described in this composition is a garden that happens to be a sacred precinct of Hera (Dioscorides *Palatine Anthology* 7.351),[100] who is the goddess of seasonality, equilibrium, and completion in both nature and society (puberty, marriage, and so on).[101] Yet the Epode is preoccupied with the themes of unseasonality, disequilibrium, and incompleteness. For example, one girl is presented as sexually unripe, and the other, as overripe; also the sex act, with the unripe girl as participant,

---

Greek analogue of the Saturnalia, the feast of Kronos, exhibits a similar tradition of nostalgia for the Golden Age: cf. Rösler 1986.36. The theme of Saturnalian nostalgia is also reflected in the *Works and Days* of Hesiod: cf. N 1979.168–172.

97. I use the term *grotesque* in the sense outlined by Bakhtin, pp. 30–58, especially 31–32. On the correlation of the grotesque with the notion of fertility, I cite in particular his following observation on the traditional imagery of the grotesque: it is a "system [. . .] in which death is not a negation of life seen as the great body of all the people but part of life as a whole — its indispensable component, the condition of its constant renewal and rejuvenation" (p. 50; cf. also pp. 326–328, 405). This thought pattern, which Bakhtin sums up in the formula "death is included in life" (p. 50), amounts to a system of opposition between life and death where life is the unmarked and inclusive member (on the terms *marked* and *unmarked*, see p. 5). In Bakhtin's scheme this opposition is a sign of fertility: "Even the struggle of life and death in the individual body is conceived by grotesque imagery as the struggle of the old life stubbornly resisting the new life about to be born, as the *crisis* of change" (p. 50; emphasis mine).

98. See Miralles and Pòrtulas 1983.135–157, especially p. 135n15.

99. See Zink 1972.93, 102.

100. Commentary by Miralles and Pòrtulas, p. 136 and nn16, 17.

101. Cf. Pötscher 1961; also N 1979.303.

is itself incomplete. I suggest that the unseasonality dramatized within the precinct of Hera serves to define the seasonality that is encompassed by the potency of Hera, just as the unseasonality of the hero Herakles, caused by Hera, serves to define the goddess's power of seasonality: the disequilibrium of the hero leads to his famed Labors, earning him the name **Hēra-kleēs** 'he who has the glory [**kleos**] of Hera'.[102] Thus a sacred framework, the precinct of Hera, encompasses the deviant behavior within the narrative; likewise there is a proper ideology, presumably integrated into rituals sacred to Hera, that encompasses the improper self-characterization of Archilochus. In this connection I draw attention to certain similarities between Archilochus and what folklorists describe as trickster figures:[103] within the narrative the trickster consistently deviates from the norms of society, but outside the narrative and within the society that serves as context for the narrative, the trickster figure's pattern of deviation from social norms reaffirms the pattern of these norms.[104]

In the case of Archilochus, the 'iambic' function is manifested in his dramatized alienation from his own here and now. This fact of alienation can be accepted as part of the undifferentiated past by the community that embraces Archilochus as the present guarantor of its fertility. In the case of comedy, especially the Old Comedy of Aristophanes, there is an analogous stance of dramatized alienation from everything that happens to be current. That includes the conventions in the craft of poetry and song as it was current in the time of Aristophanes.

The criticism of current poetry and song in Aristophanes operates on a solid foundation: a thorough education in the Classics of poetry is presupposed, as we can see from the parodic references to such canonical masters as Alcman (*Lysistrata* 1248–1320), Stesichorus (*Peace* 796–816), and Anacreon (*Birds* 1373–1374).[105] But the critical area for criticizing what is current in terms of the Classical is the theater itself, the medium par excellence for the composition and performance of poetry and song in the time of Aristophanes. The theater, as it developed within the City Dionysia, had absorbed the repertoire of epic, as we can readily see from such individual tragedies as the *Seven against Thebes* of Aeschylus and more generally from the overwhelmingly epic themes of most of the tragedies composed by Aeschylus and other early dramatists who followed in his wake.[106] As with epic, so also with lyric: the evolving predominance of Athenian theater as the primary poetic medium played a major role in the obsolescence of lyric poetry in other media and, by extension, in other genres. We have already had

---

102. Cf. again N 1979.303.
103. Cf. Miralles and Pòrtulas, pp. 11–50.
104. See Radin 1956.
105. Cf. Herington 1985.254n9, with special reference to Fraenkel 1962 ch. 10.
106. Cf. Herington 1985.138–144.

occasion to note the complaints about **theatrokratiā** in Plato's writings (*Laws* 701a) and about the intoxication of pleasure in the poetry of theater (700d), leading to 'transgressions' of genre (700e).[107] To be contrasted are the good old days, as in the earlier era that followed the Persian Wars (*Laws* 698b), when there were still distinct genres (700a), five of which are specified as examples: **humnos** 'hymn', **thrēnos** 'lament', **paiān** 'paean', **dithurambos** 'dithyramb', and **kitharōidikos nomos** 'citharodic nome' (700b).[108] These genres, as well as other genres left unspecified (ibid.), are the structurally distinct aspects of lyric poetry, parallel to the structurally distinct aspects of **aristokratiā** in Plato's good old Athenian society (701a). In contrast, as we have seen, the progressive leveling by Athenian theater of generic distinctions in lyric poetry is for Plato parallel to the leveling by Athenian democracy of class distinctions in society.[109] Precisely such generic distinctions characterize the lyric poetry of Pindar, composer of such genres as the **humnos**, the **thrēnos**, the **paiān**, the **dithurambos**, and so on.[110]

Given that the Theater of Dionysus at Athens is the predominant context of poetry as current poetry, it follows that contemporary comedy singles out the current poetics of the theater as the main target of its criticism of poetry. Specifically the current comedy of theater attacks the poetics of current tragedy. One of the clearest examples is the great **agōn** 'contest' between Aeschylus and Euripides in Hades, as dramatized by Aristophanes in the *Frogs* (905–1098).[111] That tragedy is the **tekhnē** 'craft' of poetry par excellence — and this concept recurs frequently —[112] is the one given that is held in respect by both sides in the contest.[113] What is at issue is the superiority or inferiority of the old and current ways of practicing that craft, as represented by Aeschylus and Euripides respectively:

> The two great professionals are made to discuss the correct proportion of song to dialogue, and the character of that dialogue (905–91); then the moral impact of tragedy and poetry (1003–98: the two arts are not distinguished, at least by Aeschylus, who invokes the precedents of Homer, Hesiod, and other early epic composers); iambic prologues, together with the questions of clarity in diction (1119–99) and of the avoidance of metrical/syntactical monotony (1200–1247); choral lyric technique (1248–1329); solo lyric technique (1329–64); and weight of diction (1365–1414).[114]

107. Cf. p. 108.
108. Cf. p. 87.
109. Cf. p. 108.
110. Cf. p. 111.
111. The word **agōn** is actually used in self-references at *Frogs* 785, 867, 873, 882.
112. Aristophanes *Frogs* 93, 766, 770, 780, 786, 793, 811, 831, 850, 939, 961, 973, 1369, 1495.
113. Herington 1985.106.
114. Ibid.

The old-fashioned Aeschylus wins over the innovative Euripides in the judgment of the god Dionysus himself (1467 and following), who is after all the
raison d'être of the City Dionysia.

In short the fundamental reason for the loss of Euripides to Aeschylus in
the *Frogs*, and in general for his being singled out as a special target for the
comedy of Aristophanes, is that his poetics are *current*. The definitive statement on what is current in the poetics of tragedy is treated as a foil by the
poetics of comedy. Thus Euripides cannot even be a runner-up to Aeschylus:
that honor is reserved for Sophocles (Aristophanes *Frogs* 787–794,
1515–1519). That it is Aeschylus who wins the contest in the *Frogs*, thus
winning the chance to be brought back to the contemporary world of the living by the god of theater himself, is the wish fulfillment of a nostalgia for the
undifferentiated Dionysiac essence of Drama.

The contest of Aeschylus and Euripides in *Frogs* 905–1098 takes the
form of an **agōn**, and this word is actually used in self-references at lines
785, 867, 873, 882. The very format of the **agōn** is indicative of an undifferentiated phase of drama as it must have existed before the differentiation
of the City Dionysia. It has been argued that the functional part of comedy
known as the **agōn** resulted from an undifferentiated choral **agōn** consisting
of two antagonistic **antikhoria**, "each combining the aggressive entrance of
the parodos with the primitive features of the parabasis: self-presentation and
self-praise, invocation and invective, 'literary' polemics."[115] Ironically, however, the very notion of **agōn** as 'contest' is the basis for the ongoing differentiation of poetics in the theater. The **agōn** of a poetic contest requires a
judgment, the word for which is **krisis**, and the two words actually occur
together at *Frogs* 785 (**krisis** and its verb **krīnō** also at 779, 805, 873, 1467,
1473).

At an earlier stage we had observed that the Alexandrian concept of
krisis, in the sense of *separating, discriminating, judging* (verb **krīnō**) those
works and those authors that are to be preserved and those that are not, is crucial to the concept of *canon* in the Classical world.[116] The Alexandrian scholars who were in charge of this process of separation, discrimination, judgment, were the **kritikoi** 'critics', while the Classical authors who were meant
to survive the **krisis** were called the **enkrithentes**.[117] We also observed that
the **krisis** of the **enkrithentes** starts not with the Alexandrian scholars, nor
even with the likes of Aristotle: the *crisis* of this **krisis** is already under way
in the Archaic and Classical periods of Greece, where songs and poetry were
traditionally performed in a context of competition. The premier example of

---

115. Seaford 1977–1978.86. Again we may compare the Aeginetan example of choruses subdivided into rival halves, as discussed at pp. 365 and following.

116. Cf. p. 61.

117. Ibid.

such competition is the tradition of dramatic festivals at Athens, with the krisis 'judgment' of winners by kritai 'judges'.[118] What we see in the agōn of the *Frogs* of Aristophanes is a dramatization of that competition between drama and drama, and this time the competition is happening *within* drama. This way the ontogeny of drama is recapitulating its own phylogeny as a competitive medium, an agōn calling for the krisis of selection.

The craft of theater is one of continual crisis, of innovation. Even the older features of the craft, perceived by Comedy as old-fashioned, reveal earlier stages of poetic innovation in the theater. The stage-Aeschylus may be ridiculed by the stage-Euripides for his old-fashioned and monotonous lyric rhythms, as parodied by the lyre-strumming onomatopoeia tophlattothrat tophlattothrat (*Frogs* 1286, 1288, 1290, 1292, 1294), and yet the form of these rhythms, from an earlier perspective, represents an innovative appropriation, by the poetics of theater, of the distinct genre of the kitharōidikos nomos 'citharodic nome'. The stage-Euripides says that these old-fashioned Aeschylean rhythms are taken from kitharōidikoi nomoi 'citharodic nomes' (*Frogs* 1282). It is precisely the appropriation and hence domination of such genres by the poetics of theater that led Plato to condemn the poetic innovations of the theater as a degeneration of genres: for Plato, the usurpation of the kitharōidikos nomos (*Laws* 700b) by theater is an example of theatrokratiā (701a). Thus the Aeschylean use of the kitharōidikos nomos may be old-fashioned synchronically, but it is an innovation diachronically. It represents an earlier stage of the same sort of innovations practiced by Euripides, who is accused by the stage-Aeschylus of freely appropriating to drama such nondramatic forms as skolia and thrēnoi (*Frogs* 1301–1303). Such theatrokratiā, it seems, goes back to the early days of the City Dionysia, and there is no reason not to take it all the way back to the era of the Peisistratidai, tyrants of Athens. In sum the Theater of Dionysus at Athens, with its theatrocracy of genres, has been appropriating and assimilating, ever since its inception, the traditions of song making that we can still see as independent and unassimilated forms in the repertoire of a figure like Pindar.

Ironically this innovative process of appropriation and assimilation induces a sense of nostalgia, as articulated by Old Comedy, for the older phases of song making. In Aristophanes' *Wasps*, for example, the old Philokleon is described as spending all night singing and dancing the choral parts of old-fashioned tragedies that Thespis himself had once upon a time composed when he had entered the competition or agōn (ἠγωνίζετο 1479). Turning time upside down, the old man claims that his choral singing and dancing can make contemporary tragōidoi 'players of tragedy' seem old-fashioned by comparison, as if the modern were ancient, and the ancient,

118. For the wording, see again the description in Plato *Laws* 659ab.

modern (1480); in this context the notion of *old-fashioned* is described as **kronoi**, that is, 'Kronos' in the plural (κρόνους 1480). The era of Thespis is the era of the Peisistratidai, the dynasty of tyrants that founded the City Dionysia. That the notion of old-fashioned **tragōidoi** should be represented as the incarnation of Kronos shows that the ideological attitude toward the old tyranny on the part of the newer democracy combines feelings of revulsion and nostalgia. Shaped by the tyrants, the institution of Athenian Theater as later reshaped by democracy teaches against the internal threat of tyranny.[119] So much for the aspect of revulsion. It is true that Kronos, with his horrors of violence and guile, is a suitable negative model for the state's older phase of existence, under the reign of the tyrants. But Kronos is also a figure of nostalgia, as ruler of the Golden Age. Thus the comic description of primordial players of tragedy as the incarnation of Kronos amounts to an Athenian version of nostalgia for the Golden Age of the Saturnalia.[120]

Such nostalgia for the old forms of poetry and song, which reaches the level of ideology in the Old Comedy of Athenian Theater, helps explain the survival of Pindar's compositions as Classical examples of independent and unassimilated traditions in song making.

These considerations bring us back to my argument that the very evolution of what we know as the Classics — as both a concept and a reality — was but an extension of the organic Panhellenization of oral traditions. The evolution of ancient Greek canons in both poetry and song need not be attributed primarily to the factor of writing.[121] Writing would have been essential for the ultimate preservation of these canons once the traditions of performance were becoming obsolete, but the key to the actual evolution of canons must be sought in the social context of performance itself. I argue that the performance traditions of the Classics, as an extension of the Panhellenization of oral traditions in poetry and song, were preserved in the social context of private education for the élite, including the institution of private schools.

For the Greek city-states, the primary mode of education was public, through the performance of song and poetry at festivals. In the case of poetry, performance at festivals tended to be left to professionals such as the rhapsodes at the festival of the Panathenaia at Athens.[122] In the case of song, the situation was more complex, as we have seen in the case of a festival like

---

119. A crucial work on this theme is Lanza 1977. According to Lanza (see especially p. 178), the tyrant of tragedy is born of the Reform of Kleisthenes, which cancels the political need for the tyrant in the here and now. When the people inherit the apparatus of the aristocracy, they also inherit the enemy of the aristocracy, the tyrant.

120. For a direct comparison of the era of the Peisistratidai with the Age of Kronos, see "Plato" *Hipparchus* 229b.

121. Cf. p. 84. On writing as a medium not for performance but for the 'demonstration' of performance in Herodotus, see p. 220.

122. Cf. p. 21.

the City Dionysia at Athens, where poetry was performed by professional actors while song was performed by the nonprofessional chorus.[123] Here the performance by the chorus was a central form of civic education, not only for the audience at large but also for the members of the chorus. The numbers of chorus members selected each year for the annual production of the City Dionysia convey the pervasiveness of the institution: for example, the three competing choruses of the tragedies required a total of not less than thirty-six new chorus members each year, while the ten competing choruses of the dithyrambs, with separate men's and boys' divisions, added up to a yearly total of 500 men and 500 boys.[124] Wherever the traditions of making song and poetry are still alive, as in the documented cases of the City Dionysia and the Panathenaia,[125] we have reason to think that the process of civic education through song and poetry is also alive. But we have also seen that the traditions of public education in song making and poetry at the City Dionysia tended to absorb or displace older traditions of aristocratic education in song making and poetry, such as those represented by Pindar.[126] Here we see a fundamental impetus for the very institution of private schools: if aristocratic education in the public performance of songs was becoming less and less available by way of the chorus, since the State was transforming the old aristocratic poetics into the new popular poetics of the City Dionysia, then the older ways of choral education in the older traditions of song making had to be compensated by way of increased private schooling for the élite. Once State Theater, the creation of tyrants, becomes transformed into the democratic self-expression of the polis, the concept of the private school can become the nondemocratic self-expression of aristocrats, the new breeding ground of tyrants.

Even private schools, however, serve as a setting for changes in the old traditions of song making. In the older poetics we would naturally expect the traditions of composition in performance to survive from one generation to the next through the factor of performance. Yet if the traditions of composition in performance were breaking down, then the need for sample performances would become greater and greater. Which means that education itself would become gradually transformed: the learning of techniques in composition through performance could shift to the learning of sample compositions through reading. Once the performance tradition becomes obsolete, the text is no longer a demonstration of ability to perform: rather the text

---

123. Cf. pp. 85, 378, 379 and following.

124. Herington 1985.96 and 252n83, following Pickard-Cambridge 1968.234–236.

125. Timotheus was famed for a performance of a composition of his, known as the *Persians* (Timotheus PMG 788–791), at the Feast of the Panathenaia at Athens, around 408 B.C. (cf. p. 89).

126. Cf. p. 400.

becomes simply a sample piece of writing, potentially there to be imitated by other sample pieces of writing.

Still the written text can present itself as not just a sample composition but a sample composition *as potential performance*. It is a privately teachable demonstration of what could be publicly performed, and its accessibility depends on power, political power. To gain access to such a sample composition is to gain knowledge, from a privileged vantage point. The composition, as a mimesis of recomposition in public performance, is a paradigm of authority that is as hard to come by as some treasure in a treasure box, accessible to the rich and powerful.[127] The silent reading of such a sample composition, such a *script*, is symptomatic of the tyrant's power to control the performance of a composition.[128] The reading out loud of such a script, in contrast, is the metaphor for performance, and in fact the very act of reading out loud is the ultimate metaphor of State Theater.[129]

In order to illustrate the effects of private education on the transmission of the Classics, I now turn to two passages in particular, one from the *Clouds* of Aristophanes and another from the *Protagoras* of Plato. Let us begin with the *Clouds* of Aristophanes, with its informative description of old-fashioned Athenian **paideiā** 'education' (τὴν ἀρχαίαν παιδείαν: 961), the kind that purportedly produced the men who fought at the Battle of Marathon (985–986),[130] where boys learn selected compositions of old lyric masters[131] in the house of the **kitharistēs** 'master of the **kitharis**' (964), who teaches them to learn by heart (**promathein**: 966) the performance of famous lyric compositions (967) and who insists on their adherence to performing these compositions in the proper **harmoniā** 'mode' that had been 'inherited from their fathers' (968; cf. 969–972).[132] This precious glimpse of old-fashioned **paideiā** 'education' in Athens provides us with a model for understanding the gradual metamorphosis of oral traditions into the institutions of private schooling in the "Classics."[133] The oral traditions of the boys' chorus are giving way to the written traditions of the boys' school. Further, if the chorus becomes dispensable in a school for performing choral lyric, then the idea of the chorus as the primary medium of education will also have become dispensable. In which case, it is only a matter of time before the performance itself of choral lyric becomes dispensable. With the passage of time, the per-

---

127. Cf. pp. 171 and following.

128. Cf. p. 172.

129. Cf. pp. 171 and following.

130. See p. 97. The "old" **paideusis** 'education' (*Clouds* 986) is explicitly associated with the era that produced the fighters at Marathon (985–986).

131. I say "selected" in light of my earlier discussion of the limited repertoire reflected by references in Old Comedy to the lyric masters: see pp. 108 and following.

132. Cf. p. 97.

133. Further discussion at p. 97.

formance of choral lyric need no longer be the primary curriculum of boys' schools. Thus the progression from an old-fashioned education in the chorus toward an innovative education in the school inexorably leads to still newer patterns of education in a school that may no longer have anything to do with the chorus. The differentiated new concept of "schools" becomes further differentiated into "old schools," which had taught the performance of choral lyric, and "new schools," with a curriculum emancipated from the medium of chorus altogether. By the time of the late fifth century, in a rapidly changing polis like Athens, schools were in fact becoming divorced from the traditions of performance in choral lyric. A prime example is the school of Socrates and his disciples, as ridiculed in the *Clouds* of Aristophanes.[134]

With the increasing complexity of society in the context of the polis comes a pattern of differentiation in the passing on of traditions from generation to generation, and the institution of private schools, as we have just seen described in the Aristophanic passage about the good old days of **paideiā** 'education' in the era of the Battle of Marathon, may be considered an early reflex of this pattern. Already in this era, schools are not a phenomenon merely confined to Athens but seem to appear throughout Archaic Greece. The earliest attested mention of schools is in Herodotus 6.27.2, alluding to an incident that occurred in Chios around 496 B.C., where a roof collapsed on a group of 120 children as they were being taught **grammata** 'letters'; only one boy survived.[135] This disaster is explicitly cited by Herodotus as an omen presaging the overall political disaster that was about to befall the whole community of Chios in the wake of the Ionian Revolt against the Persians (6.27.1), namely, the attack by Histiaios (6.26.1–2) and then the atrocities resulting from the occupation of the island by the Persians (6.31–32). Moreover, the disaster that befell the school at Chios is explicitly coupled by the narrative of Herodotus with another disaster, likewise presaging the overall political disaster about to befall Chios: at about the same time that the roof fell in on the children studying their **grammata** 'letters' in school (again 6.27.2), a choral ensemble of one hundred young men from Chios, officially sent to Delphi for a performance at a festival there, fell victim to a plague that killed ninety-eight of them, so that only two returned alive to Chios (ibid.). We have already noted that the oral traditions of the chorus, throughout Archaic Greece, were giving way to the written traditions of the school. In this narrative of Herodotus, then, we see two symmetrical disasters befalling the song-making traditions of a community, presaging a general political disaster befalling the community as a whole: first to be mentioned are the old-fashioned and élitist oral traditions of the chorus, to be followed

---

134. See p. 107.

135. Cf. the anecdote recorded by Pausanias 6.9.6 about the mass murder of sixty children in a school at Astypalaea in 492 B.C.; cf. also Thucydides 7.29.5.

by the newer and even more élitist written traditions of the school.[136]

That the **grammata** 'letters' that are being taught to these select children of Chios as the roof caves in on them are the belles-lettres or liberal education of song and poetry is made clear if we compare the portrait of old-fashioned education in the *Protagoras* of Plato. Here again, however, as in the *Clouds* of Aristophanes, this kind of education is in fact considered no longer new but already old-fashioned. In the *Protagoras*, with its dramatization of the way things supposedly were in the second half of the fifth century, we can see how schooling is a matter of differentiations in the passing on of traditions from generation to generation. The subject is introduced as we find an old Protagoras debating with Socrates in a company of young Athenian intellectuals that pointedly includes two sons of Pericles himself (314e). In his description of **paideiā**, the figure of Protagoras specifically says that the wealthy can afford more of it: they extend the education of their children by starting it earlier and continuing it longer (326c).[137] There are at least three stages to what Protagoras describes. First, there is a period of education at home, where father, mother, **trophos** 'nurse', and **paidagōgos** 'tutor' all play a role in one's early ethical *formation* (325cd). Second, the child is sent to school, where he is taught letters for the explicit purpose of memorizing poetry (325e-326a); that this memorization is for the explicit purpose of performing and interpreting this poetry is made clear in Protagoras' description of the third stage of schooling, where the child is taught to sing compositions of lyric poets while accompanying himself to the lyre (326ab).[138] Whereas the poetry that is taught in the earlier stage when the child is still learning his letters is described only generally as **diexodoi** 'descriptions', **epainoi** 'praises', and **enkōmia** 'encomia' concerning 'noble men of the past' (326a), it is clear that the poetry taught at the later stage is specifically lyric poetry (the compositions of **melopoioi** 'lyric poets': ibid.). From the standpoint of Protagoras, the most important aspect of **paideiā** (his word) is to acquire skill in the performance and interpretation of poetry (339a), and it is clear that he is thinking in particular of song, that is, lyric poetry: illustrating his point about the primacy of poetry in education, he begins his debate with

136. The symbolism of these symmetrical disasters is signaled by the words προσημαίνειν 'make a sign [**sēma**] in advance' at Herodotus 6.27.1 (cf. also σημήια μεγάλα 'mighty signs' ibid.).

137. On this kind of élitism within the social context of the polis, see Dover 1968.lx, who adduces passages like Demosthenes *On the Crown* 265.

138. This passage, Plato *Protagoras* 325e-326a, in conjunction with the earlier passage in Herodotus 6.27.2 alluding to the learning of letters by children in Chios, can be used as the most explicit available testimony to the effect that the medium of writing could indeed be used for the teaching of song and poetry. Still we note that the learning of letters is linked with the notion that such learning is a means for preserving traditions of performance. In any case this sort of testimony is the best evidence for the existence of school texts that could have been passed down to the time of the Alexandrian editors. On which topic see p. 112.

Socrates by citing and then interpreting a lyric composition of Simonides (339b and following: Simonides PMG 542),[139] having just made an earlier reference to a famous lyric passage from Pindar (337d: Pindar F 169a.1–5 SM).[140]

After Protagoras and Socrates have a contest of wits in interpreting the meaning of the composition by Simonides (and Socrates comes off with the seemingly superior interpretation), Alcibiades challenges Protagoras to continue his debate with Socrates by abandoning the use of poetry as the framework for the discussion (347b and 348b), in the context of a particularly significant remark of Socrates: to use poetry as a framework for the debate between Protagoras and himself is analogous, says Socrates, to the hiring of girl musicians, either string or wind, or girl dancers to entertain at symposia (347cd). Such participants in the symposium reveal their lack of **paideiā** 'education' (**apaideusiā**: 347c), whereas those who are noble and 'educated' (**pepaideumenoi**) can entertain themselves with their own conversations (347d). Plato could have had Socrates say, as does the poetry of Aristophanes, that the educated participants in the symposium can also entertain themselves by performing and interpreting lyric compositions, as opposed to the ill-educated participants who hire girl musicians to play for them. But Plato is the champion of a new education where dialogue supplants the primacy of poetry, and Socrates in fact goes on to set up "the poets" as a bad thing that is parallel to the girl musicians (347e). In other words, instead of having girl musicians as a foil for "the poets," Plato has both the girl musicians and "the poets" serving together as a foil for the medium of the dialogue that Socrates and Alcibiades are advocating. The stance of Alcibiades here is particularly suggestive: his generation is ridiculed in the *Clouds* of Aristophanes for abandoning the ideals of old-fashioned **paideiā**. According to these ideals, a sign of the highest achievement was the performance, at a symposium, of a lyric composition by one of the old masters. There is a vivid contrast to these ideals in the *Alcibiades* of Plutarch (2.6), where the young Alcibiades refuses to learn how to play the reed: let the Thebans, says he, play the reed, since *they* do not know how to have a conversation at a symposium.

Given the obsolescence, lamented already in the days of Aristophanes, of the old-fashioned **paideiā** at Athens, it follows that the survival of the Classics in old lyric poetry, with their antiquated traditions of composition and even performance, was severely threatened.[141] Other cities, such as Thebes in the anecdote that precedes, would doubtless have held on to the

139. On the portrayal of Simonides in the *Protagoras* of Plato: Privitera 1965.100–10.

140. On this Pindaric passage, cf. p. 112.

141. This is not to say that efforts in such education had ceased altogether: cf. Isocrates *Antidosis* 267 (τὴν μουσικὴν καὶ τὴν ἄλλην παιδείαν); also Plato *Laws* 654a–b, 809b; *Republic* 376e.

antiquated traditions for a longer period, what with their more conservative traditions of **paideiā**. Such traditions, it seems, were not so much a matter of composition any longer, and more a matter of performance only.[142] In Athens, by contrast, where traditions in actual composition seem to have survived for a longer time, these traditions could have contributed to the relative sparseness of the Archaic lyric traditions that have survived, in that the Classics of Archaic lyric were being replaced in Athens by the new Classics, as it were, of State Theater. Such trends in Athens, what with the overarching cultural prestige of this polis, surely had a profound effect on other cities as well, as we can see from occasional traces of a given city's educational repertoire in the performance of song.[143]

As we have seen, the occasional lyric poetry of Pindar, Simonides, and Bacchylides, unlike other types of old lyric poetry, does not lend itself to an ongoing process of recomposition in performance, so that its references to a given composition's setting — as also the self-references of the composer — retain a higher degree of historicity than we find elsewhere. Such occasionality is at least partly incompatible with the institutions of public performance in song and poetry as fostered by the polis. The polis, as we have seen, tends to promote its own Panhellenic prestige by fostering a Panhellenic perspective in the public performing of song and poetry, and such a perspective discourages ad hoc references that would become politically obsolete with the passage of time.[144] Only with the rise of the individual above the polis, in the first instance through the advent of tyrants, can ad hoc references to special individual interests in the song and poetry of the polis at last become compatible with the Panhellenization of this song and poetry.[145] Moreover, it is the institution of tyranny that provides an impetus, in the Archaic era, for the Panhellenization of compositions that are linked with specific occasions or persons.[146]

To overreach the polis, then, is to become an individual, from the hindsight of recorded history.[147] But the model of the individual, in order to assert itself in the first place, must still conform to the ideals of the polis, as encoded in the traditions of the chorus; in fact the prime metaphor for the individual and the polis is the chorus itself, in its articulation of a complementarity between the **khorēgos** 'chorus leader' and the rest of the chorus, the aggregate.[148]

142. Cf. p. 83, with a discussion of the Boeotian traditions attributed to Corinna. On the Spartan traditions of reperforming the masterworks of local traditions in song making, see pp. 343 and following.

143. See p. 106.

144. Cf. pp. 67 and following; pp. 144 and following, especially p. 145.

145. Cf. pp. 174 and following.

146. Ibid.

147. Cf. pp. 153 and following.

148. Cf. pp. 344 and following.

As a self-expression of the polis, the chorus tends to accentuate the least occasional and most catholic aspects of its seasonally recomposed choral self-presentation, in order to live up to the proper degree of admiration from outside and consequently from within.[149] In the eyes of the polis, the content of a choral composition must look beyond local interests in order to achieve a Panhellenic prestige in the eyes of whatever Hellenes from the outside may be looking in.[150]

Like the polis, the chorus is a mechanism of rotating deindividualization and individualization, where the member of the chorus can move up from the status of egalitarianism in the aggregate, the chorus, into the status of leadership in the hierarchy, the status of the **khorēgos** 'chorus leader', thereafter potentially rotating back down into the status of membership in the aggregate. The necessity of being part of a group is balanced by the desire to have one's day in the sun: in an aristocratic choral model of society, everyone wants a chance to be at the head of the chorus, to become a **koruphaios** (cf. Herodotus 3.82.3).[151]

This choral model is important for understanding not only a new kind of authority sought by tyrants but also a new kind of authority for poets, which approaches the notion of historically verifiable authorship. As we have seen, there is a relationship between the authority of the role model who is represented as leading the choral group and the authority of the composer who is credited with the representation.[152] This relationship is visualized as the authority of Apollo over song in his function as **khorēgos** 'chorus leader', which is the fundamental model for the authority of the composer in choral lyric. The key to choral performance is the 'public presentation', the **apodeixis**, of the **khorēgos**.[153] The authority of the **khorēgos** is *presented* through the performance of the chorus. What is presented, through **apodeixis**, and represented, through **mīmēsis**, is authority. From this authority a newer and more specialized notion, that of authorship, can develop in the so-called age of tyrants and thereafter. The institution of tyranny, then, was for ancient Greece a watershed in the evolution of authorship as we know it.[154]

As we shift our attention from the Archaic to the Classical period, with its realities of historically attested authorship, we must ask ourselves where to draw the line between the generic composer and the real author. From the standpoint of Archaic Greek traditions, what has to happen, for a composer to preserve his historicity, is either (1) the arresting of the process of recomposition in performance — wherein any self-reference by the composer is itself

149. Cf. pp. 349 and following.
150. Ibid.
151. Cf. pp. 368 and following.
152. Cf. pp. 364 and following.
153. Cf. pp. 364, 369.
154. Cf. p. 174.

vulnerable to recomposition — or (2) the commissioning of occasional poetry by an authority that goes beyond the polis. As long as the polis is the sole authority presiding over the performance of song and poetry, (1) the factor of recomposition is not likely to be arrested and (2) occasional compositions have little chance of transmission beyond their original occasion. Only with the rise of tyrants can the individuality of a composition and of a composer begin to be protected from being recomposed in the context of performance in the polis.[155] Granted, those who publicly championed the polis against the tyrant held that the truth of poetry must be protected from private possession, since such possession leads to tampering by tyrants.[156] The opposite standpoint of the tyrant, however, held that the truth of poetry must be protected from public recomposition.[157]

These two conflicting standpoints are indirectly reflected in the symmetrical account in Herodotus of the twin disasters befalling the community of Chios, the death of the chorus boys and the death of the schoolboys (6.27.2).[158] One particular detail in the story of the schoolboys, that the roof caved in on them as they were being taught **grammata** 'letters' (ibid.), can be connected with a general attitude that we have found in the *Histories* of Herodotus, namely, that the medium of writing encourages the private possession of the public media of singing or making speeches, and that such private possession is a characteristic of tyrants.[159]

It is the institution of tyranny, I argue, that makes the difference between such figures of Archaic lyric poetry as Stesichorus and Ibycus. If the *vita* tradition of Stesichorus, both extrinsic and intrinsic to the compositions attributed to him, strikes us as generic[160] while the corresponding *vita* tradition of Ibycus strikes us as at least in part historical, it is due, I submit, to the historical fact that Ibycus became a protégé of the tyrant Polykrates of Samos.[161] Just as the tyrant fixes his individuality in the collective memory, so too does the poet as the tyrant's protégé.[162]

Throughout this presentation I have been developing the argument that the Panhellenic diffusion of occasional compositions like Pindar's victory odes cannot be attributed to the medium of writing alone. Even though they were originally occasional poems, they kept on being performed as master-

155. In this connection I cite again Ford 1985, where the **sphrāgis** 'seal' of Theognis (19–20) is interpreted as an affirmation of authorship through an authority analogous to that of the tyrant Hipparchus of Athens; further discussion at pp. 169 and following.

156. Cf. pp. 169 and following.

157. Ibid.

158. See p. 407.

159. Ibid.

160. Cf. pp. 362, 363; cf. further at p. 427. I agree with Burnett 1988.137 that Stesichorus was "a public poet."

161. Cf. pp. 187 and following, especially p. 189.

162. Cf. pp. 174 and following.

pieces in the canon of old lyric poets.[163] True, the medium of writing was on hand to record the ultimate phases of performance tradition in the evolving canons of song and poetry. Still, in the case of occasional song and poetry, what was needed in addition was an authority that went beyond the polis — an authority that could make even an occasional composition definitive enough to be performed as if it were already Panhellenic in stature, so that it could be reperformed from then on as a Classic, beyond its original occasion. Such authority was pioneered by the tyrants, and this authority in turn conferred the first traces of authorship.[164]

163. Pp. 107 and following.
164. For the conceptual linking of *authority* and *authorship*, see pp. 79, 350, and following.

14 ▢▢ Pindar's Homer

As a lyric poet who flourished in an age when emerging patterns of individual power within the Greek polis had already established corresponding patterns of individualism, marking the poet as well as the poet's powerful patrons, Pindar was an author.[1] As a figure who served to connect the heroic past with the present, he was a master of the mode of discourse known as the **ainos**. In this discourse the poet's references to the present identified him as much as his patrons. But this identification had to be expressed in terms of the past, in terms of Homer and the age of heroes.[2] And the question remains: what exactly was Homer to Pindar?

To begin, Pindar's lyric poetry seems to make no distinction between the heroes of the Homeric *Iliad* and *Odyssey* on the one hand and the heroes of other epic traditions, most notably those of the so-called Epic Cycle, on the other. Within but the briefest space, for example, in *Olympian* 2.81–83, Pindar's words recount how Achilles vanquished three heroes, Hektor (81–82), Kyknos (82), and Memnon (83). Whereas Hektor was the main opponent of Achilles in the *Iliad*, Kyknos figured prominently as his antagonist in the Cyclic *Cypria* (Proclus, p. 105.2–3 Allen) and Memnon, in the *Aithiopis* (Proclus, p. 106.1–7). One expert on Pindar remarks about *Olympian* 2.81–83: "These lines illustrate Pindar's indebtedness to the post-Homeric epics: from the [*Cypria*] he draws the episode of the slaying of [Kyknos], and from the *Aithiopis* of [Arctinus] he derives the translation of Achilles and his slaying of Memnon, a story that haunted Pindar's imagina-

---

1. Ch.6.
2. Ch.6, Ch.7.

tion, for he recurs no less than six times to Memnon in the odes."[3] Instead, what I propose to emphasize is that Pindar's lyric poetry treats Cyclic heroes as equivalents of Homeric heroes. At *Isthmian* 5.39–42, for example, the victims of Achilles are enumerated as Kyknos (39), Hektor (39), Memnon (40–41), and Telephos (41–42); the last of these figures is yet another hero of the Cycle (*Cypria*/Proclus, p. 104.5–7 Allen). Again at *Isthmian* 8.54–55, Memnon and Hektor are equated as heroic opponents of Achilles.[4] Even more, Pindar's lyric poetry seems at times not to distinguish the authorship of the *Iliad* and *Odyssey* from the authorship of the Cycle. From Pindar F 265 SM (by way of Aelian *Varia Historia* 9.15), for example, it appears that Pindar's words had ascribed the *Cypria* to Homer.[5] Similarly the words of Callinus (F 6 W) explicitly ascribed the epic *Seven against Thebes* tradition to Homer, according to Pausanias 9.9.5, who rates this epic as a poem so superior that it is second only to the *Iliad* and *Odyssey* (ibid.).[6]

This poetic convention, as practiced by Pindar, of equating the themes of Homeric and Cyclic epos may at first seem surprising in view of the clear differences between these two poetic traditions. The nature of these differences, as also the reasons for them, has already been formulated: the Cycle is more localized, less Panhellenic, than the Homeric *Iliad* and *Odyssey*.[7] The fact that Pindaric song refers to epic traditions that cross over from the Homeric to the Cyclic, traditions of varying stages in the development of epic, suggests that Pindaric reference is diachronic, stretching across the span of development in epic traditions. The fact that the diachronic differences in the epic medium are not sorted out by Pindaric song implies that Pindar's own medium contains within itself the metamorphoses of epic. If indeed the different epic heroes from different epic phases are treated as multiforms, parallel variants, then it follows that different epic phases are likewise mere

---

3. Farnell 1932.21. Cf. Stoneman 1981, especially p. 63.

4. While taking into account these passages, Nisetich 1989.70–72 nonetheless argues for "Pindar's preference of the *Iliad* over the poems of the epic cycle" (p. 70). I prefer to say, instead, that Pindar's *tradition*, evolving as it does well into the fifth century, is therefore responsive to the evolution of epic tradition, crystalized at a much earlier stage. The basic fact in the evolution of early Greek epic tradition is that the *Iliad* and *Odyssey* achieved a preeminence over the Cycle: see Ch.2. Accordingly, we may expect cases where this preeminence is reflected in Pindaric references to epic. The point remains, however, that there are also cases where Pindar's wording makes no distinction between versions proper to the *Iliad* and those that we find in the Cycle (as Nisetich concedes at pp. 71–72).

5. Nisetich, p. 73n2, concedes that we may indeed have here a case where the authorship of the Cycle is being attributed by Pindar to Homer, but he insists that Pindar would still have thought the *Iliad* to be superior to the *Cypria*. I prefer a different perspective: if indeed we understand Aelian correctly, and Pindar's words had really referred to Homer as the poet of the *Cypria*, I would interpret this reference to mean that Pindar's tradition accepts the rhapsodic tradition of performing the *Cypria* as the genuine *Homeric* tradition.

6. See pp. 22, 75, 78.

7. Cf. pp. 70 and following.

multiforms from the standpoint of Pindar's poetics. I am proposing then that there is in Pindaric song an ongoing nondifferentiation of epic traditions — traditions that we see otherwise attested only in their already differentiated forms, for example, the *Iliad* as distinct from the *Odyssey*, or, more generally, Homeric poetry as distinct from Cyclic poetry.[8]

Pursuing this line of thinking, I shun the common opinion that the Pindaric references to the traditions that survived in the Cycle are merely borrowings from the Cycle.[9] Rather I suggest that Pindar is drawing upon a continuum of epic tradition. I suggest in addition that Pindar's tradition can draw upon such a continuum because it actually contains Homer's tradition within itself.

In support of this suggestion that the diachronic mode of Pindar's references to epic reveals something about the diachronic relationship of Pindar's own medium to epic, we have already had recourse to the references of Pindar's lyric tradition to itself and to epic, where the medium of epic is conventionally treated as an outgrowth of Pindar's own traditional medium.[10] The lyric poetry of Pindar represents epic as extending into the epinician **ainos** of Pindar, thereby presenting itself as the ultimate authority of tradition.[11]

The relationship between the Pindaric tradition and the Homeric is also apparent on the level of metrics. In the case of Pindar we have seen that the heritage of his rhythmical repertory centers on the so-called dactylo-epitrite meters, as attested in the Dorian tradition of Stesichorus, and on the Aeolic meters, as attested in the Aeolian tradition of Sappho and Alcaeus.[12] Of Pindar's epinician songs, roughly half (twenty-three) are composed in Doric dactylo-epitrite meters, and half (twenty) in Aeolic meters.[13] There is one solitary occurrence, *Olympian* 2, of a song composed in distinctly Ionic meters. In considering the half-and-half proportion of Doric dactylo-epitrite and Aeolic meters in Pindar, we may note an important analogue in the dactylic hexameter of epic, which can be explained as a synthesis of dactylo-epitrite and Aeolic metrical traditions.[14] Roughly half of the hexameters in Homeric poetry are built with phraseology where the main word break (") occurs immediately after the sequence $- \overline{\cup\cup} - \overline{\cup\cup} -$, which can be traced back

8. On the notion of evolutionary differentiation in Homeric and Hesiodic poetry, see pp. 53–54.

9. Cf. again Farnell 1932.21.

10. Detailed discussion at pp. 202 and following. For reinforcement from the self-references of epic, see pp. 197 and following.

11. Cf. pp. 202 and following.

12. Cf. pp. 47 and following.

13. In reaching these figures, I am counting *Isthmian* 3 and 4 as one composition; also I am including the fragmentary *Isthmian* 9. In *Olympian* 13, there is an exceptional case of coexistence between dactylo-epitrite and Aeolic, with Aeolic modulating into dactylo-epitrite.

14. Cf. pp. 456 and following.

to dactylo-epitrite patterns, and roughly another half where it occurs after the sequence $- \cup\cup - \cup\cup - \cup$, which can be traced back to Aeolic patterns.[15] These two sequences, $- \cup\cup - \cup\cup -$ " and $- \cup\cup - \cup\cup - \cup$", account for the main caesura, or word break, in 99% of Homeric hexameters.[16] To restate in terms of the colon,[17] the cola of the hexameter as defined by the so-called masculine caesura ($- \cup\cup - \cup\cup -$ ") seem to be built from the cola of dactylo-epitrite meters as attested in Pindar and of prototypical dactylo-epitrite meters as attested in Stesichorus. As for the cola defined by the so-called feminine caesura ($- \cup\cup - \cup\cup - \cup$ "), these in turn seem to be cognate with the cola that we find in the so-called Aeolic meters of Pindar, as also in the Aeolic repertory of Sappho and Alcaeus.

Thus the two metrical patterns that combine as one in Homeric diction, namely, the dactylo-epitrite and the Aeolic, are still by and large separate and autonomous in the diction of Pindar. To put it more strongly: Pindar's lyric poetry still preserves the separateness of the prototypical components of epic poetry.

The dactylo-epitrite heritage of dactylic hexameter, however, is not specifically Doric, as in the case of Stesichorus or Pindar. The poetry of Archilochus, a prominent representative of Ionic traditions, is distinguished by metrical building blocks that can be described as cognate with those of the Doric dactylo-epitrite.[18] In other words there is an Ionic as well as Doric tradition of dactylo-epitrite patterns. Still, in the wake of the overlap between Doric dactylo-epitrite patterns and the Ionic patterns that are cognate with them, the term *Ionic*, as applied to the lyric poetry of Pindar, tends to be restricted to categories not covered by *Doric*. In other words Ionic is a default category in describing the metrics of Pindar. Thus *Olympian* 2 is the only Pindaric composition where the meters can be described as overtly Ionic because it is the only Pindaric composition where the meters are *exclusively* Ionic. I would summarize the hierarchy of Pindar's metrical heritage as follows: dominant Doric, recessive Aeolic, and residual Ionic. It seems to me that this proportion of Doric/Aeolic/Ionic meters in Pindaric composition corresponds to the dialectal synthesis of Pindaric diction: again we see a pattern of dominant Doric, recessive Aeolic, and residual Ionic.[19]

15. In the survey of Archaic hexameters by West 1982.36, the overall ratio of occurrences in word breaking shaped $- \cup\cup - \cup\cup -$ " and $- \cup\cup - \cup\cup - \cup$" is respectively 3:4. On the dactylo-epitrite and Aeolic associations of the patterns $- \cup\cup - \cup\cup -$ " and $- \cup\cup - \cup\cup - \cup$" respectively in hexameter, see pp. 456 and following.

16. West ibid. gives the following statistics for the nonoccurrence of the main caesura: 1.4% in the *Iliad*, 0.9% in the *Odyssey*.

17. On this term, see p. 439.

18. Cf. p. 451.

19. On the dialectal hierarchy of dominant Doric and recessive Aeolic in Pindaric diction, see Palmer 1980.123–127. On the Ionisms in Pindar, see, for example, Palmer, p. 125. These Ionisms need not be interpreted as direct borrowings from "Homer" but rather as reflexes of an Ionic tradition cognate with the Homeric.

The proportions of this metrical and dialectal synthesis in Pindaric song correspond to the hierarchy established by the traditional story of Terpander's coming to Sparta (Hellanicus FGH 4 F 85; Pindar F 191 SM).[20] The background for this story is a story, originating from the native Aeolic tradition of the Lesbian poets, that claims Terpander as the ancestor of this same Aeolic tradition (Sappho F 106 V). We know from the attested diction of Sappho and Alcaeus that this Aeolic tradition is actually a blend of two dialects, dominant Aeolic synthesized with recessive Ionic.[21] A similar description seems apt for the meters of Sappho and Alcaeus: a synthesis of dominant Aeolic and recessive Ionic (where the Ionic is cognate with the meters of Anacreon and even Hipponax). This blend in traditions as represented by Terpander, that is, dominant Aeolic synthesized with recessive Ionic, is then further blended in the Doric context of Sparta. As myth has it, Terpander brings with him to Doric Sparta the Aeolic traditions of Lesbos.[22] Thus the story of Terpander's arrival at Sparta accounts for the final and definitively dominant stage, the Doric, in the traditional diction of figures like Alcman and even Pindar.[23]

Another way to approach the relationship between the traditions of Pindar and Homer is to compare them both with other traditions that reveal close affinities with both. What follows is a brief survey of a few such traditions, including those of Stesichorus, Theognis, Archilochus, Alcaeus, and Sappho. This survey, it is hoped, will yield a final overview of the effects of Panhellenism on the heritage of ancient Greek song and poetry.

Let us begin with Stesichorus. On the level of form, the dactylo-epitrite meters of Stesichorus are clearly related to what we see in roughly one-half of Pindar's metrical repertory.[24] Also the way in which these dactylo-epitrite meters of Stesichorus frame traditional phraseology is clearly related to the way in which roughly half of the verses in Homeric poetry are built, that is, where the main word break occurs immediately after the sequence $- \overline{\cup\cup} - \overline{\cup\cup} -$ ("masculine" caesura).[25] Paradoxically the dactylo-epitrites of the earlier figure, Stesichorus, seem to be less conservative at least in one respect than those of the later figure, Pindar, in that the rules of Stesichorean meter are moving in the direction of epic by tolerating the substitution of $\underset{\cup\cup}{\cup} - \cup\cup - \cup\cup - -$ for $\underset{\cup}{\cup} - \cup\cup - \cup\cup - -$.[26]

---

20. On which see pp. 86, 93.

21. On the evidence for Ionic in Lesbian poetic diction, see the summary in Bowie 1981.136.

22. Cf. p. 93.

23. I cite again, for an overview of the dialectal texture of choral lyric traditions, Palmer 1980.119–130.

24. Cf. p. 416.

25. Cf. p. 417. Rо̨ ᵗ ᵗly another half of Homeric hexameters is taken up by phraseological patterns where the main word break occurs immediately after the sequence $- \overline{\cup} - \overline{\cup} - \cup$ ("feminine" caesura).

26. Cf. pp. 456 and following.

The comparison of Homer and Pindar with Stesichorus is also pertinent on the level of theme: the repertory of themes to be found in the more localized Cycle, as distinct from the more Panhellenic *Iliad* and *Odyssey*, is remarkably parallel to what we find in the compositions attributed to Stesichorus. Given that the lyric poetry of Stesichorus is related to that of Pindar on the level of form,[27] we may pursue the question, what is Homer to Pindar, by considering the affinities of Stesichorus and Pindar on the level of theme, and, further, the relationship of their shared lyric tradition to the concept of epic in general and Homer in particular.

A singularly useful point of departure is the Stesichorean rendition of the *Helen* story, which contrasts its own adherence to one particular localized version with the syncretism of the Homeric *Helen* tradition of the *Iliad* and *Odyssey*. In the Stesichorean version Homer is blamed for representing Helen as having allowed herself to be seduced by Paris: the Homeric version, which says that Helen went with Paris all the way to Troy, is specifically rejected (Stesichorus PMG 193.2–5), as is what seems to be the Hesiodic version, which says that she went as far as Egypt, while her **eidōlon** 'image-double' was taken to Troy (Stesichorus PMG 193.5–7, 12–16).[28] The rejected story about the **eidōlon** 'image-double', with the detail concerning the voyage of Paris and Helen to Egypt (cf. Stesichorus PMG 193.15–16 in conjunction with Hesiod F 176.7 MW), affirms the seduction of Helen since the actual adultery of Paris and Helen traditionally took place during their voyage from Sparta to Egypt (cf. *Iliad* III 445). The celebrated theme of the **palinōidiā** 'recantation' of Stesichorus has to do with the story that told how this poet had previously blamed Helen, like Homer and Hesiod, by virtue of telling stories about her that were parallel to theirs, only to recant later and then be rewarded with the restoration of his eyesight, which had been taken away by the supernatural powers of Helen as punishment for defamation (Isocrates *Helen* 64, Conon FGH 26 F 1.18, Plato *Phaedrus* 243a, Pausanias 3.19.11).[29]

It could be argued that the words of the recantation, as a composition, actually presupposed the story of how Stesichorus was blinded and how he then had a change of heart: this way the restoration of vision would be a

27. Cf. pp. 47 and following.

28. Cf. Cingano 1982.32. On the **eidōlon** 'image-double' of Helen at Troy (Stesichorus PMG 193.5 and 14), see also Hesiod F 358 MW. On the faulting of Helen for being seduced by Paris, see also Stesichorus PMG 223 in conjunction with Hesiod F 176.7. Cf. Kannicht 1969 I 38–41.

29. Kannicht 1969 I 28–29 argues, from the wording of Isocrates *Helen* 64, that the blaming and the recantation would have taken place not in two separate poems but within a single poem, where Stesichorus shifts from blaming to recantation. Cf. also Woodbury 1967. In the discussion that follows, I propose to build on this argument by positing a dramatized change of heart within the framework of the composition. For other sources concerning the recantation of Stesichorus, see Cingano 1982.22–23, who argues that Stesichorus was traditionally credited with two, not one, recantations offered to Helen.

given of the composition, that is, something that is ostensibly caused by the dramatized here and now of the recantation. The recantation of Stesichorus, featuring the restoration of his vision, not only denies the Homeric tradition but also reaffirms another tradition that happens to acknowledge explicitly the thought patterns associated with the cult of Helen as a local goddess. According to Pausanias 3.19.11, the story of Helen and the blinding of Stesichorus is a tradition stemming from the city-state of Kroton, also shared by Himera, the traditional provenience of Stesichorus; in this version Helen abides on the sacred Island of Leuke, as consort of Achilles, through the agency of the gods; from there she sends word to Stesichorus that he compose a recantation. Thus the recantation of Stesichorus seems to be a theme that also reaffirms the traditions native to Kroton and Himera. More important for the moment, the recantation of Stesichorus presupposes the distinctness of Stesichorus and his lyric poetry from the likes of Homer and his epic poetry, in light of another tradition claiming that Homer himself had been blinded as punishment for *his* having defamed Helen through his story of Helen at Troy (*Life of Homer* VI 51–57 Allen; Plato *Phaedrus* 243a).[30]

This juxtaposition of Homer and Stesichorus within the tradition of Stesichorus is important in understanding a genuine distinction between two traditions of poetry. The central point of reference, even for Stesichorus, is Homer and the version of Homer in telling the story of Helen. We have already noted the juxtaposition of Homer and Stesichorus in traditional references, such as Simonides PMG 564 and Isocrates *Helen* 64–65, which I interpret to imply the appropriateness of conventionally juxtaposing performances of Homeric and Stesichorean poetry at given festivals.[31]

The variability of the Helen story in fact served as a touchstone in ancient controversies over the attribution of given compositions to Homer. For example, Herodotus has to go out of his way to argue, apparently against beliefs held within certain traditions in his own time, that the poet of the *Cypria* is not Homer (2.116–117). Herodotus makes his argument on the grounds that the *Cypria* has Paris and Helen sail directly, within the space of three days, from Sparta to Troy (2.117). The version of the *Cypria* known to Herodotus is different from the one summarized by Proclus, where we do find the elaboration of one sidetracking: a storm sent by Hera blows Paris and Helen off course and they land at Sidon, but then they sail from there directly to Troy (*Cypria*/Proclus, p. 103.9–12 Allen). In contrast the Homeric poems, as Herodotus points out, allow for at least two sidetrackings, one at Sidon and one in Egypt (2.116, quoting from *Iliad* VI 289–292 and *Odyssey* iv 227–230, 251–252), though these sidetrackings are clearly subordinated by the narrative (as Herodotus also points out: 2.116.1). It is the more complex pattern of

30. Other references in Cingano, p. 31n42.
31. Cf. p. 23.

the Homeric poems, where one level of narrative is being subordinated to another, as contrasted with the more simple pattern of the *Cypria*, that convinces Herodotus that the poet of the *Cypria* cannot be Homer. Since "Homer" allows for variation in the Helen story and the poet of the *Cypria* does not, Herodotus infers that the latter cannot be "Homer." The greater tolerance for variation is for me a sign of relatively wider Panhellenism.[32]

In contrast with the complex and diplomatic pattern of subordination that characterizes Homer as the most Panhellenic in outlook, the story affirmed by Stesichorus in his *Helen* song is relatively simplex and uncompromising: Helen did not go to Troy, and that particular story about her is simply not **etumos** 'genuine' (Stesichorus PMG 192.1). In other words the versions of Stesichorus and the Cycle are comparable to each other by virtue of being less complex, less synthetic, than the version of Homer. In accommodating a version that pictures Helen on the sacred Island of Leuke as consort of Achilles (Pausanias 3.19.11), the tradition of Stesichorus is parallel to the less Panhellenic traditions of the Cycle: in the *Aithiopis*, the abode of Achilles after immortalization is this same sacred place, Leuke (Proclus, p. 106.15 Allen). This sacred place anchors the epic of the *Aithiopis* to the local cults of Miletus and its colonies.[33]

Besides this specific kind of thematic parallelism between Stesichorus and the Cycle, we may note that even the general organizing subjects of Stesichorean poetry coincide with those of the Cycle: for example, Stesichorus is credited with a composition called the *Destruction of Ilion* (PMG 196–205),[34] and another called the *Nostoi* (PMG 208–209), corresponding respectively to the Cyclic *Destruction of Ilion*, attributed to Arctinus of Miletus, and the *Nostoi*, attributed to Agias of Trozen. Such convergences are especially significant if the poetry of Stesichorus is indeed closely related to a prototype of the poetry of Pindar.[35] What the experts have been used to perceive as Pindaric borrowings from the Cycle are more likely to be genuine inheritances from traditions preserved in actual prototypes of Pindaric song, as represented by Stesichorean song.

Another indication that the tradition of Stesichorus is less Panhellenic than the Homeric and Hesiodic is to be found in the measuring of the truth-value of the preferred version of the Helen myth in terms of the concept **etumo-** 'genuine' (Stesichorus PMG 192.1): in Hesiodic poetry, by contrast, a plethora of local versions that are false but *seem* **etuma** 'genuine' (*Theogony* 27) is contrasted with an ostensibly unique and absolute Panhellenic

---

32. Cf. pp. 70 and following.

33. Ibid.

34. For an updated repertory, see Stesichorus SLG 88–147.

35. Cf. p. 456. I avoid saying that the lyric poetry of Stesichorus is a direct prototype of the lyric poetry of Pindar. Similarly I avoid saying that the lyric poetry of Sappho and Alcaeus is another direct prototype.

version that is described as **alēthea** 'true' (28).[36] Still another indication of the more local nature of Stesichorean lyric poetry is the privileging of the visual metaphor for poetry: the figure of Stesichorus has his vision restored by Helen, whereas Homer does not (again, Plato *Phaedrus* 243a). Homeric poetry, in contrast, is marked by the privileging of the auditory metaphor, at the expense of the visual: the inability of the the the poet to *see* is a guarantee of his ability to go beyond personal experience and thus to *hear* the true message of the Muses, which is the **kleos** 'glory' (from verb **kluō** 'hear') of Homeric poetry (*Iliad* II 486).[37]

The emphasis on the metaphor of seeing in Stesichorean lyric poetry, setting it off from the metaphor of hearing in the epic poetry of Homer, is akin to the semantics of **historiā**, with its awareness of local testimony grounded in local traditions. With its more localized orientation, Stesichorean lyric poetry can identify itself as δαμώματα Χαρίτων 'the public local performances of the Kharites' (Stesichorus PMG 212.1). The reference to Kharites or "Graces," divine incarnations of **kharis**,[38] underlines the relationship between the composition and its immediate audience, the local nature of which is conveyed by **dāmōma**, the act of 'making public', which I translate here as 'public *local* performance' in light of its derivation from **dāmos** (**dēmos**) in the sense of 'local community'.[39] Such local performances, however stylized, properly take place through the agency of the chorus, and we have noted the centrality of the chorus as the formal expression of a local community.[40] We may note as well the pertinence of the very name of Stesichorus to this formal expression: **Stēsi-khoros** means 'he who sets up the chorus.'[41]

The essence of Stesichorean lyric poetry is not that a given local version, as ordinarily formalized in the song of the chorus, has won out over the Panhellenic version, as formalized in the poetry of Homer. Rather it may be described as a local version in the process of making a bid for Panhellenic status. Such a description fits the lyric poetry of Pindar as well. A typical Pindaric composition presents itself as local in foundation, expressed through the performance of the chorus, and as Panhellenic in intent, expressed through the links of the song with the Homeric world of heroes. But the actual poetry of Homer must be made to look too compromising in face of the uncompromising standard proclaimed by Pindaric song. What we have already observed in the case of Stesichorus applies to Pindar as well: his tradition too puts a strong emphasis on its association with the visual metaphor,

36. See p. 68.
37. Fuller discussion in N 1979.16–17.
38. See p. 65.
39. See pp. 56, 251.
40. Cf. pp. 142, 144. Cf. Burnett 1988.129–147, with special reference to Stesichorus.
41. Cf. p. 362.

as distinct from the auditory metaphor that marks the Homeric tradition, and an equally strong emphasis on the truth-value of local traditions grounded in cult, as distinct from the synthetic complexities attributed to Homer. Just as the voice of Stesichorus in his *Helen* song proclaims that his version of the **logos** 'tale' of Helen is **etumos** 'genuine' by virtue of claiming that the Homeric version is the opposite (Stesichorus PMG 192.1), so also the voice of Pindar, as it proclaims in *Nemean* 7 its mission to praise what is noble, claims the control of a **kleos** 'glory' that is **etētumon** 'genuine' (verse 63).[42] Earlier in the same song, the **logos** 'tale' of and by the crafty Odysseus, as retold with commensurate craft by Homer, is described as going beyond the bounds of **alētheia** 'truth', to which most men are "blind" without the "vision" that is implicit in Pindar's lyric poetry, an uncompromising unified vision that defends the true value of heroes from the compromising complexities of **mūthoi** 'myths', which are the "hearsay" of Homer:

ἐγὼ δὲ πλέον' ἔλπομαι | λόγον Ὀδυσσέος ἢ πάθαν διὰ τὸν ἀδυεπῆ
Ὅμηρον· | ἐπεὶ ψεύδεσί οἱ ποτανᾷ ⟨τε⟩ μαχανᾷ σεμνὸν ἔπεστί τι·
σοφία δὲ κλέπτει παράγοισα μύθοις. τυφλὸν δ' ἔχει | ἦτορ ὅμιλος
ἀνδρῶν ὁ πλεῖστος. εἰ γὰρ ἦν | ἓ τὰν ἀλάθειαν ἰδέμεν, οὔ κεν ὅπλων
χολωθεὶς | ὁ καρτερὸς Αἴας ἔπαξε διὰ φρενῶν | λευρὸν ξίφος

Pindar Nemean 7.20–27

I think that the tale [**logos**] of Odysseus is greater than his experiences [**pathā**],[43] all because of Homer, the one with the sweet words. Upon his lies [**pseudea**] and winged inventiveness there is a kind of majesty; [poetic] skill [**sophiā**], misleading in myths [**mūthoi**], is deceptive. Blind in heart are most men. For if they could have seen the truth [**alētheia**], never would great Ajax, angered over the arms [of Achilles], have driven the burnished sword through his own heart.

The fame of the great hero Ajax, grounded in the local hero cult of the Aiakidai on the island of Aegina,[44] setting of Pindar's *Nemean* 7, is threatened by the **mūthoi** 'myths' of Homeric poetry and rescued by the **alētheia** of Pindaric song.[45] The local tradition, as represented by Pindar, is

---

42. Quoted at p. 147. Commentary in N 1979.222–223. For an instance of **etumos** 'genuine' as applied to **logos**, in the sense of 'what men tell', see Pindar *Pythian* 1.68, where we note that the collocation includes the verb **diakrīnō** in the sense of 'discriminate' what is genuine from what is false.

43. This word can be understood in the context of *Odyssey* i 5: **polla ... pathen algea** 'he experienced many pains'. The multiplicity of Odysseus' experiences is thematically pertinent. On the convention of juxtaposing a single absolute **alētheia** 'truth' with a multiplicity of **mūthoi** 'myths', which are deceptive, see pp. 65 and following.

44. Cf. p. 176.

45. It is typical of Panhellenic poetics to juxtapose a single absolute **alētheia** 'truth' with the multiplicity of **mūthoi** 'myths', which are deceptive because they are mutually contradictory, like the lies of Odysseus; see N 1982.47–49. Also pp. 65 and following.

making its bid for Panhellenic status by paradoxically laying claim to the kind of absolute **alētheia** already claimed by Panhellenic poetry. In the process, Pindaric song is dismissing Homer as a perpetuator of **mūthoi**. In using this word, Pindaric song turns back to the very foil used by earlier Panhellenic poetry in dismissing various uncompromising localized versions slated for displacement by way of synthetic compromise.[46] This is not to say that the poetics of Pindar can dismiss epic itself: Homer is being slighted here only to the extent that he is being accused of becoming a perpetuator of the words of Odysseus; we should note that the figure of Odysseus, whenever he is being quoted by epic, speaks not in the mode of epic but rather as a master of multiple meanings, a man of craft whose discourse is described by epic itself as **ainos** (*Odyssey* xiv 508).[47]

This point brings us back to Pindar, whose own lyric medium is called, by the medium itself, **ainos** (e.g., *Olympian* 6.12).[48] As a master of the **ainos**, Pindar is obliged to be direct and truthful toward his near and dear, the **philoi**, but at the same time he is entitled to be indirect and deceitful toward his enemies, the **ekhthroi** (e.g., *Pythian* 2.83–85).[49] The voice of Pindar, the voice of the **ainos**, can indignantly condemn the multiplicity and deceitfulness of **mūthoi** that led to the undoing of the hero Ajax, as we have just seen in the use of the word **mūthoi** at *Nemean* 7.23 (and the same situation holds at *Nemean* 8.33). At the same time it can espouse multiplicity and deceitfulness for the purpose of decoying the unrighteous **ekhthros** 'enemy'.

There is a particularly striking example of the proclaimed multiplicity of the **ainos** in a Pindaric song where the wise words of the hero Amphiaraos, who is being represented in the act of instructing his son Amphilokhos, are being directly quoted. The hero's words of instruction center on the image of an octopus:

ὦ τέκνον, ποντίου θηρὸς πετραίου | χρωτὶ μάλιστα νόον | προφέρων πάσαις πολίεσσιν ὁμίλει· | τῷ παρεόντι δ' ἐπαινήσαις ἑκὼν | ἄλλοτ' ἀλλοῖα φρόνει

Pindar F 43 SM

My son, associate with all the various cities by making your mind [**noos**] resemble, most of all, the coloring of the animal who lives in the sea, clinging to rocks. Have on your mind different things at different times, being ready and willing, for the occasion, to make **ainos** [= verb **ep-aineō**].[50]

---

46. Cf. p$_{\Gamma}$. 65 and following.

47. Further discussion in N 1979.231–242, especially p. 235.

48. N 1979.222–223.

49. N, pp. 241–242. Cf. Hubbard 1985.99–100.

50. These "quoted" words of Amphiaraos to Amphilokhos are described as a **parainesis** by Athenaeus 513c; cf. also the cognate passage, composed in dactylic hexameters and not attri-

There is a close parallel in the poetry of Theognis, another of the poetic figures whose traditions we are considering as points of comparison with the traditions of Pindar and Homer. In this parallel from Theognis, the central image is again that of an octopus, as the voice of the poet issues the following instruction:

πουλύπου ὀργὴν ἴσχε πολυπλόκου, ὃς ποτὶ πέτρῃ
τῇ προσομιλήσῃ, τοῖος ἰδεῖν ἐφάνη.
νῦν μὲν τῇδ᾽ ἐφέπου, τοτὲ δ᾽ ἀλλοῖος χρόα γίνου.
κρέσσων τοι σοφίη γίνεται ἀτροπίης

Theognis 215–218

Have the temperament of a complex octopus, who
looks like whatever rock with which he is associated.[51]
Now be like this; then, at another time, become different in your
coloring.
I tell you: skill [**sophiā**] is better than being not versatile
[**atropos**].[52]

To be **atropos** 'not versatile' is the opposite of **polutropos** 'versatile in many ways', epithet of Odysseus (*Odyssey* i 1), who is actually compared in epic to an octopus (*Odyssey* v 432–433), and whose qualities of resourcefulness and versatility are being implicitly advocated by the poetics of Theognis as a key to the survival of values worth saving even in disguise, as the figure of the speaker is moving from city to city. We see in the symbol of the octopus the very essence of **ainos**.

The **ainos** is multiple, outwardly ever-changing as the poet moves from city to city, like the disguised Odysseus who tests the inner value of the many different people whom he meets in his travels.[53] Each person who is encountered by Odysseus after his homecoming in Ithaca is effectively being challenged to look beyond the hero's outer appearance as a debased beggar and to recognize his inner reality as a noble king whose authority is eventually being reestablished in the *Odyssey*, a process that parallels the eventual reconstitution of the very identity of Odysseus through a series of encounters

---

buted to any specific author, cited by Athenaeus 317ab. In this passage, the word that designates the different communities is not **polis** but **dēmos** (on which see p. 56).

51. The verb **prosomileō** 'associate with' anticipates a person or community of persons as an object, as at Theognis 31–32, but here the language of the tenor ("a person associates with a certain kind of company") crosses over into the language of the vehicle ("just as an octopus clings to a certain kind of rock"). For the terms *tenor* and *vehicle*: Richards 1936.96. Cf. Steiner 1986, especially p. 2. Further application of Richards' terms in Petegorsky 1982.

52. This passage is cited by Athenaeus 317a, as a parallel to the anonymous passage in dactylic hexameters "quoting" the instructions of the hero Amphiaraos to his son Amphilokhos.

53. Cf. pp. 231 and following, especially p. 236.

with the population of Ithaca.[54] Thus the **ainos** is also singular, inwardly constant, bearing a true message that is hidden amidst a plethora of possible false interpretations.[55] We may compare the fable of "The Fox and the Hedgehog" as attested in Archilochus F 201 W, where the fox is said to *know* (verb **oida**) many things, while the hedgehog knows ἓν μέγα 'one big thing'. This traditional dichotomy between the multiplicity of the fox and the unitarianism of the hedgehog can be used in support of emending the textually corrupt phrase πολλῶν γνουσαν ἔτι in Theognis 670, which can be read as πολλῶν γνοὺς ἓν ἔτι 'for I know *one* thing far better than many other things'.[56] This one thing that *is* known, introduced by οὕνεκα at Theognis 671, is a riddle concerning the crisis of the Ship of State beset by a seastorm of social strife (671–680).[57] When the image of the Ship of State concludes, the poem refers to it as an **ainigma** 'riddle':

ταῦτά μοι ᾐνίχθω κεκρυμμένα τοῖς ἀγαθοῖσιν

Theognis 681

Let these things be riddling utterances [= **ainigmata**], hidden by me for the noble [**agathoi**].

As we contemplate these words, it is pertinent to observe the context of **sophiā** 'skill' in Theognis 218, the same passage that bears the symbol of the octopus (215–218), and I quote an earlier observation of mine: "This word recalls the epithet **sophos** 'skilled' applied to the man who can foresee impending misfortunes like some **mantis** 'seer' [Theognis 682][58] — a man who speaks in the mode of an **ainigma** 'riddle' (681) about a ship beset by a storm at sea."[59] In this context the same man, the figure of Theognis, is represented as a model of righteousness who had lost his **khrēmata** 'possessions' and finds himself in distress as he associates with the **agathoi** 'noble' (Theognis 667–670, with **khrēmata** at 667 and **agathoi** at 668; cf. 649–652). Implicit here is the model of Odysseus, the hidden king in beggar's disguise, intrinsically noble but extrinsically debased through impoverishment, who finds himself in distress as he associates with the extrinsically noble but intrinsically base suitors who are usurping his own realm. Moreover, the figure of Theognis, who hides his own intrinsic nobility with the extrinsic debasedness of impoverishment as he tests the worth of others (Theognis 649–652),

---

54. Cf. N 1979.231–237; also 1983.36 (with p. 52n5) and 1985.75–76.
55. Ibid.
56. See van Groningen 1966.265. We may compare Sophocles *Electra* 690: ἓν δ' ἴσθι 'I want you to know this one thing'.
57. Cf. p. 149.
58. On the implication of a **mantis** at Theognis 682, see the commentary by N 1985.24–25.
59. N, p. 76.

is directly compared to the figure of Odysseus himself (Theognis 1123–1125).[60]

In short the medium of the **ainos** may espouse the same tactics as those used by Odysseus and reported by the medium of epic. The difference is, the medium of epic may *represent* the medium of the **ainos**, as when the tactics of Odysseus are being narrated, but it cannot be **ainos** itself.[61] In contrast, a medium like that of Pindar *is* **ainos** and, as such, it claims the authority to judge what is being represented by epic, praising what is noble and blaming what is base. The **ainos** of Pindar's lyric tradition claims control over epic, as if it represented a more definitive principle of poetics. Whereas epic can just *hear,* the **ainos** claims to *see* as well. Whereas epic is Panhellenic, a delocalized synthesis of native traditions, the **ainos** purports to be both Panhellenic and local, grounding its Panhellenized truth-values in the legitimacy and authority of native traditions, which shift from city to city and which are the context for the here and now of performance.

This function of the **ainos**, as proclaimed by the poetics of Pindar, is traditional, shared by the older poetics of Stesichorus. True, these two traditions of lyric poetry are strikingly different in some respects, as we see from the contrasting principles of thematic compression in the typical Pindaric composition on the one hand and on the other of expansion, veering toward epic dimensions, in the typical Stesichorean composition. Still they are strikingly similar in their social purpose, which is to instruct and thus maintain the prestige of a given community by way of selecting those Panhellenic values that reinforce its local interests. Like Pindar, Stesichorus is an exponent of the **ainos**.

In fact the Stesichorean **ainos** can assume the specialized form of a fable, as we see from as many as four attested stories reporting various situations where the figure of Stesichorus warns a given city against violence or tyranny.[62] In one of these, as reported by Aristotle *Rhetoric* 1394b35 (Stesichorus PMG 281b), Stesichorus warns the people of Locri that they should not be **hubristai** 'men of **hubris**', and his words are described as **ainigmatōdē** 'like **ainigmata** [riddling utterances]' (ibid.). We may compare the words of warning to the people of Megara, as encoded in the celebrated image of the ship threatened by a storm at sea, in Theognis 667–682, where the poetry refers to its message as ταῦτά μοι ἠνίχθω 'let these words of mine be **ainigmata** [riddling utterances]' (681).[63] Aristotle (ibid.) specifies the image used by Stesichorus in his words of warning to the people of Locri: it is a theme from the world of fable, a riddling reference to **tettīges** 'cicadas'

60. Extensive discussion in N 1985.74–81.

61. Cf. pp. 147 and following, especially p. 197.

62. There is a list in West 1971.302–303. On the ambivalence of the **ainos** in either warning about tyranny or on other occasions praising given tyrants as "kings," see pp. 174 and following.

63. See p. 149; also N 1985.22–24.

singing on the ground (χαμόθεν; instead of trees, as in Hesiod *Works and Days* 583). In another reference to the same theme, within the larger context of a discussion of metaphor, Aristotle describes this same fable-image as an example of τὰ εὖ ἠνιγμένα 'well-made **ainigmata** [allusive utterances]' (*Rhetoric* 1412a22). We should note that the figure of the **tettīx** 'cicada' is a symbol of the poet specifically within the format of the **ainos**, as in the case of Archilochus F 223 W.[64]

Another of the four aforementioned stories where the figure of Stesichorus warns the people of a given city in the form of a fable, that is, in a specialized aspect of the **ainos**, is the story of "The Horse and the Deer," reportedly narrated by Stesichorus to the people of Himera on the occasion of their choosing Phalaris as tyrant of their polis (Aristotle *Rhetoric* 1393b8; Stesichorus PMG 281a).[65] This particular fable is cited by Aristotle as a direct parallel to the fable of "The Fox and the Hedgehog," reportedly narrated by Aesop to the people of Samos on the occasion of their impending execution of a "demagogue" (Aristotle *Rhetoric* 1093b22; Aesop *Fable* 427 Perry).[66] In yet another of the four stories, as reported by Conon FGH 26 F 1.42, Stesichorus is again telling the people of Himera the fable of "The Horse and the Deer," and the word used here by the source to designate the fable is actually **ainos** (1.42.1), but this time the fable is directed not against Phalaris but another Sicilian tyrant figure, Gelon, who is portrayed as making overtures to the people of Himera (ibid.).[67] Finally, in a fragment of a story reported by Philodemus *On Music*, p. 18 Kemke, Stesichorus is pictured as putting a stop to discord among the people of a city, by singing in their midst, just as Terpander had reputedly done in Sparta (ibid.); in another mention of this parallelism between Stesichorus and Terpander, Philodemus describes the social discord as **stasis** (*On Music*, p. 87).

Such evidence illustrates the fundamental meaning of **ainos**, as I have defined it from the start: "An affirmation, a marked speech-act, made by and for a social group."[68] As for the social group by which and for which the **ainos** is encoded in Archaic Greek poetry, it is clearly the polis. Thus, for example, the figure of Theognis, as an exponent of the **ainos**, can be portrayed as the lawgiver of his own city (Theognis 543–546, 805–810)[69] or as

---

64. N 1979.302.

65. As Lefkowitz 1981.34 points out, Phalaris was tyrant of Akragas, not Himera. But perhaps the story here concerns an invitation issued by one city to the tyrant of another, as in the story about Stesichorus and Gelon, to be discussed presently.

66. This fable of "The Fox and the Hedgehog" is cognate with what we find in Archilochus F 201 W, discussed at p. 426.

67. We may compare the stories about Aesop and his warnings to the people of Samos, by way of fables directed against the tyrant Croesus of Lydia: pp. 323 and following.

68. Cf. p. 31; also p. 147.

69. Commentary in N 1985.36–38.

the **kubernētēs** 'pilot' of the Ship of State caught in the crisis of a seastorm of social strife (667–682).[70] In this context of the storm besetting the Ship of State, the righteous man is represented as having lost his own **khrēmata** (Theognis 667). Such a righteous man, exponent of the **ainos**, is conventionally alienated from the polis of his own time and place. He can be in despair about ever having the chance to witness, in his lifetime, the **tisis** 'retribution' of Zeus (Theognis 345) against the unjust men who forcibly seized his **khrēmata** 'possessions' (346) and who seem to go unpunished. These unjust men turn out to be the false **philoi** who have betrayed the just man, the one who navigates like a **kubernētēs** 'pilot' (Theognis 575–576).[71] These are the men who seize **khrēmata** by force (Theognis 677) as they depose the **kubernētēs** (675–676) in the Ship of State afflicted by the seastorm of social strife.[72] Clearly the loss of **khrēmata** 'possessions' by the righteous man (667), speaker of the **ainigmata** 'riddles' concerning the Ship of State (681), is linked to the forcible seizure of **khrēmata** by the unrighteous (677), who have mutinied against the **kubernētēs** 'pilot' (675–676) and who have thereby caused the breakdown of the **kosmos** 'social order' (677). In Pindar's *Isthmian* 2, this same word **khrēmata** is used in a context where one of the Seven Sages,[73] in reaction to his personal loss of both property and friends (11), exclaims bitterly: χρήματα χρήματ' ἀνήρ 'Man is nothing more than **khrēmata**! Yes, **khrēmata**!' (ibid.). Another variation on this bitter reaction is quoted in the lyric poetry of Alcaeus (F 360 V), again in a context where the Sage, named here as Aristodemos of Sparta, is bewailing the equation of self-worth with purely material value.[74]

The poet's negative outlook on his own situation, as he stands bereft of his possessions and betrayed by his friends, translates ultimately into a positive message, a genuine teaching, for the polis. Thus Pindar's quotation of the Sage's bitter words, to the effect that man is nothing but material possessions, that is, **khrēmata** (*Isthmian* 2.11), is followed by the following direct address to the recipient of Pindar's words of praise and instruction: ἐσσὶ γὰρ ὦν σοφός 'for you are skilled [i.e., in decoding these words]' (2.12). That the hearer of poetry or song must be **sophos** 'skilled' in decoding its words is a mark of the **ainos**.[75] As is evident in the poetry of Theognis, the alienation that marks the poet's own there and then on the level of narrative becomes transformed, as a teaching, into the integration that ostensibly marks the audience's here and now on the level of the **ainos** conveyed by the narrative.[76] In the polis of the past, the setting of the narrative, the figure of the

70. Commentary in N, pp. 22–24, 63, 64–68.
71. Commentary in N, pp. 67–68, 71.
72. N, p. 71.
73. On the theme of the Seven Sages, see p. 243.
74. See p. 341.
75. See p. 148.
76. This point is argued at length in N 1985.27–46.

poet decries the ongoing destruction of the social order, the **kosmos** (κόσμος δ' ἀπόλωλεν Theognis 677); in the polis of the present, however, which is the audience of the **ainos** conveyed by such narrative, the same word **kosmos** means simultaneously both the sum total of its inherited social order (e.g., Herodotus 1.65.4, in the case of Sparta) and the cohesion of its poetic tradition, which upholds that social order (e.g., Pindar F 194 SM, in the case of Thebes).[77] The themes of Theognis will be sung time and again by future generations of youths, in the integrative atmosphere of feasts and symposia, 'in good **kosmos**' (εὐκόσμως 242).[78]

With this background, we turn from the traditions of Stesichorus and Theognis to those of Archilochus, as we explore further points of comparison between the lyric of Pindar and the epic of Homer. In particular, let us consider the relationship of Archilochus to the island-communities of Paros and Thasos. The poet was traditionally represented as a founder of a colony of Paros on the island of Thasos (Delphic Oracle no. 232 Parke / Wormell). We may note in passing a similar tradition about the iambic poet Semonides: he was reputed to be a founder of a colony of Samos on the island of Amorgos (*Suda* 360.7).[79] The key to understanding the importance of these traditions is the historical fact that the prevailing pattern of Greek colonizations in the Archaic period was to reduplicate the society of the mother polis in the daughter polis, even to the extent of hierarchically balancing different social strata in the daughter polis to match existing social differences in the mother polis.[80] In the case of the daughter polis at Thasos, we would expect the story of its foundation to be a reenactment, as it were, of the foundation of the mother polis at Paros. Meanwhile, the poet, as a vehicle for the education of the polis in ancestral values, becomes a representative of the polis; again I refer to the tradition about Archilochus as a chorus teacher of the polis.[81]

As a representative of the polis, Archilochus becomes a founder of a duplicated Parian society at Thasos, simply by virtue of Archilochean poetry. Archilochus becomes an expression of the function of his poetry. In that sense he is generic. So too are the other characters who figure in the Archilochus tradition. There is, for example, **Lukambēs** (as in Archilochus F 38 W), whose name is connected with the very notion of **iambos** 'iamb'.[82] Also there is **Kharilāos** (Archilochus F 168.1 W), whose name suggests the programmatic notion of 'mirth' for the community.[83] Further, the mother of

77. See p. 144.

78. For the corresponding negative situation, where social disorder is marked by the absence of **kosmos** at a feast, see Solon F 4.10 W.

79. Cf. Schmid 1947.17.

80. See Figueira 1981.192–202, especially p. 199. Also p. 71.

81. See p. 396.

82. N 1979.248–252.

83. N 1979.258–259 (and 91–93).

Archilochus is reportedly a 'slave-woman' called **Enīpō** (Critias 88 B 44 DK in Aelian *Varia Historia* 10.13), whose name is formed from the noun **enīpē**, meaning 'reproach' and specifically applicable to blame poetry.[84] The father of Archilochus is **Telesikleēs** (e.g., Archilochus T 2 Tarditi), whose name combines the notion of poetic fame or **kleos** with the notion of rites as conveyed by the element **telesi-** (related to **telea** 'rites').[85] Similarly an earlier ancestor of Archilochus is **Tellis**, husband of one **Kleoboia**, who is reputed to have introduced the rites of Demeter to Thasos (Archilochus T 121 Tarditi by way of Pausanias 10.28.3);[86] we are reminded of the Archilochus fragment where the poet is represented as participating in the rites of Demeter and Kore (F 322 W). As for **Kleoboia** 'having poetic fame [**kleos**] for cows', the name corresponds to the myth where the young Archilochus meets the Muses, who trade him a lyre, and the skill of poetry that goes with it, for the cow that he is tending (Mnesiepes Inscription, Archilochus T 4.27–30 Tarditi).[87]

In the local myth Telesikles, the father of Archilochus, 'announces' the colonization of Thasos, but Archilochus leads it. The story goes (Oenomaus, Archilochus T 116 Tarditi) that Telesikles consults the Oracle of Apollo at Delphi, where he is told:

ἄγγειλον Παρίοις, Τελεσίκλεες, ὥς σε κελεύω
νήσῳ ἐν Ἡερίῃ κτίζειν εὐδείελον ἄστυ.

Delphic Oracle no. 230 PW

Announce to the Parians, Telesikles, that I order you
to found a sunlit city on the island of Aeria [= Thasos].

The narrative goes on to say explicitly that had Telesikles not 'announced' the command of the Oracle, Archilochus would not have led a colonizing expedition to Thasos and Thasos would never have been colonized by Paros (Oenomaus ibid.). In a variant (again Oenomaus: Archilochus T 114 Tarditi), Archilochus himself consults the Oracle, after having lost his property

84. Further discussion, with bibliography, in N 1979.247–248. The lowly social status of **Enīpō** makes Archilochus a **nothos** 'bastard', the product of socially unequal parents; as such, his persona resembles that of Kyrnos, the prime recipient of loving admonition in the poetry of Theognis. As I argue at length in N 1985.51–60 (cf. also p. 183 above), the name **Kurnos** conveys the notion of 'bastard', in the transcendent sense of one who is debased by material excess; the name simultaneously conveys the notion of 'prince', as an appropriate designation of a Heraclid (N, p. 33). Thus the very name **Kurnos** is a riddle, an **ainos**.

85. Cf. West 1974.24

86. From Pausanias' description (10.28.3) of the painting of Polygnotus located in the Lesche of the Knidians (and I emphasize that Polygnotus was a native of Thasos), we note that Kleoboia is represented as offering a **kibōtos** 'box' to Demeter; she is shown crossing the Acheron in a boat, along with Tellis.

87. Cf. N 1979.303; also p. 365 above.

ἐν πολιτικῇ φλυαρίᾳ 'in the course of some political foolishness' (Oenomaus ibid.), and he is told directly to colonize Thasos:

Ἀρχίλοχ' εἰς Θάσον ἐλθὲ καὶ οἴκει εὐκλέα νῆσον

Delphic Oracle no. 232 PW

Archilochus! Go to Thasos and colonize that island of good **kleos**.

In yet another variant (Oenomaus, Archilochus T 115 Tarditi)[88] the Oracle says to Telesikles that Archilochus will be immortalized in poetry:

ἀθάνατός σοι παῖς καὶ ἀοίδιμος, ὦ Τελεσίκλεις,
ἔσσετ' ἐν ἀνθρώποις

Delphic Oracle no. 231 PW

Your son, Telesikles, will be immortal, a subject of song among men.

It is clear that the fame of Archilochus is linked with the theme of his colonizing Thasos, a theme that is also dramatized in his poetry.

Why exactly does Archilochus colonize Thasos? It is because he lost his possessions *in civil strife* (Archilochus T 114 Tarditi). We may compare the implicit theme of civil strife in the story of the foundation of Syracuse, Archilochus F 293 W. This brings us back to the central themes of Theognis 667–682, the riddling passage about the loss of a man's **khrēmata** 'possessions' (667) and about the crisis of the Ship of State beset by a seastorm of civil strife (671–680), all told in the mode of an **ainos**.[89]

Despite the self-identification of any piece of Archaic poetry or song with the polis of its origin, the strategy of the **ainos** requires, already in the Archaic period, an impact that is Panhellenic as well as local. Although the poet of the **ainos** may be addressing specifically the people of the polis, the prestige of the moment is meant to be overheard, as it were, by all Hellenes. This double-sidedness is particularly evident in the poetry of Theognis, who in the space of a single verse identifies himself as a citizen of one particular polis, Megara, while at the same time proclaiming his own Panhellenic fame (Theognis 23).[90] It is also evident that this poetry associates the uncertainties of audience reception with the here and now of performance in Megara (Theognis 24–28, 253–254), and the certainty of audience acceptance with the future of many reperformances throughout the cities of the Hellenes (19–23, 237–252, where we may note the plethora of future tenses).[91] Retro-

88. This variant is also attested in the Mnesiepes Inscription, Archilochus T 4 II 43–57 Tarditi.

89. Cf. p. 426.

90. Commentary in N 1985.29.

91. Detailed discussion at N, pp. 34–35; p. 35 §17n1, 2 on the future tenses of Theognis 19–23, 237–252.

spectively we may say that the format of **ainos** in the poetics of Theognis represents Panhellenic poetry, but even this representation must be translated into the concept of local performances for local audiences, albeit in the future.[92]

The essential point about the pre-Classical phase of the **ainos** in particular and of Greek lyric poetry in general is that local or epichoric poetry is already becoming Panhellenic through diffusion. In the case of Theognis, for example, we see local Megarian traditions becoming international, that is, inter-polis, *by way of the polis*. In this case internationalization of the native poetic tradition goes so far as to filter out the native Dorian dialect of Megara.[93]

In the earlier phases of attested Greek lyric poetry, the price of Panhellenization is that the identity of the poet as composer becomes progressively stylized, becoming ever further distanced from the reality of self-identification through performance. The key to loss of identity as a composer is loss of control over performance.[94] Once the factor of performance slips out of the poet's control, even if the performers of his poetry have a tradition of what to say about the poet as a composer, nevertheless, the poet becomes a myth; more accurately, the poet becomes part of a myth, and the myth-making structure appropriates his identity.[95]

At times it is hard to tell whether a given Archaic Greek poet is engaged in a given social function or whether it is his composition, performed and continually recomposed by others, that continues to perform that social function. In the case of Alcman, for example, we have seen indications that his choral productions kept being performed at the Spartan festival of the Gymnopaidiai for centuries after the era identified with this poet.[96] What may seem to us uncanny, as we examine the text of Alcman's surviving compositions, is that we can detect traces of self-reference beyond one single historical occasion. Specifically the persona of the poet seems to be referring to himself as being present at performances throughout the ages, continually fulfilling the social function of educating young girls to sing and dance in a chorus.[97] Not only is Alcman's lyric poetry re-created for each performance, but the figure of the creator himself keeps returning as a sort of eternal **khorēgos** 'chorus leader'.[98]

In a place like Sparta of the Classical period, one begins to wonder if there is any current activity at all in the craft of poetry and song that is not a

92. Cf. p. 374.
93. Cf. p. 53.
94. Cf. p. 80.
95. Ibid.
96. Cf. p. 344.
97. Cf. pp. 370 and following.
98. See ibid.

matter of recomposing earlier models.[99] The testimonia concerning a figure like Tyrtaeus of Sparta, for example, suggest that his poetry alone was sufficient for a wide variety of performance occasions (e.g., Philochorus FGH 328 F 216 in Athenaeus 630f; Lycurgus *Against Leokrates* 106–107).

There is a parallel phenomenon in the poetry of Theognis. The poet is dramatized as being present at crucial stages in the history of his city, Megara, though the local color is consistently screened out in favor of a generalized Panhellenic highlighting.[100] We see the phenomenon of the continually reconstituted poet, who is continually present at the events of his city. But the poet's impact is Panhellenic, even though the vantage point is the here and now of one particular locale.[101]

In the Archaic period, then, there are indeed poets of the polis. But they are from the very start more Panhellenic than local. They may be exponents of one polis, but the polis itself makes these poets Panhellenic figures, by way of diffusion in recomposition. The diffusion of a poetic tradition may be represented in myth by way of a poet's travels. The ultimate example is the figure of Homer, who is pictured in the Homeric *Hymn to Apollo* as traveling throughout the cities of humankind (174–175).[102]

Approaching the end of this retrospective survey of Panhellenism in Archaic Greek lyric, we arrive at perhaps the most subtle example, the case of Sappho and Alcaeus. Here too, as with the other traditions that we have examined, we find the claim to Panhellenic or catholic status. For example, the expression πέρροχος ὡς ὄτ᾽ ἄοιδος ὁ Λέσβιος 'outstanding like the poet from Lesbos' in Sappho F 106 V, words of praise for Terpander as the 'poet of Lesbos' who is supreme among poets,[103] presupposes the international status of Terpander, as we see from the parallel theme in a proverb associated with the traditions of Sparta, μετὰ Λέσβιον ᾠδόν 'second in rank only to the poet from Lesbos' (*Suda* s.v.).[104] By implication Sappho's lyric poetry stems

99. We may note in this connection the absence of any Pindaric epinician celebrating a Spartan.

100. N 1985.30–36.

101. Cf. pp. 370 and following.

102. N 1979.8; also above at pp. 375 and following.

103. Cf. p. 418.

104. Under the entry μετὰ Λέσβιον ᾠδόν in the *Suda*, it is explained that the proverb refers to the story that the Spartans invited, from among all the **kitharōidoi** 'lyre singers', those from Lesbos first (τοὺς Λεσβίους κιθαρῳδοὺς πρώτους προσεκαλοῦντο); that when the polis of Sparta was in disorder, an oracle told them to send for the singer from Lesbos; when Terpander arrived at Sparta, he put an end to the **stasis** 'social strife' (ibid.). On Terpander as **kitharōidos**, see p. 86. We may note another detail under the same entry in the *Suda*: tradition has it that Terpander came to Sparta while in exile from Lesbos on account of a blood guilt. This theme may imply hero cult in the making, as in the myth about Oedipus at Colonus, where the hero is exiled from Thebes on account of his blood guilt and is thereafter purified at Athens, in response to which the hero donates to the Athenians his own corpse as the talisman of his represented hero cult at Colonus; cf. p. 178.

from the traditions of the first-ranking poet of lyric, Terpander. In the Dorian tradition of Pindar, we have seen a comparable acknowledgment of Terpander, but here the stress is on the Dorian layer of the tradition, which was superimposed on the Aeolian layer of Terpander's native Lesbos when he came to Sparta (Pindar F 191 SM).[105] This superimposition is reflected in the dialectal layering of Pindaric diction: dominant Doric, recessive Aeolic, and residual Ionic.[106] But there are earlier stages of superimposition reflected in the dialectal layering of Sappho and Alcaeus: dominant Aeolic synthesized with recessive Ionic.[107] We may add the testimony of *Cologne Papyri* 5860, where Sappho is described as the 'educator' of the **aristai**, the female élite, of Lesbos *and* Ionia. To say that Sappho is an 'educator' is a prosaic way of saying that her assumed role, through her lyric poetry, is that of **khorēgos** 'chorus leader', speaking both *to* and *about* members of an aggregate of female characters who are bound together by ties that correspond to the ties that bind a chorus together.[108] The ties that bind together the circle of Sappho are not local but international, that is, inter-polis, as we see from the reference to her being an 'educator' of the élite in Lesbos and in Ionia at large. The stance of the poet is local, even personal, but the impact is Panhellenic, in that the self-expression of the lyric poetry is not exclusive, understandable only for the local community. The local color is shaded over except insofar as any detail may already have a claim to Panhellenic fame. The Panhellenic impact of Sappho and Alcaeus accounts for the reports of performances at symposia of compositions attributed to them (e.g., Plutarch *Sympotic Questions* 622c in the case of Sappho, Aristophanes F 223 Kock [= 235 KA] in the case of Alcaeus).[109]

From this overview of the effects of Panhellenism on the traditions of Archaic Greek song and poetry, we have by now seen a wide range of developments:

1. ongoing recomposition of nonlyric poetry by way of rhapsodes in formal contexts such as festivals[110]
2. ongoing recomposition of lyric poetry, that is, song, by way of choruses performing in formal contexts such as festivals[111]

---

105. Cf. p. 93.

106. Cf. p. 418.

107. Ibid.

108. Cf. p. 370. On the role of **khorēgos** 'chorus leader' as educator of the community, see the discussion of Alcman at pp. 344 and following; also of Archilochus at pp. 395 and following.

109. Cf. p. 107. Cf. the mythopoeic visualization of Terpander as he sings at the **sussitia** 'common meals' of the Spartans (*Suda* s.v. μετὰ Λέσβιον ᾠδόν).

110. For example, pp. 54 and following.

111. For example, pp. 343 and following (Alcman), p. 362 (Stesichorus).

3. ongoing recomposition of both kinds of poetry in less formal contexts, most notably symposia.[112]

The information that has been assembled in this survey encourages me to stand by a theory that I articulated in an earlier work, on the poetry of Theognis:[113] the figure of the Archaic poet represents a cumulative synthesis of a given city-state's poetic traditions. The major advantage to this theory is that the poetry of a given poet like Archilochus or Theognis may then be appreciated as a skillful and effective — maybe even beautiful — dramatization of the polis through the ages. The major disadvantage on the other hand is that the notion of a historical figure called, say, Archilochus or Theognis, may have to be abandoned. This is not to say, however, that the persona of the poet does not inform the entire corpus of his or her poetry. The poetry or song actually brings to life the integral and lively personality of one man or one woman, whose complex identity is perhaps the one constant in the changing world of his or her beloved city. If this theory is tantamount to calling the Archaic poet a "myth," then so be it, provided that *myth* can be understood as a given society's codification of its own traditional values in narrative and dramatic form.

In the earlier phases, then, of Greek lyric poetry, the trend of Panhellenization entails an ongoing recomposition of not only the poetry but also the identity of the poet, which is appropriated by the poetry. But things are changing in the later phases of Greek lyric poetry, in the era of Pindar and such contemporaries as Simonides and Bacchylides. This is the era when the system of reciprocity within the community at large, as represented by the polis, is breaking down.[114] It is an era when individuals can achieve the power to overreach the polis itself, and the pattern of overreaching extends to the realm of song. As I have argued, such power includes the specific power to arrest the ongoing process of recomposition by the polis, so that both poetry and poet can become Panhellenic and yet remain unchanging, unchanged. In this brave new world, the craft of song is ever in danger of shifting from an expression of community to an expression of the individual. That individual is the expressing poet on the one hand and the expressed patron, the "great" man of overarching power, on the other. The power of the individual is a potential threat as well as a boon to the community. In the real world, the "great" men who are being praised are the potential tyrants and quasityrants that are being generated by the aristocracy. In the ideological world of a poet like Pindar, in contrast, the aristocracy remains an ideal that must resist the degeneration that breeds tyrants. That ideal is still expressed through Pindar's traditional medium, the **ainos**. The **ainos** is not only Panhellenic.

112. For example, pp. 107, 109, 112, 113, and following.
113. N 1985.33–34.
114. Cf. pp. 189 and following.

Unlike epic, which is exclusively Panhellenic, a delocalized synthesis of native traditions, the **ainos** purports to be both Panhellenic and local, grounding its Panhellenized truth-values in the legitimacy and authority of native traditions, which shift from city to city and which are the context for the here and now of performance. The tyrant may attempt to use the **ainos** for his own political ends, but the **ainos** of a poet like Pindar is also a world apart, drawing its strength from the values of the heroic past that is Pindar's Homer.

In claiming that the form of Pindar *contains* diachronically the form of Homer, we need never forget the radical differences between Pindar and Homer. If we think of the medium, then Pindar represents song and dance performed by a chorus, while Homer is epic, performed by **rhapsōidoi** 'rhapsodes'. If we think of the author, then Pindar is a historical person of the fifth century, whereas Homer seems to be a myth-made personification, a stylized retrojection into the dark ages antedating recorded history. The point of contact can be symbolized in the medium of the **kitharōidos** 'lyre singer'. The diachronic self-references of Homeric poetry, on the one hand, picture the epic poet as a lyre singer.[115] The choral compositions of epinician poets like Pindar, on the other hand, can be reperformed at symposia as solo pieces that are self-accompanied on the lyre.[116] In fact such solo performance was the ultimate sign of education, of direct access to the true old values.[117] The meeting point between Homer and Pindar survives in the medium of the **kitharōidos**, which reflects the complex patterns of transition from choral to solo performance.

The presence of heroic narrative in Pindar is the continuation of a living tradition, not the preservation of references to lost epic texts. As for things Homeric, they do not necessarily survive in Pindar as the Homer that we know — even if Pindar calls them Homer's tradition — because the two traditions of Homeric poetry and Pindaric song, though they are cognate with each other, each have their own momentum and direction of development. This is not to say that Pindaric song cannot "cite" Homer. But the form in which Homer is "cited" is a transformation of Homer, in metrical frames that are basic to Pindar's form though admittedly cognate with Homer's form. The Homeric themes are also transformed within the poetic requirements of Pindar's cognate medium. From the lofty vantage point of Pindaric song, Homer is Pindar's Homer. Pindaric song is both staying in the present and reaching back into the past within itself. It does not have to go outside for the purpose of bringing the epic inside. Epic is within it, and from it epic shall forever flow.

115. Cf. pp. 20 and following.
116. Cf. pp. 113 and following.
117. Ibid.

▢▢ Appendix: A Comparative Survey of Pindar's Meters

In what follows, I offer a diachronic study of the two major types of meter inherited by Pindar, the so-called Aeolic and the dactylo-epitrite. My goal is to show the affinities between these meters in Greek song and the three major types of meter in Greek poetry, namely, the dactylic hexameter, the elegiac distich, and the iambic trimeter.[1] Both these meters and the dactylo-epitrites, which are described after the Aeolic, are built on the principle of the *colon*, which I define for the moment simply as a fundamental unit in the rhythmical structure of song.[3] A fundamental type of colon in the system of Aeolic meters is the so-called glyconic:

$$\underset{\smile\smile}{} - \smile\smile - \smile - \qquad\qquad = glyc.[4]$$

Both here and in the other metrical representations that follow, I show the last syllable of a given metrical unit as uniformly long, not short. This practice reflects a principle that is at the same time metrical and linguistic: I mean the neutralization, in prepausal position (that is, in the last syllable of a metri-

---

1. Earlier versions of this argument appeared in N 1979b and 1983c.

2. The following symbols are henceforth in effect: – = long syllable; ⌣ = short; ⌣̲ = anceps = long or short; ⌢ = long or two shorts; ⌣̲̆ = anceps or two shorts.

3. For more on the term *colon*: West 1982.5–6.

4. For example, Sappho F 96. In this chapter, all fragments of Sappho and Alcaeus are taken from the edition of Voigt (V). The metrical abbreviations, such as *glyc* for *glyconic*, are modifications of those found in West 1982, whose taxonomy of Greek meters I follow here, with some exceptions as noted.

cal unit), of the distinction between long and short in favor of long. This principle is commonly known as *brevis in longo*.[5]

The glyconic can be internally expanded by a unit called the choriamb

−∪∪−   = *ch*.

This expansion may involve one, two, or three choriambs, to form

⏓⏓‾−∪∪−‾−∪∪−∪−   = *glyc@ch*[6]
⏓⏓‾−∪∪−−∪∪−‾−∪∪−∪−   = *glyc@2ch*[7]
⏓⏓‾−∪∪−−∪∪−−∪∪−‾−∪∪−∪−   = *glyc@3ch*.[8]

Similarly a glyconic can be internally expanded by a unit called a dactyl

−∪∪   = *da*.

This expansion may involve one or two dactyls, to form

⏓⏓‾−∪∪−∪∪−∪−   = *glyc@da*[9]
⏓⏓‾−∪∪−∪∪−∪∪−∪−   = *glyc@2da*.[10]

Now the glyconic

⏓⏓−∪∪−∪−   = *glyc*

has a catalectic variant, called the *pherecratic*

⏓⏓−∪∪−−   = *pher*.[11]

By *catalectic* and *catalexis*, I mean the shortening of the metrical unit by way of deleting the last syllable and making the next-to-last syllable the new *brevis in longo*. Using the symbol < for catalexis, I describe the pherecratic as a catalectic glyconic:

$$pher = glyc<.$$

Like the glyconic, the pherecratic can be expanded by choriambs:

⏓⏓‾−∪∪−−∪∪−‾−∪∪−−   = *pher@2ch*.[12]

---

5. See the discussion of Devine and Stephens 1975, especially p. 204.
6. For example, Alcaeus F 112.
7. For example, Alcaeus F 343.
8. For example, Alcaeus F 387.
9. For example, Sappho F 94.
10. For example, Sappho F 44.
11. For example, Sappho F 111.1.
12. For example, Sappho F 140. I had neglected this poem in N 1974.47, where I claim wrongly that there are no pherecratics to be found with choriambic expansion.

Like the glyconic, the pherecratic can be expanded by dactyls:

⏑⏑‾⏑⏑‾⏑⏑‾‾ $= pher@da$[13]

⏑⏑‾⏑⏑‾⏑⏑‾⏑⏑‾‾ $= pher@2da$[14]

⏑⏑‾⏑⏑‾⏑⏑‾⏑⏑‾⏑⏑‾‾ $= pher@3da.$[15]

These metrical types have acephalic variants. The notions of *acephalic* and *acephaly* can be defined synchronically as the deletion of the first syllable of a given metrical line. Using the symbol > for acephaly, we may say that the glyconic has an acephalic variant known as the *telesillean*:[16]

⏑‾⏑⏑‾⏑‾ $= {>}glyc = tele.$[17]

Also the pherecratic has an acephalic variant, conventionally called the *reizianum*:[18]

⏑‾⏑⏑‾‾ $= {>}pher = reiz.$[19]

These acephalic variants, the telesillean and the reizianum, can in turn be internally expanded by choriambs or dactyls, as in

⏑‾⏑⏑‾‾⏑⏑‾⏑‾ $= {>}glyc@ch = tele@ch$[20]

⏑‾⏑⏑‾⏑⏑‾‾ $= {>}pher@da = reiz@da.$[21]

So much for a synchronic description of these Aeolic meters. Turning to a diachronic perspective, I begin by observing that the mechanics just surveyed have an Indo-European provenience.[22] For example, Brent Vine has demonstrated that cognate patterns of catalexis and acephaly are at work in Indic poetics.[23] Also I have found that the relationship between *glyc* and *glyc@ch* corresponds, within the Greek evidence itself, to the relationship

13. For example, Sappho F 110.
14. For example, Sappho F 115.
15. For example, Alcaeus F 368.
16. For the terminology, see West 1982.30.
17. For example, Alcaeus F 303.
18. Ibid. On the history of the term, see Gentili and Giannini 1977.11–12n8.
19. For example, Sappho 141.
20. For example, Alcaeus F 130.4.
21. For example, Sappho F 111.3.
22. Concerning the Indo-European heritage of Greek meters in general, I cite the pioneering studies of Meillet 1923, Jakobson 1952, and Watkins 1963. Cf. also Schmitt 1967.307–313, West 1973, 1973b, N 1974. For a survey of these works and others (such as Peabody 1975 and Vigorita 1977), see Bowie 1981.16–28. Commenting on the view of Meillet, p. 76, that the Indic and Greek correspondences in metrical patterns are too close to be coincidental, Bake 1957.195 observes that this view "is equally applicable when comparing the systems of music of the two ancient civilizations."
23. Cf. Vine 1977, 1978.

between iambic dimeter and trimeter,[24] and that there is a cognate relationship between the Indic dimeter and trimeter.[25] Like the Greek dimeter, the Indic dimeter is an 8-syllable line, or a 7-syllable catalectic variant; also the Indic trimeter is a 12-syllable line, or an 11-syllable catalectic variant.[26]

Let us take a closer look at the relationship between the Greek iambic dimeter and trimeter:

$$\underset{\smile}{\smile}-\smile-\underset{\smile}{\smile}\ -\smile- \qquad = ia\&IA \text{ iambic dimeter}^{27}$$

$$\underset{\smile}{\smile}-\smile-\underset{\smile}{\smile}\,|-\smile\ -\underset{\smile}{\smile}-\smile- \qquad = ia+ia\&IA \text{ iambic trimeter}$$

$$\underset{\smile}{\smile}-\smile-\underset{\smile}{\smile}\ -\smile\,|-\underset{\smile}{\smile}-\smile- \qquad = ia\&IA+IA \text{ iambic trimeter.}$$

In this scheme the abbreviation *ia* stands for the iamb, $\underset{\smile}{\smile}-\smile-$, in the first four syllables, or opening, of an iambic dimeter, while *IA* stands for the iamb, $\underset{\smile}{\smile}-\smile-$, in the last four syllables, or closing. The sign | stands for word break, that is, word boundary, while & stands for a combination not marked by any particular pattern of word breaking. The sign + stands for the addition of an extra opening (*ia*) or closing (*IA*).[28] The distinction between opening and closing is a matter of great importance from a diachronic standpoint. The scheme *ia+ia&IA* of iambic trimeter stands for a diachronic pattern of opening plus opening and closing, or extra opening plus dimeter. The reflex of this 4+8 pattern of syllables in a 12-syllable line is a word break (|) that leaves a pattern of 5| 7 syllables. Conversely the scheme *ia&IA+IA* of iambic trimeter stands for a diachronic pattern of opening and closing plus closing, or dimeter plus extra closing. The reflex of this 8+4 pattern of syllables in a 12-syllable line is a word break that leaves a pattern of 7| 5 syllables. In other words the synchronic description of Classical iambic trimeter as having a caesura after syllable 5 or, by default, after syllable 7 corresponds to a diachronic derivation of iambic trimeter from a combination of an extra opening plus iambic dimeter or from a combination of iambic dimeter plus an extra closing, respectively.[29] We can find a cognate situation in Indic tri-

24. N 1974.37–44. Similarly the relationship between *glyc* and *glyc@2ch* would correspond to the relationship between iambic dimeter and iambic tetrameter.

25. Ibid.

26. Ibid; also Vine 1977 and 1978. Cf. also Ananthanarayana 1973, who argues that trimeter is derived from dimeter and who posits for trimeter a basic 11-syllable unit and a derived 12-syllable unit; as the discussion proceeds, it will be clear that I disagree with the latter point and only partially agree with the former.

27. For example, Anacreon PMG 428.

28. In the present work, I have tried to be consistent in using four-letter symbols for whole dimeters (e.g. *glyc*) and two-letter symbols for openings or closings of dimeters and trimeters (e.g. *ia, ch*).

29. N 1974.37–44, 279–287; skepticism in West 1974.458, but tentative agreement in West 1982b.296n45. All this is not to say, however, that the dimeter is necessarily older than the trimeter (see the useful discussion of Vine 1978.175 and 191n7). It is only to say that the constituents of trimeter are cognate with the constituents of dimeter, and that we can therefore explain the trimeter in terms of the same constituents that we find in dimeter.

meters, where we see an older pattern 4| 8 being displaced by a newer pattern 5| 7.[30] In early Greek trimeters, moreover, we find that the pattern 7| 5 conceals further subdivision into 4| 3| 5,[31] while the pattern 5| 7 conceals further subdivision into 5| 3| 4.[32] I argue for an older pattern 4| 8 (4| 3| 5) in old iambic trimeter, with the primary alignment of 4+3&5, which is concealed by the newer pattern 7| 5 of Classical iambic trimeter, derived from a secondary alignment of 4&3+5. While the older pattern 4| 8 survives in the guise of 7| 5, it is at the same time superseded by the newer pattern 5| 7 of Classical iambic trimeter. To repeat, 5| 7 is the normal configuration of Classical iambic trimeter, while 7| 5, still retaining a hidden 4| 8 in older iambic trimeter, is the fallback alternative.[33]

Not only iambic trimeter but also other trimeters contain constituents that are cognate with dimeters other than the iambic dimeter. For example, the element *ia* can combine with a dimeter shaped *glyc*, and here again we can observe the pattern 5| 7 as an outcome:

$$\underline{\cup}-\cup-\underline{\cup} \mid \underline{\cup}-\cup\cup-\cup- \qquad\qquad = ia+glyc.^{[34]}$$

In such cases, however, the word breaking pattern 5| 7 is just one of a variety of possibilities. To use Roman Jakobson's useful distinction between *constant* and *tendency*,[35] the 5| 7 pattern is a constant in Classical iambic trimeters shaped *ia+ia&IA*, but it is only a tendency in archaic trimeters shaped *ia+glyc*. We can apply an analogous formulation to the 7| 5 pattern in Classical iambic trimeters shaped *ia&IA+IA*: again we see a constant, as distinct from a corresponding tendency in archaic trimeters shaped *glyc+IA*:

$$\underline{\cup}\underline{\cup}-\cup\cup-\cup \mid -\underline{\cup}-\cup- \qquad\qquad = glyc+IA.^{[36]}$$

So far we have considered various patterns of reapplied opening and reapplied closing. But there are also situations where the opening and the closing are inverted, that is, where a closing is fused with an opening that follows. For an illustration, let us examine what can happen when two glyconics are run together:

30. N ibid. Cf. West 1982b.295.

31. For example, Semonides F 7.12 W; *Margites* F 1 Allen, p. 156.

32. For example, Semonides F 7.3 W. Discussion in N 1974.292–293.

33. For statistics on primary 5| 7 and secondary 7| 5 patterns in iambic trimeter, see Korzeniewski 1968.45–46.

34. For example, Alcaeus F 70 and 117b.26 ff. (where the strophe is shaped *ia + glyc| glyc@ch*).

35. Jakobson 1952 passim.

36. For example, Alcaeus F 355 and F 360, which show this word break pattern, as opposed to, e.g., F 359, which does not.

$$\cup\cup-\cup\cup-\cup--\mid\underline{\cup}-\cup\cup-\cup- \qquad\qquad = glyc\ \tilde{}glyc.^{37}$$

Here I have introduced the symbol ~ to indicate a process that can be described as *dovetailing*.[38] In synchronic terms, dovetailing is when the word break is skipped at the end of one metrical unit and transferred to the position after the first syllable of the following metrical unit. As I have argued at length elsewhere,[39] this process is analogous to the synchronic pattern 5| 7 of iambic trimeter:

$$\underline{\cup}-\cup-\underline{\cup}\mid-\cup-\underline{\cup}-\cup- \qquad\qquad = ia+ia\&IA.$$

Let us now turn from the Aeolic meters to the so-called dactylo-epitrite meters, the second of the two major metrical groupings that I have undertaken to survey. A basic unit of the dactylo-epitrite meters is the so-called *prosodiakon*:

$$\underline{\cup}-\cup\cup-\cup\cup- \qquad\qquad = pros.^{40}$$

The *pros* behaves like a constituent of trimeter. Let us compare the pattern traditionally known as the *iambelegos*:

$$\underline{\cup}-\cup-\underline{\cup}\mid-\cup\cup-\cup\cup- \qquad\qquad = ia+pros^{41}$$

with an iambic trimeter that has a word break after syllable 5:

$$\underline{\cup}-\cup-\underline{\cup}\mid-\cup-\underline{\cup}-\cup- \qquad\qquad = ia+ia\&IA$$

and with the trimeter formed with a glyconic, again featuring word break after syllable 5:

$$\underline{\cup}-\cup-\underline{\cup}\mid\underline{\cup}-\cup\cup-\cup- \qquad\qquad = ia+glyc.^{42}$$

On the basis of such formal parallelisms in trimeter-formation, I propose that the prosodiakon (*pros*) is an offshoot of the Indo-European dimeter, just

37. For example, Alcaeus F 360; Bacchylides 18.9 SM.

38. For the term *dovetailing*, borrowed from the image of a dovetail joint in carpentry (so West 1982b.295), see Maas 1962.44.

39. N 1974.279–287.

40. For example, Stesichorus *Thebaid* 222 (strophe/antistrophe line 5). I refer to the version of the text (*Lille Papyri* 76abc) published by Haslam 1978.32–33, with accompanying metrical analysis. On the general subject of Stesichorean meter, the work of Haslam 1974, 1978 is essential; for important parallels illustrated by poetry that is attested in the surviving epigraphical evidence, see Gentili and Giannini 1977.19–22. On the interchangeability of ⏖ and ⏞ in Stesichorean meter, see pp. 451 and following.

41. For example, Stesichorus *Destruction of Ilion* (SLG 88–132) epode lines 6–7 in the colometry of Haslam 1978.

42. For example, again, Alcaeus F 70 and 117b.24 ff. (where the strophe is shaped *ia+glyc| glyc@ch*).

like the iambic dimeter and various other octosyllabic meters that are attested in Greek lyric:

⏓–⏑–⏓–⏑– = iambic dimeter (*ia&IA*)[43]

⏓⏓–⏑⏑–⏑– = glyconic (*glyc*)

derived from a reconstructed type

⏓⏓⏓⏓⏑–⏑– = "irregular glyconic"[44]

⏓–⏑⏑–⏑⏑– = prosodiakon (*pros*)

derived from a reconstructed type

⏓⏓⏓⏓–⏑⏑–

as attested in the type

⏓⏓–⏓–⏑⏑– = choriambic dimeter.[45]

Accordingly I withdraw my earlier suggestion that the prosodiakon (*pros*) is a resegmented derivative of the glyconic.[46] Instead I propose that both the glyconic (*glyc*) and the prosodiakon (*pros*) are independent derivatives of the Indo-European dimeter. Each Greek dimeter pattern entails various regulari-

---

43. For example, Anacreon PMG 428.

44. I say "reconstructed" because actual attestations of initial ⏓⏓⏓⏓ reveal distinct trends of patterning, not completely free variation. One such pattern is initial –⏑⏑– instead of the initial ⏓⏓–⏑ of glyconic. For example, Sappho F 95.6, where –⏑⏑–⏑–⏑– functions as a variant of ⏓⏓–⏑⏑–⏑– (cf. West 1982.31). For the term *irregular glyconic*, see Watkins 1963.203–206. Correcting some of the scansions offered by Watkins, Itsumi 1982.59n7 says that "Watkins is rash to find in Greek metres traces of initial unfixed syllables supposedly of Indo-European origin." Yet Itsumi has not disproved the existence of these traces; he has simply shown that an initial configuration ⏓⏓⏓⏓ is not attested in all the possible varieties that are expected on the basis of the comparative evidence. Cf. p. 7.

45. On the restriction of the initial pattern ⏓⏓⏓⏓ to ⏓⏓–⏑ in choriambic dimeter, see p. 7. The choriambic dimeter is most clearly attested in Anacreon PMG 349, 357; Corinna PMG 654, 655; Aristophanes *Wasps* 1457–1461, 1469–1473; *Clouds* 572. See also Merkelbach 1967.161–162, who has identified twelve consecutive lines of choriambic dimeter verse in a fragment of what seems to be the parabasis of the *Heroes* of Aristophanes. The choriambic dimeter is also found as the first part of a larger unit known as the Eupolidean verse, as most clearly attested in the parabasis of Aristophanes' *Clouds* (518–562). On the recitative (as opposed to sung) character of the Eupolidean verse, of which the choriambic dimeter is a constituent, see Poultney, pp. 140–141. For more on the choriambic dimeter, see Poultney 1979.142–144. Also Itsumi 1982 (who cites neither Merkelbach nor Poultney). This metrical unit has already been discussed at p. 6. The choriambic dimeter and the glyconic are functional variants in strophic responsion (cf. Itsumi, pp. 59, 69). On the principles of strophic responsion, see West 1982.5.

46. N 1974.294–295.

zations of various rhythmical sequences, with the general direction of regularization moving from the closing toward the opening.[47] Thus the glyconic (*glyc*), as we see in the scheme above, is a regularization of the "irregular glyconic," in that the fifth-from-last syllable of the "irregular glyconic" has been generalized as a short, forcing the sixth-from-last syllable to be generalized as a long to avoid a sequence of three consecutive shorts, which was not tolerated in early Greek metrics.[48] So also with the prosodiakon (*pros*): we could say that it is a regularization of the choriambic dimeter, with the fifth-to-last and sixth-to-last syllables generalized as two shorts, forcing the seventh-to-last to be generalized as a long to avoid a sequence of three shorts. What results is the symmetry of a rhythmical sequence

$$-\cup\cup-\cup\cup,$$

framed at each end by one syllable of indifferent quantity ($\underset{-}{\cup}$).[49]

Besides the various types of Greek dimeter that we have already seen resulting from various patterns of rhythmical generalization, I now list the following additional types:

$-\cup-\underset{-}{\cup}-\cup--$	= trochaic dimeter (*tr&TR*)[50]
$-\cup-\cup-\cup\cup-$	= trochaic-choriambic dimeter (*tr'&CH*)[51]
$-\cup\cup-\cup-\cup-$	= choriambic-iambic dimeter (*CH&ia'*)[52]

47. Watkins 1963.203–206; cf. N 1974.30–31.

48. Ibid. That the early Greek metrical law of avoiding three consecutive shorts was an outgrowth of the language itself is suggested by a residual phonological rule in classical Greek, surviving on the level of morphophonemics: I am referring to the constraint against three consecutive short syllables in comparatives and superlatives of thematic adjectives: thus, e.g., **soph-ō-teros** as opposed to **lept-o-teros**. See Householder and Nagy 1972.758.

49. To repeat, the last syllable of a line is indifferent in quantity, even though I have been writing it as a long ($-$). See p. 439.

50. For example, Anacreon PMG 347, 417. See West 1982.57. The metrical tendencies that led to this pattern are cognate with those that led to the Indic dimeter shaped $\cup\cup\cup\cup-\cup--$ and known as the trochaic Gāyatrī (on which see Vine 1977.250; cf. N 1974.170–171).

51. For example, Sappho F 95.9, 96.7. West 1982.31 recognizes this unit as a variant of the *glyc*; it is interchangeable with *glyc* in, e.g., Anacreon PMG 349 (see West, p. 57). It can be interpreted as a derivative of the choriambic dimeter. Henceforth, the symbol *tr'&CH* will indicate this particular variant dimeter.

52. For example, Sappho F 95.6. West ibid. recognizes this unit too as a variant of the *glyc*. It is clearly a derivative of the "irregular glyconic." Whereas the *glyc* generalizes the pattern long-short for the third and fourth syllables of the opening, resulting in $\underset{-}{\cup}\underset{-}{\cup}-\cup$, the unit under consideration generalizes the pattern short-long, for the third and fourth and long-short for the first and second, resulting in $-\cup\cup-$. Whereas the pattern long-short for the first and second is a *constant* for this unit, the same pattern is only a *tendency* for the *glyc* (cf. West 1982.30). Henceforth, the symbol *CH&ia'* will indicate this particular variant dimeter.

–⏑⏑–⏑– –   = aristophanean (catalectic of above)[53]

⏒–⏑⏑–⏑– –   = hagesichorean (*hage*).[54]

To posit such a plurality of categories may at first strike us as unnecessary. But the necessity is indeed there: we are dealing in each case with what amounts to independent generalizations of rhythmical patterns. I can put it another way from a comparative standpoint, juxtaposing the patterns of Greek and Indic meter: while Indic versification tends to tolerate different patterns within a single given flexible meter, Greek lyric tends to generalize the corresponding patterns as a plurality of separate rigid meters.[55] Although "Greek rigidity in meter is a more advanced phenomenon than Indic flexibility,"[56] this same rigidity is what makes the internal evidence of Greek meter particularly valuable for the comparative study of Indo-European metrics: the relatively rigid and differentiated meters of Greek lyric are *constants* that preserve phases of evolution that have been blurred by the ongoing *tendencies* of the relatively flexible and undifferentiated meters of the corresponding Indic traditions.[57]

This much said, the diachronic perspective can help us reduce the proliferation of categories in Greek lyric. Let us begin by considering again the glyconic (*glyc*) and its closest relatives:

A   ⏒⏒–⏑⏑–⏑–   = glyconic (*glyc*)

B   ⏒⏒–⏑⏑–⏑– –   = hipponactean (*hipp*)

C   ⏒–⏑⏑–⏑–   = telesillean (*tele*)

D   ⏒–⏑⏑–⏑– –   = hagesichorean (*hage*).

From the synchronic viewpoint of descriptive metrics, we may describe segments B, C, and D as derivatives of A: B by hypersyllabism, C by acephaly, and D by both acephaly and hypersyllabism. The diachronic point of view, however, is more subtle. First of all, let us observe that a 7-syllable unit like C is an inherited variant of A: the comparative evidence of Indic meter shows that dimeters could be 7-syllable as well as 8-syllable units, with matching rhythm in the closing.[58] Matching rhythm in the closing creates the perception of a missing initial syllable in a 7-syllable unit that coexists with an 8-syllable unit, whence the synchronic description of acephaly. But the comparative evidence makes it clear that 7-syllable units are inheritances parallel

53. For example, Sappho F 112; Anacreon PMG 385, 386.
54. For example, Alcman PMG 1.57. For the name, see West 1982.30n3.
55. N 1974.34, with illustrations.
56. N, p. 35.
57. N, p. 36, with illustrations. I say "relatively rigid" in describing the meters of Greek lyric because the meters of Greek nonlyric, as we shall see presently, are even more rigid.
58. Vine 1977.

to, not derived from, 8-syllable units.[59] It is possible to offer a similar formulation for matching rhythm in the openings of coexisting 8-syllable and 7-syllable units, also attested in Indic.[60] In this case, matching rhythm creates the perception of a missing final syllable in the 7-syllable unit, whence the synchronic description of catalexis.[61] Finally, I suggest that matching rhythm in the openings creates the perception of an added final syllable in 9-syllable units found coexisting with 8-syllable units, whence the synchronic description of hypersyllabism.[62] I cite the 9-syllable hipponactean (*hipp*), which functions as a dimeter in Aeolic meter.[63] Another example is the type

$$- \overline{\cup\cup} - \cup\cup - \cup - - ,^{64}$$

attested as a functioning variant of the type

$$- \overline{\cup\cup} - \cup\cup - \cup\cup -$$

in compositions attributed to Alcman.[65]

In light of this diachronic perspective, let us reconsider the process of dovetailing. For illustration, I turn to our earlier example of two dovetailing glyconics:

$$\underline{\cup}\,\underline{\cup} - \cup\cup - \cup - - \mid \underline{\cup} - \cup\cup - \cup - \qquad\qquad = glyc \,\tilde{}\,glyc.^{66}$$

In synchronic terms dovetailing happens when the word break is skipped at the end of one metrical unit and transferred to the position after the first syllable of the following metrical unit. In diachronic terms, however, what is needed to achieve such a process of dovetailing is the *systematic* juxtaposition of phraseology that is rhythmically shaped *hipp* with phraseology that is rhythmically shaped *tele* in order to achieve an overall rhythmical effect that we may still describe synchronically as *glyc ˜glyc*. In diachronic terms, then, dovetailing can evolve only in situations where the traditional repertoire features a plurality of rigid meters that allow the perception of synchronic derivation, one from the other, by way of acephaly or hypersyllabism or both. From the standpoint of the Aeolic tradition, phrases shaped *hipp* and *tele* are functional variants of phrases shaped *glyc* by the very fact that they are

59. Ibid.

60. For which see again Vine ibid.

61. In this connection, I disagree with the interpretation offered by Ritoók 1987.11n35 concerning Vine's analysis. What Vine is saying is that, whereas most Vedic heptasyllables can be described catalectic, a small residue, hitherto treated as metrical anomalies, are acephalic.

62. This discussion has been enhanced by the perspectives of Cole 1988.

63. For example, Alcaeus F 130.

64. As we see below, the pattern $- \overline{\cup}$ is a reflex of $\underline{\cup}\,\underline{\cup}$.

65. For example, Alcman PMG 1.49 (first type) and 1.35 (second type); cf. also the 9-syllable line in Alcman PMG 39.1.

66. For example, again, Alcaeus F 360; Bacchylides 18.9 SM.

traditionally combined to produce the sound-effect of double *glyc*. For this reason, we may in a given situation designate a *hipp* as *glyc~* and a *tele* as *~glyc*, provided that we have reason to think that the given phraseological repertory grew out of a *system* that produced the effect of dovetailing glyconics. Following this line of thinking, I henceforth use the sign ~ before a given symbol for a given metrical unit to designate an acephalic variant of that metrical unit, while ~ after a unit will designate a hypersyllabic variant. In other words ~ before or after a symbol will indicate that the unit designated by that symbol evolved from traditionally dovetailed combinations. For example, *ia~* can stand for a 5-syllable unit of phraseology that has evolved in the context of a following 7-syllable unit of phraseology, as in the iambic trimeter. Conversely *~ia&IA* can stand for a 7-syllable unit of phraseology that evolved in the context of a preceding 5-syllable unit of phraseology. Henceforth I write | ~ to indicate acephaly that has been disconnected from any preceding pattern of dovetailing and ~| to indicate hypersyllabism that has been disconnected from any following pattern of dovetailing.

Keeping in mind these diachronic considerations, I am ready to streamline my system of labeling for the dovetailing variants of the Aeolic units. In what follows, the left-hand column of labels presents alternatives to the right-hand column of equivalent labels:

A	⏑⏑−⏑⏑−⏑−	= *glyc*	
B	⏑⏑−⏑⏑−⏑−−	= *glyc~*	= *hipp*
C	⏑−⏑⏑−⏑−	= *~glyc*	= *tele*
D	⏑−⏑⏑−⏑−−	= *~glyc~*	= *hage*
A	⏑⏑−⏑⏑−−	= *glyc<*	= *pher*
B	none		
C	⏑−⏑⏑−−	= *~glyc<*	= *~pher* =*tele<* = *reiz*
D	none		
A	⏑−⏑⏑−⏑−	= *tele*	= *~glyc* above
B	⏑−⏑⏑−⏑−−	= *tele~*	= *hage* above
C	−⏑⏑−⏑−	= *~tele*	
D	−⏑⏑−⏑−−	= *~tele~*	
A	⏑−⏑⏑−−	= *tele<*	= *reiz* above
B	none		
C	−⏑⏑−−	= *~tele<*	= *~reiz*
D	none.		

In the case of equivalences like *~glyc* = *tele*, what decides the description is the *system* of which the unit is a constituent. Let us test this principle on some common metrical patterns in the Aeolic tradition, starting with the so-called Sapphic Strophe:

$$-\cup-\underline{\cup}-\cup\cup-\cup-- \qquad = |\;\widetilde{\;}ia+tele\widetilde{\;}|$$
$$-\cup-\underline{\cup}-\cup\cup-\cup-- \qquad = |\;\widetilde{\;}ia+tele\widetilde{\;}|$$
$$-\cup-\underline{\cup}-\cup\cup-\cup-\underline{\cup}-\cup\cup-- \qquad = |\;\widetilde{\;}ia+tele\widetilde{\;}tele<.^{67}$$

The primary word break pattern in the third unit is as follows:

$$-\cup-\underline{\cup}-\cup\cup-\cup-\underline{\cup}\,|-\cup\cup--\;.$$

This word break reflects the evolution of the constituent phraseology in terms of *tele˜tele<*, as distinct from *tele| tele<*, which would have yielded a word break pattern that is strictly avoided by the Sapphic Strophe:

$$-\cup-\underline{\cup}-\cup\cup-\cup-\,|\,\underline{\cup}-\cup\cup--\;.^{68}$$

We turn next from the Sapphic Strophe to the Alcaic:

$$\underline{\cup}-\cup-\underline{\cup}-\cup\cup-\cup- \qquad = ia\widetilde{\;}tele$$
$$\underline{\cup}-\cup-\underline{\cup}-\cup\cup-\cup- \qquad = ia\widetilde{\;}tele$$
$$\underline{\cup}-\cup-\underline{\cup}-\cup-\underline{\cup}-\cup\cup-\cup\cup-\cup-- \qquad = ia+ia\widetilde{\;}tele\widetilde{\;}|\;@da.^{69}$$

In the third unit the strict constraint against the word breaking pattern

$$\underline{\cup}-\cup-\underline{\cup}-\cup-\,|\,\underline{\cup}-\cup\cup-\cup\cup-\cup--$$

reflects the dovetailing pattern *ia˜tele*.[70]

What follows are some further examples of Aeolic combinations:

$$\underline{\cup}-\cup-\underline{\cup}\,|\,\underline{\cup}-\cup\cup-\cup- \qquad = ia+glyc^{71}$$

---

67. The Sapphic Strophe is the format, for example, of all the compositions in Sappho Book I.

68. In his synchronic metrical description, West 1982.33 provides the following interpretation of the Sapphic Strophe. For the first two units, he posits *>ia+hage*. For the third, he hesitates between *>ia+hage+adon* or *>ia+tele˜reiz*. Either way, there is a discontinuity with the first two units. To posit an adonic (*adon*, or $-\cup\cup--$) is to invoke a segmentation for which I know of no diachronic explanation. To posit *tele* clashes with the preceding *hage*. About his schematization of the third unit, West remarks (ibid.) that it "obscures the essential point that it is a distended form of the first and second." I hope that the schematization that I offer above helps establish that point.

69. For the Alcaic Strophe, see, e.g., Alcaeus F 129. Again, West (ibid.) notes that the third unit is an "amplification" of the first and second.

70. In the first two units, as West 1982b.296 points out, the word break predominantly occurs at $\underline{\cup}-\cup-\underline{\cup}\,|-\cup\cup-\cup-$. Again, a reflex of *ia˜tele*. There is an analogous type of trimeter in the Indic tradition, known as the Bhārgavā: see N 1974.180–183.

71. For example, again, Alcaeus F 70 and 117b.24 ff. (where the strophe is shaped *ia+glyc| glyc@ch*).

$−\cup−\underline{\cup}\underline{\cup}−\cup\cup−\cup−$ = ˜ia+glyc[72]

$\underline{\cup}−\cup−\underline{\cup}−\cup\cup−\cup−−$ = ia+tele˜.[73]

We see from the Sapphic and the Alcaic Strophe and from these other Aeolic examples that, just as a *glyc* allows trimeter formation with a preceding *ia* that dovetails into it, so also does the *tele* and so on. From a synchronic point of view, the *tele* functions as an actual alternative to the *glyc*, experiencing acephaly on its own like the *glyc*, as if for the very first time.

In light of the preceding discussion of dovetailing, we are ready to survey the building blocks of the dactylo-epitrite meters. I begin by reviewing the simple trimeter pattern known as the *iambelegos*:

$\underline{\cup}−\cup−\underline{\cup}\,|−\cup\cup−\cup\cup−$ = ia+pros.[74]

We find also the reverse trimeter pattern in the combination known as the *enkomiologikon*:

$−\cup\cup−\cup\cup−\,|\,\underline{\cup}−\cup−−$ = | ˜pros| ia˜| .[75]

There is also a type without initial acephaly:

$\underline{\cup}−\cup\cup−\cup\cup−\,|\,\underline{\cup}−\cup−−$ = pros| ia˜| .[76]

Moreover, there are attestations of the enkomiologikon where we see the results of dovetailing between the two units:

$−\cup\cup−\cup\cup−\underline{\cup}\,|−\cup−\underline{\cup}$ = | ˜pros˜| ˜ia˜| .[77]

We may note too this similar pattern:

$\underline{\cup}−\cup\cup−\cup\cup−\underline{\cup}\,|−\cup−\cup−−$ = pros˜| ˜ia&ia<.[78]

Having surveyed these trimeter patterns, we now have a working repertory of the major building blocks that constitute archaic dactylo-epitrite meters, as attested most clearly in the corpus of Stesichorus:

---

72. For example, Sappho F 98 (where the strophe is shaped *glyc| glyc|* ˜*ia+glyc*). I write ˜*ia+glyc* instead of ˜*ia* ˜*glyc* because the word break does not necessarily occur after syllable 4.

73. For example, Alcaeus F 384.

74. For example, Stesichorus *Destruction of Ilion* (SLG 88–132) epode lines 6–7 in the colometry of Haslam 1978.

75. For example, Stesichorus *Thebaid* strophe/antistrophe line 2.

76. For example, Stesichorus *Thebaid* epode line 2.

77. For example, Anacreon PMG 416.

78. For example, Archilochus F 168–171 W.

a $\cup-\cup-$ = *ia*

b $\cup-\cup-\cup$ = *ia*˜

c $-\cup-$ = ˜*ia*

d $-\cup-\cup$ = ˜*ia*˜

A $\cup-\cup\cup-\cup\cup-$ = *pros*

B $\cup-\cup\cup-\cup\cup--$ = *pros*˜

C $-\cup\cup-\cup\cup-$ = ˜*pros*

D $-\cup\cup-\cup\cup--$ = ˜*pros*˜

In the dactylo-epitrites of Stesichorus, there are clear signs of parallelism in the distribution of these parallel *pros* and *ia* segments: for example, both *pros*˜ and *ia*˜ tend to be placed in the closing of metrical sequences.[79] A typical sequence is the following from the *Thebaid* of Stesichorus:

$-\cup\cup-\cup\cup-|\cup-\cup--$ = | ˜*pros*| *ia*˜| = C+b.[80]

Besides trimeter formations, we also see combinations of dimeters, as in the following examples taken from the *Nostoi* of Stesichorus (PMG 209):

$-\cup\cup-\cup\cup-|\cup-\cup\cup-\cup\cup--$ = | ˜*pros*| *pros*˜| = C+B

$-\cup\cup-\cup\cup-\cup|-\cup\cup-\cup\cup--$ = | ˜*pros*˜| ˜*pros*˜| = B+D.[81]

Although some metricians prefer to distinguish such patterns from dactylo-epitrites by calling them dactylo-anapests,[82] I use the term *dactylo-epitrite* to cover both patterns.

In the immediately preceding example from Stesichorus, we must take note of a metrical innovation: it is a new metrical license, not yet marked explicitly in the schemes above for the *Nostoi*, where one long syllable is optionally substituted for two shorts ($\overline{\cup\cup}$). As I have argued elsewhere, this metrical innovation, pervasive in the diction of Stesichorus, is the reflex of the Greek linguistic innovation of contracting short vowels originally separated by intervocalic *s and *i.[83] We must also take note of the converse of this innovation, where two short syllables are optionally substituted for one long. In the corpus of Stesichorus, this pattern of substitution is restricted to those long syllables that occur in slots that traditionally allow free

---

79. Cf. Haslam 1978.56.
80. For example, Stesichorus *Thebaid* strophe/antistrophe line 2; also Alcaeus F 383.
81. Cf. Haslam 1974.46.
82. For example, Haslam 1978.
83. N 1974.49–56. Also Allen 1973.255–259 and 1987.113–114.

variation between a single long and a single short, as for example in the first syllable of the *pros.* I use the symbols A′ and B′ to reflect this metrical innovation:

```
a    ⏜ –⏑–                    = ia
b    ⏜ –⏑–⏜                   = ia~
c       –⏑–                    = ~ia
d       –⏑–⏜                   = ~ia~


A    ⏜ –⏑⏑–⏑⏑–                = pros
A′   ⏝ –⏑⏑–⏑⏑–
A″   ⏠ –⏑⏑–⏑⏑–
B    ⏜ –⏑⏑–⏑⏑– –             = pros~
B′   ⏝ –⏑⏑–⏑⏑– –
B″   ⏠ –⏑⏑–⏑⏑– –
C       –⏑⏑–⏑⏑–               = ~pros
D       –⏑⏑–⏑⏑– –             = ~pros~.
```

This innovation is attested in such compositions as the *Thebaid* of Stesichorus, where the *pros* (as also its variants) allows a new variation in the first syllable: when long, then optional two shorts instead of the single long; when short, no substitution. I draw attention to the following example:

$$-\overline{⏖} –⏑⏑– \mid \underset{⏖}{⏝}–⏑⏑–⏑⏑– – \qquad = C+B' = \mid~pros\mid pros~\mid .^{84}$$

The patterns symbolized by A″ and B″ in the scheme above reflect a further metrical innovation, attested in such compositions as the *Geryoneis* of Stesichorus (SLG 7–87), where the *pros* allows yet another new variation in the first syllable: only long, with optional two shorts instead of the single long. I cite the following example:

$$\overline{⏖} –\overline{⏖} –⏑⏑– – \qquad\qquad = pros~\mid \; = B''$$
$$\overline{⏖} –⏑⏑– \mid \overline{⏖} –⏑⏑–⏑⏑– ''\overline{⏖} –⏑⏑– – \quad = reiz\mid pros''reiz\mid \; = reiz\mid A''\mid reiz$$
$$\overline{⏖} –⏑⏑– ''\overline{⏖} –⏑⏑–⏑⏑– – \qquad = reiz''pros~\mid \; = reiz\mid B''.^{85}$$

84. For example, Stesichorus *Thebaid* strophe/antistrophe line 1, as analyzed by Haslam 1978.33. This variation (when long, then optional two shorts instead of the single long; when short, no substitution) in the first syllable of *pros* is analogously extended to the first syllable in the *ia* segments as well, as in the *Thebaid* strophe/antistrophe line 5.

85. For example, Stesichorus *Geryoneis* (SLG 7–87) strophe/antistrophe lines 1–5, as analyzed by Haslam 1974.20–22, 31; cf. West 1982.50. Henceforth, the symbol " indicates optional word break.

I indicate with the symbol *reiz* the sequences ⏕ – ⏑ ⏑ – and ⏕ – ⏑ ⏑ – –, which I take to be derivatives of ⏓ – ⏑ ⏑ – and ⏓ – ⏑ ⏑ – –. As I argue presently, such sequences as ⏓ – ⏑ ⏑ – and ⏓ – ⏑ ⏑ – – result from resegmentations of choriambic internal expansion. For now, however, the essential point to observe about the patterns in the scheme above is that the distinction between ⏕ as derived from the first syllable of the *pros* and ⏕ as derived from the double-short at syllables 3–4 and 6–7 of the *pros* is blurred. The resulting effect has aptly been described by one expert as a "river of dactyls."[86]

This term raises an important question: what is the etymology, as it were, of the dactyl? In our earlier survey, where the emphasis had been on the synchronic point of view, we had seen that dactyls (*da* = – ⏑ ⏑), like choriambs (*ch* = – ⏑ ⏑ –), figure in the internal expansion of patterns like the glyconic (*glyc*), in shapes that have been represented as *glyc@ch*, *glyc@2ch*, *glyc@da*, *glyc@2da*, and so on. But now the notion of internal expansion must be redefined from a diachronic point of view. In the case of *glyc@ch* and *glyc@2ch*, for example, the insertion of one or two choriambs (– ⏑ ⏑ – or – ⏑ ⏑ – – ⏑ ⏑ –) between the opening (⏓ ⏓) and the closing (– ⏑ ⏑ – ⏑ –) of a glyconic (⏓ ⏓ – ⏑ ⏑ – ⏑ –) is modeled on the insertion of a choriamb (– ⏑ ⏑ –) or iamb (⏓ – ⏑ –) between the opening (– ⏑ ⏑ – or ⏓ – ⏑ –) and closing (– ⏑ ⏑ – or ⏓ – ⏑ –) of choriambic and iambic dimeter patterns.[87] In the choriambic and iambic patterns, however, what is synchronically an insertion is diachronically an opening preceded by a reapplied opening, which in turn may be preceded by yet another reapplied opening. Both the single and the double reapplied openings are attested in one particular fragment of Anacreon:

– ⏑ ⏑ – – ⏑ ⏑ – – ⏑ ⏑ – ⏓ – ⏑ –	= *CH+CH+CH&ia'*
– ⏑ ⏑ – – ⏑ ⏑ – ⏓ – ⏑ – ⏓ – ⏑ –	= *CH+CH&ia'+IA*.[88]

The pattern of reapplied opening – ⏑ ⏑ – or openings – ⏑ ⏑ – – ⏑ ⏑ – that precede – ⏑ ⏑ – ⏑ – ⏑ – is reinterpreted as a pattern of opening – ⏑ ⏑ – followed by an internally expanded – ⏑ ⏑ – or – ⏑ ⏑ – – ⏑ ⏑ –. By analogy, the *glyc* ⏓ ⏓ – ⏑ ⏑ – ⏑ –, which as we have seen is a functional variant of the choriambic-iambic dimeter – ⏑ ⏑ – ⏑ – ⏑ –,[89] becomes internally expanded as the trimeter *glyc@ch* and the tetrameter *glyc@2ch*. These trimeter and tetrameter patterns have already been described in the following way from a syn-

86. Haslam 1974.32n50.

87. Examples and discussion in N 1974.39–45 (though I now distance myself from the overrestricted usage there of the terms *symmetry* and *asymmetry*).

88. Anacreon PMG 388. The pattern *CH&ia'* in these combinations is cognate with the choriambic-iambic dimeter (– ⏑ ⏑ – ⏑ – ⏑ –), a unit that functions as a variant of the glyconic. See p. 446.

89. See p. 446.

chronic point of view: the opening segment ⏑⏑ ("Aeolic base") of ⏓⏓–⏑⏑–⏑– (the glyconic) is followed by an internally expanded –⏑⏑– or –⏑⏑––⏑⏑–. Let us consider the major word break patterns in *glyc@2ch*:

⏓⏓–⏑⏑– | –⏑⏑– | –⏑⏑–⏑–   = X| Y| Z

⏓⏓–⏑⏑–– | ⏑⏑– | –⏑⏑–⏑–   = X~Y| Z

⏓⏓–⏑⏑– | –⏑⏑–– | ⏑⏑–⏑–   = X| Y~Z

⏓⏓–⏑⏑–– | ⏑⏑–– | ⏑⏑–⏑–   = X~Y~Z.[90]

I draw attention also to a common pattern of word breaking within sector X of the *glyc@2ch*:

⏓⏓ | –⏑⏑––...   = X (= V| W...)...

⏓⏓– | ⏑⏑––...   = X (= V~W...)...

By now we have seen not one but several dovetailing mechanisms leading to a "syncopated" –⏑⏑–, that is, ⏑⏑–.

Next, I draw attention to the segments that I have labeled X and X~, ⏓⏓–⏑⏑– and ⏓⏓–⏑⏑––, within the metrical pattern *glyc@2ch*. These segments are analogous to ⏓–⏑⏑– and ⏓–⏑⏑––, which I have labeled with the symbol ? earlier, in the "river of dactyls" built from prosodiaka, as in the *Geryoneis* of Stesichorus. These patterns are followed by patterns in ⏑⏑–.... We may compare the presence of "syncopated" choriambs shaped ⏑⏑– in the prosodiaka of dactylo-epitrites, as clearly attested in Pindar and Bacchylides.[91]

Having examined the basic configuration ⏑⏑– in both the Aeolic and the dactylo-epitrite metrical traditions, we now have the background that we need for examining the phenomenon generally known as dactylic expansion, which is attested in both these traditions.

Let us begin with the Aeolic metrical tradition. The XYZ components of *glyc@2ch*, I suggest, are cognate with those of a sequence that has earlier been described synchronically as *glyc@2da*, that is, a glyconic internally expanded by two dactyls. From a diachronic point of view, the expanding dactylic patterns are actually resegmented variants of choriambic patterns. In the metrical schemes that follow, I give some typical word break patterns of the type *glyc@2da*,[92] labeling the components marked off by the word breaks in terms of the XYZ components of *glyc@2ch*:

---

90. The Aeolic samples of *glyc@2ch* that I have examined are: Alcaeus F 44, 50, 115a; 296b, 340–349; cf. Theocritus 28, 30 Gow and Callimachus F 400 Pfeiffer.

91. There is an inventory of attestations in the SM edition of Pindaric fragments, p. 168, and in the SM edition of Bacchylides, p. xxvii; the sequence ⏑⏑– is labeled "d²".

92. I follow the statistics on word breaking in *glyc@2da* as compiled by Bowie 1981.35 on the basis of the following texts: Sappho F 44.5–15, 26, 30–34; 47.2, 48–52; Alcaeus F 38.3–5, 7, 9; 141.3–4; 364; 365.

$$\underline{\smile\smile}-\smile\smile-|\smile\smile-\smile\smile-\smile- \qquad = X|{\sim}Y{+}Z = glyc@2da$$

$$\underline{\smile\smile}-\smile\smile-|\smile\smile-|\smile\smile-\smile- \qquad = X|{\sim}Y|{\sim}Z = glyc@2da$$

$$\underline{\smile\smile}|-\smile\smile-\smile\smile|-\smile\smile-\smile- \qquad = V|\,Z^*|\,Z = glyc@2da$$

$$\underline{\smile\smile}-|\smile\smile-\smile\smile|-\smile\smile-\smile- \qquad = V{\sim}|{\sim}Z^*|\,Z = glyc@2da$$

$$\underline{\smile\smile}-|\smile\smile-|\smile\smile-|\smile\smile-\smile- \qquad = V{\sim}|{\sim}Y|{\sim}Y{\sim}Z = glyc@2da$$

etc.

(The * following a symbol designates a sequence where the final syllable is restricted to a short quantity.) We would expect such equivalences between constituents of *glyc@2ch* and those of *glyc@2da* to be a matter of *phraseological* correspondences in equivalent metrical slots.[93]

Let us now move from the Aeolic to the dactylo-epitrite traditions. By way of review, here are the units that we have already surveyed as the basic constituents of dactylo-epitrite meters:

a	$\underline{\smile}-\smile-$	$= ia$
b	$\underline{\smile}-\smile-\underline{\smile}$	$= ia{\sim}$
c	$-\smile-$	$= {\sim}ia$
d	$-\smile-\underline{\smile}$	$= {\sim}ia{\sim}$
A	$\underline{\smile}-\smile\smile-\smile\smile-$	$=pros$
A′	$\underset{\smile\smile}{\smile}-\smile\smile-\smile\smile-$	
A″	$\overline{\smile\smile}-\smile\smile-\smile\smile-$	
B	$\underline{\smile}-\smile\smile-\smile\smile--$	$= pros{\sim}$
B′	$\underset{\smile\smile}{\smile}-\smile\smile-\smile\smile--$	
B″	$\overline{\smile\smile}-\smile\smile-\smile\smile--$	
C	$-\smile\smile-\smile\smile-$	$= {\sim}pros$
D	$-\smile\smile-\smile\smile--$	$= {\sim}pros{\sim}.$

These units are not only prototypical of those found in the earlier dactylo-epitrite meters of Stesichorus, or the later ones of Pindar.[94] They are also identical with some of the major metrical shapes that constitute the verses of the dactylic hexameter, the elegiac distich, and the iambic trimeter. We have already observed at length the relationship of the iambic trimeter to the dactylo-epitrite meters as also to the Aeolic meters; now we may concentrate on the dactylic hexameter and the elegiac distich. The traditional phraseol-

93. This is not to say that *glyc@2da* cannot be a metrical frame for shapes other than what we find in *glyc@2ch*: for example, we may analyze Sappho F 44.10 as containing phraseology shaped *pher** followed by *~*glyc*.

94. For a useful survey of dactylo-epitrite patterns in Stesichorus, Pindar, and Bacchylides, see Haslam 1978.54–57. My one basic disagreement with Haslam is that I view the pattern $\underset{\smile\smile}{\smile}-\smile\smile-\smile\smile-$ as more archaic than $\overline{\smile\smile}-\smile\smile-\smile\smile-$.

ogy of the dactylic hexameter is distributed in such a way as to leave the following distinctive patterns of word breaking:

1. $- \overline{\cup\cup} - \overline{\cup\cup} - |\; \overline{\cup\cup} - \overline{\cup\cup} - \overline{\cup\cup} - -$ (penthemimeral caesura)

2. $- \overline{\cup\cup} - \overline{\cup\cup} - \cup\; |\; \cup - \overline{\cup\cup} - \overline{\cup\cup} - -$ (trochaic caesura)

3. $- \overline{\cup\cup} - \overline{\cup\cup} - \overline{\cup\cup} - |\; \overline{\cup\cup} - \overline{\cup\cup} - -$ (hephthemimeral caesura)

4. $- \overline{\cup\cup} - \overline{\cup\cup} - \overline{\cup\cup} - \cup\cup\; |\; - \overline{\cup\cup} - -$ (bucolic diaeresis).

Also, there is a constraint against word breaking of the type

$$- \overline{\cup\cup} - \overline{\cup\cup} - \overline{\cup\cup} - \cup\; |\; \cup - \overline{\cup\cup} - - \; .$$

This phenomenon is commonly known as Hermann's Bridge.[95] Since 99% of Homeric hexameters have either pattern 1 or pattern 2,[96] we may note with interest that pattern 1 corresponds to dactylo-epitrite formations that we have already seen, of the type

$$- \overline{\cup\cup} - \cup\cup - |\; \underset{\cup\cup}{\sqcup} - \cup\cup - \cup\cup - - \qquad = \text{C+B}' = |\; \text{\textasciitilde}pros|\; pros\text{\textasciitilde}| \; .[97]$$

The pattern 1 of hexameter could be described as C+B″, corresponding to the C+B′ pattern of the dactylo-epitrite meter immediately above:[98]

$$- \overline{\cup\cup} - \overline{\cup\cup} - |\; \overline{\cup\cup} - \overline{\cup\cup} - \overline{\cup\cup} - - \qquad = \text{C+B}'' = |\; \text{\textasciitilde}pros|\; pros\text{\textasciitilde}| \; .$$

Similarly the so-called "pentameter" of the elegiac distich could be described as

$$- \overline{\cup\cup} - \overline{\cup\cup} - |\; - \cup\cup - \cup\cup - \qquad = \text{C+C} = |\; \text{\textasciitilde}pros|\; \text{\textasciitilde}pros.[99]$$

Pattern 4 of hexameter corresponds to a common word break pattern in Stesichorean diction:

$$\ldots - \cup\cup\; |\; - \cup\cup - - \; .[100]$$

Moreover, Stesichorean diction avoids word breaks of the type

---

95. Maas 1962.60. In N 1974.72, ".01%" should read "0.1%." On the special effects achieved by the violation of Hermann's Bridge in Hesiod *Theogony* 319, see Solomon 1985.

96. Cf. N 1974.56; roughly 60% have pattern 4.

97. For example, Stesichorus *Thebaid* strophe/antistrophe line 1.

98. Cf. West 1973b.269; Gentili and Giannini 1977.28; Haslam 1978.39–40.

99. In line with my argument that the closing of the "pentameter" is particularly archaic (N 1974.99–101), it is worth noting that | *pros* patterns tend to occupy strophe-final position in Stesichorean diction; cf. *Geryoneis* (SLG 7–87) strophe / antistrophe line 9 and epode lines 7–8, as mapped out in Haslam 1974.11. As for the hexameter of the elegiac distich, its patterns are statistically distinct from those of the Homeric hexameter: see Greenberg 1985 and 1985b.

100. Data in Haslam 1978.43.

$$\ldots -\cup \mid \cup -\cup\cup --,$$

and this pattern of avoidance is directly comparable to Hermann's Bridge.[101] Pattern 3 of hexameter corresponds to yet another common word break pattern in Stesichorean diction:

$$\ldots - \mid \overline{\cup\cup} -\cup\cup --.[102]$$

And there are even sporadic traces of pattern 2:

$$-\overline{\cup\cup} -\overline{\cup\cup} -\cup \mid \cup -\overline{\cup\cup} -\cup\cup --.[103]$$

Even though these analogues in Stesichorean meter yield examples of all four major types of word breaking pattern in the hexameter, we still cannot say that the hexameter is attested in Stesichorus. In the meters of Stesichorus, a pattern like

$$-\overline{\cup\cup} -\cup\cup -\overline{\cup\cup} -\overline{\cup\cup} -\cup\cup --,$$

which looks on the surface exactly like the hexameter, is a functional equivalence of

$$-\overline{\cup\cup} -\cup\cup -\underline{\cup} -\overline{\cup\cup} -\cup\cup --.$$

Here the sequence $-\underline{\cup}-$ is incompatible with the hexameter, which regularly avoids the dactyl-thwarting pattern $-\cup-$.[104] For example, let us consider the following match:[105]

Κάστορί] θ' ἱπποδάμῳ καὶ π[ὺξ ἀγαθῷ Πολυδεύκει

Stesichorus *Oxyrhynchus Papyri* 2735.17

for Castor the horse-tamer and for Pollux, good at boxing

Κάστορα θ' ἱππόδαμον καὶ πὺξ ἀγαθὸν Πολυδεύκεα

Iliad III 237, *Odyssey* xi 300

Castor the horse-tamer and Pollux, good at boxing.

Despite the fact that the match here is both metrical and phraseological, the

---

101. Ibid.

102. Ibid.

103. For example, Stesichorus *Thebaid* 230 in the edition of Haslam 1978.33.

104. By *functional equivalence* here, I mean the same thing as what metricians call *responsion*, that is, where metrical sequences match between strophe and antistrophe. For a survey of patterns where a sequence with $\overline{\cup}$ is in responsion with an otherwise identical sequence containing $\underline{\cup}$, see Haslam 1978.39–40.

105. Pointed out by Haslam 1974.49.

Stesichorean line cannot be called a dactylic hexameter because the slot occupied here by καὶ may allow not only a long syllable (as here at line 17 of *Oxyrhynchus Papyri* 2735) but also a short syllable (as at line 10). Moreover, the Stesichorean line can allow word breaking patterns that are altogether foreign to the hexameter. In the *Nostoi* of Stesichorus, for example, we find, besides

$$- \overline{\cup\cup} - \cup\cup - \mid \underline{\cup} - \cup\cup - \cup\cup - -,^{106}$$

the following word break pattern as well:

$$- \overline{\cup\cup} - \cup\cup - \underline{\cup} \mid - \cup\cup - \cup\cup - -.^{107}$$

Thus there is a greater variety of phraseology accommodated by the meters of Stesichorus than by the hexameter of Homer.[108]

How does the dactylic hexameter maintain its frame while promoting dactylic rhythm? The answer has to do with the phraseological heritage of the hexameter. The phraseology that constitutes the repertoire of hexameter, I submit, comes from the rhythmical frame of not only the dactylo-epitrite but also the Aeolic meters.

In an earlier attempt,[109] I had argued that the framework of hexameter can be derived from an Aeolic meter:

$$\underline{\cup}\,\underline{\cup} - \cup\cup - \cup\cup - \cup\cup - \cup\cup - - \qquad\qquad = pher@3da.^{110}$$

In two later works, I went beyond my specific argument that the *pher@3da* provided the actual metrical frame for the hexameter, offering the more general argument that the hexameter was shaped by the same traditional phraseology that had shaped not only such Aeolic meters as *pher@3da*, *glyc@2ch*, *glyc@2da* but also the dactylo-epitrite meters.[111] In this book, this

106. For example, Stesichorus *Nostoi* (PMG 209) strophe/antistrophe line 3.

107. For example, Stesichorus *Nostoi* (PMG 209) strophe/antistrophe line 4; cf. Haslam 1974.46.

108. If the hexameter tends toward $- \cup\cup - \cup\cup - \overline{\cup} - \cup\cup - \cup\cup - -$ at the expense of $- \cup\cup - \cup\cup\underline{\cup} - \cup\cup - \cup\cup - -$ and of $- \cup\cup - \cup\cup\,\underset{\cup}{\cup} - \cup\cup - \cup\cup - -$, this tendency can be expected to parallel a progressive restriction of incoming phraseology. For vestigial traces of $- \cup\cup - \cup\cup - \underline{\cup} - \cup\cup - \cup\cup - -$ in hexameter, where wording shaped $- \cup\cup - \cup\cup -$ is followed by $\cup - \cup\cup - \cup\cup - -$, see, e.g., *Iliad* IV 202, XI 697 (cf. West 1982.293n41). The progressive generalization of $- \cup\cup - \cup\cup - \overline{\cup} - \cup\cup - \cup\cup - -$ over $- \cup\cup - \cup\cup\underline{\cup} - \cup\cup - \cup\cup - -$ in hexameter helps account for the absence of Homeric introductory phrases of the type *τοῖσι δὲ καὶ μετέφη, as discussed in N 1974.85. Such phrases would have been ousted by the evolving constraint against the sequence $- \cup -$ produced by fusion of wording shaped $- \cup\cup - \cup\cup -$ and o$- \cup\cup - \cup\cup - -$.

109. N 1974.49–102, following up on the suggestions of Wilamowitz 1921.98.

110. Alcaeus F 368.

111. N 1979b and 1983c. On the partially Aeolic heritage of the traditional phraseology in dactylic hexameter, there is further evidence, beyond what is offered in N 1974, in Bowie 1981, especially pp. 32–46. As I observe in N 1983c, my reservation about Bowie's work is that he undervalues his own important results by not sufficiently heeding the discovery of Parry 1928b

same general argument has been reinforced with the preceding discussion of inner expansion by dactyls, explained as a derivative of inner expansion by choriambs.

For inherited phraseology to be interchangeable between hexameter on one side and such meters as the *pher@3da*, *glyc@2ch*, and *glyc@2da* on the other, I posit two innovations on the Aeolic side, taking as an example the metrical frame of *pher@3da*:

1. optional replacement of $-\cup\cup$ by $--$ [112]

2. specialization of the initial "Aeolic base" $\underset{\smile}{\cup}\,\underset{\smile}{\cup}$ as $--$, with optional replacement of $--$ by $-\cup\cup$.

These innovations would be parallel to those already discussed in the case of the archaic dactylo-epitrites of Stesichorus:

1. optional replacement of $-\cup\cup$ by $--$

2. specialization of the initial $\underset{\smile}{\cup}$ as $-$, with optional replacement of $-$ by $\cup\cup$. [113]

The optional synchronic substitution of $--$ for $-\cup\cup$ can be explained as a diachronic reflex of vowel-contraction.[114] The substitution of $--$ for $-\cup\cup$ accords with the theory that phraseological patterns generate metrical patterns that then assume dynamics of their own and even regulate any incoming nontraditional phraseology.[115] There is internal evidence to show that the pattern $--$ is foreign to the second, third, fourth, and fifth feet of the dactylic hexameter since it involves phraseological restrictions that do not apply to the pattern $-\cup\cup$: words with a spondaic ending are shunned, whereas those with a dactylic ending are not. In the first foot of the hexameter, on the other hand, this restriction does not apply, and words with a spondaic ending are

---

that the word break patterns of hexameter are not metrical devices actively deployed by the poet but metrical effects passively reflecting the junctures where traditional phrases may begin or end (cf. N 1974.57–61). Also, I find some unnecessary presuppositions about the notions of *formula* and *oral poetry* (p. 41). At Bowie, pp. 49–60, there is a particularly important assessment, with bibliography, of the linguistic evidence for an Aeolic phase in the evolution of the hexameter. I agree with his statement at p. 55: "In the case of possible Aeolic forms in Homer, we are not dealing with Lesbian or non-Lesbian, so much as with specifically Lesbian and generally Aeolic."

112. See Allen 1987.113–114.

113. As we have seen in Stesichorus *Geryoneis* (SLG 7–87). We have also seen that, in Stesichorus *Destruction of Ilion* (SLG 88–132), initial $\underset{\smile}{\cup}$ still survives as a variant of initial $\overline{\underset{\smile}{\cup}}$: longum over biceps}.

114. N 1974.49–56. Also Allen 1973.255–259 and 1987.113–114.

115. N 1974.196, 216; cf. Allen 1973.258.

common.[116] It bears repeating that the optional substitution of $-\cup\cup$ for $--$ in the first foot of hexameter could not have happened without a preexistent pattern of optionally substituting $--$ for $-\cup\cup$ in the other feet. Then too, in a composition like the *Geryoneis* of Stesichorus, where we find no Aeolic base analogous to the first foot of hexameter, we note that phrases containing the shape $--$ can be substituted for those containing the shape $-\cup\cup$ but not the other way around.[117] Further, as in hexameter, any sequence shaped $--$ that is substituted for $-\cup\cup$ regularly avoids a following word end; instead, the word ending is bridged to the position after the next long syllable.[118]

We are ready to examine examples of phraseological interchange between hexameter and the Aeolic meters. Let us begin with an Aeolic pattern that we have already considered in detail, the *glyc@2ch:*

$$\underset{\smile}{\underline{\cup}}\,\underset{\smile}{\underline{\cup}}-\cup\cup-\,|-\cup\cup-\,|-\cup\cup-\cup- \qquad = X|\,Y|\,Z = glyc@2ch$$

$$\underset{\smile}{\underline{\cup}}\,\underset{\smile}{\underline{\cup}}-\cup\cup--\,|\cup\cup-\,|-\cup\cup-\cup- \qquad = X{\sim}Y|\,Z = glyc@2ch$$

$$\underset{\smile}{\underline{\cup}}\,\underset{\smile}{\underline{\cup}}-\cup\cup-\,|-\cup\cup--\,|\cup\cup-\cup- \qquad = X|\,Y{\sim}Z = glyc@2ch$$

$$\underset{\smile}{\underline{\cup}}\,\underset{\smile}{\underline{\cup}}-\cup\cup--\,|\cup\cup--\,|\cup\cup-\cup- \qquad = X{\sim}Y{\sim}Z = glyc@2ch\text{[119]}$$

Let us consider where these shapes could fit within the framework of a *pher@3da.* Again the * following a symbol designates a sequence where the final syllable is restricted to a short quantity:

116. N 1974.55, with references. While accepting the special status of the first foot of hexameter in allowing spondaic word endings, Berg 1978.29 argues for the special status of the second foot as well, on the grounds that this foot, unlike the third, fourth, and fifth feet, shuns dactylic word endings, not just spondaic ones (cf. Allen 1973.291–292). He claims that this constraint in the second foot is conditioned by the oncoming caesura in the third foot. It appears that Berg thinks of caesura patterns as diachronic shapers of phraseology; I prefer to follow Parry 1928b in thinking of phraseology as the diachronic shaper of caesura patterns (N 1974.57–61). In what follows, we have occasion to consider some phraseological reasons for the constraint against dactylic word ending in the second foot: that the third foot is a primary zone for syntactical boundaries in the hexameter, as reflected by the primary caesuras. When the caesura comes after the long syllable of the third foot, the second foot can have word end after the dactyl only if the next word is a monosyllable. According to Berg's own etymology of the hexameter (cf. also Tichy 1981), the first and the second feet of hexameter together reflect an earlier pattern shaped $\underset{\smile}{\underline{\cup}}\,\underset{\smile}{\underline{\cup}}\,\underset{\smile}{\underline{\cup}}\,\underset{\smile}{\underline{\cup}}\dots$, as distinct from the pattern $\underset{\smile}{\underline{\cup}}\,\underset{\smile}{\underline{\cup}}-\cup\cup\dots$ posited in my scheme. I am in partial agreement with the critique of Berg by Ritoók 1987.4–5. While I am on the subject of Berg's 1978 article, I should note in passing that I am horrified by his misunderstanding of the English idiom *hit upon* (N, p. 148), which he betrays with the placement of his bracketed sign "!" between "hit" and "upon" (Berg, p. 18); the phrase is taken from a deliberately sarcastic sentence of mine that mocks the *topos* of the "first discoverer" (ibid.).

117. Cf. Haslam 1974.15. Only at the beginning of cola can $\cup\cup$ be substituted for $-$ in the *Geryoneis* of Stesichorus, corresponding to the optional substitution of $-\cup\cup$ for $--$ in the first foot of hexameter.

118. Ibid.

119. To repeat, the Aeolic fragments that I have examined are: Alcaeus F 44, 50, 115a; 296b, 340–349; cf. Theocritus 28, 30 and Callimachus F 400.

$$\underset{\smile}{\smile}\,\underset{\smile}{\smile}-\smile\smile-|\smile\smile-\smile\smile|-\smile\smile-- \qquad = X|{\sim}Z^*|\,Y{\sim}|\,.^{120}$$

Keeping in mind the posited innovation of replacing initial $\underset{\smile}{\smile}\,\underset{\smile}{\smile}$ with $-\smile\smile$, we find that the hexameter actually accommodates phraseology corresponding to the *glyc@2ch* in exactly these slots:

$$-\smile\smile-\smile\smile-|\smile\smile-\smile\smile|-\smile\smile-- \qquad = X|{\sim}Z^*|\,Y{\sim}|\,.$$

As a case in point, I cite the hexameters in Hesiod *Works and Days* 582–593 and *Shield of Herakles* 393–401, to be compared with the stichic series of *glyc@2ch* in Alcaeus F 347. To indicate the relative metrical position of the phraseology, I propose to use the symbols # for line-initial and line-final position, 1 2 3 4 for the relevant caesuras of hexameter, and A B C D for those of the *glyc@2ch*:

$$\#-\smile\smile-\smile\smile-|\smile|\smile-|\smile\smile|-\smile\smile--\# \qquad = \text{hexameter}$$
$$\qquad\quad 1\ \ 2\quad\ 3\quad\ \ 4$$

$$\#\underset{\smile}{\smile}\,\underset{\smile}{\smile}-\smile\smile-|-|\smile\smile-|-|\smile\smile-\smile-\# \qquad = glyc@2ch.$$
$$\quad\ \ \text{A B}\qquad \text{C D}$$

Let us proceed to examine the following correspondences:

$$\underset{\smile}{\smile}\,\underset{\smile}{\smile}-\smile\smile-|-\smile\smile--|\smile\smile-\smile- \qquad = X|\,Y{\sim}Z = glyc@2ch$$
$$\qquad\quad \text{A}\qquad\quad \text{D}$$

$$-\smile\smile-\smile\smile-|\smile\smile-\smile\smile|-\smile\smile-- \qquad = X|{\sim}Z^*|\,Y{\sim}| = \text{hexameter}$$
$$\qquad\quad 1\qquad\qquad 4$$

#... δὲ σκόλυμος| A (sector X|) in Alcaeus v. 7 corresponds to #...δὲ σκόλυμος τ'| 1 in *Works* 582. A| ἄδεα τέττιξ| D (sector | Y~|) in Alcaeus v. 3 corresponds to 4| ἠχέτα τέττιξ# in *Works* 582 and *Shield* 393. #...ὑπὰ καύματος# (sector |~Z*|) in Alcaeus v. 2 corresponds to 1| ὑπὸ καύματος| 4 in *Works* 588.[121]

120. We would expect the *pher@3da* to accommodate a variety of other patterns as well. In the actual attestations of *pher@3da* in Alcaeus F 367 and 368, we find the following configurations of word breaking:

$$\underset{\smile}{\smile}\,\underset{\smile}{\smile}-\smile\smile-\smile|\smile-\smile\smile|-\smile\smile--$$
$$\underset{\smile}{\smile}\,\underset{\smile}{\smile}-\smile\smile-|\smile\smile-\smile\smile|-\smile\smile--$$
$$\underset{\smile}{\smile}\,\underset{\smile}{\smile}-\smile\smile|-\smile\smile-\smile|\smile-\smile\smile--$$
$$\underset{\smile}{\smile}\,\underset{\smile}{\smile}-\smile\smile-|\smile\smile-\smile|\smile-\smile\smile--.$$

121. Such correspondences reinforce the argument of Hooker 1977.80–81 that these Alcaic and Hesiodic compositions are independently drawing upon cognate traditions. If indeed the pattern of word breaking at position 4 in hexameter is conditioned by phraseology shaped |~Z*| at the close of glyconics, it seems pertinent that position 4 in hexameter is a common point of syn-

Now let us consider again the *glyc@2da*:

$$\underline{\cup}\,\underline{\cup}-\cup\cup-\,|\,\cup\cup-\cup\cup-\cup- \qquad = X\,|\,{\sim}Y{+}Z = glyc@2da$$

$$\underline{\cup}\,\underline{\cup}-\cup\cup-\,|\,\cup\cup-\,|\,\cup\cup-\cup- \qquad = X\,|\,{\sim}Y\,|\,{\sim}Z = glyc@2da$$

$$\underline{\cup}\,\underline{\cup}\,|\,{-}\cup\cup-\cup\cup\,|\,{-}\cup\cup-\cup- \qquad = V\,|\,Z^*\,|\,Z = glyc@2da$$

$$\underline{\cup}\,\underline{\cup}-\,|\,\cup\cup-\cup\cup\,|\,{-}\cup\cup-\cup- \qquad = V{\sim}\,|\,{\sim}Z^*\,|\,Z = glyc@2da$$

$$\underline{\cup}\,\underline{\cup}-\,|\,\cup\cup-\,|\,\cup\cup-\,|\,\cup\cup-\cup- \qquad = V{\sim}\,|\,{\sim}Y\,|\,{\sim}Y{\sim}Z = glyc@2da$$

etc.

Again we find that the hexameter actually accommodates phraseology corresponding to what we find in the *glyc@2da*, as with the placement of wording shaped $|{\sim}Z^*$ at the middle of the hexameter:

$$-\cup\cup-\cup\cup-\,|\,\cup\cup-\cup\cup\,|\,{-}\cup\cup-- \qquad = X\,|\,{\sim}Z^*|\,Y{\sim}\,|\,.^{122}$$

There is an interesting alternative pattern, where wording shaped $\cup\cup-\cup\cup-\cup\cup--$ at the end of hexameter corresponds to wording shaped $|{\sim}Z^*|$ at the end of one *glyc@2da* followed by wording that occupies the Aeolic base in a consecutive *glyc@2da:*

$$\underline{\cup}\,\underline{\cup}-\cup\cup-\,|\,\cup\cup-\,|\,\cup\cup-\cup- \qquad = X\,|\,{\sim}Y\,|\,{\sim}Z = glyc@2da$$

$$\underline{\cup}\,\underline{\cup}\,|\,\ldots \qquad\qquad\qquad\qquad = V\,|\,\ldots$$

$$-\cup\cup-\cup\cup-\,|\,\cup\cup-\,|\,\cup\cup-\cup\cup\,|\,-- \qquad = X\,|\,{\sim}Y\,|\,{\sim}Z^*|\,V = \text{hexameter.}^{123}$$

The same phenomenon occurs in wording shaped $|{\sim}Z^*|$ at the end of one *glyc@2ch* followed by wording that occupies the Aeolic base in a consecutive *glyc@2ch*.[124] Even more common in hexameter is wording shaped for

---

tactical closure. An extreme example is the end of the *Iliad*, where the scholia to the Townley manuscript report a performance tradition where the last line, 804, can be stopped at position 4, to accommodate an actual beginning of the *Aithiopis* narrative starting at this same position 4: according to this tradition, the last word at line 804, ἱπποδάμοιο 'horse-tamer', as applied to Hektor, is deleted, and a clause introducing the grand opening theme of the *Aithiopis* is substituted: ἦλθε δ' 'Αμαζών 'and there came an Amazon . . .'.

122. For example, ταχὺς ἄγγελος in Sappho 44.3 and ταχὺς ἄγγελος in *Odyssey* xv 526; ἑλικώπιδα in Sappho 44.5 and ἑλικώπιδες in *Homeric Hymn* 33.1; προγενέστεραι in Sappho 44.31 and προγενέστερος in *Iliad* IX 161.

123. Cf. Sappho F 44.7–8, where ∪∪–∪∪ ἅλμυρον#πόντον corresponds to hexameter line-final ∪∪–∪∪ ἁλμυρὸν ὕδωρ, as in *Odyssey* iv 511. The expression ἅλμυρον ὕδωρ is apparently secondary to ἅλμυρος . . . πόντος, as we can see from the expressions ἁλμυρὸς ἔτρεφε Πόντος and ἁλμυρὸς ἔνδοθι πόντος in Hesiod *Theogony* 107 and 964, respectively. In other words it seems that πόντος displaces ὕδωρ in certain environments, not the other way around.

124. Cf. Alcaeus F 347.8–9, where Σείριος#ἄσδει corresponds to hexameter line-final Σείριος ἄζει in Hesiod *Works and Days* 587. At #915, we have already examined correspondences between this Alcaic composition and the Hesiodic passage from which this line, *Works* 587, is taken.

pher sequences, which can be described as *pher** followed by * ˜*pher@da*.[125]

It is important to stress in passing that, just as Aeolic meters influence each other, we can expect hexameter, even if it is partially inherited from Aeolic meters, also to influence them.

125. Cf. p. 456, where the wording that fills *glyc@2da* in Sappho F 44.10 can be described as *pher** followed by ˜**glyc*.

▣▣ Bibliography

Alexiou, M. 1974. *The Ritual Lament in Greek Tradition*. Cambridge.

Allen, T. W., ed. 1912. *Homeri Opera* V (Hymns, Cycle, fragments, etc.). Oxford.

———. 1924. *Homer: The Origins and the Transmission*. Oxford.

Allen, W. S. 1973. *Accent and Rhythm. Prosodic Features of Latin and Greek: A Study in Theory and Reconstruction*. Cambridge.

———. 1987. *Vox Graeca: The Pronunciation of Classical Greek*. 3rd ed. Cambridge.

Aloni, A. 1986. *Tradizioni arcaiche della Troade e composizione dell' Iliade*. Milan.

Ananthanarayana, H. S. 1973. "Basic Metrical Patterns in the Poems of the Rig-Veda." *Acta Linguistica Hafniensia* 14:155–170.

Anderson, W. D. 1966. *Ethos and Education in Greek Music: The Evidence of Poetry and Philosophy*. Cambridge, Mass.

Andrzejewski, B. W., and Lewis, I. M. 1964. *Somali Poetry: An Introduction*. Oxford.

Arthur, M. B. 1983. "The Dream of a World without Women: Poetics and the Circles of Order in the *Theogony* Prooemium." *Arethusa* 16:97–116.

Austin, J. L. 1962. *How to Do Things with Words*. Oxford.

Austin, N. 1975. *Archery at the Dark of the Moon: Poetic Problems in Homer's Odyssey*. Berkeley and Los Angeles.

Bake, A. 1957. "The Music of India." In *New Oxford History of Music* I. *Ancient and Oriental Music*, edited by E. Wellesz, 195–227. London.

Bakhtin, M. M. 1963 [1984]. *Problemy poetiki Dostoevskogo*. Moscow. = *Problems of Dostoevsky's Poetics*. Edited and translated by C. Emerson, with introduction by W. C. Booth. Minneapolis, Minnesota, 1984.

———. 1965 [1984b]. *Tvorčestvo Fransua Rable i narodnaja kul'tura srednevekov'ja i Renessansa*. Moscow. = *Rabelais and his World*. Translated by H. Iswolsky, with forewords by K. Pomorska and M. Holquist. Bloomington, Indiana, 1984.

Barker, A., ed. 1984. *Greek Musical Writings* I. Cambridge.

Barnett, H. G. 1953. *Innovation: The Basis of Cultural Change*. New York.

Barrett, W. S., ed. with commentary. 1966. *Euripides: Hippolytos*. Oxford.

Barthes, R. 1973. *Le plaisir du texte*. Paris.

Bauman, R. 1977. *Verbal Art as Performance*. Rowley, Mass.

———. 1986. *Story, Performance, and Event: Contextual Studies of Oral Narrative*. Cambridge.

Bausinger, H. 1980. *Formen der "Volkspoesie."* 2nd ed. Berlin.

Beaton, R. 1980. *Folk Poetry of Modern Greece*. Cambridge.

———. 1980b. "Modes and Roads: Factors of Change and Continuity in Greek Musical Traditions." *The Annual of the British School at Athens* 75:1–11.

Beazley, J. D. 1954. *Attic Vase Paintings*, Boston II. Oxford.

———. 1963. Attic Red-Figure Vase Painters. 2nd ed. I/II. Oxford.

Becker, O. 1937. *Das Bild des Weges und verwandte Vorstellungen im frühgriechischen Denken. Hermes Einzelschriften* 4. Berlin.

Ben-Amos, D. 1976. "Analytical Categories and Ethnic Genres." *Folklore Genres*, edited by D. Ben-Amos, 215–242. Austin.

Benardete, S. 1969. *Herodotean Inquiries*. The Hague.

Benveniste, E. 1937. "Expression indo-européenne de l'éternité." *Bulletin de la Société de Linguistique de Paris* 38:103–112.

———. 1966. *Problèmes de linguistique générale*. Paris.

———. 1969. *Le vocabulaire des institutions indo-européennes*. I. *Economie, parenté, société*. II. *Pouvoir, droit, religion*. Paris = *Indo-European Language and Society*. Translated by E. Palmer. London, 1973.

Bérard, C. 1982. "Récupérer la mort du prince: Héroïsation et formation de la cité." Gnoli and Vernant 1982:89–105.

Berg, N. 1978. "Parergon Metricum: Der Ursprung des griechischen Hexameters." *Münchener Beiträge zur Sprachwissenschaft* 37:11–36.

Bergren, A. 1982. "Sacred Apostrophe: Re-Presentation and Imitation in the Homeric Hymns." *Arethusa* 15:83–108.

Bertel´s, A. Y., et al., eds. 1966–1971. *Ferdowsi: Shāhnāma*. I–IX. Moscow.

Berve, H. 1967. *Die Tyrannis bei den Griechen*. 2 vols. Munich.

Beye, C. R. 1987. *Ancient Greek Literature and Society*. 2nd ed. Ithaca.

Bickerman, E. J. 1952. "Origines Gentium." *Classical Philology* 47:65–81.

Bischoff, H. 1932. *Der Warner bei Herodot*. Marburg.

Bloom, H., ed. 1986. *Modern Critical Views: Homer*. New York.

Boardman, J. 1980. *The Greeks Overseas*. 2nd ed. London.

Boas, F. 1944. *The Function of Dance in Human Society*. New York.

Boedeker, D. D. 1974. *Aphrodite's Entry into Greek Epic*. Leiden.

———. 1987. "The Two Faces of Demaratus." *Arethusa* 20:185–201.

———. 1988. "Protesilaos and the End of Herodotus' *Histories*." *Classical Antiquity* 7:30–48.

Bornemann, L. 1884. "Über die Aegeiden, von denen angeblich Pindar stammte." *Philologus* 43:79–85.

Boulton, L. 1954. *The Eskimos of Hudson Bay and Alaska. Folkways Records, Album Notes for FE4444*. New York.

Bourriot, F. 1976. *Recherches sur la nature du Genos: Etude d'histoire sociale athénienne, périodes archaïques et classiques.* 2 vols. Lille/Geneva.

Boutière, J., and Schutz, A.-H. 1950. *Biographies des Troubadours: Textes provençaux des xiiie et xive siècles.* Toulouse/Paris.

Bowie, A. M. 1981. *The Poetic Dialect of Sappho and Alcaeus.* New York.

Bowie, E. L. 1986. "Early Greek Elegy, Symposium and Public Festival." *Journal of Hellenic Studies* 106:13–35.

Bowra, C. M. 1961. *Greek Lyric Poetry: From Alcman to Simonides.* 2nd ed. Oxford.

Bravo, B. 1974. "Une lettre sur plomb de Berezan: Colonisation et modes de contact dans le Pont." *Dialogues d'histoire ancienne.* Annales littéraires de l'Université de Besançon 166:135–141.

Brelich, A. 1958. *Gli eroi greci.* Rome.

———. 1961. *Guerre, agoni e culti nella Grecia arcaica.* Bonn.

———. 1969. *Paides e Parthenoi.* Incunabula Graeca 36. Rome.

Bresson, A. 1979. *Mythe et contradiction: Analyse de la viie Olympique de Pindare.* Annales Littéraires de l'Université de Besançon 230. Centre de Recherche d'Histoire Ancienne 29. Paris.

Bright, W. 1963. "Language and Music: Areas for Cooperation." *Ethnomusicology* 7:26–32.

Brisson, L. 1982. *Platon: Les mots et les mythes.* Paris.

Browning, R. 1963. "A Byzantine Treatise on Tragedy." In ΓΕΡΑΣ. *Studies Presented to G. Thomson on the Occasion of His 60th Birthday,* 67–81. Prague.

Brunner, H. 1970. "Epenmelodien." In *Formen mittelalterlicher Literatur: Festschrift Siegfried Beyschlag,* 149–178. Göttingen.

Bundy, E. L. 1962 [1986]. "Studia Pindarica I: The Eleventh Olympian Ode; II: The First Isthmian Ode." *University of California Publications in Classical Philology* 18.1–2:1–92. Both articles reissued 1986 as *Studia Pindarica.* Berkeley and Los Angeles.

———. 1972. "The 'Quarrel' between Kallimachos and Apollonios, Part I: The Epilogue of Kallimachos' *Hymn to Apollo.*" *California Studies in Classical Antiquity* 5:39–94.

Burkert, W. 1965. "Demaratos, Astrabakos und Herakles." *Museum Helveticum* 22:166–177.

———. 1966. "Greek Tragedy and Sacrificial Ritual." *Greek Roman and Byzantine Studies* 7:87–121.

———. 1972. "Die Leistung eines Kreophylos: Kreophyleer, Homeriden und die archaische Heraklesepik." *Museum Helveticum* 29:74–85.

———. 1979. "Kynaithos, Polycrates, and the Homeric Hymn to Apollo." In *Arktouros: Hellenic Studies Presented to B. M. W. Knox,* edited by G. W. Bowersock, W. Burkert, and M. C. J. Putnam, 53–62. Berlin.

———. 1979b. "Mythisches Denken." In *Philosophie und Mythos,* edited by H. Poser, 16–39. Berlin/New York.

———. 1983. *Homo Necans: The Anthropology of Ancient Greek Sacrificial Ritual and Myth.* Translated by P. Bing. Berkeley and Los Angeles. Originally published 1972 in German under the title *Homo Necans.* Berlin.

———. 1985. *Greek Religion.* Translated by J. Raffan. Cambridge, Mass. Originally published 1977 in German under the title *Griechische Religion der archaischen und klassischen Epoche.* Stuttgart.

———. 1987. "The Making of Homer in the Sixth Century B.C.: Rhapsodes versus Stesichorus." In *Papers on the Amasis Painter and His World,* edited by M. True, C. Hudson, A. P. A. Belloli, B. Gilman, and others, 43–62. The J. Paul Getty Museum. Malibu.

Burnett, A. P. 1983. *Three Archaic Poets: Archilochus, Alcaeus, Sappho.* Cambridge, Mass.

———. 1985. *The Art of Bacchylides.* Cambridge, Mass.

———. 1988. "Jocasta in the West: The Lille Stesichorus." *Classical Antiquity* 7:107–154.

Calame, C. 1977. *Les choeurs de jeunes filles en Grèce archaïque* I: *Morphologie, fonction religieuse et sociale.* II: *Alcman.* Rome.

———, ed. with commentary. 1983. *Alcman.* Rome.

———. 1983b. "Entre oralité et écriture." *Semiotica* 43:245–273.

———. 1986. *Le récit en Grèce ancienne.* Paris.

———. 1987. "Spartan Genealogies: The Mythological Representation of a Spatial Organisation." *Interpretations of Greek Mythology,* 1, edited by J. Bremmer, 53–186. London.

Campbell, D. A. 1964. "Flutes and Elegiac Couplets." *Journal of Hellenic Studies* 84:63–68.

———, ed. 1976. *Greek Lyric Poetry: A Selection of Early Greek Lyric, Elegiac and Iambic Poetry.* Reprint, with addenda, of the 1967 edition. Houndmills, Basingstoke, Hampshire, England.

———, ed. with translation. 1980. *Greek Lyric* I. Sappho and Alcaeus. Cambridge, Mass.

Cantilena, M. 1982. *Ricerche sulla dizione epica..* I. *Per uno studio della formularità degli Inni Omerici.* Rome.

Carson, A. 1984. "The Burners: A Reading of Bacchylides' Third Epinician Ode." *Phoenix* 38:111–119.

Cartledge, P. A. 1988. "Yes, Spartan Kings were Heroized." *Liverpool Classical Monthly* 13.3:43–44.

CEG. *See* Hansen 1983.

Chantraine, P. 1968, 1970, 1975, 1977, 1980. *Dictionnaire étymologique de la langue grecque* I, II, III, IV–1, IV–2. Paris. Abbreviated as DELG.

Chen, Li-li. 1976. "Translator's Introduction." *Master Tung's Western Chamber Romance,* ix-xxvii. Cambridge, Mass.

Cingano, E. 1982. "Quante testimonianze sulle palinodie di Stesicoro?" *Quaderni Urbinati* 12:21–33.

———. 1985. "Clistene di Sicione, Erodoto e i poemi del Ciclo tebano." *Quaderni Urbinati* 20:31–40.

———. 1986. "Il valore dell' esspressione στάσις μελῶν in Aristofane, *Rane,* v. 1281." *Quaderni Urbinati* 24:139–143.

Clay, J. S. 1984. *The Wrath of Athena. Gods and Men in the Odyssey.* Princeton.

———. 1986. "Archilochus and Gyges: An Interpretation of Fr. 23 West." *Quaderni Urbinati* 24:7–17.

Clunies Ross, M. 1986. "Australian Aboriginal Oral Traditions." *Oral Tradition* 1:231–271.

Cole, T. 1983. "Archaic Truth." *Quaderni Urbinati* 13:7–28.

———. 1988. *Epiploke: Rhythmical Continuity and Poetic Structure in Greek Lyric.* Cambridge, Mass.

Comotti, G. 1979. *La musica nella cultura greca e romana.* Torino. = *Music in Greek and Roman Culture.* Translated by R. V. Munson. Baltimore, 1989.

Comrie, B. 1976. *Aspect: An Introduction to the Study of Verbal Aspect and Related Problems.* Cambridge.

Connor, W. R. 1987. "Tribes, Festivals and Processions: Civic Ceremonial and Political Manipulation in Archaic Greece." *Journal of Hellenic Studies* 107:40–50.

———. 1988. "Early Greek Land Warfare as Symbolic Expression." *Past and Present: A Journal of Historical Studies* 119:3–29.

Considine, P. 1986. "The Etymology of ΜΗΝΙΣ." *Studies in Honour of T. B. L. Webster,* edited by J. H. Betts, J. T. Hooker, and J. R. Green, I 53–64. Bristol.

Corlu, A. 1966. *Recherches sur les mots relatifs à l'idée de prière d'Homère aux tragiques.* Paris.

Coupez, A., and Kamanzi, T. 1962. *Récits historiques rwanda. Musée royal de l'Afrique Centrale. Annales (Sciences Humaines).* Tervuren.

Crane, G. 1988. *Calypso: Backgrounds and Conventions of the Odyssey.* Frankfurt.

Crotty, K. 1982. *Song and Action: The Victory Odes of Pindar.* Baltimore.

Culler, J. 1975. *The Pursuit of Signs: Semiotics, Literature, Deconstruction.* Ithaca.

Dale, A. M. 1963. "Stichos and Stanza." *Classical Quarterly* 13:46–50. Reprinted in Dale 1969:173–179.

———. 1968. *The Lyric Metres of Greek Drama.* 2nd ed. Cambridge.

———. 1969. *Collected Papers.* Cambridge.

Darbo-Peschanski, C. 1987. *Le discours du particulier: Essai sur l'enquête hérodotéenne.* Paris.

Davidson, O. M. 1980. "Indo-European Dimensions of Herakles in *Iliad* 19.95–133." *Arethusa* 13:197–202.

———. 1985. "The Crown-Bestower in the Iranian Book of Kings." *Acta Iranica, Hommages et Opera Minora* 10: *Papers in Honour of Professor Mary Boyce,* 61–148. Leiden.

Davies, J. K. 1971. *Athenian Propertied Families, 600–300 B.C.* Oxford.

Davies, M. 1988. "Monody, Choral Lyric, and the Tyranny of the Handbook." *Classical Quarterly* 38:52–64.

Davison, J. A. 1955. "Peisistratus and Homer." *Transactions of the American Philological Association* 86:1–21.

———. 1955b. "Quotations and Allusions in Early Greek Poetry." *Eranos* 53:125–140 = 1968:70–85.

———. 1958. "Notes on the Panathenaia." *Journal of Hellenic Studies* 78:23–41 = 1968:28–69.

———. 1968. *From Archilochus to Pindar: Papers on Greek Literature of the Archaic Period.* London.

De Martino. *See* Martino.

Degani, E., and Burzacchini, G., eds. 1977. *Lirici Greci. Antologia.* Florence.

Delcourt, M. 1955. *L'Oracle de Delphes.* Paris.

DELG. *See* Chantraine 1968+.

Denniston, J. D. 1954. *The Greek Particles.* 2nd ed., revised by K. J. Dover. Oxford.

Derrida, J. 1972. *Marges de la Philosophie*. Paris.

———. 1972b. *La dissémination*. Paris. = *Dissemination*. Translated by B. Johnson. Chicago, 1981.

Descat, R. 1981. "Idéologie et communication dans la poésie grecque archaïque." *Quaderni Urbinati* 38:7–27.

Detienne, M. 1972. *Les jardins d'Adonis: La mythologie des aromates en Grèce*. Paris = *The Gardens of Adonis*. Translated by J. Lloyd. Sussex, England, 1977.

———. 1973. *Les maîtres de vérité dans la Grèce archaïque*. 2nd ed. Paris.

———. 1977. *Dionysos mis à mort*. Paris = *Dionysos Slain*. Translated by L. Muellner and M. Muellner. Baltimore, 1979.

———. 1981. *L' invention de la mythologie*. Paris.

———, ed. 1988. *Les savoirs de l'écriture. En Grèce ancienne*. Lille.

Detienne, M., and Svenbro, J. 1979. "Les loups au festin ou la Cité impossible." Detienne and Vernant 1969:215–237.

Detienne, M., and Vernant, J.-P., eds. 1969. *La cuisine du sacrifice en pays grec*. Paris.

———. 1974. *Les ruses de l'intelligence: La ΜΗΤΙΣ des Grecs*. Paris = *Cunning Intelligence in Greek Culture and Society*. Translated by J. Lloyd. Sussex, 1978.

Devine, A. M., and Stephens, L. D. 1975. "Anceps." *Greek Roman and Byzantine Studies* 16:197–215.

———. 1985. "Stress in Greek?" *Transactions of the American Philological Association* 115:125–152.

Dewald, C. 1985. "Practical Knowledge and the Historian's Role in Herodotus and Thucydides." In *The Greek Historians: Literature and History. Papers Presented to A. E. Raubitschek*, 47–63. Saratoga, California.

———. 1987. "Narrative Surface and Authorial Voice in Herodotus' *Histories*." *Arethusa* 20:147–170.

Dewald, C., and Marin:ola, J. 1987. "A Selective Introduction to Herodotean Studies." *Arethusa* 20:9 40.

DGE. *See* Schw, :r 1923.

Diels, H., and Kraṇ., W., ec's. 1951–1952. *Die Fragmente der Vorsokratiker*. 6th ed. Berlin.

Dillon, M. 1975. *Celts and Aryans*. Simla.

Dittenberger, W., ed. 1915–1924. *Sylloge Inscriptionum Graecarum*. 3rd ed. Leipzig.

DK. *See* Diels and Kranz 1951–1952.

Dodds, E. R. 1951. *The Greeks and the Irrational*. Berkeley and Los Angeles.

———, ed. 1960. Euripides: *Bacchae*. 2nd ed. Oxford.

Donlan, W. 1970. "Changes and Shifts in the Meaning of Demos." *La Parola del Passato* 135:381–395.

Dover, K. J. 1964. "The Poetry of Archilochus." *Archiloque: Entretiens Hardt* 10:183–222. Geneva.

———, ed. with commentary. 1968. *Aristophanes Clouds*. Oxford.

Drachmann, A. B., ed. 1903–1927. *Scholia Vetera in Pindari Carmina*. 3 vols. Leipzig.

Ducrot, O., and Todorov, T. 1972. *Dictionnaire encyclopédique des sciences du langage*. Paris. = *Encyclopedic Dictionary of the Sciences of Language*. Translated by C. Porter. Baltimore, 1979.

Duggan, J., ed. 1975. *Oral Literature: Seven Essays*. Edinburgh and New York.

Dumézil, G. 1978. *Romans de Scythie et d'alentour*. Paris.

———. 1982. *Apollon sonore*. Paris.

———. 1985. *L'oubli de l'homme et l'honneur des dieux: Esquisses de mythologie*. Paris.

Dunkel, G. 1979. "Fighting Words: Alcman *Partheneion* 63 *makhontai*." *Journal of Indo-European Studies* 7:249–272.

Dupont-Roc, R., and Lallot, J., eds. with commentary. 1980. *Aristote: La poétique*. Paris.

Durante, M. 1976. *Sulla preistoria della tradizione poetica greca* II. *Risultanze della comparazione indoeuropea*. Incunabula Graeca 64. Rome.

Eagleton, T. 1983. *Literary Theory: An Introduction*. Minneapolis.

Ebert, J., ed. 1972. *Griechische Epigramme auf Sieger an gymnischen und hippischen Agonen*. Berlin.

Edmunds, L. 1981. "The Cults and the Legend of Oedipus." *Harvard Studies in Classical Philology* 85:221–238.

———. 1985. "The Genre of Theognidean Poetry." Figueira and Nagy 1985:96–111.

Edwards, A. T. 1985. *Odysseus against Achilles: The Role of Allusion in the Homeric Epic*. Beiträge zur Klassischen Philologie 171. Königstein/Ts.

———. 1985b. "Achilles in the Underworld: *Iliad*, *Odyssey*, and *Aithiopis*." *Greek Roman and Byzantine Studies* 26:215–227.

———. 1988. ΚΛΕΟΣ ΑΦΘΙΤΟΝ and Oral Theory." *Classical Quarterly* 38:25–30.

Edwards, G. P. 1971. *The Language of Hesiod in Its Traditional Context*. Oxford.

Edwards, M. W. 1987. *Homer, Poet of the Iliad*. Baltimore.

EG. *See* Page 1975.

Else, G., ed. with commentary. 1957. *Aristotle's Poetics: The Argument*. Cambridge, Mass.

———. 1958. "Imitation in the Fifth Century." *Classical Philology* 53:73–90.

Elwell-Sutton, L. P. 1976. *The Persian Metres*. Cambridge.

Erbse, H. 1956. "Der erste Satz im Werke Herodots." *Festschrift Bruno Snell*, 209–222. Munich.

Fairweather, J. A. 1983. "Traditional Narrative, Inference and Truth in the Lives of Greek Poets." *Papers of the Liverpool Latin Seminar* 4:315–369.

Färber, H. 1936. *Die Lyrik in der Kunsttheorie der Antike*. Munich.

Farenga, V. 1981. "The Paradigmatic Tyrant: Greek Tyranny and the Ideology of the Proper." *Helios* 8:1–31.

Farnell, L. R. 1932. *The Works of Pindar* II: *Critical Commentary*. London.

FGH. *See* Jacoby 1923–.

Figueira, T. J. 1981. *Aegina*. New York.

———. 1983. "Aeginetan Independence." *Classical Journal* 79:8–29.

———. 1984. "The 10 Arkhontes of 579/8 at Athens." *Hesperia* 53:447–473.

———. 1985. "The Theognidea and Megarian Society." Figueira and Nagy 1985:112–158.

Figueira, T. J., and Nagy, G., eds. 1985. *Theognis of Megara: Poetry and the Polis*. Baltimore.

Finkelberg, M. 1986. "Is ΚΛΕΟΣ ΑΦΘΙΤΟΝ a Homeric Formula?" *Classical Quarterly* 36:1–5.

————. 1988. "Ajax's Entry in the Hesiodic *Catalogue of Women*." *Classical Quarterly* 38:31–41.

Finley, J. H. 1955. *Pindar and Aeschylus*. Cambridge, Mass.

Finley, M. I. 1977. *The World of Odysseus*. 2nd ed. New York.

Finnegan, R. 1970. *Oral Literature in Africa*. Oxford.

————. 1977. *Oral Poetry: Its Nature, Significance, and Social Context*. Cambridge.

Fitch, E. 1924. "Pindar and Homer." *Classical Philology* 19:57–65.

Fittschen, K. 1969. *Untersuchungen zum Beginn der Sagendarstellung bei den Griechen*. Berlin.

Flory, S. 1980. "Who Read Herodotus' *Histories*?" *American Journal of Philology* 101:12–28.

Floyd, E. D. 1980. "ΚΛΕΟΣ ΑΦΘΙΤΟΝ: An Indo-European Perspective on Early Greek Poetry." *Glotta* 58:133–157.

Fogelmark, S. 1972. *Studies in Pindar with Particular Reference to Paean VI and Nemean VII*. Lund.

Foley, H. P. 1985. *Ritual Irony: Poetry and Sacrifice in Euripides*. Ithaca.

Foley, J. M. 1985. *Oral-Formulaic Theory and Research: An Introduction and Annotated Bibliography*. New York.

Fontenrose, J. 1968. "The Hero as Athlete." *California Studies in Classical Antiquity* 1:73–104.

————. 1978. *The Delphic Oracle: Its Responses and Operations. With a Catalogue of Responses*. Berkeley and Los Angeles.

Ford, A. L. 1985. "The Seal of Theognis: The Politics of Authorship in Archaic Greece." Figueira and Nagy 1985:82–95.

Fornara, C. W. 1971. *Herodotus, An Interpretative Essay*. Oxford.

————. 1971b. "Evidence for the Date of Herodotus' Publication." *Journal of Hellenic Studies* 91:25–34.

Foucault, M. 1979. "What is an Author?" In *Textual Strategies: Perspectives in Post-Structuralist Criticism*, edited by J. V. Harari, 141–160. Ithaca.

Forssman, B. 1966. *Untersuchungen zur Sprache Pindars*. Wiesbaden.

Fraenkel, E. 1920 (1924). "Zur Form der AINOI." *Rheinisches Museum für Philologie* 73:366–370. Reprinted in his *Kleine Schriften* I, pp. 235–239. Rome, 1964.

————, ed. 1950. *Aeschylus: Agamemnon*. 3 vols. Oxford.

————. 1957. *Horace*. Oxford.

————. 1962. *Beobachtungen zu Aristophanes*. Rome.

Frame, D. 1978. *The Myth of Return in Early Greek Epic*. New Haven.

Francis, E. D. 1983. "Virtue, Folly, and Greek Etymology." Rubino and Shelmerdine 1983:74–121.

Fränkel, H. 1973. *Early Greek Poetry and Philosophy*. Translated by M. Hadas and J. Willis. New York.

Frontisi-Ducroux, F. 1986. *La cithare d'Achille. Essai sur la poétique de l'Iliade*. Rome.

Gardiner, N., ed. 1930. *Athletics of the Ancient World*. Oxford. Reprinted 1978, with preface by S. G. Miller. Chicago.

Geldner, K. F. 1951–1957. *Der Rig-Veda, aus dem Sanskrit ins Deutsche übersetzt* I–IV. Cambridge, Mass./Leipzig.

Gentili, B., ed. 1958. *Anacreon*. Rome.

————. 1979. *Theatrical Performances in the Ancient World*. London Studies in Classical Philology 2. Amsterdam.

————. 1985. *Poesia e pubblico nella grecia antica. Da Omero al V secolo*. Rome and Bari. = *Poetry and its Public in Ancient Greece: From Homer to the Fifth Century*. Translated by A. T. Cole. Baltimore, 1988.

————. 1986. "Il coro della tragedia greca nella teoria degli antichi." *Teatro e pubblico nell'antichità* (Atti del Convegno Nazionale Trento—25–27 April 1986) 27–44.

Gentili, B., and Giannini, P. 1977. "Preistoria e formazione dell'esametro." *Quaderni Urbinati* 26:7–37.

Gentili, B., and Prato, C., eds. 1979/1985. *Poetae Elegiaci* I/II. Leipzig.

Gerber, D. E., ed. 1970. *Euterpe: An Anthology of Early Greek Lyric, Elegiac and Iambic Poetry*. Amsterdam.

————. 1982. *Pindar's Olympian One: A Commentary*. Toronto.

————, ed. 1984. *Greek Poetry and Philosophy: Studies in Honour of Leonard Woodbury*. Chico, Calif.

Gernet, L. 1953. "Mariages de Tyrans." *Hommage à Lucien Febvre* 41–53. Paris. Reprinted in Gernet 1968:344–359.

Gernet, L. 1968. *Anthropologie de la Grèce antique*. Paris = *The Anthropology of Ancient Greece*. Translated by J. Hamilton and B. Nagy. Baltimore, 1981.

Giannini, P. 1982. "'Qualcuno' e 'nessuno' in Pind. *Pyth*. 8.95." *Quaderni Urbinati* 11:69–76.

Gildersleeve, B. L., ed. 1899. *Pindar: The Olympian and Pythian Odes*. 2nd ed. New York.

Gill, D. 1974. "Trapezomata: A Neglected Aspect of Greek Sacrifice." *Harvard Theological Review* 67:117–137.

Gillis, D. 1969. "Marathon and the Alcmaeonids." *Greek Roman and Byzantine Studies* 10:133–145.

Gluckman, M. 1965. *Politics, Law and Ritual in Tribal Society*. Oxford.

Gnoli, G., and Vernant, J.-P., eds. 1982. *La mort, les morts dans les sociétés anciennes*. Cambridge and Paris.

Golden, L., and Hardison, O. B. 1981. *Aristotle's Poetics: A Translation and Commentary for Students of Literature*. Gainesville, Florida.

Goldhill, S. 1984. *Language, Sexuality, Narrative: The Oresteia*. Cambridge.

Goody, J., and Watt, I. 1968. "The Consequences of Literacy." In *Literacy in Traditional Societies*, edited by J. Goody, 27–68. Cambridge.

Gow, A. S. F., ed. with commentary. 1952. *Theocritus* I/II. Cambridge.

GP, GP II. *See* Gentili and Prato.

Graham, A. J. 1983. *Colony and Mother City in Ancient Greece*. 2nd ed. Chicago.

Greenberg, N. A. 1985. "A Statistical Comparison of the Hexameter Verse in *Iliad* I, Theognis, and Solon." *Quaderni Urbinati* 20:63–75.

————. 1985b. "Appendix: Language, Meter, and Sense in Theognis (The Role of *agathos* 'noble, good')." Figueira and Nagy 1985:245–260.

Griffin, J. 1977. "The Epic Cycle and the Uniqueness of Homer." *Journal of Hellenic Studies* 97:39–53.

————. 1984. Review of Clay 1984. *Times Literary Supplement* no. 4.219, 10 February, p. 134.

Griffith M. 1983. "Personality in Hesiod." In *Studies in Classical Lyric: A Homage to Elroy Bundy*, edited by T. D'Evelyn, P. Psoinos, and T. R. Walsh. = *Classical Antiquity* 2:37–65.

Griffiths, A. 1972. "Alcman's *Partheneion*: The Morning After the Night Before." *Quaderni Urbinati* 14:7–30.

Groningen, B. A. van. 1946. *The Proems of the Iliad and the Odyssey*. Mededelingen der Koninklijke Nederlandsche Akademie van Wetenschappen 9.8:279–294.

——. 1960. *Pindare au banquet*. Leiden.

——, ed. 1966. *Théognis: Le premier livre*. Amsterdam.

Grottanelli, C., and Parise, N. F., eds. 1988. *Sacrificio e società nel mondo antico*. Rome/Bari.

Guillén, C. 1985. *Entre lo uno y lo diverso. Introducción a la literatura comparada*. Barcelona.

Habicht, C. 1985. *Pausanias' Guide to Ancient Greece*. Berkeley and Los Angeles.

Halliwell, S. 1986. *Aristotle's Poetics*. Chapel Hill.

Hamilton, R. 1974. *Epinikion: General Form in the Odes of Pindar*. The Hague.

Hamm, E.-M. 1957. *Grammatik zu Sappho und Alkaios*. Berlin.

Hansen, P. A., ed. 1983. *Carmina Epigraphica Graeca saeculorum viii–v a.Chr.n.* Berlin and New York.

Hansen, W. F. 1977. "Odysseus' Last Journey." *Quaderni Urbinati* 24:27–48.

Hardison, O. B. *See* Golden and Hardison 1981.

Hart, J. 1982. *Herodotus and Greek History*. New York, London, and Canberra.

Hartog, F. 1980. *Le miroir d'Hérodote: Essai sur la représentation de l'autre*. Paris.

Harvey, A. E. 1955. "The Classification of Greek Lyric Poetry." *Classical Quarterly* 5:157–175.

Haslam, M. 1974. "Stesichorean Metre." *Quaderni Urbinati* 17:7–57.

——. 1976. Review of Nagy 1974. *Journal of Hellenic Studies* 96:202–203.

——. 1978. "The Versification of the New Stesichorus (P. Lille 76abc)." *Greek Roman and Byzantine Studies* 19:29–57.

Havelock, E. A. 1963. *Preface to Plato*. Cambridge, Mass.

——. 1982. *The Literate Revolution in Greece and its Cultural Consequences*. Princeton.

Heath, M. 1988. "Receiving the ΚΩΜΟΣ: The Context and Performance of Epinician." *American Journal of Philology* 109:180–195.

Heesterman, J. C. 1957. *The Ancient Indian Royal Consecration: The Rājasūya described according to the Yajus Texts and annotated*. Disputationes Rheno-Trajectinae 2. The Hague.

Henderson, M. I. 1957. "Ancient Greek Music." In *New Oxford History of Music* I. *Ancient and Oriental Music*, edited by E. Wellesz, 336–403. London.

Henderson, M. I. and Wulstan, D. 1973. "Introduction: Ancient Greece." In *Music from the Middle Ages to the Renaissance*. Praeger History of Western Music I, edited by F. W. Sternfeld, 27–58. New York.

Henrichs, A. 1976. "Despoina Kybele: Ein Beitrag zur religiösen Namenkunde." *Harvard Studies in Classical Philology* 80:253–286.

——. 1979. "Greek and Roman Glimpses of Dionysos." *Dionysos and his Circle*, edited by C. Houser, 1–11. Cambridge, Mass.

——. 1980. "Riper than a Pear: Parian Invective in Theokritos." *Zeitschrift für Papyrologie und Epigraphik* 39:7–27.

————. 1981. "Human Sacrifice in Greek Religion." *Le sacrifice dans l'antiquité: Entretiens Hardt* 27:195–235. Geneva.

————. 1983. "The 'Sobriety' of Oedipus: Sophocles *OC* 100 Misunderstood." *Harvard Studies in Classical Philology* 87:87–100.

Herington, J. 1985. *Poetry into Drama: Early Tragedy and the Greek Poetic Tradition*. Berkeley and Los Angeles.

Herskovits, M. J., and Herskovits, F. S. 1947. *Trinidad Village*. New York.

Herzog, G. 1934. "Speech Melody and Primitive Music." *Musical Quarterly* 20:452–466.

————. 1950. "Song." In *Funk and Wagnall's Standard Dictionary of Folklore, Mythology, and Legend*, II 1032–1050. New York.

Heubeck, A. 1959. *Lydiaka: Untersuchungen zu Schrift, Sprache und Götternamen der Lyder*. Erlangen.

Highbarger, E. L. 1927. *The History and Civilization of Ancient Megara*. Baltimore.

Hiller von Gaertringen, F., ed. 1906. *Inschriften von Priene*. Berlin.

Hoenigswald, H. 1977. Review of Nagy 1974. *American Journal of Philology* 98:82–88.

Hohti, P. 1976. "Die Schuldfrage der Perserkriege in Herodots Geschichtswerke." *Arctos* 10:37–48.

Hooker, J. T. 1977. *The Language and Text of the Lesbian Poets*. Innsbrucker Beiträge zur Sprachwissenschaft 26. Innsbruck.

Householder, F. W., and Nagy, G. 1972. "Greek." In *Current Trends in Linguistics* IX, edited by T. A. Sebeok, 735–816. The Hague.

How, W. W., and Wells, J. 1912. *A Commentary on Herodotus*. I/II. Oxford.

Hubbard, T. K. 1985. *The Pindaric Mind. A Study of Logical Structure in Early Greek Poetry*. Leiden.

————. 1986. "Pegasus' Bridle and the Poetics of Pindar's *Thirteenth Olympian*." *Harvard Studies in Classical Philology* 90: 27–48.

————. 1987. "The 'Cooking' of Pelops: Pindar and the Process of Mythological Revisionism." *Helios* 14:3–21.

————. 1987b. "Pindar and the Aeginetan Chorus: *Nemean* 3.9–13." *Phoenix* 41:1–9.

————. 1987c. "Two Notes on the Myth of Aeacus in Pindar." *Greek Roman and Byzantine Studies* 28:5–22.

Hudson-Williams, T., ed. 1910. *Theognis. Elegies of Theognis and other Elegies*. London.

Hunt, R. 1981. "Hesiod as Satirist." *Helios* 8:29–40.

Huxley, G. L. 1969. *Greek Epic Poetry from Eumelos to Panyassis*. Cambridge, Mass.

————. 1975. *Pindar's Vision of the Past*. Belfast.

IG = *Inscriptiones Graecae*. Berlin. 1873–.

Immerwahr, H. R. 1956. "Aspects of Historical Causation in Herodotus." *Transactions of the American Philological Association* 87:241–280.

————. 1960. "*Ergon*: History as a Monument in Herodotus and Thucydides." *American Journal of Philology* 81:261–290.

————. 1966. *Form and Thought in Herodotus*. Cleveland.

Irigoin, J. 1952. *Histoire du texte de Pindare*. Paris.

————. 1956. "La structure des vers éoliens." *L'Antiquité Classique* 25:5–19.

——. 1957. "Colon, vers et strophe dans la lyrique monodique grecque." *Revue de Philologie* 31:234–238.

Itsumi, K. 1982. "The 'choriambic dimeter' of Euripides." *Classical Quarterly* 32: 59–74.

Jacoby, F. 1913. "Herodotos." *Realencyclopädie der klassischen Altertumswissenschaft* Supplement II:205–520. Stuttgart.

——, ed. 1923–. *Die Fragmente der griechischen Historiker.* Leiden.

Jacopin, P.-Y. 1981. "La parole générative de la mythologie des Indiens Yukuna." Doctoral dissertation, University of Neuchâtel.

Jakobson, R. 1939. "Signe zéro." *Mélanges de linguistique, offerts à Charles Bally* 143–152. Geneva. Reprinted in Jakobson 1971:211–219; also in Jakobson 1984:151–160.

——. 1952. "Studies in Comparative Slavic Metrics." *Oxford Slavonic Papers* 3:21–66. Reprinted in Jakobson 1966:414–463. The Hague.

——. 1957. *Shifters, Verbal Categories, and the Russian Verb.* Cambridge, Mass. Reprinted in Jakobson 1971:130–147; also in Jakobson 1984:41–58.

——. 1960. "Linguistics and Poetics." In *Style in Language*, edited by T. Sebeok, 350–377. Cambridge, Mass.

——. 1966. *Selected Writings* IV. The Hague.

——. 1971. *Selected Writings* II. The Hague.

——. 1984. *Russian and Slavic Grammar: Studies 1931–1981*, edited by M. Halle and L. R. Waugh. The Hague.

Jan, C. von, ed. 1895. *Musici Scriptores Graeci.* Leipzig.

Janko, R. 1982. *Homer, Hesiod and the Hymns: Diachronic Development in Epic Diction.* Cambridge.

Jeanmaire, H. 1939. *Couroï et Courètes.* Lille.

Jeffery, L. H. 1962. "The Inscribed Gravestones of Archaic Attica." *The Annual of the British School at Athens* 57:115–153.

——. 1976. *Archaic Greece: The City-States c. 700–500 B.C.* New York.

Jensen, M. S. 1980. *The Homeric Question and the Oral-Formulaic Theory.* Copenhagen.

Johnson, B. 1980. *The Critical Difference: Essays in the Contemporary Rhetoric of Reading.* Baltimore.

Jones, J. 1962. *On Aristotle and Greek Tragedy.* London.

Jones, N. F. 1980. "The Order of the Dorian *Phylai.*" *Classical Philology* 75:197–215.

——. 1980b. "The Civic Organization of Corinth." *Transactions of the American Philological Association* 110:161–193.

——. 1987. *Public Organization in Ancient Greece: A Documentary Study.* Philadelphia.

Jüthner, J., ed. 1909. *Philostratos über Gymnastik.* Leipzig.

Kahil, L. 1983. "Mythological Repertoire of Brauron." Moon 1983:231–244.

Kannicht, R., ed. with commentary. 1969. *Euripides: Helena.* I/II. Heidelberg.

——. 1982. "Poetry and Art: Homer and the Monuments Afresh." *Classical Antiquity* 1:70–86, with plates.

Karadagli, T. 1981. *Fabel und Ainos: Studien zur griechischen Fabel.* Beiträge zur Klassischen Philologie 135. Königstein/Ts.

Kassel, R., and Austin, C., eds. 1983–. *Poetae Comici Graeci.* Berlin.

Kelly, T. 1976. *A History of Argos to 500 B.C.* Minneapolis.

Kinkel, G., ed. 1877. *Epicorum Graecorum Fragmenta* I. Leipzig.

Kirk, G. S. 1962. *The Songs of Homer.* Cambridge.

Kirk, G. S., Raven, J. E., and Schofield, M. 1983. *The Presocratic Philosophers.* 2nd ed. Cambridge.

Kirkwood, G. M. 1974. *Early Greek Monody: The History of a Poetic Type.* Ithaca.

———, ed., with commentary. 1982. *Selections from Pindar.* American Philological Association Textbook Series 7. Chico, Calif.

———. 1984. "Praise and Envy in the Pindaric Epinician." Gerber 1984:169–183.

Kirsten, E. 1942. Review of Welter 1938 and Winterscheidt 1938. *Gnomon* 18:289–311.

Kittay, J., and Godzich, W. 1987. *The Emergence of Prose: An Essay in Prosaics.* Minneapolis.

Klusen, E. 1969. *Volkslied: Fund und Erfindung.* Cologne.

Knox, B. M. W. 1952. "The Lion in the House." *Classical Philology* 47:17–25. Reprinted in Knox 1979:27–38.

———. 1954. "Why Is Oedipus Called *Tyrannos?*" *Classical Journal* 50:97–102. Reprinted in Knox 1979:87–95.

———. 1968. "Silent Reading in Antiquity." *Greek Roman and Byzantine Studies* 9:421–435.

———. 1979. *Word and Action: Essays on the Ancient Theater.* Baltimore.

Knox, P. E. 1984. "Sappho, fr. 31 LP and Catullus 51: A Suggestion." *Quaderni Urbinati* 17:97–102.

Kock, B. 1910. *De epigrammatum graecorum dialectis.* Göttingen.

Kock, T., ed. 1880–1888. *Comicorum Atticorum Fragmenta.* Leipzig.

Koehl, R. B. 1986. "The Chieftain Cup and a Minoan Rite of Passage." *Journal of Hellenic Studies* 106:99–110.

Köhnken, A. 1971. *Die Funktion des Mythos bei Pindar. Interpretazionen zu sechs Pindargedichten.* Berlin.

———. 1974. "Pindar as Innovator: Poseidon Hippios and the Relevance of the Pelops Story in *Olympian* 1." *Classical Quarterly* 24:199–206.

———. 1975. "Gods and Descendants of Aiakos in Pindar's Eighth Isthmian Ode." *Bulletin of the Institute of Classical Studies* 22:25–36.

———. 1983. "Time and Event in Pindar *O*. 1.25–53." In *Studies in Classical Lyric: A Homage to Elroy Bundy,* edited by T. D'Evelyn, P. Psoinos, and T. R. Walsh. = *Classical Antiquity* 2:66–76.

Koller, H. 1954. *Die Mimesis in der Antike.* Bern.

———. 1956. "Das kitharodische Prooimion: Eine formgeschichtliche Untersuchung." *Philologus* 100:159–206.

Korzeniewski, D. 1968. *Griechische Metrik.* Darmstadt.

Krischer, T. 1965. "Herodots Prooimion." *Hermes* 93:159–167.

———. 1974. "Herodots Schluss-Kapitel, seine Topik und seine Quellen." *Eranos* 72:93–100.

Kullmann, W. 1960. *Die Quellen der Ilias. Hermes Einzelschriften* 14. Wiesbaden.

———. 1985. "Gods and Men in the *Iliad* and *Odyssey.*" *Harvard Studies in Classical Philology* 89:1–23.

Kunst, J. 1958. *Some Sociological Aspects of Music.* Washington.

Kurke, L. 1988. "Pindar's Oikonomia: The House as Organizing Metaphor in the Odes of Pindar." Doctoral dissertation, Princeton University.

Kuryłowicz, J. 1945–1949 [1966]. "La nature des procès dits 'analogiques'." *Acta Linguistica* 5:15–37 (1945–1949); reprinted in Kuryłowicz's *Esquisses linguistiques*, 66–86. Wrocław/Kraków (1960). Also in *Readings in Linguistics* II, edited by E. P. Hamp, F. W. Householder, and R. Austerlitz, 158–174. Chicago (1966).

Lamberton, R. 1988. *Hesiod.* New Haven.

Lanata, G., ed. 1963. *Poetica pre-platonica: Testimonianze e frammenti.* Florence.

Lane, M. G. M. 1954. "The Music of Tiv." *African Music* 1:12–15.

Lang, M. L. 1984. *Herodotean Narrative and Discourse.* Cambridge, Mass.

Lanza, D. 1977. *Il tiranno e il suo pubblico.* Turin.

Laroche, E. 1958. "Etudes de vocabulaire VII." *Revue Hittite et Asianique* 63:85–114 (especially 88–99).

Lasserre, F. 1976. "L'historiographie grecque à l'époque archaïque." *Quaderni di Storia* 4:113–145.

Lattimore, R. 1944. "Sappho 2 and Catullus 51." *Classical Philology* 39:184–187.

——. 1976. *The Odes of Pindar.* 2nd ed. Translation, with introduction. Chicago.

Laum, B. 1924. *Heiliges Geld: Eine historische Untersuchung über den sakralen Ursprung des Geldes.* Tübingen.

Leach, E. R. 1982. Critical Introduction to Steblin-Kamenskij, M. I., *Myth*, 1–20. Ann Arbor.

Lefkowitz, M. R. 1963. "ΤΩ ΚΑΙ ΕΓΩ: The First Person in Pindar." *Harvard Studies in Classical Philology* 67:177–253.

——. 1976. *The Victory Ode: An Introduction.* Park Ridge.

——. 1977. "Pindar's *Pythian* 8." *Classical Journal* 72:209–221.

——. 1985. "Pindar's *Pythian* V." *Pindare: Entretiens Hardt* 31:33–63. Geneva.

——. 1988. "Who Sang Pindar's Victory Odes?" *American Journal of Philology* 109:1–11.

Lejeune, M. 1965. "Le ΔΑΜΟΣ dans la société mycénienne." *Revue des Etudes Grecques* 78:1–22.

Lévêque, P., and Vidal-Naquet, P. 1964. *Clisthène l'Athénien: Essai sur la représentation de l'espace et du temps dans la pensée politique grecque de la fin du VIe siècle à la mort de Platon.* Paris.

Lévi-Strauss, C. 1979. *La voie des masques.* Paris.

——. 1984. "La visite des âmes." *Paroles données* 245–248. Paris.

Levine, D. B. 1985. "Symposium and the Polis." Figueira and Nagy 1985:176–196.

Lewis, J. M. 1985. "Eros and the Polis in Theognis Book II." Figueira and Nagy 1985:197–222.

Liddell, H. G., Scott, R., and Stuart Jones, H., eds. 1940. *Greek-English Lexicon.* 9th ed. Oxford.

Lidov, J. B. 1974. "Isthmians 3 and 4: Poems and Performance." *California Studies in Classical Antiquity* 8:175–185.

Lloyd, A. B., ed. 1975/1976. *Herodotus, Book II.* I/II. Leiden.

Lloyd, G. E. R. 1979. *Magic, Reason and Experience.* Cambridge.

——. 1987. *The Revolutions of Wisdom: Studies in the Claims and Practice of Ancient Greek Science.* Berkeley and Los Angeles.

Lloyd-Jones, H., and Parsons, P., eds. 1983. *Supplementum Hellenisticum.* Berlin and New York.

Lohmann, D. 1970. *Die Komposition der Reden in der Ilias.* Berlin.

Longman, G. A. 1962. "The Musical Papyrus: Euripides *Orestes* 332–40." *Classical Quarterly* 12:61–66. (Against the argument that the order of the papyrus is corrupt: see Henderson and Wulstan 1973:32.)

Loraux, N. 1981. "La cité comme cuisine et comme partage." *Annales Economies Sociétés Civilisations* 36:614–622.

——. 1982. "*Ponos:* Sur quelques difficultés de la peine comme nom du travail." *Annali del Seminario di Studi del Mondo Classico, Naples: Archeologia e Storia Antica* 4:171–192.

——. 1982b. "Les bénéfices de l'autochtonie." *Le genre humain* 3–4:238–253.

——. 1986. "Repolitiser la cité." *L'Homme* 26:239–255.

——. 1987. "Le lien de la division." *Le Cahier du Collège International de Philosophie* 4:101–124.

——. 1987b. "Variations grecques sur l'origine. Gloire du Même, prestige de l'Autre." *Cahiers de l'Ecole des Sciences Philosophiques et Religieuses* 2:69–94.

——. 1987c. "*Oikeios polemos*: la guerra nella famiglia." *Studi Storici* 28:5–35.

——. 1987d. "Cratyle à l'épreuve de *stasis.*" *Revue de Philosophie Ancienne* 5:49–69.

——. 1988. "Le 2 Boèdromion. A propos d'un jour interdit de calendrier à Athènes." In *La commémoration*, edited by P. Gignoux, 57–72. Paris/Louvain.

——. 1988b. "Poluneikēs epōnumos: le nom des fils d'Oedipe, entre épopée et tragédie." In *Métamorphoses du mythe en Grèce ancienne*, edited by C. Calame, 151–166. Geneva.

Lord, A. B. 1938. "Homer and Huso II: Narrative Inconsistencies in Homer and Oral Poetry." *Transactions of the American Philological Association* 69:439–445.

——. 1951. "Composition by Theme in Homer and Southslavic Epos." *Transactions of the American Philological Association* 82:71–80.

——. 1960. *The Singer of Tales.* Cambridge, Mass.

——. 1975. "Perspectives on Recent Work on Oral Literature." Duggan 1975:1–24.

Lowenstam, S. 1981. *The Death of Patroklos: A Study in Typology.* Beiträge zur Klassischen Philologie 133. Königstein/Ts.

LSJ. *See* Liddell, Scott, and Stuart Jones 1940.

LSS. *See* Sokolowski 1962.

Lucas, D. W., ed. with commentary. 1968. *Aristotle Poetics.* Oxford.

Lyle, E. 1986. "Whites and Reds: The Roman Circus and Alternate Succession." *Cosmos* 2:148–163.

Lynn-George, M. 1988. *Epos. Word, Narrative and the Iliad.* Houndmills, Basingstoke, Hampshire, England.

Maas, M., and Snyder, J. M. 1989. *Stringed Instruments of Ancient Greece.* New Haven.

Maas, P. 1962. *Greek Metre.* Translated by H. Lloyd-Jones. Oxford.

Maehler, H. 1963. *Die Auffassung des Dichterberufs im frühen Griechentum bis zur Zeit Pindars.* Hypomnemata 3. Göttingen.

Markey, T. L. 1982. "Indo-European Etyma for 'Left, Left-Handed' and Markedness Reversal." *The Mankind Quarterly* 23:183–194.

Martin, R. P. 1983. *Healing, Sacrifice and Battle: Amēchania and Related Concepts in Early Greek Poetry*. Innsbrucker Beiträge zur Sprachwissenschaft 41. Innsbruck.

———. 1984. "Hesiod, Odysseus, and the Instruction of Princes." *Transactions of the American Philological Association* 114:29–48.

———. 1984b. "The Oral Tradition." *Critical Survey of Poetry* (Foreign Language Series), edited by F. Magill, 1746–1768. LaCanada, Calif.

———. 1989. *The Language of Heroes: Speech and Performance in the Iliad*. Ithaca.

Martino, F. De. 1983. "Eraclito e gli Efesi 'sempre ottusi'." *Antiquité Classique* 52:221–227.

Mayo, M. E. 1973. "Honors to Archilochus: The Parian Archilocheion." Doctoral dissertation, Rutgers University.

Meid, W. 1974. "Dichtkunst, Rechtspflege und Medizin im alten Irland: Zur Struktur der altirischen Gesellschaft." In *Antiquitates Indogermanicae: Gedenkschrift für Hermann Güntert*, edited by M. Mayrhofer, W. Meid, B. Schlerath, and R. Schmitt, 21–34. Innsbruck.

Meiggs, R., and Lewis, D. 1975. *A Selection of Greek Historical Inscriptions to the End of the Fifth Century B.C.* Oxford.

Meillet, A. 1920. "Sur le rhythme quantitatif de la langue védique." *Mémoires de la Société de Linguistique de Paris* 21:193–207.

———. 1923. *Les origines indo-européennes des mètres grecs*. Paris.

Menéndez-Pidal, R. 1960. *La chanson de Roland et la tradition épique des Francs*. 2nd ed. Paris.

Merkelbach, R. 1967. "Eine Versreihe aus der Parabase der 'Heroen' des Aristophanes?" *Zeitschrift für Papyrologie und Epigraphik* 1:161–162.

Merkelbach, R., and West, M. L., eds. 1967. *Fragmenta Hesiodea*. Oxford.

Merriam, A. P. 1964. *The Anthropology of Music*. Evanston.

Merriam, A. P., and d'Azevedo, W. L. 1957. Washo Peyote Songs. *American Anthropologist* 59:615–641.

Meuli, K. 1941. "Der Ursprung der Olympischen Spiele." *Die Antike* 17:189–208. Reprinted in Meuli 1975:881–906.

———. 1968. *Der griechische Agon*. Cologne. Publication, by R. Merkelbach, of Meuli's 1926 Habilitationsschrift.

———. 1975. *Gesammelte Schriften I/II*, edited by T. Gelzer. Basel and Stuttgart.

Meyer, H. 1933. *Hymnische Stilelemente in der frühgriechischen Dichtung*. Würzburg.

Michel, R. C. 1983. "The Daughters of Zeus: Divine Brides and Helpmates in Greek Epic." Doctoral dissertation, Boston University.

Michelini, A. 1978. "ΥΒΡΙΣ and Plants." *Harvard Studies in Classical Philology* 82:35–44.

Miller, A. M. 1981. "Pindar, Archilochus and Hieron." *Transactions of the American Philological Association* 111:135–143.

———. 1982. "*Phthonos* and *Parphasis*: Nemean 8.19–34." *Greek Roman and Byzantine Studies* 23:111–120.

———. 1986. *From Delos to Delphi: A Literary Study of the Homeric Hymn to Apollo*. Leiden.

Miller, D. G. 1982. *Homer and the Ionian Epic Tradition*. Innsbrucker Beiträge zur Sprachwissenschaft 38. Innsbruck.

Mills, M. A. 1982. "A Cinderella Variant in the Context of a Muslim Women's Ritual." In *Cinderella: A Casebook,* edited by A. Dundes, 180–192. New York.

Miralles, C., and Pòrtulas, J. 1983. *Archilochus and the Iambic Poetry.* Rome.

Momigliano, A. 1971. *The Development of Greek Biography.* Cambridge, Mass.

Monroe, J. T. 1972. "Oral Composition in Pre-Islamic Poetry." *Journal of Arabic Literature* 3:1–53.

———. 1979. "Prolegomena to the Study of Ibn Quzmān: The Poet as Jongleur." *El Romancero hoy: Historia, Comparatismo, Bibliografía crítica,* 77–127. Madrid.

Monsacré, H. 1984. *Les larmes d'Achille.* Paris.

Moon, W. G., ed. 1983. *Ancient Greek Art and Iconography.* Madison.

Morris, I. 1988. "Tomb Cult and the 'Greek Renaissance': The Past and the Present in the 8th Century B.C." *Antiquity* 62:750–761.

Mossé, C. 1969. *La tyrannie dans la Grèce antique.* Paris.

Most, G. W. 1982. "Greek Lyric Poets." In *Ancient Writers,* edited by T. J. Luce, 75–98. New York.

———. 1985. *The Measures of Praise: Structure and Function in Pindar's Second Pythian and Seventh Nemean Odes. Hypomnemata* 83. Göttingen.

Mountford, J. F., and Winnington-Ingram, R. P. 1970. "Music." In *The Oxford Classical Dictionary,* edited by N. G. L. Hammond and H. H. Scullard, 705–713. Oxford.

Muellner, L. 1976. *The Meaning of Homeric* EYXOMAI *through its Formulas.* Innsbrucker Beiträge zur Sprachwissenschaft 13. Innsbruck.

Mullen, W. 1982. *Choreia: Pindar and Dance.* Princeton.

Murray, P. 1981. "Poetic Inspiration in Early Greece." *Journal of Hellenic Studies* 101:87–100.

MW. *See* Merkelbach and West 1967.

N. *See* Nagy.

Nadel, S. S. 1930. "The Origins of Music." *Musical Quarterly* 16:531–546.

Nagler, M. N. 1977. "Dread Goddess Endowed with Speech." *Archeological News* 6:77–85.

Nagy, G. 1973. "Phaethon, Sappho's Phaon, and the White Rock of Leukas." *Harvard Studies in Classical Philology* 77:137–177.

———. 1974. *Comparative Studies in Greek and Indic Meter.* Cambridge, Mass.

———. 1974b. "Six Studies of Sacral Vocabulary Relating to the Fireplace." *Harvard Studies in Classical Philology* 78:71–106.

———. 1976. Review of Edwards 1971. *Canadian Journal of Linguistics* 21:219–224.

———. 1976b. "Formula and Meter." In *Oral Literature and the Formula,* edited by B. A. Stolz and R. S. Shannon, 239–260. Ann Arbor.

———. 1979. *The Best of the Achaeans: Concepts of the Hero in Archaic Greek Poetry.* Baltimore.

———. 1979b. "On the Origins of the Greek Hexameter." In *Festschrift Oswald Szemerényi,* edited by B. Brogyanyi, 611–631. Amsterdam. Portions assimilated in the Appendix above.

———. 1981. "Another Look at KLEOS APHTHITON." *Würzburger Jahrbücher für die Altertumswissenschaft* 7:113–116.

———. 1982. "Hesiod." In *Ancient Writers,* edited by T. J. Luce, 43–72. New York.

——. 1982b. Review of Detienne 1981. *Annales Economies Sociétés Civilisations* 37:778–780.

——. 1983. "*Sēma* and *Noēsis:* Some Illustrations." *Arethusa* 16:35–55.

——. 1983b. "On the Death of Sarpedon." Rubino and Shelmerdine 1983:189–217.

——. 1983c. Review of Bowie 1981. *Phoenix* 37:273–275.

——. 1985. "Theognis and Megara: A Poet's Vision of His City." Figueira and Nagy 1985:22–81.

——. 1985b. "On the Symbolism of Apportioning Meat in Archaic Greek Elegiac Poetry." *L'Uomo* 9:45–52.

——. 1986. "Pindar's *Olympian* 1 and the Aetiology of the Olympic Games." *Transactions of the American Philological Association* 116:71–88. Reworked as Ch.4 above.

——. 1986b. "Ancient Greek Praise and Epic Poetry." In *Oral Tradition in Literature: Interpretation in Context*, edited by J. M. Foley, 89–102. Columbia, Mo. Reworked as part of Ch.6 above.

——. 1986c. "Sovereignty, Boiling Cauldrons, and Chariot-Racing in Pindar's *Olympian* 1." *Cosmos* 2: 143–147. Reworked as part of Ch.4 and Ch.6 above.

——. 1986d. "Poetic Visions of Immortality for the Hero." Bloom 1986:205–212.

——. 1986e. "The Worst of the Achaeans." Bloom 1986:213–215.

——. 1987. "The Indo-European Heritage of Tribal Organization: Evidence from the Greek *Polis*." In *Proto-Indo-European: The Archaeology of a Linguistic Problem. Studies in Honor of Marija Gimbutas*, edited by S. N. Skomal and E. Polomé, 245–266. Washington, D. C.

——. 1987b. "Herodotus the *Logios*." *Arethusa* 20:175–184, 209–210. Reworked as part of Ch.8 above.

——. 1987c. "The Sign of Protesilaos." ΜΗΤΙΣ: *Revue d'Anthropologie du Monde Grec Ancien* 2:207–213. Reworked as part of Ch.9 above.

——. 1988. "Sul simbolismo della ripartizione nella poesia elegiaca." *Sacrificio e società nel mondo antico*. Grottanelli and Parise 1988:203–209.

——. 1988b. "Mythe et prose en Grèce archaïque: *l'aînos*." *Métamorphoses du mythe en Grèce ancienne*, edited by C. Calame, 229–242. Geneva. Reworked as part of Ch.11 above.

——. 1988c. "Homerische Epik und Pindars Preislieder: Mündlichkeit und Aktualitätsbezug." Raible 1988:51–64. German version of Nagy 1986b.

——. 1988d. "Teaching the Ordeal of Reading." *Harvard English Studies* 15:163–167.

——. 1989. "Early Greek Views of Poets and Poetry." *Cambridge History of Literary Criticism* I, edited by G. Kennedy, 1–77. Cambridge.

——. 1989b. "The 'Professional Muse' and Models of Prestige in Ancient Greece." *Cultural Critique* 12:133–143. Reworked as part of Ch.6 above.

——. 1990. *Greek Mythology and Poetics*. Ithaca.

Nagy, J. F. 1985. *The Wisdom of the Outlaw: The Boyhood Deeds of Finn in Gaelic Narrative Tradition*. Berkeley and Los Angeles.

——. 1986. "Orality in Medieval Irish Narrative." *Oral Tradition* 1:272–301.

Nash, L. L. 1976. "The Aggelia in Pindar." Doctoral dissertation, Harvard University.

Nauck, A., ed. 1889. *Tragicorum Graecorum Fragmenta*. Leipzig. Revised by B. Snell et al., 1971–. Göttingen.

Nehamas, A. 1982. "Plato on Imitation and Poetry in *Republic* 10." In *Plato on Beauty, Wisdom, and the Arts*, edited by J. M. C. Moravcsik and P. Temko, 47–78. Totowa, N.J.

Nettl, B. 1956. *Music in Primitive Culture*. Cambridge, Mass.

———. 1964. *Theory and Method in Ethnomusicology*. New York.

———. 1965. *Folk and Traditional Music of the Western Continents*. Englewood Cliffs.

———. 1983. *The Study of Ethnomusicology: Twenty-nine Issues and Concepts*. Urbana.

Nicosia, S. 1976. *La tradizione dei poeti di Lesbo*. Rome.

Nilsson, M. P. 1906. *Griechische Feste*. Leipzig.

———. 1967, 1961. *Geschichte der griechischen Religion*. I 3rd ed., II 2nd ed. Munich.

Nisetich, F. J. 1975. "*Olympian* 1.8–11: An Epinician Metaphor." *Harvard Studies in Classical Philology* 79:55–68.

———. 1980. *Pindar's Victory Songs*. Translation, with introduction. Baltimore.

———. 1989. *Pindar and Homer*. American Journal of Philology Monographs 4. Baltimore.

Nussbaum, M. C. 1986. *The Fragility of Goodness: Luck and Ethics in Greek Tragedy and Philosophy*. Cambridge.

Okpewho, I. 1979. *The Epic in Africa: Toward a Poetics of the Oral Performance*. New York.

Ong, W. J. 1977. *Interfaces of the Word: Studies in the Evolution of Consciousness and Culture*. Ithaca.

———. 1977b. "African Talking Drums and Oral Noetics." *New Literary History* 8:411–429. Reprinted in Ong 1977:92–120.

———. 1981. *Fighting for Life: Contest, Sexuality, and Consciousness*. Ithaca.

———. 1982. *Orality and Literacy*. London.

———. 1986. "Text as Interpretation: Mark and After." In *Oral Tradition in Literature*, edited by J. M. Foley, 147–169. Columbia, Mo.

Oost, S. I. 1976. "The Tyrant Kings of Syracuse." *Classical Philology* 71:224–236.

Page, D. L. 1953. "Corinna." *The Society for the Promotion of Hellenic Studies Supplementary Paper* 6.

———. 1955. *Sappho and Alcaeus: An Introduction to the Study of Ancient Lesbian Poetry*. Oxford.

———, ed. 1962. *Poetae Melici Graeci*. Oxford.

———, ed. 1972. *Aeschylus*. Oxford.

———, ed. 1974. *Supplementum Lyricis Graecis*. Oxford.

———, ed. 1975. *Epigrammata Graeca*. Oxford.

Pagel, K.-A. 1927. "Die Bedeutung des aitiologischen Moments für Herodots Geschichtsschreibung." Doctoral dissertation, Berlin.

Palmer, L. R. 1979. "A Mycenaean 'Akhilleid'?" *Serta Philologica Aenipontana* III, edited by R. Muth and G. Pfohl, 255–261. Innsbrucker Beiträge zur Kulturwissenschaft 20. Innsbruck.

———. 1980. *The Greek Language*. Atlantic Highlands, New Jersey.

Papathomopoulos, M., ed. 1980. *Nouvaux fragments d'auteurs anciens*. Ioannina.

Parke, H. W., and Wormell, D. E. W. 1956. *The Delphic Oracle* I–II. Oxford.

Parry, M. 1928. *L'épithète traditionnelle dans Homère: Essai sur un problème de style homérique.* Paris. Translated in Parry 1971:1–190.

———. 1928b. *Les formules et la métrique d'Homère.* Paris. Translated in Parry 1971:191–234.

———. 1971. *The Making of Homeric Verse: The Collected Papers of Milman Parry,* edited by A. Parry. Oxford.

Pavese, C. O. 1966. "XPHMATA, XPHMAT' ANHP ed il motivo della literalità nella seconda Istmica di Pindaro." *Quaderni Urbinati* 2:103–112.

———. 1974. *Studi sulla tradizione epica rapsodica.* Rome.

Peabody, B. 1975. *The Winged Word.* Albany.

Pelliccia, H. N. 1985. "The Structure of the Archaic Greek Hymns." Doctoral dissertation, Yale University.

———. 1987. "Pindarus Homericus: *Pythian* 3.1–80." *Harvard Studies in Classical Philology* 91:39–63.

Peradotto, J. 1986. "Prophecy Degree Zero: Tiresias and the End of the *Odyssey.*" In *Oralità, cultura, litteratura, discorso,* 429–459. Rome.

Perpillou, J.-L. 1987. "Grec ὐ- pour ἐπι-: un préfixe oublié?" *Revue de Philologie* 61:193–204.

Perry, B. E., ed. 1952. *Aesopica.* Urbana.

Perusino, F. 1968. *Il tetrametro giambico catalettico nella commedia greca.* Rome.

Petegorsky, D. 1982. "Context and Evocation: Studies in Early Greek and Sanskrit Poetry." Doctoral dissertation, Berkeley. Reprinted by University Microfilms, Ann Arbor, 1982.

Petre, Z. 1975. "Le comportement tyrannique." *Actes de la XIIᵉ Conférence Internationale d'Etudes Classiques, Eirene* (Cluj-Napoca, 2–7 October 1972). Bucharest/Amsterdam.

Pfeiffer, R., ed. 1949–1953. *Callimachus.* I/II. Oxford.

———. 1968. *History of Classical Scholarship: From the Beginnings to the End of the Hellenistic Age.* Oxford.

Pfister, F. 1909/1912. *Der Reliquienkult im Altertum.* I/II. Giessen.

Piccirilli, L. 1973. *Gli arbitrati interstatali greci.* I. Pisa.

Pickard-Cambridge, A. 1962. *Dithyramb, Tragedy and Comedy.* 2nd ed. revised by T. B. L. Webster. Oxford.

———. 1968. *The Dramatic Festivals of Athens.* 2nd ed. revised by J. Gould and D. M. Lewis. Oxford.

Pinney, G. F. 1983. "Achilles Lord of Scythia." Moon 1983:127–146.

PMG. *See* Page 1962.

Podlecki, A. J. 1984. *The Early Greek Poets and their Times.* Vancouver.

Pöhlmann, E. 1960. *Griechische Musikfragmente: Ein Weg zur altgriechischen Musik. Erlanger Beiträge zur Sprach- und Kunstwissenschaft* 8. Nürnberg.

Pòrtulas, J. 1985. "La condition héroïque et le statut religieux de la louange." *Pindare: Entretiens Hardt* 31:207–235. Geneva.

Pötscher, W. 1961. "Hera und Heros." *Rheinisches Museum* 104:302–355.

Poultney, J. W. 1979. "Eupolidean Verse." *American Journal of Philology* 100:133–144.

Powell, J. E. 1938. *A Lexicon to Herodotus.* Cambridge.

———, ed. with commentary. 1939. *Herodotus Book VIII.* Cambridge.

Pretagostini, R. 1977. "Sticometria del *Pap. Lille* 76 a, b, c (Il nuovo Stesicoro)." *Quaderni Urbinati* 26:53–61.

Pritchett, W. K. 1974. *The Greek State at War* II. Berkeley and Los Angeles.

Privitera, G. A. 1965. *Laso di Ermione.* Rome.

PSI. = *Papyri Greci e Latini, Pubblicazioni della Società italiana per la ricerca dei papiri greci e latini in Egitto.* 1912–.

Pucci, P. 1979. "The Song of the Sirens." *Arethusa* 12:121–132.

———. 1982. "The Proem of the Odyssey." *Arethusa* 15:39–62.

———. 1987. *Odysseus Polytropos: Intertextual Readings in the Odyssey and the Iliad.* Ithaca and London.

PW. *See* Parke and Wormell 1956.

Raaflaub, K. A. 1987. "Herodotus, Political Thought, and the Meaning of History." *Arethusa* 20:221–248.

Race, W. H. 1979. "The End of *Olympia* 2: Pindar and the *Vulgus.*" *California Studies in Classical Antiquity* 12:251–267.

———. 1983. "'That Man' in Sappho fr. 31 L-P." In *Studies in Classical Lyric: A Homage to Elroy Bundy,* edited by T. D'Evelyn, P. Psoinos, and T. R. Walsh. = *Classical Antiquity* 2:92–101.

———. 1986. *Pindar.* Boston.

———. 1987. "P.Oxy. 2438 and the Order of Pindar's Works." *Rheinisches Museum* 130:407–410.

Radcliffe-Brown, A. R. 1948. *The Andaman Islanders.* Glencoe.

Radin, P. 1956. With commentaries by K. Kerényi and C. G. Jung. *The Trickster. A Study in American Indian Mythology.* London. Reissued 1972, with introductory essay by S. Diamond.

Radloff, W. 1885. *Proben der Volksliteratur der nördlichen türkischen Stämme* V: *Der Dialekt der Kara-Kirgisen.* St. Petersburg.

Raible, W., ed. 1988. *Zwischen Festtag und Alltag: Zehn Beiträge zum Thema 'Mündlichkeit und Schriftlichkeit'.* Tübingen.

Redfield, J. 1985. "Herodotus the Tourist." *Classical Philology* 80:97–118.

Reitzenstein, R. 1893. *Epigramm und Skolion: Ein Beitrag zur Geschichte der alexandrinischen Dichtung.* Giessen.

Rhodes, P. J. 1981. *A Commentary of the Aristotelian* ΑΘΗΝΑΙΩΝ ΠΟΛΙΤΕΙΑ. Oxford.

Richards, I. A. 1936. *The Philosophy of Rhetoric.* Oxford.

Richardson, N. J., ed. with commentary. 1974. *The Homeric Hymn to Demeter.* Oxford.

Ridgway, B. S. 1977. *The Archaic Style in Greek Sculpture.* Princeton.

Rios, R. da, ed. 1954. Aristoxenus, *Elementa Harmonica.* 2 vols. Rome.

Risch, E. 1946. "Sprachliche Bemerkungen zu Alkaios." *Museum Helveticum* 3:253–256. Reprinted in Risch 1981:290–293.

———. 1954. "Die Sprache Alkmans." *Museum Helveticum* 11:20–37. Reprinted in Risch 1981:314–331.

———. 1981. *Kleine Schriften,* edited by A. Etter and M. Looser. Berlin.

———. 1987. "Die ältesten Zeugnisse für κλέος ἄφθιτον." *Zeitschrift für Vergleichende Sprachforschung* 100:3–11.

Rissman, L. 1983. *Love as War: Homeric Allusion in the Poetry of Sappho.* Beiträge zur Klassischen Philologie 157. Königstein/Ts.

Ritoók, Z. 1987. "Vermutungen zum Ursprung des griechischen Hexameters." *Philologus* 131:2–18.

Rohde, E. 1898. *Psyche: Seelencult und Unsterblichkeitsglaube der Griechen.* I/II. Freiburg i.B. Translated by W. B. Hillis. New York, 1925.

Roller, L. E. 1977. "Funeral Games in Literature, Art, and Life." Doctoral dissertation, University of Pennsylvania.

———. 1981. "Funeral Games for Historical Persons." *Stadion* 7:1–18.

———. 1981b. "Funeral Games in Greek Art." *American Journal of Archaeology* 85:107–119.

Rose, V., ed. 1886. *Aristoteles: Fragmenta.* Leipzig.

Rosen, R. M. 1988. *Old Comedy and the Iambographic Tradition.* American Classical Studies 19, American Philological Association. Atlanta.

Rosenmeyer, T. G. 1968. "Elegiac and Elegos." *California Studies in Classical Antiquity* 1:217–231.

Rösler, W. 1976. "Die Dichtung des Archilochos und die neue Kölner Epode." *Rheinisches Museum* 119:289–310.

———. 1980. *Dichter und Gruppe: Eine Untersuchung zu den Bedingungen und zur historischen Funktion früher Lyrik am Beispiel Alkaios.* Munich.

———. 1985. "Persona reale o persona poetica? L'interpretazione dell' 'io' nella lirica greca." *Quaderni Urbinati* 19:131–144.

———. 1986. "Michail Bachtin und die Karnevalskultur im antiken Griechenland." *Quaderni Urbinati* 23:25–44.

Rossi, L. E. 1971. "I generi letterari e le loro leggi scritte e non scritte nelle letterature classiche." *Bulletin of the Institute of Classical Studies* 18:69–94.

———. 1978 [1980]. "Mimica e danza sulla scena comica greca." *Rivista di Cultura Classica e Medioevale* 1–3 (Miscellanea di studi in memoria di M. Barchiesi) 1149–1170.

Roussel, D. 1976. *Tribu et cité.* Annales Littéraires de l'Université de Besançon 193. Paris.

Royce, A. P. 1977. *The Anthropology of Dance.* Bloomington.

Rubin, N. F. 1984. "The Epinician Speaker in Pindar's First Olympian: Toward a Model for Analyzing Character in Ancient Choral Lyric." *Poetics Today* 5:377–397.

Rubino, C. A., and Shelmerdine, C. W., eds. 1983. *Approaches to Homer.* Austin.

Russo, J., and Simon, B. 1968. "Homeric Psychology and the Oral Epic Tradition." *Journal of the History of Ideas* 29:483–498.

Rusten, J. 1983. "ΓΕΙΤΩΝ ΗΡΩΣ: Pindar's Prayer to Heracles (*N.* 7.86–101) and Greek Popular Religion." *Harvard Studies in Classical Philology* 87:289–297.

Sachs, C. 1937. *World History of the Dance.* New York.

———. 1943. *The Rise of Music in the Ancient World East and West.* New York.

Saenger, P. 1982. "Silent Reading: Its Impact on Late Medieval Script and Society." *Viator* 13:367–414.

Sakellariou, M. B. 1958. *La migration grecque en Ionie.* Athens.

Sansone, D. 1988. *Greek Athletics and the Genesis of Sport.* Berkeley and Los Angeles.

Schadewaldt, W. 1928. *Der Aufbau des pindarischen Epinikion.* Halle.

Schapera, I. 1965. *Praise Poems of Tswana Chiefs.* Oxford.

Schein, S. L. 1984. *The Mortal Hero. An Introduction to Homer's Iliad.* Berkeley and Los Angeles.

———. 1987. "Unity and Meaning in Pindar's Sixth Pythian Ode." ΜΗΤΙΣ: *Revue d'Anthropologie du Monde Grec Ancien* 2:235–247.

Schmid, B. 1947. *Studien zu griechischen Ktisissagen.* Freiburg.

Schmitt, R. 1967. *Dichtung und Dichtersprache in indogermanischer Zeit.* Wiesbaden.

Schnapp-Gourbeillon, A. 1982. "Naissance de l'écriture et fonction poétique en Grèce archaïque: quelques points de repère." *Annales Economies Sociétés Civilisations* 37:714–723.

Schneider, M. 1957. "Primitive Music." In *New Oxford History of Music* I. *Ancient and Oriental Music*, edited by E. Wellesz, 1–82. London.

Schwartz, M. 1982. "The Indo-European Vocabulary of Exchange, Hospitality, and Intimacy." *Proceedings of the Berkeley Linguistics Society* 8:188–204. That Linear B -pi = /-phi/ and Homeric -φι are to be derived from a postposition *bh(e)i, as also attested in German *bei* and English *by* (I note the convergence of locative and instrumental functions here). Schwartz derives Greek **philos** from this *bh(e)i, adducing as semantic parallel Indic *priyá-* and Avestan *friia.*

Schwyzer, E., ed. 1923. *Dialectorum Graecarum exempla epigraphica potiora.* Leipzig. Reprinted, Hildesheim 1960.

Schwyzer, E. 1939. *Griechische Grammatik* I. Munich.

Scodel, R. 1982. "The Autobiography of Phoenix." *American Journal of Philology* 103:128–136.

———. 1982b. "Hybris in the Second Stasimon of the *Oedipus Rex.*" *Classical Philology* 77:214–223.

Seaford, R. 1976. "On the Origins of Satyric Drama." *Maia* 28:209–221.

———. 1977–1978. "The 'Hyporchema' of Pratinas." *Maia* 29:81–94.

———, ed. with commentary. 1984. *Euripides: Cyclops.* Oxford.

Searle, J. R. 1979. *Speech-Acts: An Essay in the Philosophy of Language.* Cambridge.

Seeberg, A. 1966. "Astrabica (Herodotus VI.68–69)." *Symbolae Osloenses* 41:48–74.

Segal, C. P. 1967. "Pindar's Seventh *Nemean.*" *Transactions of the American Philological Association* 98:431–480.

———. 1976. "Pindar, Mimnermus, and the 'Zeus-Given Gleam': The End of *Pythian* 8." *Quaderni Urbinati* 22:71–81.

———. 1982. *Dionysiac Poetics and Euripides' Bacchae.* Princeton.

———. 1983. "*Kleos* and its Ironies in the *Odyssey.*" *L'Antiquité Classique* 52:22–47.

———. 1985. "Messages to the Underworld: An Aspect of Poetic Immortalization in Pindar." *American Journal of Philology* 106:199–212.

———. 1986. *Pindar's Mythmaking: The Fourth Pythian Ode.* Princeton.

Seidensticker, B. 1978. "Archilochus and Odysseus." *Greek Roman and Byzantine Studies* 19:5–22.

Sergent, B. 1984. *L'homosexualité dans la mythologie grecque.* Paris.

Shapiro, H. A. 1983. "Painting, Politics, and Genealogy: Peisistratos and the Neleids." Moon 1983:87–96.

Shapiro, K. D. 1988. "ὕμνων θησαυρός: Pindar's Sixth Pythian Ode and the Treasury of the Siphnians at Delphi." *Museum Helveticum* 45:1–5.

Shelmerdine, S. C. 1981. "The Homeric Hymn to Hermes: A Commentary (1–114) with Introduction." Doctoral dissertation, University of Michigan.

Sifakis, G. M. 1986. "Learning from Art and Pleasure in Learning: An Interpretation of Aristotle *Poetics* 4 1448b8–19." *Studies in Honour of T. B. L. Webster* I, edited by J. H. Betts, J. T. Hooker, and J. R. Green, 211–222. Bristol.

SIG. *See* Dittenberger 1915–1924.

Silk, M. S. 1974. *Interaction in Poetic Imagery with Special Reference to Early Greek Poetry*. Cambridge.

Simpson, M. 1969. "Pindar's Ninth Olympian." *Greek Roman and Byzantine Studies* 10:113–124.

Sinos, D. S. 1980. *Achilles, Patroklos, and the Meaning of Philos*. Innsbrucker Beiträge zur Sprachwissenschaft 29. Innsbruck.

Slater, W. J. 1969. *Lexicon to Pindar*. Berlin.

———. 1969b. "Futures in Pindar." *Classical Quarterly* 19:86–94.

———. 1979. "Pindar's Myths." In *Arktouros: Hellenic Studies Presented to B. M. W. Knox*, edited by G. W. Bowersock, W. Burkert, and M. C. J. Putnam, 63–70. Berlin.

———. 1983. "Lyric Narrative: Structure and Principle." In *Studies in Classical Lyric: A Homage to Elroy Bundy*, edited by T. D'Evelyn, P. Psoinos, and T. R. Walsh. = *Classical Antiquity* 2:117–132.

———. 1984. "*Nemean* 1: The Victor's Return." Gerber 1984:241–264.

Slatkin, L. M. 1986. "The Wrath of Thetis." *Transactions of the American Philological Association* 116:1–24.

———. 1987. "Genre and Generation in the *Odyssey*." ΜΗΤΙΣ: *Revue d'Anthropologie du Monde Grec Ancien* 2:259–268.

SLG. *See* Page 1974.

Slotkin, E. M. 1978–1979. "Medieval Irish Scribes and Fixed Texts." *Éigse* 17:437–450.

SM. *See* Snell and Maehler.

Snell, B. 1924. "Die Ausdrücke für den Begriff des Wissens in der vorplatonischen Philosophie." *Philologische Untersuchungen* 29. Berlin.

———. 1954. "Zur Geschichte vom Gastmahl der Sieben Weisen." *Thesaurismata: Festschrift I. Kapp*, 105–111. Reprinted in Snell 1966:115–118.

———. 1966. *Gesammelte Schriften*. Göttingen.

———. 1982. *Griechische Metrik*. 4th ed. Göttingen.

Snell, B., and Maehler, H., eds. 1971. *Bacchylides*. Leipzig.

———, eds. 1975. *Pindarus: Fragmenta*. Leipzig.

———, eds. 1987. *Pindarus: Epinicia*. Leipzig.

Snodgrass, A. M. 1971. *The Dark Age of Greece: An Archaeological Survey of the Eleventh to the Eighth Centuries*. Edinburgh.

———. 1982. "Les origines du culte des héros dans la Grèce antique." Gnoli and Vernant 1982:107–119.

——. 1987. *An Archaeology of Greece: The Present State and Future Scope of a Discipline*. Berkeley and Los Angeles.

Sokolowski, F., ed. 1962. *Lois sacrées des cités grecques*. Paris.

Solmsen, F. 1981. Review of Nagy 1979. *American Journal of Philology* 102:81–83.

Solomon, J. 1984. "Towards a History of *Tonoi*." *The Journal of Musicology* 3:242–251.

——. 1985. "In Defense of Hesiod's 'Schlechtestem Hexameter'." *Hermes* 113:21–30.

Sommerstein, A. H., ed. with commentary. 1980/1981/1982/1983. *Aristophanes: Acharnians/Knights/Clouds/Wasps*. Warminster, England.

Sourvinou-Inwood, C. 1988. "Myth and History: On Herodotus III.48 and 50–53." *Opuscula Atheniensia* 17:167–182.

Stallmach, J. 1968. *Atē: Zur Frage des Selbst- und Weltverständnisses des frühgriechischen Menschen*. Beiträge zur Klassischen Philologie 18. Meisenheim am Glan.

Stambler, S. 1982. "Herodotus." In *Ancient Writers*, edited by T. J. Luce, 209–232. New York.

Steiner, D. 1986. *The Crown of Song: Metaphor in Pindar*. London.

Steinitz, W. 1934. *Der Parallelismus in der finnisch-karelischen Volksdichtung*. Helsinki/Tartu.

Stern, T. 1957. "Drum and Whistle 'Languages': An Analysis of Speech Surrogates." *American Anthropology* 59:487–506.

Stevens, J. 1986. *Words and Music in the Middle Ages: Song, Narrative, Dance and Drama, 1050–1350*. Cambridge.

Stewart, A. 1983. "Stesichoros and the François Vase." *Ancient Greek Art and Iconography*, edited by W. G. Moon, 53–74. Madison.

Stock, B. 1983. *The Implications of Literacy. Written Language and Models of Interpretation in the Eleventh and Twelfth Centuries*. Princeton.

Stoddart, R. C. 1980. "Pindar and Greek Family Law." Doctoral dissertation, Harvard University.

Stoneman, R. 1981. "Pindar and the Mythological Tradition." *Philologus* 125:44–63.

Striedter, J. 1969. *Texte der russischen Formalisten*. Munich.

Sultan, N. 1988. "New Light on the Function of 'Borrowed Notes' in Ancient Greek Music: A Look at Islamic Parallels." *The Journal of Musicology* 6:387–398.

Sulzberger, M. 1926. "ΟΝΟΜΑ ΕΠΩΝΥΜΟΝ. Les noms propres chez Homère." *Revue des Etudes Grecques* 39:381–447.

Svenbro, J. 1976. *La parole et le marbre: Aux origines de la poétique grecque*. Lund; 1984 Italian version, with changes and corrections, Torino.

——. 1982. "A Mégara Hyblaea: le corps géomètre." *Annales Economies Sociétés Civilisations* 37:953–964.

——. 1984. "La découpe du poème. Notes sur les origines sacrificielles de la poétique grecque." *Poétique* 58:215–232.

——. 1987. "The 'Voice' of Letters in Ancient Greece. On Silent Reading and the Representation of Speech." *Culture and History* 2:31–47, edited by M. Harbsmeier and M. T. Larsen. Copenhagen. Recast as Ch.9 in Svenbro 1988.

——. 1988. *Phrasikleia: Anthropologie de la lecture en Grèce ancienne*. Paris.

———. 1988b. "Il taglio della poesia. Note sulle origini sacrificali della poetica greca." Grottanelli and Parise 1988: 231–252.

Szegedy-Maszák, A. 1978. "Legends of the Greek Lawgivers." *Greek Roman and Byzantine Studies* 19:199–209.

Tambiah, S. J. 1981. "A Performative Approach to Ritual." *Proceedings of the British Academy, London* 65:113–169. Reprinted in Tambiah 1985:123–166.

———. 1985. *Culture, Thought, and Social Action: An Anthropological Perspective.* Cambridge, Mass.

Taplin, O. 1977. *The Stagecraft of Aeschylus.* Oxford.

———. 1978. *Greek Tragedy in Action.* London.

Tarditi, G., ed. 1968. *Archilochus.* Rome.

TGF. *See* Nauck 1889.

Thalmann, W. G. 1984. *Conventions of Form and Thought in Early Greek Epic Poetry.* Baltimore.

Thiel, H. van, ed. 1974. *Leben und Taten Alexanders von Makedonien: Der griechische Alexanderroman nach der Handschrift L.* Darmstadt.

Thomson, G. 1946. *Aeschylus and Athens: A Study in the Social Origins of Drama.* 2nd ed. London.

Thurneysen, R. 1912–1913. "Zur Wortschöpfung im Lateinischen." *Indogermanische Forschungen* 31.276–281.

Tichy, E. 1981. "Hom. ἀνδροτῆτα und die Vorgeschichte des daktylischen Hexameters." *Glotta* 59:28–67.

———. 1981b. "Beobachtungen zur homerischen Synizese." *Münchener Studien zur Sprachwissenschaft* 40:187–222.

Tod, M. N. 1913. *International Arbitration amongst the Greeks.* Oxford.

———. 1932. *Ancient Inscriptions: Sidelights on Greek History.* Oxford.

Todorov, T. 1978. *Les genres du discours.* Paris.

Tsagarakis, O. 1977. *Self-Expression in Early Greek Lyric, Elegiac and Iambic Poetry.* Wiesbaden.

V. *See* Voigt 1971.

Vallet, G. 1958. *Rhegion et Zancle.* Paris.

Vance, E. 1986. *Mervelous Signals: Poetics and Sign Theory in the Middle Ages.* Lincoln and London.

Verdier, C. 1972. *Les éolismes non-épiques de la langue de Pindare.* Innsbrucker Beiträge zur Sprachwissenschaft 7. Innsbruck.

Vermeule, E. D. T. 1979. *Aspects of Death in Early Greek Art and Poetry.* Berkeley and Los Angeles.

Vernant, J.-P. 1969. *Les origines de la pensée grecque.* Paris.

———. 1982–1983. "Etude comparée des religions antiques." *Annuaires du Collège de France, Résumé des cours et travaux,* year 83:443–456.

———. 1982. "From Oedipus to Periander: Lameness, Tyranny, Incest in Legend and History." *Arethusa* 15:19–38.

———. 1985. *Mythe et pensée chez les Grecs.* 2nd ed., recast and repaginated. Paris.

Vetta, M., ed. with commentary. 1980. *Theognis: Elegiarum Liber Secundus.* Rome.

———. 1983. *Poesia e simposio nella Grecia antica.* Roma/Bari.

Vian, F. 1963. *Les origines de Thèbes: Cadmos et les Spartes.* Paris.

Vidal-Naquet, P. 1981. *Le chasseur noir*. Paris.

——. 1986. "The Black Hunter Revisited." *Proceedings of the Cambridge Philological Society* 212:126–144.

Vigorita, J. F. 1977. "The Indo-European Origin of the Greek Hexameter and Distich." *Zeitschrift für Vergleichende Sprachforschung* 91:288–299.

Vine, B. 1977. "On the Heptasyllabic Verses of the Rig-Veda." *Zeitschrift für Vergleichende Sprachforschung* 91:246–255.

——. 1978. "On the Metrics and Origin of Rig-Vedic *na* 'like, as'." *Indo-Iranian Journal* 20:171–193.

Voigt, E.-M., ed. 1971. *Sappho et Alcaeus: Fragmenta*. Amsterdam.

Vox, O. 1984. *Solone autoritratto*. Padua.

W. *See* West 1971/1972.

Wackernagel, J. 1953. *Kleine Schriften*. I/II. Göttingen.

Wallace, M. B. 1984. "The Metres of Early Greek Epigrams." Gerber 1984: 303–315.

Waters, K. H. 1985. *Herodotos the Historian: His Problems, Methods and Originality*. Norman, Okla.

Watkins, C. 1963. "Indo-European Metrics and Archaic Greek Verse." *Celtica* 6:194–249.

——. 1976. "Observations on the 'Nestor's Cup' Inscription." *Harvard Studies in Classical Philology* 80:25–40.

——. 1976b. "Syntax and Metrics in the Dipylon Vase Inscription." In *Studies in Greek, Italic, and Indo-European Linguistics Offered to Leonard R. Palmer*, edited by A. Morpurgo Davies and W. Meid, 431–441. Innsbruck.

——. 1976c. "The Etymology of Irish *dúan*." *Celtica* 11:270–277.

——. 1979. "Is tre fír flathemon: Marginalia to *Audacht Morainn*." *Ériu* 30:181–198.

Waugh, L. R. 1982. "Marked and Unmarked: A Choice between Unequals in Semiotic Structure." *Semiotica* 38:299–318.

Wegner, M. 1968. *Musik und Tanz. Archaeologia Homerica* III, Chapter "U." Göttingen.

Wehrli, F., ed. 1944–. Die Schule des Aristoteles. Basel.

Welter, G. 1938. *Aigina*. Berlin.

West, M. L., ed. with commentary. 1966. *Hesiod: Theogony*. Oxford.

——. 1970. "Rhapsodes." In *The Oxford Classical Dictionary*, edited by N. G. L. Hammond and H. H. Scullard, 919–920. Oxford.

——, ed. 1971/1972. *Iambi et Elegi Graeci*. Oxford.

——. 1971b. "Stesichorus." *Classical Quarterly* 21:302–314.

——. 1973. "Greek Poetry 2000–700 B.C." *Classical Quarterly* 23:179–192.

——. 1973b. "Indo-European Metre." *Glotta* 51:161–187.

——. 1974. *Studies in Greek Elegy and Iambus*. Berlin.

——. 1974b. Review of Nagy 1974. *Phoenix* 28:457–459.

——. 1975. "Cynaethus' Hymn to Apollo." *Classical Quarterly* 25:61–170.

——, ed. with commentary. 1978. *Hesiod: Works and Days*. Oxford.

——. 1981. "The Singing of Homer and the Modes of Early Greek Music." *Journal of Hellenic Studies* 101:113–129.

——. 1982. *Greek Metre*. Oxford.

——. 1982b. "Three Topics in Greek Metre." *Classical Quarterly* 32:281–297.

——. 1985. *The Hesiodic Catalogue of Women: Its Nature, Structure, and Origins.* Oxford.

——. 1986. "The Singing of Hexameters: Evidence from Epidaurus." *Zeitschrift für Papyrologie und Epigraphik* 63:39–46.

——. 1988. "The Rise of the Greek Epic." *Journal of Hellenic Studies* 108:151–172.

West, S. 1988. "The Transmission of the Text." In A. Heubeck, S. West, and J. B. Hainsworth, *A Commentary on Homer's Odyssey* I. *Introduction and Books i–viii*, 33–48. Oxford.

Whitley, J. 1988. "Early States and Hero-Cults: A Re-Appraisal." *Journal of Hellenic Studies* 108:173–182.

Whitman, C. H. 1958. *Homer and the Heroic Tradition.* Cambridge, Mass.

Whitman, W. 1892. *Leaves of Grass.* 9th ed. Pagination here after the 1980 reissue, with introduction by G. W. Allen. New York.

Wickersham, J. M. 1986. "The Corpse Who Calls Theognis." *Transactions of the American Philological Association* 116:65–70.

Wilamowitz-Moellendorff, U. von. 1900. *Textgeschichte der griechischen Lyriker.* Berlin.

——. 1921. *Griechische Verskunst.* Berlin.

Will, E. 1950. "De l'aspect éthique des origines de la monnaie." *Revue Historique* 212:209–231.

——. 1975. "Notes sur ΜΙΣΘΟΣ." In *Le monde grec: Hommages à Claire Préaux*, edited by J. Bingen, G. Cambier, G. Nachtergael, 426–438. Brussels.

Willcock, M. M. 1964. "Mythological Paradeigma in the *Iliad.*" *Classical Quarterly* 14:141–154.

Willetts, R. F., ed. 1967. *The Law Code of Gortyn.* Berlin.

Williams, G. 1968. *Tradition and Originality in Roman Poetry.* Oxford.

Winkler, J. J. 1985. "The Ephebes' Song: *Tragōidia* and *Polis.*" *Representations* 11:26–62.

Winnington-Ingram, R. P., ed. 1963. Aristides Quintilianus, *De Musica.* Leipzig.

Winterscheidt, H. 1938. *Aigina. Eine Untersuchung über seine Gesellschaft und Wirtschaft.* Doctoral dissertation, Köln.

Wolff, H. J. 1946. "The Origin of Juridical Litigation among the Greeks." *Traditio* 4:34–49.

Woodbury, L. 1958. "Parmenides on Names." *Harvard Studies in Classical Philology* 63:145–160.

——. 1967. "Helen and the Palinode." *Phoenix* 21:157–176.

——. 1968. "Pindar and the Mercenary Muse: *Isthmian* 2.1–13." *Transactions of the American Philological Association* 99:527–542.

——. 1985. "Ibycus and Polycrates." *Phoenix* 39:193–220.

Wyatt, W. F. 1982. "Homeric *Atē.*" *American Journal of Philology* 103:247–276.

Wylie, J., and Margolin, D. 1981. *The Ring of Dancers: Images of Faroese Culture.* Philadelphia.

Young, D. C. 1968. *Three Odes of Pindar: A Literary Study of Pythian 11, Pythian 3, Olympian 7.* Leiden.

——. 1971. *Pindar, Isthmian 7, Myth and Exempla.* Leiden.

————. 1981. "Pindar *Pythians* 2 and 3: Inscriptional ΠΟΤΕ and the 'Poetic Epistle'." *Harvard Studies in Classical Philology* 87:31–48.

————. 1982. "Pindar." In *Ancient Writers: Greece and Rome*, edited by T. J. Luce, 157–177. New York.

————. 1983. "Pindar, Aristotle, and Homer: A Study in Ancient Criticism." In *Studies in Classical Lyric: A Homage to Elroy Bundy*, edited by T. D'Evelyn, P. Psoinos, and T. R. Walsh. = *Classical Antiquity* 2:156–170.

————. 1986. "Making the Believable Unbelievable: Pindar *Olympian* 1 and the Theory of a Kernel of Truth." Paper Presented at the 1986 Classical Association of the Middle West and South Meeting, Tampa.

Zeitlin, F. I. 1982. *Under the Sign of the Shield: Semiotics and Aeschylus' Seven against Thebes*. Rome.

Zetzel, J. E. G. 1983. "Re-creating the Canon: Augustan Poetry and the Alexandrian Past." *Critical Inquiry* 10:83–105. Reprinted 1984 in *Canons*, edited by R. von Hallberg, 107–129. Chicago.

Zink, M. 1972. *La pastourelle: Poésie et folklore au Moyen Age*. Paris.

Ziolkowski, J. 1985. "The Medieval Latin Beast Flyting." *Mittellateinisches Jahrbuch* 20:49–65.

Žirmunskij, V. M. 1965. "Syntaktischer Parallelismus und rhythmische Bindung im alttürkischen epischen Vers." *Beiträge zur Sprachwissenschaft, Volkskunde und Literaturforschung, Wolfgang Steinitz zum 60. Geburtstag*. Berlin.

Zumthor, P. 1972. *Essai de poétique médiévale*. Paris.

————. 1983. *Introduction à la poésie orale*. Paris.

————. 1984. *La Poésie de la Voix dans la civilisation médiévale*. Paris.

Zwettler, M. J. 1978. *The Oral Tradition of Classical Arabic Poetry*. Columbus.

▢▢ Index

INDEX OF GREEK WORDS

adika erga 'wrongdoings', 236
adikēma, adikiā, 'wrongdoing', 235, 312
Adrāsteia, 246; **Adrāstos,** 246, 247
adrāstos 'he from whom one cannot run away', 246
aeidō 'sing', 21, 26, 110
aethlon 'prize to be won in a contest', 137, 278